Better Money

Better Money

The Inside Story of e-gold

P. Carl Mullan

DCIA Publishing LLC.
30 N Gould St Ste R, Sheridan, WY 82801
https://www.e-goldbook.com
For more information contact: carl@e-goldbook.com
Paperback ISBN 978-1-7353569-1-4

DEDICATION

I dedicate this book to Mrs. Molly Wroth, my dear mother. Thanks, mom.

Also, a special dedication and thanks go to
Mrs. Deborah Heiman-Hughes, an exceptional teacher
and friend from Oakton High School ('82). Teachers are
indispensable leaders that play a vital role
shaping today's young minds.
Thank you, Mrs. Heiman-Hughes.

Other books by P. Carl Mullan.

A History of Digital Currency in the United States: New Technology in an Unregulated Market
Series: Palgrave Advances in the Economics of Innovation and Technology
Palgrave Macmillan, 2016
eBook ISBN 978-1-137-56870-0
Hardcover ISBN 978-1-137-56869-4
Softcover ISBN 978-1-349-93505-5

The Digital Currency Challenge: Shaping Online Payment Systems through US Financial Regulations
Palgrave Pivot, 2014
eBook ISBN 978-1-137-38255-9
Hardcover ISBN 978-1-137-38254-2

Table of Contents

List of Graphics

Case Numbers and Legal Documents

In addition to listing on the PACER system, free downloads of the court documents are available online at legalupdate.e-gold.com. All matters were before UNITED STATES DISTRICT COURT FOR THE DISTRICT OF COLUMBIA (unless otherwise annotated).
Docket numbers:
05-0664-M-01
05-cv-02497
07-167-M-01
(US Court of Appeals, DC) 07-3074
07-cv-01337
CR 07-00109 (including extensions 02, 03, 04, and 05)

Foreword to *Better Money*

By: Paul Rosenberg

I am one of the lucky few who stumbled upon e-gold in the late 1990s, as it was bursting upon the world, empowering small commerce, allowing person-to-person international transactions and creating, for lack of a better description, a planet-wide party for the motivated but unprivileged.

The e-gold economy led me to bands of brothers – talented, fascinating, and often wise bands of brothers – secretly meeting on tiny Croatian islands, in the back rooms of bars, in glitzy hotels and dark corners of the Internet. e-gold led me to raw, potent, and invigorating business deals and dealers. It brought me into a wide variety of international experiences, for both better and worse, that I wouldn't have imagined otherwise.

The e-gold era was, to me, the life of high adventure, and I loved nearly every minute of it. What 1967's Summer of Love was to my older cousins, e-gold was to me and my contemporaries, and not a bit less.

As *Better Money* notes, e-gold gave, "everyone, at all levels of society, the ability to transact financial payments online." If you've ever tried to send money to a friend or relative in a different country, you may have learned how ridiculous, expensive and time consuming that process can be. With e-gold it took only a few clicks of a mouse. In literally seconds, your friends had however much money you wanted to send them, whether it was one dollar or a hundred thousand... and for just a tiny transfer fee. And so, very quickly, billions of dollars were being transferred in precisely this way. And the reason for it was all too simple: Because the old, moribund way of officially authorized banks had always strangled this form of commerce.

As I noted above, if you were motivated, there was nothing to stop you from becoming an e-gold dealer. The whole thing was brand new; so new that there were no laws. The law-makers, in fact, hadn't the first inkling that this was even happening. There were no enforcers and no one who could grant you permission. It was completely lawless but filled with honest business.

Those of us who wanted liberation flooded in, those who didn't remained aloof. And as *Better Money* also notes, self-appointed, self-motivated dealers jumped up and began conducting, "third-party independent exchange services between national currencies and e-gold. These payment methods included bank transfers, Western Union payments, money orders, and other digital currency products." And, of course, cash. It was unfettered commerce, and it was an unmitigated gas.

If I could bottle how much fun all of this was, I'd be the world's richest man.

So, I've been waiting for this book for a long time, almost since 2008, when e-gold was taken down. Finally, we're getting the story from the inside. And I'm pleased to say that all the details you could want are in this book: The founding, the struggles, the threats, the triumphs, the overload caused by the triumphs, the back-stabbing, the big, ugly boot of the enforcer… all of it is here, and serious students of business (especially of start-ups and international business) would be well-advised to use this as a text. More than that, the entire story is told using the original sources themselves, not just recollections. This book reproduces precisely what was said at the time. This content gives us a direct view of the actors and the events, something that is still fairly rare.

Finally, I should add that the e-gold adventure was tremendously important as a precursor to Bitcoin and cryptocurrencies. As I see it – and I was involved with both spheres during this time – the e-gold adventure was definitely a motivating factor for the creation of Bitcoin. In fact, Satoshi Nakamoto, in his/her/their very few writings, exposes a rather in-depth knowledge of e-gold processes. The e-gold adventure, then, was a prologue to the Bitcoin adventure.

My thanks go to Doug Jackson for opening his files and making all this available. I especially thank Carl Mullan for undertaking the gigantic job of turning it all into a coherent story. Kudos to you both!

Paul Rosenberg

March, 2020

Introduction

In 1996, two entrepreneurs launched a revolutionary online payment system that enabled users to transfer value over the Internet without requiring a bank or credit card. The concept of Internet money, backed by gold, was untested and radically modern. This innovative private network was named e-gold®.

Non-bank Internet payments represented a contemporary approach to business in a global economy. The pioneers that designed the e-gold® platform implemented this technology on a clean slate. No other commercial Internet payment system had operated before e-gold®. By the time PayPal launched in late 1999,[1] e-gold's network had been completing online transactions for nearly three years.

e-gold® was new technology launched on top of another new technology, the Internet. The e-gold® corporate structure and financial applications were unlike any other modern commercial product in the world. From 1996 to 2007, there were no defined U.S. financial regulations that identified these digital e-metals or classified the transfer and exchange of its online units.

The existing U.S. financial regulations, established under the Bank Secrecy Act and later the USA Patriot Act, did not classify e-gold's business as a financial institution. Referring to e-gold®, a former head of the U.S. Department of Justice Computer Crime Unit, Mark Rasch, was quoted in a 2006 Businessweek article stating, "It's not like it's[e-gold] regulated by someone else; it's not regulated."[2]

With e-gold proponents unable to quickly explain the system or where digital currency belonged within the existing regulatory landscape; e-gold and its operators were at the mercy of the ignorant.[3]

As the world's first commercially successful Internet payment system, e-gold® enabled the value of gold and other precious metals to be mobilized as digital money. At all times, the unique digital units were one-hundred percent backed by precious metal. It was *Better Money*. This non-bank platform was ideally suitable as an alternative global reserve asset and international medium of settlement. Account-holders completed near-instant domestic and international payments, denominated in precious metal. E-gold® settled payments by book-entry transfer of digital units backed by precious metal held in trust by a corporate

[1] Pymnts, Staff. "The History Of PayPal: Important Company Dates." *PYMNTS.com*, PYMNTS 60 60 PYMNTS.com, 2 July 2015, www.pymnts.com/in-depth/2015/throwback-thursday-paypals-biggest-days-in-history/.

[2] White, Lawrence H. "The Troubling Suppression of Competition from Alternative Monies: The Cases of the Liberty Dollar and e-gold." *Cato Journal*, vol. 34, no. 2-5, May 2014, object.cato.org/sites/cato.org/files/serials/files/cato-journal/2014/5/cato-journal-v34n2-5.pdf.

[3] Middlebrook, Stephen T., et al. *Developments in the Law Concerning Stored-Value Cards and Other Electronic Payments Products*. Indiana University Maurer School of Law, 2007, *Developments in the Law Concerning Stored-Value Cards and Other Electronic Payments Products*.

affiliate. E-gold® digital units were not issued, measured, or insured by any government. Neither e-gold's structure nor performance fit accurately into existing U.S. financial regulations. It was the proverbial square peg for a round hole.

The co-founders of this system were Dr. Douglas Jackson, a successful oncologist from Florida, and Barry Downey, a well-known lawyer from Maryland. These two pioneers recognized that the Internet's emerging global infrastructure would soon become a worldwide virtual marketplace of goods and services. Their idea was to design and build a precious metal-backed digital currency that could service the break-out global economy and benefit all of humanity.

For billions of people around the world, their location, nationality, and language would no longer be factors that deterred trade; e-gold® could connect the world. A family in Bangladesh could instantly purchase retail products or services from a market in New York City. A tiny store in Bejing, China, could sell local items to Sao Paulo, Brazil. Account-holders would conduct all of these distant transactions using e-gold's fast, non-repudiable payments based on precious metals. The Internet gave birth to instant global commerce, and e-gold® facilitated secure transactions in this budding new online marketplace.

April 23, 2001, Barron's article, written by Jack White and Doug Ramsey, entitled *Making New Money*, described co-founder Douglas Jackson's solution for the rapidly growing Internet economy.

> Dr. Jackson also recognized that the development of the Internet had expanded the abilities of businesses to sell to a global market. Yet, he also believed that global commerce would be unable to develop in stride with the Internet so long as there were insufficient methods for merchants to be paid promptly, affordably and securely. Existing payment systems were - and are - subject to chargeback risks and high transaction costs. Furthermore, they were generally inaccessible to large segments of the world population who lacked credit cards or adequate banking arrangements.[4]

Above all else, e-gold's co-founders designed the system to serve the global economy. E-gold® delivered the convenience of sending payments anywhere, immediately, and for minimal cost. Jackson described his thought process at the time of e-gold's launch.

> The two problems I was concerned with were:
> - Payments. The emergence of commercial Internet meant that there was now a global market via which to offer one's goods and services, but there was no

---

[4] Jack White & Doug Ramsey, *Making New Money,* Barron's, April 23, 2001.

mechanism for most Internet users to receive payment online. These days this issue is known as "financial inclusion."

- Money. I was concerned that national currencies were instruments of discretionary monetary policies and would continue to degenerate into engines for debt creation, as the flood of liquidity created to address each crisis would set the stage for next, typically bigger, crisis.[5]

In an email interview, Jackson shared his analysis of government vs. private money.

The system I envisioned was informed by analysis of historic and contemporary models, one consistent flaw of all of them being the impracticability of binding a sovereign to inconvenient obligations. Even if a seemingly airtight system could be devised, a successor regime would have no qualms about repudiating it. The courts never award damages to those injured when a state reneges on its monetary obligations. Only a private enterprise can truly be held accountable to contracts of that nature.[6]

Whether e-gold® would eventually become a ubiquitous financial system capable of competing with dollars, euro, and yen would be sorted out in the decade ahead.

In April 2007, a Federal Grand Jury handed down an indictment charging e-gold Ltd., Gold & Silver Reserve, Inc., and the Directors of both companies with money laundering, operating an unlicensed money transmitter business (18 U.S.C. § 1960), and conspiracies to commit both offenses. In 2008, the defendants signed guilty plea agreements. Later, e-gold® and its operating company forfeited around $45 million of the proceeds from liquidating the massive bullion stockpile which had backed e-gold.

Before the e-gold® criminal case, no federal regulations were understood to govern this new category of digital or virtual currency. The plea agreements that resolved the e-gold® case served as templates for the U.S. Department of the Treasury in formulating new regulations for the identification and supervision of digital value moving over the Internet. After the e-gold® prosecution made headlines, U.S. lawmakers moved swiftly to decipher the various definitions of what constituted a Money Transmitter, as it related to digital currency. Shortly after e-gold's guilty plea, the government began proposing new financial guidelines and regulations targeting certain "ambiguities"[7] in U.S. laws covering Money

5   Jackson, Douglas. "2019.04.30 Observations and Comments." Received by Carl Mullan, 2019.04.30 Observations and Comments, 30 Apr. 2019

6   "Chapter 4." *The Digital Currency Challenge: Shaping Online Payment Systems through US Financial Regulations*, by P. Carl Mullan, Palgrave Macmillan, 2014, pp. 24–25.

7   Hughes, Sarah Jane; Middlebrook, Stephen T.; and Peterson, Broox W., "Developments in the Law Concerning Stored-

Transmitters and Money Service Businesses.

The e-gold® guilty plea was a tough pill to swallow for seasoned members of the global digital currency industry. Dr. Douglas Jackson was and still is today, recognized as a true pioneer and innovator who blazed a trail for thousands of future online payment systems and products. The plea agreements, along with the government's blatant money-grab halted e-gold's bright future. For a short time, Douglas Jackson's work with digital money was temporarily "on hold." However, Dr. Jackson's 1990s vision of digital payments eventually transformed the world's perception of electronic money. In 2020, Jackson's work designing global financial networks is again moving global commerce into the future.

In 2020, one hard-to-grasp concept is the sense of financial freedom that e-gold granted its users. During the late 1990s and early 2000s, banks controlled the movement of money in every country on earth. E-gold introduced a ground-breaking alternative to banks and offered this free service to anyone with an Internet connection.

Who used e-gold, and why?

Comparing consumer demand for e-gold between different income brackets provides an excellent illustration of "who" benefited from using e-gold. The ability to recognize this variance is an insight that few people had during e-gold's first decade of operation from 1996 to 2006.

It is crucial to understand "why" certain groups flocked to e-gold and why others, including most Americans, ridiculed the concept of using a private Internet version of money. This elucidation demonstrates the fundamental reason why a   virtual currency is either adopted or discarded by potential new users.

In 2020, just about every store in America has an aisle endcap display overflowing with colorful prepaid cards that satisfy consumer needs. However, when e-gold launched, financial companies were not widely issuing prepaid debit cards, and U.S. penetration was minimal. Prepaid plastic was not available on a massive scale during the early years of the Internet. Anyone shopping online needed to use a bank issue credit card, and those kinds of cards were not prevalent with low wage earners. Additionally, very few banks in Europe, S. America, and former CIS countries issued credit or debit cards. Persons residing in Russia, Belarus, or the Czech Republic had very little chance of shopping online; because they could not pay for purchases. Yes, the Internet would ultimately become a significant global marketplace. However, until prepaid debit card use began to increase with retail consumers, there were very few non-bank methods to pay for online purchases. E-gold solved this dilemma by facilitating online commerce for everyone on earth. E-gold allowed anyone to

Value Cards and Other Electronic Payments Products" (2007). *Articles by Maurer Faculty.* Paper 174.
http://www.repository.law.indiana.edu/facpub/174

transact online business and transfer value.

Another roadblock to online business in this early era was the "merchant account." Anyone desiring to receive online customer payments would have to complete the expensive process of qualifying for a card processing merchant account. For millions of users wanting to sell goods and services online and were unable to obtain a merchant account, e-gold was a brilliant alternative. E-gold merchants could open an account, and moments later, begin accepting payments from customers around the world.

Who reaped the immediate benefits of e-gold?

Well paid American workers and executives did not benefit immediately from e-gold's advantages. The market segment that appreciated e-gold's features was the unbanked or unbankable population.

Middle and upper-income American consumers with a wallet full of credit cards were not the primary beneficiaries of online e-gold payments. Every middle-class American surveyed during 2000-2008 had the same response, "E-gold, why would I use that? I'll pay with a card. I don't get it."

Most consumers did not want or need another "confusing" method of payment, and no shopper was willing to relinquish their bank cards.

The same attitude exists in 2020. An average shopper has online banking, online brokerage, mobile banking, plastic credit and debit cards, smartphone payments, and hundreds of prepaid debit cards on numerous sophisticated financial networks. This consumer does not need another way to pay, even if it is cheaper and more secure. Ask any medium to an upper-income customer why they don't use Bitcoin, and their response will be similar, "Bitcoin, why would I use that? I'll pay with a card, a cell phone, or use my bank. I don't need it."

The leading beneficiaries of innovative non-bank platforms such as e-gold were global unbanked populations. Without a bank account or card, millions of users were thrilled to conduct online business using e-gold.

The next consumer segment that gained from e-gold, and today cryptocurrency, was users in "cash-based economies." Almost all Arab countries forbid the practice of high-interest credit and borrowing, as offered by credit cards. Card penetration in these areas has been historically low, and it is accurate to say that "cash is king." If residents in any of these cash-based economies were going to shop online, they needed a secure and convenient alternative to bank issue cards. E-gold quickly became that convenient option for persons and businesses operating from Arab countries.

The federal criminal case against e-gold and the massive asset forfeitures were not games. However, to perceive the strategies depicted in *Better Money*, it is useful to think of e-gold's history from 1999 to 2009 in terms of a "game." There were three sets of players:

- the e-gold principals, who later became the e-gold defendants,
- the private cabal determined to destroy e-gold,
- the USSS and, later, other US government agencies seeking to seize/forfeit the gold and other assets and win felony convictions against the principals.

Fact vs. Fiction

Dr. Jackson asked to have several false narratives from past decades debunked before discussing the prosecutors' career-building legal moves, and the sinister USSS plans to seize e-gold's bullion. The following statements are untrue.

1. **e-gold® was shut down by the government.**
2. **The government seized physical bullion from e-gold's vaulted storage.**
3. **The government prosecuted e-gold® because the network was direct competition for the U.S. Dollar. The operators of e-gold® were antithetical to all government supervision, and opposed federal and state financial regulations.**

1. e-gold® was shut down by the government.

The e-gold® system was NEVER shut down by the government. Gold & Silver Reserve, Inc. DBA/OmniPay was able to continue exchange operations, without defaulting on any pending obligations from 2005 - 2007 even after its U.S. bank accounts were frozen. In 2008, the company revamped it's KYC and AML programs for a post-verdict relaunch. While the company was preparing to operate in compliance with all state and federal regulations, the relaunch never occurred. In 2008, both companies registered with FinCEN as Money Transmitting Businesses. But having been convicted of felonies, the company and its operators could not obtain the necessary approval from the company's home state of Florida or any other U.S. state. At the time of the plea agreement, Jackson was unaware that the felony conviction would prevent him and the company from gaining the required commercial licenses. Eventually, any plans of relaunching the original company as a licensed, registered, and regulated business, with Jackson at the helm, were shelved. Because of this unforeseen situation, e-gold's operators voluntarily closed the company. This statement, "e-gold® was shut down by the government," is FALSE. In 2019, this rumor continued to circulate through media outlets.

2. The government seized physical bullion from e-gold's vaulted storage.

Throughout the entire e-gold® legal case, no government agent or law enforcement agent ever seized any physical metal, not even one gram of gold. The precious metal bullion governed by The e-gold® Bullion Reserve Special Purpose Trust, backing the digital units, had remained secure in allocated storage. Not until late 2009, when it became apparent that the company would be unable to resume normal operations, was this bullion liquidated by Gold & Silver Reserve, Inc. Pursuant to a carefully negotiated "e-gold® Value Access Plan (VAP)" the companies initiated the return of the USD-equivalent of e-gold back to users.

3. The government prosecuted e-gold® because the network was direct competition for the U.S. Dollar.

This statement is FALSE. Despite numerous conspiracy theories, the government did not attack e-gold® because it posed a threat to the United States Dollar. Since 1996, no clear evidence backing this statement has ever surfaced, and the co-founders of e-gold® aggressively dispute this false claim.

4) The operators of e-gold® were antithetical to all government supervision, and opposed federal and state financial regulations.

This statement is also UNTRUE. Throughout e-gold's history, from 1996 through 2009, the co-founder's openly engaged members of the law enforcement community. After 2005, e-gold sought out opinions of regulators on proper licensing and guidance. The co-founders of e-gold® were not opposed to regulations; they felt the existing laws did not apply to their innovative new technology.

Other Items

e-gold, Ltd., and G&SR represented an innovative new global approach to exchanging value over the Internet. As stated in the November 14, 2008, Sentencing Memorandum, Gold & Silver Reserve, Inc. operated with a good faith belief that the company was not a money transmitting business. The co-founders were not opposed to financial regulations. The operators believed that their companies   were not subject to existing regulations applicable to a money transmitting business.

G&SR had directed its legal counsel to engage regulatory authorities and address the licensing issue as a Money Transmitter. This process had been ongoing at the time of the government's 2005 search warrant.

Their lawyers had advised the Companies and their management that this new business model, and the "digital currency" offered through e-gold, Ltd., were not subject to existing financial regulatory statutes. The co-founders believed that the older existing laws governing "money transmitting businesses" did not apply to e-gold's modern new platform.

Until the e-gold prosecution ended up in District Court, no government agency had ever challenged the company on this issue.[8]

Official documents, presented in *Better Money*, demonstrate that many other individuals working in state and federal government positions agreed with Jackson.

A 2006 interview with DOJ Attorney Courtney J. Linn contains an expert discussion of financial regulations for payment systems. The UC Davis Law Journal published this piece. It is entitled *Plugging the Gaps in the U.S. Anti-Money Laundering System How These Reforms Affect Banks and Other Financial Institutions — an interview with Courtney J. Linn of Department of Justice - U.S. Attorney.*[9] However, e-gold's co-founders do not make similar arguments.

Sinister Truths

Better Money presents unpublished emails, communications, and documents that were not previously in the public domain. Documents uncovered in 2017 blow a hole in the government's narrative, and raise questions of a cover-up. Hidden deep in this story is the ulterior motives if the USSS. After years of exhaustive research and hundreds of thousands of dollars, Jackson and his attorneys have been able to recover many of the private communications between government officials that took place before and during the e-gold® prosecution. Jackson revealed the following facts about his document search.

> The documents from FL OFR were obtained by a (series of three) FL Public Records requests. The FL Public Records law is like FOIA except in FL the legislature actually requires agencies to comply. Federal FOIA, in contrast, is a complete sham. Our expensive DC counsel had billed us over 100K over time for multiple FOIA requests to IRS, USSS, DOJ, USPIS etc. With those we received many thousands of pages of worthlessness, sometimes a thousand page run of either blank or 100% redacted pages. Altogether we received maybe 8000 pages, maybe more, which also included hundreds of my own emails sent to law enforcement and hundreds or thousands of pages of my attachments such as spreadsheets I had prepared that were then printed in a useless fashion. The FL process, while they tried to stonewall and it took three tries, was free and I did all the requests.[10]

For the first time, *Better Money* exposes internal communications and private emails,

8   Case 1:07-cr-00109-RMC Document 177. *UNITED STATES OF AMERICA v. E-GOLD, LTD*. Criminal SENTENCING MEMORANDUM OF GOLD & SILVER RESERVE, INC., 14 Nov. 2008.

9   Donald, Elizabeth, and Dina M. Randazzo. "Plugging the Gaps in the U.S. Anti-Money Laundering System How These Reforms Affect Banks and Other Financial Institutions — an Interview with Courtney J. Linn of Department of Justice - U.S. Attorney." *Business Law Journal*, vol. 10, 1 Jan. 2006.

10 Jackson, Douglas. "Re: attached." Received by Carl Mullan, *Re: attached*, 30 Apr. 2019.

evidencing the sinister actions that occurred within the investigation and prosecution. *Better Money* proposes that the e-gold prosecution was an explicit money grab.

> As a result of the offenses alleged in Counts One and Three of this indictment, the defendants E-GOLD, LTD., GOLD & SILVER RESERVE, INC., DOUGLAS JACKSON, REID JACKSON, and BARRY DOWNEY shall forfeit to the United States any property, real or personal, involved in, or traceable to such property involved in money laundering, in violation of Title 18, United States Code, Section 1956, and in operation of an unlicensed money transmitting business, in violation of Title 18, United States Code, Section 1960;including, but not limited to the following:
> (a) The sum of money equal to the total amount of property involved in, or traceable to property involved in those violations. Fed.R.Crim.P. 32.2(b)(1).
> (b) **All the assets, including without limitation**, equipment, inventory, accounts receivable and bank accounts, of E-GOLD, LTD., and GOLD & SILVER RESERVE, INC., **whether titled in those names or not, including, but not limited to all precious metals, including gold, silver, platinum, and palladium, that "back" the emetal electronic currency of the E-GOLD operation, wherever located.**[11] [emphasis added]

The United States Secret Service and DOJ Prosecutors were out to get a conviction at any cost and steal e-gold's precious metal bullion.

Additional evidence-based statements from Jackson, paint a picture of government lawyers closely aligned with a small group of USSS Special Agents. Their alleged covert efforts included vilifying Jackson in the media, and obtaining a guilty plea by any means at their disposal.

Evidence uncovered from court documents and private emails also raises questions about the actions of government lawyers and possible buried evidence that could have been helpful to the e-gold® Defendants. The trail these documents leave behind is a distinct pattern of alleged misconduct by a small group of USSS Special Agents and DOJ Attorneys responsible for prosecuting the e-gold case.

Additionally, Jackson proposes a hypothesis alleging that the District Court Judge, in his case, may have been incentivized, perhaps even pressured, to speed the case through Court to an early conclusion. Jackson propounds that career advancement for a U.S. District

---

[11] Case 1:07-cr-00109-RMC Document 1 . *UNITED STATES OF AMERICA v. E-GOLD, LTD. GOLD & SILVER RESERVE, INC. DOUGLAS L. JACKSON, BARRY K. DOWNEY, and REID A. JACKSON.* INDICTMENT, 24 Apr. 2007.

Judges is enhanced by rapidly clearing cases and speeding defendants through the Court system. In 2012, after the e-gold® case, District Court Judge Rosemary M. Collyer advanced to become the Presiding Judge of the United States Foreign Intelligence Surveillance Court (FISA), a position she occupied still in 2019. Her signature appeared on the Carter Page FISA warrants that made headlines after the election of President Donald J. Trump.

After researching incentives for federal judges to rapidly clear cases, Jackson questioned if such pressures influenced Judge Collyer's procedural decisions, particularly in denying defense requests for (and an appellate ruling mandating) an evidentiary hearing.

In Jackson's view, the introduction of evidence, through a hearing that the Judge denied, instead of reliance on the 'assumed facts' of the criminal complaint, might have had a material impact on the outcome of the case.

The facts presented in *Better Money* demonstrate that even regulators in the State of Florida, e-gold's home jurisdiction, were unwilling to join the DOJ's effort to label e-gold® as a Money Transmitter. An uncovered December 2006, official Florida internal communication shows that before the e-gold® indictment, officials generated a draft legal opinion that the Defendant Gold & Silver Reserve, Inc. was not required to obtain a local Money Transmitter license. [It was created in fulfillment of formal request and lacked only publication.]

Years after the e-gold criminal case had ended, Jackson uncovered this startling private communication through his information requests to the Florida Office of Financial Regulation (OFR).

On May 25th, 2007 Robert Beitler, General Counsel for the State of Florida, sent an email to the following Florida officials:

Robert Rosenau   –   Chief, Bureau of Financial Investigations, State of Florida
Peter Fisher – Chief Finance Attorney, State of Florida
Mike Ramsden – Financial Administrator, Money Transmitter Regulation Unit, State of Florida
Chris Hancock – FA, Bureau of Financial Investigations, State of Florida
Mark Mathosian – Investigator, Florida Office of Financial Regulation (OFR)
William Oglo – Assistant General Counsel, State of Florida

The second paragraph of the message began, "Everyone knows why they went after e-gold, but as you are aware the filing of charges is not determinative of anything."[12]

This email was part of a more massive chain circulated in late May 2007, between

---

12   Beitler, Robert. "RE: [ACAMS] Digital Currency Business e-Gold Indicted." Received by Robert Rosenau, et al., *RE: [ACAMS] Digital Currency Business e-Gold Indicted*, 25 May 2007.

Florida officials.

The State of Florida Interoffice communication containing a draft legal opinion on e-gold's business had previously circulated, a year earlier, between all of these Florida officials, during the first week of December 2006. That draft document shows conclusively that regulatory officials within the State of Florida had determined that e-gold's business did not require a Florida Money Transmitter License.

The question arises if Florida officials had already concluded that no Money Transmitter violation had occurred, what possible reason was Robert Beitler, General Counsel for the State of Florida, referencing with his statement?

"Everyone knows why they went after e-gold[…]"

The answer is simple. The e-gold® prosecution was a money grab. Prosecutors and USSS Special Agents were working to seize the precious metal bullion. Many people, familiar with this case, conclude that forfeiture is the most obvious motivation for bringing this prosecution, not the state unlicensed money transmitter violation. A primary reason for drawing this conclusion is that very few USSS guilty verdicts produce any substantial asset forfeiture. The number of assets represented by an e-gold® guilty verdict is ample motivation for the prosecutors' shameful actions.

Jackson proposes, and the evidence suggests that after Florida officials rebuffed DOJ lawyers, with the draft legal opinion, then Prosecutors went shopping for a more accommodating venue. Jackson proposes that Special Agents scouted outside of Florida for a state or jurisdiction that would support their criminal allegations. Ultimately, the USSS landed in Washington, D.C.

Jackson also shows that after the criminal verdicts, the USSS obstructed every step in the negotiation and execution of e-gold's VAP (Value Access Program). USSS Special Agents caused the refund of customer value to play out over four brutal years. This process should have lasted less than ninety days. The prolonged refund period afforded the USSS a second bite at the "gold apple." Their efforts to delay and complicate the customer notification and claims process effectively thwarted many thousands of would-be claimants from reclaiming their legal property. Through these deeds, the USSS garnered a windfall of over forty-five million dollars in unclaimed e-gold® value.

Better Money offers hundreds of pages of state and federal documents gathered through internal inquiries and the Freedom of Information Act. For several years, the author conducted of interviews and researched volumes of historical data, including Jackson's original emails and notes. All of this new material reopens the e-gold® prosecution to further investigation and scrutiny. Many of Jackson's claims are not yet proven truths, and with limited resources, exact answers to these questions may never be possible. It is up to the reader to review the evidence and form a conclusion.

The Legal Case

Jackson alleges that during the investigation and criminal prosecution of e-gold®, members of the United States Secret Service (USSS), in league with DOJ Prosecutors, engaged in misconduct, including actions if perpetrated by a private citizen, might constitute obstruction of justice. In particular, Jackson's statements focus on attorney Kimberly Kiefer Peretti, who was one of the DOJ lawyers prosecuting the e-gold® case.

Jackson believes that in early 2001, he began to see indications of a rogue element within the USSS operating "off the reservation."

Furthermore, Jackson is confident that the USSS was initially baited into aggression against e-gold® by a private group or "cabal" of industry participants. Jackson explained this reasoning, "a particular private cabal driven by malice, the interests of would-be competitors and a desire for informant rewards."[13]

Jackson identifies and detailed several critical junctures in the e-gold® case. He explained that these moments occurred when Prosecutors, tricked by sinister members of the cabal, came to a sickening realization they had been attacking "the good guys."

During the prosecution, each of these points must have required a paramount decision. Should DOJ lawyers back down and drop the charges, or close ranks and press ahead.

A most critical moment occurred in late 2006 when a classic "Boss, I've got good news and bad news" event transpired between Peretti and the USSS team she had been working with since 2003. The good news was that the USSS had discovered the identity of the most sought-after criminal hacker in modern history. The bad news that followed was the individual's name. The hacker was the government's own paid confidential informant (CI), Albert Gonzalez. The criminal sought by law enforcement around the world, turned out to be an integral part of the Peretti/USSS team. While committing crimes right under their noses for years, he had been on the government's payroll.

The truth is even more shocking because it was e-gold® investigators, personally headed up by Jackson, that discovered the crucial evidence identifying the hacker and turned it over to law enforcement. Jackson's information should have unmasked the perpetrator years before he stole the financial information of nearly 130 million Americans. However, in 2006, once the government had Jackson's intelligence, it disappeared.

One course of action would have been to arrest Gonzalez, drop the charges against the e-gold® Defendants, enabling Jackson's testimony with a clean chain of custody for the crucial evidence. This scenario did not take place.

---

[13] Ibid

19

In July 2006, DOJ Lawyer, Kim Peretti demanded the related case files and evidence from USPIS investigators working with Jackson. Gambling that Jackson had not realized the significance of his evidence, after the files arrived to Peretti, the information vanished. Gonzalez remained at large as a paid CI for the USSS, and Jackson proposes that from July 2006 forward, DOJ prosecutors closed ranks around their agency and the USSS.

Jackson believes that for nearly two years, government prosecutors covered up the Gonzalez bombshell evidence allowing him to commit these crimes. During this period, Gonzalez, aka segvec, masterminded the most massive theft of hacked personal and financial information in American history, including the Heartland breach in May 2015.

Peretti's team followed through on the e-gold® prosecution to the bitter end. A cover-up can't yet be proven. If this did occur, one might question if Peretti undertook it on her authority? How high did it reach? It is a worrisome conclusion. Did the unexpected decision to press ahead seeking Jackson's incarceration come down "from the highest levels?"

Jackson details these complaints and allegations through a historical narrative and document exhibits. As a central part of this proposed cover-up, Jackson alleges that prosecutors withheld critical information from the *Brady* materials to hide and protect their suspected malicious activity. Jackson argues that during this process, prosecutors committed a clear *Brady* violation and possible perjury related to information withheld from the Court.

Several of these unproven allegations are focused on actions taken by Kimberly Kiefer Peretti, and her associates at the USSS, DHS, and DOJ.

In the alleged case of perjury, Jackson takes specific aim at the Acting Assistant U.S. Attorney Laurel Loomis Rimon. Jackson presents evidence that appears to document his claim that Rimon was wholly complicit in the willful *Brady* violations and knowingly perjured herself in open Court.

Jackson states that as a direct consequence of actions undertaken by USSS Special Agents in league with Kimberly Kiefer Peretti, the government destroyed his business and personal life.

Jackson is seeking to undo the lingering harm caused by this alleged malicious prosecution and the conspiracy between certain USSS and DOJ officials. His ultimate goal is to have attorneys petition the Court to retroactively dismiss all charges.

During the e-gold® investigation and criminal case, the U.S. Department of Justice Computer Crime and Intellectual Property Section, Criminal Division employed Kimberly Peretti as a Senior Counsel.

As detailed by *Better Money*, in 2017, Jackson requested the then-Inspector General of DHS, John Roth, to investigate Kimberly Kiefer Peretti, her associates, and superiors, for alleged prosecutorial misconduct. Interestingly, John Roth previously had played a direct role in the e-gold® case.

In a strange twist, Jackson's 2017 investigation request crossed paths once again with Laural Loomis Rimon, who, in August 2017, was working for Roth employed as Acting Assistant Inspector General for Inspections at DHS. Roth and Rimon have both since left government service.

Actions that other Courts have labeled prosecutorial misconduct, in other cases, include:

- Using improper investigative techniques, such as "entrapment" – inducing a person to commit a crime who was not otherwise disposed to commit it.
- Bringing criminal charges in bad faith without realistic hope of winning a conviction – for example, to punish a political rival, or to retaliate against someone.
- Making statements to the media that prejudice the jury pool.
- Engaging in improper plea-bargaining– for example, convincing a defendant to plead guilty through false promises or misrepresentations about the existence of incriminating evidence.
- Failing to turn over exculpatory evidence.
- Tampering with evidence.
- Knowingly presenting false witness testimony or other false evidence to a court or grand jury.
- Asking a defendant or defense witness damaging and suggestive questions with no factual basis.
- Making improper statements in front of the jury – for example, expressing a personal opinion about the guilt of a defendant or the credibility of testimony, mentioning facts not in evidence, or criticizing the defendant for exercising his constitutional right not to testify.

Sufficiently culpable and harmful misconduct can result in the dismissal of charges or a declaration of a mistrial.[14]

Allegations

Jackson alleges that Peretti and her DOJ associates intentionally failed to disclose material facts to the Court that would have harmed their criminal prosecution. He claims that Peretti and her DOJ superiors allegedly undertook this cover-up because the undisclosed

---

[14] "What, Exactly, Is 'Prosecutorial Misconduct'?" *MoloLamken LLP (ML)*, www.mololamken.com/news-knowledge-28.html.

facts could have annulled allegations of criminal conduct by the Defendants. Specific evidence tends to confirm Jackson's claims. Relevant details were buried and hidden from the Court that had a direct impact on the state money transmitter licensing requirements. That individual charge comprised the core of the prosecution's criminal case and asset seizure.

Allegedly, supplementing the intentional acts of withholding materially important case information, DOJ prosecutors also did not provide other crucial *Brady* material to the Court. *Better Money* examines this claim and information.

Furthermore, Jackson argues that the prosecution purposely crafted a misleading and inaccurate profile of the Defendants' companies. *Better Money* presents documents and facts that allege prosecutors may have misled the Court regarding the e-gold® platform, G&SR's institutional arrangements, and the business' transaction logic. Supported by evidence, Jackson's claims demonstrate that by working with false and assumed facts, the USSS used this "bag of tricks" to deceive the Court.

Jackson's documented evidence outlines that Peretti, and her associates, conspired in overt acts that may have constituted obstruction of justice, concerning crimes committed by paid U.S. Secret Service criminal informant Albert Gonzalez a/k/a "segvec."

In the Gonzalez case, Jackson alleges that, while working for the USSS as a CI, Peretti and DOJ associates owned facts supplied by Jackson that could have identified Gonzalez as the criminal mastermind of the most massive "cybercrime heist" in U.S. history. While he was operating as a paid USSS Confidential Informant Gonzalez's crimes are estimated to have cost American companies more than $400 million. Jackson claims, that, to protect her case and reputation, Peretti buried the critical information that he had volunteered.

By burying or excluding e-gold® evidence, Jackson maintains that Peretti purposely delayed Gonzalez's arrest for nearly two years in an alleged cover-up. During this delay, Gonzalez was operating under the supervision of USSS Special Agents. The facts tend to support Jackson's claims, that it was not USSS investigative prowess that cracked the Gonzalez case. The segvec suspect was identified in 2006 by Jackson's in-house e-gold® investigations.

Better Money offers Jackson's synopsis of events that includes the government's possible motives for this alleged malicious prosecution.

Documents uncovered by Jackson, through the Freedom of Information Act (FOIA) and from the State of Florida archives, help to illustrate the DOJ Prosecutors' actions as they relate to criminal charges and seizures built on a violation of BSA regulations. The BSA rules relating to the operation of an unlicensed money transmitter were the foundation of the federal government's case. These documents illustrate that the State of Florida, e-gold's home for more than a decade, had no intention of charging e-gold® with a money transmitter violation. Furthermore, documents from Florida officials clearly demonstrate that if directed by Florida, e-gold® had been ready and willing to obtain the necessary state financial license. Official documents, later recovered from Florida, evidence these facts. Jackson believes that Prosecutors should have provided these materials, and others, according to the requirements of the *Brady* material.

Giglio Information Law and Legal Definition

In U.S. law, *Giglio* information or material refers to material tending to impeach the character or testimony of the prosecution witness in a criminal trial. The Supreme Court's 1963 decision in *Brady v. Maryland*, 373 U.S. 83 (U.S. 1963) held that the prosecution violates due process when it "withholds evidence on demand of an accused which, if made available, would tend to exculpate him or reduce the penalty. In *Giglio v. United States*, 405 U.S. 150, 153 (U.S. 1972), the Supreme Court extended the prosecution's obligations under *Brady* to disclosure of impeachment evidence. Supreme Court clarified that all impeachment evidence, even if not a prior statement by a witness falls within the *Brady* rule. *Giglio* mandated that the prosecution should disclose any and all information that may be used to impeach the credibility of prosecution witnesses including law enforcement officers. Impeachment information under *Giglio* includes information such as prior criminal records or other acts of misconduct of prosecution witness, promises of leniency or immunity offered to prosecution witnesses.[15]

Brady Material Law and Legal Definition

Brady material refers to a piece of evidence known to the prosecution that is important for establishing the innocence or reducing the punishment of a defendant. Prosecution must disclose evidence that would help in proving the innocence of a defendant and also which helps in reducing the gravity of punishment. The term '*Brady* material' comes from the U.S. Supreme Court case, *Brady v. Maryland*, 373 U.S. 83 (U.S. 1963) wherein this standard was established. For example, prosecution must reveal any agreement with the witness as to giving preferential treatment or not to prosecute him/her in return for testimony on relevant facts.[16]

Better Money presents copies of official documents that have surfaced years after the original case ended, and the guilty plea agreements were signed. Jackson proposes that this

---

[15] US Legal, Inc. "Giglio Information Law and Legal Definition." *Giglio Information Law and Legal Definition | USLegal, Inc.*, 2006, definitions.uslegal.com/g/giglio-information/.
[16] Ibid.

Brady material should have been introduced to the Defendants while the case was before the Court. However, the material and communications were buried or hidden from the Defendants and remained unknown to the Court. It is challenging to prove who concealed these documents and why.

At the core of the federal case was the charge that e-gold® violated 18 USC 1960, Operation of an Unlicensed Money Transmitting Business. The secondary charges were violations of 18 USC 1956, money laundering. However, the Prosecution never advanced any legal theory that supported the 18 USC 1956 money laundering charge. Jackson reasons that the successful money laundering violations were dependent on a fruitful 1960 Prosecution. This fact illustrates how much was riding on the government's allegation of an Unlicensed Money Transmitting Business.

The Federal statute 18 USC 1960 accompanies an earlier State charge, of the same type. Attorneys practicing in this area of federal regulation recognize there are ambiguity and contradictions in the 1960 federal statute. They use a rule of thumb, that, the only way to know if a company is a Money Transmitting Business is to approach the various relevant state regulators. It is the state financial regulators that determine whether the entity violates state law.[17]

Handwritten notes from the State of Florida, uncovered by Jackson, suggest that federal prosecutors clearly understood the importance of this initial state unlicensed money transmitter violation. Jackson suggests that during a phone call, DOJ prosecutors explained to Florida regulators the prominence of Florida's determination if the federal 18 USC 1960 charge was to succeed.

State financial laws vary across America, and the determination of whether a company requires state licensing as a money transmitter is each state's fact-intensive evaluation. In e-gold's case, a legal opinion from e-gold's home state of Florida, on whether the business required a money transmitter license, would have been a cornerstone of evidence in the Defendants' case. The state could have criminally charged the company if Florida required the license and e-gold® not obtained it.

Had the state responded with a legal opinion that Florida statutes did not cover e-gold's business, there would have been no federal violation originating from Florida. Before being indicted, e-gold® and G&SR executives informed Florida regulators that the company would obtain a license in Florida and other jurisdictions if requested by the state.

Evidence recovered by Jackson shows that in early 2007, attorneys working for the State of Florida Office of Financial Regulation had drafted a legal opinion stating that e-gold® did not require a money transmitter license under Chapter 560, Florida Statutes.

---

[17] Jackson, Douglas. "Up through 1996." Received by Carl Mullan, *Up through 1996*, 5 May 2020. 2020.05.05 draft notes pp 1-41 end 1996.docx

Unknown to the Defendants, during the investigation, and before the DOJ Prosecutors filed formal charges, competent Florida legal authorities had examined this question and concluded:

> Based upon the foregoing, the activities of e-gold and G&SR are not subject to regulation through Chapter 560, Florida Statutes. This writer has no knowledge that any other federal or state regulator has held that this activity is within the jurisdiction of their money transmitter code.[18]

During the case, this crucial evidence remained hidden from the Defendants and the Court. Jackson maintains that withholding these material facts was is a clear *Brady* violation, supporting his contention that e-gold® did not receive fair treatment under the law. *Brady* is a constitutional mandate. Had this suppressed legal opinion been available to the Defendants, a substantially more persuasive argument could have been made in the Defendants Motion to Dismiss. For the first time, *Better Money* presents a copy of this draft legal opinion rendered by the Florida Office of Financial Regulation (OFR) and the Florida Department of Financial Services (DFS).

Gold & Silver Reserve Inc., was the contractual operator of the e-gold® system. It's business, servers, and employees resided in Florida. A legal opinion from state regulators would have been critical to the Defendants' case. Additionally, USSS Special Agents instructed Florida officials not to share the draft legal opinion and not to have any contact with Jackson or e-gold®. *Better Money* also presents these private emails and interoffice communications.

Peretti ended up working with evidence obtained by the USSS local office based in Washington, D.C., just blocks from where she worked. Jackson has since requested all related documents from the D.C. Department of Insurance, Securities and Banking (DISB), along with any 2006-2007 interactions with Peretti et al. He has not received anything from the District of Columbia. Nor has he been unable to compel these officials to provide any potential material. Without evidence, Jackson can only speculate on what may have occurred between Peretti and USSS Special Agents in D.C. In a 2020 email, Jackson explained his thoughts on this situation.

I do not know whether Peretti provided false information to the DISB, or applied

---

[18] Oglo, William. "Informal Opinion Regarding Whether the Activities of e-gold, Ltd. and Gold & Silver Reserve, Inc. Are Subject to Regulation by Chapter 560, Florida Statutes Legal File No. 0009-M-6/06." Received by Bob Rosenau, and Mike Ramsden, *Informal Opinion Regarding Whether the Activities of e-gold, Ltd. and Gold & Silver Reserve, Inc. Are Subject to Regulation by Chapter 560, Florida Statutes Legal File No. 0009-M-6/06*, 5 Dec. 2006. OFFICE OF FINANCIAL REGULATION, THROUGH: Peter Fisher, Chief Finance Attorney

pressure to influence their determination, or possibly even bypassed them altogether. All I do know is that years later, in 2016, the DISB was asked to make a determination if DC license was required for another business (that I had designed, developed and financed) with the same business model, institutional arrangements and transaction model as e-gold. In the case of e-gold's successor company they determined that no license was required.[19]

Jackson notes that a competent regulatory authority created Florida's draft legal opinion in the state where the Defendants operated. As evidenced by emails between Florida officials, after initially appearing to view G&SR's business as a money transmitter, the draft legal opinion reversed that initial impression.

There is no question that the excluded materials, unavailable to the Court or the defense, could have played a significant role in the Defendants' determination whether to proceed to trial. Had these documents been available before any discussions of a plea agreement, Florida's draft legal opinion could have allowed the defense to present a much stronger motion to dismiss the 1960 charge.

Because Prosecutors withheld this critical piece of evidence from the Court, e-gold's motion to dismiss failed and received a vigorous denial from the Judge. In 2017, Jackson stated:

> As it was, the failure of the motion, and the emphatic tone of the ruling that denied it, raised the risk that a later attempt to articulate the relevant factual and circumstantial nuances necessary to frame a correct interpretation might not be permitted.
> It was the failure of the motion to dismiss, along with counseling of the defendants— whereby for the first time they were introduced to the perverse realities of the "relevant conduct" doctrine—that directly impelled the defendants to enter into plea negotiations.[20]

What was e-gold

E-gold® was a payment system, unlike any other online concept previously deployed in the world. Its   digital units served as the base money of a foreign currency without nationality and proved to be a viable global currency for Internet transactions. Jackson had created a secure medium of exchange and a store of value designed to be immune from currency debasement.

---

[19]   Jackson, Douglas. "Investigation Request." Received by John Roth, Inspector General, US Dept. of Homeland Security, 1020 Steven Patrick Avenue, 24 Aug. 2017, Indian Harbour Beach, Florida.

[20]   Ibid

Furthermore, e-gold® was unique because of its physical bullion. Gold bars and other precious metals secured every digital ounce. E-gold held its bullion reserves in allocated storage. These vaults were some of the same repositories commonly used by the international gold banks, which comprise the clearing members of the London Bullion Market Association.

e-gold® circulated by digital book-entry transfer and employed a real-time gross settlement (RTGS) protocol. Unlike most RTGS systems, hosted by government central banks, e-gold® transfers enforced a strict debit requirement. All cleared transactions entailed an increment or decrement in the user's e-metal balance. e-gold's governance and transaction models combined a dual imperative that assured the finality of settlement and freedom from default risk. The platform delivered immutable transactions absent of any chargeback risk, even precluding e-gold's management from the ability to subvert operations.

e-gold® required no bank account or credit card, yet account holders could instantly initiate and settle complicated global financial transactions. Account access was browser-based through e-gold's website. The financial inclusion afforded by e-gold® allowed individuals from any social status or economic background to send and receive immutable online payments. Starting in 1996, the platform also transacted in three other e-metals silver, platinum, and palladium. Allocated storage and strict custodial conditions protected the Bullion. All digital e-metals were proven to have been continuously backed, at all times, by a one-hundred percent reserve of precious metal.

Until 2000, e-gold's operating entity, Gold & Silver Reserve, Inc. (G&SR), provided for the issuance of the electronic currency and also executed customers' account-to-account transfer (Spend) instructions. G&SR also would buy and sell the various e-metals from/to customers in exchange for conventional money. In the company's early phase, end-users could directly bail in gold coins for digital e-gold®. Users could also redeem digital units and receive delivery of physical gold. The 2000 restructuring of corporate and institutional arrangements, brought with it multiple refinements. These changes were implemented to ringfence the core entity, responsible for issuance of the money and settlement of Spends, from any exposure to the business of currency exchange and its accompanying risks. Along with implementing the Primary Dealer model, by 2000, the bullion reserves had also migrated from gold coins to good delivery bullion bars in allocated storage.

In 2019 emails, Jackson explained a clear distinction between the pre-2000 e-gold® operation and the restructured companies that managed critical roles after that time. "The first 3 1/2 years were a steep learning curve that set the stage for the restructuring of 2000 (elements of which, such as the fully operational OmniPay site, took until 2001)."[21] Jackson identified the earliest e-gold® production model as "a work in progress that evolved radically

[21]   Jackson, Douglas. "Re: See Attached." Received by Carl Mullan, *Re: See Attached*, 17 Apr. 2019.

over the next four years."[22]

e-gold® began circulating in November 1996. The co-founders voluntarily shut down the operation in 2009.

Co-founders

Regarding e-gold's co-founders, this statement from November 2007 Court documents is accurate.

> They came together to pursue a vision to create an alternative global currency and payment system which they believed would aid society as it moved into the 21st century and evolved into a global economy. While they certainly hoped they would profit from their undertaking, they genuinely believed that this system would create legitimate commercial opportunities for people across the world - particularly those disadvantaged by poor economic conditions in their immediate surroundings - and serve the lawful interests of merchants around the globe.[23]

Dr. Douglas Jackson – Co-founder

Before pioneering online payments and co-founding e-gold®, Douglas Jackson had earned a Medical Degree from Pennsylvania State University's medical school in 1982 and was board-certified in radiation oncology. In 1986 he completed a residency in Radiation Oncology at the National Cancer Institute, Bethesda, Maryland, and was certified by the American Board of Radiology. Douglas L. Jackson, M.D., is a talented medical doctor.[24]

From 1986 through 1992, he served as a Major in the U.S. Army Medical Corps and Chief of Radiation Oncology at the Brooke Army Medical Center (BAMC) located in Fort Sam Houston, Texas. In 1992, he left active duty to be the Medical Director for Radiation Oncology at Holmes Regional Medical Center in Melbourne, Florida. Later, he was a founding partner in Florida Oncology, a group practice providing hospital-based oncology services. I a 2020 email, Dr. Jackson explained the demanding regime he endured during the new medical practice.

> My medical practice as a Radiation Oncologist entailed a 75+ hour work week. My normal day began at 5 am. My routine was to hit the gym when it opened at 5:30,

22 Ibid
23 CASE NUMBER: 07-167-M-01. *UNITED STATES OF AMERICA V. E-GOLD LIMITED, GOLD & SILVER RESERVE, INC., DOUGLAS L. JACKSON, BARRY K. DOWNEY and REID A. JACKSON.* SENTENCING MEMORANDUM OF GOLD & SILVER RESERVE, INC., Nov. 2008.
24 Ibid

work out a bit and shower/shave there as to reach the office by 07:00 to catch up on chart work before patients started arriving. [This was back in the days when there were still medical transcriptionists and it was necessary to review and edit the typed transcripts]. From about 07:30 – 16:00 the day was split between the clinic—seeing new outpatient consults, patients who were in active treatment, plus follow-up visits with previously treated folks—and active treatment planning and management. New inpatient consults were mostly then seen after 17:00 and I would normally head for home between 21:00 and 22:00.

We were a two-man practice so that meant I was on call alternate nights. You wouldn't think there would be a lot of emergency consults[25] or ER visits required with a Radiation Oncology practice but, on the average, we would be called back in about twice per week and end up spending another three hours or so in acute situations.[26]

As a practicing doctor in Melbourne, Florida, his future in medicine held great promise and financial reward. When asked what compelled him to walk away from such a promising career, Jackson confided that he had felt a sense of duty to implement his innovative monetary concepts.[27]

In 1992, Dr. Douglas Jackson, having completed his service obligation, resigned his commission at the rank of Major from the United States Army Medical Corps. It would be several years later before he conceived of an Internet platform able to facilitate the online transfer of value backed by precious metal.

Jackson's new private system could circulate monetary value outside of the banking system by connecting users through the Internet. E-gold® transactions were very different from bank payments. At the e-gold® user's instruction, the platform's software moved precise values (weights) of digital metal from one customer account to another within a closed ledger. During the creation of the e-gold® platform, Jackson took a hands-on approach and was heavily involved in creating the original software code. The company's early development and startup costs, just under $1 million, were funded primarily by Jackson and his close friend, attorney Barry Downey. To continue financing e-gold's rapid growth, Jackson drained his retirement savings and eventually sold his medical practice. When those funds were exhausted, he borrowed, accumulating substantial credit card debt. The Court sentencing memorandum detailed e-gold's start up costs.

---

[25] https://www.ncbi.nlm.nih.gov/pmc/articles/PMC2722059/ gives an overview of the types of emergencies that arise

[26] Jackson, Douglas. "Some Supplemental Material." Received by Carl Mullan, *Some Supplemental Material*, 25 Mar. 2020. attachment

[27] Ibid

[...]during the early operating years, Dr. Jackson liquidated his entire savings account balances, stock portfolio and retirement accounts, sold off all of his other substantial assets and drew heavily on all personal lines of credit and credit cards available to him. Messrs. Downey and Reid Jackson also contributed substantial assets to the Companies.[28]

Douglas revealed the new guidance that led him to create e-gold® in *Barron's* article from April 23, 2001.

I started e-gold as the outgrowth of my private study and interpretation of historical events. It appeared to me that many of the worst real-world calamities, wars, in particular, could be causally traced back to economic dislocations - booms and busts - that in turn could be traced to monetary manipulations. Over time, with discretionary control over monetary policy, such interventions - which were supposed to attenuate destructive excesses of credit cycles - ignited and amplified them instead.[29]

In December 2016, Jackson submitted public comments regarding an OCC [Office of the Comptroller of the Currency] proposal entitled *Exploring Special Purpose National Bank Charters for Fintech Companies*. In that submission, he introduced himself and offered a very brief summary of his pioneering work.

I am Dr. Douglas Jackson, founder of two companies that were the pioneers for two of the industries being contemplated as possible candidate domains for national bank charter. In 1996 I founded e-gold®, which was the first successful privately issued electronic money and direct P2P payment system, described by the Financial Times in 1999 as "the only electronic currency that has achieved critical mass on the web." Then, beginning in 2000, I and the other e-gold® founders launched and then fostered a (second) new global industry – independent businesses competing to provide Currency exchange services between privately issued alternative Currencies and conventional (government-issued) brands of money.
Originally bootstrapped with total capital investment under $4 million, by late 2000 e-gold® was settling a larger volume and value of payments every month than

---

[28] Ibid

[29] White, Jack, and Doug Ramsey. "Making New Money." *Barron's*, 23 Apr. 2001, p. 59, www.barrons.com/magazine. https://www.mail-archive.com/e-gold-list@talk.e-gold.com/msg04170.html

Digicash, Beenz, Flooz and Cybercash's Cybercoin processed *combined and cumulatively*, despite their combined equity investment exceeding $300 million. At its peak in 2006, e-gold® was backed by gold reserves exceeding 3.6 metric tonnes - more than the official gold reserves (then) backing the Canadian Dollar. The system was routinely processing over 75,000 Spends per day settling an annualized payment volume of nearly $3 billion, USD-equivalent.

Along with e-gold Ltd. and Gold & Silver Reserve Inc., I was also a pioneer in another respect. Despite proactively approaching the US government in 2005 seeking regulatory clarity and providing vital assistance to law enforcement agencies around the world in hundreds of investigations from 1999 through 2008, e-gold was singled out by the USSS for criminal indictment in 2007 as an unlicensed money transmitting business.

The government action against e-gold® was a case of first impression. As noted by the prosecutor:

> Digital currencies are on the forefront of international fund transfers. e-gold is the most prominent digital currency out there. It has the attention of the entire digital currency world. That world is a bit of a wild west right now. People are looking for what are the rules and what are the consequences.

The case was resolved by a Plea Agreement that laid out a blueprint for such rules, detailing a novel template for a compliance model consisting of a bespoke hybrid of requirements blending relevant elements of existing regimes for Money Services Businesses and Depository Institutions.

Commenting on her substantial deviation from Federal Sentencing Guidelines (which mandated a "sentence between 108 and 135 months") the presiding judge, having already noted "no doubt that Dr. Jackson has respect for law" and that "the intent was not there to engage in illegal conduct", stated in her sentencing memorandum:

> Now that legal issues are resolved, he [Douglas Jackson] has committed e-gold and G&SR to a vigorous compliance and oversight program which could only succeed if he were there to head the companies. Since there is no reason to shut down e-gold and G&SR, and every reason to have them come into legal compliance, a sentence of incarceration for Dr. Jackson would be counterproductive.

An apparently unanticipated side effect of the guilty plea, however, despite explicit

31

statements by DOJ prosecutors denying intent to shut down the business, was that it effectively disqualified the companies for the licenses required by state laws.

In 2009, due to inability to obtain required licenses, e-gold suspended the ability for customers to initiate Spends. e-gold customers received compensation for their e-gold holdings via a Value Access Plan (VAP), initiated by the companies, which was completed in 2013. VAP claimants received from two to five times the value that had been held in their accounts (at time of last access) on a USD cost basis.

Beginning in 2010, I and my team at Fulcrum IP Corporation ("Fulcrum") have developed a next generation system that merges the monetary and transactional principles of e-gold with unprecedentedly sophisticated AML and other compliance elements. Informed by nearly two decades continuous immersion as industry pioneer, refined by insightful analysis of developments in central banking and advances involving central counterparty services, the system that has been developed affords significant low risk, fee-based revenue opportunities for financial institutions that matriculate to the system.[30]

What did this ordeal cost Dr. Jackson?

At the time G&SR was launched, Dr. Jackson was an affluent physician. He financed the project's initial design and development stages with income that he earned from his medical practice. When the business' financial demands quickly outstripped revenue from his work, Dr. Jackson began liquidating his assets to pay the bills. At his November 2008 sentencing hearing, Jackson's Court-appointed attorney, Joshua Berman of Sonnenschein Nath & Rosenthal LLP, explained some of Jackson's financial burdens.

> Your Honor, Dr. Jackson did not get rich from this offense. He was, quite the contrary, he put in   approximately three quarters of a million dollars every penny between his wife and the family had from 401Ks, from savings, from his days of military service, from his operation in private practice as an oncologist. He put all of this money into this business because he believed in the vision and believed it would be an alternative from the global currency systems.

> His credit card debt currently is in the hundreds of thousand of dollars. He has an outstanding loan of over I believe a hundred thousand dollars to the corporate entities. This is a man who did not profit from this enterprise. To the contrary, he is

[30] Jackson, Douglas. "Exploring Special Purpose National Bank Charters for Fintech Companies." *Office of the Comptroller of the Currency*, Dec. 2016, occ.gov/. public comments regarding an OCC proposal entitled Exploring Special Purpose National Bank Charters for Fintech Companies.

in great and probably life time debt because of his efforts to make this work.[31]

Barry K. Downey – Co-founder

The other e-gold® co-founder, alongside Jackson, was Barry K. Downey, a prominent and respected lawyer and one of the founding partners in the Maryland based law firm Smith & Downey P.A. He practices employee benefits law in Maryland and the District of Columbia. Downey was admitted to practice before the Supreme Court of the United States and has co-authored two books on deferred compensation.[32]

Downey's resided in Maryland, and his work for e-gold was always an avocation as opposed to a profession. He did not receive a salary, and he did not take draws. Throughout e-gold's lifetime, Downey loaned the company money out of his 401-K account from his law firm.[33]

Cypherpunks & DigiCash

In a 2019 email, Jackson shared some of his thoughts on the evolution of electronic currency in the early 1990s.

> When I[Jackson] was organizing and developing e-gold, many people (pundits mostly) had fallen for the Cypherpunk conceit at the time that anonymous digital cash was the future of money and payments. [For example, David Chaum on the cover of US News and Foreign Report circa 1995 or thereabouts and, I think, some financial publications including an early Wired article that mentioned his name over 50 times].[34] DigiCash was the grand cause of the Cypherpunks.[35]

Around 1982, a brilliant young man named David Chaum at the University of California, Berkeley, wrote a notable six-page paper entitled "Blind signatures for untraceable payments."[36] The world credits Chaum with the design of Blind Signature

31 Docket No. CR 07-109. *UNITED STATES OF AMERICA vs. E-GOLD LTD, GOLD & SILVER RESERVE LTD, DOUGLAS L. JACKSON, BARRY K. DOWNEY, REID A. JACKSON.* TRANSCRIPT OF SENTENCE BEFORE THE HONORABLE ROSEMARY M. COLLYER UNITED STATES DISTRICT JUDGE, 20 Nov. 2008.

32 CASE NUMBER: 07-167-M-01. *UNITED STATES OF AMERICA V. E-GOLD LIMITED, GOLD & SILVER RESERVE, INC., DOUGLAS L. JACKSON, BARRY K. DOWNEY and REID A. JACKSON.* SENTENCING MEMORANDUM OF GOLD & SILVER RESERVE, INC., Nov. 2008.

33 Ibid

34 Levy, Steven. "E-Money (That's What I Want)." *Wired*, Conde Nast, 23 Apr. 2018, www.wired.com/1994/12/emoney/.

35 Jackson, Douglas. "Some Prelim Observations and Comments - up to p. 54." Received by Carl Mullan, *Some Prelim Observations and Comments - up to p. 54*, 1 May 2019. email attachment: 2019.04.30 observations and comments.docx

36 Chaum, David. "Blind Signatures for Untraceable Payments." *Univ. of Houston*, Department of Computer Science University of California Santa Barbara, CA, 1982,

Technology that uses public and private keys for online transfers. These cryptographic protocols were later folded into Chaum's 1989 company DigiCash, Inc. He fully implemented the technology in 1990, and many people saw DigiCash as a new kind of untraceable electronic money; or digital cash. The company's main product was a digital cash platform called eCash, and the electronic cash circulating over the Internet was known as CyberBucks. However, DigiCash was developed several years before the Internet's ecommerce revolution. While a few individuals calling themselves Cypherpunks briefly adopted it, DigiCash was never widely accepted by the public. DigiCash did not become "the future of money and payments," and in 1998, the company filed for Chapter 11 bankruptcy.[37] The downfall of DigiCash had been predicted by Jackson a year earlier.[38] In 2019 emails, Jackson shared this additional insight regarding DigiCash and Cypherpunks.

> The gist of this is that the emergence of e-gold pushed Cypherpunk pretensions of being the future of money and payments into a well-deserved decade of obscurity. Digicash failed shortly after e-gold came on the scene. Then, as long as e-gold was operational, despite incessant development and attempted promotion of new cypherpunk schemes/protocols/systems, none of them attracted any public interest or usage.[39]
>
> In 1997, I asserted that e-cash had become and was already obsolete, even before it had gained any actual traction. [A senior officer of Mark Twain Bank, where G&SR had its first foreign currency accounts, told me some years later there had only been 2 Digicash transactions that seemed to have an actual commercial purpose, both to pay for registration for the 1997 or 1998 Financial Cryptography Conference in Anguilla]. Part of the Digicash raison d'etre was a secure (encrypted) communication channel, which required installation and operation of a client program (the Digicash wallet). But, in 1996, SSL-enabled web browsers had come on the scene, such that anyone could have a secure online client-server channel with user-friendly client software (a web browser) continuously improved/updated by large companies with deep pockets, unlike the ragtag elitist approach of the cypeherpunks. [Their client program (the Digicash wallet) was rickety and required a lot of technical knowledge to get it running and keep it running. It would break whenever an operating system might update; Windows contempt was part of the schtick of true believers; if you didn't use Unix or its open source Debian variant you were an unworthy poser] –

---

sceweb.sce.uhcl.edu/yang/teaching/csci5234WebSecurityFall2011/Chaum-blind-signatures.PDF.

[37] Michael Mandel, *Money Ain't What It Used To Be*, Bus. WK., Jan. 9, 2006, at 74.

[38] Jackson, Douglas. "Some Prelim Observations and Comments - up to p. 54." Received by Carl Mullan, *Some Prelim Observations and Comments - up to p. 54*, 1 May 2019. email attachment: 2019.04.30 observations and comments.docx

[39] Ibid

similar to how laborious it was to install a Bitcoin wallet/node   before services popped up everywhere where you could simply log into a website of someone claiming to hold the Bitcoin for you. In the Digicash days, had there been customers and customer service, the response to requests for assistance would have likely been "go ask a smart person."[40]

Jackson wrote about his past thoughts regarding the origins of e-gold® as it related to the Cypherpunks.

> "Unlike the Cypherpunks then and since, I was struck by actual problems and designed e-gold to address them. [For them worrying about "untrusted third parties" as per game theory, instead of actual problems of an economic nature, was the prime directive. They also had contempt for governments in general and envisioned a more righteous world where smart people (they) made the rules].[41]
> This[e-gold] was unlike Cypherpunk stuff then and since which has always started with some sort of clever tech gimmickry where they then backfill to find a rationale for why it is needed. This especially evident in Craig Wright and Dave Kleiman's (aka Satoshi Nakamoto) original Bitcoin paper. Its only rationale was: a) new solution to the double-spending problem (a digital cash problem, not a real world problem) and some passing reference to payment repudiation (as if payment repudiation was a problem stemming from deficient tech, instead of being something purposely engineered in because of the credit nature of payment systems and the risk of default.[42]

In 2020, David Chaum remains one of the world's most gifted minds and still works in this field.

1996

In 1996, Jackson formed Gold & Silver Reserve, Inc. (G&SR) to implement his vision. Gold & Silver Reserve, Inc. (G&SR) is a domestic Delaware Corporation formed on January 24, 1996. Gold & Silver Reserve, Inc. was registered as a Foreign Profit Corporation in the State of Florida on July 12, 1999. File number:F99000003641. The principal address was: 175 East NASA Blvd. Melbourne, FL 32901. This building housed the primary office

[40]   Ibid
[41]   Ibid
[42]   Ibid

location in Florida. The state registration listed the following corporate officers.

- Douglas Jackson, President & Dir.
- Barry Downey, Secretary, Executive VP
- Charles Evans, Executive VP

The e-gold® platform was developed, deployed, and administered by G&SR. Until 2001, G&SR also maintained the network. Jackson designed G&SR with the belief that gold and silver were superior to debt instruments (such as government bonds) as the value foundation underlying money. This company was not a bank nor a licensed financial institution.

G&SR initially engaged software engineer Alex Soya, of Logan Engineering, to develop some of Jackson's envisioned programming that would control the e-gold® network. Per Jackson's requirements, Soya built the user interface and database platform that enabled account-to-account transfers within the closed e-gold® system. While managing his medical practice, Jackson devoted his free time to constructing e-gold®.[43]

> In 1996, from the time Alex Soya suggested I do some of the coding of the backend modules for transaction processing, my schedule became insane. I was still practicing medicine full time but needed to find time to accomplish the needed programming plus the myriad other tasks to launch and then singlehandedly operate the e-gold business.[44]

Because of the project's limited finances, Jackson helped code the back-end functions, including automated processing (Spends), to execute all customer orders. Dr. Jackson recalled the long hours spent launching e-gold.

> From summer 1996 through the end of 1997, I spent, on the average, an additional 35 hours per week working on e-gold. As it became evident that it would be expedient for me to do some of the coding, I bought a large library-type table and placed it in a special room of the dream home we had purchased in 1995, fondly referred to as 'River House.' River House had originally been built in 1916 as a sort of boathouse extending some 15-20 feet over the Eau Gallie River near Melbourne Florida. I liked to describe the portion that extended over the water as surrounded on four sides by water, counting the boat house dockage underneath.

---

[43] CASE NUMBER: 07-167-M-01. *UNITED STATES OF AMERICA V. E-GOLD LIMITED, GOLD & SILVER RESERVE, INC., DOUGLAS L. JACKSON, BARRY K. DOWNEY and REID A. JACKSON.* SENTENCING MEMORANDUM OF GOLD & SILVER RESERVE, INC., Nov. 2008.

[44] Ibid

Since I had no training or experience developing software, on the advice of the professional software engineer developing the CGI (Common Gateway Interface) aspects, I elected to use Borland's Delphi product. Delphi was a rapid application development tool for Windows that was much easier to work with than languages such as C++.

My typical routine for software development efforts on weekdays would begin around 22:30 – 23:00 after the kids were in bed. I would try to wrap up by about 02:00 but there were occasional weekend mornings when I would note to my dismay that dawn was imminent – a time we used to refer to as BMNT (Begin Morning Nautical Twilight) back in my Army days.

The way my mind works in relation to problem solving relies heavily on working things out while asleep and realizing solutions in the morning. One way I would capitalize on this was to make use of my short commute to work, being sure to bring along my dictation device to capture insights while they were still fresh. I stopped listening to music to such an extent that I was completely out of touch with new music from 1996 – 2000.[45]

E-gold completed its first online transactions in November 1996. In addition to e-gold® (gold-backed), G&SR also offered digital e-silver, e-platinum, and e-palladium. The network labeled its process of exchanging conventional (government-issued) currencies for digital e-metal units as an "InExchange." The movement of digital e-metal units back into fiat currency was called an "OutExchange."

Between 1996 and 1999, the system accepted direct transfers of value—payments of fiat money or bailments of physical precious metal—from customers. All of these funding payments or bailments were sent directly to G&SR through its Melbourne, Florida office. G&SR was also responsible for issuing new digital e-gold® units, a process known as "digital minting." G&SR responsibilities included:

- Selling e-gold® to customers (InExchange)
- Buying e-gold® from customers (OutExchange)
- Bailment (customers depositing bullion in exchange for digital units)
- Redemption (customers could redeem digital units for physical metal)

During those initial years, the e-gold® concept attracted only a few active customers, and the business operated at a loss. However, Jackson and his team never slowed their

[45] Ibid

forward progress and continued working feverishly to enhance the company's position.

> At the time I still attended church regularly but I recall becoming completely oblivious to what was being said as ideas would come to me during Sunday morning services. Often I would fail to remember to bring along paper to jot notes on and would end up writing in every spare margin of the paper bulletins that were handed out or, once that was full, ripping open the little offering envelopes to take advantage of the blank paper inside.[46]

After the business launched, G&SR subcontracted much of the daily administration work to Jackson Trading Company Inc, a Florida Corporation owned and operated by Dr. Douglas Jackson. The two companies had a current business arrangement until December 31, 2000.[47]

In January 2000, management devolved the core e-gold® roles of Issuance and Settlement to e-gold Ltd., a new Nevis W.I. Company. This new company served as the General Contractor responsible for the performance of the e-gold® Account User Agreement.   e-gold Ltd.'s computer servers remained in co-location facilities in Florida.

Mechanics of e-gold®

E-gold® mobilized the value of gold as money for Internet payments. As a financial tool, e-gold® provided all people of the world, particularly those in impoverished areas underserved by traditional financial services, a convenient and secure way to transfer value, down the block or across the globe. The co-founders did not design e-gold® as a replacement for national currencies or conventional financial tools. The G&SR platform functioned alongside fiat money to complement rather than compete.

E-gold's system for instantaneous account-to-account transaction settlement was analogous to the realtime gross settlement (RTGS) systems offered by central banks, such as Fedwire in the United States.

However, unlike other renowned RTGS systems, e-gold® was directly available to the public, with no obligatory financial intermediary (bank) whose involvement added only additional cost and delay. E-gold's Internet transactions outperformed bank payments at every level. This innovative benefit was due to an absence of credit risk in the e-gold® system. The platform was not a bank and did not extend credit.[48]

---

[46] Ibid

[47] (Filed December 29, 2000, and effective December 31, 2000)

[48] CASE NUMBER: 07-167-M-01. *UNITED STATES OF AMERICA V. E-GOLD LIMITED, GOLD & SILVER RESERVE, INC., DOUGLAS L. JACKSON, BARRY K. DOWNEY and REID A. JACKSON.* SENTENCING MEMORANDUM OF GOLD & SILVER RESERVE, INC., Nov. 2008.

The company trademarked e-gold® as Better Money,™ and users compared e-gold® transactions to bank payments such as credit cards. This challenge became a successful marketing tool for the company. A quick comparison with bank cards, shown on the website, proved e-gold® to be safer, cheaper, and free of chargebacks. The e-gold® system separated online customer transactions from an assortment of expensive issues that plagued modern banking. Additionally, customer value, held in an e-gold® account, was protected against inflation, currency devaluation, and other deep-rooted fiat currency risks.

A highly beneficial feature of e-gold® was the ability of any customer to operate more than one account. Allowing users to open multiple online accounts instantly was a benefit that no bank could match.

e-gold® afforded these features to all users at every level of society. Users were not required to provide any previous bank account, credit card, or credit rating. Additionally, all e-gold® accounts were the same. Businesses receiving e-gold® payments did not need an expensive or exclusive merchant account. An individual user's e-gold® account was identical to a large merchant's account.

Jackson believed that e-gold Ltd.'s business did not meet the definition of a money transmitter. In a 2019 email, Jackson shared some additional information on this position.

> The canonical act of a money transmitter was receiving money payments (especially cash) from customers and paying out money (again typically cash) to someone else. Once we had accomplished the restructuring, e-gold Ltd. did not (and had no capability of—lacking so much as a bank account, or employees, or a physical office—receive or make any money payments (or transfers of value in any form) from/to customers or anyone else. Even Primary Dealers, when they delivered bullion to the repository, were bailing it into the Trust holdings.[49]

Jackson also saw e-gold's business as being quite different from a bank in terms of the necessity of confirming customer identity. Payments through the banking system—credit card payments in particular (but also ACH transfers) —are based on credit. When receiving a payment, the bank treats the customer as if it has borrowed the money. In the event of payer default, with such credit-riddled payments, the bank will either claw back the money from the recipient or go after the payer. In either case, it had a strong business requirement to verify both identities to facilitate its ability to avoid absorbing losses due to payer non-performance.

In contrast, with e-gold's strict debit rule, a customer couldn't fail to meet obligations

---

49   Jackson, Douglas. "Some Prelim Observations and Comments - up to p. 54." Received by Carl Mullan, *Some Prelim Observations and Comments - up to p. 54*, 1 May 2019. email attachment: 2019.04.30 observations and comments.docx

and cause a default that might lead to either the recipient or e-gold Ltd. itself suffering a loss. Therefore, in the early years, Jackson's view on a customer providing inaccurate identity or contact information was that such a customer was only hurting themselves. He based this reasoning on the fact that people, even tricky and dishonest people, sometimes lose track of passwords or other authentication tokens required for account access. The protocol e-gold® had at the time to recover account access entailed customer service reaching out to the customer using the identity and contact information supplied. The would-be anonymous customer would be out of luck if they submitted false documents.

Other Differences

There were no fees charged for opening an e-gold® account, and there was no customer obligation to transact future business. There were no monthly or yearly account fees. G&SR only charged fees for transactions and precious metal storage. Unlike a bank, e-gold® users had to transact some business before accruing a fee.

An e-gold® transaction moving from one account to another, within the closed digital ledger, was not labeled a "Payment." An existing e-gold® balance transferred, per the payer's instructions, was a "Spend." Users were "spending" an amount of digital metal by weight to another user's account. Strong non-repudiation (finality of settlement) and a strict debit rule concluded all transactions. The e-gold® terms stipulated that all "Spends" were final. Unlike credit cards, there was no possibility of reversing an e-gold® transaction. With no charge-back risk, merchants were happy to accept the payments.

G&SR highlighted the distinction between "Spends" and traditional payments by contrasting the differences. E-gold measured transactions denominated by weight in precious metal and banks tallied payments in fiat currency. E-gold® metal balances were accounted for by the metal's weight, which was precise to 0.000001 oz, normalized to 100% purity. E-gold® also offered the capability of using a numeraire for specifying a Spend amount that differed from the native units of the settlement currency.

For example, it was possible to Spend $10 worth of e-gold®. At the time of the transaction, a calculation would automatically take place determining the actual metal weight using a table of reference exchange rates maintained by the company. The business supervised these rates and updated them every few minutes during the day and every few hours at night. The Spend preview screen displayed the reference exchange rate and final calculated transaction. A German user spending 10 Euros to an American user was, in reality, spending a small weight of gold, not an amount of € or $. Spending orders exemplified fungibility. A user did not order "pay two silver eagles to Account___" or "pay $15 worth of silver eagles to Account___." An order might instead specify "pay 2.8571 oz of silver to Account___" or "pay $15 worth of silver to Account__."

40

The platform measured quantities of metal in decimal fractions of either (troy) ounces or grams. The customer's transactional unit was discretionary and priced transactions using whatever unit of account the parties mutually agreed. If fiat amounts priced e-gold® goods or services, such as the U.S. dollar, G&SR's posted exchange rates calculated the precise weight of metal. This feature was extremely efficient and convenient for all users worldwide. Organized using a transaction model, G&SR's computerized book-entry system afforded practically unlimited divisibility. While e-gold's display truncated transaction amounts to 0.0001 oz, the actual quantities stored in database tables were accurate to fifteen decimals.

The only information required to initiate an e-gold® Spend was the receiver's account number. Transactions incurred a small fee paid in e-metal at the time of the Spend.

E-gold® transactions exposed little identifying information about the sender or receiver. The only possible release of user information occurred during a Spend when the preview showed the payer the designated recipient's display name. Unlike credit cards, no valuable information was ever at risk of being stolen during or after an e-gold® Spend. Not requiring personal or financial information to complete transactions proved to be beneficial for e-gold® users. Archive.org has the complete capture of the very earliest e-gold site located at https://web.archive.org/web/19980627133859/http://www.e-gold.com/.

Unlike credit card transactions, that pull funds from the cardholder account balance, e-gold® users "pushed" transaction value to the recipient's account. The mechanics of an e-gold® transfer required the sender to engage the system at the time of the transaction, granting instant approval for the outgoing e-metal value.

If the account holder was not present and online at the time of a Spend, then the value could not be "pushed" or "pulled" out of the account. E-gold® accounts could not make automatic monthly payments. All order details were instantly presented for review and required the user to manually approve the final transaction.

G&SR was required to purchase all precious metal before minting[issuing] new digital units. G&SR bought the vast majority of the gold bullion (and silver, platinum, palladium) and bailed it into the system minting new digital units of e-metal. G&SR sought to maintain a large enough balance of digital units in its company trading account to enable the timely fulfillment of all customer orders. The company always purchased and stored precious metal before issuing its e-metal digital representation.

The e-gold Account User Agreement specifies that:
"All e-metal in circulation shall be backed 100% at all times with unencumbered metal in allocated storage".
Examiner is a real-time report of Issuer's compliance with this definitive provision.

e-gold® Examiner Page header July 1, 2004[50]

Transparency

Jackson designed the e-gold® platform for maximum transparency. From December 1996, the operating system's total real-time precious metal account balances were visible on a website page entitled Examiner.

Examiner showed the details of an automated query that retrieved live data from internal transaction tables and inventory records. The page displayed three account tables:

- Total quantity (weight) of metal in electronic circulation
- Total reserves (fine) weight of physical metal serving as the digital units' backing
- An exact number of pieces of the various metal types comprising reserve

This page offered an unprecedented real-time indicator of e-metals in circulation (liabilities) and a detailed real-time inventory of the underlying precious metal assets backing the digital units. The following image shows an Examiner E-metal Balance Sheet from July 1, 2004.[51]

(data current as of: 7/1/04 9:06:25 PM ET)

e-metal Balance Sheet							
The e-gold Bullion Reserve Special Purpose Trust (Assets)			e-metal in Circulation (Liabilities)				
Metal	Fine Troy Ounces	Fine Grams	e-metal	Xxx		xxG	
Gold	55,460.98	1,725,029.30	e-gold	XAU	55,459.21	AUG	1,724,974.32
Silver	123,353.08	3,836,709.66	e-silver	XAG	123,327.39	AGG	3,835,910.47
Platinum	400.00	12,441.39	e-platinum	XPT	396.99	PTG	12,347.86
Palladium	396.47	12,331.69	e-palladium	XPD	394.09	PDG	12,257.55

Examiner E-metal Balance Sheet from July 1, 2004.[52]

---

[50] "Gold Examiner." Edited by Douglas Jackson, *e-gold Examiner*, 1 July 2004, web.archive.org/web/20040702013712fw_/http://www.e-gold.com/examiner.html.

[51] Ibid

[52] Ibid

Examiner was a tool described as G&SR's real-time public audit utility. Any visitor could drill down on the identifying details of the bullion reserves showing factual information for each bar, including vault location, serial number, refiner, purity, and fine weight. These calculations provided the total quantity of e-metal in electronic circulation at all times (all customer accounts combined) vs. total physical reserves held by G&SR. "Real-time" indicated that once any user pressed the 'Examine' button, CGI automatically queried the e-metal transaction database as well as current inventory records. The following text is a 2001 description from the e-gold® Examiner Page.

> Try this: Bring up the Examiner screen. Print it out. Enter a redemption order [Seeing and handling physical precious metal is a worthwhile experience. You gain a visceral sense of why people spontaneously adopted the use of gold and silver as money. If you decide not to retain it in your physical possession you can readily bail it back into the Reserve]. Bring up Examiner again. You will see that the inventory has already been updated reflecting your order. When your shipment of metal arrives by registered mail, note the date it was shipped. Figure out how incredibly difficult it would be to fake that sequence.[53]

Never before had any financial company presented such up-to-date and accurate transparency. Additionally, G&SR owned all physical metal outright, free of liens, before it appeared in the Examiner reserves list. The e-gold® website also hosted a real-time statistical reports (Stats) page that displayed the total number and value of all transactions over the previous 24 hours. In 2001, the e-gold website presented the following statement about the transparent real-time metal records available to the public. "We are proud of Examiner and challenge all other issuers of payment media to develop mechanisms affording similar transparency."[54]

E-gold's highly divisible precise digital transactions circumvented some old issues of using physical metals. The e-gold® computerized book-entry system allowed transactions as small as one ten-thousandth of a gram. Account-holders were able to Spend e-gold® in amounts more modest than a penny, and the fees charged were meager. Through this feature, e-gold® became the world's only successful micropayment system of its time. The company's published payment statistics showed hundreds of thousands of micro-transactions

53 Jackson, Douglas. "e-gold Is...." Wayback Machine, e-gold.com, 7 Feb. 2003, web.archive.org/web/20030207053358/http://www.e-gold.com/unsecure/qanda.html.
54 Jackson, Douglas. "e-gold Homepage." *e-gold Home Page*, Gold & Silver Reserve, Inc., 27 June 1998, web.archive.org/web/19980627133859/http://www.e-gold.com:80/.

through the platform's API. Unlike other attempts at online micropayments, e-gold® afforded a convenience that encouraged retail consumer use.

1997

e-gold® was the first commercial system to attract and serve a global customer base successfully. During 1997, G&SR transacted InExchanges and OutExchanges using various national currencies, including USD, CAD, AUD, GBP, DEM, CHF, JPY, and FFR. Customers wired federal money to G&SR accounts at various bank branches around the world. These deposit options included AmSouth, Hong Kong Bank of Canada, Commerzbank AG, Midland Bank plc, and Hong Kong Bank of Australia.

In 1997, e-gold® began receiving favorable press coverage. One of these articles was published on January 31, 1997, in Grant's Interest Rate Observer.[55] Grant's publication is an independent and contrary-minded journal of the financial markets founded by James Grant in 1983. The January article offered some well deserved positive press coverage on e-gold's new system.

Grant detailed how e-gold's features had "solved the divisibility problems: Its computer easily translates dollar values into metallic weights, and back again." The article also discussed some e-gold® issues stating, "but, of course, it[e-gold] has not solved the confidence problem."[56]

This new article illustrated the momentous task of expanding this new digital gold business and the many obstacles ahead for the co-founders. In 1997, the successful adoption of any private Internet "money" system was a tremendous challenge. While e-gold® met this challenge head-on, the added job of integrating digital gold within the framework of existing financial institutions was profoundly difficult. In January 1997, there were just 31 e-gold® accounts, and the e-gold® Examiner reported $160,000 worth of precious metal.

During a 2018 email interview for the book *A History of Digital Currency in the United States: New Technology in an Unregulated Market*[57], Jackson discussed some of these early challenges.

> For the first year or so of operations we faced mostly suspicion and cynicism. We wanted to embody robust good business assurances such as third-party auditing by a high profile accounting firm – but they wouldn't even return our calls. We wanted to

[55] Grant's Interest Rate Observer. "Bullish on Gold." *Grant's Interest Rate Observer*, vol. 15, no. 2, 31 Jan. 1997, pp. 10–11.

[56] Ibid

[57] Mullan, Philip Carl. *A History of Digital Currency in the United States: New Technology in an Unregulated* Market . Palgrave Macmillan, 2016.

establish direct relationships with larger wholesale providers for specie acquisition and storage, but they were disinterested.[58]

◆

Bulky Bullion

To store the growing physical volume of metal, during those initial years of operation, Jackson opened safe deposit boxes with several banks around Melbourne, Florida. Each secure storage box was just a few minutes from the e-gold® offices located at 175 East NASA Blvd.[59] Jackson explained:

> Things became more challenging after e-gold launched as I would need to fulfill exchange orders, take delivery of precious metal shipments and respond to customer service requests. By late 1997 I realized my average sleep had dropped to three and a half hours per night and my weight had dropped from around 180 lbs. into the low 160s.
> By the summer of 1997 it was no longer possible to get by without an office and I leased office space from Huntington Bank (location later acquired by and rebranded as Bank of America) a few blocks away from my hospital-based practice. I recall the anxiety I would feel trying to find time to slip away for a few minutes from the hospital to the e-gold office. There was always concern that I would miss post office or bank operating hours that could lead to delay in fulfilling exchange, bailment or redemption orders. I was also worried the software would hang or the server might crash. A downside of having used Delphi was that some of its Visual Component Library (VCL) components such as drop-down lists had serious 'memory leaks' that would require periodic reboots of the web server(s) to avoid them locking up due to running out of memory."[60]

Jackson later acknowledged that his original method of securing customer bullion was not a viable long-term solution. Jackson also revealed that he was somewhat unfamiliar with the infrastructure arrangements that existed for gold banks and central banks. However, the local convenient bank box option had been helpful during the company's early years. Additionally, he confided that due to e-gold's innovative new digital e-metal concept, the

---

[58] Ibid

[59] The e-gold office location from 1997 until 2013 (after VAP was completed).

[60] Jackson, Douglas. "Some Supplemental Material." Received by Carl Mullan, *Some Supplemental Material*, 25 Mar. 2020.

business had significant difficulties in forming relationships with standard financial institutions. With a growing bullion inventory, by 1998, e-gold® was faced with a severe depository overload. As e-gold's metal reserves grew, a physical audit of the bullion became increasingly difficult. Jackson explained this situation.

> Our accountant, initially Dale Cox, later Peggy Hill, would periodically (probably once in 1997, once in 1998 – not sure) personally oversee an accounting of the physical reserves. This was a matter of counting and inspecting each bullion coin or other item. The first time we did this, it entailed driving around town, getting the boxes and going though contents in the bank's vault area for as long as it took. The second time, the accountant didn't want to traipse around town and I instead brought everything to the office to count.[61]

Jackson further described this issue:

> The other problem was simply bulk, especially as we also began to accumulate 100oz silver bars and, worse yet, bags of "junk silver" – pre-1965 90% silver US coins that came in bags each containing $1000 face which worked out to a fine content of 715 oz. troy per bag. In 1997 or early 1998 I acquired a safe. It weighed about 2500 lbs – which meant that we had to have a representative of the elevator company present when it was first delivered, and when we moved from 2nd floor to third floor, and when we ultimately got rid of it when we were closing that portion of the office. It was configured with an even more secure (TR 30 – if I recall correctly), but smaller, safe welded inside the larger outer safe.[62]

Mocatta Delivery Orders (MDOs)

Jackson was familiar with Mocatta Delivery Orders (MDOs) long before the launch of e-gold®. MDOs were certificates of title to good delivery gold bars, located in allocated Zurich storage, issued by a reputable third party. Since taking delivery of large amounts of physical metal entailed considerable risk and created storage issues, Jackson recognized the Mocatta delivery system as an excellent alternative.[63]

Using MDOs, the metal buyer would receive a document (certificate) identifying the new owner and proving title to the bullion. The MDO owner could hold a certificate titled to serially-numbered gold bars. The owner could choose a storage location for their bullion in

---

[61] Jackson, Douglas. "e-gold Fiduciary Safeguards." Received by Carl Mullan, *e-gold Fiduciary Safeguards*, July 2019.
[62] Ibid
[63] The good delivery silver bars represented by silver MDOs were held in Basel.

Zurich, Switzerland, or Wilmington, Delaware. The depository institution countersigned the certificates as proof of its receipt. Lloyds of London fully insured the stored bullion. Jackson explained his thoughts on MDOs.

> For a period of time prior to the 2000 restructuring and the elimination of direct customer Bailment and Redemption, though the bulk of reserves were in the form of MDOs, we did need to maintain the ability to ship out Redemption orders. So we kept bullion coins and silver bars at the office. The gold and platinum coins, palladium bars and the MDO certs were in the safe within a safe. The bigger problem was the many 100 oz silver bars and the bags of junk silver – several tons worth. We at one point had them stacked near the walls closest to the stairwell, figuring those walls were highest load bearing. We did not want to come in some morning and discover we had collapsed the floor and dropped our safe and the silver into the bank directly below us.[64]

The delivery order (MDO) held by the buyer is a certificate issued by the Mocatta Metals Group, one of the world's most respected trading groups with offices in New York, London, and Hong Kong. The certificate could be sold, assigned, or used as collateral. The delivery order certificate is itself a non-negotiable instrument, protecting its owner against loss or theft. In November 1999, the e-gold® website explained it this way.

What is a Mocatta Delivery Order (MDO)?
When you view the e-gold Examiner you will see that a large proportion of e-metal reserves are held in the form of MDOs issued by ScotiaMocatta. Each MDO is a non-negotiable warehouse receipt signifying title to a particular bar held in allocated storage by a third party custodian. The metal is insured by Lloyds of London.[65]

The e-gold® changeover from locally held physical metal (bulky bullion) to MDOs began in March 1997. By December 1998,[66] less than 30% of the gold reserves were in the form of non-standard items such as bullion coins, and over 70% was held as MDOs. By October 1999, the e-gold® examiner page revealed that MDOs comprised over 90% of the gold bullion reserves.[67] An e-gold® web page from October 9th, 1999,[68] even displayed and

---

[64]   Ibid

[65]   Jackson, Douglas. "Gold MDOs." *e-gold Mocatta Delivery Orders* , e-gold.com, 3 Nov. 1999, web.archive.org/web/19991103000759/http://www.e-gold.com/mdo.html.

[66]   Jackson, Douglas. "e-gold Examiner." *e-gold Examiner*, e-gold.com, 6 Dec. 1998, web.archive.org/web/19981206163732fw_/http://www.e-gold.com:80/examiner.html.

[67]   Jackson, Douglas. "e-gold Examiner." *e-gold Examiner*, e-gold.com, 8 Oct. 1999,

image of MDO certificates held by the company. The following image is picture of e-gold's MDOs representing gold bullion.

E-gold website image from 10.9.99 shows the stack of gold MDOs.[69]

Ernst & Young

Throughout years of operation, particularly the early ones, e-gold's co-founders continually attempted to hire and employ the largest most well known "big six" accounting

web.archive.org/web/19991012214957fw_/http://e-gold.com:80/examiner.html.
68   Jackson, Douglas. "e-gold Mocatta Delivery Orders ." *e-gold MDOs*, e-gold.com, 9 Oct. 1999,
       web.archive.org/web/19991009043145fw_/http://www.e-gold.com:80/mdo.html.
69   Ibid

firms. In April 1997, an archived email from Downey to Jackson evidenced at least one of these big six proposals.

> Date: Sat, 26 Apr 1997
> Doug:
> Thanks for continuing to respond to the questions from Potential customers. I will make a concerted effort to obtain low cost but comprehensive bonding coverage next week. Also, I will try to obtain big 6 accounting auditors for e-gold next week. I will let you know as soon as I have willing parties.
> Barry[70]

A few days later, on the 28th, Downey faxed Jackson, a document entitled "Proposal for Ernst & Young to Monitor and Report Fidelity of the Gold & Silver Reserve." Downey sent the solicitation to Mr. Greg Repas, a Senior Manager at Ernst & Young. The following text is a majority of the content from that proposal and details showing the company's attempt to hire the well-known accounting firm.

Background

Gold & Silver Reserve, Inc. administers e-gold; a monetary (payments) system which enables individuals and businesses to use gold (and other precious metals) as money. An e-gold balance is title to a precise weight of metal in the custody of G&SR. Proprietary solutions to divisibility and conversion (between weight and other monetary units of account) impediments enable automated execution of payment orders. Payment is processed as a book entry transaction - the metal stays put but its ownership changes. Customers access the system and conduct transactions via the World Wide Web. SSL (secure socket layer) technology assures privacy and security. A fundamental requirement of the system is custodial fidelity. G&SR holds physical metal - fungibly, as bailee - backing 100% of metal in electronic circulation. In the interest of maximum transparency, G&SR displays details of its reserve adequacy on a real-time basis, on a Web page referred to as "Examiner."

Outline of Proposal

G&SR   proposes a contract with Ernst & Young to monitor the Reserve adequacy of   G&SR on a continuous basis and make audit data available on the World Wide Web.   Specifically, Ernst & Young would check and report on the accuracy of the information in G&SR's "Examiner" page, using frequent random on-site inspections.

Examiner Data Series

---

[70] "Forwarded Questions." Received by Douglas Jackson, and Barry Downey, *Forwarded Questions*, 26 Apr. 1997

Examiner contains 3 tables, which afford every customer the ability to assess whether G&SR is fulfilling its 100% Reserve requirement.

Table 1: total amount of each metal in electronic circulation (oz of e-metal)

Table 2: total physical metal in G&SR's custody

Table 3: details of inventory; type and number of coins and other specie

Audit Methods

e-metal: the issue here is; How does one know there is not more e-metal in circulation than indicated in the Examiner table? The auditor would become intimately familiar with the table structure and organization of G&SR's main transaction database and transaction processing algorithms. The auditor would be able to log into physical network and query the system as desired. In addition the auditor could arrange for certain accounts (unknown to G&SR) to be created for the purpose of spot checking the completeness of data captured in database queries.

Physical Inventory

The issues here are:

Is the data regarding physical inventory accurate?

Is the inventory held free of encumbrance or lien?

Is the inventory genuine?

Physical Data

Auditor personally physically counts metal pieces. Initially, while system is small, the entire physical inventory would be periodically counted. As the quantity of metal increases, random spot checks would be employed. The current physical security protocol requires that metal be dispersed in multiple safe deposit boxes in multiple separate bank locations, with no more than 200oz gold or equivalent at any physical site. Auditor could select as many sites as desired for on-site inspection, with frequency determined by the prudence of Ernst & Young. It is G&SR's intention to migrate from bank storage to a contract with a secure storage contractor offering (at least partial) indemnification against storage-related loss.

Lack of Encumbrance

The auditor would have free reign to investigate any personal financial records and other business records of all of G&SR's (or its first echelon contractors') principals and employees.

Detection of Counterfeit Specie

G&SR will make available lab equipment and reference material for determining the specific gravity of specie items.

Reporting

G&SR will be permitted to advertise that Ernst & Young serves as our auditor.

Ernst & Young will post digitally signed audit reports accessible via its web server. These reports will describe the methods employed in monitoring and audit findings, using a report format negotiated as mutually acceptable.

Other Requirements

G&SR uses an outside contractor to operate its computer network and act as agent and bailee for inventory operations such as acquisition/liquidation, storage, and order fulfillment. Physical security is a critical priority. Ernst & Young should not reveal the name of G&SR's contractor(s) or the location of any physical operations. It should not identify specific identifying information of the Ernst & Young branch (or subcontractor, if applicable) conducting the monitoring, or even reveal the state the branch is located in.

Payment for audit services will be in gold, payable via the e-gold system. This stipulation will help assure alignment of incentives. Unlike a typical corporate audit on behalf of shareholders, these audits are designed to primarily protect the interests G&SR's customers.[71]

Ernst & Young rejected the proposal and offer of new business.

1998

The co-founders' efforts to achieve positive cash flow during the early years was not easy for Downey and Jackson. In April 1998, after almost two years of online operations, the Examiner showed there were just 850 active e-gold® accounts.[72] In 1998 Dr. Jackson sold his interest in the Florida Oncology business and devoted full-time attention to the e-gold® enterprise.

That year, the e-gold® co-founders began to seek a path that would allow the precious metals platform to emerge as a global leader. This goal led the company to implement specific measures to assure e-gold's fiduciary integrity and eliminate any need to trust the company or its principals. Becoming a global enterprise would eventually mean moving a significant component of e-gold's company structure out of the United States. Dr. Jackson stated:

We realized that institutional arrangements that would demonstrably thwart insider

---

[71] Downey, Barry. "Proposal for Ernst & Young to Monitor and Report Fidelity of the Gold & Silver Reserve." Received by Mr. Greg Repas, a Senior Manager at Ernst & Young, One W. Pennsylvania Ave. Suite 950, 28 Apr. 1997, Baltimore, Maryland.

[72] Jackson, Douglas. "e-gold Examiner." *e-gold Examiner*, e-gold.com, 21 June 2000, web.archive.org/web/20000511160944fw_/http://www.e-gold.com/examiner.html.

malfeasance would also serve to protect against error or external coercion. Our survey of potential risks also took into account jurisdictional and political risks, both from the standpoint of where to store reserves and where to locate the company.[73]

In March 1998, Jackson approached Ian Grigg of Systemics, Inc. during Bob Hettinga's Philodox Symposium on Digital Bearer Transaction Technology. After discussions, Jackson purchased three licenses from Grigg for the use of his Ricardo technology. Ricardo is Systemics' architecture for Internet payment systems, that was available for licensed use.

In a March 16, 2001 Hansa Bank press release, Grigg described his Ricardo technology "The Ricardo architecture was originally designed in 1995-1996 and was launched into live usage with the creation of the DigiGold currency, issued by DigiGold Ltd in 1999. (See http://www.digigold.net for more details)."[74]

The release proclaimed issuance of a 'Hansa Bank dollar' backed by deposits in an offshore bank run by an expat named Lynwood Bell. Dr. Jackson later provided additional color:

> "Ian had always been inordinately impressed by Lynn Bell, who was one of the sponsors of the annual Financial Cryptography Conferences held in Anguilla. Ian obviously felt there was more to gain by hitching his wagon to Bell, who had all the mannerisms and gold watch atmospherics that have always been the stock in trade of offshore operators. My sense though was that Bell was the sort of guy who was allergic to having any 'skin in the game', preferring to finance everything with OPM (Other People's Money). The Hansa Bank dollar apparently didn't generate much of a cascade. For all intents and purposes, their 2001 Press Release was the only mention of the project that ever surfaced."

> Indeed, as Grigg described in a 2018 blog post: "in 2008 I found myself again in deep poverty in the rich country of Austria. This time I had a job doing community auditing, which worked out at about €1 per hour, comfortably well below the poverty line, but alive".[75]

Jackson deployed one of the licenses for DigiGold Inc., a new enterprise that had been e-gold's planned second-generation bearer system. A second license went to e-gold.com for

[73] Jackson, Douglas. "Re: See Attached." Received by Carl Mullan, *Re: See Attached*, 17 Apr. 2019.
[74] "Recent Intertrader and Systemics Alliance Brings Forth Digital Dollar from Hansa Bank." Systemics, Hansa Bank, 15 Mar. 2001, www.systemics.com/legal/digigold/discovery/extras/20010316_hansa.html.
[75] Jackson, Douglas. Received by Carl Mullan, *Evans and Grigg Analysis and Write-Up*, 8 Apr. 2020.

an unspecified project.

That month, Jackson also reconnected with Ian Grigg regarding a transition for e-gold® from a "US-based prototype to a worldwide system."[76] Jackson emailed Grigg expressing an interest in hiring him as a consultant. Grigg's proposed work, to be detailed through a future business plan, would outline a "more coherent division between functions and enabled more rapid recoupment of initial development costs utilizing a licensing arrangement."Other proposed e-gold® changes discussed with Grigg included: a new offshore corporate structure, licensing Reserve Institutions as legal bailees with marketing rights in the U.S. and Canada, and the construction of a foreign server farm. Showing his intention to move quickly on this project, Jackson stated in an email, "I want to have the system in place at identified plateau of capacity, security and functionality by year end 1998."[77]

Through personal interviews, granted more than a decade after this original 1998 email, Jackson disclosed that his reconnection with Grigg was the "beginning of relationship which ultimately turned out so ruinously."[78] In summer 2001, Jackson and e-gold® sued Grigg and Systemics, Inc. The lawsuit eventually ended in arbitration, with the arbitrator finding in favor of Grigg and Systemics.[79]

Early Buy-Out Offer

As early as 1998, the e-gold® co-founders were entertaining their first buyout offer. The potential buyer had been an individual named Ross Palmer.[80] However, in talks with Palmer, it became clear that he was only interested in purchasing the e-gold® platform if the company and operations migrated out of the United States. His proposal was contingent upon the creation of a new offshore company named EGT that retained all e-gold® assets titled through a foreign jurisdiction. The knowledge gained from these talks, would fuel Jackson and Downey's future ideas on protecting and securing e-gold's customer assets using offshore trusts.

Several of the emails received by Jackson in March 1998 extolled the substantial benefits of offshore financial operations. One of these emails, from James Bennett,[81] included several pages of text entitled *"The Wind from Anguilla."* This document referenced

---

[76] Jackson, Douglas. "It's Time." Received by Ian Grigg, et al., *It's Time*, 24 Mar. 1998.

[77] Ibid

[78] Jackson, Douglas. "e-gold Fiduciary Safeguards." Received by Carl Mullan, *e-gold Fiduciary Safeguards*, July 2019.

[79] The DigiGold license contract never stated or implied any ownership transfer of the Ricardo software or the intellectual property of Grigg or Systemics.

[80] Jackson, Douglas. "Ross, Cyber Freetrade Zone, Offshore Server Net." Received by Jalon Q. Zimmerman, et al., *Ross, Cyber Freetrade Zone, Offshore Server Net*, 1 Apr. 1998.

[81] In 1998, James C. Bennett was a Technology Editor of Strategic Investment, and President of Internet Transactions Transnational, Inc.

the Financial Cryptography 98 Conference, held in Anguilla, and the advantages of locally-based corporate services. Mr. Bennett's opening statement read:

> I recently returned from the Island of Anguilla where I attended the Financial Cryptography 98 conference. Anguilla is one of the world's most aggressive tax havens. As a British Dependent Territory, it has enjoyed very substantial autonomy since it rebelled against independence as part of St. Kitts and Nevis. It [Anguilla] has used this autonomy to enact very substantial banking secrecy provisions, and a complete abolition of income and capital gains taxes.[82]

Jackson and Downey's principal concern that led them to explore re-establishment offshore was the precedent set in the United States in 1933 when the FDR administration took the U.S. off the gold standard.

On April 5, 1933, President Franklin D. Roosevelt signed Executive Order 6102 "forbidding the hoarding of gold coin, gold bullion, and gold certificates within the continental United States." The U.S. Government seized all privately held gold and criminalized the private ownership of gold except for narrow numismatic exceptions. Roosevelt made the order under the authority of the Trading with the Enemy Act of 1917. The enormous stock of gold coins, which, over many decades, had accumulated in bank vaults enabling their most effective monetary use – as a reserve asset backing more useful media of payment – were nationalized and melted down. The United States Bullion Depository, often known as Fort Knox, was erected as a repository for the bullion bars fabricated from melted gold coins. Treasury officials provided rewards to informants that would identify citizens who had not surrendered their gold coins in exchange for U.S. dollars. Furthermore, the government had just devalued those same dollars from a gold value of 1/20th troy ounce to 1/32nd.

Furthermore, during gold confiscations in Russia after the Bolshevik takeover, bank safe deposit boxes were drilled open based on informant denunciations. Private debt contracts with clauses requiring repayment in gold were over-ridden and re-interpreted to allow for reimbursement in "lawful money."

Although e-gold launched more than half a century after FDR's confiscation, and the U.S. had already decriminalized the private possession of gold, Jackson was still concerned about his customers' precious metal.

Another consideration for Jackson, at the start of e-gold®, was the new policy of the United States government classifying strong encryption as a munition subject to

---

[82] "Fwd: Thought You Might like to Read This, Nameste Kevan." Received by Douglas Jackson, and R. Ambre, *Fwd: Thought You Might like to Read This, Nameste Kevan*, 23 Mar. 1998.

International Traffic in Arms (ITAR) export regulations. Only the brave actions of Phil Zimmerman, risking imprisonment, to release the source code of PGP had thwarted their gambit to prohibit private access to this critically important, liberty-protecting capability.

With the assistance of counsel, Jackson and Downey set out to find jurisdictions with a strong tradition of respect for British common law and its principle of the sanctity of contract. Around the same time, Jackson was introduced to the concept and advantages of an 'eleemosynary trust' by Philip Spicer, the principal of the Central Fund of Canada. Spicer explained that titling the gold reserves to such a trust would protect them from legal claims brought against the e-gold® system administrator or customers. In a later interview, Jackson shed light on this decision process.

> As we progressed toward formation of a suitable offshore Trust it was evident that certain functions could only be accomplished by non-US persons. The most important was the "grantor," a person who would declare the trust and provide the initial trust assets (corpus) with their own money. This not uncommonly was done with some nominal sum such as a few dollars deposited into a bank account.[83]

On April 27, 1998, Jackson sent an email to Stefan Metzeler inviting him to the U.S. for talks about serving as Grantor for a new offshore trust.

> Dear Stefan,
> Barry Downey and I are working through a business plan for re-deploying the e-gold system http://www.e-gold.com offshore, using an entirely new non-US company. We need a reliable and honest person who is not a US citizen to serve as Grantor for the trust(s) which will be the vehicle of ownership.[84]

In late 1998, Downey and Jackson began reviewing a possible e-gold® business model using Bermuda-based trusts to own the newly planned offshore company and its assets. The jurisdiction of Bermuda was an attractive location for private trusts and also provided an additional level of asset protection for the e-gold® customer bullion. Eventually, Metzeler became Grantor of the trusts that owned the new offshore company, e-gold Ltd. More importantly, Metzeler became Grantor of the e-gold Bullion Reserve Special Purpose Trust (Bermuda), which held title to the bullion backing e-gold® and the other e-metals. Later, court documents detailed this trust arrangement.

83   Jackson, Douglas. "e-Gold Fiduciary Safeguards." Received by Carl Mullan, e-Gold Fiduciary Safeguards, 14 Jan. 2019. ref. -book1-e-gold fiduciary safeguards.odt
84   Jackson, Douglas. "Grantor." Received by Stefan Metzeler, *Grantor*, 27 Apr. 1998.

4. The e-gold bullion reserve special purpose trust

e-gold is further unique in that every ounce is secured by actual gold bullion held in allocated storage at repositories owned by members of the London Bullion Market Association. Title to that bullion is held by the e-gold Bullion Reserve Special Purpose Trust (the "Special Purpose Trust"), which exists for the express "purpose of holding precious metal bullion on behalf of and for the exclusive benefit of all e-metal account holders collectively, pursuant to the e-gold, e-silver, e-platinum, and e-palladium currency contracts." Declaration of Trust, The e-gold Bullion Reserve Special Purpose Trust ("Trust Agreement'), § 4.1; *see* http://www.e-gold.com/contracts/egold-sptl11899.htm. A recent audit of all bullion titled to the Special Purpose Trust has confirmed, as required by the Plea Agreement, that e-gold® is what it purports to be, i.e. "100% backed at all times by gold bullion in allocated storage," and that all gold bars identified by e-gold® as backing the e-gold® in circulation are maintained in allocated storage facilities in repositories in London and Dubai. *See* http://www.e-gold.com/unsecure/ganda.html.

Significantly, as a result of the governance model established to protect Users of egold, the e-gold in the e-gold system is insulated from physical, legal and political risks. Indeed, throughout the course of these proceedings, and the resulting turmoil caused to the e-gold system and its customers, the Special Purpose Trust fulfilled its purpose and ensured that the Special Purpose Trust's gold continued to be available to back all e-gold in circulation. Thus, e-gold continues to be as valuable as the gold by which it is backed even though it temporarily lacks the money-like attribute of being readily exchangeable for national currencies, as was the case prior to these proceedings.[85]

e-gold account holders hold an indirect fungible and non-allocated ownership interest in gold via the Special Purpose Trust [The e-gold Bullion Reserve Special Purpose Trust] and may transfer that ownership interest (or portions thereof) to other e-gold account holders by making Spends.[86]

E-gold® posted the full trust agreement online for anyone to view, and it is still

---

[85] CASE NUMBER: 07-167-M-01. *UNITED STATES OF AMERICA V. E-GOLD LIMITED, GOLD & SILVER RESERVE, INC., DOUGLAS L. JACKSON, BARRY K. DOWNEY and REID A. JACKSON.* SENTENCING MEMORANDUM OF GOLD & SILVER RESERVE, INC., Nov. 2008.

[86] Ibid

available in 2020.[87] The most critical element of the document was section 4.1.[88]

> [...] purpose of holding precious metal bullion on behalf of and for the exclusive benefit of all e-metal account holders collectively, pursuant to the e-gold, e-silver, e-platinum, and e-palladium currency contracts, all of which explicitly require 100% physical reserves backing all e-metal in circulation. The physical assets shall be held in allocated storage by secure third party repositories with each individual bullion bar uniquely and explicitly identified and cataloged. All precious metal shall be held free and clear of all liens and encumbrances whatsoever.   The safekeeping arrangements with secure repositories shall require dual signature (i.e., authorization by both e-gold Ltd. and by the designated third party contracted to serve as Escrow Agent) before any bullion may be removed for any purpose.[89]

The Grantor, Stefan Metzeler, established the Trust. The document also designated a "Protector." According to the terms of the Trust, the Protector could declare an emergency and appoint Emergency Trustees. The original Protector appointed to the Trust was Ian Grigg. Jackson later had reason to regret Grigg's assignment to that role. Here are Jackson's statements regarding Grigg and the Trust.

> In early 2001, as we realized he[Grigg] was part of cabal betraying us, we remembered to ask the Trustees to un-appoint him and appoint someone else. It was fortunate we did that. In 2007, we learned from Jeroen Van Gelderen, a protégé of Grigg's, that Grigg did attempt to hijack the Trust to enable the US Secret Service to take it over and seize the bullion reserves.[90]

From the start of operations, e-gold's co-founders dedicated themselves to combating fraud and the illegal use of online payments. In October 1998, e-gold® helped organize and underwrite the Lex Cybernetoria Conference in Reykjavik, Iceland. The event examined private sector solutions to cross border issues of Internet fraud and criminality; legacy law enforcement mechanisms had poorly addressed. Iceland's Minister of Education, Science and Culture, Mr. Bjorn Bjarnason, addressed visitors at the opening of the conference on

[87]   Jackson, Douglas. "Gold Bullion Reserve Special Purpose Trust." *THE E-GOLD BULLION RESERVE   SPECIAL PURPOSE TRUST*, e-gold.com, 5 June 2005, web.archive.org/web/20030605160747/http://www.e-gold.com:80/contracts/egold-spt-111899.htm.

[88]   Ibid

[89]   Ibid

[90]   Jackson, Douglas. "Crackers in the Gtloaming." Received by Douglas Jackson, et al., *Crackers in the Gtloaming*, 29 May 2007.

October 16, 1998.

> At this conference here in Iceland you will discuss what rules are necessary to govern cyberspace. We want to be able to protect lawful users from criminals we also want to ensure intellectual property rights and we want to be able to to use cyberspace to do business in a secure way. The question is who shall have the authority to set the rules and enforce them. Shall we put our trust in public government or private or community governance?[91]

Sponsoring this event and other related industry conferences demonstrated e-gold's commitment to a fraud-free Internet. Jackson wrote about this conference in 2019 email communications.

> The focus of Lex Cybernetoria was a survey of historic and proposed private law concepts and institutions that had emerged or been proposed in circumstances where state judicial arrangements were lacking or ineffective. With the then on-going emergence of the commercial Internet, it was rapidly becoming apparent that existing jurisdiction-based (national, local) justice systems were too slow to deal with Internet crime and other legal issues because the Internet was global, with flows of information and money transcending national borders more or less at light speed. It might take weeks or months for a writ initiated in one country to be executed in another. Meanwhile, proceeds of crime might be long gone.
>
> The main thread was the idea of an international Internet court, organized by private sector entities, similar in logi to private/international arbitration. A particular concept, previously unfamiliar to me, was the notion of an interpleader. An interpleader was a court or arbitrator that could make a disposition of value when approached by a plaintiff such as an entity holding value on behalf of third parties (but to which the plaintiff itself had no claim) where the disposition of that value was being (or would be) contested by multiple claimants. This was highly relevant to us because of a number of unique challenges we faced.
>
> To start, consider the case of a bank, where the bank becomes concerned that a depositor is up to something crooked, such as operating an investment scam. The bank would simply exercise its right of association, close the customer's account and send her a check, washing its hands of the matter. Under no circumstance would the bank unilaterally freeze the funds without court order.

---

[91] "Internetið - Stjórn á Því (Enska)." *Björn Bjarnason - Bjorn.is*, Minister of Education, Science and Culture: Conference Arranged by CSEI and SUS., 16 Oct. 1998, www.bjorn.is/greinar/nr/535.

In our case, in such a matter, the issue was that we, like a bank, could not freeze an account without due process. We thought we needed a court order or some legal writ (such as a valid subpoena). Circumstances might arise, however, where someone may have compromised someone else's account login credentials and made an unauthorized Spend to another account, or any other situation where we might have suspicions that an account contained value that originated as the proceeds of crime, but where no court would take timely action. We could neither get police agencies to take action if we ourselves were not a victim nor ourselves get a court to proceed with a criminal action. [I may have provided emails where federal LE agencies declined to take on the Van Dinh matter because e-gold Ltd. wasn't (and could never be) the victim]. The best we believed we could do on our own was to block an account from receiving additional Spends.

Moreover, in our case, the idea of closing an account and sending someone a check did not compute. e-gold only circulated within the system and we were already starting the process of implementing a separation of roles such that the system operator (e-gold Ltd.) was not going to be engaged in exchange activities and would have no capability of closing the account, forcibly exchanging   the e-gold for conventional money and sending a check.[92]

During November 1998, the e-gold® team introduced an assortment of new services geared toward attracting and serving retail customers. One ingenious service was a payment tool, created by G&SR, called OutExchange with Directed Payment (OEDP). OEDP was a tool that could OutExchange e-metal and use the fiat currency balance for general bill payments. The e-gold® account holder directed G&SR to send checks in specific amounts drawn from the proceeds of an OutExchange. The checks were drawn on a Gold & Silver Reserve Inc. bank account and made payable to the third-party, as directed by the e-gold® customer. OEDP remained popular for several years.

That month, the company also created the e-gold® discussion mailing list. This popular utility operated through a public website email list and proved to be a ubiquitous discussion platform for many topics, including gold, online payments, and related digital currency subjects. Interaction between the e-gold® operators and the public, through this list, helped to overcome some early issues. In 2020, this online archive of facts, comments, and materials is a treasure trove of historic e-gold® information. The e-gold® Mail Archive list is still available online through the Internet Archive.[93]

92   Jackson, Douglas. "Comments Re: Interpleader." Received by Carl Mullan, 1 May 2019, Melbourne, Florida.
93   "e-gold List." Edited by Public List, *The Mail Archive*, The Mail Archive, 18 Aug. 2000, web.archive.org/web/20000818005359/http://www.mail-archive.com:80//.

In November, the company launched an e-gold® Shopping Cart Interface and also provided an API for automating outbound Spends. When deployed, the shopping cart and automation interfaces respectively allowed for the specification of an incoming Spend, and automatic entry of an outbound Spend instruction. Text from the 1998 e-gold® website discussed these new innovative tools for online commerce.

How do you implement e-gold into online shopping carts?

e-gold is excellent for online shopping carts. In less time than it takes to receive an automated credit card confirmation, you receive confirmation of cleared payment. There's no such thing as a "charge back". [Refunds, if appropriate, are entirely under your control - no one can pull from your e-gold account]. The fee for receiving payment in e-metal [1%, in metal, deducted from payee, subject to maximum of 50 cents (equivalent value)] is much less than what credit card companies charge for fiat money. In fact, even if you OutExchange all the metal you receive, the combined fees/commissions are still likely to be significantly less. Unlike the hassles of setting up a merchant credit card account, there is no application process, no initiation fee. We don't even distinguish a so-called merchant account; an account is an account. You can implement and test the protocol entirely on a self-service basis. Download our Shopping Cart Interface specification demo.e-gold.com/docs/e-gold_SCI.doc We frankly can't imagine why anyone would accept credit cards when they can be paid in gold... at lower cost![94]

This Shopping Cart Interface integrated with several popular shopping cart software programs circa 1998. The tool afforded both large and small merchants the ability to receive e-gold® Spends and notification via email or HTTPS of any payments.[95]

In November 1998, e-gold® had already integrated its platform with online merchant payments (Spend transactions) and popular e-commerce software. E-gold® launched all of these products before PayPal.

The co-founders of e-gold® were the original pioneers of online payments and digital currency. In 1998, Jackson walked away from a secure medical career earning $500,000 a year to exclusively pursue the dream of secure global payments backed by precious metal. His vision wasn't a bigger paycheck; he envisioned this work as a solution to many of the world's problems. His intent was always to do the right thing.

[94] Jackson, Douglas. "Questions and Answers." *FAQ*, e-gold.com, 27 June 1998, web.archive.org/web/19980627133917/http://www.e-gold.com/unsecure/faq.htm#SCI.

[95] Jackson, Douglas. "Gold vs. Credit Card." *e-gold Credit Card Comparison Calculator*, e-gold.com, 17 Aug. 2000, web.archive.org/web/20000815214630fw_/http://www.e-gold.com:80/unsecure/cc.htm.

The last and perhaps most crucial e-gold® 1998 addition was the e-gold® Incentive Plan. Alongside the Shopping Cart Interface, e-gold® rolled out a new referral incentive plan that would attract more new e-gold® customers. The incentive plan eventually became an enormous success for the company, yielding tens of thousands of new users. Regarding the Incentive Plan, the e-gold® website shared this news.

> By directing others to the e-gold system, you can share in the growth of the system. Become an account originator today. May your progeny be many![96]
> Terms of the incentive plan:
> New e-gold Account Referral Incentive Program
> Beginning November 1998, every time anyone clicks an e-metal payment, the payment processing fee will automatically be split three ways:
> - 25% of the fee (up to 12.5 cents (US$-equivalent) worth of e-metal) will be credited to the account of the person or company who originally referred the payer to us,
> - 25% of the fee (up to 12.5 cents worth) will go to whoever originally referred the payee to us,
> - 50% of the fee (up to 25 cents worth) will go to the Reserve Institution of the payee.
>
> The e-metal payment processing fee is not being increased. It is being divided up. It remains 1%, in metal, deducted from payee, subject to a maximum of 50 cents (US$-equivalent) worth of e-metal... a fraction of what credit card companies charge.[97]

That year also ushered in the e-gold® Stats page showing details of the preceding 24 hours system usage. The Stats page displayed the total number of accounts, broken down by balance, and the total number of spends delineated by values and aggregated by totals.

Relationship with Ian Grigg, origins
July 1998: The Philodox Symposium on Digital Bearer Transaction Settlement, Boston

In April 1997, as cypherpunks in general were gnashing their teeth in outrage against (what they regarded as) Dr. Jackson's ignorance and temerity as displayed by his "Debunking ecash" post, Ian Grigg (and Robert Hettinga) had posted more constructive comments. A year later, Reid Jackson brought an upcoming symposium in Boston to Douglas and Barry's attention, noting that Ian Grigg was one of the speakers and suggesting

---

[96] Ray, Jim. "e-gold News." Recent / *Noteworthy Items about e-gold*, e-gold.com, Nov. 1998, web.archive.org/web/19991009074300fw_/http://www.e-gold.com:80/news.html.
[97] Ibid

it might be a convenient venue to meet and compare notes.

Dr. Jackson and Barry Downey elected to attend and found Grigg's presentation highly insightful. They invited Grigg to lunch to discuss possible collaboration. As Jackson later noted:

> "I don't recall the specific content of that lunch discussion but I do remember it being the first time I'd ever eaten sushi. Grigg, to his credit, warned me that wasabi is not as innocuous as it appears rather than allowing me to blithely ingest a big dollop and discover that the hard way.
>
> The more important outcome of the meeting however was that Barry and I concluded that both Ian and another presenter, Ryan Lackey, were on the side of the angels, devoted to the development and emergence of payment systems that were not dependent on banks as obligatory financial intermediaries. Ryan indicated he was in his final semester at MIT but was so keen to implement the so-called "Brands protocol"[98] in computer code as to be willing to abandon his studies for the opportunity to pursue the project. Ian, in turn, was determined to resurrect a digital cash project he had begun in collaboration with Gary Howland, called Ricardo—under the auspices of a company he called Systemics—but which had gone dormant due to lack of capital. As Grigg himself later recalled "My startup had just failed - in 1998 nobody wanted to issue hard cryptographically-protected secure instruments that could describe any money at all. Go figure. But those weren't my worries then, what I was worried about then was … money… For about 6 months I was in this state of poverty".
>
> Barry and I ended up proposing to sponsor their respective development efforts. Ryan lingered in Boston a few days to tidy up loose ends with MIT while Ian flew back to Melbourne, Florida with me to start fleshing out a plan." [99]

Systemics in Anguilla

Jackson goes on to describe the situation.

> "Ian turned out to have a pretty detailed plan already in mind which involved renting a house in the 'The Valley' district of Anguilla in the general vicinity of 'Crypto Hill' where Vince Cate had established an outpost for renegade

---

[98] David Chaum had patented the original blinded digital cash protocol to attract widespread attention. Stefan Brands came up with an alternative approach that appeared to not be covered by the Chaum patent.

[99] http://financialcryptography.com/mt/archives/001638.html "Zooko Buys Groceries". The post makes no mention of Jackson stepping in at that time and financing Griggs Ricardo/Systemics venture for the next two years.

cryptographers seeking to circumvent US restrictions that treated strong cryptography as "munitions" under ITAR[100] regulations. In retrospect, it should have raised suspicions that Ian happened to have all these arrangements already waiting in the wings, lacking only a credulous investor ready to open his wallet.

And credulous I was. Right off the bat I provided Ian with $3,200 cash and airfare to get underway as well as permission to charge expenses to my personal credit cards. For the first few tens of thousands I wasn't even keeping close track, assuming the eventual return on investment would be such as to make such outlays part of the background noise.

Over the next two years, this open checkbook arrangement should surely go into the Guinness Book of Records for the most trusting patron, relative to available resources, in history. It wasn't until 1999 that it became apparent that some more orderly auspices for these outlays should be put into place, enabling the Anguilla-based company to book revenue and G&SR to book expenses. What ensued was the classic situation where one party to a contract is proceeding on a high trust basis, seeing it as a draft vehicle to be better formalized when conditions warrant, but the other has a specific design in mind.

Moreover, in retrospect, it also appeared that Ian had nurtured the sort of classic resentment harbored by Michelangelo-like geniuses faced with the repugnant necessity of accepting support from sponsors whom they deemed inferior species in every defining metric of the Renaissance Man ideal they envisioned themselves as embodying.

There was also likely some degree of cognitive dissonance stemming from the fact that, by early 2000, e-gold was exhibiting exponential growth while there was continued intense disinterest in Grigg's more crypto-oriented Ricardo project. A particularly discouraging indicator of this disinterest occurred at the first Edinburgh Financial Cryptography Exposition (EFCE) in June 2000. As Grigg noted in his after-action report [bolding added for emphasis]:

> "bob [Hettinga] continues to ignore everything we have done, even though we showed non-vapourwear that was as bearer as the vapour that Tyler Close showed.   A few observations on that - TC will need to rewrite his stuff again - he claims - and may not be ready for months.   he continues to fuck off all and sundry around him, so i continue to rule him out as a workable business. he may come good, but nobody succeeds without substantial help, and nobody helps after being insulted more than once or twice.

---

[100] International Traffic in Arms Regulations

back to bob.   it is a mystery to me.   **He didn't care about our stuff and neither did the CrestCo guys**.   the audience ratings for the competition were also very low.   **so that was bad for me, and i've been scratching my head trying to figure out why it is that the rating was so bad**.

One thing was that there was zero marketing in there, I refused to break ranks on the "running code" concept, whereas most others did a marketing presentation with running code (i was of course papers chair and it would be bad form for me to drown the audience in marketing.) that's a vexing problem in itself, as the conference only works because it is running code, which filters out the nonsense.   And, we can only attract people based on our rigour in applying the standard.   so maybe the answer is that i shouldn't be papers chair next time as well.

but i don't think a poor presentation explains it all. one thing that was told to me was that the demo simply wasn't clear - there was, for example, no belief in what had been done, no appreciation that a complete trading cycle had been shown.   It might have been better if I had spent more time on the recovery features and shown a lost transactions.

Also, i didn't say what I was going to do up front.   **So people didn't pick it up.   this has me wondering, is our audience that dumb, that they can't see the thing in front of them that we've talked about all these years? maybe, as ben laurie scored more than me in the competition** for demonstrating a coded up formula. anyways, i guess i'll have to toe the line and do some marketing in the talks next time.

Another unconfirmed report is that CrestCo, the bearded guy with the big research budget, was not only impressed with James Milner, but was also impressed with Bob's micromint nonsense.   rumour has it that he might give money to bob.   I'm missing something here, as the guy was *very* knowledgeable, to a radical flavour and extent, yet, he didn't pick up the obvious failure of bob's idea (money likes to be efficient, not inefficient)."

But through all of this, the money spigot from G&SR supporting Systemics remained open. I recall once when Ian was in Melbourne—possibly for the first Indian River Summit "(IRS I", in October 1999), when resources had become painfully scarce—going for a long walk to discuss progress and funding. I specifically recall it being near the railroad tracks and a cemetery close to the hospital where I had practiced as recently as two years prior, an eternity ago it seemed. I described that we were running on fumes but pledged to keep the funds flowing to Anguilla as long as we had a roof over our heads. (No longer able to afford my two mortgages I did subsequently need to sell my home in 2003 and have lived in rentals ever since)."[101]

History

E-Dinar FZ-LLC
DIC-building 01 office 113
P.O Box 500237
Dubai Internet City, Dubai UAE
Trade Licence N-19909

The e-dinar operation began around 1992-1993, minting pure gold dinar and silver dirham coins for Islamic countries. Like millions of other worldwide businesses, by 1996, the group was establishing an online presence for the gold and silver economy. 1999 was the e-dinar organization's first contact with Florida based e-gold®. By the end of that year, a business concept and strategy had developed along with a solid investment plan. This interaction facilitated the first work session with e-gold® in Florida and a second May 2000 meeting in London.

By May 2000, there was a 1st release of the online e-dinar interface. By the third quarter, the business had opened a banking relationship with both HSBC and Standard Charter. A month later, the company established mints in UAE and Indonesia and received permission to mint coins from the central bank of UAE. The platform officially launched in September 2000, and by December, there had been a significant upgrade to the e-dinar website offering enhanced account tools and functions.

Based on the Islamic Model

In October 2006, Dr. Umar Ibrahim Vadillo, President of the Board (UK) E-Dinar FZ-LLC, published a noteworthy   seventy-eight-page paper entitled, *Fatwa on Banking - The Use of Interest Received on Bank Deposits.*[102] The paper included details on the function of the e-dinar platform. Copied here are selected portions of the document illustrating how Islamic Law governed the digital e-dinar.

---

[101] Jackson, Douglas. Received by Carl Mullan, Evans and Grigg Analysis and Write-Up, 8 Apr. 2020.

[102] Vadillo, Umar Ibrahim. *FATWA ON BANKING AND THE USE OF INTEREST RECEIVED ON BANK DEPOSITS.* Umar Ibrahim Vadillo, 2006, pp. 1–78, *FATWA ON BANKING AND THE USE OF INTEREST RECEIVED ON BANK DEPOSITS.*

Islam has its own economic model. This model is not capitalist, nor is it socialist. It stems from the Qur'an and the Sunna. It has a history of 1400 years, from the beginning of Islam up until the   dissolution of the Khalifate in the 20th century. This model protects and acknowledges private property as well as property of Allah (awqaf) and it is based on Islamic contractual law.

The Islamic model uses physical commodities as money. The Gold Dinar and the Silver Dirham are known as the Shari'ah currency. These two commodities (gold and silver) have a special status because they are mentioned in Qur'an and they are the measure for fundamental matters such as Zakat and issues concerning hudud. The Dinar and the Dirham are fundamental in preserving a stable currency, that is a currency that fluctuates in value but does not suffer inflation. It does not suffer inflation because it cannot be substituted by credit money (inflated), since credit money has no validity in Islamic Law.

A payment system based on the Dinar and the Dirham that facilitates payment across the world strictly following Islamic Law was established in 1999. It is called e-dinar. It is a practical alternative to banking transfers and allows individuals to avoid the use of credit money if they wish to. The legal implication of the development of these tools is that the case of darurah is no longer justified. There is an alternative way. It further demonstrates that there is no need to remain inside a system which is not acceptable, and that to establish the Halal is certainly possible.[103]

The Islamic model uses physical commodities as money. E-gold® proved to be the perfect digital platform for Islamic finance. The Gold Dinar and the Silver Dirham are known as Shariah currency and comply with Islamic Law. Islam dictates that the precious metal Dinar and the Dirham are fundamental to preserving a stable currency. Credit money is inflated fiat currency and has no validity in Islamic Law. Gold and silver are not affected by fiat currency inflation. Copied below is text from the e-dinar website, circa 2001, describing the benefits of e-dinar as recognized in the Islamic world. The message illustrates how the digital platform afforded users the ability to circumvent Western banking and digital "credit money" used by conventional banks.

A payment system based on the Dinar and the Dirham that facilitates payment across the world strictly following Islamic Law was established in 1999. It is called e-dinar. It is a practical alternative to banking transfers and allows individuals to avoid the use of credit money if they wish to. The legal implication of the development of

---

[103] Ibid

these tools is that the case of darurah is no longer justified. There is an alternative way. It further demonstrates that there is no need to remain inside a system which is not acceptable, and that to establish the Halal is certainly possible.[104]

The e-dinar system had a familiar description. It was labeled an Internet-based electronic payment and exchange system that enabled the use of gold as money. E-dinar was also used to identify the digital unit corresponding to an exact, fixed weight of 4.25 grams of pure 24k gold and title to the precise weight of physical gold. e-dinar Ltd. was incorporated in Labuan, Malaysia. The company acted as administrator of the system and bailee for all e-dinar bullion held in allocated storage by third-party custodians. Account holders had the option of exchanging their digital e-dinar into any popular fiat currency or redeeming the digital units for an equivalent amount of gold dinar.[105]

Board Members[106]
- Dr. U. Vadillo, President of the Board (UK)
- Dr. H. Dahinden, CEO (Switzerland)
- Mr. A. Rahman Shariff, CFO (Malaysia)

Operations[107]
- Mr. Y. Cattanach, COO (Dubai – UAE)
- Mr. M. Hirsch, CTO (Germany)

Banking Partners
- HSBC in Labuan
- Standard Chartered Banks in Labuan and Dubai

Precious Metals Repository Services
- Transguard Dubai UAE

Settlement Through e-gold (Original before a spinoff from e-gold platform)
- Settlement services, US-based in/out-exchanges
- Melbourne Florida (USA)

Software support from Dynac
- Software development and operations Johore Bahru, Malaysia[108]

---

[104] "Edinar." *e-Dinar*, E-Dinar FZ-LLC, 26 Apr. 2012, web.archive.org/web/20120426122259/https://www.e-dinar.com/cgi/?page=edinar&a=_1.

[105] "Dinar Questions & Answers." *e-Dinar*, E-Dinar FZ-LLC, 19 Apr. 2001, web.archive.org/web/20010419175902/http://www.e-dinar.com/en/index_7.html.

[106] "Dinar about Us." *e-Dinar: the Company*, E-Dinar FZ-LLC, 19 Apr. 2001, web.archive.org/web/20010419161632/http://www.e-dinar.com/en/index_4.html.

[107] Ibid

E-dinar was established through the e-gold platform by a cooperative partnership with Jackson, and e-gold Ltd. Both organizations promoted similar benefits. E-dinar's key strengths and features that differentiated the digital units from "credit money" included:

- Focus on B2B transactions
- Transactions 100% backed by physical gold
- Low costs
- The Immediate settlement, no credit & no fraud
- Immediate global fund transfers
- No currency conversion
- Universal means of exchange
- Minimal restrictions by local regulations
- Local bullion repositories close to major depositors
- Addressed well-known e-payment issues

E-dinar offered e-gold's innovative platform plus, under Islamic Law, the digital dinar gold and silver-backed units were an acceptable form of Islamic finance. The original e-dinar software platform was hosted for several years from Orlando, on the e-gold AT&T servers, before moving overseas.

A October 28, 2000 screenshot from e-dinar.com.[109]

---

[108] Ibid

[109] "e-Dinar." *e-Dinar*, E-Dinar FZ-LLC, Oct. 2000, web.archive.org/web/20001028150900/http://www.e-dinar.com/.

In 2001, e-dinar attempted to launch a more sensible approach to the exchange of e-dinar, fiat currency, and precious metal. This plan involved exchange providers called "e-kiosks." These independent exchange providers addressed high transaction costs and slow service. Like an e-gold® independent exchange provider, anyone could have operated an e-dinar mobile "e-kiosk." Website content from April 17, 2001, explained the company's direction. The e-dinar digital unit is compared to interest-bearing banks, a practice that the Islamic world forbids. E-dinar online content regularly disclosed that the system did not offer credit or pay interest.

e-kiosk
How to become an e-Kiosk Operator
e-Kiosks are mobile 'exchange offices' offering convenient in-exchange (cash for e-dinars) and out-exchange (e-dinars for cash or gold coins). Kiosks have their own e-dinar account with a stock of e-dinars that can be sold to or bought from other account holders. The beauty is that all kiosk transactions occur on the spot – there are no delays. Anybody can become an e-kiosk operator if they accept the following

terms:

- no franchise or territorial rights (we want a competitive chain of free-lance kiosk operators)
- min. initial deposit 10'000. - USD, min. yearly turnover 20'000. - USD
- Operators of e-kiosks receive special terms
- reduced agio: 0.5% savings on agio for in-exchange (3.5% rather than 4% above spot)
- 3.5% savings on out-exchange: customers click e-dinars to the kiosk account for out-exchange at spot, kiosks re-circulate e-dinars at spot and thus avoid the agio for in-exchange!
- additional fees are charged as appropriate (e.g. fees for conversion of local into international currencies, currency transfers for in-exchange, shipping costs for coin redemption, time & effort spent). Fees are ultimately be regulated by the market.
- e-kiosk operators receive kiosk accounts with special account logic and configurable fee structure.

The key advantage of the e-dinar kiosk network is increased customer convenience: on the spot transactions coupled with lower cost overhead for smaller accounts. If you want to become an e-dinar kiosk operator, please contact us for necessary arrangements. It is your opportunity to make a real difference while doing some very healthy business. We no longer have to worry about credit cards and bank rates or what to do about the accumulated interest on our bank accounts. The e-dinar on-line exchange system is the first system enabling correct financial transactions.[110]

E-kiosks offered more services than just the exchange of digital currency. Some exchange providers attempted to generate new business using smart cards and local bill payment services. Additionally, several independent e-dinar exchange providers also traded e-gold®.

E-dinar operated online from 2000 through early 2018. In January 2018, the company's management posted a letter on the e-dinar website stating, because of slowing interest in precious metals and increased adoption of blockchain currency, the business was closing its doors. Copied here is the closing notice from e-dinar's Managing Director Mr. Zeno Dahinden.

Dear customers,

[110] "Dinar Questions & Answers." *e-Kiosk How to Become an e-Kiosk Operator,* E-Dinar FZ-LLC, 17 Apr. 2001, web.archive.org/web/20010417041134/http://www.e-dinar.com/en/index_8.html.

Kindly be informed that the shareholders decided to liquidate the e-dinar FZ LLC company in Dubai Internet City and to pay out its customers by the end of January 2018. Please do not worry - all accounts are 100% covered by precious metals and can be converted and paid out in full. As a consequence, we will not accept or process any new purchase orders. We took this difficult step with great regret. Now entering the sixth year of an ongoing lull in the precious metal market - all the "fast" money seems to have moved into crypto-currencies - e-dinar has under performed for several years, thus forcing its closure. To terminate your account with e-dinar, kindly proceed as follows:

1. Login to your account at www.e-dinar.com and use the "Sell Gold/Silver" transaction to convert your account(s) into cash. In case you have several accounts, all accounts will be converted simultaneously.
2. When you outexchange your account(s), please verify that your banking details are correct in order to ensure a smooth fund transfer. Note that funds can only be transferred to a bank account in your own name and not in the name of a third party (important: small errors in the banking details can lead to endless delays). Please provide your IBAN account number and SWIFT code of your bank if that exists in your country.
3. Your precious metal will then be sold at the following day's London fixing.
4. E-dinar will credit your bank account with the proceeds (minus the agreed out-exchange and bank transaction fees) within five to max. eight business days of your outexchange.
5. Accounts containing less than 50 USD will not be refunded since the transaction and handling fees would exceed the principal.

Our Managing Director Zeno Dahinden will contact the larger customers personally to answer their questions and assist them as required. All other customers can send questions and concerns to our email address support@e-dinar.com which will be responded to expediently either by email or phone. We would like to use this opportunity to thank you for your year-long trust in our company and wish you all the best for the future.
With kind regards,
Zeno Dahinden Managing Director e-dinar FZ-LLC[111]

1999

E-gold, Ltd. (Nevis) was established in 1999 as the contractual Operator for the e-gold

---

[111] "e-Dinar Home." *e-Dinar*, E-Dinar FZ-LLC, 19 Mar. 2018, web.archive.org/web/20180319171826/https://www.e-dinar.com/cgi/.

system and assumed responsibility for its roles of Issuance and Settlement. E-gold, Ltd. was organized as a virtual company that performed operational and fiduciary roles by contracting with other businesses. Brinks (located in London) and Transguard (a division of Emirates Air located in Dubai) provided vaults where gold bullion was stored. A third-party escrow agent controlled the physical disposition of the gold and precious metals bullion. Dr. Jackson, Barry Downey, and Reid Jackson were the three directors of e-gold, Ltd.

In February 1999, e-gold® sponsored the third annual Financial Cryptography Conference (FC99) hosted on the Island of Anguilla, British West Indies.[112] The goal of FC99 was to bring together individuals and companies involved in both the financial and data security fields to foster cooperation and the exchange of ideas. The International Financial Cryptography Association (IFCA) organized the conference. The 1999 conference solicited original works focused on securing commercial transactions and systems, along with fundamental as well as applied real-world deployments surrounding commerce security. The FC99 meeting was another opportunity for Jackson to advance the ideas and innovations that grew from the e-gold® platform.

During the FC99 event, Max Levchin approached Jackson to solicit investment for his new payment system called PayPal. Maksymilian Rafailovych "Max" Levchin is a Ukrainian-born American computer scientist who co-founded the company that became PayPal.[113]

After the 1999 conference, cryptographer Ian Goldberg, who ported SSL (secure sockets layer) encryption to a 3com "Palm Pilot," executed the first known online e-gold® payment from a Palm Pilot mobile device. Mobile payments were not only possible in 1999; they became popular with many e-gold® users.

June introduced several crucial new e-gold® tools and features. These included a sample online e-gold store, an in-house e-gold Directory, and a world map displaying countries that contained e-gold® users.

The sample e-gold store was an example of how a very simplistic e-gold online shop might look as displayed on a third-party website. This implementation targeted users that did not have access to their web servers or cgi/asp capability. The example store utilized the e-gold shopping cart interface specification.

The e-gold Directory was a section of the e-gold® website that listed businesses and organizations (Merchants) that accepted e-gold®. During that early 1999-2001 period, it was not easy to obtain a Directory listing. Only established and well-known companies appeared on the e-gold® website. Gaining a Directory listing proved to be an essential marketing tool.

---

[112] "Third International Conference 22-25 February 1999, Anguilla, BWI." Edited by -- --, *Financial Cryptography '99*, International Financial Cryptography Association (IFCA)., 22 Feb. 1999, ifca.ai/fc99/.

[113] Wikipedia. "Max Levchin." *Wikipedia*, Wikimedia Foundation, 19 Aug. 2019, en.wikipedia.org/wiki/Max_Levchin.

In 2000, as the marketplace for e-gold® expanded, all Directory listings experienced increased traffic and sales. A few years later, many of the listed companies came under fire from U.S. Congressmen during Jackson's congressional testimony in a House Subcommittee hearing.

The publicly viewable e-gold® Account Balance Option, introduced in June 1999, was a beneficial new feature designed explicitly for e-gold® based financial institutions. Because transparency is always a critical means for any financial institution to demonstrate trustworthiness, the new Account Balance Option was popular with users. The tool allowed any e-gold® customer purporting to hold value on account, to continuously publish the e-gold® balance for public viewing. Many e-gold® merchants, clients, and potential customers investigating a new e-gold® service used this tool to monitor e-gold® account balances.

In mid-1999, e-gold® received some welcome positive press coverage. On July 13, The Financial Times column entitled "On The Web," written by Tim Jackson, introduced readers to the digital gold platform by concluding that "e-gold® is the only electronic currency that has achieved critical mass on the web." The article stated, "For merchants, eGold has a further bonus: unlike credit cards, which are liable to chargebacks, the system guarantees payment once ordered."[114]

In August, e-gold Ltd. appointed a new escrow agent, The Central Group Ontario Ltd., to manage the gold, silver, platinum, and palladium bullion held in allocated storage.[115]

Early G&SR Business Relationships

During the company's development and early years from 1996 to 1998, individual prestigious financial institutions ignored and rejected this new company. However, by 1999, a shift in the public's perception of e-gold® began to emerge. A significant breakthrough for e-gold® occurred with Claude Cormier and Philip Spicer. In 1999, Philip Spicer was the principal of the Central Fund of Canada (CEF), and Claude Cormier was editor of The Ormetal Report.[116]

In later emails, Jackson described Philip Spicer's fund in these terms "Central Fund was a mutual fund offering a pure play on gold, with something like 98% of assets held in the form of good delivery bullion bars in allocated storage."[117]

On July 1, 1999, Jackson was a guest the Spicer's home in Ancaster, Ontario. The house

---

[114] Tim Jackson, When Gold Makes Cents: It May Sound Crazy, but the eGold Payment Mechanism Based on Deposits of Precious Metal, Is Cheap, Efficient and Easy, FIN. TIMES, July 13, 1999, at 18.

[115] e-gold Ltd, et al. "Archives of Douglas Jackson/e-gold." Ancaster, Ontario, 24 Aug. 1999.

[116] Ormetal Inc. was in the precious metals business since 1995. The Ormetal Report was a newsletter produced by French-Canadian small-cap gold analyst Claude Cormier. It began in 1995.

[117] Jackson, Doug. "e-Gold Fiduciary Safeguards." Received by Carl Mullan, *e-Gold Fiduciary Safeguards*, 19 July 2018. 7-19-2018-book1-e-gold-fiduciary-safeguards.odt

also contained the CEF offices. This statement from Jackson recounted the significant events of that evening.

> It was while I was a guest in the Spicer home that I learned that Phil had been the one who, sometime in the early 90s, originally came up with core elements, and the name, for what later became Goldmoney. He described his surprise when, some months after his germinal discussion with James Turk, he discovered Turk had unilaterally trademarked the name and filed a provisional patent. As it turned out, when Goldmoney was actually launched as an online service (in 2001), it bore no resemblance to the original scheme but rather had more or less emulated the e-gold model. The critical aspect which had been jettisoned was a notion of making a distinction between gold stored in various locations – loco London, loco Hong Kong etc. – which would have prevented Goldmoney from being fully fungible. It would have been analogous to the way a balance of USD in one bank differs from the balance in another. For example, if you have $200 in Citi and $200 in BoA you can't make a single payment of $300. Actually, it was worse than that. In the bank example, once two USD-denominated payments reached the recipient account they could be combined. With Goldmoney however, as originally conceived and claimed in the patent filing, the recipient would have also had an immiscible quantity of the London money and a quantity of the Hong Kong version.[118]

Philip Spicer was one of Jackson's original information sources on the development of vital elements in e-gold's sound financial model. One of those concepts was the need to establish a trust for holding title to metal assets. History had shown that a suitably organized trust could separate e-gold's precious metal assets from any legal action against the company's corporate administrative entities or customers. This strategy proved to be a critical factor in the post-1999 structure of the e-gold® business. Jackson provided further insight into this development.

> Such a trust would not have individual named beneficiaries but rather would hold title on behalf of a defined class and/or pursuant to a defined purpose. Later, as we delved into trust arcana, we learned that a purpose trust was ideal and that, terminology-wise, it was more common to use the eleemosynary terminology in relation to a charitable, often non-profit, purpose. The original aspect of what we hoped to accomplish with the Spicer collaboration was an arrangement for a dual signatory for any releases of bullion. This second signatory would also be notified as

[118] Ibid

to all additions to reserves, which basically meant being cc'ed on all reports from bullion dealers and repositories when new bullion was bailed into the trust. We elected to frame this in terms of an Escrow Agent function, since the independent external party serving as second signatory would effectively have sufficient control over assets as to be able to make representations as to their quantity and composition in perfect confidence.[119]

In October, G&SR lowered the fees charged per OutExchange down to a fixed cost of 0.1 gram for Gold/Platinum/Palladium or 5 grams for Silver. In the fourth quarter of 1999, Gold & Silver Reserve Inc. also lowered fees on exchange services. After this event, in December 1999, e-gold® implemented a new account block feature that was designed as a security utility to prevent designated accounts from receiving incoming e-gold® Spends.

During each year of e-gold's growth, the company introduced additional features and other tools that helped integrate the platform into everyday commercial use. Before 1999 ended, e-gold® had introduced a commercial feature that gave all e-gold® account holders the ability to Spend e-gold® using a mobile device. Below is a copy of the news published on the e-gold® website.

> Wireless Phone access to e-gold now available
> Pay off your dinner tab right in the restaurant?
> Check your e-gold account balance on the city bus?
> You can do it now.
> e-gold now provides wireless access via its pcs.e-gold.com site. Use your SprintPCS Wireless Web phone (or other compatible HDML/WAP browser) to access http://pcs.e-gold.com. To see how the phone interface works, visit our e-gold wireless demo.[120]

By year's end, all e-gold® accounts were accessible through mobile devices. This e-gold® mobile feature was operating seven years before mobile payments were an option on PayPal accounts.

◆

Jackson alleges that throughout 2001, 2002, and 2003 at least one fired e-gold® rogue employee, who previously worked in management, collaborated with others to bring down

---

[119] Ibid
[120] "Gold News." *Recent / Noteworthy Items about e-gold*, e-gold.com, 9 Apr. 2000, web.archive.org/web/20000815053908fw_/http://www.e-gold.com/news.html.

e-gold®. Jackson makes some compelling allegations, supported by documents that Charles Evans conspired with Ian Grigg and engaged in an activity that would cause harm to Jackson and e-gold®. In addition to Jackson's claims, circumstantial evidence, along with some strong opinions, surfaced to support this conspiracy. The information presented here, along with the documentation is for the reader's evaluation and consideration.

Ian Grigg and the Digigold Case Summary

In October 1999, DigiGold.net, Ltd., which was owned by the same family trusts that owned e-gold Ltd. and operated by the same contractor as e-gold®, began issuing a new innovative digital cash product, backed by e-gold®. The units were named DigiGold_AUG. G&SR, Dba Omnipay, was the primary dealer between e-gold® and DigiGold_AUG and exchanged these digital units on a gram for gram basis. One gram of e-gold® equaled one gram of DigiGold_AUG.

In a 1999 letter to Philip Spicer, Jackson explained some details behind DigiGold and its relationship to e-gold®:[121]

> "Simultaneous with efforts directly involving e-gold, we are also moving ahead with a technically fascinating digital cash. The financial cryptography community was initially slow to embrace e-gold because its technology is not much different than the book entry systems already commonplace in banking. The digital cash however, is at the head of the class in terms of technical interest. The system it embodies extends the Ricardo system described on http://www.systemics.com. I look forward to detailing how the two systems complement one another.[122]

In a May 22, 2000 response to a post on the Webfunds users discussion list, Ian Grigg lauded the benefits of his Ricardo technology.

> There are several advantages for WebFunds over e-gold. Or, Ricardo over e-gold technology:
> - Ricardo can do infinitely complex currencies, e-gold will be limited to the four metals. Dollars, shares, bonds, loyalty, etc.
> - Ricardo is designed to be fast and programmatic. e-gold hasn't got that, although will get a limited version of this access method in the next generation.
> - Ricardo has special features that make it ideal for new applications. At least

---

[121] Jackson, Douglas. "Follow-up ." Received by Philip Spicer, *Follow-up*, 1 July 1999.
[122] Ibid

one of those new applications is in the works now.

- WebFunds is a platform for multiple systems, rather than just the one that is there now, and work is being undertaken now to add a different payment type on to it, one that is sufficiently exciting to its fans that they are forking out the cash to have it done. In theory, one could add a wallet to WebFunds to also do e-gold, so if WebFunds were to take off in a big way, we would not be faced with competition, but cooperation.

Iang[123]

In a 2020 email, Dr. Jackson reflected on his past experiences with Ian Grigg and Digigold. He acknowledged Grigg's positive contributions as well as several negative experiences.

> The negative aspects of Grigg's involvement with e-gold were offset to significant degree by insights he contributed: The two most critical insights that informed the restructuring of e-gold's institutional arrangements and business model at the turn of the millennium related to establishment of a trust and to separation of roles. Phil Spicer, as I've described, introduced me to the logic and merits of the bullion reserves being held in trust. But the other critical element and, quite frankly, the distinction that differentiated e-gold from all its gold-mongering would-be imitators (then or since) and set the stage for exponential growth, was the decision to "ringfence" (Ian's term) the core functions of issuance and settlement from the exchange function.[124]

> Over the next few years, Grigg went from one would-be backer to another. I don't know if he ever faced up to the fact that our Digigold and nascent digitalbearer projects turned out to have been the high water mark of his Ricardo scheme. Certainly the vengeance Grigg and Evans wreaked on us was ruinous for us, and possibly humanity (time will tell), but an honest appraisal would surely conclude he 'blotted his copy book' big time by pissing in the rice bowl we had provided.[125]

An Arbitrator did not uphold the claims brought by DigiGold[Jackson] and delivered the

---

[123] Grigg, Ian. "[Webfunds-Users] [Fwd: e-gold: DigiGold]." *[Webfunds-Users]*, Webfunds.org, 22 May 2000, linas.org/mirrors/www.webfunds.org/2001.04.16/pipermail/webfunds-users/2000-May/000148.html.

[124] Jackson, Douglas. "Evans and Grigg Analysis and Write-Up." Received by Carl Mullan, *Evans and Grigg Analysis and Write-Up*, 8 Apr. 2020.

[125] Ibid

final award on 28th August 2002.   The Arbitrator's award to Systemics was paid out in full by DigiGold, in late January 2003.

Early Praise for DigiGold

The following September 16th, 1999 article by author Claire Wolfe is reprinted here, with permission, conveys her clear insight on digital gold. Claire is a well-respected writer and privacy advocate. Her concise understanding of modern politics and human nature are always worth sharing. This piece is an excellent view of what e-gold® represented to many users during its early years.

Will this replace banking?

Money, in Hardyville, is a private matter -- just as it used to be everywhere. What you have and what you do with it is between you and your banker, you and the shopkeeper, you and you alone.

Unless the government has take-to-the-judge evidence that the $10,000 you just deposited is a payoff for rubbing out your lawyer's brother's mother-in-law (You know, like, actual harm has been done to an actual victim), it has no cussed business sticking its nose into your financial affairs -- not to tax you, not to keep statistical tables on you, not "for your own good," and not to go on fishing expeditions about such non-crimes as "money laundering" or that silliest bureauspeak crime of all – "structuring."

If there were a Bank of Hardyville, the tellers wouldn't question you about why you were making withdrawals, wouldn't file Suspicious Activity Reports, wouldn't demand your National ID number or fingerprints, wouldn't routinely report your account to the tax vampires, and wouldn't sniff down their quasi-governmental noses at you. They'd treat you as a valued customer, not a crook or a peasant.

Besides all that, the confidentiality of your relationship with your banker would be as sacrosanct as that with your lawyer.

It goes without saying that there's no bank in Hardyville. Are you kidding? Any banker who tried to set up that kind of operation would be arrested just ahead of his customers. So here in town we mostly use cash, money orders, barter and even the occasional bit of gold or silver. But these methods have their limitations and inconveniences.

e-gold -- and soon, DigiGold

Bob-the-Nerd -- he of the No Name (and Mostly Out-To-Lunch-Back-in-20-Minutes) Computer Store -- has for several years been beating the drum for a different type of store-and-spend currency option, called e-gold.

e-gold has been offered on the Net for about three years -- which makes it about as established as Lloyds of London. Well, in cyberspace terms, anyway. Because of the bankruptcy of an earlier, much-ballyhooed electronic money system -- David Chaum's Digicash (now ignominiously known as Digicrash) -- e-gold has had a struggle establishing a major market base or getting coverage from the once-burned wired press.

Though I've written about e-gold in my books, I've personally ignored it because it didn't offer the one thing Internet commerce ought to enable -- truly, totally anonymous transactions. So, a couple of months ago, when James Ray -- "chief mouth" of e-gold started nagging me (Yes, Jim, you nagged) to write about e-gold, I said nope, no way, not interested, ho hum.

Then two things happened. First, a whole raft of orders for my books turned up missing in the mail under circumstances that pointed at theft, rather than mere postal incompetence. One of those orders was from an e-gold advocate, who kindly refrained from saying, "I told you so." Second, at a conference, I heard one of e-gold's techno-mavens, Douglas Jackson, (another is Ian Grigg) refer to something new -- something called DigiGold. DigiGold, he said, will be a "strongly privacy enabled" electronic medium of exchange that uses e-gold as its backing. An anonymous currency with a metal base!

As soon as I heard that, I said, "Hey, Jim! Tell me more." Now (though I stop short of endorsing either of these systems and urge you to investigate for yourself) I'm kind of excited.

First, a little on e-gold

Before getting to DigiGold, here's some quick background on e-gold. If you want to know more, just follow the link to their website.

Unlike other electronic exchange media, e-gold isn't just fiat government notes turned into bookkeeping blips. The stuff is real money. When you open an e-gold account, you can opt to store your currency as gold, silver, platinum or palladium -- metal in a warehouse. Everything in your account is 100-percent metal-backed. If you want verification that the metal is there, and assurance that these guys aren't going to take your money and run, check their website. (Jim Ray doesn't mind answering those questions -- but he does wonder why we don't ask our local bankers just how much real money they keep in their empty vaults!)

To open an account, you give minimal information about yourself -- information even a privacy freak like me considered non-invasive. Though they want an actual, physical address, it doesn't even have to be yours. No ID. No SSN. No fingerprints, either.

Of course, e-gold isn't banking as they'd be the first to note. It's a currency system. You won't be paid interest on the metal in your account. In fact, you'll have to pay small transaction and storage fees. That's how they make their money. (Opening the account is free and you don't have to put in any money to start with.)

What can you do with e-gold?

- Pay money to other e-gold account holders.
- Purchase items from vendors who have e-gold accounts.
- Through a process called OutExchange, pay your bills or make pre-arranged payments to merchants that don't have e-gold accounts.
- (You still can't go into the drugstore and write an e-gold check.)
- Make transactions of any size.
- Make transactions in any major currency or by weight of any of the four metals.

You can also donate to worthy causes. One of the finest, Jews for the Preservation of Firearms Ownership, has account number 105440. Or there's Texans Against Intrusive Government; they're bringing suit against the use of SSNs on drivers licenses. TAIG holds account number 105988. Tons, ounces or grams of gold will also be welcome in an account I'm uncommonly fond of, 106974. (Only kidding, only kidding. Well, about the tons, anyway.)

It's necessary to have account numbers to make transactions, so I'm not giving away any secrets here. Security comes through password protection, secure servers and such. And that brings us to....DigiGold.

e-gold is private in the sense that they don't sell customer information, and that you can open an account using personal information of your choice. But being physically located in the U.S., with its leagues of financial enforcers, they don't dare offer an anonymous transaction system.

DigiGold -- debuting soon -- is a different critter.

DigiGold is, first of all, a bearer system. Whoever holds DigiGold can spend it. And as with cash or gold coins purchasers don't have to identify themselves to vendors and (this being the Internet) it's even possible for vendors to be unknown to purchasers. It's private. Unlike e-gold, DigiGold will have no transaction fees. That also means it has the same vulnerabilities as cash. As Jim says, "Light a cigar with a $100 bill -- and that bill's gone." If you sent a DigiGold payment unencrypted and it was snagged by a stranger, that stranger would be richer by X-amount of DigiGold. So there are certainly risks. Unlike most gov-cash, however, it's got a metal backing.

DigiGold is 100 percent e-gold backed. (Later, that will change to 25 percent e-gold,

75 percent commercial notes; DigiGold intends to be a profitable operation.) While e-gold is a Delaware corporation that must remain "pure as the driven snow" in the eyes of the fedgov, DigiGold will be an offshore entity -- in fact, an entity that exists only in cyberspace.

"Ah, yes," some gov-o-snoop is muttering right now, "Another cyberspace purveyor of money laundering, dope-dealing, terrorism, right-wing extremism, smut and all those other wonderful things that let me build my agency's budget. Oh, goody."

And of course DigiGold could be used by criminals -- for instance, by the CIA to hide payments for one of its drug-smuggling operations. It could be used exactly -- as Jim Ray notes -- the way "Alan Greenspan money is used by criminals every day. The fact is, unimaginative people use anonymity irresponsibly. Responsible people use anonymity to solve real problems." (Like the problem of bureaucrats sticking their noses into private affairs.)

Are governments everywhere going to hate DigiGold? Is Bill Clinton a womanizer? Of course, those who love to control others, and who see "crime" in every expectation of privacy, are going to detest DigiGold -- and it will be quite interesting to see whether the power of the state or the power of the sovereign individual prevails (as James Dale Davidson and Lord William Rees-Mogg predict in the linked book of that name).

Bottom line: No amount of government intrusion will halt crime. But impenetrable financial privacy may halt government intrusion.

"If DigiGold was sold as the best thing ever to happen to Murder Inc. (or the CIA), that would be terrible," Jim agrees. "But this is going to be the best thing that ever happened to liberty. Think about it; Thomas Jefferson would have been horrified by a government that snooped into everyone's record books." If DigiGold is all its promoters say, it could give us back something our ancestors accepted as a given.

"Something like DigiGold is technologically and mathematically inevitable," Jim concludes. "Trying to build barriers against it is like trying to build sand castles against tidal waves. If they destroy this system, someone else will build another one. I just hope to see it happen peacefully and for prosperity."

To find out more, DigiGold is currently in "late alpha or early beta" testing stage. It isn't yet ready for marketing -- though it could go live in the next few months.

© 1999 Claire Wolfe

WND originally published this article. However, it is no longer online. A copy was retrieved from Marc.info.[126]

[126] Hettinga, Robert. "Will This Replace Banking?" *Cypherpunks*, Marc.info, 16 Sept. 1999,

2000

From 1996 through 1999, the e-gold® platform had formed and hardened its credible institutions.

- 100% reserve
- Immediate settlement
- Non-repudiation
- Real-time transparency
- Decoupling of numeraire

This focus was later summarized in a 2008 memorandum to the court for the sentencing of Gold & Silver Reserve, Inc. "Having stoically battled the financial adversity of the formative years, beginning in 2000 the Companies finally began to see growing acceptance of their product."[127]

By 2000, e-gold® was experiencing explosive growth in the number of new customers, the amount of stored precious metal, and the number of daily e-metal transactions. Several critical influences were driving this growth.

- The establishment and emergence of independent providers of exchange services.
- The first privately owned online casino accepting e-gold®.
- E-commerce software tools that supported e-gold® payments.
- Thousands of new debit cards accepting e-gold® deposits facilitating instant access to fiat currency.

This breakout year was a time when the co-founders looked inward to refine their doctrines and logic. Jackson's innovations became a catalyst for significant positive change to the e-gold® platform.

By the end of February 2000, account holders had completed a cumulative total of 50,000 Spend transactions. By April, that figure had risen to 100,000, and as September ended, customers had performed more than 1,000,000 Spends. E-gold® had become the first successful digital currency system to gain widespread merchant adoption and a global user base. E-gold® was also the first payment service provider to offer an application

---

marc.info/?l=cypherpunks&m=95280154629767&w=2.

[127] *https://legalupdate.e-gold.com2008/11/sentencing-memorandum-of-gold-silver-reserve-inc-second-submission-2008-11-17.html UNITED STATES OF AMERICA V. E-GOLD LIMITED, GOLD & SILVER RESERVE, INC., DOUGLAS L. JACKSON, BARRY K. DOWNEY and REID A. JACKSON.* 17 Nov. 2008, SENTENCING MEMORANDUM OF GOLD & SILVER RESERVE, INC.

programming interface (API), enabling third-party businesses and software components to interact with the e-gold® platform. Customers and merchants had adopted digital gold for metals trading, online auctions, online casinos, shopping carts, web hosting, and even a donation platform. The past three years of calculated efforts had shaped G&SR and guided e-gold® toward an inevitable, more refined stage of institutional arrangements.

> During this period, the Companies initiated efforts to develop a strategic relationship with a suitable and prominent merchant who could benefit from and highlight e-gold's secure transactions, low cost and global reach.[128]

Restructuring

The 21st century ushered in several crucial platform changes that marked a clear-cut separation between G&SR's pre-2000 operation and the company's new, more institutional architecture. Multiple factors aided this system wide expansion.

- The deployment of major platform refinements
- Separation of currency exchange from the core functions of issuance and settlement
- Global acceptance of the new competitive independent third-party exchange provider model

From the e-gold® Statistics pages, available in the Internet Archive, here is a chart showing the surge in new accounts from January 2000 through January 2001.[129]

---

[128] Ibid

[129] "Gold Statistics." *e-gold Examiner*, e-gold.com, 28 Nov. 1999, web.archive.org/web/19991128161421/http://www.e-gold.com:80/stats.html.

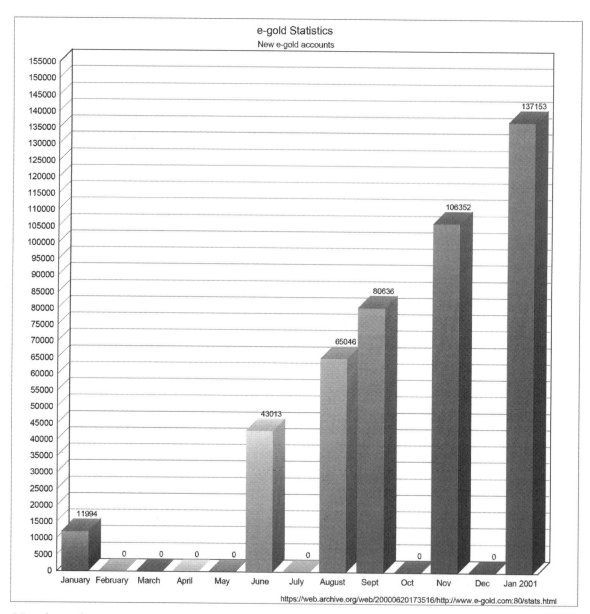

e-gold Statistics
New e-gold accounts

https://web.archive.org/web/20000620173516/http://www.e-gold.com:80/stats.html

Number of new e-gold accounts during the month. Data from the e-gold® statistics page in the Internet Archive[130] shows the massive increase in spends during the same time period.

[130] "Gold Statistics." *e-gold Examiner*, 20 June 2000, web.archive.org/web/20000620173516/http://www.e-gold.com:80/stats.html.

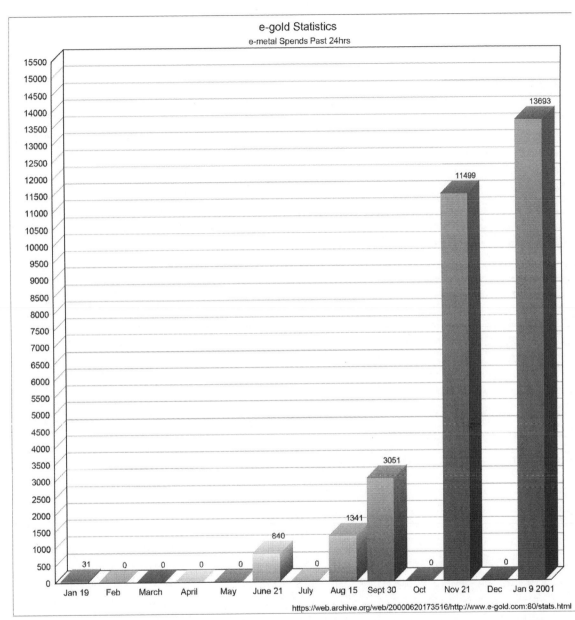

e-gold Statistics
e-metal Spends Past 24hrs

https://web.archive.org/web/20000620173516/http://www.e-gold.com:80/stats.html

Number of daily e-gold spends on one day. A zero (0) indicates no data was available for that month from the archive.[131]

---

[131] Ibid

In December, a technical issue prevented the system from managing a higher transaction load, and the pace of growth briefly slowed.

Risk

Financial assets such as direct loans or, as commonly held by monetary authorities, debt securities are subject to risk.

- Performance risk – Risk, the debtor does not pay in full or on time
- Interest rate risk – Fluctuation of a debt instrument's market value, particularly the fall in price of a bond with a rise in interest rates
- Market risk – The risk that during times of market disruption even sound securities may be unsalable except at fire-sale prices

The ability to separate these potential risks from the dual roles of issuance and settlement safeguarded the e-gold® platform and all customer assets. Restructuring isolated e-gold® client operations from possible payment defaults and other well-recognized risks that accompany all bank transactions. E-gold Ltd. assumed the following responsibilities:

- Performance of the e-gold Account Agreement
- The integrity of the e-gold balance sheet
- Governance of the e-gold system

The post-restructuring arrangement allowed G&SR to focus exclusively on exchange operations. Before devolving exchange operations, the early years' experiences had taught Jackson a few lessons. First, any entity offering exchange services, by accepting payment through conventional means, was at risk of loss from payment reversal. So when Jackson established OmniPay as a separate business, it imposed a universal identity verification requirement based on the account holder's ability to receive a 'secret' via postal mail and enter it online while logged into the OmniPay site.

G&SR's newly formed OmniPay division effectively became the 'Primary Dealer' for the e-gold community, as elaborated below. Issuance and settlement became the responsibility of a Nevis, West Indies Corporation named e-gold Ltd. The foreign company served as a general contractor responsible for the performance of the e-gold® Account User Agreement and also took over as bailee. e-gold Ltd. assumed responsibility for the e-gold® family of currencies.[132] In 2020 emails, Jackson shared this insight regarding e-gold's restructuring.

The original e-gold implementation entailed a single entity that not only issued the money and settled Spends between system participants. It also made a market for exchange - transactions termed 'InExchange' and 'OutExchange'. But this is not how other issuers of real money—in particular government monetary authorities—structure their monetary systems. A person that wishes to obtain USD does not approach the US Federal Reserve to buy some. They can only obtain USD by receiving payment from someone else who already has some (or an existing line of credit).

The biggest, most obvious problems with the issuer of money also making a market for exchange is that it ends up exposed to the business risks of currency exchange. It may be exposed to exchange rate risk. But worse, it also finds itself receiving payments of conventional money through conventional remote payment systems. A major rationale for e-gold in the first place was the fact that such systems are slow, expensive and, worst of all, repudiable.

But the other compelling reason for the issuer of money and the entity responsible for settlement of transfers to avoid the exchange business is that it enables emergence of an extensive and ever-more liquid market for exchange, offered by independent providers on a competitive basis. The emergence of such a network leads to a number of businesses for which it is in their best interests if significant demand for the new money emerges. The result is that the core entity itself has greatly reduced need to engage in marketing – the providers of exchange services do the heavy lifting."[133]

Restructuring coincided with a corporate merger between the Jackson Trading Company (Florida Corporation) and G&SR, Inc. Filed with the State of Florida on December 29, 2000, and effective December 31, 2000.[134]

The company announced its restructuring goals on the website, "more clearly delineating the separateness of the currency exchange services offered by G&SR (the U.S. company) and the e-gold® payment system (the non-U.S. Company)."[135]

---

[132] Nevis is the smaller of the two islands comprising the nation of Saint Kitts and Nevis in the Caribbean. The islands are part of the Leeward Islands chain of the West Indies.

[133] Jackson, Douglas. "Evans and Grigg Analysis and Write-Up." Received by Carl Mullan, *Evans and Grigg Analysis and Write-Up*, 8 Apr. 2020.

[134] "Article of Merger, Merger Sheet." *State of Florida Division of Corporations*, State of Florida, 29 Dec. 2000, search.sunbiz.org/Inquiry/CorporationSearch/ConvertTiffToPDF?storagePath=COR%5C2001%5C0118%5C30533793. tif&documentNumber=P95000073027.

[135] "Gold Transition Progress." *e-gold Transition Progress*, e-gold.com, 5 Dec. 2000,

In a 2018 email, Jackson described how the company restructuring advanced the business, "The circa-2000 restructuring, implementing separation of roles - where the core entity (e-gold Ltd) was ringfenced off, responsible for the Issuance and Settlement functions, leaving exchange for third parties - was what set the stage for the subsequent exponential growth."

This innovative corporate architecture, designed by Jackson, afforded e-gold® account holders a significantly higher level of customer asset protection than previously available. Retail buyers could no longer go directly to the e-gold® Issuer to obtain e-metals, just as people seeking to get US dollars do not buy them from the Federal Reserve. Soon after the restructuring, dozens of large and small independent exchange providers launched in various countries around the world. These exchange providers served retail customers exchanging digital currency for federal money. Many existing exchange providers for other currencies, such as WebMoney Transfer, added e-gold® to their lineup. Consequently, the e-gold® restructuring established a small army of new global vendors willing to buy and sell e-gold®. The emerging marketplace blossomed.

After this transformation, exchange providers began offering e-gold® on a more competitive basis, and the market gained liquidity. Some were willing to accept new world currencies and new methods of payment. These advances opened up the market to many previously excluded individuals. The time required to exchange federal money into e-gold® (and vice versa) was reduced dramatically along with individual exchange fees.

As more entities around the world exchanged e-gold®, and more funding options emerged, the e-gold® consumer market evolved into a highly liquid community. The restructuring of G&SR had been a remarkably successful mechanism for developing e-gold's global customer base. G&SR began offering a new innovative set of hybrid currency exchange services under its new OmniPay® brand.

The OmniPay System

After the restructuring, e-gold® balances were identified as non-allocated, indirect, and fungible ownership interest in gold® bullion through the Special Purpose Trust. Account-holders had the option to transfer their ownership interest (or portions thereof) to other e-gold account holders. The act of transferring digital e-gold between accounts was called a "Spend."

However, to move value out of the e-gold platform, or make a payment to persons or businesses that did not directly accept e-gold, an account holder would use a third-party independent exchange provider. OmniPay was one of these entities, and quickly grew to become the largest independent exchange provider in the world. Thus, OmniPay, and other exchange providers, helped to deliver e-gold's money-like attribute. The liquidity afforded through these exchange providers translated into e-gold being readily exchangeable for national currencies through multiple countries.

OmniPay became the primary dealer of e-metals to the public, with the obligation to make a market at all times. OmniPay exchanged national currency for e-metal, transacting between the issuer, e-gold Ltd., and all other third-party independent exchange providers. As the primary dealer, OmniPay had the full-time responsibility of maintaining cash and e-metal liquidity, effectively serving as the external market of last resort for any retail exchange service facing an imbalance in customer demand resulting in the need to replenish depleted trading balances.

7. The exchange orders that OmniPay processes

There are three types of exchange orders that OmniPay processes:

a. "InExchange" (National Currency toe-metal):

A User remits national currency (for example, USD) to OmniPay via bank wire. Upon receipt of remittance, OmniPay pays the User in e-gold via the e-gold system, according to the terms of the exchange order.

b. "Metal-to-Metal" (e-metal toe-metal):

A User remits e-metal (for example, e-silver) to OmniPay via the e-gold system. Upon receipt of remittance, OmniPay pays the User in a different e-metal (such as egold) via the e-gold system, according to the terms of the exchange order.

c. "OutExchange" (e-metal to National Currency):

A User remits e-gold to OmniPay via the e-gold system. Upon receipt of remittance, OmniPay pays the Payee, as specified by the User, in national currency (for example, USD) via the banking system, according to the terms of the exchange order.[136]

◆

Regarding Early Investigative Work

In 2019 email discussions, Jackson explained some of e-gold's in-house investigative work, before and after the organization's restructuring.

Prior to March 2000 I personally performed all the investigative work and liaised

---

[136] CASE NUMBER: 07-167-M-01. *UNITED STATES OF AMERICA V. E-GOLD LIMITED, GOLD & SILVER RESERVE, INC., DOUGLAS L. JACKSON, BARRY K. DOWNEY and REID A. JACKSON.* SENTENCING MEMORANDUM OF GOLD & SILVER RESERVE, INC., Nov. 2008.

with outside law enforcement, while Barry handled the actual correspondence and submission of responses to subpoenas etc. When Randy Trotter came on, I trained him re SQL queries. He quickly mastered all that and went on to develop a number of rapid query templates enabling him, and subsequently his team, to track down and exhaustively evaluate leads much faster than I had ever managed. [His role was Head of Due Diligence and Investigations]. [137]

♦

World Gold Council

In November 2000, Dr. Jackson spoke at an international conference in Rome called "The Euro, The Dollar and Gold" - organized by the World Gold Council. European central bankers, gold bankers and monetary economists from the academic community, including Nobel Prize winner Robert Mundell, Ph.D. (the "father of the Euro") attended the conference. During his presentation, Dr. Mundell remarked favorably about the emergence and nature of e-gold®. Professor Steve Hanke, one of the world's leading experts in currency boards (an alternative to the traditional central bank model), also echoed these comments and began to yield favorable attention for the e-gold®.

At the conference, a senior executive in the gold banking operations at JP Morgan (which was then in the process of merging with Chase) approached Dr. Jackson to suggest the formation of a relationship between e-gold, Ltd. and his bank. Dr. Jackson went to London to meet further with JP Morgan executives (including Thanksgiving dinner at one executive's home in Chelsea) and discuss the framework for such a relationship. JP Morgan urged Dr. Jackson to use JP Morgan's facilities to store gold bullion and to enter into a dealing relationship with the bank. During his JP Morgan meetings, Jackson met the CEO of the London Bullion Market Association (LBMA). Subsequently in the UK, Jackson was invited to speak at the LBMA conference in Istanbul.[138]

Additionally, e-gold® appeared in the 2000 World Gold Council Study on Digital Gold. The publication stated, "The first company offering digital gold (e-gold) is now in existence."[139] In February 2000, e-gold® continued its sponsorship of the annual Financial Cryptography conference FC00.

---

[137] Jackson, Douglas. "Notes for Carl." Received by Carl Mullan, *Notes for Carl*, 1 June 2019.

[138] CASE NUMBER: 07-167-M-01. *UNITED STATES OF AMERICA V. E-GOLD LIMITED, GOLD & SILVER RESERVE, INC., DOUGLAS L. JACKSON, BARRY K. DOWNEY and REID A. JACKSON.* SENTENCING MEMORANDUM OF GOLD & SILVER RESERVE, INC., Nov. 2008.

[139] Rahn, Richard W., B.R. MacQueen and M.L. Rogers (2000): "*Digital Money and Its Impact on Gold: Technical, legal and economic issues*", World Gold Council, London

X.com & PayPal

According to her 2019 online bio, Kathleen Donovan is an Accomplished Risk Management Executive in the San Francisco Bay Area. From 1999 through 2002, she was the Chief Credit Officer for X.com and PayPal.[140]

In March 2000, X.com merged with a company named Confinity. X.com was the surviving entity. Its largest shareholder and CEO was Elon Musk. In September 2000, Peter Thiel, the co-founder of Coinfinity, replaced Elon Musk, and in June of 2001, X.com took the new name PayPal.

In early 2000, employees at e-gold Ltd. were able to detect and interdicted $28,000 worth of fraudulent wire transfers used for the purchase of e-gold®. The funds had originated with x.com, and third party independent e-gold® exchange providers received them.[141]

After identifying the fraud, e-gold® had the funds returned to X.com. Email records from Omnipay/e-gold® later explained the reason for quickly repatriating the $28,000, without any legal order. Douglas Jackson stated he did it because returning the money "makes them [x.com] whole."

Immediately following this action, the e-gold® co-founders proposed a cooperative investigation arrangement to executives at x.com that would involve an interpleader. In 2019 emails, Jackson describes his version of an interpleader and his view of PayPal during those early years.

> The interpleader concept (I had learned of at the Lex conf) came to mind in the Paypal case because it seemed expedient to develop an efficient process to: share investigative data; arrest any improperly diverted value by freezing an account (if it could be done without harm to an innocent third party); and returning/restoring stolen value to its rightful owner. As noted though, they weren't interested in catching bad guys. They were in the business of raising round after round of investment, which required suppressing any public revelation of the rampant criminality infesting their system.[142]

From 1996 through 2000, e-gold® had developed the tools and skills required to detect, track, and often prevent, various types of electronic payment fraud. As the following email

---

[140] Kathleen Donovan graduated from Georgetown University in 1969 and later received an MBA in International Finance from The New York University Leonard N. Stern School of Business. Her resume includes past employment at Citibank FSB and the SunFund Corporation. https://www.linkedin.com/in/kathydonovan/

[141] In March 2000, X.com merged with a company called Confinity. The surviving entity was also named X.com; it's largest shareholder and CEO was Elon Musk. In September 2000, Peter Thiel, the co-founder of Coinfinity, replaced Elon Musk, and in June of 2001, X.com was renamed PayPal.

[142] Jackson, Doug. "Notes for Carl." Received by Carl Misty, *Notes for Carl*, 1 May 2019. 5-1-2019-Notes-for-Carl.odt

demonstrated, in 2000, e-gold's management appeared ready and willing to share their knowledge and tools to fight fraud with X.com. Around April 19, 2000, e-gold's co-founder Barry Downey sent a formal email to the person identified as the fraud manager for both X.com and PayPal. Her name was Kathleen Donovan.

> Dear Kathy:
> Your name and e-mail address was provided to me today by Virginia in your fraud department. I spoke to Virginia by calling 650-251-XXXX.
> I am General Counsel to Gold & Silver Reserve, Inc. (a Delaware company), the wholesale exchange provider for e-gold (R) (www.e-gold.com). I have been contacted by several of the retail exchange providers for e-gold who accept PayPal payments from Confinity, Inc. From my conversations with the retail exchange providers, it appears that Confinity has received a significant number of fraudulent payments from its customers, who have been the "Sender" of PayPal payments to the "Recipient" retail exchange providers. These retail exchange providers fulfill orders for e-gold, pay e-gold to the Senders of the PayPal payments and later are notified by Confinity that Confinity has taken the payments back out of the Recipient's PayPal account. After reviewing the Terms of Use at the www.paypal.com site, it appears that Confinity has not reserved the right to take back these payments under these circumstances and a different procedure should be implemented immediately for the e-gold retail exchange providers to avoid legal action against Confinity.
> While I do not represent the retail exchange providers, it seems that it would be in both of our company's interests for us to meet to discuss better procedures for dealing with the fraudulent credit card payments.
> With the technologies available to both companies, I am certain we can work together to implement appropriate procedures that will reduce the losses incurred by this fraud, limit the criminals' ability to commit this type of fraud against Confinity and more likely lead to the arrest and conviction of the criminals' committing this fraud.
> Please contact me at your earliest convenience to discuss these issues. If at all possible, I would like to discuss these issues with you sometime today or tomorrow.
> Very truly yours, Barry K. Downey[143]

After a phone call between Downey and Kathy Donovan, Downey followed up the conversation with the detailed proposal.

---

[143] "Proposal." Received by Kathy Donovan, *Proposal*, 26 Apr. 2000

Barry Downey <bdowney@smithdowney.com>
Wed 4/26/2000 10:05 AM
To: Kathy Donovan <XXXX@x.com>

Kathy:

The following is the proposal we discussed last week that would allow x.com, Confinity, Inc., Gold & Silver Reserve, Inc., e-gold Ltd. and other similar entities to work together to curtail fraudulent activities while avoiding liability to innocent parties.

I would like to discuss this proposal this week, if at all possible. I also would like to discuss two specific sets of circumstances involving two retail exchange providers of e-gold to see if we can resolve the existing problems for these providers. Are you available any time today before 11:30 a.m., your time, or anytime Thursday or Friday?

Thank you.

Barry K. Downey

(410) 321-9351

General Counsel, Gold & Silver Reserve, Inc.

PROPOSAL

A cooperative mechanism to combat fraud is proposed for PayPal, x.com, e-gold and other providers of online electronic currencies or payment systems. The proposed mechanism would provide effective means for investigating fraudulent exchanges and potentially enable:

- apprehension of check kiters and credit card fraudsters,
- stabilization and recovery of value that has crossed institutional/transactional boundaries,
- limitation of the liability of participants.

Problem

PayPal and x.com engage in two distinct businesses:

- a core business, settling transfers of value between participants who use their system,
- exchange, accepting national currency payments as a means of loading value into their settlement space.

e-gold was also initially organized to perform these separate functions but split the core currency business from exchange specifically to isolate core functions, that must be risk free, from exchange, which is a profit center, but entails risk.

The recurring problem is that criminals take advantage of the ineffectiveness of transaction authentication mechanisms used for credit card transactions and for drawing from bank accounts. The criminal will establish an account in one or several of the systems using bogus or stolen identity information. The perp then funds an account via a fraudulent bank transfer or credit card payment. The perp then waits until the system makes funds available and uses the funds to buy another form of electronic currency from an innocent third party. The initial provider then becomes aware of the fraud and discovers that the identity of the criminal is unknown to them. **It is at this point that an effective mechanism is needed.** Lacking an appropriate mechanism, some of the providers have repudiated payments that were transmitted via their payment system and accepted in good faith by innocent third parties. This is a class action suit waiting to happen and defeats the major purpose of offering an electronic currency, that is, to make means available for accepting payment at low cost and not having payment rolled back despite no fault of the recipient.

Constraints

In the e-gold system, the electronic transfer – an e-gold payment – is non-repudiable. [e-gold Ltd. avoids exposure to the costs, risks and other inadequacies of bank administered payment systems by abstaining from any exchange activity whatsoever. Third parties perform the functions of loading/distribution at their own risk and for their own profit]. The e-gold Account User Agreement provides that

a) e-gold will not freeze without court or arb order

b) e-gold will not release customer information without court or arb order.

OmniPay, the primary market maker for e-gold exchange activities, will not stop payment or refuse to honor an exchange unless ordered by an arbitrator/court or indemnified by the party requesting these actions.

Details

All parties participating in this agreement should engage an arbitrator who would serve as an   Interpleader. At the first indication of a fraudulent transfer, the party that accepted the fraudulent payment would notify the Interpleader. The Interpleader would direct all parties to:

 - exchange information relating to the fraud,
 - attempt to stabilize value,
 - return information to the Interpleader regarding disposition of funds.

Stabilization of value would entail freezing the account only of the perp himself or of other accounts clearly controlled by the same person.

Customer agreements would make it clear that an account can be frozen only by order of suitable arbitrator or court. Acting in compliance with the Interpleader's order would therefore not expose the payment system provider to additional liability. In the case where recovery could be made without loss, the Interpleader would order return of funds.

In the case where investigation identifies outside entities that might have further information that could lead to identification, apprehension and conviction of the perp, the Interpleader would contact the outside parties with an information request or obtain a court order for release of information and/or stabilization of value. Examples of an inquiry or order to an outside entity would be if the group generates a list of IP numbers and timestamps that might enable the perp's ISP to identify the perpetrator. Another example might be where the perp has made payment to a merchant who might have delivered goods to the perp and may have a copy of the delivery address.

Advantages

Most courts are unfamiliar with emerging ecommerce facilities. They would require extensive coaching regarding procedures and possibly even the legal nuances. There is a risk that a government agency would make the problem worse by demonizing and persecuting the electronic payment system, or of imposing ill-advised regulations that would impair customer privacy. Routine use of the same arbitrator would have the benefit of expertise and experience leading to more rapid response and probably lower cost since the Interpleader could reuse procedures and documents.

The cooperative group could also control dissemination of data to the press, such that for instance successful busting of an international conspiracy could be parlayed into positive press while the risk of negative press from freezing the accounts of innocent parties would be minimized.

Next steps

Conference of inhouse legal counsel of concerned parties.

Identification and recruitment of suitable arbitrator [we know of several candidates that are quite interested in developing this niche].

Exchange of contact numbers of in-house fraud staff. Possible coordination of research and review of customer agreements.[144]

Kathy did not respond to Mr. Downey's email, and Paypal did not acknowledge or discuss this proposal with e-gold®.

Peter Thiel

Peter Thiel, a former hedge fund manager, conceived of the idea that became PayPal in the fall of 1998, after giving a speech at Stanford University. After the speech, he

[144] Ibid

met up with Max Levchin, a 23-year-old programmer with experience at three start-ups. After throwing around a few ideas for how to mix their talents, they decided to focus on digital payments.[145]

On February 24, 2001, Salon magazine published an article by Damien Cave entitled *Losing faith in PayPal*.[146] In this article, the founder of PayPal, Peter Thiel, is quoted making several remarks that mentioned e-gold's business. Here is the extracted text from that article.

> Thiel believes that the vast majority of the people whose accounts have been closed or back-charged deserve some of the blame for taking money from "sketchy" customers. Thiel noted that one of the companies that Stoney Brody purchased gold from was e-gold, an offshore company based in the Caribbean that had been a favorite target of the previous summer's gangsters, many of whom attempted to launder funds by buying gold certificates. "While I doubt this person [Brody] is engaged with the Russian mafia, I don't think [he and other merchants] are totally innocent either," Thiel says. "They certainly know that much of the money they're receiving is from suspicious sources."

While describing e-gold® customers as "sketchy," Thiel failed to grasp the bigger picture; those same people were also X.com (PayPal) customers and account holders. Moreover, nearly a year previously, e-gold® had approached Paypal as it was ramping up and proposed a solution (the Interpleader arrangement) that could have thwarted these later incidents of fraud!

Thiel's puzzling comments evolved to nothing more than a classic case of "the pot calling the kettle black." Jackson issued a very public response through a letter to the editor of Salon.com. The e-gold® discussion list published the letter.[147]

> Douglas Jackson Fri, 23 Feb 2001
> Peter Thiel, according to today's salon.com article (correctly) describing the repudiable nature of PayPal payments, apparently regards it as appropriate to make reckless allegations that depict e-gold(r) http://www.e-gold.com as some sort of system to "launder funds." This (probably actionable) remark is especially ironic

---

[145] Cave, Damien. "Losing Faith in PayPal." *Salon*, Salon.com, 25 Sept. 2011, www.salon.com/2001/02/23/pay_pal/.
[146] Ibid
[147] Jackson, Douglas. "Thiel's Sloppy Libel." [e-gold List], The Mail Archive, 23 Feb. 2001, www.mail-archive.com/e-gold-list@talk.e-gold.com/msg02560.html.

given the multiple attempts that Gold & Silver Reserve, Inc. and other companies have made to help PayPal address PayPal's severe fraud problems. Gold & Silver Reserve, Inc. was the original developer and operator of the e-gold system. It now functions as the primary distributor of e-gold with its OmniPay service http://www.omnipay.net, a system of online exchange that functions as a hybrid payment system in its own right. OmniPay, by the way, accepts national currency payments only by wire transfer (subject to a $3000 minimum) because wire is the only non-repudiable method for receiving payments that involve the banking system. The first time we heard of x.com and PayPal was around November 1999 when our fraud detection protocols were triggered by a series of suspicious wires from x.com. We contacted Kathy "I guess I'M the fraud manager!" Donovan and informed her of our suspicions. x.com (shortly afterward merged with PayPal) never was able in that episode to even reconstruct how funds had been taken from their bank account. We actually had to explain to them that available funds and good funds are not synonymous and that their practice of ACH debit for funding accounts was an invitation for fraudsters. They mentioned to our amazement that they did not even capture IP numbers with the online application they were using at the time.

Since then we have detected and thwarted multiple episodes of would-be crooks who, having already taken PayPal to the cleaners, attempted to rip off our company or companies we do business with. In several incidents we have offered to help PayPal identify and prosecute obvious crooks but the attitude of their responses (like many banks) was that they would rather cover up the fact that they are being inundated by fraud rather than risk loss of investor confidence. Like so many dotcoms they seem to be in the business of raising money from investors, as opposed to earning profits (the former they have excelled at, the latter I doubt will ever occur).

To set the record straight regarding what e-gold is and how ridiculous it would be to use it as a system to hide the proceeds of crime...

e-gold enables people to use gold like they would money. e-gold is backed 100% by gold in allocated storage* under the signatory control of a third party escrow agent, titled to the e-gold Bullion Reserve Special Purpose Trust for the exclusive benefit of all e-gold account holders collectively. A person with an e-gold balance can click some to another account holder. These transfers settle immediately and, unlike PayPal or credit card transactions, are non-repudiable. e-gold is account based, so the entire lineage of any value stream is logged - right back to the time that value entered the e-gold universe via exchange. Sophisticated pattern matching protocols detect activities such as smurfing (attempts to structure transactions in a way to disguise large flows of value).

Please note that the e-gold shopping cart interface enables automation that enables a recipient to programmatically post accounts as paid and to deliver goods and services with total confidence that payment (including micro payments) is fully and irreversibly settled. The maximum cost of receiving an e-gold payment is 50 cents (US$-equiv.). For values under $50 the fee for receiving payment is 1%. There have been over 2 million e-gold transactions** even though, unlike PayPal, e-gold never needed to give money away as an inducement to open accounts, and in fact has never done much of anything in the way of marketing/promotion.
Douglas Jackson, MD
Chairman, OmniPay
Melbourne, FL 32901

In October 2001, e-gold Ltd. sued Paypal for libel. That following spring, the case was settled out of court with PayPal compensating e-gold® with an unknown amount of money. There is a "gag order" on this case, and neither party can comment. No further information is available.

However, in 2013, Peter Thiel again mentioned e-gold® in a negative light during an interview.

At paypal, one of the companies we encountered was this company called e-gold, which had anonymous sort-of certificates for gold that you could be traded anywhere in the world. At paypal, we made paypal operable with e-gold in March of 2000. We disconnected it from paypal three months later, when we found the main use for e-gold was people finding stolen credit cards, and charging the stolen credit card holders, and then laundering the money with anonymous gold certificates.
And in April of 2001, there was an interview with Wired magazine where they asked me about e-gold, and I said they were a sketchy company. The e-gold people then sued me for libel [the audience breaks out in laughter]. In October of 2001, we settled. You know, whenever we get sued in a company. What happens is you never negotiate...plaintiff's lawyers are like terrorists, and you never negotiate with terrorists...except in every specific instance. And so of course we settled with them in sort-of the spring of 2002. And then, sort of the aftermath was that around 2008, the FBI got around and arrested all the people, and they went to jail.[148]

Throughout this case, no employee at G&SR, e-gold®, or Omnipay received a jail sentence.

---

[148] Sitver, Michael. "Exclusive: Peter Thiel on Bitcoin." *The App Store Chronicle*, 7 Nov. 2014, www.appstorechronicle.com/2013/11/exclusive-peter-thiel-bitcoin.html.

One significant issue with PayPal's operation circa 2000-2001 stemmed from the practice of freezing the account of any PayPal user that received funds from a dubious or questionable PayPal sender's account. Even if the receiver did not know the individual, when the sender's account is suspect, PayPal froze the receiver's account. According to a September 10th, 2002 article by Matthew Humphries for Geek.com entitled *PayPal disputes can be taken to court:*

> "The biggest complaint made–and part of a current class-action suit against the company [PayPal]–is that Paypal has over 100,000 unanswered complaints, and instead of dealing with them just palms off the customers, locks their accounts, and keeps the interest."[149]

In that same February 24, 2001, Salon magazine published an article by Damien Cave entitled *Losing faith in PayPal* [150], Thiel discussed this inconvenience.

> Thiel says he regretted having to freeze the accounts, and wishes he didn't have to put in place other anti-fraud measures that incited further complaints, such as a more complicated sign-up and verification system. But he says PayPal had no choice: "PayMe, PayPlace, PayPro, ExchangePath -- they all went out of business because of the fraud issue. The fact of the matter is that people use our service because it's easier to use than anything else. As a result, there are more responsibilities that people have to assume," says Thiel.[151]

Thiel never mentions the non-repudiable nature of e-gold® spend transactions. This mechanism blocks the possibility of reversing a payment that eliminates the critical issue of fraudulent credit card payments and chargebacks.

In May 2001, Peter Thiel appeared to take advantage of a new meme that depicted e-gold® as being criminal friendly. Jackson later alleged that he believed Peter Thiel was attempting to denounce e-gold® as part of a misdirection strategy. Jackson asserts that the Thiel's efforts were likely part of lame attempts to hide a growing awareness of PayPal's "tsunami of fraud." Jackson speculated that Thiel was working to preserve PayPal's funding capability via round after round of private placements, in the presence of PayPal's mounting

[149] Humphries, Mathew. "PayPal Disputes Can Be Taken to Court." *Geek.com*, Ziff Davis, LLC. PCMag Digital Group, 10 Sept. 2002, www.geek.com/news/paypal-disputes-can-be-taken-to-court-550795/.

[150] Cave, Damien. "Losing Faith in PayPal." *Salon*, Salon.com, 25 Sept. 2011, www.salon.com/2001/02/23/pay_pal/.

[151] Ibid

deficits.[152]

E-gold® operated online for more than ten years through 165 different countries. Its business was privately funded and established through the personal investments of its co-founders and close associates.

From 1999 through February 2002, PayPal raised more than $210 million in venture capital financing from prominent financial backers including Sequoia Capital, Nokia Ventures and Madison Dearborn Partners.[153]

The e-gold® platform is estimated to have cost around $4 million for its development. Most of the funding came from the co-founders' saving. The company had no "first," "second," or "third" round of venture capital financing. After its launch, e-gold® funded its rapid expansion only using internally generated funds. Despite these money challenges, e-gold® stayed true to its original mission.

During that same ten year period, numerous other payment platforms, including PayPal, attempted to enter the marketplace with varying degrees of success. According to the Washington Post, in 2000, PayPal lost $127 million on revenue of $14.5 million. During it's first three years of operation, PayPal accumulated $264.7 million in losses.[154] A February 16th, 2002 article by Nicholas Johnston for the Washington Post detailed the massive losses PayPal incurred during it's start up period.

> The Palo Alto, Calif., provider of online payment services raised more than $60 million, giving it a market value of $1.2 billion. This happened despite accumulating $264.7 million in losses over the past three years, drawing scrutiny from banking regulators and facing lawsuits that threaten to shutter the firm.[155]

E-gold® thrived where others failed due to the knowledge of its co-founders, a robust business structure, and evolving self-governance. E-gold's non-repudiable settlement protocol and global reach delivered early market penetration and a worldwide customer base. These advanced gains, combined with e-gold's refined capabilities for detection and interdiction of illicit payments, could have ultimately provided significant benefits to any institution accepting online payments, such as the U.S. Postal Service or the Internal

---

[152] Jackson, Douglas. "*Re:*" Received by Carl Mullan, *Re:* 20 Jan. 2019.

[153] Johnson, Nicholas. "Shades of Yesteryear: PayPal IPO Gains 55%." *The Washington Post*, The Washington Post, 16 Feb. 2002AD, www.washingtonpost.com/archive/business/2002/02/16/shades-of-yesteryear-paypal-ipo-gains-55/102de841-3c85-47fa-90d5-5e5846eb2ac9/

[154] Johnson, al IPO Gains 55%." *The Washington Post*, The Washington Post, 16 Feb. 2002AD, www.washingtonpost.com/archive/business/2002/02/16/shades-of-yesteryear-paypal-ipo-gains-55/102de841-3c85-47fa-90d5-5e5846eb2ac9/.

[155] Ibid

Revenue Service.

In early 2000, online casinos were primarily accepting credit card deposits, and players had no fast method of withdrawing casino funds. It was common for players to wait for one to three business days to receive a casino credit or debit card deposit and three to six business days for bank transfers. In February 2000, a new online operation opened called The Gold Casino (TC). The only accepted method of funding or withdrawal for TGC was e-gold®. All TGC betting was denominated by weight in e-gold®. In 2000, the market value of one gram of gold was about ten dollars, which made the unit a popular wager. TGC operated 24/7, offering e-gold® players traditional casino games, including slot machines, poker, and blackjack.

Online gambling and betting in the unregulated 2000 Internet marketplace were risky for both the players and casinos. Three of the most significant issues at online casinos were:

- Players disputing credit card charges
- Players threatening to dispute card charges
- Scammers fraudulently using someone else's credit card

Because e-gold® did not expose casinos to chargeback risks, digital gold began gaining popularity with online gaming and wagering businesses. A February 25th, 2000 Wired.com article entitled *There's gold in That E-Casino* discussed The Gold Casino in these terms.

> The Gold Casino differs from rival online casinos by allowing gamblers to use e-gold, a true gold-backed Internet currency, to place bets and collect earnings. That may solve one of the thornier problems plaguing other virtual casinos: How lucky customers can escape with instant winnings.[156]

Incorporating a non-bank alternative method of payment, such as e-gold®, in a casino was a bold innovation that gave TGC the early first-mover advantage. Players enjoyed receiving their withdrawn e-gold® funds moments after winning or anytime during play. TGC was an instant success, and the use of e-gold® digital currency paved the way for thousands of other online digital gaming platforms.

On October 13th, 2006, the Unlawful Internet Gambling and Enforcement Act was signed into law by George W. Bush as a separate add-on to the SAFE Port Act of 2006. These new rules focused attention on the ability of e-gold® and other digital currencies to become a dynamic substitute for credit cards and bank transfers. However, Jackson was

---

[156] Staff, WIRED. "There's Gold in That E-Casino." *Wired*, Conde Nast, 5 June 2017, www.wired.com/2000/02/theres-gold-in-that-e-casino/.

quick to comply with the Act.

In 2019, he explained that once Congress passed the Act, e-gold immediately informed all known gambling sites that the company would not allow them to continue using e-gold. E-gold® would block all access to the platform for any gambling business that continued using the payment system.

Jackson further detailed the process by which e-gold® supervised individual accounts after the passage of the 2006 SAFE Port Act.

> When the SAFE Port bill was enacted we still understood e-gold to be an offshore company since it was incorporated in Nevis and any of its dealing that required it to make payments to G&SR (which were in e-gold since e-gold Ltd. had no bank account and never owned any USD or any other national currency) were accounted as taxable income for G&SR. So we developed and deployed a protocol to detect and prevent gambling sites from accepting e-gold payments. Any non-compliant casino was blocked from receiving e-gold Spends. See https://blog.e-gold.com/2007/02/e-gold-empowers.html[157]

In May 2000, Jackson met with the Minister of Finance for the Island nation of Nevis. In later discussions, Jackson revealed that his meeting had been an attempt to strengthen the relationship with a sovereign entity. Jackson had hoped of opening dialog with the country regarding the acceptance of e-gold® for certain official payments, particularly international payments on items such as ship registry and import duties.

Through the forming of the e-gold Bullion Reserve Special Purpose Trust, the Spicers, under their established reputation for integrity, were able to open previously closed doors for e-gold®. Since the Spicers already had maintained billions of dollars worth of gold in secure storage, they could introduce e-gold® and G&SR to some of the larger banks that maintained Treasury grade vaults. In emails, Jackson shared some of these details.

> Initially, they[Spicers] undertook to help us establish a relationship with CIBC, a bank where their largest bullion stores were held. This dragged on for months – even their sterling reputation was unable to overcome the presumption which dogged us from day one that an online entity purporting to back a digital currency with gold had to be shady in some way. So they opened up a second line of discussion with Bank of Nova Scotia, with whom we already had an established dealing relationship. This also dragged on for months. But then, on May 4, 2000, I received a call from Drummond Gill, Head of Trading, North America, ScotiaMocatta, memorialized in

---

[157] Jackson, Doug. "Notes for Carl." Received by Carl Mullan, *Notes for Carl*, 1 May 2019. 5-1-2019-Notes-for-Carl.odt

the email of same date. It was evident (though not stated) that, most likely in relation to the 1997 acquisition of Mocatta Bullion by BoNS, that the Lloyds arrangement had slipped through the cracks.[158]

The email appears below.[159]

> Subject: MDO's held by e-gold
> Date: Thu, 4 May 2000
> From: Drummond Gill <XXXXXX@scotiamarkets.com>(by way of Sylvia Berndt)
> To: Doug <XXXXXX@mindspring.com>
> Mr. Jackson -
> It was a pleasure to speak to you today. With regard to our phone call this e-mail is confirmation that:
> ScotiaMocatta Toronto will swap gold and silver Mocatta Delivery Orders (MDO's) held by e-gold for 400 oz. gold bars (plus some smaller bars if necessary to match the ounces) and 1000 oz. silver bars respectively at no cost to e-gold.
> ScotiaMocatta will reduce the regular storage fees it charges e-gold to a level matching that currently paid with MDO's. This fee reduction only applies to the equivalent number of ounces currently held as MDO's by e-gold. The current fee for material held in custody in Toronto and any other new business will be charged at the agreed rate of $24.00/bar/month for gold and $6.00/bar/month for silver or platinum or palladium.
> e-gold will remove all references to "Lloyd's of London" insurance from it's web-site and advertising material. Thank you for your business. I hope our relationship continues to grow mutually beneficial.
> If you have any questions, call us on our toll free line: 1-888-BULLION (888-285-5466).
> – Drummond Gill, Head of Trading, North America, ScotiaMocatta

Copied below is a list showing how many good delivery bars were swapped for MDOs by the Bank of Nova Scotia. Toronto vaults stored these bars.[160]

Manifest of MDOs:

---

[158] Ibid

[159] Gill, Drummond. "MDO's Held by e-gold." Received by Douglas Jackson, *MDO's Held by e-gold*, 4 May 2000.

[160] Jackson, Douglas. "MDOs - See Attached Spreadsheet." Received by Charles Davis, *MDOs - See Attached Spreadsheet*, 2 Mar. 2000.

Au 400s – 10 Bars
Au 100s – 29 Bars
Ag 1000s – 56 Bars

In June 2000, e-gold® achieved a significant milestone. The company surpassed $7 million worth of e-metal in circulation. $7 million worth of bullion translated to over 1/2 ton of physical gold along with more than 3.5 tons of silver bullion reserves.

Charles Evans

In 1998, Jackson had hired Charles Evans as an independent consultant to explore promoting e-gold®. It was Evans who had organized the first and second Lex Cybernetoria conferences, respectively, in Reykjavik Iceland and Nevis. In 1999, Evans was hired by G&SR as director of marketing and became a close confidant of Jackson. However, by June 2000, Charles Evans had become enraged at e-gold's co-founders, convinced that e-gold's Directors, Barry Downey and Reid Jackson, were supplanting his influence. Evidence of his behavior was on full display in this June 29th email to Reid Jackson.

> From: Charles Evans <XXXX@chyden.net>
> Sent: Thursday, June 29, 2000 10:26 PM
> To: Reid Jackson
> Subject: pity
> Dearest Reid:
> You and Doug have been absolute angels over the past couple of years. I have enjoyed working with Doug, and I have enjoyed the few moments that I have spent with you. That Barry has an issue with me is utterly irrelevant.   Barry has enjoyed a cushy life in his law practice, and has never felt the fear of the lights going out. ▇▇▇▇ and I have been through THREE (3) Ends-of-the-World. Doug pulled e-gold out of thin air.   Doug nearly lost his family over e-gold. Doug had the vision. We owe our paper-wealth to Doug. Barry has hidden up in Baltimore in his legal practice and never felt our fear.
> *YOU* created OEDP --> OmniPay.   Please help me.
> *I* Introduced Doug to:
>> JW Zidar
>> Paul Vahur
>> Elwyn Jenkins
>> Mohammed Ojaroodi
>> Richard Rahn

Bill Frezza

I organized the following conferences:

Iceland

IRS (Melbourne)

Nevis

I initiated the following projects:

PCS/WAP

AGIO

GoldChanger

I developed the following proofs-of-concept:

RealGoldLotto

FlyingRat

I am working on the following projects, currently:

OmniPay Japan

OmniPay India

Standard Reserve

AGIO

FlyingRat

If you cannot rise to the occasion, and protect me from Barry's childish wrath, then my job falls on your shoulders. My job is among the shittiest on the planet. I am not a Jackson, but I have supported the Jackson Legacy for the past few years. I do not understand what bug is up Barry's ass about me, but I NEED your help. Please defend me. If Barry bent me over a rail, then you would be left to pick up the piece, alone.   And it WOULD be a lot of sharp, little pieces. Please!   I am not joking. CE[161]

The following information, provided by Jackson, suggests that while employed at G&SR, Charles Evans, held secret meetings with outside companies and members of the digital currency industry unaffiliated with G&SR. Evans' purposeful actions allegedly illustrate underhanded attempts to establish his own branded version of a new digital gold company. Furthermore, evidence suggests that Evans was also engaged in some malicious activity designed to harm e-gold® and its operators. Uncovered emails and personal communications show that Evans appeared to have been motivated by a bitter hatred toward the Jackson family and even the company that employed him; G&SR/e-gold.

Jackson believed that many associates interacted with Evans, including James Fayed of e-bullion.com/Goldfinger Coin & Bullion, James Turk of GoldMoney.com, Ian Grigg of

---

[161] Evans, Charles. "Pity." Received by Reid Jackson, *Pity*, 29 June 2000.

Systemics.com, the principals of e-dinar, and the operators of Standard Reserve.

Evans' actions suggest that he was confident in his knowledge of e-gold's operation, and intended to use that experience to form his own digital gold company. It is unknown if Evans tried to flee with e-gold's technology, business model, or customers. Fortunately, Jackson discovered this plan and terminated his employment along with other alleged conspirators.

> As late as 10/9/2000, Jackson and Grigg were very actively engaged in efforts to implement a demo of the trading utility that Systemics, financed entirely by G&SR, had been developing. The idea of the trading utility was to enable issuance, distribution and direct P2P trading of digital securities against digital money. Jackson had worked out sample contracts for demo shares and was developing the institutional arrangements for an entity called digitalbearer to facilitate a standardized issuance process. The digitalbearer model, developed by Jackson, was precisely what Evans, unknown to his employers, was duplicating under the name of PicoIPO.[162]

While scheming to form a separate digital gold company, Evans had sought introductions to funding sources and angel investors. He set up a company named PicoIPO; in 2000, describing it as an investment fund focused on small-cap projects.[163] In a 2019 email, Jackson provided these details on Evans' activity.

> Picoipo was Evans' own scheme, where he was working in collusion with Grigg to use the Ricardo tech to do securities issuance and trading, taking advantage of my groundbreaking work in developing sample contracts and logic for GDRs (Global Depositary Receipts) and other smart-contract-defined securities. https://www.sec.gov/Archives/edgar/data/1073091/000101041202000295/to.txt relates to all this in that the plan was to roll the picoipo IP into one of James Nesfield's pink sheet listed shell companies and relocate the company to the Freeport Bahamas location the cabal was then living in (partly because of Charles's continued effort to avoid service of process in re our suit against him for corporate espionage and other tortious acts).[164]

Partial details from an SEC document, referenced by Jackson, are copied below and include

[162] Jackson, Douglas. "Evans and Grigg Analysis and Write-Up." Received by Carl Mullan, *Evans and Grigg Analysis and Write-Up*, 8 Apr. 2020.

[163] Staff, Wired. "THERE'S GOLD IN THAT E-CASINO." *PicoIPO : Making the World a Better Place, One IPO at a Time*, Condé Nast., 25 Feb. 2000, web.archive.org/web/20001206204400/http://www.picoipo.com/index2.html.

[164] Jackson, Doug. "Notes for Carl." Received by Carl Mullan, *Notes for Carl*, 1 May 2019. 5-1-2019-Notes-for-Carl.odt

both Evans and Grigg.[165]

Schedule TO -- Tender Offer Statement Under Section 14(d)(1) or 13(e)(1) of the
Securities Exchange Act of 1934
(Amendment No. --)
Freerealtime.com, Inc.
8001 Irvine Center Drive Suite 330
Irvine, CA 92618
Business Phone 949-754-3085

(Name of Subject Company [Issuer])
Nesfield Acquisition Corp., Offeror
c/o Nesfield Capital, Inc.
32 Goshen Road
Engelhard, NC 27824

Item 3. Identity and Background of Filing Person

Nesfield Acquisition Corp. ("NAC") is a wholly owned subsidiary of Nesfield
Capital, Inc. ("NCI").   NCI is a Broker Dealer registered on Form BD with the
Commission, and is a member of the NASD.   NCI maintains minimum net capital
of $5,000.00, and offers trading execution in mutual fund issues. NCI does not hold
customer funds.   NCI believes Freerealtime.com Inc.'s business compliments NCI's
existing business activity.

Management of NCI

Charles W. Evans, (CEO & President) Age 40

Mr. Evans has over 15 years experience in customer service and marketing, with
emphasis on Latin America and Europe. Mr. Evans has lectured to business and
advocacy groups in the USA, Scandinavia, and Eastern Europe on Internet
marketing, and has been cited in The Economist and newspapers in Estonia, Iceland,
and Sweden as an expert on Internet usage.   For the past 5 years, Mr. Evans has
served at the executive level in business development and marketing strategy of
online payment systems including e-gold® and GoldMoney, as well as electronic
currency exchange providers that trade in those systems. More recently, Mr. Evans
has been involved with the establishment of an online microfinance marketplace, and
continues to be active in the development and promotion of online payment systems.
After running several entrepreneurial ventures in the USA and Germany, Mr. Evans

---

[165] Nesfield, James. "Tender Offer Statement Under Section 14(d)(1) or 13(e)(1)." *SEC.gov*, James Nesfield c/o Nesfield
Capital, Inc., 3000, www.sec.gov/Archives/edgar/data/1073091/000101041202000295/to.txt.

earned his MS Economics at George Mason University in 1994.

Ian Grigg - Chief Technology Officer Age 41

Mr Grigg has worked as an independent consultant in the Unix systems field from 1985 to 1995, acting as project leader and other roles for many different companies in Australia and in Europe. In 1995, Mr Grigg started Systemics, a company dedicated to Financial Cryptography, an emerging field to manage digital value such as money and assets on the Internet. He architetured and built the Ricardo system, a payment system that describes and transfers value using the techniques developed by Systemics. He was responsible directly for the "backend" programming, having built the bespoke double entry accounting engine, as well as the complete (stock) exchange server for Systemics' trading architecture. Mr Grigg is a consultant to ventures in Financial Cryptography, and has published 4 papers in the field. Mr. Griggs holds a BSc(Hons) Computer Science (1984 University of New South Wales) MBA (1996 London Business School)

James Nesfield -Secretary Age 44

Mr. Nesfield is a specialist in the art of investing in distressed companies primarily companies in bankruptcy. Mr. Nesfield has worked in the financial service field since 1978 in various capacities such as trader of government bonds, corporate bonds, market maker, and analyst. Recently Mr. Nesfield founded Nesfield Capital for the purpose of developing a Mutual Fund retailing firm. In the past Mr. Nesfield has been featured on Sixty Minutes and various articles due in large part to his fundamental approach to investment analysis. Mr. Nesfield is an advocate of the Vulture Style of investments whereby assets acquired cheaply enough can be made profitable. Mr. Nesfield has worked in the Former Soviet Union building Depositories and Exchanges as well as in South Africa. In consultation for institution building in less developed nations Mr. Nesfield worked to form broker organizations and shareholder rights organizations.

Item 9.

b.   Employees and Corporate Assets.

Charles Evans, President Nesfield Acquisition Corp., has been retained on a tender offer success basis by NAC; Mr. Evans' biographical information, and his intended management role, are set forth in Item 3.

Ian Grigg, Chief Information Officer Nesfield Acquisition Corp., has been retained on a tender offer success basis by NAC; Mr. Grigg's biographical information, and his intended management role, are set forth in Item 3.

James Nesfield has been retained on a tender offer success basis by NAC; Mr. Nesfield's biographical information, and his intended management role, are set forth in Item 3.[166]

The gambit to repackage PicoIPO as a public company was unsuccessful. Nesfield went his separate way.

Only in 2001 did the possibility begin to dawn on the Jackson's that Ian and Charles might have been planning the Fall 2000 rupture in relations from the early months of 2000. Indications surfaced that both Grigg and Evans had met with would-be competitors James Fayed in Los Angeles and James Turk in London while Evans was still drawing his salary as Head of Business Development at G&SR.

An additional troubling element also began to emerge. Throughout 2000, Grigg, in his conversations with Jackson, had been critical of Evans, beginning with a report that he had represented e-gold very poorly at the February 2000 Financial Cryptography Conference. [This was later borne out in a deposition from Peter Thiel describing his February 2000 meeting with an e-gold representative that left him with a highly unfavorable opinion of the company]. But at the same time, Evans was continually making jibes to Dr. Jackson noting the large outlays of badly needed funds to Grigg in return for software that as late as October 2000 was still not ready for commercial deployment.

Was this apparent antipathy between Grigg and Evans a ruse? If so, were any of Grigg's subsequent protestations of growing resentments genuine? Indications soon surfaced that the alienation had been staged as a ploy to enable Grigg to walk away from exclusivity understandings and hook up with a more prestigious strategic partner.[167]

Jackson alleges that Evans and Grigg continued their efforts to destroy e-gold®. They worked out of their shared household in the Bahamas, seeking a new partner to re-implement the Ricardo system, the original commercialization of which, DigiGold, had been funded by G&SR.

In an interesting postscript, James Nesfield later re-surfaced concerning a highly publicized scandal involving crooked trading in mutual funds.[168] Nesfield was hired as a "capacity consultant" for a newly formed hedge fund. His job was to find mutual funds that would allow "late trading." This practice was likened by then-New York State attorney general Elliot Spitzer to "betting on a horse race after the horses have crossed the finish line."[169]

[166] Ibid

[167] Jackson, Douglas. Received by Carl Mullan, Evans and Grigg Analysis and Write-Up, 8 Apr. 2020.

[168] Quigley, Winthrop. "Wall St. Money Manager Helped Expose Madoff Ponzi Scheme, 2003 Mutual Fund Scandals." *Albuquerque Journal*, 7 Nov. 2011.

[169] Elkind, Peter, et al. " The Secrets of Eddie Stern If You Think You Know How Bad the Mutual Fund Scandal Is, You're Wrong. It's Worse." *The Secrets of Eddie Stern If You Think You Know How Bad the Mutual Fund Scandal Is, You're Wrong. It's Worse. - April 19, 2004*, Fortune Magazine, 19 Apr. 2004,

But returning to the events of fall 2000, according to Jackson, the extent of Evans' actions to undermine e-gold® didn't fully register until October. The crisis had occurred during the second Indian River Summit (IRS2), an event hosted by G&SR in Melbourne, Florida, that brought together the proprietors of over a dozen recently established exchange services. Jackson's primary goal was to impose conduct standards for exchange transactions, particularly concerning acceptable payment methods for funding exchanges in which the customer was buying e-gold®. Jackson regarded it as imperative that exchange services not accept payment via notoriously repudiable payment methods, especially credit cards and credit card intermediaries such as Paypal.

Evans, who had a flair for organizing such events, was, per usual, tasked with arrangements for IRS2, which included setting the agenda.

As the event unfolded, it became apparent that Evans had been working to organize resistance akin to a union pitted against management rather than articulating and implementing the prohibition. Exchange providers formed an organization. Rather than preventing credit card and Paypal fraud, the providers took the position that e-gold® should bail them out of fraudulent transactions by freezing e-gold® accounts on their demand and reversing fulfillment Spends to alleged fraudsters.

♦

In conjunction with the October Indian River Summit event, multiple former e-gold strategic partners had gathered in this same Florida location. Charles Evans, who was at the time employed by G&SR, met in secret with these partners during the event. Jackson clarified that two parties had independently reached out to clue him in that Charles Evans was conspiring against e-gold. Jackson stated:

> It was fall 2000 when, concurrently, Zeno Dahinden (CEO of e-dinar) and Elwyn Jenkins (of Standard Reserve infamy) separately contacted me, Jenkins by email, Zeno in person (he was still in town after the disastrous IRS II summit), to report meetings that they felt I needed to know about because they interpreted them as treachery on the part of Evans and his sidekick, ███." [footnote]

These private emails reveal details of the events. Jackson wrote Downey:

> At Sat, 21 Oct 2000 22:37:41 -0500 (EDT), implacable@hushmail.com[Jackson] wrote:

archive.fortune.com/magazines/fortune/fortune_archive/2004/04/19/367348/index.htm.

Zeno spent some time with me this morning. He had just come from a secret meeting with Charlie and ▮▮▮. He felt awkward in raising the subject but thought we should know that Charles is exerting himself to undermine G&SR. He suggested we would be best off dismissing Charlie, ▮▮▮, and Steve immediately. Steve is not part of the cabal but Zeno indicates that Mujahid had described Steve right off as utterly ineffective.

I met with Reid and Corina today. Monday the ax falls. I will dismiss Steve first and walk him outside the suite, followed by Charlie and ▮▮▮. I'm still not 100% sure about ▮▮▮ but this note from Elwyn indicates she is fully involved and has at the least lied to us. I'm thinking probably a clean sweep is in order. Corina indicates we won't miss a beat and will probably make faster progress lacking Steve.

Attached to this message, Jackson also forwarded the note he previously received from Elwyn Jenkins detailing Jenkins' earlier meeting with Evans and ▮▮▮.

> Douglas
> Re: Charles
> He is considering moving on to picoIPO -- see it on the net --
> http://www.picoipo.com/index2.html
> He is looking for funding. He would involve: himself, his wife, and one other from G&SR -- ▮▮▮
> The idea is a great idea, but whether it flies for investors is another thing. He is looking to me to help him become introduced to some angel investors. That may be a tall order. I do not know whether this is possible? I have some serious questions about this idea whether it can be put together to support the three people he has identified in the development time. He would look towards the Gold Economy as providing the payment system -- possibly SR with debit cards being ideal (his words). He will move when he gets funding. I do not think this will be as quick as he thinks. He will give notice when he has funding and then will give one month's notice. That is as much as I know. I appreciate confidentiality unless you need to ensure the longevity of G&SR.
> Ej [Elwyn Jenkins]

The following day, October 22nd, Downey emailed Jackson for details on this situation.

At Sun, 22 Oct 2000 09:37:04 -0500 (EDT), bdowney@hushmail.com wrote:

Did Zeno give specifics about how Charlie is undermining G&SR. Is there any threat he has taken, or is taking, anything to someone like Turk?

I think the clean sweep is what we should do and it should include ████. The risk is too great when she has indicated already that she is willing to lie to us to protect Charlie.

The one thing we have never done is to get everyone to sign a non disclosure agreement. I had thought I would get ████ to get all employees to sign one first thing Monday morning. Then we could go in and fire everyone we need to. I think it probably is too late at this time and we have common law on our side on this point anyway.

I can e-mail the document to ████ with instructions to get all to sign it first thing if you have strong feelings we should do this. Maybe we should discuss this one. I don't want it to delay the terminations.

Barry

Later that Saturday, Downey met with Reid Jackson and Corina, another employee of G&SR, and shared that Douglas Jackson would be firing both Charles Evans and ████ ████ the following Monday. Downey also indicated that Charles Evans' wife, ████, would likely also be dismissed at the same time. A few days later, on Monday, all three employees were terminated.

At the time of the e-gold restructuring in 2000, Reid Jackson—having wound down the medical billing practice (Jackson & Escher Inc.) he had established in 1992 to handle billing for Florida Oncology— was hired by G&SR as a full-time contractor.

Reid also became a director of G&SR. Initially, a systems analyst primarily engaged in computer work, Reid assumed responsibility as de facto Chief Operating Officer for G&SR. He established and managed OmniPay operations and supervised an overhaul of G&SR's accounting processes to conform with GAAP. Reid dedicated 7-8 years of his life to G&SR and achieving his brother's vision.[170]

Jackson & Escher, Inc. is still an active Florida for-Profit Corporation. (Originally filed on October 5, 1992 (Document #V69720).[171] Beginning in 2000, this entity provided services to G&SR.

Jackson also released CTO Steve Foerster around December 18, 2000. After leaving the company, he partnered with Bernard von Nothaus [Liberty Dollar] in early 2001. They

---

[170] Docket No. CR 07-109. UNITED STATES OF AMERICA vs. E-GOLD LTD, GOLD & SILVER RESERVE LTD, DOUGLAS L. JACKSON, BARRY K. DOWNEY, REID A. JACKSON. TRANSCRIPT OF SENTENCE BEFORE THE HONORABLE ROSEMARY M. COLLYER UNITED STATES DISTRICT JUDGE, 20 Nov. 2008.

[171] "State of Florida Division of Corporations." *Detail by Entity Name*, Sunbiz.ort, 2020, https://bit.ly/3cGvoxb

launched 3Pgold.com.[172] This new platform was another digital gold system with a few strange similarities to e-gold®. In 2002, 3PGold.com was sold to associates of Terry Neal, including Sean Trainor, and renamed Crowne Gold.

The Crowne Gold operation was also plagued by legal matters including the government's well-known attacks focused on money transmitting. On July 21, 2008, all of the e-gold® and Gold & Silver Reserve defendants pleaded guilty. Only days later, that same month, Crowne Gold announced it was closing all operations. Crowne's business officially ended in December 2008.[173]

Regulations

Advances in technology, over the past several decades, have driven virtual currency innovation. This fact was evident in the e-gold® case. Our world had never enjoyed such indulgent financial freedom as e-gold® delivered. Unfortunately, this new disruptive technology also allowed bad actors to exploit gaping holes in outdated U.S. Financial Regulations.

E-gold® was the first Internet-based monetary and payments system to enable "remote" payments—i.e. payments which, unlike cash, do not require physical proximity of payer and recipient—external to and independent of traditional bank platforms. Regulations established under the 1970 Bank Secrecy Act, before the USA Patriot Act of 2001, did not define the acts of issuing, transferring, or exchanging digital currency.

As e-gold® was innovative new technology, it was not yet defined or categorized under existing financial regulations. This absence of existing laws for the legal identification and supervision of digital currency products was the basis of e-gold's trouble. Digital gold was a square peg, and U.S. financial regulations were only offering round holes.

The success of e-gold® launched a tidal wave of interest in controlling and supervising digital currency products.

2001

GoldMoney

Mr. James Turk, the creator of GoldMoney, has stated that he envisioned an online digital gold payment system as early as 1993. He even filed patents on a version of his digital gold payment system in the 1990s. However, it was not until 2001, nearly five years after e-gold®, when he launched GoldMoney.com.

---

[172] "Welcome to 3PGold.Com!" *3PGold.Com: Buying and Selling Gold, Around the World, Around the Clock*, 3PGold.Com, 1 Mar. 2001, web.archive.org/web/20010301223709/www.3pgold.com/.

[173] "Notice, Crowne Gold Will Be Officially Closed on Dec 21st, 2008." *Crowne Gold*, Crowne-gold.com, 16 Dec. 2008, web.archive.org/web/20081216152053/www.crowne-gold.com/.

After opening his version of online digital gold, many excited onlookers were speculating that GoldMoney would quickly become e-gold's dominant competition. Notwithstanding Turk's excellent industry reputation and GoldMoney's leading governance model, no direct e-gold® rivalry materialized. Compared to e-gold®, Turk's company never garnered a large global base of individual retail users. Additionally, online commercial merchants never flocked to GoldMoney, and online merchants did not extensively adopt the platform.

Having a strong background in the banking industry, Mr. Turk operated GoldMoney with identification requirements and account restrictions that were similar to a bank. Turk never suggested that GoldMoney, a foreign corporation, was required to abide by the Bank Secrecy Act (BSA) Regulations or needed to institute strict Know Your Customer (KYC) requirements. However, opening a new GoldMoney account required similar documentation and verification as necessary to open a U.S. bank account.

The Know Your Customer (KYC) verification and restrictions prevented abuse of the GoldMoney platform. However, the significant "bank-like" requirements also blocked GoldMoney from being widely adopted. Only a handful of retail merchants accepted GoldMoney, and Turk did not permit unregistered independent third-party exchange providers. Consequently, GoldMoney lacked some of the liquidity that grows from multiple methods of exchanging funds in and out of digital currency.

Jackson designed e-gold® to offer everyone, at all levels of society, the ability to receive and make payments online. It was independent providers of exchange services that helped e-gold® achieve this goal. By 2001, several dozen well-funded exchange providers and other individuals were conducting third-party independent exchange services between national currencies and e-gold®. These payment methods included bank transfers, Western Union payments, money orders, and other digital currency products such as WebMoney. However, GoldMoney restricted all clients to wire transfer deposits through GoldMoney's banks. GoldMoney restricted exchange transactions to bank deposits and withdrawals, limiting significantly "who" could operate an account.

It is the multiple deposit and withdrawal options that widely facilitates the exchange of any digital currency. Fiat money choices and unique payment options translate to higher liquidity and greater customer acceptance.

Without a cadre of independent third party exchange providers, GoldMoney did not attract smaller retail customers or online sellers. However, there was a silver lining under all the bank-like restrictions. Ultimately, it was the red tape that prevented GoldMoney from attracting or being used by bad actors. Turk offered a Hobson's choice.

As GoldMoney's principal, James Turk, repeatedly and insistently framed the logic of his system in a way that contained at least one grave flaw. Industry insiders conceptually described the problem as a "liability and balance sheet issue."

All issuers of real money maintain electronic ledgers on which the money they have issued and which is outstanding, is carried as a current liability. The value of these monetary liabilities derives from assets, the other side of the ledger or balance sheet, held against them. This asset portfolio enables the amount of money outstanding to be reduced by selling assets and de-issuing the funds received as proceeds of such sales, thereby symmetrically shrinking the balance sheet.

Using the US Federal Reserve as an example, their direct monetary liabilities—paper cash in circulation plus deposits of commercial banks at Federal Reserve Banks—are balanced by an asset portfolio. Those assets consist of US Treasury securities, gold, and (these days) a LOT of mortgage-backed securities. These assets do NOT belong to a money holder. Stated differently, the money holder does not hold title to any of these assets. The money holder's asset is money.[174]

Here is why this fact matters. Suppose a civil lawsuit is brought against a holder of money, resulting in attachment of assets. Or perhaps a government agency seizes the assets of a money-holding individual or entity alleging probable cause that he/she/it is a criminal and his/her/its assets are the proceeds of crime.

If the assets backing the money belong to the money holder (in addition to the money) and those assets, consist of gold bullion, the vault door swings open. This paradigm could be quite a problem. For example, let's say the money holder has one or two grams worth of the money, but the bullion bars backing the money are 400 oz. good London good delivery bars. The agents conducting the seizure are unlikely to err of the side of taking too little (i.e., nothing, since there are no small bars), and the result of taking too much would be that all of the remaining money would be under-backed. The Issuer's reciprocal obligation is to fulfill the terms of its contract or mandate that constitute the auspices under which it issues money.

But this scenario is trivial compared to legal action against the issuer or administrator responsible for the entire monetary system.

Suppose an agency such as the US Secret Service, which historically had never gained much usable loot from asset seizures, is convinced by a would-be confidential informant to undertake the arrest of the reserves backing an entire currency. The CI's allegations might be used to support a claim that the operation is a criminal enterprise, and all its customers are accomplices guilty of criminal conspiracy. The bar for getting a magistrate judge to sign a seizure warrant, after all, is quite low – an allegation of probable cause. Additionally, as will be detailed in later chapters, once the government seizes the property, there is no 'innocent until proven guilty' concerning property seizure/forfeiture. To have the assets returned, the

---

[174] The reciprocal obligation of the Issuer is to fulfill the terms of its contract or mandate that constitute the auspices under which it issues money.

subject of an asset forfeiture must prove the seized assets are innocent.

As will be seen, the prolonged shock and awe campaign conducted against e-gold® failed to breach the integrity of its fiduciary and custodial arrangements for the gold reserves. After the case, the gold bullion was still in the vaults, titled to the Purpose Trust, and all e-gold® continued to be 100% backed.

Consider what would have happened if e-gold had owned the bullion according to the ownership arrangement asserted below, and throughout GoldMoney's history.

A May 4, 2001 email from James Turk to Matthew Turner of the World Gold Council vehemently asserted:

> "GoldGrams are not backed by gold, they ARE gold…with GoldMoney the person who owns the Holding is the person who owns the gold in that Holding…with GoldMoney you own the gold in the Vault in the physical world."[175]

G&SR's annual report with the State of Florida, filed on January 26, 2001, reflected the departure of Charles Evans, and the addition of Douglas Jackson's brother Reid, as an officer/director.

During 2001, James Fayed (e-bullion.com) and James Turk (goldmoney.com) were busy launching their own online digital gold platforms. During their startup phase, each of these companies employed Charles Evans for a short time.

Van Dinh of Phoenixville, PA

Unfortunately, as an almost inevitable byproduct of its rise in popularity, e-gold also began to attract the undesired attention of unsavory figures engaged in perpetuating fraudulent schemes and selling unlawful materials. Just as such persons have used credit cards and other payment methods - much as they use U.S. currency when feasible -to facilitate their crimes, criminal elements began exploiting e-gold for the very features that had begun to make it popular, including the finality of settlement and perceived levels of anonymity.[176]

In January 2001, e-gold's primary dealer OmniPay detected a series of suspicious e-gold® exchanges. Out of an abundance of caution, OmniPay held off on fulfilling the exchange transactions and escrowed the e-gold® it had received, stabilizing $1.1 million worth of e-gold® pending investigation. In-house investigators tracked the source of these

---

[175] Jackson, Douglas. "Re: Attached Copy." Received by Carl Mullan, *Re: Attached Copy*, 27 Feb. 2020. Ref: email May 4, 2001, from James Turk to Matthew Turner of the World Gold Council DJ redlines 3 second try-final.pdf

[176] CASE NUMBER: 07-167-M-01. *UNITED STATES OF AMERICA V. E-GOLD LIMITED, GOLD & SILVER RESERVE, INC., DOUGLAS L. JACKSON, BARRY K. DOWNEY and REID A. JACKSON*. SENTENCING MEMORANDUM OF GOLD & SILVER RESERVE, INC., Nov. 2008.

funds to suspected criminal activity. Indications that control over the suspect account had passed to an initially unknown third party complicated the process of evaluating the transactions. The sleuthing that ensued illustrated the level of sophistication e-gold's investigative staff had already developed circa 2001.

E-gold investigators had tracked the IP number for the logged-in session of the exchange transactions' funding spends to a regional planning commission in a mid-western state. Suspecting this government server had been exploited and used as an unauthorized proxy server, Jackson contacted the facility's IT systems administrator. The system administrator confirmed that during a recent operating system upgrade, they had accidentally configured the server with the (insufficiently secure) default settings. This standard environment had enabled unrestricted third-party access as a proxy server. The administrator supplied weblogs for the relevant time interval, which revealed the trespasser's upstream IP number. This IP number uniquely matched the one used by Van Dinh of Phoenixville, PA, to access his e-gold® account and the one he had opened for his mother.

OmniPay immediately relayed this critical evidence to the USSS and FBI. Discovering evidence that Van Dinh had also used a stolen driver's license to impersonate a young woman from Philadelphia, OmniPay reached out to the Philadelphia PD. However, after receiving the data implicating Van Dinh in these fraudulent activities, none of the law enforcement agencies contacted took action to arrest or even question him.

OmniPay obtained a court order enabling it to turn over the exchange proceeds of the escrowed e-gold® to a court-appointed receiver who distributed the value back to the victims. However, Van Dinh remained at large. Subsequently:

> On October 10, 2003 in Boston Massachusetts, 19 yr old, Van Dinh of Phoenixville, PA was arrested for hacking into another person's online brokerage account to trade options. The U.S. attorney's office in Boston and the Securities and Exchange Commission said they filed criminal and civil securities fraud charges. At the age of 19, Dinh became the first person to be charged in the U.S. with an identity-theft crime instrumented through computer hacking.[177]

In 2003, on seeing news of Van Dinh's arrest, Jackson reached out to the SEC, indicating that their perp, in this relatively low value ($35,000) caper, had previously committed crimes involving over thirty   times as much value. The SEC expressed no interest in this relevant prior conduct.

---

[177] "Teenager Charged with Hacking into Brokerage Account." *Chicago Tribune*, 10 Oct. 2003, "Teenager Charged with Hacking into Brokerage Account." Chicago Tribune, 10 Oct. 2003.

In December 2008, according to the FBI, Van T. Dinh, from Phoenixville, Pennsylvania was arrested and charged with two counts of computer fraud after he hacked into an administrative account of a currency-exchange service and transferred money into another one, set up with the same company. The hacker had previously spent 13 months in prison for a stock-market scheme.[178]

It was OmniPay's internal procedures that first identified Dinh's criminal activity in 2001. This case lends credibility to Jackson's steadfast claims regarding the usefulness of e-gold's internal investigation procedures.

Valid User Project

As early as fall 2000, it had become apparent to Jackson and the other e-gold® directors that a robust identity verification capability would aid in deterring illegal usage of e-gold® and also yield reputational benefits. The goal was to balance the requirements for system integrity against a reasonable expectation of privacy. Ideally, the solution could be used on multiple platforms, reducing the need for duplicative identity verification processes as well as the need to secure personal identifying information in numerous databases. The concept, dubbed "Valid User," was similar to WebMoney Transfer's Passport service. Mainly, a third party would identify and authenticate a user, then issue them an "authentication token." e-gold® users would present the token at the time of an e-gold® commercial transaction.

The initial project lead, left G&SR in January 2001 and Jay Wherley took over the task. Copied here are some details from his first round of refinements, dated February 15, 2001.

> author: Jay Wherley
> email: XXX@squires-eng.com
> for: Ancien Ltd.
> date: February 15, 2001
> version: 1.2
>
> 1.3. Overview Valid User provides a general purpose, internet based user validation service. Valid User will offer its user validation services and defined software interfaces to end customers for use at approved third party merchants. These third party merchants are thus relieved of the effort placed in checking identities of users. Valid User will collect, verify, and store user identification information for each user that chooses to use its service. It will charge a fee to do so. Valid User will validate the email address, postal mail address, and identification documents of its

---

[178] Constantin, Lucian. "Former Teen Hacker Charged with New Cybercrimes." *Softpedia News*, Softpedia News, 1 Apr. 2009, news.softpedia.com/news/Former-Teen-Hacker-Charged-with-New-Cybercrimes-108337.shtml.

users. Successfully validated users will be presented with an authentication device (initially a "session card") that can then be used at a merchant site accepting Valid Users. Internet merchant sites that accept valid users will utilize the software interfaces to and from Valid User to pass authentication information. These sites will not have access to the user identity information – only Valid User itself will have access to this information.

1.3.1. Levels of User Validation Users can achieve three levels of validation via Valid User. Each level provides a successively higher amount of "know your customer" information.

1.3.1.1. Level 1 – Email Email address validation is the lowest level of validation. Every user of the system is required to have a validated email address to become a user of the system.

1.3.1.2. Level 2 - Postal Address Postal mailing address validation is the next step up the validation staircase from email address validation. It is expected that every user will proceed to this level as it will be the minimum required level to receive an authentication device for use at Merchant sites utilizing Valid User services.

1.3.1.3. Level 3 – Identification Documentation A third and highest level of validation is obtained by supplying Valid User with notarized documentation such as drivers license, passport, utility bills etc. A Merchant might require users to achieve this validation level to perform the most privileged operations at their site.

1.4.   Business Context The Valid User development will be funded by Ancien Ltd. The first third party merchant to utilize Valid User's services will be e-gold Ltd. (http://www.egold.com) which will take advantage of the higher authentication security offered by the authentication device provided by Valid User, yet remain ignorant of actual user identities. (e-gold Ltd. must assure that some particular entity has adequate and accurate identifying information on file that can be discovered and divulged in appropriate legal circumstances; Valid User solves this problem.)[179]

Unfortunately, other urgent technical and resource issues cropped up, requiring the assignment of a lower priority to the Valid User Project and it was not completed.

The exponential growth in e-gold® transactions accelerating into December 2000 overwhelmed system capacity and led to an unacceptable number of transactions timing out. It was at this time that the last sections of Jackson's legacy computer code, some of it dating back to 1996, were finally retired and replaced by more robust and efficient software. The

---

[179] Wherley, Jay. "Valid User Project, Requirements Specification." 15 Feb. 2001.

company brought higher capacity web and database servers online and moved core resources to a more secure co-location facility. Valid User was postponed, pending marshaling of adequate resources to see the project through. As it turned out, it was not until 2005 that e-gold® was finally able to earmark funds for Valid User, enabling it to engage an outside contractor with extensive experience in software for financial institutions.

On February 22, 2001, the Central Escrow Agency inspected the e-gold® bullion reserve. The results of that inspection were published online, and the public could view details all of the e-gold® physical bullion held in secure vaults.

A month later, in March, e-gold Ltd. moved the audited bullion reserves to new storage facilities operated by JP Morgan Chase and Transguard in London and Dubai, respectively. The London Bullion Market Association (LBMA) has certified both of these repositories.

That same month, John Rubino published an article on TheStreet.com that offered a brief glimpse into digital gold payment systems, including e-gold®. The piece quoted Jackson, describing the booming e-gold® business "We finally hit our millionth transaction in November" "and we hit a million and a half in December." Rubino stated, "All, notes Jackson, with a marketing budget of zero."[180]

During March, another opening in communications with government investigators occurred. This event marked one of the earliest occasions where Jackson was able to connect directly with the DOJ. In March 2001, e-gold® provided service of process information and investigative contact numbers to Ed Broton at the U.S. Department of Justice (DOJ).

Fake News

After building upon Jackson's successful industry relationships from previous conferences, e-gold® company representatives scheduled a 2001 London meeting to discuss a closer strategic relationship with JP Morgan Chase.

After London, Jackson planned to visit representatives in Dubai for second stage talks with Emirates Air. That strategic program could have enabled Emirates the ability to accept online e-gold® payments and also offer employees e-gold® as an elective component of their salary.

Before the e-gold® team traveled to London, the U.S. Secret Service conducted a raid on a digital currency exchange business located in New York called Gold-Age. The firm had been a victim of credit card fraud.[181]

---

[180] Rubino, John. "Digital Gold Offers Liquidity to Dollar-Spooked Investors." *TheStreet.com*, Systemics.com, 19 Jan. 2001, www.systemics.com/legal/digigold/discovery/postings/20010119_rubino.html.

[181] CASE NUMBER: 07-167-M-01. *UNITED STATES OF AMERICA V. E-GOLD LIMITED, GOLD & SILVER RESERVE, INC., DOUGLAS L. JACKSON, BARRY K. DOWNEY and REID A. JACKSON.* SENTENCING MEMORANDUM OF GOLD & SILVER RESERVE, INC., Nov. 2008.

However, on Friday, March 30, 2001, Wired.com published an article written by Declan McCullagh entitled "*U.S. Secret Service Raids e-gold.*"[182]

The Wired.com article's title was erroneous. E-gold® had not been the subject of any raid by the U.S. Secret Service or any other law enforcement agency. The USSS raided a New York business named Gold-Age, not e-gold®.

According to Jackson, the false headline, published by Wired.com, remained online, discoverable by search engines and the public, for about eight hours. By Saturday, a member of the staff at *Wired.com* had replaced the title with an accurate version, "*Secret Service Raids Gold-Age.*"

Wired.com's falsely titled article had been actively copied and re-posted across dozens of high-profile industry websites, discussion forums, and email lists. The blow to e-gold's growing reputation, caused by the alleged mistake, was appalling. In a 2018 email, Jackson recalled the damage.

> But the worse harm to us was the erroneous Wired headline "Secret Service raids e-gold". It would be impossible to overstate the harm this did to us[e-gold], even though the erroneous headline was corrected to "Secret Service raids Gold-Age" after 8 hours. Our[e-gold's] brief interval of exponentially improving success, which included my Rome talk Nov 2000 and the resulting relationship with JP Morgan Chase, ended within six months.
> Emirates Air, Reuters, Hypercom – virtually every entity with which strategic relationships were being discussed – all broke off discussions."[183]

In 2020, original text copies of this wrongly titled article are still online. [184]

> From that moment, e-gold lost all the nascent constructive relationships that had been emerging. JPMorgan Chase canceled the scheduled meetings and in the following months abrogated first the dealing relationship with G&SR and then the storage arrangement for the Special Purpose Trust. From that date forward, the Companies struggled to counter the negative press and image that had suddenly arisen through little fault of their own. They did recognize that they would have to do their best to prevent such illicit use of e-gold, and they set off to do what they could within the

[182] McCullagh, Declan. "Secret Service Raids Gold-Age." *Wired*, Conde Nast, 5 June 2017, www.wired.com/news/politics/0,1283,42745,00.html.

[183] Jackson, Douglas. "Re: Attached Cover Sample." Received by Carl Mullan, *Re: Attached Cover Sample*, 24 Feb. 2020. Attachment: DJ redlines 3.docx

[184] McCullash, Declan. "Secret Service Raids e-gold." *Interesting People: IP: U.S. Secret Service Raids e-gold Currency Exchanger*, Seclists.org, 31 Mar. 2001, seclists.org/interesting-people/2001/Mar/120.

limits of their small enterprise.[185]

A few weeks later, in April, e-gold® rebounded with some positive exposure in Barron's. The article "Making New Money" was published on April 23, 2001, in Barron's. Barron's heralded the emergence of e-gold® for precisely the reasons advanced by Jackson.

> With the global expansion of the Internet and eCommerce, the world needs a new type of currency. It needs an asset backed, high-tech monetary standard, without the political machinations that hobble the euro, the dollar, the yen and all other traditional currencies ...
>
> One company, e-gold, already allows online users to settle payments using its currency, which is 100% backed by gold. Ownership of the gold changes, but the physical bullion stays put with the company, which is based on the Caribbean island of Nevis. The system also is transparent: Holders have real-time access to the total amount of e-gold in circulation, and the company's total bullion reserves.[186]

On March 30, 2001, the e-gold blog shared more good news.[187]

> Read About e-gold in the book *"Money"*
> "[e-gold] is a fascinating concept and it merits the attention of everyone interested in helping to resolve the world's monetary dilemma."

> That's what James W. Ewart has to say about e-gold in his book "Money". Head on over to Principia Publishing and use e-gold to pick up a copy of the book for yourself. You'll have the same edition (the first printing of the first edition) on your coffee table as the founder of e-gold has on his. Gorgeous large color photographs of US paper currency. Discover the difference between "currency" and "money" among other topics.[188]

---

[185] CASE NUMBER: 07-167-M-01. *UNITED STATES OF AMERICA V. E-GOLD LIMITED, GOLD & SILVER RESERVE, INC., DOUGLAS L. JACKSON, BARRY K. DOWNEY and REID A. JACKSON.* SENTENCING MEMORANDUM OF GOLD & SILVER RESERVE, INC., Nov. 2008.

[186] White, Jack, and Doug Ramsey. "e-gold Covered in Recent Barron's." *e-gold Covered in Recent Barron's*, e-gold Blog, Apr. 2001, blog.e-gold.com/2001/04/e-gold-covered.html.

[187] Jackson, Douglas. "Read About e-gold in the Book 'Money.'" *Read About e-gold in the Book "Money"*, e-gold Blog, 30 Mar. 2001, blog.e-gold.com/2001/03/read-about-e-go.html.

[188] Jackson, Douglas. "e-gold News." *e-gold News*, e-gold Blog, Apr. 2001, web.archive.org/web/20011212164904fw_/www.e-gold.com/news.html.

With an advertising budget of zero, these little mentions created big excitement for the emerging e-gold® business.

e-gold® Online Interface

Detailed information on interacting with the e-gold® website was available in early 2001.[189]

- e-gold Shopping Cart Interface (SCI) - The e-gold SCI provides checkout capability to any e-gold account holder by allowing them to place a button on their web page to accept e-gold payments.
- e-gold Automation Interface - These defined methods allow programmers to perform e-gold actions (spend, balance, history) via their own program.

The shopping cart interface enabled other online businesses to build applications on top of the e-gold® platform and greatly expanded the company's e-commerce capabilities.

In June and July 2001, e-gold® landed some additional coverage from mainstream sources.

Some positive press appeared in Reuters through a July 10th, 2001, online report. One quote from the piece read, "In theory a grandmother in Bangladesh with a few grams of gold could get access to the global financial system for the first time."[190]

Not all of the new articles were flattering. On June 14, 2001, Wired.com published an article by Declan Mccullagh, entitled *Digging Those Digicash Blues.*[191] Later, in July, Mccallagh wrote another piece for Wired.com entitled *Nothing that Glitters is Digigold.* This piece hammered Jackson and reported on e-gold's project called Digigold.

> Hurt feelings, financial disputes and bizarre sexual allegations have led to a legal tiff between a high-profile digital currency firm and its software developer. After the once-friendly relationship between DigiGold and Systemics soured this spring, DigiGold sued the software company in an attempt to keep its servers online. Systemics' computers, which maintain DigiGold's customer accounts, are located on the West Indies island of Anguilla. Systemics' Ian Grigg claims he wants to pull the plug on the server since DigiGold has paid only $370,000 of the $500,000 it owed

---

[189] Jackson, Douglas. "e-gold Programmer's Information." *e-gold Programmer's Information*, e-gold Blog, 2001, web.archive.org/web/20011212171010fw_/www.e-gold.com/unsecure/sci_home.html.

[190] Jackson, Douglas. "e-gold News." e-gold News, *e-gold Blog*, Apr. 2001, web.archive.org/web/20011212164904fw_/www.e-gold.com/news.html.

[191] McCullagh, Declan. "Digging Those Digicash Blues." *Wired*, Conde Nast, 5 June 2017, www.wired.com/2001/06/digging-those-digicash-blues/.

him under a 1999 contract.[192]

Phishing

E-gold's digital store of value, immutable transactions, and massive international customer base created a prime target for online malware and scams. Organized transnational criminal syndicates increasingly conducted this type of malicious activity.

The first known phishing attacks against an online payment system occurred on the e-gold® system. The June 2001 attacks focused on members of the e-gold mailing list. This new technique was later refined during attacks against new digital gold systems. By 2003, phishing had become a primary malware tool targeting mainstream online financial institutions.[193]

> In addition to phishing, the attackers made widespread use of flaws in the Microsoft Windows operating systems and Internet Explorer web browser to collect account details from millions of computers to compromise e-gold accounts.[194] [195]

◆

2001 Patriot Act

More than five years after e-gold® had launched, Congress passed the USA Patriot Act.[196] These new 2001 regulations, made it a federal crime to operate a money transmitter business without a state money transmitter license, in any state that required such a permit. Due to the ambiguity of these new rules, practically speaking, the only reliable way to know if a business was in violation of the federal statute would be if a state first determined the party was in violation of state laws governing a money transmission business. The federal government could then use that determination to build a federal case.

Most U.S. States identified money transmitters as operations that cashed checks or accepted cash to fund remittances in which money from one person was sent to another person, either domestically or   across an international border. Prime examples of money

[192] McCullagh, Declan. "Nothing That Glitters Is DigiGold." *Wired*, Conde Nast, 5 June 2017, www.wired.com/2001/07/nothing-that-glitters-is-digigold/.

[193] "Financial Cryptography." *Financial Cryptography: GP4.3 - Growth and Fraud - Case #3 - Phishing*, Financialcryptography.com, 30 Dec. 2005, financialcryptography.com/mt/archives/000609.html.

[194] Dixon, Julia. "The e-gold Story." *DGC Magazine*, 27 June 2013, dgcmagazine.com/the-e-gold-story/.

[195] 2/27/2020 Jackson commented "I know this has been asserted but we never saw any evidence. There were fake sites to harvest passwords, key stroke loggers but we never encountered any plausible claim that operating system or browser vulnerabilities played a role."

[196] Uniting and Strengthening America by Providing Appropriate Tools Required to Intercept and Obstruct Terrorism (USA PATRIOT) Act of 2001

transmitters were Western Union and MoneyGram. No agents of the federal government (or, for that matter, any state) had ever applied the new money transmitter laws to any business that did not accept or disburse cash. However, the new federal statute was the tool used to prosecute civil and criminal cases against e-gold®.

November 2001, marked the commencement of an Internal Revenue Service (IRS) audit of G&SR that ultimately encompassed thirteen years of e-gold's operation. To comply with repeated IRS document requests, G&SR's expenditures for accountants and lawyers grew to outstrip its entire payroll costs for customer service and operating functions such as hosting and bandwidth from early 2002 until revenues finally skyrocketed in 2005.

A promising development occurred when Jackson received an introduction to senior officials at the World Bank. Their discussion centered on how e-gold® might lower the cost of guest worker remittances and advance financial inclusion for unbanked global citizens. This hopeful initiative was cut short though by a potentially fatal health crisis for Dr. Jackson.

A Broken Heart

Since his years in college, Jackson had been aware he had a congenital heart anomaly of the aortic valve. In preparation for being commissioned as an Army officer, military doctors had discovered the defect. The anomaly had never caused any symptoms as, for example, Jackson had recently completed the physically demanding US Army Ranger School. However, the valve issue posed a risk factor for heart infection. This condition warranted prophylactic antibiotics for most medical procedures, which is a common precaution against "subacute bacterial endocarditis (SBE)."

Of note, Maynard Keynes was progressively disabled by, and eventually died from, SBE, his heart valve having been damaged initially by a bout of rheumatic fever in childhood.

Risk became a reality in September 2001 when in the aftermath of an under-treated urinary tract infection (concurrent with initial depositions on the Thiel libel case), Jackson experienced the sudden onset of fever, muscle and joint aches, and lassitude. Symptoms quickly progressed to include drenching night sweats and drastically diminished exercise tolerance. By October, in the second round of depositions in the Thiel matter, Jackson, who was an avid runner, could not manage the hilly terrain of San Francisco without stopping to pant for breath.

Initially misdiagnosed as a "post-viral syndrome" and treated with NSAIDs, the situation reached the crisis point in December with fevers spiking to 104 degrees, and Jackson was unable to walk across a room. Upon Emergency Room admission, multiple blood cultures confirmed sepsis, and imaging studies revealed a crumbling aortic valve.

Jackson urgently required heart valve replacement.

As 2001 came to an end, Jackson's progressively degraded physical condition from October 2001 through January 2002 severely impaired his abilities to deal with the crises brewing with e-gold®.

2002

By 2002, the e-gold® system was rapidly approaching one million user accounts. New year's day began with an article by Julian Dibbell, for Wired.com, entitled *In Gold We Trust*. The piece profiled e-gold® and some of the company's management, including Douglas Jackson. Some readers viewed the article as favorable as it included this memorable quote:

> Invulnerable to government manipulation and subject to the kinds of market forces only a worldwide, 24/7 open-ended network can bring to bear, e-gold promises not simply Better Money but the best: a money supply kept so straight and narrow that it has room for neither bubbles nor crashes.[197]

Jackson, reading the article from a hospital bed as he was recovering from open-heart surgery, viewed it quite differently. He perceived the piece as ridiculing e-gold® with its emphasis on eccentric users and an excessive focus on e-dinar.

♦

On April 24, 2002, attorneys associated with James Turk at the Bermuda law firm of Conyers Dill & Pearman, sent a letter to attorney Michael J. Mello, a partner in the Bermuda law firm Mello Jones & Martin. Mello was a Trustee for the e-gold Bullion Reserve Special Purpose Trust registered in Hamilton, Bermuda.

It contained inflammatory content and a laundry list of items attacking the character of Jackson, G&SR, Inc. and e-gold Ltd. The first paragraph of the document is below.

> Our client [GM Network Ltd./GoldMoney] has become increasingly concerned by recent reports in the Press concerning the propriety of the activities and management of the e-gold system, and the effect of these activities on public confidence in digital gold currency systems.[198]

---

[197] Dibbell, Julian. "In Gold We Trust." *Wired*, Conde Nast, 4 June 2017, www.wired.com/2002/01/egold/.

[198] Pearman, Conyers Dill. "e-gold Bullion Reserve Special Purpose Trust." Received by Michael Mello, Clarendon House, 2 Church St., 24 Apr. 2002, Hamilton, Bermuda.

Jackson alleges that Turk's reputation attack was just one of numerous such denunciations being coordinated by Turk in cahoots with Charles Evans and Ian Grigg. The trust was the legal entity holding title to e-gold's bullion. In 2002, e-gold® was the industry's leading digital gold currency with the most significant number of users, fastest growth, and the highest number of transactions. Industry participants considered GoldMoney could be direct competition for e-gold®. Jackson believed that the law firm's accusations were a direct assault on e-gold® and an attempt to intimidate the firm handling the trust. The letter appeared to have been a malicious attempt to shut down e-gold® and, in the process, eliminate GoldMoney's possible competition. If that was Turk's goal, the scheme was not successful, or rather not immediately.

But as it turned out, the Turk-initiated letter to e-gold's Bermuda counsel was just one of the "sharp little pieces" as threatened by Charles Evans before his sabotage of the IRS2 Conference in October 2000. Throughout 2001-2003, the Turk, Evans and Grigg cabal was flinging allegations in every direction attempting to instigate a cascade of suspicion regarding the integrity of the e-gold® system. Turk's threat to e-gold's Bermuda lawyers was carefully coordinated with denunciations of e-gold® to the Bermuda Monetary Authority (BMA) by Grigg. A November 2003 email from Downey to Mello Jones partner Hil DeFrias provided a summary update:

> "Hil: This is a copy of the latest e-mail [to the e-gold discussion list] written by James Turk, who is the founder of GoldMoney, the competitor of e-gold Ltd. that instituted the patent lawsuit and that tried to smear Mello Jones in Bermuda.
>
> I expect that what he is saying probably sounds like the words that are being used by the BMA and have been heard by the partners of Mello Jones. If so, I believe this ties the genesis of the concerns to calls and other communications from Turk (and his coconspirators--Ian Grigg and Charles Evans) to the BMA and the partners. In the discovery process in the patent case, we received hundreds of emails that had gone out from James Turk with the same kind of false accusations, innuendo and questions to everyone they knew we had dealt with in the past or would be expected to deal with in the future. They literally have said in writing that the purpose of the patent lawsuit was to drive e-gold out of business. Having failed at that attempt, they continue to try to do this by spreading lies to the public, users of e-gold, the trustees and other governance partners. Further evidence of why we need to have that meeting with BMA and the partners to counter these continued attacks."[199]

[199] Downey, Barry K. "Mello." Received by Hil DeFrias, and Douglas Jackson, *Mello*, 20 Nov. 2003.

The cabal members had made substantial progress in poisoning the relationship between e-gold Ltd and its Bermuda-based lawyers during the 18-month interval between their last attack. For example, learning that Michael Mello was seeking to abandon his responsibilities as Trustee, the cabal tipped off a prominent Cypherpunk lawyer (who had an e-gold account) to call Mello. This attorney contacted e-gold inquiring:

> "Sirs/Mesdames:
> Your trust document (http://www.e-gold.com/contracts/egold-spt-111899.htm) lists Michael Mello as one of the original trustees. Mr. Mello informs me that he is no longer acting in that capacity.
>
> If you would be so kind, I would appreciate it if you would e-mail me the names and contact information for the current trustees of the e-gold bullion reserve special purpose trust."

The actual situation was summarized in a December 2003 email update from Downey:

> "I spoke with Hil on Friday. He called me back. He said it would be fruitless to talk to Peter Martin, making me think it may be Peter driving the termination of the relationship. Hil assured me that he and Michael would be the ones championing our cause with the firm and that they were required to ensure an orderly transition to new trustees of all the trusts, including helping us find new trustees. He told me he was extremely busy but we should rest assured that he and Michael will not suddenly stop serving as trustee before a new trustee is found."

But throughout Fall 2003, the rumor mill alleging Trustee resignations was being stoked vigorously by Turk et al. On October 21, 2003, Ken Griffith, then publisher of "The Gold Economy Magazine" emailed:

> I have it from a reliable source that the current trustee for the e-gold trust has or is in the process of withdrawing. When does the company plan to announce the new trustee?[200]

Similarly, at a gold industry conference in New Orleans the following week, Turk was hard at work disseminating the rumor. The principal of a prominent exchange service emailed

---

[200] Jackson, Douglas. "Re: Attached Copy." Received by Carl Mullan, *Re: Attached Copy*, 27 Feb. 2020. FJ redlines 3 second try.pdf

that he had been told at the conference that Mello had resigned:

> "It appears that he did write an e-mail, which is quoted in part below. I have not spoken to Mr. Mello and I have not spoken to or corresponded with the person who sent him the e-mail. So, what I have is third-hand. Here is what he is said to have written:
> "I regret to inform you that we have had to exit the e-gold relationship, not because of any differences with the client, but because of difficulties experienced in operating the alternative payment system."…
> I also contacted the person who talked to me at the New Orleans Conference. The reply I got back included a request to keep confidential my source."

Turk also busied himself, broadcasting the rumor of Mello's resignation on various online discussion lists. A notable example was this exchange on November 18, 2003:

> "Turk: Trustees don't resign unless there is a good reason. Trusts are an easy business, and the fees are a reliable annuity. Trustees don't walk away from that business. It would be interesting to know why the trustee resigned.
>
> >If there is something else maybe you could say more about why you think there is some reason to be suspicious about the trustee resigning?
>
> Turk: I have nothing to say about this specific situation because I only know what I've heard, and it is second hand. But I have a lot of years of experience working in and dealing with financial institutions and trustees. So if I sound "suspicious", it's probably because I've never in my experience seen a trustee resign unless he has had cause. But I suppose there is a first time for everything."[201]

Turk's remark, "It would be interesting to know why the trustee resigned," vividly illustrated his disingenuousness, having been the principal instigator of the whole affair.

The actual outcome of the Trustee imbroglio was that Mello's partner Hil DeFrias continued to serve as Trustee for the e-gold Bullion Reserve Special Purpose Trust until the e-gold Value Access Plan (e-gold VAP) was completed in 2013)

However, as with multiple other avenues of attack made by the cabal, dealing with the Bermuda lawyers was a costly distraction, requiring attention and effort that could otherwise have been applied to more beneficial and proactive matters. More ominously, a March 1,

---

[201] Ibid

2004 update email from Downey to the Jackson highlighted an element that ended up being highly material, almost serendipitously, at a later critical juncture involving the USSS:

> Michael Mello and Hil S. de Frias no longer are directors of e-gold Ltd. and DigiGold.net Ltd. They simply have been faxing the subpoenas they receive to Randy. Nevis is the agent for service of legal process. Hil was uncomfortable with the prior process of having subpoenas sent to him, because they were simply accepting on behalf of the shareholders. It will be a much better process this way to have the subpoenas going to Nevis. He does not want to tell the Nevis corporate attorney that he is receiving pressure from outside regulatory bodies. Hil says that the BMA was saying why is this "issuance of electronic currency" going on in Bermuda. He has nothing concrete on why the BMA was concerned…[It appears] BMA is concerned about the unknown, which means they are concerned with the issuance of electronic currency. (I think they are confusing digigold with e-gold.)
>
> Until Hil transitions this, we are to continue to tell people to send subpoenas to Hil. He will immediately send them to Randy.[202]

The evident reluctance of the Bermuda attorneys to perform their duties ultimately resulted in their negligent failure to forward the most critical subpoena ever to be served on e-gold Ltd. before the legal attacks that commenced in December 2005. As we will see, the lawyers' failure, in December 2004, to forward a USSS subpoena regarding ringleaders of Shadowcrew, directly resulted in the cancellation of a crucial USSS scheduled meeting with Jackson in DC. The meeting had been arranged to educate USSS officials on how best to take advantage of the cyber-forensic capabilities of e-gold's in-house investigative unit.

The Litany

Jackson alleges that Turk, Evans and Grigg incessantly denounced e-gold to whoever would listen. Stating:

> Their poison pen attacks always included the following litany:
> - e-gold turned a blind eye to criminal activity on the part of its customers, especially investment scams,
> - the Trustee(s) for the e-gold Bullion Reserve Special Purpose Trust had resigned (as discussed above),
> - e-gold refused to have the gold reserves audited, probably because of some

---

[202] Ibid

130

sort of fraud,

- G&SR had knowingly accepted investment funds from a Ponzi-scheming criminal, JohnWayne Zidar.[203]

The Zidar matter

Not uncommonly, private companies do not publish the names of their investors, especially if the investor is passive, i.e., with no operating role or representation on the board. The only way Turk had of knowing that G&SR had an investor named John Wayne Zidar was that Charles Evans told him when, after a brief stint helping James Fayed launch e-Bullion, he had moved on to help James Turk launch GoldMoney.

In his June 2000 email in which Evans threatened Reid Jackson with "a lot of sharp, little pieces", Evans had highlighted his most signal accomplishment as "*I* Introduced Doug to: [a list of names, headed by] JW Zidar."[204]

To be certain of receiving the credit due, this action was also spelled out in a self-initiated performance review sent by Evans (also in June 2000) to Dr Jackson and seven other of the G&SR staff and directors:

> "To date, I have:
> introduced Doug and Barry to:
> JW Zidar"[205]

Zidar was eventually convicted in 2003 of mail fraud, wire fraud and money laundering.[206]

Did G&SR accept money from a known criminal? Were the investment funds taken, with no questions asked?

Following Evans' August 1999 "introduction" to Zidar, Jackson took no immediate action. Notes from October 2000 memorializing a discussion between G&SR's then-counsel and the Assistant US Attorneys heading up a grand jury investigation of Zidar relate:

> "He first called us in 1999 and talked to Charles Evans. Doug was supposed to call back and he was interested in investing, but Doug did not call back because it

---

203 Ibid

204 Evans, Charles. "Pity." Received by Reid Jackson, *Pity*, 29 June 2000.

205 Jackson, Douglas. "Re: Attached Copy." Received by Carl Mullan, *Re: Attached Copy*, 27 Feb. 2020. DJ redlines 3 second try.pdf

206 "UNITED STATES SECURITIES AND EXCHANGE COMMISSION." John Wayne Zidar, Et Al.: Lit. Rel. No. 18267 / August 4, 2003, UNITED STATES SECURITIES AND EXCHANGE COMMISSION, 4 Aug. 2003, www.sec.gov/litigation/litreleases/lr18267.htm.

sounded too good to be true. Zidar then called back and talked to Doug and told Doug he had resources at his disposal and he could make the investment decisions."[207]

Jackson traveled to Phoenix, Arizona, in August 1999 to check out Zidar. As Jackson relates in a later email:

Zidar met with me in his home which was also where he maintained his office in two rooms separated from the residential portion. One was his office, which was well-appointed and decorated with pictures that included a race car sporting his company logo. Another was a work area with two men busy at what appeared to be multi-screen Bloomberg terminals. Zidar described his business as a private hedge fund for qualified high net worth investors plus a handful of long-term clients of more modest means. He described his investment strategy as assembling a portfolio of long-term holdings—capital appreciation—rather than active trading to try to beat the market. I was pleased to hear this because our limited experience in talking with potential investors such as venture capital firms had always been frustrating with their emphasis on "exit strategies" such as IPOs.

I returned home and we did a lot of snooping around the web looking for indications of prior indictments or injunctions. Finding none, we accepted what turned out to be his first round of investment, $450,000 in September 1999, supplementing our 1999 'family and friends' round. At the time, he requested that if we found ourselves needing more capital that we talk to him before approaching additional investors.

In February 2000 the racing car/team Zidar's firm was sponsoring competed in a Le Mans-style event at Daytona, an hour north of our Melbourne office. He dropped by the office and I described the break-out in e-gold usage we were starting to observe. After some negotiation we agreed to a second round of investment, $2 million, at a higher valuation for G&SR.

Our next interaction was when he invited me to come to Las Vegas the first week of May 2000 to make a presentation at an event he was organizing. My understanding was that it was for his investors to get an update on portfolio companies. I went, along with Evans and his assistant and made a presentation about e-gold and Digigold and demonstrated a live transaction.

At that conference however, we developed misgivings. The presentations we heard, mostly rambling discourses by Zidar himself, were more focused on what

[207] Jackson, Douglas. "Re: Attached Copy." Received by Carl Mullan, *Re: Attached Copy*, 27 Feb. 2020. DJ redlines 3 second try.pdf

could be called 'patriot movement' topics such as home-schooling or even stashing money offshore.

The following week, we learned that on May 10, 2000 search and seizure warrants had been served on Zidar and a civil action had been filed in Federal court alleging securities and wire fraud.[208]

Over the next several years, Jackson, Downey, and G&SR investigative staff had multiple interactions with the SEC, FBI, and the Assistant US Attorneys developing the case against Zidar. In September 2000, G&SR responded to a subpoena from an AUSA in Seattle, looking for any value he or associates might have in e-gold accounts. He then forwarded the G&SR issued Zidar stock certificates. In October 2000, Downey engaged in an extended phone conference concerning the grand jury investigating Zidar.

In July 2002, attorneys called Jackson as a defense witness. Because Jackson's schedule conflicted with the court date, he was allowed to testify from Melbourne via remote video conference. As Jackson later related:

> "In preparing to testify, I developed the impression that the investment made in G&SR was felt by his defense team to be the most economically justified expenditure Zidar had made. His counsel was trying to make the case that at least some of the funds had indeed been invested prudently. Of note, while Zidar had also invested in Bernard von Nothaus's NORFED (later called "Liberty Dollar") scheme, I was left with the impression that they'd determined that highlighting that investment would not cast Zidar in a favorable light. The actual questions asked were quite straightforward - the nature of our business, usage and revenue statistics. The prosecution in turn, elected not to cross-examine."[209]

On August 14, 2002, the Court convicted Zidar after a seven-week trial on multiple counts of fraud and money laundering. Several million dollars of assets were recovered, including the G&SR shares. Those were turned over to a court-appointed receiver, the Seattle law firm McKay Chadwell. After extended negotiations, G&SR repurchased the shares.

It is noteworthy that in years of interaction with the law enforcement agencies and DOJ attorneys investigating and prosecuting Zidar, at no time did any of these agencies threaten any legal action against G&SR or accuse it of impropriety in accepting these investments.

Turk, Grigg, and Evans, in contrast, with their relentless moralizing and spin on the

[208] Ibid
[209] Ibid

topic, made it clear they allegedly answered to a higher standard: to destroy e-gold by any means.

Ernst & Young

By February 2001, Jackson had hired Ernst &Young, to inspect e-gold's bullion at the Bank of Nova Scotia in Canada. Ernst & Young's report showed that all audited amounts of vaulted precious metal were congruent with the published Examiner statistics. The accounting firm's Dubai business office also inspected the e-gold® bullion held through Transguard. During the first quarter of 2001, all of the e-gold® precious metal bullion stored in Canada was moved from the Canadian vault facility at Bank of Nova Scotia to Transguard facilities in Dubai and JP Morgan Chase vaults in London.

Additionally, Ernst & Young was employed to prepare an audit report for e-gold Ltd. in July 2001. That document included all gold bullion and other metal holdings of the e-gold Bullion Reserve Special Purpose Trust currently vaulted at the Transguard facilities in Dubai. Barry Downey met with representatives of Ernst & Young in the firm's Dubai, UAE office.

E-gold had previously employed Ernst & Young, for select tasks, through the company's offices in Northern Virginia and Dubai. By October 2001, e-gold® and G&SR were vigorously trying to hire the firm as full-time auditors. As U.S. Counsel to e-gold Ltd. and General Counsel to Gold & Silver Reserve, Inc. Barry Downey was trying to appoint Ernst & Young, through the London office, precious metals accounting, and auditing services. Downey had requested verification of ownership along with an audit and report from the Ernst & Young London office on all of the e-gold® bullion vaulted at the London JP Morgan Chase vaults.

An October 17, 2001 email from Downey, to Ernst & Young Senior Manager Colin Copel, detailed the extensive list of requested services.

Subject line: Re: e-gold Ltd. And e-gold Bullion Reserve Special Purpose Trust

1. An audit of the bullion vaulted at the London vault of JP Morgan Chase. You can coordinate this audit through me and Peter Smith at JP Morgan Chase (20 777 xxxx). We would like to have you perform this audit at the earliest possible date.
2. Engagement of E&Y to control the liability side of the balance sheet.
3. Engagement of E&Y to serve as the Escrow Agent.
4. Recommendation by E&Y of an e-gold interface to E&Y e-commerce and regular business clients.

5. A meeting this year in your London office to discuss all of these items.[210]

Also included in this letter was an invitation for the E&Y along with the firm's business clientele, to meet with e-gold's management and learn more about its beneficial services.

> Finally, I would like to arrange a meeting with you and with other partners in the e-commerce and general corporate departments of E&Y to more fully brief you on the companies and the e-gold currency. This would allow us to discuss in detail the additional services we would like E&Y to provide to e-gold Ltd. In addition, I am certain that upon seeing the extent of an e-gold interface by many of your corporate clients (both e-commerce and general corporate) would be highly beneficial to their business.[211]

Following this letter, G&SR provided hundreds of documents used for due diligence during consecutive rounds of audits over four months. However, E&Y rejected e-gold® as a client. In 2019 emails, Jackson offered one conclusion that may have led to the rejection.

> Their rejection seemed in part to be due that they had served as auditor for (what I could tell to be a patently fraudulent) gold scheme that had blown up in their face shortly before we re-approached them. Ironically it made headlines on the day, 2/28/2002, of their rejection of us.[212]

In February 2002, an article by Jeff D. Opdyke in the Wall Street Journal labeled the accounting firm Ernst & Young LLP as the unwitting accomplice in a gold financial scheme that defrauded Well Fargo & Co. of $14.5 million. At the time, Ernst & Young LLP was the fourth-largest auditor in the United States.

Opdyke's article, along with other court files detailed that the owner of a small gold jewelry business in Oceanside, California, had defrauded Wells Fargo & Co. The scheme occurred when the jewelry company forged fraudulent documents showing inflated annual sales and then filled the company's storage vaults with fake gold. E&Y had signed off on the jewelry company's phony accounting, and Wells Fargo had approved a healthy line of credit based on the fraudulent audits. Allegedly, the scheme succeeded, in part, because of the lax

---

[210] Downey, Barry. "Re: e-Gold Ltd. and e-Gold Bullion Reserve Special Purpose Trust." Received by Colin Copeland, *Re: e-Gold Ltd. and e-Gold Bullion Reserve Special Purpose Trust*, 17 Nov. 2001. BY OVERNIGHT DELIVERY. Colin Copeland, Senior Manager, Ernst & Young, Rolls House 7 Rolls Buildings, Fetter Lane, London, EC4A lNH

[211] Ibid

[212] Jackson, Douglas. "e-Gold Fiduciary Safeguards." Received by Carl Mullan, *e-Gold Fiduciary Safeguards*, 16 July 2018.

standards employed by Ernst & Young.

When the story surfaced in the Wall Street Journal,[213] there were no allegations that Ernst & Young had intentionally engaged in fraudulent activity. No one has made this kind of claim. However, the fake gold case proved to be a severe embarrassment for the accounting firm. This strange turn of events did not help e-gold's chances to employ Ernst & Young. The date of the articles that appeared in the paper was February 28, 2002. e-gold® was never mentioned in the article and had no involvement with the company.

On February 28, 2002, the same day of the article, Downey received an email letter from Simon Michaelson, the Senior Manager in Ernst & Young LLC's London office.

> 2/28/2002
> Dear Barry,
> Further to our recent correspondence and discussions, having now made significant progress with our internal client acceptance procedures, we are unfortunately unable to accept e-gold and its associated companies as a client of the UK firm. I apologise for any inconvenience this may have caused you.[214]

♦

Giacomo Furlan

In addition to underwriting day-to-day operating expenses and safeguarding bullion reserves, e-gold® and G&SR had to fight off miscreants attempting to scam account holders. As early as 2001, bad actors began trying to scam e-gold® account holders and steal their digital assets. The hackers used every possible tool and trick they could develop.

One individual named Giacomo Furlan registered a series of domains containing words with similar spelling to e-gold®. This scam is known as typo-squatting.

Furlan copied and cloned publicly viewable pages of the e-gold® website to be successful with this scam and hosted a copy of the clone on one or more misspelled domains, notably e-qold.com (spelled with a Q instead of a G). The cloned fake site could trick unwitting visitors into entering their private e-gold® access information. The scammer then recorded the details. Once in possession of the login access information, the bad guys would log in to the real e-gold® websites and clean out the customer's value. Since e-gold transactions could not be modified or reversed, once stolen, the funds were in the wind.

Furlan also tried to extort money from G&SR. Some partial details of his activities,

[213] Opdyke, Jerry. "Aspiring Midas Enmeshes Auditors in Gold Chain." *Wall Street Journal*, 28 Feb. 2002.
[214] Michaelson, Simon. Received by Barry K. Downey, Rolls House, 7 Rolls Building, 28 Feb. 2002, London, United Kingdon.

copied from a G&SR arbitration document, are shown here.[215]

> *Gold & Silver Reserve, Inc. v. Giacomo Furlan* Claim Number: FA0204000109054
> PARTIES Complainant is Gold & Silver Reserve, Inc., Wilmington, DE
> ("Complainant") represented by Michael F. Snyder, of Drinker Biddle & Reath LLP.
> Respondent is Giacomo Furlan, Bruino, Torino, ITALY ("Respondent")
> REGISTRAR AND DISPUTED DOMAIN NAMES The domain names at issue are
> e-yold.com, e-vold.com, e-qold.com, e-gpld.com, e-gopd.com, e-golx.com, e-
> gols.com, e-golr.com, e-gole.com, e-golc.com, e-glox.com, e-glld.com, egkld.com, e-
> gild.com, e-g9ld.com, e-g0ld.com, and 3-gold.com, registered with Verisign, Inc.
> Respondent registered <e-qold.com> on April 8, 2001.   Respondent registered the
> remaining sixteen disputed domain names on April 7, 2001.   Respondent links each
> of the disputed domain names to a website that not only offers similar services, but
> uses Complainant's e-gold mark on the corresponding websites.   According to the
> Complaint, Respondent's websites are a complete replica of the website associated
> with Complainant's e-gold mark, <e-gold.com>, and Respondent's use of the
> disputed domain name is to drain the e-gold account of Complainant's customers.
> Respondent[Furlan] has sent an e-mail to Complainant[G&SR/e-gold] stating that he
> is the owner of "more of 30 e-gold mistyped web site" and that Respondent "could
> change web hosting service everyday until you close your e-gold web site."
> Respondent then requested $3,000 "every Monday" to "suspend all the attacks
> against" Complainant.

On April 4, 2002, G&SR electronically submitted a complaint to the National Arbitration
Forum, and the organization resolved the dispute in favor of G&SR.

> RELIEF SOUGHT Complainant requests that the domain names be transferred from
> Respondent to Complainant.
> Respondent has registered seventeen disputed domain names, which incorporate
> various misspellings of Complainant's e-gold mark.   It has been held that this
> practice of "typosquatting" has been recognized as a bad faith use of domain names
> under the UDRP, therefore Respondent has used the disputed domain names in bad
> faith.
> DECISION Having established all three elements required under the ICANN Policy,
> the Panel concludes that the requested relief should be hereby granted.

---

[215] National Arbitration Forum. *Gold & Silver Reserve, Inc. v. Giacomo Furlan Claim Number: FA0204000109054.* 8 Apr.
2002. http://www.adrforum.com/Domaindecisions/109054.htm

137

Accordingly, it is Ordered that the following domain names: e-yold.com, e-vold.com, e-qold.com, e-gpld.com, e-gopd.com, e-golx.com, e-gols.com, e-golr.com, e-gole.com, e-golc.com, eglox.com, e-glld.com, e-gkld.com, e-gild.com, e-g9ld.com, e-g0ld.com, and 3-gold.com be transferred from Respondent to Complainant.[216]

This G&SR arbitration was not Furlan's first illicit act; nor his last. During his criminal career, e-gold® had attempted to provide law enforcement with additional significant evidence on this individual. If law enforcement had used the information obtained from his e-gold® account history, it might have led to an earlier prosecution. However, for several years, e-gold's offer of assistance was rejected or ignored by law enforcement, and this offender, and others, continued committing crimes. LE Investigators' desire to catch Furlan changed in 2008.

> Perp [Giacomo Furlan] remains active year by year (Interpol refuses to help as late as 2006) until finally gov contacts Jackson in 2008 in desperation to track him down after he makes extortion threat to FL governor. e-gold devises a real time tracking that pinpoints location and supplies in real time to FBI.[217]

Years later, Jackson summarized his thoughts regarding law enforcement's efforts to pursue Furlan, saying, "One can only imagine how swiftly the wheels of justice might have turned if the misspelled domains had been similar to PlayPal.com or PayPal.com."

Reserve Bank of India

As early as year-end 1999, Dr. Jackson had become aware that a growing number of people were opening e-gold® accounts and encouraging family members abroad to do so as well. The families were using e-gold for international remittances. Some of these customers volunteered anecdotal information regarding international bank wires that would sometimes go unfulfilled for weeks. They expressed their dissatisfaction with the exorbitant fees charged by banks and traditional remittance services such as Western Union.

By 2002, three remittance corridors appeared to be the most active; the U.S. to the Philippines, the U.S. to India, and the United Arab Emirates (UAE) to India. Active exchange providers served the Philippine and UAE markets, but it was unclear whether or how customers could exchange e-gold® for Indian Rupee (INR) or vice versa. Despite this, the number of accounts in India was growing by thousands per year from 2001-2003.

---

[216] Ibid

[217] Jackson, Douglas. "Re: Attached Cover Sample." Received by Carl Mullan, *Re: Attached Cover Sample*, 24 Feb. 2020. DJ redlines 3.docx

In the summer of 2002, the proprietor of a gold and jewelry dealership in Calcutta (now Kolkata) contacted Dr. Jackson and proposed to make introductions to officials of the Reserve Bank of India (RBI). This government central bank issues INR and is the primary regulator of the banking system in India. The hope was to formalize arrangements whereby exchange provider services could support e-gold<--->INR on a licensed basis.

In August 2002, Jackson had face-to-face meetings in Mumbai with Dr. TC Nair and other mid-level RBI officials. During the discussions, Dr. Nair showed an interest in e-gold®. He advised Jackson to return later that year for a meeting with the Reserve Bank's senior officials, including the Deputy Governor. Jackson's recovered 2002 emails reveal a strategy for expanding e-gold® around the globe to friendly nations that could benefit from the innovative e-metals structure. Jackson was to begin traveling through Asia and the Middle East in October 2002.

Jackson discussed his return to India in a September 2002 email with to Dr. TC Nair.[218]

> Following the Dubai leg, I would be interested in returning to Mumbai and possibly other Indian cities in order to make further presentations to familiarize a broader group of decision makers with the advantages of this alternative global medium. I plan to finish up with visits to Bangkok, Kuala Lumpur and Jakarta.
> My questions are these:
> 1. Would it be possible to meet with you and additional senior officials at the RBI in early/mid-October? I have been advised to seek appointments with Mr. Rakesh Mohan and Mrs. Grace Koshie.
> 2. Are there specific issues or questions regarding which I should develop and submit documentation in advance? You had suggested working up a "FAQ" sort of document. I am attaching a basic FAQ but would be happy to prepare additional materials.
>
> In recent weeks there has been a gratifying level of institutional engagement on the related topic of a global clearinghouse enabling clearing of dissimilar liabilities using e-gold as a common medium of settlement. I am meeting next week with Dr. Benjamin Friedman at Harvard to elicit critical review of the topic, in view of his expertise and prior analyses of alternative settlement arrangements http://post.economics.harvard.edu/faculty/friedman/papers/decouplingmargin.pdf and http://post.economics.harvard.edu/faculty/friedman/papers/futureofmonetary.pdf
> Sincere regards,
> Douglas Jackson

---

[218] From: Douglas Jackson <djackson@omnipay.net>, Sent: Tuesday, September 17, 2002 2:32 PM, To: tcnair@rbi.org.in Cc: nairtc@yahoo.com, Subject: e-gold; guidance requested

The following FAQ responses were provided by Jackson in connection with e-gold's due diligence. Jackson sent this 2002 email to Dr. Nair for representatives of the Reserve Bank of India.

FAQs Attached to the email (partial list)
What is the e-gold standard?
The term "e-gold standard" refers to all monetary and financial liabilities denominated in AUG, meaning that they are defined as ultimately payable in e-gold. The e-gold standard is a stricter standard than the classic gold standard. The base money issuer is bound by explicit contract and accountable under the rule of law.
How does the e-gold Standard differ from the classic gold standard?
Under the gold standard, gold did not circulate as a currency. Gold was a commodity used as an external benchmark for a multitude of currencies. Instead of standard weight units, each currency was denominated in customary units of account, solemnly defined in terms of a fixed quantity of gold. A recurring problem, however, was that there was no way to prevent governments from redefining the gold content of national currency units or even from suspending obligations to redeem monetary liabilities in gold. Not only would sovereigns repudiate their own obligations but would also permit or even force third parties [banks, bond issuers] to abrogate theirs. Under the gold standard, in every country, the most basic form of monetary liability capable of being circulated via a remote payment system was financial in nature – a bank deposit. Even bank notes were fiduciary instruments, backed partially by the putative redemption medium, but partly by remunerative assets. In such an arrangement it was impossible to entirely eliminate default risk.
With specie serving as the reserve asset underlying notes and deposits, procedures that would enable a depositor to determine the adequacy of reserves of any particular financial institution were inconvenient and difficult to verify.
The fact that the legislatively defined base money, specie, was incapable of being circulated efficiently external to the banking system meant that a critical feedback loop - diminishing reserve ratios leading to a tightening of credit -were dysfunctional due to excess latency.
The most telling weakness of the alleged discipline imposed by the gold standard was the fact that it could be abolished.
In contrast, e-gold manifests the following characteristics:
- The unit of account cannot be tampered with.
- A remote payment system, offering freedom from default risk and finality of

settlement, is directly accessible by end Users.

- Efficient circulation of base money [the medium used as reserves by the banking system] external to the banking system subjects banks to zero-latency discipline governing broad money supply in a fashion that inhibits booms and the resultant busts.

Why is the present moment in history ideal for the emergence of e-gold?

e-gold is timely because of the convergence of two unprecedented historic phenomena:

1) The emergence of the Internet enables universal access to a secure global communication/transaction network.
2) Western governments, dating back to World War I, evince their continuing determination to dissociate legacy monetary systems from gold. Gold reserves are no longer husbanded by central banks in OECD countries but rather are treated as an anachronistic burden and cost center.

This combination provides an unprecedented opportunity for private enterprise to take the lead in implementing a robust, sustainable and global gold-based monetary infrastructure; the "e-gold Standard".

As noted by Barron's, a leading US financial publication:

> "With the global explosion of the Internet and e-commerce, the world needs a new type of   currency. It needs an asset-backed, high-tech money standard, without the political machinations that hobble the euro, the dollar, the yen and all other traditional currencies.... One company, e-gold, already allows online users to settle payments using its currency, which is 100% backed by gold."[219]

Perceptively, the authors single out e-gold as the only example of such a monetary undertaking, and follow-up with the recommendation:

> "… a strong but economically backward country, such as China or India, could try to leapfrog the developed world by endorsing and protecting the use of a convertible e-currency."

How are payment orders transmitted to the e-gold system?

The e-gold system supports one type of transaction, called a Spend. This is a transfer, authorized by the payer, from the e-gold account of the payer to the e-gold account of a designated recipient. The system enforces a strict debit rule – there must be a positive e-gold balance in the payer's account equal to or greater than the amount specified for a Spend. There is one exception to the strict debit rule; a Mint account

---

[219] White, Jack, and Doug Ramsey. "e-gold® Covered in Recent Barron's." *e-gold Covered in Recent Barron's*, e-gold Blog, Apr. 2001, blog.e-gold.com/2001/04/e-gold-covered.html.

specially enabled to make overdraft Spends for the purpose of increasing the total quantity of e-gold in circulation. This Mint function is described in greater detail below.

A Spend is technically constrained to occur in its entirety—both credit and debit committed in a single transaction—or to roll back to the preceding state. The Spend is also irreversible, by contract, strengthening finality of settlement and consistent with the classification of the e-gold system as an RTGS (real-time gross settlement) system.

There are currently three basic interfaces for initiating a Spend:

1. Spend initiated by a logged-in User from the User's Account Manager screen. See https://www.e-gold.com/acct/login.html . In this instance, the Payer specifies all details; the recipient account, the value of the spend and optional posting information in a memo field. The system returns a Preview screen to minimize risk of error. If acceptable to the Payer, clicking a "commit" button authorizes the payment.

2. Mobile Spend – this is essentially the same as a Spend initiated from the payer's computer, but is performed using a web enabled mobile phone, provided the payer's mobile phone service supports secure (SSL) protocol. See http://mobile.e-gold.com.

3. Automation Interface – referred to as the e-gold Shopping Cart Interface. See http://sci.e-gold.com .This Spend is typically initiated from the website of a User intending to accept payment in e-gold, for example, a merchant. The recipient supplies information fully specifying the payment details. The prospective payer is passed seamlessly to the e-gold secure server where the payment specification is previewed and, if acceptable, authorized by the Payer. The interface entails cryptographically authenticated server-to-server notification, enabling the recipient to know with certainty that good funds have been received in settled payment. This automated immediate notification allows the recipient, for example, to post an invoice as paid and release goods for delivery.

Additional interfaces are under development, including a bill presentment interface directly accessed by a logged-in e-gold User. The bill presentment interface is intended to facilitate use of e-gold in a point-of-sale context (mCommerce).

An additional capability under development entails the concept of pending payment, with a specified value date, supporting virtual equivalence to letters of credit and other facilities that extend the utility of e-gold.

What are the requirements for becoming an e-gold User?

Anyone, regardless of creditworthiness, net worth, physical location or other characteristic may become an e-gold User. Account creation entails no cost. An account is funded by the acceptance of an e-gold payment from another User who already has an e-gold balance. The e-gold system, by virtue of its strict debit protocol, is not exposed to credit risk from any source. Unlike a bank depositor, there are no actions an e-gold User can commit that would expose the e-gold system to credit risk.

The next generation e-gold system differentiates between Users based on the quality of due diligence information supplied by the User. A User who has been postally validated, for example, enjoys greater permissions than an entry level User (who is email validated). The postally validated User is also empowered to use stronger authentication protocols to authorize Spends.

By what means does the circulation of e-gold increase or decrease?

Increased Circulation by means of Bailment and Mintage

Circulation increases when a User has caused acceptable good delivery gold bars to be delivered to one of the allocated storage accounts titled to the e-gold Bullion Reserve Special Purpose Trust. Upon notification of delivery, the e-gold Comptroller instructs the Mint to issue additional e-gold in an amount equal to the fine gold content of the delivered material. The Mint is specially enabled to make overdraft payments, thereby increasing the total circulation of e-gold. The Mint is only able, by programmatic constraint, to direct these overdraft spends to the e-gold Comptroller. The Comptroller in turn spends the newly minted e-gold into the e-gold account of the User on whose behalf the gold was bailed in.

It should be noted that in the normal event a User who is in possession of a quantity of gold and who desires to exchange it for e-gold would sell the physical material to a counterparty offering payment in e-gold or some other currency that could be exchanged for e-gold. Bailment is typically a relatively uncommon event undertaken at the wholesale level by an entity such as OmniPay® in the event it needs to replenish e-gold balances because of an imbalance in trading activity that has led to accumulation of national currency balances and depletion of e-gold. It is also anticipated that commercial banks, central banks and participants in the gold industry, already in possession of significant quantities of good delivery gold bars, may tend to prefer bailment over currency exchange as a means of funding their e-gold accounts.

Decreased Circulation by means of Redemption and Extinguishment

The e-gold Account User Agreement entitles any e-gold User to redemption on demand, subject to two conditions; 1) The redemption medium must be bars already held in allocated storage on account of the e-gold Bullion Reserve Special Purpose Trust. In other words, since the Trust holds only LBMA certified good delivery bars, it can not deliver some other sort of material, such as kilo bars or bullion coins. This, of course, means that redemption orders must entail an amount of e-gold in at least the range of approximately 400 oz troy, the nominal weight of a good delivery bar. 2) Reasonable fees may be assessed.

The User desiring redemption notifies the e-gold Operator of intent and of the approximate quantity of e-gold to be redeemed (for example, the number of good delivery bars desired). The e-gold Operator will request the storage facility to identify specific bars in order to calculate a precise total of fine weight. The User is then instructed to Spend an amount of e-gold to the e-gold Comptroller account equal to the sum of fine weight plus any relevant fees. The Comptroller spends an amount of e-gold to the Mint account equal to the fine weight of the bullion being redeemed, thereby reducing the negative balance of the Mint account, extinguishing that amount of e-gold and reducing the total quantity of e-gold in circulation. Following the reduction in circulation, the Escrow Agent and Trustee are notified of the delivery order. The Escrow Agent verifies that the e-gold circulation has been reduced, authenticates the instruction, instructs and authorizes the Storage vault to make delivery. Dual authorization is required, in order to prevent the risk of coercion of the Escrow Agent or malfeasance.

It should be noted that in the normal event, a User with an e-gold balance that wishes to exchange it for physical gold, whether bars, coins, or jewelry would use the e-gold as money in order to buy the physical material as goods. Redemption is typically an uncommon event undertaken at the wholesale level by an entity such as OmniPay® that may find itself with an imbalance in trading balances that is best addressed by redemption followed by liquidation of physical bars.

What role does e-gold Ltd. play in the e-gold system

e-gold Ltd. serves as the General Contractor responsible for performance of the obligations memorialized in the e-gold Account User Agreement.

See http://www.e-gold.com/unsecure/e-g-agree.htm The primary functions of e-gold Ltd. are Issuance and Settlement. e-gold Ltd. uses sub-contractors to carry out the following roles and responsibilities:

- Operator
- Mint
- Escrow Agent
- Trustees
- Storage Facilities

The Operator performs the technical functions of; maintaining the e-gold website, system development and   customer service. G&SR currently serves as Operator. The Mint contractor is solely capable of increasing the total quantity of e-gold in circulation. G&SR currently serves as interim Mint.

The Escrow Agent is one of two signatories exercising control over the physical assets that back e-gold. Baker, Baxter, Conn, and Sidle, a law firm in Baltimore Maryland, currently serves as Escrow Agent. See http://www.e-gold.com/contracts/egold-bbsc.3.htm.

All physical assets that back e-gold are titled to the e-gold Bullion Reserve Special Purpose Trust. This trust is domiciled in Bermuda and exists to hold bullion assets for the exclusive benefit of all e-gold Account Users collectively. See http://www.e-gold.com/contracts/egold-spt-111899.htm.

Secure storage facilities currently used by the Trust are JP Morgan Chase, in London, and Transguard, a subsidiary of the Emirates Group, in Dubai. See http://www.e-gold.com/contracts/egold-jpmorganchase.htm and http://www.e-gold.com/contracts/egold-transguard.htm.

How can one know whether e-gold is backed 100% by gold?

See attached description of the e-gold governance model. The basic principle is that there is no need to rely on trust. Every element of fiduciary responsibility is objectively and readily verifiable - delegated to third parties of high reputation, further strengthened by separation of roles, automated transparency mechanisms and cryptographic safeguards.

How would a commercial bank exploit the existence of e-gold?

The best way to visualize the role of e-gold in the banking system is to think of it as the base money of a foreign currency referred to as AUG – gold, as currency, denominated in grams and decimal fractions, payable in e-gold.

Banks benefit from the emergence of e-gold and AUG by offering services in the areas of currency exchange and financial intermediation. They offer e-gold [AUG] deposits and participate in payments systems.

There are four basic means by which a bank would create or add to an AUG deposit:
- Accepting e-gold payments from the depositor's e-gold account to the bank's e-gold account,
- Accepting AUG payments through a clearinghouse for the benefit of a designated depositor,
- Fulfilling a customer's order to exchange a deposit denominated in another currency for an AUG balance,
- Extending credit to a depositor and creating an AUG balance for the borrower

145

to draw on.

In all cases, the commercial bank would hold settlement balances in the form of e-gold in an e-gold account, directly analogous to maintaining reserves in an account with the central bank (in the case of deposits denominated in the domestic currency) or in a correspondent bank (in the case of foreign currency deposits).

What attributes of e-gold make it suitable to serve as the base money of a global currency?

1) e-gold can be directly accessed by any payer and payee, regardless of location or jurisdiction, to effect a payment that is settled instantaneously.
2) e-gold may be held as a reserve asset by any bank or financial intermediary worldwide.
3) e-gold is designed to be suitable for use as a medium of settlement supporting global clearinghouse operations.

What is the significance of e-gold's global characteristics as they relate to clearinghouse operations?

The characteristics of e-gold enable the global clearing and settlement of dissimilar liabilities using e-gold as a common medium of settlement. A global clearinghouse based on e-gold could involve not only bank intermediaries but any sufficiently credit worthy institution with a need to process multiple inbound or outbound payments, on its own account or for third parties.   For example, a payer, holding value in the form of shares in a closed ended mutual fund in the UK, quoted in GBP, could authorize a payment of a sum defined in terms of a specified quantity of USD to a merchant recipient that holds a current account denominated in INR at an Indian bank. This protocol offers substantial efficiencies and economies exceeding, for example, the recently deployed Continuous Linked Settlement scheme http://www.cls-bank.com/ . In many instances the need for actual FX transactions would be eliminated by the ability to effect cross-currency remittance.

How can the emergence of e-gold alleviate some of the dysfunctional elements of globalization?

The most dysfunctional element of globalization as currently manifest is overgrowth of financial activity at the expense of growth in the real economy. A much higher proportion of monetary velocity is attributable to purely financial activities such as trading in currencies and other debt instruments than to commercial payments. Concurrently, capital malinvestment occurs and debt ratchets upward to unsustainable levels.

A strong case can be argued that the use of USD instruments as the predominant international reserve asset functions as the vector that disseminates these financial excesses globally. Discretionary US monetary policy assigns high priority to the attenuation of economic downturns in the US. This includes lender-of-last-resort support of OECD-based financial institutions, exacerbating injection effects that effectively subsidize overly aggressive international lending.

In contrast, the availability of e-gold, an alternative global medium of settlement:

- Substitutes the predictability of an explicit contract for the unpredictable impact of a discretionary medium,
- Precludes the moral hazard of a lender of last resort,
- Eliminates the distortions of injection effects that preferentially foster and subsidize aggressive international lending on the part of too-big-to-fail Western banks, and,
- Reduces the need for interbank FX operations by supporting cross currency payments through a global clearinghouse capable of processing dissimilar liabilities.

How can a central bank benefit from the emergence of e-gold?

e-gold is designed to be highly suitable as a reserve asset, the 'hardest' of all foreign currency reserves. It is precisely equivalent to physical gold, in terms of value, but is superior in terms of fungibility, divisibility and transferability.

The emergence of e-gold usage as a foreign currency, suitable for routine commercial transactions, will lead to the emergence of gold-denominated securities markets. It will also increase the exchange value of existing official gold stocks.

The use of a non-national currency asset also levels the playing field among central banks, reducing the anomaly of using the fiat liabilities of selected OECD nations as reserve assets – a situation that causes poorer nations to finance the fiscal and current account deficits of wealthier nations.

Why does India especially stand to benefit from the emergence of e-gold?

India, like many Asian nations, has a cultural affinity for gold… and a lot of gold. The World Gold Council estimates private stocks of gold exceed 13,000 tonnes – nearly 10% of all above ground gold on the planet. The emergence of e-gold, especially beginning in the Indian economy, will lead to:

- Upward revaluation of gold,
- Eventual mobilization of privately held gold,
- Decreased exposure to USD fluctuation,
- 'First mover' advantage for Indian financial institutions.

Monetization of gold, via the emergence of e-gold, taps into the largest potential reservoir of demand conceivable – People Who Use Money. This reservoir has ample capacity to absorb dishoarding of official reserves from Western central banks. To

147

put this matter in perspective, it is estimated that flight capital from Argentine alone exceeds USD 75 billion – an amount exceeding the current market value of the entire official gold holdings of the US government.

Irreversible upward revaluation of gold relative to major currencies is the key to an "invisible hand" mobilization of privately held gold in India, enabling it to circulate in routine commercial transactions.

An overly simplistic perspective would be to view the emergence of e-gold as a phenomenon similar to prior historic episodes where attempts have been made to "corner" gold. The analogy is entirely faulty. Attempts to corner gold have always been done with a motive to realize capital gains, that is, to eventually "sell" gold with the goal of capturing a greater quantity of money than expended in the effort to acquire and accumulate control of gold. By contrast, in this instance, the emergence of progressive efficiencies relating to the global qualities of AUG assure that the flow of value from OECD currencies into AUG tends to be largely self-reinforcing and irreversible. Also dissimilar is the fact that historic efforts to corner gold were perpetrated by relatively small groups, personifying the attitude of the perverted golden rule, that "whoever has the gold makes the rules". In the emergence-of-AUG scenario, no particular insider group "has" the gold. Ownership and control is dispersed among an enormous group; the entire population of Users worldwide with e-gold balances or AUG deposits.

It should be noted that no factor could ease the burden of USD-denominated debt more effectively than being long gold and owing dollars when gold is revalued upward relative to USD.

Although such a suggestion far exceeds the intent of this document, India alone, by replacing a significant proportion of its nearly USD 60 billion foreign currency reserves with e-gold could singlehandedly dethrone the US dollar as the world's preferred reserve currency. It should also be obvious that were such an event to commence, all other Asian countries with significant gold holdings [non-OECD countries in general] would voluntarily or of necessity reduce their exposure to USD, adding momentum to the irreversible markdown of USD denominated assets. While exploring this vein, it should also be noted that a serious and sustained spike of gold exchange rates relative to USD would force the Federal Reserve and likely the ECB into open market gold operations, releasing their gold into a market fully capable of absorbing all they had to offer and more, leaving the US dollar and EUR with less gold backing.

Although these considerations far exceed the intent of this document, the nature of emergent events suggests a non-trivial likelihood of such outcomes regardless of

148

whether official institutions participate. At the time of Bretton Woods, the vast majority of above-ground gold was sequestered in official holdings, approximately 75% of all gold ever produced being held by the US government. Since then, official gold holdings have declined both on an absolute basis and even more so in percentage terms. Currently, the sum of all official gold holdings worldwide, approximately 34,000 tonnes, amounts to less than a quarter of above ground stocks.

What role could RBI play to facilitate the emergence of e-gold in India?

- Authorize banks and licensed exchange providers to offer exchange between e-gold and national currencies
- Authorize banks to offer e-gold deposits
- Commission and publish interval audits of the e-gold currency balance sheet
- Accumulate e-gold reserves, gradually effecting a substitution of a portion of USD reserves with e-gold

What role might the Ministry of Finance play to facilitate the emergence of e-gold in India?

- Offer incentives to channel inbound current account flows – remittances from non-resident Indians, and, revenue from IT sector exports - into AUG-denominated bank deposits.
- Accept e-gold for selected categories of payments to government – especially payments amenable to the online environment.
- Offer e-gold for designated categories of disbursements – government employee savings programs, tax refunds.
- Assist in bootstrapping the AUG-denominated securities market by issuing limited quantities of AUG bonds.

In October 2002, Jackson returned for the second round of talks with the RBI, starting with an initial productive meeting with Mrs. Grace Koshie, Chief General Manager. He also booked a session with Deputy Governor Rakesh Mohan for three weeks later. Then, everything came off the rails.

One factor that played a role in the adverse outcome, which followed was that the Indian gold and jewel dealer who had played such a vital role in organizing and facilitating meetings did not take part in the second trip. The dealer had proposed an exclusive arrangement, per which his dealership would be the only exchange provider for the Indian market. Jackson was inexperienced, and by his admission, an inept negotiator probably could have found some basis for a compromise, such as exclusivity for a limited period. But instead, an impasse quickly developed. Jackson found himself on his own, not only for the

Indian discussions but for all other meetings during the same trip, in Singapore, Taipei, and Dubai.

The more glaring problem was a tactical blunder on Jackson's part. Restive from delays in obtaining this and other meetings, Jackson turned to a more active gambit. In early morning runs around the Nariman Point district of Mumbai, Jackson had observed the process of assembling thousands of copies of the Times of India on a nearby street corner for local distribution. Jackson got the bright idea of doing some guerrilla marketing on the cheap. He wrote up an e-gold promotional flyer and had two thousand copies printed. He then paid a modest sum to the workers assembling the Sunday newspaper and worked with them to insert a flyer into two thousand.

As a direct result of the flyer, Deputy Governor Rakesh Mohan canceled his meeting with Jackson, and the RBI sent an advisory to the Economic Times for publication: "The RBI had correctly clarified that e-gold is not a currency of any sovereign state and that its usage as money in India would be violative of current   regulations."

This note wasn't such a lousy clarification, because it was entirely correct and accurate. Although, one might fail to gather in reading it that Indian currency controls at the time did not allow for usage of ANY foreign currency for routine domestic transactions.

But in time-honored journalistic tradition, the author of the Economic Times article reporting the RBI statement elected to embellish it, characterizing e-gold in pejorative terms such as "dubious schemes," "dubious concepts," "The RBI got a whiff" [implying a bad odor] and so forth.

The situation improved a bit when that author's editor published a response from Jackson as a letter to the editor:

> "As the CEO of Gold & Silver Reserve. Inc., the US company that has operated the e-gold® system since 1996, I would like to express my disappointment with the way the Economic Times reported the recent statement from the RBI regarding e-gold. The RBI had correctly clarified that e-gold is not a currency of any sovereign state and that its usage as money in India would be violative of current regulations.
> It is not the desire of the e-gold Directors to short circuit the legal restrictions that govern currency exchange in India. We seek rather to establish a dialog with government institutions and business leaders in India to explore benefits of an official embrace of e-gold.
> Our position is that the emergence of e-gold usage in India would be of   enormous benefit to the national economy. Integration of e-gold into the banking system would facilitate mobilization of privately held gold in a coordinated fashion that would foster growth of gold deposit banking and ultimately transform this national treasure

from a 'sterile' asset into capital."

No more RBI meetings were scheduled and Jackson returned home discouraged. Within a month, an exchange service offering AUG/INR launched in India, initially unaware of the RBI statement. But then, on being informed of it by prospective customers, the founder reached out to Dr. Jackson:

> "Hello e-gold,
> We are from www.IndiaGold.biz <http://www.IndiaGold.biz> - India's first e-gold exchanger. [220]
> We came across an article on the internet -
> http://in.biz.yahoo.com/021021/26/1woqo.html
> Please read it and tell what to do?. We are from India, so should we continue with our business? Should we allow our India Peoples to have Egold account? What was your (GS&R)'s response towards this Article?"

> Monday October 21, 11:58 PM
> RBI bans gold money as payment channel
> *By Our Banking Bureau MUMBAI, 21 October*
> The Reserve Bank of India (RBI) today disallowed "e-gold", a payment channel which along with "goldgrams" has slowly been emerging as an alternate currency. The central bank sounded out warning bells to the general public against the use of "e-gold" as a currency.
> "Use of e-gold in any transaction is violative of current regulations in force in the country. The public, banks, money changers and other financial institutions are, therefore, cautioned against the use of e-gold as a currency in their transactions," a RBI release said.
> The RBI said an impression had been created among the public by some agencies or persons that transactions involving "e-gold", purportedly an electronic currency, were freely permitted in the country and that it had the status of a foreign currency. Replacing a currency with anything else was not done, said RBI officials.
> "e-gold" was not a currency of any sovereign state, pointed out RBI. How does an "e-gold" account work? One just needs to go to the website and open an account by buying gold. Gold in this form can be used to make payment for transactions on the

---

[220] Jackson, Douglas. "India's Premiere e-gold Exchanger." *India Gold: India's Premium e-gold Exchanger*, Archive.org, 30 Sept. 2003, web.archive.org/web/20030930030749/http:/indiagold.biz/.

Net. e-gold can also be used as any other form of foreign currency provided someone is willing to accept it.

"e-gold" professes that non-resident Indians use it to make remittances directly to their families in the country. The popularity of GoldMoney has gained ground since most people have access to an Internet connection.

It was an open system, available to individuals or businesses anywhere in the world who wanted to use GoldGrams as currency, Turk said.

"The response so far has been very good, with the maximum interest from Europe, North America and Australia, and from Asia, particularly Hong Kong. By interest not only do I mean users who have opened a holding account, but also merchants, particularly online merchants, who see the usefulness and many advantages of our payment system," he said.

GoldGrams were the result of combining gold with 21st century technology, thereby bringing new efficiencies to global commerce by enabling the world's oldest money, gold, to once again circulate as currency, Turk said.[221]

Jackson advised:

"As far as our response to the asinine article(s), the Economic Times of India, Mumbai print edition, published my reply 24 October p. 12., text pasted below. The RBI statement, as best I can tell, was personal retribution from a mid-level manager named Padmanabham, in the foreign exchange department. I think what happened was he felt slighted one day in early October when I was re-directed to his office after his boss, Mrs. Grace Koshie, canceled an appointment with me at the last minute. [which was re-scheduled and went well]

I don't want to be in a position of advising you to undertake actions that might be "violative of current regulations", even if the odds are that the same regulations will be conveniently re-interpreted in a few months after discussion at the appropriate levels."[222]

Having just launched, Indiagold.biz shut down.

In the aftermath of the RBI missteps, multiple avenues for potential engagement opened

[221] Bureau, Banking. "RBI Bans Gold Money as Payment Channel." *RBI Bans Gold Money as Payment Channel*, Archive.org, 21 Dec. 2002, web.archive.org/web/20021221053946/in.biz.yahoo.com/021021/26/1woqo.html.

[222] Jackson, Douglas. "Re: Attached Copy." Received by Carl Mullan, *Re: Attached Copy*, 27 Feb. 2020. Ref. DJ redlines 3 second try-returned2.pdf

up in India. Some of the most prominent academic authorities in monetary economics reached out to offer advice on how to advance the project through civil society and academic engagement and offered to arrange speaking engagements. By this point, however, the e-gold® directors were stretched too thin by the defensive efforts required to survive unremitting reputation attacks to muster the resources to re-vitalize the opportunities in India.[223]

In December 2002, a second growth breakout had begun for e-gold®. Unfortunately, this leap ahead was again derailed after twelve months of exponential growth by a combination of technical issues involving the inability to scale, combined with the emergence of Internet-wide criminal exploits for harvesting user log-in credentials. All online payment systems begin to slump manifested by declining Alexa ranks.

2003

After nearly seven years, it seemed the world was finally recognizing the vision of e-gold's co-founders. While Jackson's original design had endured a lengthy startup, unlike many new companies, e-gold's mission had not changed during those early years. In the third week of November 2003, a new customer created e-gold® account number 1,000,000.

In February 2003, e-gold® began offering a convenient new tool to accept e-gold® payments, that simplified merchant sales. The e-gold® website shared the news.

> February 2003 -- Quick way to accept e-gold
> The e-gold Shopping Cart just got even easier to use. How can you accept e-gold online? It's now as easy as putting up a link like this: http://100998.e-gold.com/ on your web page. Users clicking the link will be taken straight to a payment form at the e-gold site ready to pay your account. Visit the e-gold Programmer's Information page to generate your own shortcut link.[224]

◆

On June 9th, 2003, Douglas Jackson received an email from an unknown sender calling him or herself William Amzallag that offered some shocking information. The subject line read, *"Charles Evans has been supplying the IRS with information."*

Mr. Evans while working with Bob Nugent has been supplying information to the

[223] Jackson, Douglas. "DJ Redlines 3 Second Try." Received by Carl Mullan, DJ Redlines 3 Second Try, 27 Feb. 2020.

[224] Jackson, Douglas. "e-gold News." *e-gold News*, e-gold.com, Feb. 2003, web.archive.org/web/20040712005041fw_/www.e-gold.com/news.html.

IRS about GSR and Egold. It seems that private information was removed from your offices in Florida via Mr. Evans personal computer. Mr. Evans is located in Freeport the Bahamas and is about ready to leave to go to Florida since his venture with Mr. Nugent has not produced results. Mr. Evans is broke and without funds. Mr. Evans is actively speaking to people in your office and has an active campaign to destroy you.[225]

In July 2003, Jackson had approached the IRS and requested a list of third parties that had made contact with the agency regarding e-gold® or G&SR. In a 2019 email, Jackson detailed this activity "In response to our 7206(c) filing with the IRS of 7/18/2003 requesting a list of all third parties they had been in contact with, Ian and Charles were listed."[226] The men had made contact with the IRS regarding information about e-gold® and G&SR. What information the men discussed with America's tax agency is unknown.

The government has never charged e-gold® or G&SR with a criminal tax offense. The IRS has never alleged any wrongdoing by Jackson, e-gold®, or G&SR.

In July 2003, Nevis officials removed e-gold Ltd. from the Island's Corporate Registry for failing to pay the annual registration fee of $220. The media overemphasized this simple event, which was attributable to negligence on e-gold's Bermuda attorneys. Jackson alleges that this event was a result of the cabal's mischief.

Jackson has stated on many occasions, that for more than a decade, he had made substantial proactive inquiries, on e-gold's behalf, to financial regulators and members of the law enforcement. Jackson has established that through these interactions, he volunteered his personal assistance toward combating crime on dozens of occasions, maybe hundreds. Jackson demonstrated that e-gold's "war chest" of knowledge, experience, and digital forensic tools were available to any law enforcement agency willing to communicate and work with e-gold®. Physical evidence such as archived emails, court documents, and press statements prove these offers of assistance.

AUSTRAC Introduction Letter

The following 2003 communication with AUSTRAC is an excellent example of Jackson's proactive style. On Friday, July 18, 2003, the Joint Committee of the Australian Crime Commission, met to discuss cybercrime in Australia. This organization reported on recent trends in practices and methods of cybercrime with particular reference to:

1. Child pornography and associated paedophile activity

[225] Amzallag, William. "Charles Evans Has Been Supplying the IRS with Information." Received by Douglas Jackson, *Charles Evans Has Been Supplying the IRS with Information*, 9 June 2003.
[226] "Comments." Received by Carl Mullan, *Comments*, 21 July 2019.

2. Banking, including credit card fraud and money laundering
3. Threats to national critical infrastructure

These Senators and members were in attendance: Mr. Baird (*Chair*), Mr. Sercombe (*Deputy Chair*), Senators Denman, Ferris, Greig, Hutchins, and McGauran and Mr. Baird and Mr. Sercombe. While e-gold® was not the primary focus of the dialog, the discussion mentioned e-gold®. Select text from a transcript of this 2003 event, as it related to e-gold®, is copied below.[227]

COMMONWEALTH OF AUSTRALIA
Official Committee Hansard
JOINT COMMITTEE ON THE AUSTRALIAN CRIME COMMISSION
Reference: Cybercrime, Friday, July 18, 2003

Page 15
Mr McLeod—One of the areas which the submission touched on was what has been termed online money laundering—and this is probably mirrored in the submission from AUSTRAC—and the cash to electronic barrier. The cash to electronic barrier refers to a person converting cash, from drugs sales or another criminal act, into an electronic form either by placing it in a bank or going through another cash dealer to have it in a form which can then be electronically transferred overseas or used by things such as e-gold, PayPal or a number of other electronic pseudobanking type facilities available on the Internet. I cannot specifically comment on e-gold and those other facilities.

Page 64
CHAIR—What do you think is the impact on Australia of the use of non-financial Internet
institutions, such as e-gold, on funds movement?
Ms Atkins—AGEC has a number of focus groups. Two of them have relevance in this area:
one is about new technologies and the other is about the financial system. In that, we are looking at ways of avoiding the financial system as well. e-gold and other similar types of mechanisms have been of great interest, particularly to the Australian

227 Commonwealth of Australia, Official Committee Hansard, et al. "JOINT COMMITTEE ON THE AUSTRALIAN CRIME COMMISSION." *JOINT COMMITTEE ON THE AUSTRALIAN CRIME COMMISSION*, By Authority of the Pariliament, 2003, pp. 15–73. Transcript

Taxation Office. People use them to avoid our reporting mechanisms, which Mr Jensen mentioned earlier, on international funds transactions. It is quite easy to use these mechanisms by buying e-gold and then having credit cards or debit cards on international accounts so that our reporting systems are completely avoided. There is quite a large amount of concern within the broader law enforcement agencies, including revenue and regulatory agencies, about those sorts of mechanisms.

Page 73

Ms Atkins—The alternative payment systems that we have already talked about, like e-gold and that sort of thing, used in combination with an overseas credit card are the main ways. Really, that is not new; it is just that there are lots of different alternative payment systems—but they are all very similar.[228]

Upon learning that the committee had mentioned e-gold®, in early September, Jackson sent an introductory email offering assistance to Benjamin Richards, the AUSTRAC Policy and Publishing Officer.

Email to:
Benjamin Richards
Policy and Publishing Officer, Policy and Coordination Section
AUSTRAC, PO Box 5516, West Chatswood,   NSW   1515
Email: XXXXX@austrac.gov.au
September 3, 2003
Douglas Jackson <djackson@e-gold.com>
Please forward to the office of Mr. Jensen or Ms. Atkins.
Dear Mr. Jensen and Ms. Atkins
I read with concern today the following report
http://australianit.news.com.au/articles/....
which depicts the e-gold(r) system as posing a risk for the facilitation of money laundering and financial crime. The article describes testimony before the joint parliamentary committee on the Australian Crime Commission that indicates discussions have taken place among various regulatory and law enforcement agencies - "There is quite a lot of concern within the broader law-enforcement agencies, including revenue and regulatory agencies, about these sorts of mechanisms."
I am the founder of the e-gold enterprise, which has been online since 1996, and

[228] Ibid

Chairman of e-gold Ltd., the Nevis W.I. company that serves as general contractor for the e-gold Account User Agreement http://www.e-gold.com/unsecure/e-g-agree.htm. I am puzzled that no one in your agency has made any attempt to contact me to discuss your concerns or to obtain more precise details regarding the internal logic and systematic safeguards that we have designed into the e-gold system.

There are several elements in the design of the e-gold system that make it wholly unsuited for the obfuscation of money trails or otherwise disguising the proceeds of crime. These same elements also would definitively solve a problem that has hindered legitimate gambling vendors, including Australian based lotteries with sovereign beneficiaries, from fully exploiting the global capabilities of the Internet. Briefly stated, the use of e-gold could definitively eliminate any possibility of a casino, lottery or global bank serving as the unwitting patsy of money launderers. Ultimately, e-gold is designed to serve as the base money of an alternative global currency that plays a complementary role to conventional national currencies. I would be pleased to forward you a draft of a fairly extensive exegesis on this topic. I would like to encourage a more constructive dialog. Instead of rushing to judgment with legislation and its likely unintended consequences you could be fostering strategic relationships, especially between e-gold and the Australian banking community, that might advance the material welfare of all Australians.
sincere regards,
Dr. Douglas Jackson[229]

In a July 2006 email, Jackson explained his reasons for contacting the agency "I was trying to initiate constructive dialog with AUSTRAC, Australia's version of FINCEN."[230]

Kimberly Kiefer Peretti

Attorney Kimberly Peretti began working for the Justice Department's Computer Crime and Intellectual Property Section shortly after September 11, 2001. In 2020, Peretti is a partner in the Washington, D.C.-based law firm Alston & Bird, LLP.[231] She was one of the DOJ attorneys in the 2003 Operation Firewall case that included hacker Albert Gonzalez. According to the NY Times Magazine, she had lobbied the DOJ for that Operation Firewall

[229] Jackson, Douglas. "From the e-gold Chairman." Received by Benjamin Richards, From the e-gold Chairman, 3 Sept. 2003.

[230] Jackson, Douglas. "[Fwd: Re: from the e-Gold Chairman]." Received by Mitchell Fuerst, et al., [Fwd: Re: from the e-Gold Chairman], 13 July 2006.

[231] "Kimberly Kiefer Peretti: Cyber and Data Security Lawyer." Alston & Bird, 2020, www.alston.com/en/professionals/p/peretti-kimberly-kiefer/.

assignment.[232] 2003 is believed to be the year that Gonzalez became a salaried confidential informant for the Secret Service.

The Gonzalez case fit neatly into the e-gold® prosecution. While Gonzalez operated as a U.S. Secret Service confidential informant (CI), he was responsible for the most massive hacks and thefts of personal information in the world. He also sometimes used e-gold®. James Verini writing for *The New York Times Magazine* in a November 10th, 2010 article entitled *The Great Cyberheist,* offered his thoughts on Peretti after interviewing her.

> Over the course of several years, during much of which he worked for the government, Gonzalez and his crew of hackers and other affiliates gained access to roughly 180 million payment-card accounts from the customer databases of some of the most well known corporations in America: OfficeMax, BJ's Wholesale Club, Dave & Buster's restaurants, the T. J. Maxx and Marshalls clothing chains. They hacked into Target, Barnes & Noble, JCPenney, Sports Authority, Boston Market and 7-Eleven's bank-machine network. In the words of the chief prosecutor in Gonzalez's case, "The sheer extent of the human victimization caused by Gonzalez and his organization is unparalleled."[233]

> Peretti made a point of getting to know the agents in the Secret Service's Electronic Crimes Task Force because she knew that they were, like her, eager to make a name in going after cybercriminals.[234]

Peretti participated in the TJX/Heartland case involving Albert Gonzalez. She had previously worked with him in 2003 during Operation Firewall, and she also later prosecuted him. The same James Verini article described Peretti's close association with Gonzalez.

> Much of what Peretti knows about cybercrime she learned from working with Gonzalez. "Albert was an educator," she said, describing their experience on Operation Firewall. "We in law enforcement had never encountered anything like" him. "We had to learn the language, we had to learn the characters, their goals, their techniques. Albert taught us all of that." They worked as well together as any investigative team she has been a part of, she said.[235]

[232] Verini, James. "The Great Cyberheist." *The New York Times*, The New York Times, 10 Nov. 2010, www.nytimes.com/2010/11/14/magazine/14Hacker-t.html.

[233] Verini, James. "The Great Cyberheist." *The New York Times*, The New York Times, 10 Nov. 2010, www.nytimes.com/2010/11/14/magazine/14Hacker-t.html.

[234] Ibid

By the time she was 35, thanks to Operation Firewall and Gonzalez, Peretti was the Justice Department's chief prosecutor of cybercrime in Washington.[236]

Peretti was the Senior Counsel for the United States Department of Justice Criminal Division overseeing the e-gold® prosecution. On April 29, 2010, Tom Field, writing for *BankInfoSecurity.com*, published an interview with Kim Peretti.[237] The piece introduced Peretti with a detailed description.

> Peretti is a former Senior Counsel in the Computer Crime and Intellectual Property Section of the Criminal Division of the United States Department of Justice, located in Washington, DC.
>
> At the Department of Justice, Peretti investigated and prosecuted multi-agency and multi-district computer crime and financial fraud cases, especially those involving large scale data breaches, identity theft, and online payment systems. She was co-lead prosecutor in the Department's largest hacking and identity theft case ever prosecuted - a case in which several members of an international retail hacking ring were convicted of stealing over 40 million credit and debit cards. She also co-led the benchmark prosecution of a global internet-based payment system convicted of money laundering and illegal money transmitting.[238]

There is no question that Kimberly Peretti is an accomplished individual. The 2010 article references the career-building e-gold® prosecution, "She also co-led the benchmark prosecution of a global internet-based payment system convicted of money laundering and illegal money transmitting."[239]

Regarding Peretti, Jackson disagrees with these portrayals. In Jackson's August 24, 2017 letter to John Roth, Inspector General, U.S. Department of Homeland Security, entitled "Investigation Request," Jackson delivered a substantially different opinion of Peretti's legal work during the e-gold® prosecution.

> I am providing evidence that Ms. Peretti, almost certainly with the full knowledge of her associates and her superiors, likely including her chain of command up to and

---

[235] Ibid

[236] Ibid

[237] Field, Tom. "Inside the TJX/Heartland Investigations." *Bank Information Security*, Information Security Media Group, Corp., 29 Apr. 2010, www.bankinfosecurity.com/interviews/inside-tjxheartland-investigations-i-500.

[238] Ibid

[239] Ibid

possibly beyond then-US Attorney Jeffery Taylor as well as senior officials at main Justice, conspired in overt acts that may have constituted obstruction of justice in relation to criminal acts committed by Albert "segvec" Gonzales, a Secret Service criminal informant (CI). The essence of my allegation is that Ms. Peretti et al, having learned (from the work product of egold's own in-house investigatory unit, headed up by me) no later than July 2006 that their own CI was the perpetrator of the largest "cybercrime heist" on record, purposely delayed the arrest and prosecution of Gonzalez for nearly two years in order to cover up that it was my personal efforts that cracked the case. During this two year delay, and while continuing to operate under the noses of Peretti and his USSS handlers, Gonzalez perpetrated additional massive cybercrime exploits eclipsing his own personal world's record.[240]

Albert Gonzalez aka Segvec - Hacker and U.S.S.S. Confidential Informant

Statements about e-gold's in-house cooperation with law enforcement, from the August 24, 2017 letter to John Roth, provide some background on the investigation of Gonzalez's criminal activity.

> Suffice it to say that the Gonzalez investigation was just one of many collaborations with law enforcement, a continuity of engagement dating back to 1999.

> This particular investigation (which I initiated) renewed a collaboration with a senior agent of the US Postal Inspection Service, Greg Crabb, with whom I had worked another case circa 2000. In preparation for this collaborative effort, Crabb had invited me to participate in an Interpol cybercrime conference in Lyon, France where I was also introduced to his associate "Agent X". [In the course of this case (May 2006), we also went to Moscow to liaise with other international law enforcement agencies, especially Russia and the UK].[241]

As reported by James Verini in *The New York Times Magazine*, Gonzalez's crime spree, most of which occurred while he was a paid confidential informant, was one of the largest in U.S. History.

> According to Attorney General Eric Holder, who last month presented an award to Peretti and the prosecutors and Secret Service agents who brought Gonzalez down,

---

[240] Jackson, Douglas. "Investigation Request." Received by John Roth, Inspector General, US Dept. of Homeland Security, 1020 Steven Patrick Avenue, 24 Aug. 2017, Indian Harbour Beach, Florida.
[241] Ibid

Gonzalez cost TJX, Heartland and the other victimized companies more than $400 million in reimbursements and forensic and legal fees. At last count, at least 500 banks were affected by the Heartland breach.[242]

ShadowCrew & Operation Firewall

Gonzalez was a recidivist who authorities arrested in 2003. He had been participating in computer hacking, data theft, and the sale of stolen financial information through an online organization called ShadowCrew. This online group was a virtual criminal supply house. Its members offered encryption software and hardware for encoding credit card magnetic strips. ShadowCrew sold counterfeit passports, driver's licenses, Social Security cards, credit & debit plastic cards, birth certificates, college student identification cards, health insurance cards, and many other hard-to-obtain contraband items. On the ShadowCrew website (http://www.shadowcrew.com), Gonzalez became one of the site's trusted administrators using the alias "CumbaJohny."

The ShadowCrew case involved law enforcement agencies and police units from the United States, Bulgaria, Belarus, Canada, Poland, Sweden, the Netherlands, and Ukraine. The U.S. Secret Service labeled the ShadowCrew investigation "Operation Firewall" and this probe included other 'carder' websites.[243] During this investigation, the United States Secret Service swarmed websites promoting criminal activity including www.shadowcrew.com, www.carderplanet.com, and www.stealthdivision.biz.

Albert Gonzalez First Arrest 2003

On July 1, 2003, the Vice President of Global Corporate Security of Chase Manhattan Bank notified the USSS of an apparent fraud scheme where individuals had been illegally withdrawing cash through local ATMs. He stated that the bank had photographs of the alleged criminals taken by security cameras during the withdrawals. On July 24, 2003, the USSS identified Albert Gonzalez as participating in this activity and arrested him while he was withdrawing cash. In his possession, Gonzalez had around $3,000 cash and more than fifteen counterfeit ATM cards. Photograph evidence from other suspicious ATM withdrawals also showed Gonzalez making withdrawals that totaled approximately $50,000.

A criminal complaint was filed in the U.S. District Court of New Jersey, charging Albert Gonzalez with violating Title 18, United States Code, Sections 1029(a)(3), and 2.[244]

[242] Verini, James. "The Great Cyberheist." *The New York Times*, The New York Times, 10 Nov. 2010, www.nytimes.com/2010/11/14/magazine/14Hacker-t.html.

[243] Lemos, Robert. "Secret Service Busts Suspected ID Fraud Ring." *CNET*, CNET, 29 Oct. 2004, www.cnet.com/news/secret-service-busts-suspected-id-fraud-ring/.

[244] UNITED STATES DISTRICT COURT DISTRICT OF NEW JERSEY. *UNITED STATES OF AMERICA V. ALBERT*

While under arrest, Gonzalez openly admitted to USSS Special Agents that he possessed the fraudulent cards and made illegal cash withdrawals on May 15, May 23, and on or about July 24, 2003, in New York. On July 25, 2003, he appeared before a Judge, who released him on a $50,000 bond.

The investigating USSS Special Agent, David Esposito, stated in the criminal complaint, that in Essex County, New Jersey, and elsewhere, Albert Gonzalez knowingly and with intent to defraud, possessed more than fifteen counterfeit and unauthorized access devices.

The Judge ordered Attorney Donald McCauley from the Office of the Federal Public Defender for the District of New Jersey to be Gonzalez's court-appointed attorney in this case.[245]

> After he agreed in 2003 to become an informant, Gonzalez helped the Justice Department and the Secret Service build, over the course of a year, an ingenious trap for Shadowcrew. Called Operation Firewall, it was run out of a makeshift office in an Army repair garage in Jersey City. Gonzalez was its linchpin.[246]
> Gonzalez worked alongside the agents, sometimes all day and into the night, for months on end. Most called him Albert. A couple of them who especially liked him called him Soup, after his old screen-name soupnazi. "Spending this much time with an informant this deeply into a cybercrime conspiracy — it was a totally new experience for all of us," one Justice Department prosecutor says. "It was kind of a bonding experience. He and the agents developed over time a very close bond. They worked well together."[247]

> On Oct. 26, 2004, Gonzalez was taken to Washington and installed in the Operation Firewall command center at Secret Service headquarters. He corralled the Shadowcrew targets into a chat session. At 9 p.m., agents began knocking down doors. By midnight, 28 people across eight states and six countries had been arrested, most of them mere feet from their computers. Nineteen were eventually indicted.[248]

Before being shut down by law enforcement, it is estimated the 4,000 members of

GONZALEZ. CRIMINAL COMPLAINT, 25 July 2003.

[245] UNITED STATES DISTRICT COURT DISTRICT OF NEW JERSEY. *UNITED STATES OF AMERICA V. ALBERT GONZALEZ*. ORDER, U.S. Magistrate Judge Patty Shwartz, 25 July 2003.

[246] Verini, James. "The Great Cyberheist." *The New York Times*, The New York Times, 10 Nov. 2010, www.nytimes.com/2010/11/14/magazine/14Hacker-t.html.

[247] Ibid

[248] Ibid

ShadowCrew trafficked approximately 1.5 million stolen card numbers and allegedly robbed cardholders and banks of more than $4 million. To obtain the stolen card information, organization members, including Albert Gonzalez, hacked the retail companies' networks and took personal customer information, which included credit and debit card numbers. Albert Gonzalez paid out and received funds during these illegal transactions through a variety of online methods, including e-gold®.

A March 22, 2019 article by Kim Zetter for Wired.com entitled *Secret Service Paid TJX Hacker $75,000 a Year*, detailed what occurred after Gonzalez's 2003 arrest.

> For his part, Gonzalez began working for the Secret Service when he was arrested making fraudulent ATM withdrawals in New York. Under the nickname "Cumbajohnny," he was a top administrator on a carding site called Shadowcrew. The agency cut him loose and put him to work undercover on the site, where he set up a VPN the carders could use to communicate – a supposedly secure communications channel that was actually wiretapped by the Secret Service's New Jersey office.[249]
>
> That undercover operation, known as "Operation Firewall," led to the arrest of 28 members of the site in October 2004. After the site went down, Gonzalez changed his nick to "Segvec" and moved to Miami where he resumed his life of crime under the noses of the agents who were paying him. Authorities finally arrested him in May 2008.[250]

Jackson shared his thoughts on this arrangement in a 2019 email "It is important to remember that the USSS AND KIM PERETTI had been working directly with Gonzalez since 2003."[251] Because of his participation as a USSS Confidential Informant, Peretti did not prosecute Gonzalez for his 2003 felony charges. The government did not indict him for any of the other crimes committed by the ShadowCrew organization. Prosecutors did not incarcerate Gonzalez, Peretti allowed him to walk free under court supervision. After his direct USSS involvement had resulted in more than a dozen indictments within the ShadowCrew network, Gonzalez was encouraged by his USSS handlers to move back to his home town of Miami; for his safety.[252]

[249] Article for Wired.com, Secret Service Paid TJX Hacker $75,000 a Year, by Kim Zetter, March, 22, 2019 https://www.wired.com/2010/03/gonzalez-salary/

[250] Ibid

[251] Jackson, Douglas. "Re: Attached for Short Important Read." Received by Carl Mullan, *Re: Attached for Short Important Read*, 13 Feb. 2019.

[252] Verini, James. "The Great Cyberheist." *The New York Times*, The New York Times, 10 Nov. 2010, www.nytimes.com/2010/11/14/magazine/14Hacker-t.html.

The mastermind did not go to prison. Instead, Albert Gonzalez moved to Miami, with the government's blessing, and the USSS employed him full-time as an informant. Not only did he receive a $75,000 annual salary, also paid in cash, he even delivered educational speeches to groups of law enforcement agents on how to combat hacking crimes. All of this occurred after the government helped him kick his drug addiction!

Before moving to Miami, Gonzalez had to garner the consent of Pretrial Services and approval from the U.S. Department of Justice. Senior Counsel Kimberly Kiefer Peretti was assigned to the case. Gonzalez became the USSS's CI "poster boy" of the decade under the watchful eye of Kim Peretti.

Over the during the next four years, Gonzalez would plan and commit some of the nation's most extensive thefts of consumer personal information while living in Miami and employed by the USSS. Gonzalez engineered network intrusions in TJX (TJ Maxx), Office Max, Hannaford Brothers, 7-Eleven, and Heartland Payment Systems, exposing the magstripe data on 130 million credit and debit cards. He accomplished these criminal acts while under pretrial supervision with Kim Peretti in the loop.

The 2010 article by Kim Zetter in Wired.com revealed details of cash paid to Gonzalez by the USSS.

> Convicted TJX hacker Albert Gonzalez earned $75,000 a year working undercover for the U.S. Secret Service, informing on bank card thieves before he was arrested in 2008 for running his own multimillion-dollar card-hacking operation. The information comes from one of Gonzalez's best friends and convicted accomplices, Stephen Watt. Watt pleaded guilty last year to creating a sniffer program that Gonzalez used to siphon millions of credit and debit card numbers from the TJX corporate network while he was working undercover for the government.[253]

> Gonzalez's salary highlights how entwined he was with the government at the time he participated in the largest identity theft crimes in U.S. history.[254]

Jackson Identified the Criminal in 2006

In 2019 emails, Jackson elaborated on the 2006 information volunteered by e-gold®, which should have allowed the USSS to identify and arrest the person using the alias "segvec."

I provided all the data (to USPIS, which they passed on to the USSS Miami field

[253] Ibid
[254] Ibid

office summer 2006) needed for them to have absolute certainty that their criminal informant Gonzalez was the criminal everyone was after. Moreover, Peretti demanded USPIS provide all the records of our work together, to her, July 2006.[255]

In an August 2017 letter, Jackson summarized the egregious results that emerged from the government's failure to prosecute Gonzalez.

> The essence of my allegation is that Ms. Peretti et al, having learned (from the work product of e-gold's own in-house investigatory unit, headed up by me) no later than July 2006 that their own CI was the perpetrator of the largest "cybercrime heist" on record, purposely delayed the arrest and prosecution of Gonzalez for nearly two years in order to cover up that it was my personal efforts that cracked the case. During this two year delay, and while continuing to operate under the noses of Peretti and his USSS handlers, Gonzalez perpetrated additional massive cybercrime exploits eclipsing his own personal world's record.[256]

♦

New Press Attacks

In a 2019 email, Jackson stated that in Los Angeles, Fox TV News had contacted e-gold® in November 2003, alleging that criminals were using e-gold® to pay for online child pornography. Fox also requested a response from the company.

On November 19th and 20th, Jackson had phone conversations with a Producer for FOX UNDERCOVER in Los Angeles named Dan Leighton. He had been working up a story that portrayed e-gold as being used for payments for child porn. As it turned out, the "evidence" Fox had was a website phishing ploy leading people to a counterfeit e-gold site in an attempt to trick them into divulging their e-gold account number and passphrase.

An internal e-gold® investigation determined the Fox claims to be 100% false after reviewing the information presented by Fox. Jackson sent the following letter, by email and FedEx:

21 November 2003
Dan Leighton

---

[255] "Re: Attached for Short Important Read." Received by Carl Mullan, *Re: Attached for Short Important Read*, 13 Feb. 2019.

[256] Jackson, Douglas. "Investigation Request." Received by John Roth, Inspector General, US Dept. of Homeland Security, 1020 Steven Patrick Avenue, 24 Aug. 2017, Indian Harbour Beach, Florida.

Producer, Fox11 UNDERCOVER
KTTV FOX 11
1999 South Bundy Drive
Los Angeles, California 90025-5235
Dear Mr. Leighton,
I am writing to follow-up on our conversations of 19 and 20 November 2003. On 19 November, you described alleged instances of entities selling child pornography over the Web and accepting e-gold in payment. The example you provided, however, seemed to be a site that was purporting to sell kiddie porn but in actuality was engaged in tricking would-be customers into divulging their e-gold passphrase in order to subsequently access and loot their e-gold account.

I have no doubt that there is also criminal activity of substantially greater magnitude seeking to trick would-be child porn customers into divulging credit card numbers and other identity theft data by means of fake interfaces simulating iBill, PayPal and other payment processors that serve as intermediaries for credit card payments.

Pretending to sell illegal goods is an effective strategy for identity theft and password stealing ("phishing") because the victims are extremely unlikely to contact the police.

The public's f ear of being associated in any way with child porn, in f act, gives rise to an even more devious angle for phishing as detailed in www.zdnet.com.au/newstech/communications/story/0,2000048620,20280570,00.htm

In our follow-up conversation today I asked if you had in fact in the course of your investigation succeeded in acquiring actual illegal goods using e-gold as the payment mechanism. Although your answer was unclear I was careful to emphasize that unless your investigator has a suff icient balance of e-gold in an e-gold account it would have been impossible for him or her to purchase anything using the e-gold system. I further of fered, and renew my of fer, to provide a limited quantity of e-gold for the purpose of funding the e-gold account of an investigator who wishes to ascertain if it is indeed possible to obtain illegal goods with e-gold. If such an illegal purchase can in fact be consummated, we would take immediate remedial action and welcome a subpoena that would enable us to cooperate in a criminal investigation. You would f ind that our investigative abilities are quite powerful, based on the fundamental design of e-gold as a system for transferring value by book entry from payer to recipient. As such, the entire lineage of every particle of value circulating in

166

the e-gold system can be traced back to where value first entered the e-gold universe. With e-gold, there would be no place to hide the proceeds of crime.

I checked and confirmed that e-gold Ltd. has never received any subpoena involving alleged child porn activities. Given that every law enforcement agency in the world assigns a high priority to the detection and apprehension of child pornographers and that considerable, possibly even inordinate, resources are devoted to tracking down these perpetrators, the absence of such subpoenas suggests that if, in fact, child porn exists on the Web it is being paid for with something other than e-gold. It is my understanding that the medium of choice for paying for most criminal goods is US dollars, in the form of cash, since Federal Reserve Notes, unlike e-gold, are anonymous and untraceable.

In our conversation today you vigorously affirmed that your investigation has turned up actual instances of hard core pornography involving children as well as sites where children could actually be purchased, presumably for sexual slavery. I attempted to discuss the improbability of such crimes being conducted *via the Web* based on the difficulties a seller of such goods would face in attempting to be paid and stay paid while also avoiding detection. I would think that *offering* to sell a child, or pornographic images of children, while in and of itself heinous, is quite a different matter than actually *delivering* such "goods". If a criminal can trick someone into paying for illegal goods, but defaults on the actual delivery, he could be regarded as guilty of false advertising. This (as is the case with phishing) would also be an economically more rational crime since the victim of false advertising is unlikely to seek legal remedy and the risk of prosecution for false advertising is minuscule compared to the exertions that law enforcement officials would undertake to convict the purveyor of kiddie porn.

There was an additional alarming aspect in our initial conversation, the risk of defamation of e-gold. You spoke of e-gold as a "system for processing porn". I corrected you, pointing out that e-gold is a system for processing payments. You then referred to e-gold as a "system for processing payments for porn". I replied and wish to re-emphasize, that for a Fox Underground viewer learning of e-gold for the first time, to hear it referred to in such a fashion would be both factually incorrect and damaging to our reputation, and, therefore, defamatory. The analogy I used would be to describe dollars (to a person previously unfamiliar with them) as a medium for

167

buying illegal drugs. Such a description would be defining by example, and by highlighting a highly aberrant and rare possible abuse one would convey the impression that such usage was the intended purpose of the system.

I look forward to the opportunity to discuss these matters with you further at your convenience.
Dr. Douglas Jackson
Chairman, e-gold Ltd.
CEO, OmniPay[257]

2004

The next year brought some new changes to e-gold® transaction fees. The lowering of specific costs was a concerted effort to stimulate e-gold's use for micropayments. Text from the website confirms these events.

> In January, e-gold Ltd. will announce its new Micropayment Initiative for Online Digital Content. To better support enhanced micropayment capabilities, a new formula for calculating e-gold Spend fees will be put into effect January 1, 2004, the first substantive adjustment since 1996.[258]

♦

On March 9th, in compliance with an IRS Summons, both Jackson and Downey were deposed. Representatives from the IRS international audit team were present in addition to local IRS agents.

Also in March, the same Los Angeles Fox News station (TV), that had worked on a false CP story in November 2003, released a video news piece with very similar harmful e-gold content. The information about CP had been removed and replaced with different content and a new alleged threat. Instead of a malicious "kiddy porn" angle, the news outlet has substituted hypothetical abuses alleging possible use of the e-gold® system for terrorist payments. Stock footage of Islamic guerrillas firing AK-47 rifles in the air and shouting "Allah Akbar" had replaced the CP story. The fake news Fox item had falsely presented the idea that terrorist enemies of America could be using e-gold®.

When other media and so-called "watchdog organizations" followed suit with negative

[257] Jackson, Douglas. "Fox LA Leighton Email and FedEx." Received by Dan Leighton Producer, Fox11 UNDERCOVER, 1999 South Bundy Drive, 21 Nov. 2003, Los Angeles, California.

[258] Jackson, Douglas. "e-gold News." *e-gold News*, e-gold.com, 1 Jan. 2004, web.archive.org/web/20040712005041fw_/www.e-gold.com/news.html.

e-gold stories based on the erroneous Fox report, Jackson was quick to respond.

> In January 2003, the ADL had run an irresponsible headline and story portraying e-gold as a "possible terrorist tool". We immediately undertook to contact them via Aron Raskas, our Baltimore counsel, and via a local physician named Craig Deligdish, both of whom had contacts within the organization. ADL took down the story.

As in all cases when the media misrepresented the uses of e-gold, Jackson responded quickly with sensible facts and accurate details on e-gold®. The text copied below is Jackson detailing his reactions   followed by email dialog with Mark Pitcavage, a member of the Anti-Defamation League (ADL).

> "I attempted to contact all of the third parties who had been quoted in this (first of several) Fox smear piece(s). I am attaching the extensive follow-up correspondence with one of the quoted experts who, not surprisingly, turned out to be sincere and highly competent but who had been misled and probably quoted out of context."

> One such contact was Mark Pitcavage of the Anti-Defamation League (ADL). The email thread that follows illustrates the challenge and time-consuming nature for an innovative initiative seeking to build a positive image in the face of default assumptions of ill intent.

As Jackson later related:

> "You can see from some of these email threads such as with the ADL—or a legion of public policy or libertarian think tanks, academics and institutions such as the World Bank—that reversing negative assumptions and seeking positive engagement absorbed such time and effort as to impede more proactive efforts. Day by day we were scrambling to deal with the mortal threat du jour, stuck on defense, even as we recognized that nothing would help more than moving the ball forward on Valid User and other refinements of a preventive nature. In terms of lessons learned from over a decade of operational experience, the main one was that timely implementation of even the most conventional KYC measures would have radically reduced our vulnerability to reputation attacks. Our failure to marshal the needed resources, or even to proceed in piecemeal fashion with a less ambitious upgrade path was on me and my lack of the skills required of a CEO."

The ADL dialogue

169

-----Original Message-----
From: Douglas Jackson [mailto:djackson@e-gold.com]
Sent: Thursday, March 04, 2004 3:06 PM
To: XXXX@adl.org Subject: regarding e-gold

Mark

I understand that Fox 11 Los Angeles ran a story about e-gold portraying it as a sinister thing that could be used for obfuscating money trails for various pernicious purposes.

Also, in January 2003, the ADL had posted what I regarded as a pretty irresponsible piece referring to e-gold as a potential terrorist tool.

I can't help but think you guys (ADL, that is... Dan Leighton of Fox certainly knew he was misrepresenting e-gold) have been more or less led down the primrose path by people who have an unrevealed (to you) agenda/ax to grind. Stated differently - I think ADL may well have been unwittingly manipulated by folks acting on behalf of a rather vicious wannabee competitor of ours.

A simple assertion that I would be pleased to discuss with you and defend/develop is that one could scarcely conceive of a less suitable mechanism than e-gold for a bad guy to attempt to hide money trails. To really understand why I say this (despite the fact that someone can create an account saying he's Mickey Mouse living at 999 Pine) I would propose to walk you through the logic and any scenario that you might think of as constituting a loophole.

One especially ironic aspect of all this is that e-gold would be a terrific additional alternative payment system for ADL to accept donations online. It wouldn't interfere with any other systems you already use. It would be cheaper and would enable you to accept payments in perfect confidence from anywhere in the world, including from places where people don't have credit cards, or whose checks could not be negotiated by your bank, or who might be unbanked altogether [like about half the world's adult population].

sincere regards,
Dr. Douglas Jackson[259]

Jackson further clarified his interpretation of the ADL's response. "Pitcavage's reply[copied below] demonstrated that he had not been acting in bad faith but rather illustrates the tendency people have of forming opinions based on uninformed assumptions."

"Dr. Jackson, thank you for your e-mail. I can't speak to what Mr. Leighton or Fox

[259] Jackson, Douglas. "Subject: Regarding e-Gold." Received by Mark Pitcavage, *Subject: Regarding e-Gold*, 4 Mar. 2004.

News may believe or have said about e-gold. I have not seen the Fox 11 story--or even knew that it had aired until your e-mail. I cannot find it on their website. It seemed from my limited conversation with Mr. Leighton that his concerns and issues went beyond those ADL may have had.

I may be able to reassure you regarding your statement about a competitor. Our concerns about e-gold have not been influenced by external sources, but are based more on our awareness of the history of nonelectronic predecessors to e-gold, such as the barter/warehouse banks of the 1980s and early 1990s, which were abused by many domestic extremists; and based to some degree as well as the apparent basic lack of transparency in e-gold accounts.

Our desire, therefore, is merely to make sure government officials dealing with money laundering and other illegal means of financially supporting extremists and terrorists do not unintentionally overlook ecurrencies in their efforts. As we said on our Web site, we do not suspect e-gold of illicit activities.

Best regards,
Mark Pitcavage Director, Fact Finding Department Anti-Defamation League"[260]

Encouraged by Pitcavage's reply, indicating at least a potential willingness to engage, Jackson hoped to transform what had been an effectively hostile stance into a more real understanding or even institutional relationship. That day the email discussion continued between Jackson and Pitcavage.

"Mark

Thanks for your note, but I was hoping you might want to understand better how e-gold® is really organized. It is not accurate to assume on the basis of seeing similarities that we do in fact embody the troubling characteristics of these historic entities. e-gold® is not a rehash of the gold standard or any other legacy model. Are you interested in learning, or would you prefer to continue to offer public advice and analysis on the basis of relatively uninformed assumptions?

I recognize that simply being well-intentioned (as we are) does not necessarily correlate with beneficial outcomes. [It sometimes seems like there is an inverse correlation - I'm reminded of Malkovich's insight expressed in "The Dancer Upstairs"]. But the systemic logic of e-gold®, which entails substantive subtleties not articulated on the e-gold® website, quite realistically could end up advancing the material welfare of mankind. The primitives that e-gold® is built on are freedom from

[260] Pitcavage, Mark. "Subject: Re: Regarding e-Gold." Received by Douglas Jackson, *Subject: Re: Regarding e-Gold*, 4 Mar. 2004.

default risk and finality of settlement. You might find the elaborations and ramifications of these basic elements more logically elegant and profound than one would expect at first glance.

If I can entice you into somewhat more critical engagement, my proposed mechanism of discourse would be interactive and iterative, rather than dumping a lengthy document on you. I know you are busy. I am too. But I perceive that you are a person of principle and it distresses me that my life's work would be ill-regarded by people of intelligence and goodwill.

Douglas Jackson

ps - A memo is attached. [The November 2003 letter to Leighton and the attorney notes regarding the content of the February 2004 Fox broadcast]"[261]

Pitcavage:

"Dr. Jackson, thanks for your reply. I would be happy to receive any information on e-gold that you would care to send. Because I will be traveling for most of the next five weeks, I am uncertain that I would be able to engage in any sustained dialogue, for which I apologize in advance."[262]

Jackson's email reply on March 8, 2004, illustrated that e-gold® was not anonymous, even if a user-provided false identifiers or contact information:

"Thanks for your continued patience/indulgence. Since sustained dialog is impracticable at this time, I propose to revert to Plan B - a sort of draft "white paper" that lays out the business model in more detail. The middle "Governance" section speaks to the money laundering issue.

To briefly supplement that part, I add that no payment system or currency could possibly proactively exclude usage by terrorists/criminals. That would essentially require the ability to discern their intentions before they commit their crimes. The key thing is the ability to sort out flows retrospectively [which may lead to real-time recovery if the investigation is timely] in the context of investigation. In this regard it's important to recognize that a currency like e-gold®, where the base money circulates only via a closed book entry system, is a wholly different animal than national currencies that can circulate in bearer form. Cash is anonymous and untraceable. e-gold isn't cash. The only cash-like economic quality e-gold exhibits is immediate settlement, with no need for clearing and collection."

[261] Ibid email chain
[262] Ibid

172

Another element that is not immediately obvious is that the ability to create an e-gold account with bogus contact data hurts the account User who does it but is useless to them if they imagine it achieves anonymity. This is because the account remains empty until some other account User who has some e-gold clicks some to the account in question. From that moment on it is connected to a continuous chain of transactions of which there are permanent records. There are, of course, subtleties and challenges to investigation, for example the need to sort out constellations of accounts that are under unified control. But any payment connects the account to someone who had some discoverable reason for pushing payment to the account in question and who is himself connected to a very sticky web of value flow that is exquisitely traceable. To clarify this further it is useful to work through scenarios, which can be classified in terms of:

1. bad guy already has proceeds of crime, in the form of a non-e-gold money quantity, and wants to exchange it to another medium through a process that obscures the original source
2. bad guy is trying to obtain value by offering or purporting to offer good or services that are themselves illegal, in other words he is trying to perform the crime that yields proceeds of crime in the form of e-gold [later phase of this is another starting point of money laundering concern, only the proceeds of crime in this case would already be in the form of e-gold]
3. bad guy steals value by tricking an e-gold User into divulging data that gives him access to victim's e-gold account.

Each entails nuances that differ from the other categories, but all of them are as good as busted virtually the moment they accept their first e-gold payment and thereby enter that closed universe.

I'm sorry my notes are always too long but one other point worth noting is that the gold-related schemes that were used by patriot movement loons were run by people who tended to be in some way philosophically in tune with anti-government goals. Their concept of privacy in some cases encompassed resistance to legitimate investigation. Even if we wanted to offer anonymity [which we don't for a variety of straightforward business reasons], to deliver it would require some very complex technology along the lines of so-called digital cash. The possible business case for mounting a digital cash system is an interesting discussion [that none of the entities who undertook to offer it seemed to grasp] but is inapplicable to a system like e-gold, based on conventional book entry settlement.

Again, please forgive me for a long note. If you read over this or the attached material and desire clarification I would be delighted to follow up further."[263]

This prolonged back and forth thawed relations to the extent that a few weeks later, Pitcavage alerted Jackson and forwarded headers of an email detected by ADL technical staff, which contained malware targeting e-gold® users. But the ADL never did undertake to accept donations in the form of e-gold®.

AccSent

To further help e-gold® customers protect their accounts, beginning in May 2004, e-gold® implemented the AccountSentinel (AccSent) feature as a powerful phishing countermeasure.

AccSent enhanced customer e-gold® account security. By enabling customers to direct the circumstances for the entry of their e-gold® account. Copied here is website text detailing the benefits of this new feature.

> e-gold "AccSentuates" Security
>
> e-gold Users now have some serious protection against "phishing" attacks, and its name is Account Sentinel™ (a.k.a. AccSent™)
>
> AccSent empowers you to restrict browser access to your account to a single IP address (or range of IP addresses) and/or to a single web browser based on settings you can configure to best meet your needs - simply log in to your account, click Account Info, and scroll down to AccSent's browser access settings. AccSent monitors account access attempts and issues a one-time PIN challenge to those coming from IP address ranges or browsers that differ from the last authorized account access. The AccSent advantage is that e-gold Users need not take any action - or even understand what an IP address or a phishing attack is - to immediately benefit from this innovative new feature. However, as powerful as AccSent is, the best protection against phishing and other criminal attacks is user education.[264]

After e-gold® added this security feature, the network resumed its exponential growth. For the first time in the company's history, e-gold's hardware supported an improved ability to scale. This exponential growth continued until January 2006. Jackson has stated that through this new growth, by late 2005, e-gold® had attained an annualized transaction volume greater than $2 billion (USD-equivalent).

---

[263] Ibid

[264] Jackson, Douglas. "Gold's Account Sentinel." *e-gold's Account Sentinel™*, e-gold.com, May 2004, web.archive.org/web/20040624234647if_/www.e-gold.com:80/accsent.html.

Australian Regulatory Actions

Due to the stricter application of Financial Services Licensing regulations, in September 2004, several popular Australian digital currency exchange providers voluntarily closed. The independent entities, transacting e-gold® that closed because of the Australian Securities and Investments Commission (ASIC) new requirements included:

- goldex.net
- sydneygoldsales.com
- ozzigold.com

2004 was the first time, in any jurisdiction, that government regulators had required a digital currency business to obtain state-issued licensing. New Australian regulations had called for digital currency exchanges to institute rules and regs similar to a bank. While these Australian exchange providers could have increased their KYC, AML, and applied for the required licensing, they quickly determined it was too expensive and impractical.

Because e-gold® was a tool of the Internet, the local Australian customers moved their business to foreign operating exchanges in Europe, Asia, and other countries. The action was a significant move for ASIC. However, across the growing digital currency industry, news of these closures ended up as a one-line item on page ten of the paper. A massive worldwide marketplace of digital currency had developed, and services were available in dozens of countries.

In 2004, there were no U.S. regulations that accurately defined digital currency products, issuers, or exchangers. The laws had not yet caught up with the new financial technology. National and state-level governments had not established regulations that covered digital currency businesses. In November, Jackson had located a USSS contact, Special Agent Eric Winter, that seemed receptive to being trained on how to interact with e-gold's investigative capabilities.[265]

Jackson also urged a Department of Justice attorney, named Todd Hinnon, to attend the meeting. Hinnon had recently written an article in the Columbia Law Review that discussed e-gold®. The report was a reflection of an industry outsider looking inward.

e-gold® Interaction with USDOJ and USSS

Long before G&SR was the subject of any government investigation, the operators had forged productive relationships with many law enforcement agencies around the world. They provided records of transactions, affidavits, and certifications to help further such investigations and assist in the prosecutions of criminals using the e-gold® system. Jackson

---

[265] Jackson, Douglas. "Subject: Fw: USSS Blurb." Received by Carl Mullan, *Subject: Fw: USSS Blurb*, 15 Jan. 2020.

had worked hand-in-hand with government investigators from the Federal Bureau of Investigation (FBI), United States Postal Inspection Service, Federal Trade Commission (FTC), Securities and Exchange Commission (SEC), Commodity Futures Trading Commission (CFTC), and Assistant United States Attorneys. His work was transparent, and he made a practice of forging connections that would facilitate the identification and apprehension of potential bad actors attempting to use e-gold®. These relationships were an inherent element of Jackson's business style. He had always tried to fulfill the business's responsibility and provide law enforcement with customer account information.

In 2004, Jackson initiated, on behalf of e-gold® and G&SR, a dialogue with the United States Secret Service to discuss further measures to locate abusers of the e-gold® system. Unlike other agencies of the international law enforcement community, a working relationship between the United States Secret Service (USSS) and e-gold® had been slow to materialize. In court documents, Jackson explained this situation "the USSS had always stood out as obtusely refusing to engage with our investigators, on several occasions appearing to prefer to turn a blind eye to criminal exploits rather than engage with us to bring identified perpetrators to justice."[266]

In late 2004, the USSS was continuing to rebuff Jackson's outreach. That year, this pattern of rejection had reached a level bordering on absurdity.

However, on Monday, November 22, 2004, it appeared a breakthrough might be possible. USSS Special Agent Eric Winter[267] provided the e-gold® technical staff a heads-up regarding some malware targeting e-gold® users: "Link to malicious code analysis ref. E-gold." Recalling Jackson's frequent complaints regarding the seeming hostility of the USSS toward e-gold®, the Lead Developer alerted Jackson to the email, which contained Special Agent Winter's phone number. Jackson immediately gave Winter a call thanking him for the alert and describing his concerns about the conspicuous lack of constructive engagement between USSS and e-gold®.

Jackson proposed coming to Washington to brief USSS cybercrime investigators regarding e-gold's in-house investigative capabilities and potential strategies for greater coordination of efforts. Special Agent Winter followed up and set a meeting between Jackson and the USSS at the agency's L Street office in Washington at 10:00 AM on December 13, 2004. The email was very cordial, and Special Agent Winter stated he was looking forward to meeting with Jackson and their future cooperation.

---

[266] Jackson, Douglas. "Investigation Request." Received by John Roth, Inspector General, US Dept. of Homeland Security, 1020 Steven Patrick Avenue, 24 Aug. 2017, Indian Harbour Beach, Florida.

[267] In 2004, Eric S. Winter was a United States Secret Service Special Agent working as a Federal Criminal Investigator focused on financial crimes including counterfeit, I.D. theft, Credit Card Fraud, Check Fraud, Bank Fraud, Money Laundering, and Computer Crimes. In 2019, Mr. Winter is the Assistant Vice President Enterprise Security at Cox Enterprises in Atlanta, Georgia. https://www.linkedin.com/in/eric-winter-0abb44/

Subject: Link to malicious code analysis ref. e-gold
From: "Eric S. Winter" <XXXXX@usss.dhs.gov>
Date: Mon, 22 Nov 2004
To: <djackson@omnipay.net>
CC: "Ruskowski, Paul" <XXXX@usss.dhs.gov>, "'Christopher Williams, David'" <XXXX@usss.dhs.gov>, "'Jay L. Perry'" <XXXX@usss.dhs.gov>
Mr. Jackson,
Thank you for your time today. I will contact the National Hi-Tech Crimes Unit and Australian Federal
Police regarding our meeting on December 13th at 10:00am. Our office is located at 1100 L St. NW Suite 6000, Washington, D.C. 20005. You can reach me directly at 202-406-8589, or 202-406-8500 (Squad number). In addition, our fax number is 202-406-8503.
I have attached a link to the new malicious code that appears to target e-gold account holders. I look
forward to the meeting and future cooperation in investigations.
Thank you, Eric Winter
http://www.lurhq.com/grams.html[268]

Winter's email also forwarded a link to details of the malicious code, discovered November 2, that would allow illegal software to drain the accounts of an infected e-gold® user. It was named Win32.Grams e-gold Account Siphoner.

Win32.Grams e-gold Account Siphoner Analysis
Win32.Grams e-goldAccount Siphoner Analysis by LURHQ Threat Intelligence Group
URL http://www.lurhq.com/grams.html
Release Date: November 4, 2004
A-V Names: Win32.Grams, TrojanSpy.Win32.Small.bl, Troj/Agent-AF, TROJ_GETEGOLD.A
Filenames: NewLoginPass.vbe, media.exe, svhost.exe
With the prevalence of phishing trojans designed to log keystrokes and steal passwords, financial institutions have taken measures to enhance the security of their account portals. Measures such as blocking eastern-European IP addresses,

---

[268] "Link to Malicious Code Analysis Ref. e-gold®." Received by Douglas Jackson, *Link to Malicious Code Analysis Ref. e-gold®*, 22 Nov. 2004.

password-entry applets, photo-passwords and other methods have been employed to keep fraudsters from capturing account information using spy trojans. While some institutions haven't taken any measures at all, plain-old password-stealing trojans are still problematic for the phishers themselves, as they are then left with the task for logging into all those accounts through proxies in order to hide their origins. Members of the phishing underground have solved these problems by creating a new type of trojan - an account siphoner that uses the victim's own web browser to empty the target account. LURHQ's Threat Intelligence Group has analyzed such a trojan that targets e-gold account holders.[269]

On December 1, 2004, Winter emailed Jackson with instructions and the appropriate paperwork to reimburse Jackson's travel expenses.

> Subject: RE: Link to malicious code analysis ref. e-gold
> From: "Eric S. Winter"
> Date: Wed, 1 Dec 2004 11:24:14 -0500
> To: "Douglas Jackson"
> I am forwarding the appropriate paperwork to pay for your air travel.
> Eric[270]

On or about December 3, 2004, Todd Hinnen[271] from the USDOJ also responded to Jackson with a positive email indicating his interest in learning more about e-gold®.

> From: Todd M. Hinnen XXXX@usdoj.gov
> Date: Fri, 03 Dec 2004 11:49 -0500 (EST)
> To: "djackson@e-gold.com"
> Thank you for your phone call. I will try to attend the meeting December 13th if you send me the details, as I would be very interested to learn more about e-gold's ability to respond to law enforcement requests for information. If my schedule prevents me from attending the meeting, I would like to impose upon your time to talk about it over the phone at some convenient future time.

[269] LURHQ Threat Intelligence Group. "Win32.Grams e-gold Account Siphoner Analysis." *Win32.Grams Trojan Analysis - LURHQ*, Lurhq.com, 4 Nov. 2004, web.archive.org/web/20041109065937/www.lurhq.com/grams.html.

[270] Ibid

[271] In 2004, Todd M. Hinnen was employed at the United States Department of Justice as a prosecutor in the Department's Computer Crime & Intellectual Property Section. He later served in the National Security Division as both Deputy Assistant Attorney General for Law and Policy and Acting Assistant Attorney General. In 2019, Mr. Hinnen was a partner at the Perkins Coie Law Firm in the firm's Washington, DC office.

Thanks again for the call.
Regards,
Todd Hinnen[272]

On Friday, December 3, 2004, Jackson responded to Hinnen informing him that USSS Special Agent Eric Winter was unable to confirm the date, and had postponed the meeting till January 2005. Jackson's message also affirmed his company's open invitation to discuss e-gold® or any associated pending issues at any time. He also extended an offer for the Special Agents to visit the e-gold® operation in Melbourne, FL.

> Subject: Re: e-gold investigative capability and coordination
> From: Douglas Jackson <djackson@e-gold.com>
> Date: Fri, 03 Dec 2004 12:13:26 -0500
> To: Todd M. Hinnen <XXXX@usdoj.gov>
> Todd
> Thanks for your note. I just now had a call (literally about an hour ago) from Eric Winter, the Secret Service agent coordinating the meeting. He was unable to nail things down with the UK guys for the Dec 13 date and is now looking instead at early/mid January.
> I would be delighted in the meanwhile or whenever to discuss these issues. My contact info is below.
> Also, my office (Melbourne, FL) is about an hour from Orlando International Airport in case you happened to be in the neighborhood sometime.
> sincere regards,
> Douglas Jackson[273]

On or about December 9, 2004, Jackson received an email from Hinnen informing him that, because of another engagement, Hinnen could not attend the proposed meeting.

> Subject: FW
> From: Todd M. Hinnen XXXX@usdoj.gov
> Date: Wed, 08 Dec 2004 12:52:10 -0500 (EST)
> To: "djackson@e-gold.com"
> Dr. Jackson -

---

[272] Jackson, Douglas. "Re: FW:" Received by Todd M. Hinnen, *Re: FW:* 9 Dec. 2004.
[273] "Re: e-gold Investigative Capability and Coordination." Received by Todd M. Hinnen, *Re: e-gold Investigative Capability and Coordination*, 3 Dec. 2004.

As it turns out, I have to be in NH for an arraignment on the 13th. Would still be interested in learning more about e-gold, however. Don't suppose you all have a white paper, or something, that explains your service.
Regards,
Todd Hinnen

A day later, Winter again tried to reschedule.

Subject: Meeting Date
From: "Eric S. Winter" <XXXX@usss.dhs.gov>
Date: Thu, 9 Dec 2004 10:09 -0500
To: djackson@omnipay.net
CC: "Ruskowski, Paul" <XXXX@usss.dhs.gov>
Mr. Jackson,
I was wondering if you had a chance to check your calendar for availability in early January. With Inauguration on the 20th, the sooner the better for us. We will get busier as that date approaches. Please let me know which day(dates) work for you.
Thank you,
Eric Winter[274]

Subject: Re: Meeting Date
From: Douglas Jackson <djackson@e-gold.com>
Date: Thu, 09 Dec 2004 11:17:26 -0500
To: "Eric S. Winter" <XXXX@usss.dhs.gov>
Eric
My best would be Friday 7 January because I'll be in southern Pennsylvania for a wedding. Next best would be anytime 11th-14th.
Douglas Jackson[275]

On December 9, 2004, Jackson responded to Todd Hinnen with a lengthy email attempting to finalize the meeting's date. Responding to Hinnen's request for information, Jackson included details on the e-gold® operation.

Subject: Re: FW:

[274] Winter, Eric S. "Link to Malicious Code Analysis Ref. e-gold." Received by Douglas Jackson, *Link to Malicious Code Analysis Ref. e-gold*, 22 Nov. 2004.
[275] Jackson, Douglas. "Re: Meeting Date." Received by Eric Winter, *Re: Meeting Date*, 9 Dec. 2004.

From: Douglas Jackson <djackson@e-gold.com>
Date: Thu, 09 Dec 2004 12:37:10 -0500
To: "Todd M. Hinnen" <XXXX@usdoj.gov>
Todd
I've been in contact with Eric Winter again this morning to try to nail down a convenient time for early January. My best is Friday 7 January but he's checking availability of the other parties.
I'm attaching a 'big picture' whitepaper laying out the general logic of e-gold. The more pertinent parts may be the mid-section where I walk through the logic of our governance model. The foundation of my assertion that e-gold would be an imprudent choice for bad guys seeking to obfuscate
money trails or otherwise hide the proceeds of crime is two-fold:

1. it is impossible for a general user of e-gold to send/add money (value in any form) into the system... he can only get e-gold by receiving a payment from someone who already has some.
2. there's a permanent record of all transfers.

   The application of these entails some subtlety. When someone sees that they can create an e-gold account with bogus contact information it is non-obvious how that fails to keep them anonymous in any useful way.
One is a step closer to seeing it though when you note that such an account has nothing in it. The moment the account has some e-gold clicked into it, it becomes tied into a web of transactions, all of which had some discoverable reason, generally a flow of consideration in the opposite direction. When we are doing an actual investigation it can of course get complex as we have to test propositions of things like boundaries between a constellation of accounts controlled by a unified entity vs. transactions that pass value to genuine third parties. An investigation often requires iterative interaction where data we supply may lead to new data from the external agency that gives us grist for an additional round of queries.
Someone like that anonymous gold guy though is basically a charlatan. It is technically extremely hard to create systems that afford anonymity remotely akin to bearer tokens. [e-gold is designed to afford cash-like finality of transfers but as a book entry system couldn't possibly be construed as digital cash].
To expose his uselessness though it may be worthwhile to walk through scenarios in real-time discussion.
I hope some of this is useful, or at least interesting.
sincere regards,
Douglas Jackson

The scheduling continued.

> Subject: Re: Meeting Date
> From: "Eric S. Winter" <XXXX@usss.dhs.gov>
> Date: Thu, 9 Dec 2004 12:57:36 -0500
> To: Douglas Jackson <djackson@e-gold.com>
> Let's plan on Friday, January 7th at 10am. Sound good?
> Thanks, Eric

> Subject: Re: Meeting Date
> From: Douglas Jackson <djackson@e-gold.com>
> Date: Thu, 09 Dec 2004 13:40 -0500
> To: "Eric S. Winter" <XXXX@usss.dhs.gov>
> Excellent. I'll be there.[276]

No December meeting took place between the USSS and e-gold®. On December 29, 2004, Jackson sent another email to SA Winter and Todd Hinnen at the United States Department of Justice. His message referenced an earlier phone call with Winter from the previous day, December 28, 2004 In which Winter canceled the meeting, explaining that when he tried to obtain routine approval for Jackson's travel voucher, his superiors insisted he cancel the meeting on grounds that the e-gold people were bad actors who had not responded to some particular subpoena.[277] Jackson stated that he was looking forward to possibly meeting agents that did not have preconceived notions about e-gold®.

Having investigated the alleged non-response to a subpoena and discovering the Bermuda attorneys had negligently failed to forward it in a timely fashion, he also addressed the incident.[278]

Regarding a January meeting in Washington with the USSS, Jackson planned on still heading to Washington.

> Subject: e-gold related subpoenas
> From: Douglas Jackson <djackson@e-gold.com>
> Date: Wed, 29 Dec 2004 14:49:02 -0500

---

[276] Ibid

[277] Jackson, Douglas. "Pp. 108-196." Received by Carl Mullan, *Pp. 108-196*, 20 May 2020.

[278] The errant subpoena was then immediately forwarded from the Bermuda attorneys, followed by the normal timely investigation and response.

To: "Eric S. Winter" <XXXX@usss.dhs.gov>
CC: "Todd.M.Hinnen" <XXXX@usdoj.gov>

Eric

I am grateful that you called yesterday. I hope that we can get the people who jumped to the conclusion that we (e-gold) are bad guys will re-consider their opinion in the light of facts. I would encourage proceeding with the meeting of 7 January as planned, ideally to also include whoever interpreted the   actions of our obviously worthless Bermudan counsel as indicative that we are less than cooperative. It simply isn't so. I'm trying to find out what the hell the problem is with our Bermuda counsel that would prompt them to sit on subpoenas. But, as we would have reviewed in detail had we met 13 December, there are expeditious ways to cut through any delays and cc/fax subpoenas/court orders to our investigative staff directly. Our lead investigator, by the way, who you talked with yesterday, Randy   Trotter is at 321 956 1200 ext 106 and our fax is 321 951 0790. He loves to nail bad guys, and he's very good at it. Its as simple as that.
I still have my tickets etc. for the 7 January meet and plan to come even if I'm turned away at the door.
sincere regards,
Douglas Jackson[279]

Subject: RE: e-gold related subpoenas
From: "Eric S. Winter" <XXXX@usss.dhs.gov>
Date: Wed, 29 Dec 2004 15:06 -0500
To: "Douglas Jackson" <djackson@e-gold.com>
CC: "Ruskowski, Paul" <XXXX@usss.dhs.gov>
I forwarded Randy's information to the appropriate people. That is all I can do for now. I will let you know when I have more information. Thank you for your efforts.
Eric[280]

On January 7, 2005, Jackson traveled to Washington, D.C., in the hope of meeting with USSS Special Agents, and others to provide helpful in-house information on e-gold's methods for combating potential criminal activity. To his shock, the USSS refused to admit

---

[279] Jackson, Douglas. "e-gold Related Subpoenas." Received by Eric S. Winter, e-gold® Related Subpoenas, 29 Dec. 2004.
[280] Winter, Eric S. "Link to Malicious Code Analysis Ref. e-gold." Received by Douglas Jackson, *Link to Malicious Code Analysis Ref. e-gold*, 22 Nov. 2004.

him into the building. No meeting ever took place.

In a November 2008 email to Attorney Machalagh Carr at Sonnenschein Law, Jackson summarized previous conversations he had with USSS Special Agent Eric Winter. The discussion includes details regarding contact with the Agency and possible USSS reasons for a canceled December 2004 meeting in Washington, D.C. Jackson wrote:

> On 12/28/04, Winter called again and informed me that his superiors had ordered him to cancel our meeting for January. They had told him that e-gold was not responding to subpoenas and that we were bad guys. [Months later we indeed learned that Hil de Frias, for inexplicable reasons did in fact sit on several subpoenas from the USSS, at that critical time, neglecting to inform us in any way that they existed]. As I pointed out to Winter, a major element of what I had been planning to tell them about was how to reach us any time 24/7 and bypass formal channels to avoid delays. I had also put Winter in touch with Randy Trotter on 12/28 the moment I heard that these subpoenas had not reached us.[281]

In 2004, The Columbia Science and Technology Law Review published an article by Todd M. Hinnen entitled *The Cyber-front in the War On Terrorism: Curbing Terrorist Use of the Internet by* Todd M. Hinnen[282]

B. *Internet-Based Banking Alternatives*

The Internet provides several new financial services and means of transferring value. Internet users can avail themselves of online non-bank payment systems such as AnonymousGold, PayPal, and   StormPay; electronic currencies such as E-Bullion, Edinar, e-gold®, and Evocash; electronic checks such as those offered by PayNow and BankServ; and electronic debit cards such as "smartcards." Dollar-based electronic currencies such as Evocash and electronic checks are dependent on the banking system. Transactions involving these value transfer mechanisms must eventually pass value into or out of the traditional banking system, subjecting these transactions, at least secondhand, to the record-keeping and reporting requirements imposed on the banking industry.[283]

---

[281] "USSS Blurb." Received by Machalagh Carr, USSS Blurb, 5 Nov. 2008.

[282] The author is a Trial Attorney with the United States Department of Justice's Computer Crime & Intellectual Property Section. His duties with the Department of Justice include serving as a consultant in federal terrorism investigations and prosecutions involving the Internet and co-chairing an inter-agency working group on online terrorist financing with Juan C. Zarate, Deputy Assistant Secretary of Treasury for Terrorist Financing and Financial Crime. The views expressed in this Article are those of the author and do not necessarily represent the views of the Department of Justice.

[283] The Columbia Science and Technology Law Review 2004 Vol. V p.32 www.stlr.org Article by Todd M. Hinnen

Hinnen was incorrect in his 2004 risk assessment and comparison of e-gold® to other online non-bank payment systems, otherwise known as digital currency or virtual currency. His working knowledge of digital currency was limited, and he over-simplified the claim. This document was the outsider's view. He separated non-bank payment platforms (e-gold®) from dollar-based payment systems, such as EVOcash (also categorized as fiat-backed digital currency). He stated that dollar or fiat-backed digital currency was more likely to be tracked because dollars moved through banks which keep records and have reporting requirements. This statement infers that the movement of value through bullion-backed digital currency would be riskier because bullion deposits do not move through banks and are less likely to be reported.

> Dollar-based electronic currencies such as Evocash and electronic checks are dependent on the banking system. Transactions involving these value transfer mechanisms must eventually pass value into or out of the traditional banking system, subjecting these transactions, at least secondhand, to the record-keeping and reporting requirements imposed on the banking industry.[284]

This claim is untrue. All centralized digital currency platforms, bullion-backed and fiat-backed, are dependent on the banking system. The value does not enter the e-gold® system from thin air. Any amount from .01 cent to $1mil must enter or exit the closed e-gold® system through a fiat currency source.

E-gold's bailment feature, accessible to end-users, had been deprecated by 2000, and G&SR had exchanged all of the gold reserves for good delivery bullion. Also, with the restructuring of the institutional arrangements at that time, the core e-gold® functions of Issuance and Settlement were ring-fenced off from any exposure to activities that entailed receiving or making fiat money payments—transfers of value in ANY form—directly from or to customers.

With Bailment deprecated, e-gold® became a closed system where the only way to obtain e-gold® was to receive a Spend from someone who already had some, forming a permanent highly traceable link. The only linkages to the outside world were via currency exchange, and the bank link and interaction during this exchange process would have required previous bank KYC and AML. This movement of money through a bank would have created a traceable legal record on the source of funds and further identified the owner. If a 2004 e-gold® user wanted to obtain $300,000 worth of e-gold via currency exchange,

---

entitled *The Cyber-front in the War On Terrorism: Curbing Terrorist Use of the Internet* By Todd M. Hinnen
[284] Ibid

then a wire transfer or a bank check would have been used to make a payment into the bank account of an exchange provider. No fiat currency was ever able to enter or exit e-gold®. The exchange portals linking "dollar-based" and "bullion-backed" digital currency required the use of banks.

Furthermore, when EVOcash and other early dollar-backed platforms were in operation, all of these popular digital currencies could be instantly exchanged in and out of any other digital currency. In 2020, a crypto exchange will swap any virtual currencies such as Bitcoin for any other online payment system or digital currency. In 2004 independent exchange providers could swap between values of EVOcash, StormPay, E-Bullion, E-Dinar, Pecunix, e-gold®, Crowne Gold, Virtualgold, V-cash, 1MDC, Moneybookers, NetPay, Paymer, WebMoney, and FriendlyPay.

A WebMoney account holder could have easily, and instantly, swapped WebMoney for EVOcash at any time, through a third party exchange agent. This fluid movement of value between various digital currency brands, whether dollar or bullion based, significantly increased the risk of criminal proceeds moving through Dollar-based electronic currencies such as Evocash. Hinnen's inference that one category of digital money is less likely to be used for illegal activity is false.

All brand name digital units were exchangeable with other platforms; through the hundreds of online third-party independent exchange providers.[285] Law enforcement would have no easier time tracking funds through EVOcash than through e-gold® because value always moved back and forth between the different brands of digital currencies without any reporting. However, Hinnen, was not likely to understand this activity because he was not an active participant in these markets. He was an outsider looking inward.

Without hands-on trading and exchange experience, during 2004, many people "looking in" at digital currency made significant mistakes in their assumptions about how these platforms functioned and interacted.

This anonymous exchange risk is still present across all 2020 virtual currency markets. A user can instantly exchange Bitcoin for WebMoney, instantly exchange WM for PerfectMoney, and instantly exchange PM for Ether (ETH). A user can finally sell the ETH tokens for cash through https://localethereum.com/ In this example, it takes just 30 minutes for digital value to move through two centralized digital currency systems in Russia and Iceland and two decentralized platforms. Tracing these funds is extremely difficult.

---

[285] Virtually all of the reputable exchange services maintained extensive records and were also responsive to not only subpoenas and other lawful requests, but also investigative requests from e-gold Ltd. or other exchange providers, analogous to the information sharing between US financial institutions under the safe harbor provisions of the FinCEN 314(b) mechanism https://www.fincen.gov/sites/default/files/shared/314bfactsheet.pdf

2005

In the aftermath of the USSS rebuff, several OmniPay customers reported that a Tampa-based Bank of America Risk Management officer named Paula Tritschler was circulating rumors that the United States government was planning to shut down e-gold in February 2005. As later (March 2006) recollected in an email from Reid Jackson:

> G&SR once had a BOA account with full treasury mgmt capabilities configured that it used in support of the OmniPay line of business.
>
> That account was closed by the Corporate Security Dept. Doug thinks it must have been Risk Management, but my recollection is Corporate Security (i.e. the same Dept as Doug's contact). The person in this department who Barry, [redacted] and I had interactions with is named Paula Tritschler. She seemed to have a real vendetta against G&SR that went above and beyond risk management. We heard reports of her making slanderous comments to other banks and other bank of America customers about G&SR and e-gold. For instance, she supposedly told some BOA customers that G&SR and/or e-gold were not going to be around for long because the Feds were going to shut one or both of them down. Supposedly she was pretty specific about when this was supposed to happen. That time frame came and went without incident, but events similar to those she allegedly described did eventually transpire as we all well know.[286]

This combination of indicators suggestive of government antipathy toward e-gold prompted Jackson and Downey to seek out counsel to establish a more constructive dialogue with US federal agencies. A former colleague of Downey's, Ben England, endorsed his new law partner, Mitchell Fuerst as a suitable candidate:

> My partner, Mitchell Fuerst, is one of the foremost authorities. He does a lot of international tax, patriot act, bank secrecy act, and anti-money laundering compliance and litigation work. Eight years as an IRS prosecutor with 20 plus years in private civil and criminal litigation.[287]

On the strength of this endorsement, Jackson then reached out:[288]

---

[286] Jackson, Douglas. "Some Supplemental Material." Received by Carl Mullan, *Some Supplemental Material*, 25 Mar. 2020.

[287] Ibid

[288] Jackson, Douglas. "Request for Consultation - Patriot Act, e-Gold." Received by Mitchell Fuerst, *Request for*

Fri 1/21/2005
To: mfuerst@rofgw.com <XXXXX@rofgw.com>;
Cc: Barry Downey <bdowney@smithdowney.com>;
XXXXX@MFUERSTLAW.COM <XXXXX@MFUERSTLAW.COM>
Subject: request for consultation - Patriot Act, e-gold
Mitchell,

My pathway to you: Barry Downey, one of our Directors and a Principal of Smith & Downey www.smithdowney.com in Baltimore contacted Ben England.

I am the Chairman of e-gold Ltd., a company incorporated in Nevis (West Indies), that is the Issuer of e-gold(r), an alternative payment system that mobilizes the value of gold for Internet payments. e-gold has been online since 1996 and currently serves Users in over 165 countries. Since inception, the e-gold system has settled over 40 million user-to-user transfers via its online interface, accessed at www.e-gold.com

I am also CEO of Gold & Silver Reserve, Inc. (G&SR), a Delaware Corp. with its office in Melbourne, Florida. G&SR originally developed and deployed the e-gold system but devolved the core functions (Issuance, Settlement) to e-gold Ltd. effective 1/1/00. G&SR continues to serve as the contractual Operator of the e-gold system and also makes a market for exchange between e-gold and various national currencies with its OmniPay service www.omnipay.com

In the past week, rumors have been circulated that the US government is planning to shut down e-gold (and/or possibly G&SR) in February, allegedly for non-compliance with Patriot Act provisions, possibly relating to it being interpreted as a Money Services Business. We have had no direct communication from any agency suggesting someone has a beef with us, although we have had occasion to cooperate with hundreds of investigations of various abusers of e-gold.

We have of course repeatedly and extensively reviewed the various provisions of 31 CFR 103, 12 USC 1813 and guidance relating to registration, reporting and other compliance issues and can articulate why we believe that neither e-gold Ltd. or G&SR fall under the Patriot Act or other Bank Secrecy rubric.

We need at least two things, initially.

1. We need to find out if there is indeed some sort of active process underway where e-gold or G&SR are targets of some sort of investigation or enforcement action

2. We desire to establish a constructive dialog with US (and eventually Australian, UK, euroland) regulators that takes cognizance of the unique

character of e-gold.

Can we talk about this? If useful I can forward a draft of why we think our round pegs do not fit these square holes, but it may be expedient to rehearse all this in realtime.

My best contact tonight through weekend is my mobile 321 223 XXXX. Barry's mobile is [XXX]

sincere regards,

Douglas Jackson

Chairman, e-gold Ltd, and CEO, OmniPay

175 East Nasa Blvd. Suite 300 Melbourne, FL 32901[289]

Mitchell Fuerst was subsequently engaged. The engagement letter of February 13, 2005, specified:

> Nature of Legal Services. This is a joint representation of Gold & Silver Reserve, Inc., Jackson Trading, Inc., (for 1999), E-Gold Limited, Barry K. Downey and Douglas Jackson in reference to: (a) an Internal Revenue Service income tax examination; (b) an Internal Revenue Service Bank Secrecy Act/Patriot Act/anti-money laundering examination; (c) an Internal Revenue Service examination/investigation of the customers of Gold & Silver Reserve, Inc., and E-Gold, Ltd.; (d) a Commodities Futures Trading Commission summons based inquiry of the business activities of Gold & Silver Reserve, Inc., and possibly E-Gold, Ltd.; (e) possible other regulatory interest/inquiries of governmental agencies, including FinCen, OFAC, the Secret Service, other bureaus, agencies and divisions of the United States Treasury Department and bureaus, agencies and divisions of the Department of Homeland Security; (f) questions/concerns of governmental bodies of other nations that may rise to the level of investigations.

From the beginning, Fuerst emphasized that the most appropriate and urgent focus should be the IRS. He explained that the IRS Small Business and Self-Employment Division (IRS-SBSE) was the agency tasked with determining the appropriate regulatory rubric for novel businesses with respect to Bank Secrecy Act (BSA)/Patriot Act/anti-money laundering requirements. This seemed plausible as the first "U.S. Money Laundering Threat Assessment (MLTA)" issued later in 2005 specified:

---

[289] Jackson, Douglas. "Some Supplemental Material." Received by Carl Mullan, *Some Supplemental Material*, 25 Mar. 2020. 3-25-2020-Supplemental insertions.docx

On the civil side, the IRS established a new organization within its Small Business/Self-employed (SB/SE) Division, the Office of Fraud/BSA, which has end-to-end accountability for BSA oversight of certain non-bank financial institutions. There are over 300 examiners and managers who are fully trained and dedicated full time to the BSA program.

Similarly, the international Financial Action Task Force (FATF), in its THIRD MUTUAL EVALUATION REPORT ON ANTI-MONEY LAUNDERING AND COMBATING THE FINANCING OF TERRORISM (2006) subsequently noted:

> IRS Small Business and Self-Employment Division (IRS-SBSE): The IRS-SBSE has been delegated examination authority for civil compliance with the BSA for all financial institutions that do not have a federal functional regulator as defined in the BSA, including MSBs (as broadly defined), insurance companies, credit card companies, non-federally insured credit unions, casinos (tribal and non-tribal) and dealers in precious metals, stones and jewels. It also has responsibility for auditing compliance with currency transaction reporting requirements that apply to any trade or business.

Fuerst persuaded G&SR to transition its representation in relation to the ongoing IRS audit, already in its third year, from Miriam Fischer of Morgan Lewis to Fuerst's new firm and to formally request the IRS-SBSE to perform a BSA examination.[290]

BSA Compliance Exam for Gold & Silver Reserve, Inc.

The 2008 e-gold® sentencing memo contained the following statements.

> G&SR genuinely believed – and had good faith reason to believe -- that the nature of these businesses left them outside the regulatory scheme governing money transmitting businesses.[291]

> Counsel for the Companies openly engaged on this issue with the necessary representatives of the United States Department of Treasury, yet as late as May 2005, the Treasury Department- including, specifically, the Bank Secrecy Act (BSA)

---

[290] Ibid

[291] CASE NUMBER: 07-167-M-01. *UNITED STATES OF AMERICA V. E-GOLD LIMITED, GOLD & SILVER RESERVE, INC., DOUGLAS L. JACKSON, BARRY K. DOWNEY and REID A. JACKSON.* SENTENCING MEMORANDUM OF GOLD & SILVER RESERVE, INC., Nov. 2008.

examiners primarily responsible for such assessments - had not concluded that the Companies were subject to BSA requirements.[292]

On March 23, 2005, G&SR's attorney Mitchell Fuerst received a letter from Lisa Moffit. Moffit worked as an AML Revenue Agent for the Department of the Treasury, Internal Revenue Service Small Business / Self-employed Division in Washington, D.C.[293] The letter confirmed a scheduled appointment for May 2, 2005, at 11 a.m. in the G&SR Melbourne, Florida offices regarding the BSA Compliance Exam[294] for Gold & Silver Reserve, Inc. The letter stated that on May 2nd, 2005, the IRS was to hold an "Initial Interview" with the company's officers and make a Documents Request for detailed information on G&SR's business operations.

The requested records were to aid the IRS in determining whether the government considered G&SR a Money Service Business (MSB). If applicable, the IRS would also decide whether BSA regulations, as they pertain to MSBs, were being followed. The parties listed here were to be present for the interview:

- One or more corporate officers from G&SR
- IRS Manager Steven F. Anderson
- One or more BSA Technical Advisors
- Lisa Moffit, AML Revenue Agent

A later April 7, 2008 email sent by DOJ Attorney Kimberly Kiefer Peretti from the U.S. Department of Justice Criminal Division confirmed that attorneys for e-gold Ltd. and G&SR had been in contact FinCEN in March 2005. Furthermore, Mitchell Fuerst had asked BSA examiner Lisa Moffitt to determine whether their platform was considered a Money Service Business. Below is a partial section from the April 7th DOJ letter substantiating this 2005 contact.

> In addition, in a report dated March 21, 2005, BSA examiner Lisa Moffitt indicates that Mitchell Fuerst stated that he had spoken with FinCEN regarding whether the defendant businesses were an MSB. In addition, in a report dated May 3, 2005, Ms.

---

[292] Ibid

[293] Moffitt, Lisa. Received by Mitchell Fuerst, 1001 Brickell Bay Drive, 23 Mar. 2005, Miami, Florida.

[294] The Bank Secrecy Act (BSA), also known as the Currency and Foreign Transactions Reporting Act, is legislation passed by the United States Congress in 1970 that requires U.S. financial institutions to collaborate with the U.S. government in cases of suspected money laundering and fraud. The Bank Secrecy Act (BSA) is the primary U.S. anti-money laundering (AML) law and has been amended to include certain provisions of Title III of the USA PATRIOT Act to detect, deter and disrupt terrorist financing networks.

Moffitt reported that:

"Since there were no more questions by anyone present the meeting was concluded. [Donna]
Dohrman stated she would summarize her notes and forward those to FinCen to ask them to make a determination whether they are an MSB. In the interim Moffitt will prepare and issue a Document Request and make arrangements to review these records the purpose of which is to corroborate their oral testimony as told to Fuerst at an earlier date. [Steve] Anderson emphasized that we want to make an expeditious but also accurate determination of whether they are or are not an MSB and if so what BSA requirements should apply to them."[295]

These documents and these meetings confirm that in early 2005, long before any criminal indictment or warranted search, the principals of e-gold, Gold & Silver Reserve, Inc. were engaged with the IRS in determining whether the government considered G&SR a Money Service Business (MSB). If applicable, the IRS would also decide whether BSA regulations, as they pertain to MSBs, were being followed.

◆

As early as Spring 2005, Jackson began to work intensively with Agent Shaun McLeary, of New Scotland Yard in the United Kingdom. Jackson's goal was to assist in any pending investigations. Agent McLeary and an FBI Special Agent, Thomas Sloan, accepted Jackson's invitation to visit G&SR's office in Florida. Both Agent McLeary and Special Agent Sloan visited the e-gold offices and met with Jackson. During that two day trip, the men learned how the e-gold system operated and interacted with Jackson as he conducted searches to further their current investigations.[296]

◆

New York Times
On June 21st, 2005, the New York Times published an article, that mentioned e-gold®, written by Tom Zeller Jr. entitled, *Black Market in Stolen Credit Card Data Thrives on Internet.*[297] Two lines of the article named e-gold® and WebMoney.

[295] "Re: *United States v. e-Gold, Ltd., Et al.*, Crim. No. 07-109 (RMC)." Received by Joshua G. Berman, et al., Re: *United States v. e-Gold, Ltd., Et al.*, Crim. No. 07-109 (RMC), 7 Apr. 2008.

[296] Case 1:07-cr-00109-RMC Document 177. *UNITED STATES OF AMERICA v. E-GOLD, LTD.* Criminal SENTENCING MEMORANDUM OF GOLD & SILVER RESERVE, INC., 14 Nov. 2008.

[297] Zeller, Tom. "Black Market in Stolen Credit Card Data Thrives on Internet." *The New York Times*, 21 June 2005,

Payments often change hands in relative anonymity (and with little regulation) by, an electronic currency that purports to be backed by gold bullion and issued by Ltd., a company incorporated on the island of Nevis in the Caribbean. (Secret Service agents have expressed skepticism over the gold backing.) Transactions might also be made in WMZ's, electronic monetary units equivalent to American dollars and issued by WebMoney Transfer, a company based in Moscow.[298]

This Zeller article, allowed the USSS to use a private news media and purposely cast doubt over whether e-gold® had physical gold bullion backing its digital units. This piece illustrates one of the many frequent USSS attempts to discredit e-gold® and vilify Jackson using public media.

Additionally, the article provided details on individuals known as "carders." This term is a slang phrase describing individuals that illegally sell stolen credit cards and personal identity information through the Internet. Carder communities operate online around the world. These groups are generally coordinated and controlled by transnational criminal organizations.

Jackson has repeatedly stated, over many years, that Zeller's article was the first time he had encountered these various slang terms of art associated with illegal credit card sales. Terms including "carders" "dumps" "fullz" "COB" and "CVV" are language used in the sale of stolen credit card and identify information.

After reading the article, Jackson was confounded as to why the USSS was not making use of e-gold's in-house investigative capabilities in this case. Immediately, Jackson used 2004 email contact information and called the USSS cybercrime unit. Learning that his previous contact, Special Agent Eric Winter had left the USSS, Jackson persisted in his efforts and finally connected with USSS Special Agent Paul Ruskowski, who had been Winter's former boss. In an October 2005 email, Jackson described his feelings that during the call. He said, Ruskowski seemed like a "decent sort [but] I never learned who in USSS had decided they preferred for us[e-gold] to be regarded as bad guys regardless of facts."[299]

E-gold® accounts were spider webs. Every user's Internet connection to the e-gold® platform irreversibly linked that user to their online account, along with all other transacting accounts. Finding just one e-gold® account containing a carder phrase could lead Jackson's investigations to an entire connected carder account network and all participants. During the

www.nytimes.com.

[298] Ibid

[299] Jackson, Douglas. "e-Gold Follow-Up." Received by Brian Grow, and Bill Cunningham, e-Gold Follow-Up, 13 Oct. 2005.

summer 2005, after Zeller's article, Jackson experimented with full-text queries of the e-gold® transaction database. His goal was to learn if these "carder associated" slang terms were present in any other user accounts. The theory was that if any of these terms appeared in a search query, it might pinpoint accounts involved with this kind of criminal activity. Jackson realized that, if present in the database, accessing carder accounts through the filtered information would have been a massive benefit to the law enforcement community.

However, initial database searches were unsuccessful because the search would time-out before returning data. The technical roadblock preventing the completion of a full database term search was due to the platform's hardware and the growth in new e-gold activity. Due to the recent growth in users and transactions, the operation had pushed the database server hardware to near capacity levels. Even though Jackson attempted complex searches, the full database search failed. He was unable to successfully compete a database search for the carder terms due to the network stress.

In October 2005, e-gold® ordered multi-core processors capable of easing these capacity constraints and enabling more CPU-intensive searches of all database information. This slowdown had been a product of e-gold's soaring popularity. With the new hardware ordered, the company would soon be searching for all slang carder terms and any connected account networks.

◆

According to the existing 2005 U.S. Financial regulations, neither G&SR nor the e-gold® business was required to operate under the strict financial laws for U.S. money transmitting businesses. Jackson had created a new technology and category of online value transfer mechanisms the world had previously not encountered. The operation of e-gold® was breaking no existing rules or regulations. However, the media sought to wrongly impeach the company and its operators through malicious press reports and wild untrue stories.

Jackson's personal life was also interrupted by multiple false allegations leaked through the press. Evidence suggests, and Jackson agrees, that rogue USSS Special Agents planted numerous deceitful claims with the media to advance the government's prosecution and asset forfeiture. On October 13th, 2005, Douglas Jackson and Bill Cunningham of G&SR, met with Mr. Brian Grow and were interviewed for an upcoming Businessweek article.

After the interview, Jackson emailed Grow a follow-up letter to thank him. In the email, Jackson provided additional information, contacts, and details to assist Grow in completing the e-gold® article. Jackson's email, shown here, also offered insight into the USSS investigation, including a long list of associated law enforcement individuals that had worked with e-gold®.

Subject: e-gold follow-up[300]
From: Douglas Jackson
Date: Thu, 13 Oct 2005 17:25:42 -0400
To: "Grow, Brian (Businessweek)"
CC: Bill Cunningham

Brian

We enjoyed meeting with you today and appreciate your insightful questions. Here's the first round of other things we said we'd look up. Jim and Bill are contacting customers and checking with other exchange providers.

One exchange provider we know very well since she is local (and very personable)

Jane Anderson
GitGold Worldwide Inc.
2117 S. Babcock St.
Melbourne, FL
321 723-7XXX

Secret Service debacle (the recent one, not the 2001 "Secret Service Raids e-gold" one) The Secret Service guy who let us know about the e-gold targeting trojan Fall '04 and who tried to set up an educational session for USSS, and NHTCU plus Australian counterparts was Eric Winters. Later when I tried to figure out why unnamed sources in USSS were casting aspersions about us I learned he was gone and I spoke to the guy who had been his boss, Paul Ruskowski. Paul also seemed a decent sort. I never learned who in USSS had decided they preferred for us to be regarded as bad guys regardless of facts. Other USSS people who had been cc'ed on Eric's emails to me were Christopher Wiliams and Jay Perry but I never had direct contact with them and don't know where they fit in. I was also trying to get Todd Hinnen, an attorney at DOJ, to attend. He had written a lengthy piece in Columbia Law Review about Internet payment that got most things right but was off target when it came to e-gold. 'The Cyber-Front in the War on Terrorism: Curbing Terrorist. Use of the Internet.' Columbia Science and Technology Law Review Vol. 5 2004.[301]

---

[300] Jackson, Douglas. "e-gold Follow-Up." Received by Brian Grow, *e-gold Follow-Up*, 12 Oct. 2005.

[301] The Columbia Science and Technology Law Review 2004 Vol. V   p. 32 http://www.stlr.org *The Columbia Science and Technnology Law Review* The Cyber-front in the War On Terrorism: Curbing Terrorist Use of the Internet By Todd M. Hinnen

NCMEC contacts
Michelle K. Collins
Exploited Child Unit, Director National Center for Missing & Exploited Children
Ernie Allen, President & CEO
National Center for Missing & Exploited Children
699 Prince Street, Alexandria, Virginia 22314
Some of Randy's current favorite law enforcement contacts
Jon Tyboroski U.S. Immigration and Customs Enforcement, Seattle, WA
Timothy J. Schmitz, Federal Bureau of Investigation, Oklahoma
Trish Gomersall, Commodity Futures Trading Commission
Thomas Cohn, Federal Trade Commission, New York
Joan Cronier, Federal Bureau of Investigation, Atlanta GA
Michelle Harden, Postal Inspector, Detroit, Michigan
Deborah N. Murphy, Special Agent, IRS-CI, Boston Field Office
Harold Loftin, Securities and Exchange Commission, Ft. Worth, TX

◆

By November 2005, no regulatory or law enforcement agency had filed any criminal charges against e-gold® or G&SR. Furthermore, the e-gold® co-founders had been actively interacting with the law enforcement community and U.S. Financial regulators. On November 17th, 2005, Wired.com published an article, by Kim Zetter, entitled *Guilty Pleas in ID Theft Bust*.[302]

Zetter's article referenced the USSS's investigation code name "Operation Firewall." The content of the material discussed Shadowcrew.com and stated that Shadowcrew criminals used e-gold® and Western Union as methods of paying for illegal goods. This Wired.com article was just the beginning of multiple e-gold® media attacks lasting more than two years.

Despite vicious media assaults, e-gold's online business continued to expand. Heading into 2006, the company was booming. In November 2005, the average number of e-gold® Spends per day was 44,054, and the average daily transaction value was $8,312,682.72 (on a cost basis).[303] By December 2005, e-gold® had processed over 55M individual transactions, and the majority of those Spends appeared to be from accounts owned by U.S. Citizens.

---

[302] Zetter, Kim. "Guilty Pleas in ID Theft Bust." *Wired*, Conde Nast, 17 Nov. 2005, www.wired.com/2005/11/guilty-pleas-in-id-theft-bust/.

[303] CASE NUMBER: 07-167-M-01. *UNITED STATES OF AMERICA V. E-GOLD LIMITED, GOLD & SILVER RESERVE, INC., DOUGLAS L. JACKSON, BARRY K. DOWNEY and REID A. JACKSON.* SENTENCING MEMORANDUM OF GOLD & SILVER RESERVE, INC., Nov. 2008.

Fighting Online Child Porn

In 2005, e-gold® became a founding and active member of the Financial Coalition Against Child Pornography (FCACP) organized by the National Center for Missing and Exploited Children (NCMEC). While a member, Jackson continuously provided information to agents of this organization about persons using the e-gold system who were believed to be involved in child exploitation.

Jackson also revealed that bank credit card processors, transacting 99.99% of Visa and MasterCard payments, did not join the Coalition until several months after e-gold's matriculation.

Before becoming an active member, Jackson noted that e-gold® had experienced some privacy issues that had created barriers to its legal investigative ability.

> Prior to the formation of NCMEC's Financial Coalition Against Child Pornography, NCMEC was refusing to help with alerts and we were hamstrung by the fact that our investigators could not look for offending sites without that act being a crime.[304]

For anyone online, it is a severe crime to visit any website containing Child Pornography (CP). Even if an in-house e-gold® investigator received a tip about a CP website accepting e-gold®, it was impossible to visit the website without breaking the law.

The fight against Child Pornography was always a high-level priority for all individuals associated with e-gold® and G&SR. As Jackson explained, "In looking at the crime-fighting, CP was the first area where a systematic breakthrough in cooperation with law enforcement occurred."[305]

An extract from 2007 expose, drafted by Dr. Jackson for Brian Krebs, who was then a journalist at the Washington Post reveals:

> "On August 17, 2005 I received an invitation to come to NCMEC and participate in the formation of the FCACP. Upon arrival at NCMEC's headquarters August 24, 2005, I was expressing my enthusiasm and gratitude to John Sheehan (Cybertipline Director) and proposed that NCMEC add e-gold as an alternative payment option for accepting donations on the ncmec.org website. His visibly surprised but measured reaction was to say words to the effect that prior to my arrival they (NCMEC staff) were under the impression that e-gold was complicit in child pornography. During

---

[304] Jackson, Douglas. "Fw: Add'l Backgrounders." Received by Carl Mullan, *Fw: Add'l Backgrounders*, 15 Jan. 2019.
[305] Ibid

the same initial visit I showed Michelle Collins and John Sheehan how to determine if a site that appeared to be accepting e-gold was actually linked to an e-gold account and demonstrated [via real-time telephone link to e-gold investigators] that any such account could be blocked instantly. They expressed surprise and described the complex, confusing and unreliable drill that credit card companies and law enforcement must go through to attempt to determine if a site displaying credit card logos is actually receiving credit card payments. I made my first of many invitations for NCMEC staff to make a site visit to the e-gold Operator facility in Melbourne Florida to learn more of our capabilities and to better coordinate with e-gold's investigators.

We followed up with a series of emails wherein I detailed service of process procedures, which Michelle Collins forwarded in August 2005, with my approval, to hundreds of law enforcement agencies, plus 24/7 rapid response workarounds to avoid any possible delay."[306]

Many of the in-house techniques for eradicating CP payments, initially developed and refined at e-gold®, were later adapted to fight other potential online criminal activity. Jackson shared his belief about the lack of cooperation between e-gold® and the USSS on fighting CP. Jackson always watched for any illegal attempt to use e-gold® for the purchase of CP. During Congressional testimony before a House Committee, Jackson provided the following partial statement, including these charts.

During this time period e-gold received adverse press that came close to implying complicity in this problem, but it was press that was not justified. Based upon the financial size of the CP trade identified by the NCMEC and our review of historical transactions, e-gold has been the payment mechanism abused in less than one hundredth of one percent of the CP payment dollar volume since this problem surfaced. The NCMEC CyberTipLine sends alerts to Financial Coalition members and alerts are received from other third party sources as well. Since collaborative efforts started the activity has decreased dramatically. When an alert is investigated, 95% of the time the account has already been identified and blocked through e-gold's own internal investigative efforts, almost always detected upon the first payment or before a single payment has been received. The following chart represents all CP alerts from all sources since December 2005.[307]

306 Jackson, Douglas. "DJ Redlines 4." Received by Carl Mullan, *DJ Redlines 4*, 27 Feb. 2020.
307 Ibid

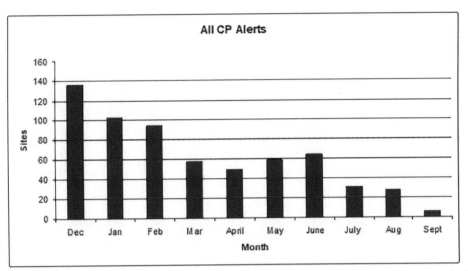

e-gold investigators estimate that 90-95% of the alerts received are for CP websites for which e-gold has already blocked the applicable account.

The very favorable trend shown in the chart is not by accident. e-gold continues to refine its protocols to detect and interdict CP. payments Investigative protocols are routinely upgraded as more is learned about behaviors of the perpetrators and enormous personnel resources are applied. e-gold's cost for investigative and preventive actions to stop the use of e-gold for illicit activity, especially CP, is the single largest element of expense in its business. e-gold will continue to apply this attention and resource until the problem no longer exists.

The following graph illustrates the declining dollar volume that unfortunately had escaped detection before the accounts were ultimately identified and blocked. It is evident that the visibility we gained from our association with NCMEC in the fall of 2005 was a turning point in our efforts to prevent e-gold being used at all for CP payment. The declining value depicts the evolving capability of our investigative techniques and show we have reduced e-gold abuse to a background noise level.[308]

---

[308] Ibid

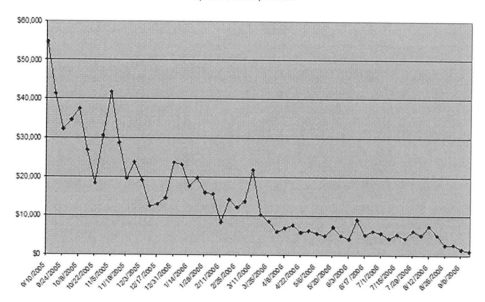

Abuse of e-gold for Child Pornography Payment Volume per Week[309]

e-gold is not limiting its efforts to its own database. Whenever a CP buyer account is identified e-gold investigators alert the exchange provider from whom the perpetrator purchased their e-gold. The exchange providers are proving very helpful in suppressing CP from the demand side. It has been highly encouraging to see how strongly these organizations are supporting the efforts.

As low as the escape payments have become, we will still remain very vigilant; we know full well that these criminals will not stop until the the risks of their activity outweigh any possible commercial incentive. We will continue to strenuously support the NCMEC and law enforcement until the problem is gone.[310]

[309] Jackson, Douglas. "e-gold 4Q06 Interim Progress in Detection and Interdiction of CP-Related Payment Transactions." Melbourne, Oct. 2006.

[310] "DELETING COMMERCIAL PORNOGRAPHY SITES FROM THE INTERNET: THE U.S. FINANCIAL INDUSTRY'S EFFORTS TO COMBAT THIS PROBLEM." - DELETING COMMERCIAL PORNOGRAPHY SITES FROM THE INTERNET: THE U.S. FINANCIAL INDUSTRY'S EFFORTS TO COMBAT THIS PROBLEM HEARING BEFORE THE SUBCOMMITTEE ON OVERSIGHT AND INVESTIGATIONS OF THE COMMITTEE ON ENERGY AND COMMERCE HOUSE OF REPRESENTATIVES ONE HUNDRED NINTH CONGRESS SECOND SESSION SEPTEMBER 21, 2006 Serial No. 109-141 Printed for the Use of the Committee on Energy and Commerce Available via the World Wide Web: http://www.access.gpo.gov/Congress/House U.S. GOVERNMENT PRINTING OFFICE 31-467 WASHINGTON : 2006, [House Hearing, 109 Congress] [From the U.S. Government

Jackson has always taken pride in sharing the fact that e-gold/G&SR had been one of the founding members of the National Center for Missing and Exploited Children's Financial Coalition Against Child Pornography. The e-gold® staff and employees at G&SR dedicated themselves to identifying and stopping the payment methods used by online sellers of child pornography. Jackson was accommodating and often met with other professional industry organizations for discussions on how to solve this ongoing problem.

It is worth noting, that in 2020, criminals widely use blockchain currencies as payment tools for Child Pornography. Unlike the co-founders and staff of e-gold, who were committed to preventing this activity, there is no comparable concerned group in the blockchain world. On April 21, 2020, Danny Nelson, writing for Coindesk.com published an article entitled, *Crypto Payments for Child Porn Grew 32% in 2019: Report.*[311] The article included this opening text.

> Nearly $1 million in bitcoin and ethereum flowed into child pornography-linked wallet addresses in 2019, continuing a multiyear upward trend that captures the complicated realities of mass crypto adoption.[312]

In November 2005, Jackson attended the "Protecting Children Online" conference in Belfast, Ireland. This meeting was the first of CEOP Command's Virtual Global Taskforce (Child Exploitation and Online Protection Command).[313]

Thanks to contacts made at the Belfast VGT Conference, e-gold® began also receiving timely notifications from the Association of Sites Advocating Child Protection (ASACP). The Association of Sites Advocating Child Protection (ASACP) is a non-profit organization dedicated to eliminating child exploitation from the Internet.

Mr. Keven Zuccato, the newly appointed head of the Australian High Tech Crime Centre (AHTCC), met with Jackson during that conference.[314] The image below, taken in the fall 2005 CEOP conference shows Jackson and Zuccato.[315] This picture was taken about

---

Printing Office], 21 Sept. 2006, www.govinfo.gov/content/pkg/CHRG-109hhrg31467/html/CHRG-109hhrg31467.htm. Serial No. 109-141

[311] Nelson, Danny. "Crypto Payments for Child Porn Grew 32% in 2019: Report." *CoinDesk*, CoinDesk, 21 Apr. 2020, www.coindesk.com/crypto-payments-for-child-porn-grew-32-in-2019-report.

[312] Ibid

[313] The Child Exploitation and Online Protection Command, or CEOP Command, is a command of the UK's National Crime Agency (NCA).

[314] The Australian High Tech Crime Centre (AHTCC) is a policing initiative to coordinate the efforts of Australian law enforcement in combating serious, complex and multi-jurisdictional Internet-based crimes.

[315] Former director of the Australian Federal Police's high-tech crime centre in 2019 leads IBM's Canberra-based national cyber security centre.

a month before the USSS raids on the Florida offices of e-gold®, G&SR, and Jackson's residence.

Unidentified female, Kevin Zuccato, and Douglas Jackson[316]

Of note, Jackson learned at the conference that Mr. Zuccato had been one of the international law enforcement members scheduled to participate in the December 2004 USSS meeting Jackson had sought to arrange. In 2019 emails, Jackson shared his thoughts regarding the USSS activity around the e-gold® business.

> I recall at the time feeling as if the SS [USSS] was desperately stepping up its attacks (the Brian Grow matter) and afterwards realized they were in a panic for fear my bridge building to LE[Law Enforcement] was going to foil their plot to use us as their meal ticket.[317]

As it related to fraud and child pornography, Jackson and Zuccato routinely discussed the U.S. Secret Service; as did other industry professionals. Below is a December 2005 email chain between Jackson and Zuccato just weeks before the e-gold® raid. Zuccato wrote:

Hi Douglas

Thanks for the email, I am just getting back to work following my travel to Belfast,

316 Zuccato, Kevin. "Kevin Zuccato on LinkedIn." *LinkedIn*, 2010, au.linkedin.com/in/kevin-zuccato-b61aa9a4.
317 Jackson, Douglas. "Fw: Add'l Backgrounders." Received by Carl Mullan, *Fw: Add'l Backgrounders*, 15 Jan. 2019.

London, Perth, Melbourne and Adelaide during November. Christmas can't come soon enough. Thanks for this information and your participation in Belfast. I found your input into the summit very useful and informative especially regarding how e-gold works and what we can do to access e-gold information if we need to. I will circulate your advice to other Australian law enforcement participants in the AHTCC and hopefully generate some further interaction with you. Have a great holiday season and thanks again for making the time to come to Belfast.
Kevin Zuccato[318]

From: Douglas Jackson
Sent: Monday, 5 December 2005 12:02 PM
To: Zuccato, Kevin
Subject: Re: e-gold service of process and contacts
Thanks for your note. Our investigative staff is standing by ready to rock'n'roll if we see an Australian subpoena. Weirdly, I've been making another attempt to establish a more constructive working relationship with the USSS this past week but the guys at cybercrime squad level have been told by their higher-ups that they aren't allowed to talk to me. They were instructed to refer me to their Public Relations dept.?! I asked if WE were under investigation but they said that wasn't it. I get the impression it's some sort of political weirdness involving a need for spin doctoring or some such.[319]

Subject: RE: e-gold service of process and contacts
From: "Zuccato, Kevin"
Date: Wed, 14 Dec 2005 15:58:09 +1100
To: "Douglas Jackson"
Thanks Douglas
Sorry to hear your approaches to USSS fell on deaf ears. Rest assured that if we come across an investigation that has some sort of connection with e-gold we will be in touch and see whether we can help one another. Have a safe holiday season.
Kevin Z[320]

Jackson had an amicable relationship with many members of the law enforcement

[318] Zuccato, Kevin. "e-Gold Service of Process and Contacts." Received by Douglas Jackson, *e-Gold Service of Process and Contacts*, 5 Dec. 2005.

[319] Jackson, Douglas. "Re: e-Gold Service of Process and Contacts." Received by Kevin Zuccato, *Re: e-Gold Service of Process and Contacts*, 5 Dec. 2005.

[320] Zuccato, Kevin. "RE: e-Gold Service of Process and Contacts." Received by Douglas Jackson, *RE: e-Gold Service of Process and Contacts*, 14 Dec. 2005.

community. Records filed by G&SR attorney's detailed some of this cooperation.

Agent Shaun McLeary, of New Scotland Yard in the United Kingdom, advised the government that Dr. Jackson "was cooperative and helpful in supplying information related to e-gold" in connection with an investigation that New Scotland Yard was conducting. Kiefer Letter, p. 4. In fact, G&SR began to work intensively with Agent McLeary and others as early as the Spring of 2005. To assist them in their investigations, Dr. Jackson invited Agent McLeary and an FBI agent, Thomas Sloan, to G&SR's office in Florida and spent the better part of two days showing them how the e-gold system operates and conducting searches to further their investigations. According to Agent McLeary, Dr. Jackson was so interested in furthering these investigations that he implored on Agents McLeary and Sloan to keep working late into the evenings, even when they were ready to quit for the day.[321]

After instituting multiple company initiatives to detect and prevent any possible CP payments, Jackson documented this ground-breaking work in a 2006 e-gold® report. Here are some parts of the document submitted to the NCMEC in preparation for the January 2007, quarterly Financial Coalition.

e-gold 4Q06 Interim Progress in Detection and Interdiction of CP-related Payment Transactions
Core elements of CP payment detection
- With e-gold's comprehensive book-entry settlement database, and permanent records, the best way to find the sellers of CP is to find a buyer. The best way to find the buyers of CP is to find a seller. This network phenomenon enables iterative discovery.
- Every identifier, every forensic characteristic, of every buyer and every seller of CP is captured into permanent databases.
- Notifications of sites purporting to accept e-gold serve to refresh the profiles in the event sellers "shape shift" using completely new identifiers.
Interdiction and response protocol as of 2Q06
- New e-gold accounts are screened for identifiers that raise suspicion of control by a previously identified buyer or seller of CP.
- Transaction registers of these identified accounts are reviewed.

---

[321] CASE NUMBER: 07-167-M-01. *UNITED STATES OF AMERICA V. E-GOLD LIMITED, GOLD & SILVER RESERVE, INC., DOUGLAS L. JACKSON, BARRY K. DOWNEY and REID A. JACKSON.* SENTENCING MEMORANDUM OF GOLD & SILVER RESERVE, INC., Nov. 2008.

- Generalized transaction database is screened for payments with characteristics known to correlate with CP payment, special emphasis on memo text strings and target strings (URLs, email addresses) in Shopping Cart notifications.
- If a CP payment is detected:
- block and freeze the seller,
- block and freeze the buyers,
- find all other accounts controlled by buyers and seller and block/freeze them,
- review all other accounts spent to by buyers and all other accounts that paid sellers
- iterate until trail is exhausted.

Protocol enhancements 3Q06
- If buyer obtained e-gold via exchange, notify the exchange service they used so the exchanger can blacklist the e-gold user and alert other exchangers.
- If payment made it through to seller and seller then exchanged for Webmoney, notify Webmoney investigations.
- Uniform data re-coding enabling auditable interdiction performance metrics.

Protocol enhancements 4Q06
- SheriffBot deployed that captures transaction in realtime before seller can exchange value for Webmoney.
- Routine screen of new accounts looking for password hashes with high specificity for sellers.
- Draconian reduction of pool of value potentially available for CP purchase by detection of historic yet-unfrozen buyer accounts and freezing them.

Statistical series
Cumulative gross (USD-equiv.) total of all CP payments that went through e-gold [first one was Aug 2003] through year-end 2006: $ 2,959,537
Gross total CP payments 4Q06 - $16,537 (annualized would be $65,000 or 0.00033% of global commercial CP)
Cumulative total (USD-equiv. at $620/oz) value of e-gold impounded from CP buyers and sellers - $193,000

Attachments
Chart 1 – Comprehensive historic monthly volume of CP payments through e-gold system
Chart 2 – 4Q06 weekly volume of CP payments, and volume arrested by SheriffBot program[322]

[Blank]

[322] Jackson, Douglas. "Fw: Add'l Backgrounders." Received by Carl Mullan, *Fw: Add'l Backgrounders*, 15 Jan. 2019.

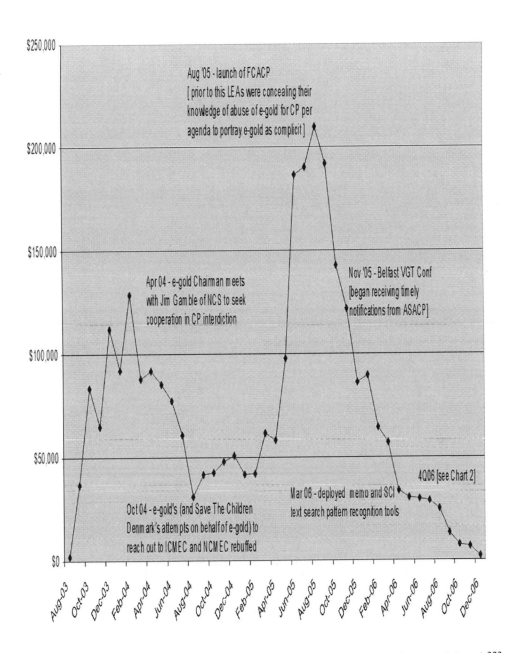

Chart 1, Abuse of e-gold® for Child Pornography Payment Value per Month[323]

[323] Jackson, Douglas. "e-gold 4Q06 Interim Progress in Detection and Interdiction of CP-Related Payment Transactions." Melbourne, Oct. 2006.

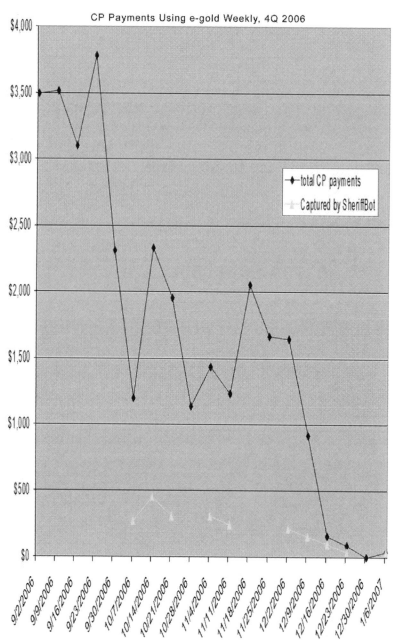

Chart 2: 4Q06 weekly volume of CP payments, and volume arrested by SheriffBot program[324]

---

[324] Ibid

In later 2019 emails, Jackson explained the significance of this document and the graphs.

> It constitutes the only instance where any financial firm ever provided a report, verifiable or otherwise, of actual retrospective historic data. The graph was an update of one I'd produced for a report I had prepared for my Congressional testimony in Sept 06. The attached NCMEC Q406 report was copied and re-distributed to all attendees of the January 07 meeting.[325]

The National Crime Squad (NCS) was a British police organization that dealt with national and transnational organized and major crimes. Jackson had previously met with Jim Gamble of the NCS, in April 2004, to offer e-gold's assistance and cooperation with the interdiction Child Pornography.

Operation Goldwire

Around December 5, 2005, the Nevis Financial Services Regulation & Supervision Department posted a notice inexplicably, on its website, stating that e-gold® had disseminated "misleading information" about the organization's legal status. No statements or explanations accompanied this notice, and for the next eleven days, the item persisted as an open question.

On December 14, 2005, behind sealed federal courthouse chambers, Magistrate Judge John Facciola of the United States District Court for the District of Columbia signed an Order authorizing the freeze of Gold & Silver Reserve, Inc. U.S. based bank accounts. Here is a partial statement from Judge Facciola that was copied from later Court documents, stating his reason for signing the seizure warrant.

> [...]based on my initial conclusion that the government had made a sufficient showing of probable cause to believe that defendants had violated Title 18 U.S.C. § 1960,[326] the statute which makes it unlawful to operate an "unlicensed money transmitting business.[327]

---

[325] Jackson, Douglas. "Add'l Backgrounders." Received by Carol Van Cleef, *Add'l Backgrounders*, 12 Feb. 2009.

[326] All references to the United States Code are to the electronic version that appears in Westlaw and Lexis.

[327] Case 1:05-cv-02497-RMC. *UNITED STATES OF AMERICA v. ALL FUNDS SEIZED FROM OR ON DEPOSIT IN SUNTRUST ACCOUNT NUMBER 1000028078359, IN THE NAME OF GOLD AND SILVER RESERVE, INC. AND ALL FUNDS ON DEPOSIT IN REGIONS BANK ACCOUNT NUMBER 67-0919-4851, IN THE NAME OF GOLD AND SILVER RESERVE, INC. . CLAIMANT GOLD & SILVER RESERVE, INC.'s FIRST NOTICE OF FILING IN PARALLEL PROCEEDINGS* , 2 Feb. 2006.

The Court blocked all access to G&SR's U.S. daily operating bank accounts, and all funds on deposit were frozen, preventing any further business transactions. This legal action, by DOJ Prosecutors, was an attempt to shut down the e-gold® business. The total amount of money locked up by the Judge's order was $841,897.46. Here is a list of the frozen accounts and dollar amounts.

- $590,306.59 – Regions Bank Account No. 6709194851
- $115,678.55 – Regions Bank Account No. 6709194878
- $135,912.32 – SunTrust Bank Account No. 1000028078359

The money contained in those bank accounts became the subject of the Government's Civil Action No. 05-02497.[328] Jackson has explained that the 2005 seizure froze all of the money in G&SR's domestic bank accounts.

G&SR operators were unaware of the government's legal action and only learned of the bank account seizures when OmniPay customer service staff began receiving frantic calls from customers alerting them that company checks were bouncing. While they continued to receive and freeze incoming wires from customers (funding payments for pending exchange orders) over the next few days, Regions and Suntrust denied knowledge of any problems with the accounts.

Two days later, on Friday, December 16, 2005, the USSS executed a Search Warrant for the offices of Gold & Silver Reserve, Inc. DBA OmniPay, 175 East Nasa Boulevard, Suite 300, Melbourne, FL 32901, concurrent with searches at Dr. Jackson's home and the ATT Orlando co-location facility where both e-gold Ltd. and G&SR maintained their primary servers.[329]

During the warranted search of G&SR's offices, United States Secret Service Special Agents surprised G&SR employees by talking to them during the investigation. Through discussions, the USSS Special Agent made multiple references to conversations, the USSS had previously with a past fired rogue employee [Charles Evans] of e-gold®. This evidence demonstrated that the USSS had been in contact with Charles Evans. Furthermore, almost

---

[328] DEFENDANTS' MOTION TO VACATE SEIZURE WARRANT AND TO MODIFY RESTRAINING ORDER AND REQUEST FOR AN EVIDENTIARY HEARING. *UNITED STATES OF AMERICA v. e-gold LIMITED, GOLD & SILVER RESERVE, INC., DOUGLAS L. JACKSON, BARRY K. DOWNEY and REID A. JACKSON.* Case 1:07-cr-00109-RMC Document 35, 1 June 2007.

[329] Gold & Silver Reserve, Inc "Gold & Silver Reserve, Inc." included the following parties Barry K. Downey, Director, Jackson Trading Company; Douglas L. Jackson, President, Jackson Trading Company; Barry K. Downey, Director, Gold & Silver Reserve, Inc.; Douglas L. Jackson, President, Gold & Silver Reserve, Inc.; Barry K. Downey; and, Douglas L. Jackson.

certainly the contact had been initiated by Evans. E-gold® employees present during the search recognized that the Special Agents' comments and questions were "out of the ordinary" and, at that time, made notes to memorialize their fresh recollection of these interactions.

During the same visits, Special Agent Sherri Dunlop also made a casual inquiry to Dr. Jackson regarding e-gold's would-be competitor GoldMoney. As Jackson later related: "Her question was along the line of 'Doesn't James Turk's Goldmoney system do the same thing as e-gold?' I pointed out that it was different, noting that e-gold Ltd. itself neither received nor made money payments or transfers of value in any form from/to customers."[330]

That same Friday, December 16th, a group of government Chevy Suburbans, transporting more than a dozen FBI and Secret Service Special Agents, executed another Search Warrant nearby at the Jackson family home. The local media was quick to report that the U.S. Department of Justice nicknamed the e-gold® investigation "Operation Goldwire."

Government agents took the hard drives of every computer at the G&SR offices (over fifty computers) and more than one-hundred boxes of paper files (approximately 288,000 pages). At Jackson's residence, agents seized such significant evidence as family members' birth certificates, vintage family photos, and even the Jackson family burial plot deed.

At the Orlando co-location facility, USSS technicians took the e-gold® and OmniPay websites offline as they proceeded to clone the hard drives of each database server. Special Agents assured Jackson the outage would be brief. However, on Saturday morning, over twelve hours later, the sites remained offline, and Jackson drove to Orlando to take a first-hand look. As Jackson related:

> I approached the technicians and chatted them up without identifying myself, allowing them to assume I was just another customer or tech with servers in the facility. I inquired with words to the effect of 'Wow, looks like a big job!' They responded along the lines of 'There's terabytes of data here! We had no idea there was so much. We had to break into shifts to avoid all of us doing an all-nighter. And indeed, I got the impression the USSS, despite whatever investigation they had done, was completely unaware that the e-gold system retained all data, dating back to when the system went online in 1996. It was only a few months later that I learned this was unique among payment systems. In the September 2006 Congressional Hearing regarding the progress of the FCACP, I discovered that Paypal and the credit card banks deleted transaction data as soon as the law allowed, which was somewhere in the 12-18 month range. But anyway, altogether the e-gold site ended up being offline for over 18 hours.[331]

[330] Jackson, Douglas. "Chunk 4." Received by Carl Mullan, *Chunk 4*, 27 Feb. 2020. DJ redlines 4.pdf

However, the precious metal bullion, backing customers' digital accounts, remained intact, stored in secure vaults. Throughout these 2005 events, the government seized no precious metal, made no arrests, and charged no one with a crime.

The launch of Operation Goldwire would ultimately mark the beginning of a significant long-term offensive against co-founders Douglas Jackson and Barry Downey. The outcome and legacy of these events would motivate the government to change U.S. Financial Regulations. Ironically, the day of the raids was also the day that e-gold's new multi-core processor hardware arrived at the Melbourne offices.

♦

A Few Days After the e-gold Warranted Search

The e-gold raids took place Friday, December 16th, and the servers remained offline through most of Saturday. Because both e-gold.com and Omnipay.com websites were down, Jackson could not announce or explanation the service interruption. But on Saturday afternoon, Jackson received a call on his cell with caller ID indicating it was from Brian Grow. Smelling a rat, Jackson let it go to voicemail. Sure enough, Grow left a message seeking comment, meaning he'd heard rumors of a federal law enforcement raid on e-gold.

After a second similar voicemail on Sunday, Jackson consulted the other Directors and determined to take steps to prevent any public announcement or disclosure of the 'raid' by either company. Grow was working in cooperation with the USSS, and Jackson wanted to preclude any fig leaf that might enable Grow to pose as if his knowledge of the raid came from the companies. Jackson and Downey coordinated with the handful of staff members aware of the event to prevent disclosure and flush Grow into the open.

After yet another voicemail from Grow, Wednesday, his fifth attempt, Grow sent the following email. Jackson did not respond.

-------- Original Message --------
Subject: Secret Service/FBI visit Dec. 19/Nevis corporate registration for e-Gold Ltd.
Date: Wed, 21 Dec 2005 15:08:03 -0500
From:"Grow, Brian \(Businessweek \)" <xxxxxxx@businessweek.com>
To:<djackson@e-gold.com>, <djackson@omnipay.com>
CC:<bcunningham@omnipay.com>, <xxxxxx@mfuerstlaw.com>
Doug –
Per my call earlier this afternoon, we would like to get your responses to the

following questions regarding recent events and information pertaining to e-Gold and its related entities:

Secret Service/FBI visit of Dec. 19 –

1. We understand that the Secret Service and FBI, in a joint operation, visited your home and the G&SR office on Dec. 19. We understand that the agents took paper and computer files. In addition, they froze certain bank accounts and seized some funds. Is this correct? What files did they specifically take? What bank accounts did they freeze? What $ value of funds did they seize?

2. The affidavits for search warrants in the case are sealed to date. What other items did the Secret Service and FBI seek during their visits?

3. Did the FBI or Secret Service indicate why they served search warrants on the G&SR office and your home? Did they indicate that the search was the precursor to any indictment of G&SR, e-Gold and its operators?

4. Do you or G&SR or any of its entities intend to contest the freezing of bank accounts or seizure of assets? If so, when is that hearing scheduled to occur and in what court?

5. What is your comment regarding the Secret Service and FBI visits? Were they warranted?

Nevis corporate registration for e-Gold Ltd. –

1. Regulators in Nevis informed BusinessWeek that, in fact, e-Gold Ltd. was struck from the company registry there in July 2003 for failure to pay annual registration dues. The company has not, they say, been a registered Nevis company since then. Were you aware of this? What happened?

2. Further, regulators in Nevis informed BusinessWeek that they put out an announcement on their web site --
http://www.nevisfinance.com/Announcements.cfm?Idz=4&MIdz=36 – on Dec. 5th, warning that e-gold.com contains "inaccurate and misleading information" as to its legal status. They cite the statements on your web site that e-Gold Ltd. is a Nevis company and governed by Nevis law. Were you aware of this?

3. Why did e-Gold continue to advertise itself as a Nevis company if it was not registered there for more than two years?

4. How does this affect jurisdiction for e-Gold's account user agreement when law enforcement seeks data?

Thanks for your earliest reply. Our deadline is this Friday, December 23.
Regards, Brian
Correspondent, BusinessWeek Atlanta bureau

Grow's questions were so precise, it was obvious that he had been coached by Special Agents about the government's activity. After receiving Grow's inquiring email, Jackson emailed his lawyer.

From: Douglas Jackson [mailto:djackson@OmniPay.com]
Sent: Thursday, December 22, 2005 9:13 AM
To: Mitchell Fuerst; Barry Downey
Subject: [Fwd: Secret Service/FBI visit Dec. 19/Nevis corporate registration for e-Gold Ltd.]
The assertions in item #1 did not come from our company or anyone in our circle of correspondents. This journalist and his publication could only have heard such an assertion from government sources. To me it seems improper for the government to use the press in this fashion, as an adjunct to their direct intervention, apparently in order to undermine public confidence in e-gold and purposely damage our revenue base.

Grow went ahead and published his article detailing the raid, apparently having decided no one would care enough to recognize he was acting as the USSS's mouthpiece.

♦

On December 27, 2005, Gold & Silver Reserve, Inc. filed a petition to vacate the freeze on its bank accounts, and lawyers moved for an emergency hearing on its request.

It is worth noting that the court was under no obligation to grant such a hearing. The English common law precedent known as habeas corpus protects a person from being arrested and held in the absence of a hearing and arraignment on criminal charges. The arrest of physical goods, in contrast, derives from British Admiralty laws dating back to the reign of Queen Anne, which does not require any hearing until forfeiture proceedings are undertaken, which may be months after the seizure.

In this case, however, the request for an emergency hearing was immediately granted, for reasons that became clear when Judge Facciola expressed his indignation at the government's tactics.

Two days later, on the 29th, an emergency hearing took place in D.C. District Court, with Magistrate Judge John Facciola. During the emergency hearing, Magistrate Judge Facciola stated that, when seeking the original search warrant, he believed government lawyers had initially deceived him with their ex parte allegations of probable cause. In a

2017 letter to John Roth, Jackson discussed this deception.

> The pattern of misleading the court that I allege in this document was first evident in relation to the December 2005 asset seizures and search warrant that preceded the indictment. It is my belief—evidenced by the remarks of Magistrate Judge Facciola at an emergency hearing on December 29, 2005, in which he expressed indignation and outrage at the willful deceit of the government attorneys—that the government attorneys knowingly misled him in their allegations of probable cause. At the outset of the hearing, speaking of the government's application for the search and seizure warrants, Magistrate Judge Facciola related (Exhibit 39):

> "In the ordinary course I would review it on the spot and sign it or not sign it. But in that particular instance I immediately expressed to Mr. Cowan [sic Cowden] my concern with this matter, because it seemed to be a quite unusual matter," going on to relate "I anticipated a day like today would come."

> As the hearing proceeded, Judge Facciola, speaking of "the representations that were made to me with the search warrant" reprimanded Ms. Peretti's associate, Laurel Rimon, "This was part of an investigation into what I was told was related to a child pornography ring, and that this money was being used. It never occurred to me in my wildest dreams, until counsel explained it to me, that far from operating surreptitiously, there have been negotiations with this company and the Internal Revenue Service as to the precise issue you raise about transmitting money and being subject to that statute, the Bank Secrecy Act. That's not true."[332]

Kimberly Keifer Peretti, a lawyer working for the Criminal Division of the Department of Justice, was one of the two lawyers that appeared in court on behalf of the government.

Before the judge, and also in their petition, e-gold's lawyers argued strenuously that their client's operation was not a "money transmitting business" and that, as a result of the government freezing the funds, their client's business came to a virtual standstill. Counsel also indicated that the lack of customer access severely harmed users. Finally, the Defendants stated for the Court, that they had willingly responded and fulfilled numerous information requests from government agencies regarding the nature and appropriate regulation of their unique type of business.[333] These organizations included the Commodity

[332] Jackson, Douglas. "Investigation Request." Received by John Roth, Inspector General, US Dept. of Homeland Security, 24 Aug. 2017, Indian Harbour Beach, FL.
[333] Case 1:05-cv-02497-RMC. *UNITED STATES OF AMERICA v. ALL FUNDS SEIZED FROM OR ON DEPOSIT IN*

Futures Trading Commission and the Internal Revenue Service.

In this emergency hearing, the Defendants' lawyers disclosed that G&SR also had engaged in dialog with agents of the U.S. Treasury regarding possible licensing of the e-gold® business.

Nevertheless, at that hearing, Judge Facciola ruled that he lacked authority to revoke the search and seizure warrants. Shortly after this hearing, Facciola turned the case over to Chief Judge Hogan for procedural determination. The dice were cast.

G&SR had previously made a formal request during Spring 2005 for the IRS SB/SE Division to conduct a Bank Secrecy Act Compliance examination. This review could have determined a possible basis for regulating the company's activity. These facts and others showed that Gold & Silver Reserve executives had been openly talking with government agents and regulatory agencies about the future direction and possible licensing of e-gold's digital currency business.

The Verified Complaint for Forfeiture and Warrant of Arrest in Rem was filed the following day on December 30, 2005. This follow-up legal action, telegraphed the government's intent to snatch e-gold's precious metal bullion reserves. This was the DOJ's "money grab." Government lawyers repeated their claims that under 18 U.S.C. § 981(a)(l)(A), the property "Involved" in a transaction in violation of 18 U.S.C. § 1960 was subject to forfeiture, and that, under 18 U.S.C. § 981(b)(2), the government had a right to seize it using a warrant issued according to the Federal Rules of Criminal Procedure. The government also argued that neither defendants' business nor their clients were being prejudiced in the manner alleged. The government further indicated that they intended to file a civil complaint within thirty days.

This early point in the criminal case, did not illustrate a deductive process, where the government claims that a crime has been committed and moves forward to prosecute. No, this stage in the e-gold case illustrates an inductive process, where the government identified what assets to seize, and only later would Prosecutors attempt to build a criminal case. The e-gold case was an unmistakable instance of the tail wagging the dog.

♦

The Internal Revenue Service Investigation

In 2004, Deenanauth P. Ganesh was a duly commissioned Revenue Agent employed in the Small Business/Self Employed Division of Area 5 of the office of the area manager of

SUNTRUST ACCOUNT NUMBER 1000028078359, IN THE NAME OF GOLD AND SILVER RESERVE, INC. AND ALL FUNDS ON DEPOSIT IN REGIONS BANK ACCOUNT NUMBER 67-0919-4851, IN THE NAME OF GOLD AND SILVER RESERVE, INC. . CLAIMANT GOLD & SILVER RESERVE, INC.'s FIRST NOTICE OF FILING IN PARALLEL PROCEEDINGS , 2 Feb. 2006.

the Internal Revenue Service in Melbourne, Florida. (Badge #59-06970)

In February 2004, Revenue Officer Examiner Ganesh was seeking to inspect relevant tax records and determine the correct federal tax liabilities of the Jackson Trading Company and Gold & Silver Reserve, Inc. for the taxable years 1999, 2000, and 2001 along with Douglas L. Jackson for the taxable years January 1, 1999, through December 31, 2000.

On February 2, 2004, both Jackson and Downey were served with summons requesting their appearance to testify and produce books, records, and other documents identified in the IRS request. The meeting took place on March 9, 2004; Jackson and Downey appeared as directed, gave testimony, and produced records. However, Examiner Ganesh determined that the men failed to produce some of the documents requested by the government's summonses. Agent Ganesh claimed that the following items were not present and that the respondents had refused to comply with the summonses.

- Records and testimony concerning the e-gold system
- Financial transactions concerning the flow of funds
- Identities of customers[334]

Court records reveal an aggressive IRS approach to uncover identifying personal and financial information on all e-gold® users. The following text is from Attachment "B" to the IRS request for e-gold® customer information.

To include but not limited to:
1. All records maintained for each e-gold subscriber account for the period January 1, 1999 through December 31, 2001 including but not limited to records that reflect the following information:
- Name
- Address
- Length of service
- Logon username
- Account Number
- Source of payment including any credit card or bank account number
- Records of any payments made on the subscribers behalf

---

[334] CLAIMANT GOLD & SILVER RESERVE, INC.'s FIRST NOTICE OF FILING IN PARALLEL PROCEEDINGS . *UNITED STATES OF AMERICA v. Barry K. Downey, Director, Jackson Trading Company; Douglas L. Jackson, President, Jackson Trading Company; Barry K. Downey, Director, Gold & Silver Reserve, Inc.; Douglas L. Jackson, President, Gold & Silver Reserve, Inc.; Barry K. Downey; and, Douglas L. Jackson;* Case 1:05-cv-02497-RMC Document 9-2, 2 Feb. 2006.

- Records of income earned from each transaction

2. Communications and records of communications related to the accounts identified in item #1 here in above for the period January 1, 1999 through December 31, 2001.[335]

However, Jackson & Downey had cited the e-gold® Customer User Agreement and, while ready to comply with lawful requests regarding specific customers, refused to allow a fishing expedition. They did not provide the IRS with open information about e-gold's entire customer base – millions of people who had not been accused of any wrongdoing. In the Court filing, Agent Ganesh stated:

> The testimony and documents sought by the above-described summons are not presently in the possession of the Internal Revenue Service. The taxpayer has refused to produce the database of its customer records citing its user agreement that states customer records will not be disclosed unless ordered by a court of law. Records of communications between the taxpayer and its customers were not produced.[336]

In addition to requesting details about e-gold® customers, the IRS asked for a large number of items directly related to the operation of e-gold®, Gold & Silver Reserve, Inc., and other associated entities. April 2004, documents also reflected that there had not been a DOJ criminal referral regarding tax matters. "There is no "Justice Department referral," in effect with respect to Respondent or any other persons whose tax liability is at issue with regard to this summons for the tax years 1999, 2000 and 2001, as that term is defined in 26 U.S.C. § 7602(d)."[337]

Seeking to obtain the missing e-gold® documentation, on June 13, 2005, a trial attorney for the U.S. DOJ Tax Division named Robert L. Welsh filed a Petition to Enforce the February IRS Summonses. Welsh asked the court for the following:

> WHEREFORE, the petitioner respectfully prays:
> 1. That the Court issue an order directing the respondents to show cause, if any, why they should not fully comply with the aforementioned summons;
> 2. That the Court enter an order directing the respondents to appear before Revenue Officer Ganesh or any other proper officer of the Internal Revenue Service and provide the testimony and produce the books, papers, records, and other data identified by the summons at such time and place as may be fixed by Revenue

---

[335] Ibid
[336] Ibid
[337] Ibid

Officer Ganesh or any other proper officer of the Internal Revenue Service; and
3. That the Court grant such other and further relief as is just and proper.
PAUL I. PEREZ
United States Attorney
ROBERT L. WELSH
Trial Attorney, Tax Division, U.S. Department of Justice[338]

On July 7, 2005, the Court granted this Petition to Enforce the February IRS Summonses. On August 15, 2005, the Court compelled the respondents to appear, give testimony, and produce certain documents required by the IRS. Following the Court's request, all parties engaged in good faith efforts to allow the Petitioner to enforce and the Respondents to comply with the terms of the order. The parties scheduled meetings in Melbourne on November 21, 2005, and December 5, 2005. However, due to scheduling conflicts on the part of both parties, those meetings were canceled. The parties scheduled another meeting to take place in Melbourne, Florida, on January 9, 2006.

Ironically, on December 16, 2005, following its receipt of an affidavit prepared by U.S. Secret Service Special Agent Roy Dotson, the same Court signed a Search Warrant for the offices of G&SR Inc., DBA OmniPay. On December 16, 2005, USSS Special Agents executed the Search Warrant at the location mentioned above. During the execution of the search warrant at the G&SR's offices, government agents removed every paper, folder, and file that was present. The confiscated files and documents included all of the materials that G&SR had compiled ahead of their IRS meeting.

Because there were no documents in the GS&R offices after the execution of the search warrant, G&SR couldn't comply with the Court's August 15, 2005 order producing any records for the IRS. Consequently, the parties canceled the January 9, 2006, IRS meeting. The warranted seizures had left Jackson and Downey no possible means of meeting in good faith with the IRS to resolve the ongoing matter. In Court documents, G&SR's attorney explained the irony of their current situation.

> As the direct and natural result of the execution of the Search Warrant in Case No. 05-M-3201, all of the documentation that the IRS sought through its Petition to Enforce Internal Revenue Service Summonses is *already* within the possession of the IRS.[339]

---

[338] CLAIMANT GOLD & SILVER RESERVE, INC.'s FIRST NOTICE OF FILING IN PARALLEL PROCEEDINGS . *UNITED STATES OF AMERICA v. Barry K. Downey, Director, Jackson Trading Company; Douglas L. Jackson, President, Jackson Trading Company; Barry K. Downey, Director, Gold & Silver Reserve, Inc.; Douglas L. Jackson, President, Gold & Silver Reserve, Inc.; Barry K. Downey; and, Douglas L. Jackson;* Case 1:05-cv-02497-RMC Document 9-2, 2 Feb. 2006.

The G&SR attorney's asked the Court to vacate the Consent Order because the seizure had rendered compliance with the Order impossible.

♦

The Government's End Game

> Asset forfeiture is a powerful tool used by law enforcement agencies, including the FBI, against criminals and criminal organizations to deprive them of their ill-gotten gains through seizure of these assets. -FBI.gov [340]

> [...]the ability to generate revenue is a significant motivator of police forfeiture activity, lending weight to critics' claims that law enforcement agencies use forfeiture to police for profit. -Institute for Justice [341]

Forfeited assets, such as gold bullion and large bank accounts, are the government's reward for successful criminal prosecutions. The U.S. policy of confiscating criminal assets to control crime and recover illicit wealth occupies a central position in America's courts. Governments understand that disrupting illegal activity requires depriving the bad guys of their criminal profits. Prosecutors share this nugget of wisdom, "by seizing valuable assets associated with a crime, the bad actors have no incentive to engage in illegal activity." This process is how modern U.S. law works.

Any federal defendant, attempting to navigate an asset forfeiture case, will be thrust into a complicated and expensive legal process. In simple terms, the Court Asset Seizure results in the defendant's lack of access to their daily operating funds. If available, a Defendant could use this money to pay for a more robust legal defense. Consequently, the government moves a Defendant's money out of the legal equation and the Prosecution team benefits greatly. The legal and technical difficulties of fighting a federal court asset seizure are staggering.

It is also important to understand that Prosecutors can selectively choose which cases to prosecute. The value of a possible asset forfeiture can shape the government's decision. Choosing one case over another can be influenced by the size of the forfeiture and not the seriousness of the crime.

---

[339] Ibid

[340] FBI. "Asset Forfeiture." *FBI*, FBI, 29 Mar. 2017, www.fbi.gov/investigate/white-collar-crime/asset-forfeiture.

[341] Kelly, Brian D. "Fighting Crime or Raising Revenue?" *Institute for Justice*, Institute for Justice, June 2019, ij.org/report/fighting-crime-or-raising-revenue/.

It was no accident that the USSS along with Prosecutors targeted e-gold® and G&SR. The potential asset seizures, including the business bank accounts and precious metal, were substantial. Some observers contend that government Prosecutors initiated the e-gold® seizures and only later developed their criminal case later. Details and documents uncovered years after the e-gold® case closed, clearly show that DOJ lawyers hurriedly changed the Defendant's jurisdiction from Florida to Washington, D.C.

◆

2006

2006 began on an ugly note for e-gold® with Brian Grow's January 8ᵗʰ Businessweek article entitled *Gold Rush.* He announced, *"Online payment systems like e-gold Ltd. are becoming the currency of choice for cybercrooks."* Despite a lengthy and open interview with Jackson, the article was   overwhelmingly negative. The piece landed a sharp knife in Jackson's back. Grow's written words, no doubt coached by government agents, viciously attacked e-gold® and its co-founders. As the new year began, bad news, bad press, and manipulation of the truth enveloped the e-gold® business. Despite clear public responses by Jackson through the e-gold blog, the company was hammered by the media.

In this Businessweek Investigative Report[342] by Brian Grow, the following inaccurate information appeared in the first paragraph.

> e-gold is a "digital currency." Opening an account at www.e-gold.com takes only a few clicks of a mouse. Customers can use a false name if they like because no one checks. With a credit card or wire transfer, a user buys units of e-gold. Those units can then be transferred with a few more clicks to anyone else with an e-gold account. For the recipient, cashing out - changing e-gold back to regular money - is just as convenient and often just like anonymous.[343]

However, one critical point that could not be hidden, came shining through the muck. The section of the article that discussed current U.S. financial regulation included this notably truthful statement. As late as 2006, the e-gold business was not operating illegally nor was it overstepping any existing U.S. financial regulation.

---

[342] Gold Rush, By Brian Grow, with John Cady, Susann Rutledge, and David Polek, BusinessWeek, Monday, January 9, 2006 original link http://www.businessweek.com/magazine/content/06_02/b3966094.htm
[343] Ibid

Federal officials reluctantly confirm this loophole: e-gold and other digital currencies do not neatly fit the definition of financial institutions covered by existing self-monitoring rules established under the Bank Secrecy Act and the US Patriot Act. "It's not like it's regulated by someone else, it's not regulated," says Mark Rasch, senior vice president of Internet Security firm Solutionary Inc. and former head of the Justice Dept.'s computer crime unit. The Treasury Dept.'s Financial Crime Enforcement Network (FinCEN) is studying ways to close the regulatory gap. Meanwhile, US officials say e-gold and similar companies should voluntarily do more to deter crime.[344]

♦

During his earlier interview with Brian Grow, Jackson made a statement that Grow directly quoted in the January *Gold Rush* article. Jackson said, "We want e-gold® to be recognized as a privately issued currency and to be treated as a foreign currency by the U.S. and other governments." [345]

Furthermore, the idea of a gold-based currency seemed natural. A monumental legal change in regulations for e-gold® may have enabled G&SR to register as a legal currency exchange and fit neatly into the government's existing financial landscape.

However, the government had no intention of categorizing e-gold®, or any other private digital product, as "currency" under the Code of Federal Regulations (CRF). On January 12, 2006, the United States Department of the Treasury released its 2005 U.S. Money Laundering Threat Assessment. This annual report is the product of an inter-agency working group composed of financial experts from various U.S. Government agencies and organizations. The group's ambitious purpose is to find effective ways for the U.S. government to combat money laundering. This document reaffirmed the government's interpretation of CRF currency definitions.

♦

Jackson was quick to respond to Grow's Businessweek article and posted this open letter on the e-gold® website.[346]

---

[344] Ibid

[345] Gold Rush, By Brian Grow, with John Cady, Susann Rutledge, and David Polek, BusinessWeek, Monday, January 9, 2006 original link http://www.businessweek.com/magazine/content/06_02/b3966094.htm

[346] Jackson, Douglas. *"Letter from Dr. Douglas Jackson; Chairman, e-gold, Ltd." Letter from Dr. Douglas Jackson; Chairman, e-gold, Ltd.*, e-gold.com, Jan. 2006, web.archive.org/web/20060304203545if_/http://www.e-gold.com:80/letter.html.

January 2006
e-gold® founder responds to slanderous Business Week article
Letter from Dr. Douglas Jackson; Chairman, e-gold, Ltd.

e-gold® has recently been the subject of a slanderous and unfounded article in Business Week. e-gold® strongly refutes the allegations and presumptions of this article. The article chose to focus through anecdote and suspicion only on an exception - criminal abuse - and ignores the overwhelming majority of e-gold® usage. It also fails to note that all online payment mechanisms including credit cards and intermediaries such as PayPal are targeted by criminals, likely at a much greater magnitude than e-gold®, and fails to relate the very proactive steps e-gold® takes to eliminate any criminal behavior involving e-gold®.

e-gold® and its Operator, Gold & Silver Reserve (G&SR®), including G&SR's exchange service OmniPay® in cooperation with the United States Government and pursuant to a lawfully issued written request, did allow an examination of the e-gold® and OmniPay computer systems and data. The examination occurred on December 16th after normal business hours so as to avoid disrupting access to the system. The examination utilized the full resources of e-gold's system and prevented customer access. We were told by the government examiners that the outage would be for a few hours, however, due to the volume of data maintained by e-gold® for its customers' protection, a surprise to the examiners, the examination occupied e-gold's computing capacity for 36 hours. e-gold® apologizes for any inconvenience of the system down time caused by the government's request. No charges have been filed against e-gold®, G&SR, OmniPay or any of its principals.

e-gold® operates legally and does not condone persons attempting to use e-gold® for criminal activity. e-gold® has a long history of cooperation with law enforcement agencies in the US and worldwide, providing data and investigative assistance in response to lawful requests.

I'm proud of what we have accomplished so far with e-gold®. e-gold®, now in its 10th year online, is growing exponentially because of a network effect, a global cascade of Users telling their friends who then tell their friends. For the first time since our launch in 1996, this growth is providing the revenue and resources needed for e-gold® to accelerate technical development and other refinements to make it more reliable and even less hospitable to those who would seek to abuse it.

We are processing the same volume of transactions and growing at the same exponential pace that PayPal was in the second quarter of 2000. One difference, though, is that they had to give away $tens of millions of their investors' money to build a critical mass of user balances and were continuing a burn rate of about $10 million per month during this period. Altogether they burned through about $275 million of capital losses before their IPO.

e-gold®, in contrast, lacking significant outside investment:

- has attained a circulation larger than Canada's official gold reserves (currently 3.46 metric tonnes of gold, equivalent to about $55 million at current exchange rates).
- has web traffic surpassing etrade.com and citi.com and is neck and neck with kitco.com as the most heavily trafficked gold related site on the Web
- settles 50 to 60 thousand user-to-user payments per day, a daily value of about $10 million
- has active Users in every country, (including more than 150,000 in China) despite our lack so far of foreign language versions - a high priority on our to-do list

e-gold® is the only payment mechanism that is truly global, enabling any merchant to accept payment online even if the payer lives in a third world country, has no credit card, or is perhaps 'unbanked' altogether.

e-gold® enables the migrant worker of modest means to send value back to his family in Mexico or Bangladesh at a fraction of the cost of conventional international remittance mechanisms. e-gold® alone is free of chargeback risk, yet the fee for receiving payment in e-gold® is a tiny fraction of those charged by any other systems.

Thanks to e-gold®, for the first time in history, normal people of modest means worldwide have the option of using currency that is designed from the ground up to be immune to debasement, with a governance model that precludes even its management and founders from having the power to subvert it.

Gold & Silver Reserve has been operating for over nine years. Seeking to comply with every applicable law, G&SR has reached out to the Government dozens of times, has repeatedly met with officials from the Internal Revenue Service, the FBI, SEC and a variety of other Federal agencies, and has been told – in no uncertain terms – that we were operating legally and in full compliance with all laws, rules and regulations. Additionally, the Government has requested from us – on more than three hundred occasions – information regarding individuals it believed to be lawbreakers. Gold & Silver Reserve complied with every single request in a professional and timely fashion. Numerous Government officials have gone so far as to commend us in writing for our efforts in complying with their requests and aiding them in their investigations.

Very recently, however, the Government concluded that it was unable to "regulate" our business under any current statutes or regulations. Rather than moving Congress to enact legislation, the Government apparently chose to undertake to regulate us under pre-existing statutes which are totally and utterly inapplicable to our business. To do so, the case the Government brought against Gold & Silver Reserve centered around false statements and fabrications made to a Magistrate Judge in Washington , D.C. A week later, when challenged by that Judge, the Government, fearing it would lose its case filed a second suit against Gold & Silver Reserve. We are now addressing that action and are confident that we will be victorious in a very short time.

Both OmniPay and e-gold® have been substantially harmed. Both sites were off-line altogether for 36 hours - an interval during which we were at a loss to know what to announce or even how to announce it. There were other direct interventions as well that I am not yet at liberty to discuss that nearly crippled OmniPay's ability to honor its obligations to and on behalf of users. The worst effect of course is on our reputation. This irresponsible smear piece will surely impair our efforts to build strategic relationships with the host of businesses and individuals that would benefit from an embrace of e-gold®.

Let me be very clear, e-gold® in no manner condones persons or organizations attempting to use e-gold® to support criminal acts. The exact opposite is true. e-gold® limits accounts that are suspect of illicit activity and has a long history of cooperation with law enforcement agencies.

There are two elements that make e-gold® about the dumbest choice a criminal could make if seeking to obfuscate a money trail or otherwise hide the proceeds of crime.

225

- it is impossible for a general user of e-gold® to send/add money (value in any form) into the system... he can only get e-gold® by receiving an e-gold® Spend from someone who already has some.
- there's a permanent record of all transfers, that is, a permanent record of the entire lineage of every particle of value in the e-gold® system.

There is nothing "anonymous and untraceable" about e-gold®. e-gold® Spends settle by book entry - it isn't so-called "digital cash".

e-gold® is not about crime. e-gold® is not a hospitable environment for criminals. e-gold® maintains an efficient and highly capable investigative staff to aid in the identification, apprehension and prosecution of any criminal abusing the system. Our staff has participated in hundreds of investigations supporting the FBI, FTC, IRS, DEA, SEC, USPS, and others. This is the reality of every payment system, the need to aid in rooting out criminal abuse, whether it is child pornographers taking advantage of the multiple layers and indirection of credit card middlemen, or smurfs aggregating cash via international remittance processors or even state lotteries.

e-gold® has taken a proactive approach, reaching out to law enforcement agencies and NGO's (Non-Governmental Organization) to foster closer cooperation in combating crime online. For example, e-gold® is a charter member of the Financial Coalition to eradicate Child Pornography, organized by the National Center for Missing and Exploited Children, along with Visa, MasterCard, Microsoft, AOL, PayPal, First Data and some of the major banks.

I hope to have additional and useful facts shortly and will communicate them when appropriate. I can assure you e-gold® is up and running, supporting its customers, and continuing to grow.
Dr. Douglas Jackson[347]

On January 20, 2006, Jackson published an astonishing notice on the e-gold® website, regarding the company's ongoing investigation by the federal government.[348]

[347] Jackson, Douglas. "*Letter from Dr. Douglas Jackson; Chairman, e-gold, Ltd.*" *Letter from Dr. Douglas Jackson; Chairman, e-gold, Ltd.*, e-gold.com, Jan. 2006, web.archive.org/web/20060304203545if_/http://www.e-gold.com:80/letter.html.

[348] Jackson, Douglas. "e-gold® Welcomes US Government Review of Its Status as a Privately Issued Currency." *e-gold*, e-gold.com, 20 Jan. 2006, web.archive.org/web/20060322134922if_/https://www.e-gold.com/letter2.html.

e-gold® welcomes US Government review of its status as a privately issued currency

Starting in mid-December 2005, Gold & Silver Reserve, Inc. (G&SR), contractual Operator and primary dealer for e-gold®, has been the subject of a warranted search of its premises and records, had its domestic bank accounts frozen, and been the target of a precisely timed, extraordinarily misleading attack by a major business publication.

In an emergency hearing in US District Court January 13, 2006, the freeze order on G&SR's bank accounts was lifted. Though numerous criminal claims had been made in obtaining the search and seizure warrants, the Government has not sustained these allegations and the only remaining claim is a contention that G&SR has operated as a currency exchange without the proper license. G&SR had previously proposed to the Government that e-gold® be classified for regulatory purposes as a currency, enabling G&SR to register as a currency exchange. In a Treasury report released January 11, 2006, however, the Department of Treasury reaffirmed their interpretation of the USC and CFR definitions of currency as excluding e-gold®.

G&SR, for nearly a year, has been engaged with an agency of Treasury in a BSA (Bank Secrecy Act) compliance examination it had voluntarily initiated. G&SR, though preferring that the venue was not a courtroom, welcomes the opportunity to extend its discussions with the Government on how best to achieve appropriate statutory or regulatory cognizance of e-gold while continuing to build e-gold's market share as a medium of international commerce.

Despite the unfounded charges and adverse misleading publicity that have severely damaged both e-gold® and G&SR, G&SR has continued to meet all financial obligations and remain completely operational. e-gold® remains highly committed to its goal of bringing, for the first time in history, to people of any financial means across the globe, a secure payment mechanism at a fraction of the cost of any other system. e-gold® fully expects to transcend the unfortunate events of the past month and resume its exponential growth.[349]

◆

---

[349] Ibid

Beginning in January 2006, online auction leader, eBay changed its customer terms of service. These new rules stated that the only method of payment accepted through eBay auctions was PayPal. Accompanying this news, eBay published a list of alternative payment methods, the company would no longer permit in the online auction house. This list included e-gold®. Later that week, several articles surfaced, referencing the fact that all e-gold® transactions were final. In the case of non-delivery by an eBay seller, the finality of e-gold® transactions extended no consumer protection.

♦

Tracking Carders

Any e-gold user's activity would irreversibly link that user to other e-gold accounts. Who got paid, when, by whom, how much, and any other notes left by the users could later be uncovered. By mid-January 2006, e-gold® had installed the upgraded hardware, and Jackson was very busy with in-house text searches of the e-gold® customer database. Jackson stated:

> I didn't resume direct investigative activity myself until 2006 when we found the Rosetta stone for detecting and tracing carders (after we installed multi-core processors in the database server – I have the emails time stamping that event). Since we had no legal cover for that work (we were repeatedly promised a pen register type writ, but never received it) he preferred not to act in what amounted to violation of our User Agreement so I took that on myself. He[e-gold's head of investigations] continued to handle all the subpoena and court order work while I spent over 500 hours on investigative work in 2006.[350]

If he discovered a slang carder term, the e-gold® account would be marked (flagged or tagged) accordingly, and in-house investigators could later examine all linked accounts. Just like touching a spider web, this in-house investigating could potentially identify entire criminal networks; if such activity existed. Jackson was still unsure if this process would lead to any potential illegal activity.

Much to Jackson's surprise, the full database search for slang terms such as "dumps," "fullz," "COB," and "CVV" revealed a web-like network of e-gold® accounts containing these slang phrases.

While the vast majority of e-gold® accounts and users had nothing to do with carding,

---

[350] Jackson, Douglas. "Re: Attached for Short Important Read." Received by Carl Mullan, *Re: Attached for Short Important Read*, 13 Feb. 2019.

Jackson discovered that a small subset of accounts contained the target words and terms. Those small clusters offered a jackpot of carder information. Realizing how this treasure trove of potential illegal information might help identify and prosecute carders, in January 2006, Jackson undertook to engage with law enforcement for a more coordinated investigation. Jackson first reached out to an investigative contact at Visa Inc. he knew from their joint participation in the Financial Coalition Against Child Pornography (FCACP). This organization had formed in the summer 2005 and e-gold was a founding member. The first suggestion, from his Visa associate, was to reach out to USSS Special Agent Wayne Peterson. On January 24, 2006, Jackson emailed Peterson:

> "Wayne,
> Eric Sites of Sunbelt Software gave me a lead this morning for a trojan kit that targets various online payment systems including e-gold®, something called 'rat systems'.
> On my first pass looking for this bad guy's tracks in the e-gold® database, I found what seems to be a ring of people selling/buying cc data, cobs, ebay log-ins etc. The query results I'm looking at are chock full of hacker nyms, email addresses they use, (in some cases) their icq, plus beaucoup of our normal traffic/transaction analysis data. This data, in the context of an iterative interaction with law enforcement, could nail not only the seller of stolen cc data but also the cohort of people who are buying the stuff from him/her/them.
> We should talk to figure out best wording for a subpoena so it is broad enough to chase the bunny trails. This may well also be an instance where monitoring and a well-timed sting would be productive.
> Our general service-of-process instruction is pasted below. Please note particularly to cc fax the order to the 321 number as well [avoids delay as the official version makes its way through channels]."[351]

Initially, this USSS Special Agent responded enthusiastically:

> "Dr. Jackson,
> Thanks for your call earlier and the email. I have made contact with our guys at HQ and they will be in contact with you or your staff concerning this matter.
> Thanks again!
> Wayne"[352]

[351] Jackson, Douglas. "DJ Redlines 4." Received by Carl Mullan, DJ Redlines 4, 27 Feb. 2020.
[352] Ibid

Ready to help, Jackson followed up:

"Wayne

We have continued our investigation into this ring and are finding that they are substantial, with participants in Canada, Germany, Indonesia, Israel, Russia, Ukraine, Sweden, Estonia, US, Lithuania, Macedonia, Poland, Romania. Many of them are presumably experts in identity theft but by working in conjunction with e-gold exchange providers around the world we have already succeeded in nailing down several confirmed physical addresses and bank accounts that the perps control. [We've also identified one of their more catchy names which would sound sexy in the press and might suffice for phrasing the subpoena]. For the moment we're concentrating on traffic analysis identifying account activity since confirmation of meatspace locations/connections is somewhat more labor intensive.

If this is handled properly it also appears that significant asset recoveries are possible. They don't hold much value in e-gold but appear to have substantial deposits in Bank of America and WebMoney. We have also identified an entity they are using for apparent ML who is certain to have reams of physical addresses because he has helped them buy physical consumer goods which had to be shipped. He is also one of their portals to BoA and MoneyGram.

I need a lead law enforcement agency. For the moment we have not blocked/expelled the group. Once we take action under our Right of Association there will be no loss of data—e-gold and reputable exchange providers who deal in e-gold keep permanent records—but once they know we're on to them the assets currently being held in banks are probably at risk of being dispersed."

However, shortly after that email, Special Agent Peterson went silent. Jackson explained:

As was the norm with our efforts to engage with the USSS, when he escalated the matter to his superiors, they apparently read him in on the agency policy of not working with us. A dead end. But then my Visa contact mentioned another possibility – a familiar name, a Postal Inspector of the US Postal Inspection Service with whom I'd worked in an investigation back in 2000.[353]

◆

[353] Ibid

On January 12, 2006, G&SR lawyers filed three items: Verified Statements of Interest, an Answer to the Government's Verified Complaint for Forfeiture, and a motion for judgment on the pleadings and summary judgment.

The purpose of the Verified Statements of Interest was to identify G&SR as the owner of the seized funds.[354] These statements also affirmed to the Court that G&SR obtained the frozen money through legal business activity. G&SR maintained that the company was not in the business of transmitting money and did not need to be licensed or registered.

That same day, G&SR lawyers filed the Answer to the Government's Verified Complaint for Forfeiture and a motion for judgment on the pleadings and/or summary judgment. G&SR's attorney presented these statements to the court. The following partial text includes sections of this motion that help to illustrate G&SR's core arguments.

> **Claimant Gold & Silver Reserve, Inc.'s Motion for Judgment on the Pleadings and/or Motion for Summary Judgment Pursuant to Rules 12(c) and/or 56 of the Federal Rules of Civil Procedure and Incorporated Memorandum of Law**[355]
>
> 8. To be sure, as previously stated, 18 U.S.C. § 1960 provides that it is a felony to operate an unlicensed money transmitting business. The term "money transmitting business" is defined in three parts in 41 U.S.C. § 5330. The Government has not and cannot plead that any of those three parts describes or characterizes Gold & Silver Reserve, Inc.'s business.
>
> 9. First, under § 5330(1)(A), Gold & Silver reserve, Inc. does not provide check cashing, currency exchange, or money transmitting services, and neither issues nor redeems money orders, travelers checks or any other similar instruments. Gold & Silver reserve, Inc. is not "a non-bank financial institution that sells money orders, cashes checks, and sends money by wire outside the United States," and the Government's Verified Complaint does not allege otherwise; see, Puche, supra. As stated by the Court in *United States v. 47 10-Ounce Bars, et al.*, 2005 U.S. Dist.

---

[354] GOLD & SILVER RESERVE, INC.'s NOTICE OF FILING PHOTOCOPIED VERIFIED STATEMENTS OF INTEREST. *UNITED STATES OF AMERICA v. ALL FUNDS SEIZED FROM OR ON DEPOSIT IN SUNTRUST ACCOUNT NUMBER 1000028078359, IN THE NAME OF GOLD AND SILVER RESERVE, INC. AND ALL FUNDS ON DEPOSIT IN REGIONS BANK ACCOUNT NUMBER 67-0919-4851, IN THE NAME OF GOLD AND SILVER RESERVE, INC.* Case 1:05-cv-02497-RMC Document 3-2, 12 Jan. 2006.

[355] CLAIMANT GOLD & SILVER RESERVE, INC.'s MOTION FOR JUDGMENT ON THE PLEADINGS AND/OR MOTION FOR SUMMARY JUDGMENT PURSUANT TO RULES 12(c) AND/OR 56 OF THE FEDERAL RULES OF CIVIL PROCEDURE AND IN CORPORA TED MEMORANDUM OF LAW. *UNITED STATES OF AMERICA v. ALL FUNDS SEIZED FROM OR ON DEPOSIT IN SUNTRUST ACCOUNT NUMBER 1000028078359, IN THE NAME OF GOLD AND SILVER RESERVE, INC. AND ALL FUNDS ON DEPOSIT IN REGIONS BANK ACCOUNT NUMBER 67-0919-4851, IN THE NAME OF GOLD AND SILVER RESERVE, INC.* Case 1:05-cv-02497-RMC Document 15, 12 Jan. 2006.

LEXIS 2906, 16 (D. Or. 2005), "[m]any businesses receive and transmit funds as payment as a part of their business." Not all of those businesses, however, are in the business of transmitting money.

10. Second, under § 5330(1)(B), Gold & Silver Reserve, Inc. is not required to file reports under 31 USCS § 5313, and the Government's Verified Complaint does not allege otherwise § 5313 provides as follows:

> When a **domestic financial institution** is involved in a transaction for the payment, receipt, or transfer of United States coins or currency (or other monetary instruments the Secretary of the Treasury prescribes), in an amount, denomination or amount and denomination, or under circumstances the secretary prescribes by regulation, the institution and any other participant in the transaction the Secretary may prescribe shall file a report on the transaction at the time and in the way the Secretary prescribes.

[Emphasis added].

11. Additionally, Gold & Silver Reserve, Inc. is not a "domestic financial institution" as defined by 31 U.S.C. § 5312(a)(2) and the Government's Verified Complaint does not allege otherwise. In fact, the Verified Complaint ignores that essential element altogether. (The Verified Complaint similarly ignores the third and final essential element of "money transmitting business," i.e. whether Gold & Silver Reserve, Inc. is a depository institution as defined in 31 USCS § 5313(g)).

12. Although Gold & Silver Reserve, Inc. has been openly and notoriously operating in the United States for nine (9) years, the Department of Treasury has never required Gold & Silver Reserve, Inc. to file reports of any kind on any of its transactions. Indeed, § 5313 is applicable only to cash and cash-equivalent transactions, and Gold & Silver Reserve, Inc. engaged exclusively in wire transactions directed solely to the named payee of the e-gold® account for deposit to a bank account. As such, Gold & Silver Reserve, Inc. cannot be held to be a money transmitting business under 31 U.S.C. § 5330 and therefore cannot be held to be an unlicensed money transmitting business under 18 U.S.C. § 1960.

13. As presented to Magistrate Judge Facciola during the December 29, 2005 hearing addressing Gold & Silver Reserve, Inc.'s emergency motion to vacate the order freezing the bank accounts at issue in this action, over the past two years, Gold & Silver Reserve, Inc. had responded to approximately 300 summonses, subpoenas and other requests for information from a variety of Federal agencies both within and separate from the Department of the Treasury. Each and every one of these responses has been timely and complete, and the comprehensive record of these compliance efforts, i.e. seven 5-inch binders worth of information, will be available for this

232

Court's inspection when the parties appear before it on January 13, 2006.

14. Gold & Silver Reserve, Inc.'s flawless compliance efforts are central to this discussion because they weigh so heavily on the Government's failure to artfully plead a prima facie violation of 18 U.S.C. § 1960 in its Verified Complaint for Forfeiture. The Government has not only known of Gold & Silver Reserve, Inc.'s business since Gold & Silver Reserve, Inc.'s inception, but the Government has been requesting crucial information from Gold & Silver Reserve, Inc. throughout that time. However, at no time during that 9-year history has any Government office or agent informed Gold & Silver Reserve, Inc. that it was either a) operating as an unlicensed money transmitting business, b) neglecting to file § 5313 reports, or c) acting in any other illegal or unlawful way. Now, in an effort to regulate Gold & Silver Reserve, Inc.'s business activities, the Government has moved this Court for the forfeiture of the *res* of Gold & Silver Reserve, Inc.'s bank accounts - i.e. funds intended for the benefit of all three interested represented in the several Verified Statements of Interest filed in conjunction with this motion - pursuant to a Federal criminal statute that has simply no application to Gold & Silver Reserve, Inc.'s business activates. The Government's efforts are transparent and not well taken.

15. Today, consistent with its inability to do so for the past 9 years, the Government cannot artfully plead that Gold & Silver Reserve, Inc. is an unlicensed money transmitting business. Regardless of whether this Court views this motion as one for judgment on the pleading or one for summary judgment pursuant to Rule 12(c) or Rule 56, respectively, of the Federal Rules of Civil Procedure, Gold & Silver Reserve, Inc. is entitled to the dismissal of this action **with prejudice**.

WHEREFORE, for the forgoing reasons, the Claimant, GOLD & SILVER RESERVE, INC. respectfully requests that this Court enter a judgment on the pleadings or, in the alternative, summary judgment.[356]

On January 13th, the Defendants received a mixed ruling from U.S. District Judge Rosemary Collyer. The court order unfroze G&SR's two bank accounts, and the Defendants could again access each bank account. However, more than $800,000 of funds that had been seized were not returned and remained under the government's control. Both Regions Bank and Suntrust then hastened to close the accounts.

Civil Action No. 05-2497 (RMC)
As agreed by the parties in open court on January 13, 2006, it is hereby **ORDERED**

[356] Ibid

that Suntrust Account Number 1000028078359 and Regions Bank Account Number 6709194851 shall be unfrozen; however, the United States shall retain control of the funds previously seized from those accounts pursuant to the warrant issued by Magistrate Judge Facciola in Case No. 05-664 M-01[357]

Additionally, Judge Collyer stated that the merits of G&SR's motion for judgment on the pleadings and/or summary judgment were unripe, and the Court could not rule on them. Less than a week after Judge Collyer's decision, Attorneys William Rakestraw Cowden and Kimberly Kiefer Peretti submitted notices of Appearance on behalf of United States.[358]

◆

Even with U.S. bank accounts frozen and the government's seizure of all business files, computer drives, and other office property, throughout this ordeal, G&SR managed to pay its ongoing financial obligations. G&SR, along with e-gold, both remained open and fully operational. Despite the lethal press reports, transactions in the e-gold® system moved along without so much as a slow down. Amazingly, clients did not seem to mind. On January 20th, 2006, Douglas Jackson published an open letter on the e-gold® website, highlighting facts regarding the company's interaction with the government.

e-gold® welcomes US Government review of its status as a privately issued currency
January 20, 2006

Starting in mid-December 2005, Gold & Silver Reserve, Inc. (G&SR), contractual Operator and primary dealer for e-gold, has been the subject of a warranted search of its premises and records, had its domestic bank accounts frozen, and been the target of a precisely timed, extraordinarily misleading attack by a major business publication.
In an emergency hearing in US District Court January 13, 2006, the freeze order on G&SR's bank accounts was lifted. Though numerous criminal claims had been made

---

[357] ORDER. *UNITED STATES OF AMERICA v. ALL FUNDS SEIZED FROM OR ON DEPOSIT IN SUNTRUST ACCOUNT NUMBER xxxxxxxx8359, IN THE NAME OF GOLD AND SILVER RESERVE, INC., AND ALL FUNDS ON DEPOSIT IN REGIONS BANK ACCOUNT NUMBER xxxxxx4851, IN THE NAME OF GOLD AND SILVER RESERVE, INC..* Case 1:05-cv-02497-RMC Document 4, 13 Jan. 2006.

[358] Case 1:05-cv-02497-RMC Document 7. *05-2497.* Notice of Appearance Kimberly Kiefer Peretti, 17 Jan. 2006.

in obtaining the search and seizure warrants, the Government has not sustained these allegations and the only remaining claim is a contention that G&SR has operated as a currency exchange without the proper license. G&SR had previously proposed to the Government that e-gold be classified for regulatory purposes as a currency, enabling G&SR to register as a currency exchange. In a Treasury report released January 11, 2006, however, the Department of Treasury reaffirmed their interpretation of the USC and CFR definitions of currency as excluding e-gold.

G&SR, for nearly a year, has been engaged with an agency of Treasury in a BSA (Bank Secrecy Act) compliance examination it had voluntarily initiated. G&SR, though preferring that the venue was not a courtroom, welcomes the opportunity to extend its discussions with the Government on how best to achieve appropriate statutory or regulatory cognizance of e-gold® while continuing to build e-gold's market share as a medium of international commerce.

Despite the unfounded charges and adverse misleading publicity that have severely damaged both e-gold® and G&SR, G&SR has continued to meet all financial obligations and remain completely operational. e-gold® remains highly committed to its goal of bringing, for the first time in history, to people of any financial means across the globe, a secure payment mechanism at a fraction of the cost of any other system. e-gold® fully expects to transcend the unfortunate events of the past month and resume its exponential growth.[359]

After the December 2005 raids, the media began a long-lasting campaign to discredit e-gold®, and worst of all, press outlets were desperately trying to connect e-gold® with the sale of child pornography. The earlier January 8th, 2006 article by Brian Grow for Businessweek (Bloomberg Business) contained the following statements.

Crime courses through the internet in ever-expanding variety. Hackers brazenly hawk stolen bank and credit-card information. Pornographers peddle pictures of little boys and girls. Money launderers make illicit cash disappear in a maze of online accounts. Diverse as they are, many of these cybercriminals have something important in common: e-gold Ltd.[360]

Law enforcement officials worry that the little-known digital currency industry is becoming the money laundering machine of choice for cybercriminals.

[359] Jackson, Douglas. " e-gold Welcomes US Government Review of Its Status as a Privately Issued Currency." *e-gold*, e-gold.com, 20 Jan. 2006, web.archive.org/web/20060304203618if_/www.e-gold.com:80/letter2.html.

[360] Grow, Brian, et al. "Gold Rush." *BusinessWeek*, Bloomberg.com, 9 Jan. 2006, www.bloomberg.com/news/articles/2006-01-08/gold-rush.

Some sites pushing child pornography have recently dropped Visa and MasterCard in favor of e-gold, according to the National Center for Missing & Exploited Children, which tracks underage pornography.

There is one crime, however, to which Jackson has reacted more aggressively: child pornography. In August, he attended a conference in Alexandria, Va., Organized by the National Center for Missing & Exploited Children. The center is trying to enlist banks and credit card companies in a crackdown on payment schemes used by child porn Web sites. "There are fewer and fewer sites with Visa - and more and more with e-gold," says the center's chief executive, Ernest E. Allen. The center has a policy of not publicly identifying child porn sites it tracks. Jackson says he was appalled to find e-gold on the list of institutions used by the porn sites. He provided the center with instructions on how to find e-gold records, and the group says it is pleased with e-gold's cooperation.[361]

♦

On January 26, 2006, Nick Szabo, published a short post and a follow-up comment in support of e-gold®.

Egold challenges forfeiture
The U.S. government has confiscated some egold related funds on the pretext of failure to obtain a license as a "money transmitter," as Ian Grigg reports. Apparently egold has already had to put up with "approximately 300 summonses, subpoenas, and other requests for information." Unless they are counting routine stuff, that sounds rather like harassment. The feds are arguing that the U.S. portion of egold, G&SR, is a "money transmitter" even though the U.S. Treasury has refused to recognize egold as a "currency."

Thanks to the out-of-control Washington D.C. bureaucracy, the U.S. is becoming a poor place to do business if you have an innovative business that rubs some people in D.C. the wrong way. For example, if you claim that you have a new form of money that competes with inflating U.S. dollars.

Another thing that may rub feds the wrong way is the embarrassing fact that egold

[361] Ibid

has appreciated by over 100% compared to the U.S. dollar since 1999. In other words, if you held $1,000 worth of egold since 1999, it would be worth over $2,000 now. It's closer to the truth to say that the dollar is worth about half what it was in 1999 than to say that egold is worth twice as much. Which currency is the funny money?

Interestingly, Yahoo Finance considers gold (although not egold in particular) to be a "currency" for the purposes of their currency converter.[362]

(Follow up comment)
Nick Szabo said:
The burden of proof in criminal cases is on the government, Mike. Here they came nowhere near meeting this burden. That is why I "cast aspersions" on the fed's handling of this case. My comments are directed at the prosecutors themselves, and to the politicians and voters who uncritically support them, not to any potential jury in this case. Every time prosecutors screw up like this, they do indeed make it easier for real criminals to get away with fraud. Making this kind of case against an innocent (as far as we can tell from their complaint) and innovative company reduce the "ethos" of the Justice Department (see Aristotle). It also reduces American competitiveness, as it encourages innovative companies to base themselves overseas.

As for for fraud, the company still has a strong incentive, both for business reasons and because of other laws they and their customers must follow involving tax, fraud, etc. not to allow their system to be used for such things. Protection against fraud does not require grossly disproportionate seizures without trial for mere alleged failure to figure out, given the confusing information provided to them by Treasury, what the proper licenses they need. Vigilance against fraud is worthwhile, and egold already has strong incentives to exercise such vigilance itself, but the irrational fear, which rather than protection against fraud is what the Justice Department seems to have an incentive to generate, is very destructive of efforts to provide innovative solutions to fraud, inflation, and other ills of commerce.[363]

In Court
In response to the January 2006, G&SR Motion for Judgment on the Pleadings and/or

---

[362] Szabo, Nick. "Egold Challenges Forfeiture." *Unenumerated*, Unenumerated, 26 Jan. 2006, unenumerated.blogspot.com/2006/01/egoldchallengesforfeiture.html.
[363] Ibid

237

Summary Judgment, government lawyers filed an aggressive fifteen-page opposing statement on January 30, 2006.[364] It was signed by the government's A team.

PLAINTIFF'S OPPOSITION TO CLAIMANT'S MOTION FOR JUDGMENT ON THE PLEADINGS, OR IN THE ALTERNATIVE FOR SUMMARY JUDGMENT

Kenneth L. Wainstein	United States Attorney District of Columbia
William R. Cowden	Assistant United States Attorney
Laurel Loomis Rimon	Assistant United States Attorney, Criminal Division, D.C.
Kimberly Kiefer Peretti	Senior Counsel, DOJ, Computer Crime and Intellectual Property Section[365]

Copied below are Paragraph C. and the concluding text of the government's opposition to G&SR's January Motion. This summary is the last section of the material from the government's complex response to the Court.

G&SR's Motion for Summary Judgment Should Be Denied Because It Has Not Established The Absence of Disputed Material Facts.

In its Verified Complaint, the Government describes in detail how it understands the defendant funds to have been used (or to have been intended for use), and how such use or intended use would violate the provisions of 18 U.S.C. § 1960. In its Answer, claimant denies that the funds were to be used in violation of law, and even denies knowing much at all about how e-gold® operates. Through such denials, G&SR establishes only that many of the material facts that it would have to establish as uncontested before this case could be deemed ripe for summary disposition in its favor are, currently, contested. See Answer ¶¶ 6-28 (where claimant generally "[d]enies for lack of knowledge or information" almost every paragraph of the Verified Complaint). Claimant's failure to submit a "Statement of Uncontested Material Facts" may be consistent with its effort to deny facts that it is in the best position to know, but not in accordance with this Court's standards for entertaining motions for summary judgment. See Local Rule 56.1. Indeed, G&SR offers no evidentiary support for its bald assertion that it is not operating its business in

---

[364] PLAINTIFF'S OPPOSITION TO CLAIMANT'S MOTION FOR JUDGMENT ON THE PLEADINGS, OR IN THE ALTERNATIVE FOR SUMMARY JUDGMENT. *UNITED STATES OF AMERICA v. ALL FUNDS SEIZED FROM OR ON DEPOSIT IN SUNTRUST ACCOUNT NUMBER xxxxxxxxx8359, IN THE NAME OF GOLD AND SILVER RESERVE, INC., AND ALL FUNDS ON DEPOSIT IN REGIONS BANK ACCOUNT NUMBER xxxxxx4851, IN THE NAME OF GOLD AND SILVER RESERVE, INC..* Case 1:05-cv-02497-RMC Document 8, 30 Jan. 2006.

[365] Ibid

violation of 18 U.S.C. § 1960, and no legal support for its assertion, again, that this case should end before any more facts are revealed.

III.   CONCLUSION

For the foregoing reasons, the United States respectfully submits that G&SR's motion should be DENIED.[366]

Shortly after this filing, Judge Rosemary M. Collyer issued an Order denying G&SR's Motion for Summary Judgment.

◆

Violation of State Law is Violation of Federal Law

Jackson obtained this document from FL OFR (Florida Office of Financial Regulation) through a series of three Florida Public Records requests.

He explained these tasks in an email: "The FL Public Records law is like FOIA except in FL the legislature actually requires agencies to comply. The FL process, while they tried to stonewall and it took three tries, was free and I did all the requests."[367]

Jackson believes the following hand-written memo, memorialized a phone call received by the Florida Office of Financial Regulation in January 2006. Jackson suggests that during the call Special Agent Dotson explained the Prosecutors' specific reasons for reaching out to FL. The Prosecution needed a state regulator to declare that e-gold and G&SR required a license under state law. Florida was the only state where G&SR ever maintained an office or servers, and a Florida legal opinion would carry the most weight. Without a state charge, there was no federal case or any basis to justify the forfeiture of assets.

This document showing handwritten notes was uncovered Jackson from the Florida Office of Financial Regulation long after the case ended.

The following image is the upper right hand corner of the full page, enlarged slightly to show the full detail. Handwritten notes from Florida Office of Financial Regulation received by Jackson years after the case.

[366] Ibid

[367] Jackson, Douglas. "Re: Attached." Received by Carl Mullan, *Re: Attached*, 30 Apr. 2019.

18
↓
§ 1960 -

Violation of State

Law is violation

of Federal Law.

Ⓚ Kimberly Peretti
   (202) 353 - 4249
   DOJ, Criminal Div.

Ⓛ Laurel Rimon
   AUSA
   (202) 514 - 7788

◆

On February 2, 2006, in the United States District Court for the Middle District of Florida, Orlando Division, in Case No. 05-M-3201, G&SR lawyers filed a forty-two-page Motion for the Return of Property Pursuant to Rule 41(g) of the Federal Rules of Criminal Procedure and Request for an Evidentiary Hearing on the Matter. In support of this motion to return the seized funds, attorneys for G&SR provided the following arguments. The detailed material presented here is only partial text extracted from Exhibit 1.[368]

3.   In open Court on December 29, 2005, before Magistrate Judge Facciola, upon the Respondent's request that the Order seizing their bank accounts be vacated, the parties discussed the merits of the Freeze Order signed by the Magistrate.[369] The Magistrate expressed, in no uncertain terms, that he was very seriously "concerned" about both the application for and issuance of the seizure order. The Magistrate explained that upon application he was told that a) the Respondents were knowingly furthering the child pornography business, and b) no third party would be injured by the issuance of the seizure order.

4.   Each piece of information provided to the Magistrate was false. First of all, at the hearing before Magistrate Judge Facciola, the Government could offer no proof - reliable or otherwise - that the Respondent was in some way engaged in the knowing trade or distribution of child pornography. The Magistrate openly recognized that the statements made to him concerning that subject were fabrications.

5.   Secondly, the Magistrate further determined that the Secret Service lied when they informed him that no third parties would be injured as a result of the Freeze Order. Magistrate Judge Facciola expressed his concerns regarding this issue in his January 3, 2006 Memorandum Order:

> I hasten to add that I have been concerned about the nature of the seizure sought in this case from the moment that warrant was presented to me. Among other matters, I was most specifically concerned that third parties

---

[368] Case 1:05-cv-02497-RMC Document 10-2 . *In the Matter of the Search of Gold & Silver Reserve, Inc. DBA OmniPay 175 East Nasa Boulevard, Suite 300 Melbourne, FL 32901.* MOTION FOR THE RETURN OF PROPERTY PURSUANT TO RULE 41(g) OF THE FEDERAL RULES OF CRIMINAL PROCEDURE AND REQUEST FOR AN EVIDENTIARY HEARING ON THIS MATTER, 2 Feb. 2006.

[369] The proceeding before Magistrate Judge Facciola was filed under seal as Case No. 05-664 M-01 (JMF). The Respondent has since moved the Court to unseal the proceeding for purposes of transcribing it, but the Court has yet to rule on the issue. As such, the Respondent is currently unable to furnish a copy of that transcript to this Court.

would have their checks and other negotiable instruments dishonored if the seizure order was issued. I was assured by government representatives that this would not occur. At the hearing, however, counsel for GSR consulted with his clients, the principals of GSR, and indicated to me that hundreds of its clients' negotiable instruments had been dishonored or were about to be. I am, therefore, referring this matter to the Chief Judge immediately.

-----

9. "Generally, the government is not required to demonstrate probable cause for seizing property until the forfeiture trial. However, if a claimant challenges the validity of a seizure, as the Petitioners have done here, then the merits of the forfeiture trial are expedited and the government must establish probable cause for the forfeiture prior to the forfeiture trial. Accordingly, the Government must demonstrate here that it had probable cause to believe that the accounts seized are subject to forfeiture." In re the Seizure of All Funds ... , 887 F.Supp.435, 449 (E.D.N.Y. 1995) (internal citations omitted) [Emphasis added]; citing, *Marine Midland Bank, N.A. v. United States*, 11 F.3d 1119, 1124-26 (2d Cir. I 993).

10. The Respondent moves this Court for the immediate release of the property seized pursuant to an illegal Search Warrant and thereby challenges the Government to demonstrate that it had probable cause to believe that the property ultimately seized from the offices of Gold & Silver Reserve, Inc. was either the fruit or the evidence of a crime or any criminal activity. The Respondent respectfully argues that the Government lacked the requisite probable cause and, as such, the warrant executed at the offices of Gold & Silver Reserve, Inc. was illegal.

11. To be sure, as detailed earlier in this motion, Magistrate Judge Facciola from the District Court for the District of Columbia has previously expressed his concern and distaste for the manner in which the Government secured his signature on the Order that led to the freeze of the Respondent's several bank accounts. It appears likely that this Court was persuaded to sign the search warrant in the same illegal and unconstitutional way that Magistrate Judge Facciola was; see, ~~ 3-5, supra; Franks, supra.

12. Furthermore, even ignoring the issue of whether this Court was furnished with false, misleading, material statements prior to its signing of the search warrant, the Government cannot establish that probable cause exists to believe that the Respondent committed any crime at any time.[370]

---

[370] The Respondent was never noticed of the legal bases - if any - of the Search Warrant. All the Respondent received was the cover page of the Warrant, which included this Court's signature and an extremely generic description of the location to be searched. That being said, the proceedings in Washington, D.C. noticed the Respondent that the

13.   The Government cannot establish that probable cause exists to believe that the Respondent has acted as an unlicensed money transmitting business in violation of 18 U.S.C. § 1960. That statute provides that "[w]hoever knowingly conducts, controls, manages, supervises, directs, or owns all or part of an unlicensed money transmitting business, shall be fined in accordance with this title or imprisoned not more than 5 years, or both." [Emphasis added].

-----

15.   Consequently, in order to parry a motion for the return of property pursuant to Rule 41 (g), the Government must establish at a hearing that it has probable cause to believe that the Respondent demonstrates each of the three elements of a money transmitting business. The Government cannot accomplish that task. The Respondent does not provide check cashing, currency exchange, or money transmitting or remittance services and has never been required to file reports under 31 U.S.C. § 5313; see, 31 U.S.C. 5330(1). The Respondent is not a money transmitting business and has never purported to be one.

16.   In open court on December 29, 2005 and January 13, 2006, counsel for the Respondent provided the Court (Magistrate Judge Facciola and District Judge Collyer, respectively) with the record of the Respondent's compliance with approximately 300 summonses, subpoenas and other requests for information from a variety of Federal agencies both within and separate from the Department of the Treasury. This record proved that the Government had not only known of Gold & Silver Reserve, lnc.'s business since Gold & Silver Reserve, Inc.'s inception, but that the Government had been requesting crucial information from Gold & Silver Reserve, Inc. (concerning third parties and Gold & Silver Reserve, Inc.) throughout that time. However, at no time during that 9-year history did any Government office or agent inform Gold & Silver Reserve, Inc. that it was either a) operating as an unlicensed money transmitting business, b) neglecting to file § 5313 reports, or c) acting in any other illegal or unlawful way.

17.   It is thus intriguing that the plain language of the cover page of the Search Warrant reveals that, upon signing the Search Warrant, this Court was "satisfied that the affidavit(s) and any record testimony establish probable cause to believe that the person or property so described is now concealed on the person or premises above-described and establish probable cause for the warrant." See, Exhibit 1; [Emphasis added]. Indeed, that language reveals that further false statements were

Government was moving to forfeit the Respondent's property pursuant to 18 U.S.C. § 1960. As such, the Respondent proceeds *sub judice* using the notice it received in that case as constructive notice of the Government's theory of prosecution in this one.

presented to this Court prior to its signing of the Search Warrant in this case.

-----

19.   Ultimately, it is beyond dispute that the Application for the Search Warrant in this case was presented to this Court while the parties (the United States and the Respondent) were working in the utmost good faith to comply with this Court's Consent Order in Case No. 6:05-mc-71-Orl-KRS. It is also beyond dispute that the Respondent has complied with approximately 300 summonses, subpoenas and other requests for information from a variety of Federal agencies both within and separate from the Department of the Treasury over the past two years. In light of that transparency, it necessarily follows that the Agent's statement that evidence of a crime was "concealed" at Gold & Silver Reserve, Inc.'s offices was either false or told with a reckless and willful disregard for the truth. There was simply no other way for that statement to have been made.

20.   In conclusion, it appears that because the Government could not establish that probable cause existed to believe that the Respondent ever acted as an unlicensed money transmitting business in violation of 18 U.S.C. § 1960, it provided false statements to this Court in an effort to illegally search the Respondent's offices and seize the contents of same. Therefore, following an evidentiary hearing on the matter, everything seized pursuant to that illegal search warrant should be immediately returned to the Respondent.

WHEREFORE, for the foregoing reasons, the Respondent, GOLD & SIL VER RESERVE, INC., respectfully requests that this Court order the return of the property seized pursuant to the December 16, 2005 search warrant signed in this case and hold an evidentiary hearing on this matter.[371]

Just days later, on February 6th, G&SR lawyers also filed a Motion for the Release of Seized Property Under 18 U.S.C § 983(f) and a Request for Oral Hearing.[372] Some of the document is shown below and illustrates the facts presented in G&SR's legal arguments.

4. While the Claimant appreciates the Government's concession and this Court's consideration of same, the Claimant respectfully submits that this Court's order did little to ameliorate the disastrous effects of the previously entered freeze and arrest orders. At this point, Gold & Silver Reserve, Inc. can access to its bank accounts, but

---

[371] Ibid

[372] MOTION for Release of Funds Pursuant to 18 U.S.C.S. 983. *United States of America v. All Funds Seized From or on Deposit in Suntrust Account Number 1000028078359, in the Name of Gold and Silver Reserve, Inc. Et Al.* Case 1:05-cv-02497-RMC Document 11, 6 Feb. 2006.

it cannot touch, move or otherwise affect any of the contents of those bank accounts. Consequently, its business continues to hemorrhage.

5. 18 U.S.C. § 983(f) provides for the release of seized property in certain circumstances:

> (f) Release of seized property.
>
> (1) A claimant under subsection (a) is entitled to immediate release of seized property if –
>
>> (A) the claimant has a possessory interest in the property;
>>
>> (B) the claimant has sufficient ties to the community to provide assurance that the property will be available at the time of trial;
>>
>> (C) the continued possession by the Government pending the final disposition of forfeiture proceedings will cause substantial hardship to the claimant, such as preventing the functioning of a business, preventing an individual from working, or leaving an individual homeless;
>>
>> (D) the claimant's likely hardship from the continued possession by the Government of the seized property outweighs the risk that the property will be destroyed, damaged, lost, concealed, or transferred if it is returned to the claimant during the pendency of the proceeding; and
>>
>> (E) none of the conditions set forth in paragraph (8) applies.

6. The Claimant in this case is entitled to the immediate release of the funds contained in the previously frozen bank accounts. First of all, the Claimant has a unquestionable possessory interest in the property and has notified this Court of same.

7. Second, the Claimant has sufficient ties to the community to provide assurance that the property will be available at the time of trial. The Claimant (a nine year resident of Melbourne, Florida) has previously presented to this Court evidence of its timely and professional responses to approximately 300 summonses, subpoenas and other requests for information submitted to the Claimant by agencies both within and separate from the Department of the Treasury over the past two years. These requests and responses reveal that the Claimant is well known among these governmental agencies, interacts with them with the utmost good faith, and has no plan to abscond – physically or otherwise – with the funds constituting the *res* of this civil forfeiture action.

8. Third, the Government's continued control over the contents of the Claimant's bank accounts is very seriously harming the Claimant and the Claimant's customers .

Because the Claimant is still unable to complete the wire transactions that allow its business to operate, many of its customers continue to suffer the grievous effects of bounced checks and other forms of non-payment.

9. Fourth, because the risk of the Claimant absconding with the contents of its bank accounts is so minimal, and because the Government's continued control over these funds is so damaging, the Claimant's (and the Claimant's customers') ongoing hardship substantially outweighs the risk that the property will be destroyed, damaged, lost, concealed, or transferred if it is returned to the Claimant during the pendency of this proceeding.

10. Finally, none of the conditions set forth in 18 U.S.C. § 983(f)(8) applies in the instant action.

11. 18 U.S.C. § 983(f)(8)(A) does not apply in the instant action because the funds which the Government currently possesses are the assets of a legitimate business. While the Government has alleged in its Verified Complaint for Forfeiture that the Claimant is nothing more than an unlicensed money transmitting business acting in violation of 18 U.S.C. § 1960, the Government's application of § 1960 is erroneous.

12. To be sure, § 1960 provides that "[w]hoever knowingly conducts, controls, manages, supervises, directs, or owns all or part of an **unlicensed money transmitting business**, shall be fined in accordance with this title or imprisoned not more than 5 years, or both." [Emphasis added].

13. 31 U.S.C. § 5330 defines the term "money transmitting business" as having the following three essential elements:

> (1) Money transmitting business. The term "money transmitting business" means any business other than the United States Postal Service which –
> (A) provides check cashing, currency exchange, or money transmitting or remittance services, or issues or redeems money orders, travelers' checks, and other similar instruments or any other person who engages as a business in the transmission of funds, including any person who engages as a business in an informal money transfer system or any network of people who engage as a business in facilitating the transfer of money domestically or internationally outside of the conventional financial institutions system;
> (B) is required to file reports under [31 USCS § 5313]; **and**
> (C) is not a depository institution (as defined in [31 USCS § 5313(g)]).

[Emphasis added]; *see, United States v. Puche*, 350 F.3d 1137, 1141, n.2 (11th Cir.

247

2003) ("A money transmittal company is a non-bank financial institution that sells money orders, cashes checks, and sends money by wire outside the United States."

14. Gold & Silver Reserve, Inc. is not an *unlicensed* money transmitting business under § 1960 because, under § 5330, it is not a money transmitting business (licensed or otherwise) in the first place. While the Claimant concedes that it is not a depository institution, the Claimant respectfully notes that it is not – and has never been – required to file reports under 31 U.S.C. § 5313 because it does not conduct cash or cash-equivalent transactions. Furthermore, the plain language of § 5330(1)(A) is plainly inapplicable to Gold & Silver Reserve, Inc.'s business. As the Court stated in *United States v. 47 10-Ounce Gold Bars*, 2005 U.S. Dist. LEXIS 2906, "[m]any businesses receive and transmit funds as payment as a part of their business." However, not all of these businesses are "'network[s] of people who engage as a business in facilitating the transfer of money;'" *quoting*, 31 U.S.C. § 5330(d)(1)(A).

15. Consequently, the Claimant is entitled to the immediate return of the contents of its bank accounts. The Claimant has a possessory interest in the property and substantial ties to the community to provide assurance that the property will be available at the time of trial. Also, the hardships that the Claimant is currently suffering as the natural result of the Government's possession of the property substantially outweigh the risk that the property will be destroyed, damaged, lost, concealed, or transferred if it is returned. Furthermore, because the Claimant is not a money transmitting business – unlicensed or otherwise – it has not acted in violation of 18 U.S.C. § 1960 and the arrested contents of its bank accounts cannot be characterized as the fruits of any criminal act.

WHEREFORE, for the foregoing reasons, the Claimant, GOLD & SILVER RESERVE, INC., respectfully requests that this Court, pursuant to 18 U.S.C. § 983(f)(6), order the return of the contents of the Claimant's previously frozen bank accounts and hold an oral hearing on the matter.373

◆

DOJ Letter

A February 2006, DOJ letter from Kenneth L. Wainstein, United States Attorney for the District of Columbia, is an excellent illustration of the USSS attempting to block any assistance from Jackson and e-gold. On February 10, 2006, Assistant United States Attorney

---

373 Ibid

William Cowden wrote a letter to the Defendants' counsel about ongoing interaction between Jackson and USSS Special Agents during a law enforcement conference in Russia.

In the letter, Cowden noted that "contacts at the United States Secret Service have informed me that Dr. Jackson recently attempted to contact the USSS (and potentially other law enforcement agencies) to provide information about potential criminal activity of which he is aware."[374]

> U.S. Department of Justice
> Kenneth L. Wainstein
> United States Attorney
> *District of Columbia*
> *Judiciary Center*
> *555 Fourth St., N.W.*
> *Washington, D. C. 20530*
> February 10, 2005
> By Fax: (305) XXX-XXXX and E-mail
> Mitchell S. Fuerst, Esq.
> Andrew S. Ittleman, Esq.
> Rodrigues O'Donnell Ross Fuerst
> Gonzalez Williams & England, P.C.
> 1001 Brickell Bay Drive, Suite 2002
> Miami, FL 33131
> Dear Messrs. Fuerst and Ittleman:
> I write inform you that contacts at the United States Secret Service (USSS) have informed me that Dr. Jackson recently attempted to contact the USSS (and potentially other law enforcement agencies) to provide information about potential criminal activity of which he is aware. Specifically, I understand that Dr. Jackson may have information concerning a ring of thieves selling confidential credit card information and using e-gold to secure payment.
> Rule 4.2(a) of the District of Columbia Bar's Rules of Professional Conduct provides that: "During the course of representing a client, a lawyer shall not communicate or cause another to communicate about the subject of the representation with a party known to be represented by another lawyer in the matter, unless the lawyer has the prior consent of the lawyer representing such other party or is authorized by law to

---

[374] Wainstein, Kenneth L., and William R. Cowde. "U.S. Department of Justice." Received by Mitchell S. Fuerst, and Andrew S. Ittleman, *U.S. Department of Justice*, 10 Feb. 2005. Signed by William R. Cowden Assistant United States Attorney 2-10-2005-Feb-2005-Cowden-DOJ-USSS-ltr-178-4LETTER-81.pdf

do so." This Rule may be inapplicable because the attempted communication about e-Gold activity was initiated by Dr. Jackson, because he indicated that the subject matter of the communication concerns a third party's potential criminal activity, and because the communication at issue may be authorized by law. Nevertheless, in an abundance of caution, I write both to inform you of this recent contact and to seek from you written consent for law enforcement agents to follow-up with Dr. Jackson (or other representatives within G&SR or OmniPay who have similar knowledge) about potential third-party criminal activity.

It should be understood that at this time neither a willingness to share information with the USSS (or with any other agency or entity), nor the quality of any information provided, will have any bearing on the pending civil case, the pending criminal investigation, or any future civil or criminal litigation concerning your client(s). The Department of Justice is not obligated to enter into any future plea bargain with Dr. Jackson (or any affiliated entity) or to file any motion regarding cooperation provided by him (or by any affiliated entity) and, to date, no promises have been made. To ensure that there is no confusion concerning the independent tracks of the pending civil case and criminal investigation, I suggest referring Dr. Jackson to a Special Agent other than one working on either of the pending matters. At your earliest convenience, please let me know, in writing, if this proposal is agreeable.

Very truly yours
KENNETH L. W AINSTEIN
United States Attorney
WILLIAM R. COWDEN [Signed]
Assistant United States Attorney
cc: Andrew Levchuk, Esq.
S.A. Roy Dotson[375]

◆

After being rebuffed once again by the USSS, Jackson had contacted USPS Agent Greg Crabb. On February 9, 2006, they held a preliminary discussion by phone. Jackson then sent an email providing service of process information and some tips for crafting subpoenas that would be maximally productive.

The following day, Crabb invited Jackson to participate in an Interpol law enforcement conference scheduled for February 16, 2006, in Lyon, France. Jackson attended the meeting

---

[375] Ibid

and made a presentation describing e-gold's investigative capabilities and provided guidelines for fast-tracking international legal inquiries. The Lyon conference presented the opportunity to meet not only Crabb (previous collaboration had been only by email and phone) but also Crabb's superior officer, Buddy Lane, Assistant Chief Inspector of the USPIS.

Upon returning to the US, Jackson again met with Crabb and his team at their Arlington, VA headquarters. He continued to negotiate terms of a court order that would provide for ongoing collaboration. The precedent type orders discussed were "trap and trace" or "pen register" orders that law enforcement investigators had used for decades with phone taps. Sticking points were Jackson's insistence that transaction data not be provided carte blanche, and that e-gold® investigative staff would perform the analysis.

On the promise of the immediate issuance of a proper court order, Jackson proceeded to gather and provide intel, working with database queries and also drawing on the resources of his global network of correspondents, the e-gold® exchange providers in multiple countries. Jackson and the head of e-gold's in-house investigations agreed that, pending service of the appropriate legal writ, Jackson would be working the investigation on his own.

♦

On February 23, 2006, Jackson sent an email to Agent Crabb requesting a subpoena for the pending investigations.

-----Original Message-----
From: Douglas Jackson [mailto:djackson@e-gold.com]
Sent: Thursday, February 23, 2006 8:45 AM
To: Crabb, Gregory S
Cc: peterXXXX@bankofamerica.com
Subject: carder ring
Greg
So far I've held off on blocking the e-gold accounts of the carder ring we talked about in order to maximize the possibilities for asset recovery. But I am getting anxious to lower the boom on these people and expel them from the e-gold universe. Our initial discovery of this ring, and attempt to engage law enforcement in the matter [email/phone to WayneXXXX@usss.dhs.gov] was 1/24/06.
Can you offer an estimate of when a subpoena might be forthcoming, especially with a view to picking up the Long Beach, CA kingpin who I believe has data regarding the various carder stashes at BoA?

Peter - if delays are expected, is there a chance that BoA could proceed with a John Doe civil case? e-gold can certainly comply with civil subpoenas as well.
sincere regards,
Douglas Jackson[376]

◆

The last week in February 2006, the official e-gold blog posted the following news item reflecting the proactive approach e-gold® had taken against bad actors attempting to misuse the e-gold® platform. This new tool was big news for e-gold® users.

e-gold® Empowers Users to Refuse Payments from "Blocked Accounts"
e-gold® is pleased to deploy a feature empowering e-gold® Users to refuse payments from "Blocked accounts". "Blocked accounts" are blocked from receiving payments due to insufficient identifying information and/or e-gold® invoking its Right of Association. The new feature enables Users to reduce the possibility of receiving payments from potentially unscrupulous counterparties. The default setting (User may view/change via "Account Info") refuses payment from Blocked accounts.[377]

◆

On February 21st, government prosecutors requested that the Court deny G&SR's Motion. A week later, on February 28th, G&SR lawyers hammered back. The Court received a fresh 15-page response to the government's opposition to defendants' previous motion for the release of their property, complete with four exhibits.

Three of the exhibits contained copies of bank account debit receipts, which detailed the money taken through the seizure. The total amount of funds initially frozen by the government's action was $841,897.46. However, after the seizure dates, all outstanding checks on the accounts bounced, and new incoming deposits continued to flow in the account and disappeared into the government's coffers. Here is the actual summary of the account activity.[378]

---

[376] Jackson, Douglas. "Carder Ring." Received by Gregory S. Crabb, *Carder Ring*, 23 Feb. 2006.

[377] Jackson, Douglas. "E-Gold Empowers Users to Refuse Payments from 'Blocked Accounts.'" *e-gold® Empowers Users to Refuse Payments from "Blocked Accounts"*, e-gold.com, 28 Feb. 2006, blog.e-gold.com/2006/02/e-gold-empowers.html.

[378] CLAIMANT GOLD & SILVER RESERVE, INC.'s REPLY TO THE PLAINTIFF'S OPPOSITION TO CLAIMANT'S MOTION FOR RELEASE OF SEIZED PROPERTY. *UNITED STATES OF AMERICA v. ALL FUNDS SEIZED FROM OR ON DEPOSIT IN SUNTRUST ACCOUNT NUMBER 1000028078359, IN THE NAME OF GOLD*

252

- Frozen $499,754.09 (Dec. 19, 2005) Seized $590,306.59 (Dec. 22, 2005) – Regions Bank Account No. 6709194851
- Frozen $115,678.55 (Dec. 22, 2005)   Seized $705,985.14 (Jan. 13, 2006) – Regions Bank Account No. 6709194878
- $135,912.32 – SunTrust Bank Account No. 1000028078359

Here is some partial text copied from that document stating G&SR's opposition.

a. The Regions Bank account

As the caption of this case makes clear, the Defendant funds were all contained in two separate bank accounts.[379] The first bank account, Regions Bank Account No. 67-0919-4851 served two primary purposes. First, the Claimant used that account to receive the numerous wires for InExchange orders made by the Claimant's customers on a daily basis. Second, the Claimant used that account to send wires in fulfillment of its customers' OutExchange orders on a daily basis.[380] When this account was frozen on December 19, 2005, it contained $499,754.09. However, although it was frozen, between December 19 and December 22, 2005, inclusive, two Automated Clearing House (ACH) credits totaling $0.55 and fourteen wires totaling $142,277.50 were credited to the account. On December 22, 2005, the Government seized $590,306.59 from that account.[381]

Between December 23, 2005 and January 13, 2006, inclusive, $10,000 was debited from the account via the Automated Clearing House (ACH) system[382] and an

---

AND SILVER RESERVE, INC. AND ALL FUNDS ON DEPOSIT IN REGIONS BANK ACCOUNT NUMBER 67-0919-4851, IN THE NAME OF GOLD AND SILVER RESERVE, INC. . Case 1:05-cv-02497-RMC Document 19, 28 Feb. 2006.

[379] The caption does not reveal, however, that the Claimant lost a third bank account as a result of these proceedings. Shortly after the freeze order was entered in this case, Regions Bank closed the Claimant's treasury account which the Claimants used to pay tax liabilities and employee retirement plan contributions. Consequently, the Claimant was unable to pay its retirement plan contributions or payroll taxes using the required payment methods. The IRS has thus notified the claimant that, because it was paying its taxes in an unauthorized manner (via money order), the Claimant would be penalized 25% per payment.

[380] The Claimant respectfully reiterates that any and all exchanges of currency for e-gold or e-gold for currency which passed through the Claimant's Regions account were conducted through bank wires which are fully regulated by the Bank Secrecy Act (BSA). The Claimant only accepts non-repudiable forms of payment (i.e., e-gold and bank wires) and is also not required to file currency transaction reports under 31 U.S.C. § 5313. Indeed, currency transaction reports are only required for payment methods where there is not necessarily any record of value changing hands (as with Federal Reserve notes).

[381] The Government's December 22, 2005 seizure was based on a December 20, 2005 intra-day balance. (Attached hereto as Exhibit 1 is a copy of the Regions Bank checking debit slip evidencing the first seizure of the Claimant's Regions Bank account).

additional six wires totaling $73,953 were credited to the Claimant's frozen and previously-seized Regions Bank account.[383] On January 13, 2006 – the date of the last hearing before this Court – $115,678.55 was removed from the Claimant's Regions Bank account.[384] As such, every dollar that had accumulated in the Claimant's Regions Bank account after the original December 22, 2005 seizure of that account disappeared. The total amount thus seized by the Government from the Claimant's Regions Bank account was $705,985.14.

b. The SunTrust Bank account

The second bank account seized was SunTrust Bank Account No.1000028078359. Prior to the freeze and seizure, the Claimants used that account to issue checks in fulfillment of OutExchange orders and kept it solvent via periodic wires sent from the Regions account previously discussed. Thursday, December 15, 2005 was an ordinary day for the SunTrust Bank account. On that date, $115,866.14 in checks cleared while no money entered the account. At the close of that business day, $112,912.32 remained in the account. Friday, December 16, 2005 was the day of the search and seizure at the Claimant's offices (and the home of Dr. Douglas Jackson) and was a most extraordinary day for the SunTrust account. Despite the fact that the account was backing in excess of two hundred outstanding checks, not one of those checks cleared. However, $30,000 managed to enter the account pursuant to a wire from the Claimant's Regions Bank account ordered earlier that day. Accordingly, at the close of the December 16 business day, $142,912.32 remained in the Claimant's SunTrust Bank account.

---

[382] The Claimant assumes, in the absence of confirmation from Regions Bank, that the $10,000 debit was the result of the Claimant's pre-freeze rejection of a customer's attempt to send remittance for an InExchange order via ACH. (ACH is a type of repudiable payment which the Claimants, as a matter of course, do not accept.) The Claimant never attempted to move or otherwise affect the funds which the Government left over in the Regions Bank account once the freeze was in effect.

[383] The Claimant's officers and employees colloquially refer to these additional funds as "stragglers." These stragglers entered the Regions account contrary to the Claimant's efforts to stop them. In short, when a customer desires to exchange his currency for e-gold®, he conducts that exchange over the Internet and receives a confirmation sheet that includes wiring instructions. The stragglers fell into two groups. The first group included customers who had placed an order prior to the freeze but did not send the wire until after the freeze and pursuant to the original wire instructions. The second group included customers who, because they were so accustomed to wiring to that particular Regions Bank account, sent their wires there as a matter of course and did not notice that the wiring instructions on the confirmation sheet had changed.

[384] Whether those funds were seized by the government or *sua sponte* turned over by Regions Bank remains a mystery to the Claimant. All that the Claimant has evidencing the turnover is a copy of a $115,678.55 Regions Bank debit slip which was issued to the United States Secret Service on January 12, 2006. Regardless of whether the Government seized those funds, it was unmistakably willing to accept them without notifying either the Claimant or undersigned counsel. (Attached hereto as Exhibit 2 is a copy of the Regions Bank checking debit slip evidencing the January 12, 2006 "seizure" of the Claimant's Regions Bank account).

The Claimant's SunTrust Bank account was not actually seized until Tuesday, December 20, 2005. (Attached hereto as Exhibit 1 is a copy of the SunTrust Bank deposit account debit slip evidencing the first seizure of the Claimant's SunTrust Bank account).

The total amount seized by the Government from the Claimant's SunTrust Bank account was $135,912.32.[385] Following the seizure, as the result of checks that cleared on December 20, the SunTrust account had a negative balance of ($2,542.54).[386]

CONCLUSION

The Government has not and cannot articulate that the Claimant is a money transmitting business as that term is defined by statute; see, 18 U.S.C. §1960 and 31 U.S.C. §5330. Nevertheless, due to slanderous allegations it made and subsequently withdrew, the Government took control of the Claimant's bank accounts and business and is currently attempting to choke the Claimant into submission. Should this Court deny the Claimant's request for the return of its seized property, there exists a very strong likelihood that the Government may succeed in doing so. Albeit unfairly, these proceedings would be rendered moot. The bandages that the Claimant has placed over the wounds in its hemorrhaging business were not designed to be permanent, and they are being stretched towards their breaking point with every passing day.

That being said, the Claimant has displayed in its pleadings that it carries the burden articulated in 18 U.S.C. § 983(f) and is therefore entitled to the immediate return of its seized property. The Claimant has an unquestionable possessory interest in the seized funds and has sufficient ties to the community to provide assurance that the funds will be available at the time of trial. Such ties are vividly evidenced by a nine year history of good faith relations with Federal agencies both within and removed from the Treasury Department. Furthermore, because the Claimant's suffering as the necessary and proximate result of the Government's possession of the defendant funds is so great, and because it would be impossible for the defendant funds to "dissipate" if returned to the Claimant at this time, the Claimant's suffering

---

[385] The Government's December 20, 2005 seizure of the Claimant's SunTrust Bank account was based on that account's December 19, 2005 closing balance. On Monday, December 19 and Tuesday, December 20, 2005, a total of $9,542.54 left the Claimant's SunTrust account. Of that amount, $847.54 was withdrawn by SunTrust for treasury management services unrelated to this case. The remainder left the account when three outstanding checks – in the amounts of $7,000.00, $1650.00, and $45.00, respectively – cleared. Following an in-house investigation, the Claimant has no explanation as to why these checks cleared. At the close of the December 20, 2005 banking day, more than two hundred checks remained outstanding.

[386] Congress's use of the terms "violation of the law," "illegal," and "criminal" in § 983(f)(8) clearly evinces its intent to speak of something that is "illegitimate" in a very different light.

outweighs the risk of dissipation. Lastly, the defendant funds are the assets of a legitimate business, earned in relation to the Claimant's business of purchasing and selling liability contracts on the open market. The burden set forth in § 983(f) is thus carried, and the Claimant is therefore entitled to the return of the Defendant funds at this time.

WHEREFORE, for the foregoing reasons, the Claimant, GOLD & SILVER RESERVE, INC., respectfully requests that this Court enter an order releasing the seized property in this case to the Claimant at this time.

Also included in the exhibits was daily information on the price of gold, which had increased during that period. The Court heard the parties' motions, oppositions, and replies at a Hearing on March 16, 2006. The next day, March 17, 2006, Judge Rosemary M. Collyer issued another order denying G&SR's motions. (Doc. 21)

> **ORDERED** that Defendant Gold & Silver Reserve Inc.'s Motion for Judgment on the Pleadings or, in the alternative, for Summary Judgment [Dkt. #15] is **DENIED**; and it is
> **FURTHER ORDERED** that Defendant Gold & Silver Reserve Inc.'s Motion for the Release of Seized Property pursuant to 18 U.S.C. § 983(f) [Dkt. #11] is **DENIED**; and it is
> **FURTHER ORDERED** that this matter shall promptly be set for an Initial Scheduling Conference, via telephone, at a date and time to be selected by the Deputy Clerk. The parties are further advised that the Court remains willing to treat this matter, insofar as is practicable, on an expedited basis.[387]

◆

On March 15th, 2006, the NCMEC published its inaugural press release (though FCACP meetings, attended by Dr. Jackson, had occurred regularly since August 2005) listing e-gold® as a founding member of the NCMEC's Financial Coalition to Combat Child Pornography.[388]

---

[387] ORDER. *UNITED STATES OF AMERICA v. ALL FUNDS SEIZED FROM OR ON DEPOSIT IN SUNTRUST ACCOUNT NUMBER xxxxxxxx8359, IN THE NAME OF GOLD AND SILVER RESERVE, INC., AND ALL FUNDS ON DEPOSIT IN REGIONS BANK ACCOUNT NUMBER xxxxxx4851, IN THE NAME OF GOLD AND SILVER RESERVE, INC..* Case 1:05-cv-02497-RMC Document 21, 17 Mar. 2006.

[388] "FINANCIAL AND INTERNET INDUSTRIES TO COMBAT INTERNET CHILD PORNOGRAPHY." *News and Events*, International Centre for Missing & Exploited Children, 15 Mar. 2006, web.archive.org/web/20060515090017/http://icmec.org/missingkids/servlet/NewsEventServlet?LanguageCountry=en_

Financial and Internet Industries to Combat Internet Child Pornography

ALEXANDRIA, VA, March 15, 2006 – Eighteen of the world's most prominent financial institutions and Internet industry leaders have joined with the National Center for Missing & Exploited Children (NCMEC), and its sister organization, the International Centre for Missing & Exploited Children (ICMEC) in the fight against Internet child pornography. The goal is to eradicate commercial child pornography by 2008.

The new Financial Coalition Against Child Pornography includes leading banks, credit card companies, third party payment companies and Internet services companies. Founding members of the Coalition include America Online, American Express Company, Bank of America, Chase, Citigroup, Discover Financial Services LLC, e-gold®, First Data Corporation, First National Bank of Omaha, MasterCard, Microsoft, North American Bancard, PayPal, First PREMIER Bank/PREMIER Bankcard, Standard Chartered Bank, Visa, Wells Fargo, and Yahoo! Inc.

The Coalition will work in collaboration with Child Focus of Belgium, the European Federation for Missing and Sexually Exploited Children, the International Association of Internet Hotlines (INHOPE), the U.S. Office of the Comptroller of the Currency, and law firm DLA Piper Rudnick Gray Cary.

Child pornography has become a multi-billion dollar commercial enterprise and is among the fastest growing businesses on the Internet. The Internet has enabled instant access to child pornography by thousands and possibly millions of individuals around the world. And the ability to use credit cards and other payment methods has made purchasing child pornography easy.

Senator Richard C. Shelby (R-AL), Chairman of the Senate Banking, Housing and Urban Affairs Committee, was the catalyst in bringing these industry leaders together to address the problem. In challenging them to join with NCMEC and ICMEC in this effort, Senator Shelby said, "If people were purchasing heroin or cocaine and using their credit cards, we would be outraged and would do something about it. This is worse."

The exact number of child pornography web sites is difficult to determine. In 2001,

X1&PageId=2315.

the CyberTipline operated by NCMEC had received more than 24,400 reports of child pornography. By the beginning of 2006, that number had climbed to more than 340,000.

"Not only have we seen an increase in reports of Internet child pornography, but the victims are becoming younger and the images are becoming more graphic and violent," said Ernie Allen, President and CEO of NCMEC and ICMEC, and Chairman of the Coalition. "To eliminate the commercial viability of child pornography, we must stop the flow of money. To do that, we need the involvement of the world's leaders in the payments industry and the Internet. The founding members of the Financial Coalition Against Child Pornography are to be commended for joining this critical fight."

If members of the public have knowledge of a child pornography web site they are encouraged to report it immediately to the CyberTipline managed by the National Center for Missing & Exploited Children (www.cybertipline.com or 1-800-843-5678). Citizens outside the United States can call the CyberTipline or can contact any number of hotlines around the world. To learn more about these hotlines, visit the website of the International Association of Internet Hotlines (INHOPE) at www.inhope.org.

About the National Center for Missing & Exploited Children
NCMEC is a 501(c)(3) nonprofit organization that works in cooperation with the U.S. Department of Justice's Office of Juvenile Justice and Delinquency Prevention. NCMEC's congressionally mandated CyberTipline, a reporting mechanism for child sexual exploitation, has handled more than 365,600 leads. Since its establishment in 1984, NCMEC has assisted law enforcement with more than 117,100 missing child cases, resulting in the recovery of more than 99,500 children. For more information about NCMEC, call its toll-free hotline at 1-800-THE-LOST or visit www.missingkids.com.

About the International Centre for Missing & Exploited Children
ICMEC, the sister organization of NCMEC, is a private, nonprofit 501 (c) (3) nongovernmental organization. It is the leading agency working on a global basis to combat child abduction and exploitation. For more information visit www.icmec.org.[389]

[389] "FINANCIAL AND INTERNET INDUSTRIES TO COMBAT INTERNET CHILD PORNOGRAPHY." *News and Events*, International Centre for Missing & Exploited Children, 15 Mar. 2006,

♦

March 27, 2006, Jackson received a list of high priority e-gold® target accounts for investigation from USPIS Agent Gregg Crabb. To assist with the identification, location, and apprehension of these high-priority criminal suspects, Jackson gathered technical account data from the e-gold® server. These in-house investigations offered details such as login emails, access time, and IPs.

One of the targeted accounts was titled "Maksik." On the same day, Jackson discovered a significant counterparty account, which he proposed would best be referred to as "segvec" that was the nym used by the person controlling the account. From that day forward, this second account carried the name segvec, and the moniker identified this particular e-gold® user in future investigations with the USPIS and Crabb.

Jackson's work also included additional detailed information he was able to uncover from the e-gold® accounts' activities. This data included details he tracked offline, outside of the e-gold database. Segvec's account had been Spending e-gold® to a third-party business that was loading funds, in fiat currency, to a prepaid debit card. These types of cards are common in the digital currency industry and provide instant access to cash through ATM transactions. Jackson reached out to the card agent, responsible for loading funds, and made an informal request for details on the card's use. The agent had access to more information, such as ATM withdrawal information and POS locations that the carder had previously accessed. Jackson's in-house investigative work was rewarding. Within a few hours, he had gathered and delivered a substantial amount of critical user data on all of Crabb's high-priority e-gold® target accounts.

♦

On April 20, 2006, Jackson attended the "International Conference to Combat Cybercrime and Terrorism" in Moscow, Russia. The conference included around two-hundred experts from over fifty countries, coming together to discuss ways of jointly fighting online crimes and regulating Internet content. Jackson had planned meetings with agents of the Interior Ministry's Department K (Hi-Tech Crimes Fighting). While attending the conference, Jackson and Crabb negotiated a fast-track conduit for exchanges of cybercrime intel between the USPIS (and the umbrella National Cyber-Forensic Training Alliance (NCFTA) in which USPIS was a key participant) and Russia's Department K.

web.archive.org/web/20060515090017/http://icmec.org/missingkids/servlet/NewsEventServlet?LanguageCountry=en_X1&PageId=2315.

The strategy was for e-gold® and Webmoney investigators to act as intermediaries and both organizations would further coordinate their mutual investigative efforts. Though these actions, they could help the respective law enforcement agencies overcome the sometimes several-week delays of formal requests between jurisdictions.

Jackson related a humorous event that highlighted the low regard that law enforcement agencies around the world seemed to have for the USSS.

> As we were wrapping up our meeting at the headquarters of Department K in the Russian Interior Ministry, we noticed a handful of more junior agents clustered at the window visibly trying to suppress mirth about something. Cueing off the fact that they now had the attention of the room, rather than trying to feign innocent seriousness, the agent who had apparently incited the disruption decided the most expedient course of action was to share the joke. He then did the impromptu schtick that had given them the giggles. He affected an exaggerated tough guy strut and in hilarious Russian accent was singing the jingle from a popular cop show that had gone into international syndication: "Bad boys, Whatcha gonna do, whatcha gonna do When they come for you". We all rushed to the window and saw the USSS contingent coming up the sidewalk for the meeting scheduled to follow ours.[390]

Jackson provided some additional color concerning the Moscow conference:

> Early on, during a break between meetings, I finally got a chance to meet Andy Auld, an agent in the UK who had just recently transferred from the NHTCU to the newly formed Serious Organized Crime Agency (SOCA), and who was part of the international coalition I was working with. The scene that ensued reminded me of the famous late-1970's commercials that showed people at a cocktail party all leaning over and straining to overhear a conversation. The tagline was "When E.F. Hutton talks, people listen." In this case, it was folks from the USSS and DOJ who all knew of the breakthroughs our coalition was achieving, hoping to overhear some snippet of intel.

> There was also a surreal experience at the breakout session regarding internet payment systems. USSS Special Agent Sherri Dunlop—the agent who had asked me the weird questions about Goldmoney during execution of the December 2005 search warrant—gave a presentation in which she mentioned e-gold. The session moderator then, on an impromptu basis, gave me the opportunity to make my by-then usual

[390] Jackson, Douglas. "DJ Redlines 5." Received by Carl Mullan, DJ Redlines 4, 29 Feb. 2020.

comments regarding e-gold's in-house investigative capabilities and how to most efficiently engage with us.

That same trip, I was invited to stop by London and meet with senior SOCA people at their gleaming new (and relatively secret) Docklands facility. I discovered Andy Auld's boss was Sharon Lemon who I had previously met at the Belfast conference in November 2005. The highlight of the meeting was when they thanked me for the data that had directly led to the arrest of Renu Subramanian, aka "Jilsi."[391] They revealed that when the NHTCU was re-organized into SOCA and CEOP that other agencies had resented that SOCA got the posh new facilities. They described that busting Jilsi had greatly helped in demonstrating that they were deserving of such high-end amenities.[392]

Regarding Crabb's high-priority target accounts and the segvec investigation, Jackson made this statement in an August 24, 2017, Investigation Request letter to John Roth confirming his past activity.

This particular investigation (which I initiated) renewed a collaboration with a senior agent of the US Postal Inspection Service, Greg Crabb, with whom I had worked another case circa 2000. In preparation for this collaborative effort, Crabb had invited me to participate in an Interpol cybercrime conference in Lyon, France where I was also introduced to his associate "Agent X". [In the course of this case (May 2006), we also went to Moscow to liaise with other international law enforcement agencies, especially Russia and the UK].[393]

◆

In April 2006, Nadia Oehlsen published an article in *Cards & Payments* entitled *U.S. Law Enforcers Are Cold on Gold*. Once again, lacking any understanding of current U.S. financial regulations, members of the press ignorantly cast another negative characterization of the e-gold® business.

[391] Davies, Caroline. "Welcome to DarkMarket – Global One-Stop Shop for Cybercrime and Banking Fraud." The Guardian, Guardian News and Media, 14 Jan. 2010, www.theguardian.com/technology/2010/jan/14/darkmarket-online-fraud-trial-wembley.

[392] Jackson, Douglas. "DJ Redlines 5." Received by Carl Mullan, DJ Redlines 4, 29 Feb. 2020.

[393] Jackson, Douglas. "Investigation Request." Received by John Roth, Inspector General, US Dept. of Homeland Security, 24 Aug. 2017, Indian Harbour Beach, FL.

Digital currencies in general, and e-gold in particular, however, developed poor reputations in some circles and one commentator called the payment systems "at best, lax on financial crime."[394]

Skeptics, though, charge that efforts to create currency based on the value of metals seem designed to skirt standard banking and money-transfer rules while providing few customer protections and inadequate checks of account-holder identities. They also point to high fees typically charged by third party companies that support prepaid card programs and that exchange gold value for traditional currencies.[395]

♦

On May 2, 2006, a letter[396] arrived by fax and courier to e-gold's Miami lawyers from the Office of United States Attorney for the District of Columbia. This extraordinary document referenced Jackson's out-of-court interaction with the Department of Justice prosecutors and other law enforcement personnel.

U.S. Department of Justice
By Facsimile and U.S. Mail
May 2, 2006
Mitchell S. Fuerst, Esq.
Andrew S. Ittleman, Esq.
Rodrigues O'Donnell Ross Fuerst
Gonzalez Williams & England, P.C.
l001 Brickell Bay Drive, Suite 2002
Miami, FL 33131

Dear Messrs. Fuerst and Ittleman:
Kenneth L. Wainstein
United States Attorney
District of Columbia

---

[394] Nadia Oehlsen, U.S. Law Enforcers Are Cold on Gold, CARDS & PAYMENTS, Apr. 2006, https://www.paymentssource.com/news/us-law-enforcers-are-cold-on-gold

[395] Ibid

[396] Wainstein, Kenneth L. Received by Mitchell S. Fuerst Esq., Andrew S. Ittleman Esq., l001 Brickell Bay Drive, Suite 2002, 2 May 2006, Miami, FL. Laurel Loomis Rimon & William R. Cowden, Assistant United States Attorneys Kimberly Kiefer Peretti, Senior Counsel United States Department of Justice Memorandum in Aid of Sentencing November 14, 2008 Exhibit 5

Judiciary Center
555 Fourth St., N. W.
Washington, D.C. 20530

The purpose of this letter is to alert you to a recent contact with your client, Dr. Jackson, and Department of Justice ("DOJ") prosecutors and other law enforcement personnel, and to clarify our understanding of your letter to Mr. Cowden, dated February 15, 2006, agreeing to our proposal concerning certain communications that Dr. Jackson might initiate with law enforcement agents.

First, as we are sure you are aware, on April 19-20, 2006, Dr. Jackson attended a conference in Moscow that was also attended by DOJ prosecutors and other law enforcement personnel. It is our understanding that Dr. Jackson introduced himself to DOJ prosecutors, but that no further contact occurred between Dr. Jackson and the DOJ prosecutors. Because we had previously agreed that any contact would be with law enforcement agents only, DOJ attorneys will continue to avoid conversations with Dr. Jackson.

Second, based on your February 15th letter, you agreed that law enforcement agents could follow up with Dr. Jackson concerning third-party criminal activity and that Dr. Jackson would avoid direct contact *with* law enforcement agents involved in the pending civil and criminal investigations. You expressed no objection to Dr. Jackson providing law enforcement agents not involved in the pending investigations with information on criminal activity of E-Gold account holders. Dr. Jackson continues to have contact with the United States Postal Inspection Service ("USPIS") (among other law enforcement agencies) and has recently provided a USPIS agent with information concerning the criminal activity of many E-Gold account users.

Please note that we did not propose, or agree, to prohibit the sharing of information voluntarily provided by him (or G&SR) with agents or prosecutors involved in either the pending civil case, or the ongoing criminal investigation. We have not agreed to any timitation or conditions on how information that Dr. Jackson might provide to law enforcement would be used. An awareness of the criminal activity of third-party users (or customers) of a money transmitting business may impact the liability of the business or related individuals/entities.

In sum, while Dr. Jackson's cooperation is appreciated, we want it to be clear that, to date, we have extended no offer of immunity (of any sort) for any information he may provide.

Any information provided by Dr. Jackson to law enforcement agents can be used against him. Regardless of whether he continues to provide someirifom1ation voluntarily, we expect G&SR will comply with any legal Process served upon it. If

you have any questions or concerns, or would like to dfacuss this matter further, or any matters relating to the pending litigation/investigation, please do not hesitate to contact Laurel Loomis Rimon at (202) XXX-XXXX, Kimberly Kiefer Peretti at (202) XXX-XXXX, or Bill Cowden at (202) XXX-XXXX.
Laurel Loomis Rimon
William R. Cowden
Assistant United States Attorneys
Kimberly Kiefer Peretti
Senior Counsel
United States Department of Justice[397]

Grand Jury

While the Defendants quietly went about their daily business, Court records indicate that on May 11, 2006, the prosecution convened a Federal Grand Jury to hear evidence against the e-gold/G&SR Defendants in a criminal case. These jurors eventually returned the original indictment.

After impaneling the grand jury, government prosecutors rapidly moved forward on the criminal case and seemed to change their tactics in the civil forfeiture. On June 16, 2006, Government lawyers called G&SR's counsel to discuss a stay in the civil forfeiture case and ascertain whether the claimant would consent to a stay. G&SR lawyers opposed any stay.

♦

United States Postal Inspection Service Assistance

The United States Postal Inspection Service is the law enforcement arm of the United States Postal Service. The USPIS defines its jurisdiction as crimes that may adversely affect or fraudulently use the U.S. Mail, the postal system or postal employees. November 2008, Sentencing Memo to the Court detailed Jackson's connection to the USPIS.

> Dr. Jackson also worked closely with the U.S. Postal Inspection Service Agents Gregory S. Crabb and Agent X, supplying a steady stream of financial and other information related to individuals involved in buying and selling stolen credit cards.[398]

Jackson uncovered several new critical facts and dates regarding the segvec investigation and shared the information with Crabb. Two of these new significant items are

---

[397] Ibid
[398] Ibid

listed below.

Item 1

The third-party exchange provider loading the segvec debit card supplied Jackson details on the last two ATM withdrawals. Both locations were in South Florida. The ATM withdrawals were less than two-weeks old, and the banks' ATM footage would still have been available to law enforcement for review. The critical information shared by Jackson with Crabb could have unmasked the person withdrawing cash using the segvec card in Miami, Florida. Around May 3, 2006, Crabb received these details.

Item 2

Through in-house investigations, Jackson uncovered that segvec had used a Tokyo maildrop to receive physical mail, including the debit card. The operator of this particular Tokyo maildrop forwarded box items to a second box location in another country. Jackson learned this fact and continued searching.

Further investigation revealed that the Tokyo box operator was forwarding all of segvec's Tokyo mail to a Miami, Florida P.O. Box address rented under the name Leo Peralta. At the request of Agent Crabb, in May 2006, Jackson uncovered and provided the U.S. Maildrop P.O. Box located at 11762 S.W. 88 Street, Miami, FL 33186. On or about May 16, 2006, Jackson sent all of this critical segvec identifying information to USPIS Agent Crabb. Jackson was unmasking the mysterious segvec to the law enforcement community.

From Jackson's in-house investigative work, by June 2006, government agents had received direct evidence identifying that segvec operated from Miami, not Europe or Russia (their previous assumption). Furthermore, Jackson has supplied segvec's local Miami mailbox drop address and debit   card withdrawals from two bank ATMs that would have still had recent footage the segvec withdrawals. Finally, Jackson profiled the segvec suspect, to USPIS Investigator, as having been previously arrested and released.

This evidentiary intelligence, uncovered by Jackson, established that segvec was operating in Miami, Florida. Bank ATM videos and surveillance of the maildrop should have quickly and easily located the segvec suspect. Jackson shared his reaction to the news about segvec in a later email.

> On October 19, 2006, perplexed as to how segvec could still be at large after I had provided evidence that should have led to ATM camera data and surveillance of his known maildrop, I provided another update (Exhibit 24) with yet more time stamped IP data and additional email addresses and domain names under his control.

265

And then things went silent – no further feedback from our law enforcement partners regarding the segvec case. We never heard the outcome of the case. We actually figured segvec had been found and compelled to become a CI. This presumption was based on our observation in another case, Ali Beldjouheur of Marseille, France, aka "kaisersose", where in March 2006 we had uncovered and provided verified high resolution images of his driver's license. The USSS had subsequently issued a showy press release noting that they had caught kaisersose in Marseille…but never then or since revealed his name.

The next we heard of segvec was August 5, 2008 when, two weeks after I entered my guilty Plea, a DOJ press release (Exhibit 25) announced arrests involving "the largest hacking and identity theft case ever prosecuted by the Department of Justice". It revealed that segvec was actually Albert Gonzalez and adding (buried down in the 6th paragraph) "During the course of this investigation, the Secret Service discovered that Gonzalez, who was working as a confidential informant for the agency, was criminally involved in the case."[399]

In July 2006, all of the e-gold® in-house information, shared by Jackson with the USPIS, was forwarded to Kimberly Peretti at the Department of Justice. Below is the July 9th DOJ email request received by USPIS Agent Crabb from the DOJ.

Subject: Request From Main Justice To The Postal Inspection Service Concerning Our Cooperation
From: "Crabb, Gregory S" <XXXXX@uspis.gov>
Date: Sun, 9 Jul 2006 16:07:54 -0400

To: "Douglas Jackson" <djackson@e-gold.com>
CC: "Agent X" <XXXXX@uspis.gov>, "Agent Y" <XXXXX@uspis.gov>
Douglas,
On Friday, I received a request from Kimberly Kiefer Peretti, Senior Counsel, Computer Crime and Intellectual Property Section, Department of Justice inquiring as to the cooperation that you have provided to the Postal Inspection Service. I have been asked to provide her with a summary of all of the communications that we have had.

---

[399] Jackson, Douglas. "Chunk 5 plus a Few Things." Received by Carl Mullan, *Chunk 5 plus a Few Things*, 29 Feb. 2020. DJ redlines 5.pdf

I am going to provide her with a schedule summarizing our communications. The schedule will include date, time, parties involved in the communication and the nature of communication. In the event the communication included the exchange of subscriber or transaction records, I will provide her with a list of the number of records by type that you have provided.

Mrs. Kiefer Peretti requested that I provide her with a draft of this schedule by Wednesday.
If you have any specific questions or concerns, please don't hesitate to contact me.
Take care,
Greg[400]

In a 2019 email, Jackson expressed his distaste for sharing the work results of the productive alliance with Inspector Crabb with the USSS.

At the time I was outraged, interpreting this as indicative that the USSS was once again planning to hijack and claim credit for solving some hard cases. They had an established pattern of acting on the work product of my investigative team (or other law enforcement agency cases), arresting the culprit (often prematurely, even if it meant compromising an ongoing investigation) and taking credit in press releases, often gratuitously badmouthing e-gold in the process. As detailed below, however, there is reason to suspect that this intervention was for a more sinister purpose. A cover-up.[401]

DOJ attorney Kimberly Peretti was now in possession of the segvec evidence and was aware that he operated from the Miami area. Jackson had uncovered, and profiled segvec as having been previously arrested and released; matching Gonzalez! This information was enough to track, identify, and arrest the suspect quickly.

However, no one rushed to identify, detain, or arrest the Miami segvec suspect based on Jackson's evidence. Furthermore, the detail information provided by Jackson seemed to have been ignored or buried. Why would the DOJ prosecuting attorneys and the USSS ignore or conceal this critical evidentiary information? Why didn't Peretti or the USSS have him arrested? What did Peretti do with Jackson's fresh intelligence on segvec?

[400] Crabb, Gregory. "Request From Main Justice To The Postal Inspection Service Concerning Our Cooperation." Received by Douglas Jackson, *Request From Main Justice To The Postal Inspection Service Concerning Our Cooperation*, 9 July 2006.
[401] Jackson, Douglas. "Investigation Request." Received by John Roth, Inspector General, US Dept. of Homeland Security, 24 Aug. 2017, Indian Harbour Beach, FL.

Only years later, the world learned that "segvec" was the alias used by hacker Albert Gonzalez. In 2006, Gonzalez was a paid confidential informant for the USSS.

In a February 15, 2019 email, Jackson summed up the critical evidence he had shared with Crabb and, ultimately Peretti.

> I believe three datapoints enabled Peretti and the SS to know with certainty no later than August 2006 that their CI, Gonzalez was the perp.[segvec]
>
> 1. I put Maksik's major counterparty in international law enforcement radar in February 2006, referring to him as "segvec" based on his frequent usage of that nym for himself. That alone would have told both SS and Peretti it was Gonzalez since that was the nym by which they had know him as far back as 2003.
> 2. I found he had a Tokyo drop box that forwarded to an address in Miami.
> 3. I found he had a debit card that had seen usage in Kendall and Miami proper, as recently as two weeks prior to my detection and reporting, where he definitely would have still been on ATM camera footage.[402]

In 2006, USSS CI Albert Gonzalez (segvec) was under pretrial court supervision through the U.S. Probation Office in Miami. Kimberly Peretti was the DOJ Attorney connected with that previous Gonzalez case. Even more shocking, USPIS Agent X indicated that USSS Special Agents located in South Florida received all of Jackson's segvec data. This group of Miami USSS Special Agents included members of the team supervising paid confidential informant Albert Gonzalez.

Gonzalez and his associates, hacked into large computer networks and stole customer credit card data from some of America's most popular retail businesses. The list included BJ's Wholesale Club, DSW, Office Max, Boston Market, Forever 21, Barnes & Noble, Sports Authority, and T.J. Maxx. Nearly two years after Jackson had provided details on segvec, in 2008, Gonzalez was finally arrested, and indicted for multiple felonies. During a Boston press conference on the Gonzalez prosecutions, U.S. Attorney General Michael Mukasey called the case, "single largest and most complex identity theft case ever prosecuted in this country."[403]

While receiving a cash salary from the USSS, Court records indicate that Gonzalez committed his most significant criminal acts. Gonzalez was engaged in massive illegal electronic intrusions and the most significant theft of personal information in America.

---

[402] "Re: K. Peretti." Received by Carl Mullan, *Re: K. Peretti*, 15 Feb. 2019.
[403] Mayville, Casey. "11 Indicted In Largest ID Theft Case Ever." *CBS News*, CBS Interactive, 6 Aug. 2008, www.cbsnews.com/news/11-indicted-in-largest-id-theft-case-ever-05-08-2008/.

A majority of these crimes were committed while Gonzalez was a paid USSS confidential informant. Jackson shared details showing how e-gold's investigative evidence landed with USSS Agents in the Miami office. He explained:

> The matter rested there until September 2, 2009 (Exhibit 28), when I[Jackson] related to Agent X (by then in private sector) that the USSS had yet again claimed credit for one of my cases, Egor Shevelev of Kiev, aka "Esk" who I had tracked down to true name and other locating data.

> His[USPIS Agent X] response on this occasion was more pointed: 'On the Segvec stuff, where we worked with you[Jackson] and the exchanger out of Salt Lake, we sent all of that stuff to our Miami office to work it. They sent an Inspector with the information (unbeknownst to us) to a USSS task force meeting in Miami where all of that info was brought up in the meeting. The Inspector said "The SS there was really interested in all that information. They seemed like they had a handle on it so I turned it over to them."[404]

The Shadowcrew case, which launched the career of Albert Gonzalez as a confidential informant, and his later infamous crime wave, became cornerstones of Kimberly Peretti's burgeoning DOJ career. April 29, 2010, Tom Field's interviewed Peretti for BankInfoSecurity.com.

> She was co-lead prosecutor in the Department's largest hacking and identity theft case ever prosecuted - a case in which several members of an international retail hacking ring were convicted of stealing over 40 million credit and debit cards.[405]

It was a beaming interview, showing that Peretti is genuinely an accomplished prosecutor/attorney. However, there was no mention of her interaction with recidivist Albert Gonzalez.

Gonzalez planned the intrusions, recruited accomplices, committed the hack, and attempted to launder millions in illegal cash. All of this criminal activity took place while Gonzalez was walking around a free man courtesy of the USSS.

USSS Confidential Informant Gonzalez's 2003 criminal case, was purposely stalled in pre-trial while he was allowed to move to Miami and carry out his South Florida crime

---

[404] Received by Douglas Jackson, and Agent X, *Subject: Re: Esk*, 3 Sept. 2009.

[405] Field, Tom. "Inside the TJX/Heartland Investigations." *Bank Information Security*, 29 Apr. 2010, www.bankinfosecurity.com/interviews/inside-tjxheartland-investigations-i-500.

spree. Tom Field's article never mentioned any of the in-house investigations shared by Jackson that should have led directly to Gonzalez. Finally, the material in BankInfoSecurity.com never indicated that Gonzalez had been receiving a cash salary from the USSS while committing these infamous hacking crimes.

The New York Times reported that Gonzalez had been shuttled around the country by USSS Special Agents to give presentations at law enforcement conferences. Gonzalez gave presentations or briefings to rooms full of federal agents and law enforcement officers. His topic was, of course, hacking.[406]

Additionally, Court documents revealed that during his career as a USSS confidential informant, Gonzalez shared sensitive law enforcement intelligence, obtained from his USSS handlers, with other criminals. He warned associates that the government was investigating them! The Gonzalez Indictment (Boston) filed August 5, 2008, details his illegal activity.[407]

> [In furtherance of the conspiracy]
>> n. Used sensitive law enforcement information, obtained by GONZALEZ during the course of his "cooperation" in a U.S. Secret Service undercover investigation, to warn off conspirators and ensure that they would not be identified and arrested in the course of that investigation.[408]

Why didn't the USSS work with Jackson?

> "Rather than attack him, Justice officials and the Secret Service should have been working with him, says Jackson. Because all the while they were trying to build a case against e-gold, he was gathering evidence that could help them battle the real criminals."[409]

By the end of 2006, e-gold® workers had honed their skills and tools for preventing misuse of the platform. A December 11th, 2006, article in Wired.com described how changes in e-gold's commercial practices were laser-focused on identifying and preventing illegal activity. E-gold® had instituted breakthrough software that automatically took action to block and blacklist suspicious accounts.

---

[406] Verini, James. "The Great Cyberheist." The New York Times Magazine, 10 Nov. 2010.

[407] U.S. District Court of Massachusetts. *UNITED STATES OF AMERICA v. ALBERT GONZALEZ, Alkia Cumbajohny, a/k/a Cj,Alk/a UIN 20 I 679996, a/k/a CIN 476747, a/k/a Soupnazi, a/k/a Segvec, Aik/a k 1 Ngchilli,Alk/a Stanozololz, Defentant.* Indictment, 5 Aug. 2008.

[408] Ibid

[409] Staff, WIRED. "e-gold Gets Tough on Crime." *Wired*, Conde Nast, 4 June 2017, www.wired.com/2006/12/e-gold-gets-tough-on-crime/.

"In the last month, he's[Jackson] blocked about 2,000 accounts from his system, and he's voluntarily turned over detailed account and transaction histories to federal law enforcement."[410]

"In November [2006], Jackson began running an automated script to blacklist accounts he identified as suspicious. The digital funds aren't frozen, and the account holder can conceivably get the money out by transferring it to another account he controls, or to a different e-gold   customer. But then those accounts get blocked, too."[411]

By late November, no one in the industry doubted that Jackson was committed to working with the authorities toward preventing e-gold® from being used by malicious parties. However, the USSS was still ignoring his offers. Did the USSS have a predetermined bias toward a conviction and asset forfeiture in the e-gold® case?

From examination of documentary evidence obtained through the Freedom of Information Act (FOIA), and Jackson's email records archived over the past decade, a sinister pattern of USSS activity emerges.

Furthermore, after his plea agreement, redacted emails obtained by Jackson expose internal communications between State of Florida financial regulators discussing e-gold®, Jackson, and GS&R. Statements found in these newly uncovered official documents support many of Jackson's previous claims.

These documents establish that regulators within the State of Florida examined whether e-gold Ltd. or GS&R were required to obtain a Florida Money Transmitter License. Several of the state's internal documents indicate that G&SR and e-gold's business did not fall within the scope of activities subject to state regulations, and the state would not have required e-gold® or G&SR to obtain a Florida Money Transmitter License.

A majority of this documented information was acquired in later years after the criminal case had   concluded. This evidence is compelling.

Text from the 2008 Sentencing Memo illustrates that G&SR was actively working to prevent the e-gold® platform from being used by bad actors.

Indeed, materials disclosed by the government pursuant to *Brady v. Maryland,* 373 U.S. 83 (1963) and *Giglio v. United States,* 405 U.S. 150 (1972), demonstrate that, notwithstanding the picture painted by the Indictment, defendants were indeed

[410] Ibid
[411] Ibid

271

concerned with and sought to combat illegal activity in the e-gold system and worked cooperatively with law enforcement personnel to do so.[412]

In August 2017, Jackson sent a detailed letter to Mr. John Roth, Inspector General, United States Department of Homeland Security requesting an official investigation into misconduct by individual members of the USSS and officials in the United States Department of Justice involved with the previous investigation of e-gold Ltd., Gold & Silver Reserve, Inc.; as well as the asset seizures and forfeiture actions undertaken in conjunction with the case. Jackson wrote the following text copied from that letter.

Gold & Silver Reserve Inc., the contractual "operator" of the e-gold system was located in Florida, as well as its computer servers and all employees, and had been since e-gold went online in November 1996. There can be no question that the opinion of Florida's financial regulators would have been the most pertinent and would have carried the most weight. e-gold at no time ever had any physical facilities or operational resources in any other state (or the District of Columbia).[413]

Supporting Evidence

The following documents are copies of 2006 emails, official interoffice communications, and email list messages circulated between the State of Florida officials, the DOJ, and the USSS. Also listed here are the individuals' job titles in 2006.

Robert Rosenau "Bob" –   Chief, Bureau of Financial Investigations, State of Florida
Robert Beitler "Rob" – General Counsel, State of Florida
Chris Hancock "Chris" – FA, Bureau of Financial Investigations, State of Florida
David M. Burley –   Investigator, Florida Department of Financial Services
Mike Ramsden "Mike" – Financial Administrator, Money Transmitter Regulation Unit, State of Florida
William Oglo "Bill" – Assistant General Counsel, State of Florida
Peter Fisher – Chief Finance Attorney, State of Florida
Roy Dotson – United States Secret Service Special Agent Orlando Field Office
Jo Schultz –   Attorney Supervisor, State of Florida
Rick White – Director of Securities and Financial Regulation, State of Florida

---

[412] CASE NUMBER: 07-167-M-01. *UNITED STATES OF AMERICA V. E-GOLD LIMITED, GOLD & SILVER RESERVE, INC., DOUGLAS L. JACKSON, BARRY K. DOWNEY and REID A. JACKSON.* SENTENCING MEMORANDUM OF GOLD & SILVER RESERVE, INC., Nov. 2008.

[413] Jackson, Douglas. "Investigation Request." Received by John Roth, Inspector General, US Dept. of Homeland Security, 1020 Steven Patrick Avenue, 24 Aug. 2017, Indian Harbour Beach, Florida.

Kathy Norris – Florida Attorney working for the State of Florida
Mark Mathosian[414] – Investigator, Florida Office of Financial Regulation (OFR)
John Harper[415] – Florida Office of Financial Regulation (OFR) [Deceased 12-01-2008]

Roy Dotson

In 2006, Roy Dotson was a United States Secret Service Special Agent working in the Orlando Field Office. The nine years before working for the USSS, Dotson was employed by the Brevard County Florida Sheriff's Office. Brevard Country Florida is an area to the East of Orlando, including Melbourne, Florida. Dotson was the USSS Special Agent that signed the Affidavit in Support of Complaint For Forfeiture in e-gold's case (18 U.S.C. §§ 981, 1960, 1957).[416]

Jackson wrote the next two paragraphs in an August 2017, letter to John Roth, Inspector General, United States Department of Homeland Security.

> In the course of this case and in subsequent years the defendants learned (the hard way) that the only way for any company to know whether its business activities constitute Money Transmission would be to contact every state in which potential customers reside and seek a determination by that state's competent regulatory authority. [The Plea Agreement in this case memorialized this understanding]. In Exhibit 1, you will even note a telltale handwritten memo memorializing a phone call (Exhibit 1, page 7), clearly indicative that the federal prosecutors understood this from the beginning and had verbally explained to their Florida regulatory correspondent the necessity of getting a state to make such a determination if an 18 USC 1960 charge were to succeed.[417]

> Accordingly, beginning in January 2006, the USSS agent doing Peretti's legwork, reached out to Florida, corresponding with both the DFS and OFR. The DFS and OFR have (so far) failed to produce any records of the correspondence prior to May 5, 2006 but Exhibit 3.[418]

---

[414] Mathosian, Mark. "Mark Mathosian." *LinkedIn*, 2019, www.linkedin.com/in/mark-mathosian-88349a1b/.   [retired]

[415] "John B. Harper Obituary." *The Florida Times-Union*, 6 Dec. 2008, www.legacy.com/obituaries/timesunion/obituary.aspx?n=john-b-harper&pid=121213409.

[416] UNITED STATES DISTRICT COURT FOR THE DISTRICT OF COLUMBIA. *UNITED STATES OF AMERICA, Plaintiff, v. ALL PROPERTY IN/UNDERLYING E-GOLD ACCOUNT NUMBER(S): 352900, 2325383, AND 2449745, Defendant.* 25 Nov. 2008.

[417] Jackson, Douglas. "Investigation Request." Received by John Roth, Inspector General, US Dept. of Homeland Security, 24 Aug. 2017, Indian Harbour Beach, FL.

[418] Ibid

Shown below is an unsigned "Draft Legal Opinion" rendered by the Florida Office of Financial Regulation (OFR) and Florida Department of Financial Services (DFS). Jackson obtained a copy of this document through the Freedom of Information Act (FOIA) or similar State of Florida information requests. Also copied below is email correspondence between State officials regarding their actions during the e-gold Ltd. and Gold & Silver Reserve, Inc. federal case.

In May 2006, emails between Investigator David Burley (Investigator, Florida Department of Financial Services) to Kathy Norris, Bob Rosenau, and Chris Hancock, Burley explained that he was awaiting a return call from US Secret Service Special Agent Roy Dotson. In this text, Burley suggested that independent e-gold® exchange providers, operating in Florida, including G&SR, could be operating a business that required the Florida Money Transmitting License.

> From: David Burley
> Sent: Thursday, May 04, 2006 12:56 PM
> To: Kathy Norris; Robert Rosenau
> Cc: Chris Hancock
> Subject: RE. IV Gold and Silver Reserve
> Importance: High
> Bob and Chris:
> Although I am still waiting for a return call from the local lead case agent in the federal investigation of Gold and Silver Reserve (GS&R), SA Roy Dotson of the Secret Service, I have checked with GS&R and e-gold, Ltd. directly by phone to see if the company was operational and still allowing new accounts to be created. The customer service rep answering my call asserts that the company is operational and still accepting new e-gold accounts. They also refer you to their website at www.e-gold.com <http://www.e-gold.com> to an create an account and learn more about the company. I checked the website this morning and found many of the links active, including external links to other e-gold exchange outlets offering to buy or sell e-gold currency units for a fee ranging from 2% to 5% of the dollar amount exchanged. These outlets, plus GS&R, could possibly be deemed to be operating as currency exchangers under Ch. 560 of the Florida Statutes and require registration. One of these independent exchange outlets, R.L. Wahl Tampa Exchange, Inc., has placed a notice on their website stating that they were informed by the State of Florida that they needed to be registered as a Money Transmitter Bureau has been in contact with this specific outlet. www.tampaexchange.com <http://www.tampaexchange.com>

P.S. Two articles linked to e-gold's website are helpful in covering the U.S. Treasury's press release of their investigation, and GS&R's response to the investigation and their status as a currency exchanger. Please refer to www.treas.gov/press/releases/reports/js3077_0111205_MLTA.pdf and <http://e-gold.com/letter2.html>[419]

In this next email, Kathy Norris follows up with her State of Florida associates regarding the U.S. Treasury's press release referencing e-gold®.

From:	Kathy Norris
Sent:	Thursday, May 04, 2006 1:25 PM
To:	David Burley: Robert Rosenau
Cc:	Chris Hancock
Subject:	RE: IV Gold and Silver Reserve

In regard to the information below, it appears that the website for Tampa Exchange is not operational. The U.S. Treasury's press release references businesses such as e-gold in Chapter 3, pages 34-36 of the release but I did not see specific information regarding their investigation of GS&R.[420]

The following day, May 5, 2006, Robert "Bob" Rosenau Chief, Bureau of Financial Investigations, State of Florida emailed Kathy Norris and Chris Hancock declaring that the State of Florida has a "regulatory responsibility" to investigate [e-gold] and that in his opinion, G&SR is likely an unregistered money transmitter.

From: Robert Rosenau
Sent: Friday, May 05, 2006 9:12 AM
To: Kathy Norris
Cc: Chris Hancock
Subject: RE: IV Gold and Silver Reserve
I don't see why we could not conduct our investigation concurrent to whatever the fed's are doing. We do have regulatory responsibility and as best I can tell this company is likely an unregistered money transmitter. However, if they[Federal

---

[419] Burley, David. "RE. IV Gold and Silver Reserve." Received by Kathy Norris, and Robert Rosenau, *RE. IV Gold and Silver Reserve*, 4 May 2006.

[420] Norris, Kathy. "RE: IV Gold and Silver Reserve." Received by David Burley, et al., *RE: IV Gold and Silver Reserve*, 4 May 2006.

Agents] have a compelling reason to keep us "on hold" maybe we should wait. R[421]

Rosenau's May 5th email is revealing because this is the first time an email statement confirms that federal agents may have directed the State slow or stop its regulatory investigation and interaction with the native Florida company. He wrote, "However, if they [Federal Agents] have a compelling reason to keep us "on hold" maybe we should wait."[422] This statement was the first evidence of this fact, but not the last.

This May 5th email illustrates the OFR's initial presumption regarding G&SR's status as a Florida Money Transmitter. Rosenau wrote, "as best I can tell this company is likely an unregistered money transmitter." These email statements provide critical insight into the state regulators' initial opinions on the licensing status of e-gold, Ltd. and G&SR Inc.

If the state's initial May 2006 opinion was that e-gold® required a Money Transmitter License, then strong consideration should be given to the state's later conclusion that the business was not a Money Transmitter. It is a serious matter for the State of Florida to assert one claim, investigate, then reverse the opinion. These emails reveal that after a severe effort reviewing the facts and circumstances of e-gold® and G&SR, the State concluded that neither company's activities fell under Florida statutes.

Later that afternoon, Rosenau asked Ramsden for a legal opinion on the G&SR business model.

From:	Robert Rosenau
Sent:	Friday, May 05, 2006 1:12 PM
To:	Mike Ramsden
Subject:	IV Gold and Silver Reserve

Mike,

We discussed this briefly this morning. Before I ask my folks to do lots of work on this, have you asked legal for an opinion on their business model? If not, would you? tks,

r[423]

On Friday, May 19, 2006, Special Agent Dotson, sent an email to Investigator David Burley of the Florida Department of Financial Services.

---

[421] Rosenau, Robert. "RE: IV Gold and Silver Reserve." Received by Kathy Norris, and Chris Hancock, *RE: IV Gold and Silver Reserve*, 5 May 2006.

[422] Ibid

[423] Rosenau, Robert. "IV Gold and Silver Reserve." Received by Mike Ramsden, *IV Gold and Silver Reserve*, 5 May 2006.

From: Roy Dotson, Daniel
Sent: Friday, May 19, 2006 12:58 PM
To: David Burley
Subject: Interviews
Dave,
Thanks for all the help. The AUSA is wondering if any notes were kept from interviews with Douglas Jackson (GSR). If so, can you get me copies of them.[424]

Investigator David Burley emailed back about two hours later.

From: David Burley
Sent: Friday, May 19, 2006 3:04 PM
To: Roy Dotson, Daniel
Subject: RE: Interviews
Importance: High
Roy:
I believe you are confusing our Tampa Office's interview with Richard Wahl of the Tampa Exchange. This interview was in February and conducted by Danielle Brooks, a Financial Crimes Investigator with our Tampa Office, in connection with a complaint involving a high yield investment program (Atlantis Society) using e-gold accounts. We have not interviewed Douglas Jackson or any of the employees at G&SR or OmniPay due to your request in late January to not correspond with Mr. Jackson or his staff. You explained that your investigative team did not want to give Mr. Jackson the opportunity to boast about his cooperation in resolving complaints and assisting government regulators.
I have talked recently with my supervisor and our administrators in Tallahassee about trying to pursue the two complaints I have complaining of missing funds from their e-gold accounts, including the latest complaint I forwarded to you regarding Robert Donald, the investment trader from New York. They have asked me to not pursue my complaints directly with G&SR or e-gold, Ltd., until a decision is made by our Legal Department on whether we have jurisdiction over their business operations.
Please feel free to address Robert Donald's complaint and allegations of insider theft directly with Mr. Jackson and/or G&SR, as the administrator of the e-gold system.
I hope we will soon have a legal opinion determining whether they and all of the exchange outlets meet our definition of a funds transmitter and/or currency

---

[424] Dotson, Roy Daniel. "Interviews." Received by David Burley, *Interviews*, 19 May 2006.

exchanger, under Chapter 560 of the Florida Statutes.

I hope this information helps,

David[425]

This May 19, 2006, email from David Burley to Dotson is explosive. Once again, the evidence shows that during the previous contact, federal authorities handling the e-gold® case directed Florida's Regulators to have no contact with Jackson or the business. Burley stated, "We have not interviewed Douglas Jackson or any of the employees at G&SR or OmniPay due to your request in late January to not correspond with Mr. Jackson or his staff."

Burley's statement continued and offered this perverse reasoning for the government's request "You explained that your investigative team did not want to give Mr. Jackson the opportunity to boast about his cooperation in resolving complaints and assisting government regulators."[426]

This email proves that in January 2006, Dotson had asked that employees working in Florida's Department of Financial Services not to have contact with e-gold®, OmniPay, G&SR, Douglas Jackson, or his staff.

This content supports Rosenau's May 5th email, establishing that federal agents had requested the state slow or stop its interaction with the e-gold®.

Why did the USSS and Dotson block the State of Florida lawyers and regulators from interacting with Jackson, G&SR, and OmniPay? This date was a year before any Court charged the entities with a crime. Could have e-gold® applied and received a Money Transmitter license during that time?

Another 2006 email chain shows State documents and emails that evidenced the official request for a financial opinion regarding the e-gold® operation and the company's possible classification as a "Funds Transmitter" with the State of Florida. This classification would have required e-gold® to obtain a State Money Transmitter License. An up or down on this classification was precisely the opinion that e-gold® needed. Florida assigned the task of writing this legal opinion to Attorney William Oglo.

INTEROFFICE COMMUNICATION
OFFICE OF FINANCIAL REGULATION
DATE: May 15, 2006
TO: Jo Schultz, Attorney Supervisor
FROM: Mike Ramsden, Financial Administrator

[425] Burley, David. "RE: Interviews." Received by Roy Daniel Dotson, *RE: Interviews*, 19 May 2006.
[426] Ibid

THRU: Rick White, Director
Issue: Legal Opinion Regarding e-gold
Recommended Action:
Assign an attorney to review the concept of e-gold and give an opinion on whether companies that offer e-gold should register to be a licensed Money Transmitter.[427]

A week later, SA Roy Dotson emailed Investigator Burley for contact information within the State of Florida's legal department to determine the status of e-gold®.

From: Roy Dotson, Daniel
Sent: Monday, May 22, 2006 11:08 AM
To: David Burley
Subject: Legal Contact
David,
The AUSA and DOJ attorney would like a contact in your legal department to reference determining where e-gold falls. Can you send me a name and number please?
Thanks,
Roy[428]

Days later, Investigator Burley sent another email to Dotson and cc'd Jo Schultz, Peter Fisher, Mike Ramsden. The email stated that Burley had spoken to Mike Ramsden Financial Administrator in the Florida Money Transmitter Regulation Unit. Mike had suggested contacting Ms. Jo Schultz, Chief Counsel, and Peter Fisher, Chief Counsel for an opinion on e-gold's classification as a Money Transmitter under Florida Statutes.

From: David Burley
Sent: Monday, May 22, 2006 3:10 PM
To: 'Roy Dotson, Daniel'
Cc: Jo Schultz; Peter Fisher; Mike Ramsden
Subject: RE: Legal Contact
Importance: High
Roy:
I spoke with Mike Ramsden, the Administrator of our Money Transmitter Unit,

---

[427] Ramsden, Mike. "Legal Opinion Regarding e-gold." Received by Jo Schultz, *Legal Opinion Regarding e-gold*, 15 May 2006. INTEROFFICE COMMUNICATION OFFICE OF FINANCIAL REGULATION, THRU: Rick White, Director

[428] Dotson, Roy Daniel. "Legal Contact." Received by David Burley, *Legal Contact*, 22 May 2006.

regarding his referral to our Legal Department for an opinion on whether the business operations of e-gold, Ltd, and the e-gold exchange outlets, fall under our money transmitter statutes found in Chapter 560, of the Florida Statutes. He advised that you should refer your AUSA and the DOJ attorneys to our General Counsel's office in Tallahassee, more specifically to either of the following persons:
Ms. Jo Schultz, Chief Counsel
Peter Fisher, Chief Counsel
Take care,
David[429]

On July 26, 2006, the following month, Investigator Burley sent communication from the Florida Office of Financial Regulation to Bob Rosenau, Chief, Bureau of Financial Investigations and Chris Hancock, FA, Bureau of Financial Investigations. This document was an official State of Florida reques for a legal opinion. The interoffice communication included these legal questions:

1) Whether e-gold was acting as a bank or financial institution subject to regulation under the Florida Statutes
2) A legal opinion on whether GSR's activities as the primary currency exchange provider for e-gold and other electronic or digital currencies, could be deemed as a "currency exchanger" under Part III of Chapter 560 of the Florida Statues is also requested.

INTEROFFICE COMMUNICATION
OFFICE OF FINANCIAL REGULATION
DATE: July 26, 2006
TO: Chris Hancock, FA and Bob Rosenau, Bureau Chief
FROM: David M. Burley, FICE
SUBJECT: Request for legal opinion regarding jurisdiction over e-gold, Ltd. and Gold & Silver Reserve, Inc.
Please read and review the attached "Operational Summary" describing the methods and operational practices of e-gold, Ltd., and Gold & Silver Reserve, Inc., the administer and primary currency exchange provider for e-gold, Ltd., and Gold & Silver Reserve, Inc., the administer and primary currency exchange provider for e-gold, Ltd. e-gold, Ltd. (e-gold) is the issuer of an account-based electronic gold-backed currency used primarily to store value and facilitate payments on a global basis through the Internet. Gold & Silver Reserve, Inc. (GSR) operates the system

---

[429] Burley, David. "RE: Legal Contact." Received by Roy Daniel Dotson, *RE: Legal Contact*, 22 May 2006.

software from Melbourne, Florida, and is responsible for recording and retaining records of all transactions performed through the e-gold automated computer program. These records are not required to be monitored, audited or forwarded to any federal or state agency, including the IRS.

Given the depository and stored value functions of e-gold, and similar gold-based currencies, the legal question has arisen as to whether e-gold is acting as a bank or financial institution subject to regulation under the Florida Statutes. A legal opinion on whether GSR's activities as the primary currency exchange provider for e-gold, and other electronic or digital currencies, could be deemed as a "currency exchanger" under Part III of Chapter 560 of the Florida Statues is also requested.

In connection with the attached research report describing e-gold, I have included several related exhibits to further clarify the business practices of e-gold, GSR, and those independent currency exchange providers, such as SpaceGold. These currency exchangers are needed and required in order to fund and redeem the value held in accounts with e-gold. The exhibits are as follows:

1. Pages printed from the e-gold website found at www.e-gold.com
2. Pages printed from the OmniPay (GSR) website found at www.omnipay.com
3. Pages printed from the SpaceGold website found at www.spacegold.com
4. Copy of an article published by BusinessWeek in April of 2000
5. Copy of an Investigative Report published in BusinessWeek Online in January of 2006
6. Copy of the rebuttal open letter to the BusinessWeek report published by FreemarketNews.com on January 23, 2006[430]

◆

On August 23, 2006. U.S. Prosecutors formally requested a six-month stay of the instant civil forfeiture proceeding against the bank accounts.

Court documents show that the Government and Defendants disagreed on stipulations of fact as to how G&SR's business operated. During these civil forfeiture proceedings, G&SR affirmed to the Court that it could stipulate to the necessary facts so that the Court

---

[430] Burley, David. "Request for Legal Opinion Regarding Jurisdiction over e-gold, Ltd. and Gold & Silver Reserve, Inc." Received by Chris Hancock, and Bob Rosenau, *Request for Legal Opinion Regarding Jurisdiction over e-gold, Ltd. and Gold & Silver Reserve, Inc.*, 26 July 2006.

would be able to determine whether its business activities constituted an unlicensed money transmitting business. The prosecution refused to accept G&SR's proposal declaring that any stipulations drafted by the defendants would be hypothetical and allegedly incomplete.

Additionally, G&SR's counsel indicated that given the existence of the criminal investigation, lawyers would not permit the government to depose G&SR's controlling officials in the civil case. With discovery so curtailed, the United States responded that it could not proceed with the civil forfeiture and, therefore, it requested a stay. Ultimately, the government requested that the Court postpone Civil Action No. 05-2497 while conducting the "companion" criminal case against the defendants.

On September 6th, 2006, G&SR lawyers filed a Memorandum in Opposition aggressively objecting to the stay.[431]

♦

On September 14, 2006, there was another message from Rosenau to Chris Hancock regarding a legal opinion on e-gold® and G&SR. This message requested the same information and advice.

> e-gold, Ltd. Administered by Gold & Silver Reserve, Inc.
> OPERATIONAL SUMMARY
> DATE: September 14, 2006
> TO: Robert J. Rosenau, Chief, Bureau of Financial Investigations
> FROM: Chris Hancock, FA, Bureau of Financial Investigations
> SUBJECT: Request for Legal Opinion – e-gold/Gold & Silver Reserve
>
> e-gold, a Nevis based corporation, provides on-line payment systems using "digital currency" purportedly backed by gold or other precious metals. Gold & Silver Reserve (GSR), based in Melbourne, Florida, apparently created e-gold and runs the e-gold system.
> The types of services provided by e-gold through GSR have characteristics which resemble the deposit taking function of a financial institution and the funds transmission services typically provided by a financial institution or an entity registered pursuant to Chapter 560. (see attached material provided by Orlando FICE David Burley)

---

[431] Case 1:05-cv-02497-RMC Document 30. *UNITED STATES OF AMERICA v. ALL FUNDS ON DEPOSIT IN SUNTRUST ACCOUNT NUMBER XXXXXXXXX8359, IN THE NAME OF GOLD AND SILVER RESERVE, INC., And ALL FUNDS ON DEPOSIT IN REGIONS BANK ACCOUNT NUMBER XX-XXXX-4851, IN THE NAME OF GOLD AND SILVER RESERVE, INC.* CLAIMANT'S OBJECTION TO PLAINTIFF'S MOTION FOR STAY, 6 Sept. 2006.

To our knowledge, e-gold and GSR are not chartered as, or subsidiaries of, any national or state bank or other financial institution. Neither are they registered in any capacity pursuant to Chapter 560 F.S. No governmental authority regulates the activities of e-gold or provides oversight to protect consumers or merchants. Lack of regulation or digital currency dealers has also been identified by a U.S. Government working group as a money laundering threat.[432]

Later that same day, Rosenau sent almost the same request to Robert B. Beitler, General Counsel.

OFFICE OF FINANCIAL REGULATION INTEROFFICE MEMORANDUM
FROM: Robert J. Rosenau, Chief, Financial Investigations
TO: Rob Beitler, General Counsel
DATE: September 14, 2006
SUBJECT: Request for Legal Opinion – E Gold/Gold & Silver Reserve
Find attached interoffice communication and information packet from FA Chris Hancock.
It would be helpful to obtain legal guidance in attempting to answer the following:

- Can the State of Florida assert any jurisdiction over the activities f e-gold?
- If so, do the business practices of e-gold fall under Chapter 560 or any of the Florida banking statutes?
- Do the business practices of GSR fall under Chapter 560 or any of the Florida banking statutes?[433]

-----Original Message-----
CONFIDENTIAL: Agency attorney mental impression not subject to disclosure under public records law until conclusion of imminent litigation pursuant to Section 119.071 (1), Florida Statutes
Peter,
Enclosed is a revision of my e-gold informal opinion draft. Also enclosed for your convenience are Rob's comments. Please let me know if you have additional suggestions, then I'll send it to Pury.
I have to warn you, the more you think about gold bullion, the more you want to get

432 Hancock, Chris. "Request for Legal Opinion – e-gold/Gold & Silver Reserve." Received by Robert Rosenau, *Request for Legal Opinion – e-gold/Gold & Silver Reserve*, 14 Sept. 2006.

433 Rosenau, Robert. "Request for Legal Opinion – E Gold/Gold & Silver Reserve." Received by Bob Beitler, *Request for Legal Opinion – E Gold/Gold & Silver Reserve*, 14 Sept. 2006.

your hands on some if it. Bullion is defined as bars, ingots, and plates. Ingots is defined as a mass of metal (gold) shaped in a bar or block. On the other hand, when people with high moral standards (Gregg) think of bullion, they think of the soup that you take when you are ill.
Bill[434]

Peter and Gregg,
I added another footnote (#5) which I believe helps to respond to Rob's first comment. Please review the newest revision.
Thanks.
Bill[435]

The following day Bill Oglo, acting as a lawyer for the State of Florida, sent out his informal opinion on e-gold®. The draft document was dated October 25, 2006, and went through Peter Fisher, Chief Finance Attorney to Bob Rosenau, and Mike Ramsden, who worked in the Money Transmitter Regulation Unit. The document included the following statements.

"There is no evidence that e-gold is money of the United States or of any other country which is designated as legal tender. Thus, when G&SR takes currency from a customer and exchanges it for e-gold units, this activity is not encompassed by the definition of Section 560.103(6), Florida Statues.

"If G&SR received e-gold units from a merchant for conversion to domestic currency, it would not be not receiving currency that is the legal tender of a government. Thus, G&SR would not be operating as a transmitter of funds from the merchant either."

"Based upon the description of the e-gold business model as it is currently known and described herein, this writer believes first position, that funds are not being transmitted, is more appropriate."

"Thus, when G&SR converts e-gold units into domestic or foreign currency for a merchant, it is not receiving a "payment instrument" -which needs to involve money- for purposes of transmission to another location. Based upon the foregoing, the

---

[434] Oglo, William. "e-gold." Received by Peter Fisher, and Gregg Morton, *e-gold*, 24 Oct. 2006.
[435] Ibid

activities of e-gold and G&SR are not subject to regulation through Chapter 560, Florida Statutes."

It seems evident that from this Office of Financial Regulation Interoffice Memorandum Florida lawyers and regulators determined that e-gold® and G&SR were not subject to regulation under Florida Statutes as a Money Transmitter. Two critical paragraphs in this document are shown below.[436] The full document is discussed later in the book.

> Pursuant to Sections 560.204(1) and 560.303(1), Florida Statutes, e-gold and G&SR cannot engage in the businesses of acting as funds transmitters or exchanging of foreign currency, among other things, without first being registered with the Office.

> Based upon the foregoing, the activities of e-gold and G&SR are not subject to regulation through Chapter 560, Florida Statutes. This writer has no knowledge that any other federal or state regulator has held that this activity is within the jurisdiction of their money transmitter code. This opinion is based upon the following materials provided to Legal. The Money Transmitter Regulation Unit provided a Business Week magazine article about e-gold as well as copies of material from e-gold's website. Investigations provided Legal with an operational summary of e-gold, Ltd. Prepared by an investigator, printouts of a digital currency exchange service's website, and a chapter about online payment systems from the U.S. Money Laundering Threat Assessment December 2005, among other things.
> Approved by:
> _____ Robert B. Beitler, General Counsel
> _____ Mike Ramsden, Financial Administrator, Money Transmitter Regulation Unit
> _____ Robert Rosenau, Chief, Bureau of Investigations
> _____ Rick White, Director of Securities and Financial Regulation[437] [438]

---

[436] Oglo, William, Assistant General Counsel. "Informal Opinion Regarding Whether the Activities of e-gold, Ltd. and Gold & Silver Reserve, Inc. Are Subject to Regulation by Chapter 560, Florida Statues Legal File No. 0009-M-6/06." Received by Bob Rosenau, Chief, Bureau of Investigations, and Mike Ramsden, Financial Administrator, Money Transmitter Regulation Unit, *Informal Opinion Regarding Whether the Activities of e-gold, Ltd. and Gold & Silver Reserve, Inc. Are Subject to Regulation by Chapter 560, Florida Statues Legal File No. 0009-M-6/06, 25 Oct. 2006.* THROUGH: Peter Fisher, Chief Finance Attorney

[437] This document dated October 25, 2006 was labeled DRAFT and did not contain any signatures.

[438] Oglo, William, Assistant General Counsel. "Informal Opinion Regarding Whether the Activities of e-gold, Ltd. and Gold & Silver Reserve, Inc. Are Subject to Regulation by Chapter 560, Florida Statues Legal File No. 0009-M-6/06." Received by Bob Rosenau, Chief, Bureau of Investigations, and Mike Ramsden, Financial Administrator, Money Transmitter Regulation Unit, *Informal Opinion Regarding Whether the Activities of e-gold, Ltd. and Gold & Silver Reserve, Inc. Are Subject to Regulation by Chapter 560, Florida Statues Legal File No. 0009-M-6/06, 25 Oct. 2006.* THROUGH: Peter Fisher, Chief Finance Attorney

In a later email, dated August 2017, Jackson made this statement about the draft opinion.

> "The Florida legal opinion was the work product of the competent regulatory authority of the state where the defendant businesses were located. The OFR's conclusions were reached after significant inquiry and evaluation, the findings of which in fact caused the FL OFR to reverse its initial impression that the business of the companies probably fell within the scope of the Florida statute."[439]

◆

On October 12th, 2006, District Judge Rosemary Collyer granted the government's motion for a stay in the G&SR forfeiture proceeding Case 05-2497 and postponed it for six months.

> The Government has shown that proceeding with civil discovery would adversely affect its criminal investigation. If the civil case continued, the Government would be subject to the breadth of civil discovery from GS&R. Such discovery could compromise any existing confidential informants and/or interfere with the Government's ability to obtain confidential information from others. The Government also states that responding to civil discovery would burden law enforcement officials who are otherwise conducting a contemporaneous criminal investigation.

> In response, G&SR presents a host of arguments that assail the way the Government has, and is, pursuing this case. None of them has any bearing on whether civil discovery could interfere with the criminal investigation. For this reason, the Court does not believe oral argument would be helpful to its determination and denies the G&SR request for oral argument. See LCvR 7(f) (oral hearing is within court's discretion).[440]

> Accordingly, it is hereby ORDERED that GS&R's motion for a hearing [Dkt. # 33] is DENIED; and it is FURTHER ORDERED that the Government's motion to stay this

---

[439] Jackson, Douglas. "Investigation Request." Received by John Roth, Inspector General, US Dept. of Homeland Security, 24 Aug. 2017, Indian Harbour Beach, FL.

[440] The Government's argument that the refusal of officials of GS&R to be deposed would interfere with its civil case is not relevant.

case [Dkt. # 29] is GRANTED; and it is FURTHER ORDERED that this civil forfeiture case is STAYED for a period of six months from the date of this Order. On or before April 12, 2007, the Government shall file a status report.[441]

◆

Lord Kaisersose Unmasked by Jackson

"Kaisersose" or Keyser Söze references a fictional criminal mastermind character in the 1995 Kevin Spacy movie entitled *The Usual Suspects*. The following e-gold® information details a real-life 2006 case were a criminal used the online alias "Lord Kaisersose."

Jackson's evidence provided to USPIS Agents identified the perpetrator Mr. Ali Beldjouheur of Marseille, France.

Before March 2006, e-gold® had voluntarily participated extensively in discussions regarding the establishment of a protocol for continuous interaction with law enforcement in pursuit of criminal carder activity. As previously discussed, on March 27, 2006, USPIS Investigator Greg Crabb had emailed Jackson requesting assistance with several investigations. Jackson provided the USPIS with preliminary intelligence on the requested high-priority target e-gold® accounts. This detailed information contained data on what first appeared to be two criminals using the aliases "Napalm" and "Lord Kaisersose." During that day's investigation, Jackson had also reached out to an e-gold® exchanger in France for any helpful information on the user of this e-gold® account.

Soon after his inquiry, Jackson received a response from the French agent, which included conclusive data and documents establishing the bad actor's identity, location, and partial criminal history. Jackson's intelligence concluded that one person was using the two separate aliases Lord Kaisersose and Napalm. Jackson was able to quickly identify the individual as Ali Beldjouheur of Marseilles, France. Jackson immediately forwarded this information to Crabb at the USPIS. In that brief email, Jackson characterized Kaiser as "Low hanging fruit, but a prolific one man crime wave." The first email date was Monday, March 27, 2006, from Crabb.[442]

> Doug,
> Thank you for taking the time to examine this activity with us in this iterative

[441] Case 1:05-cv-02497-RMC Document 35. *UNITED STATES OF AMERICA, v. ALL FUNDS ON DEPOSIT IN SUNTRUST ACCOUNT NUMBER XXXXXXXXX8359, IN THE NAME OF GOLD AND SILVER RESERVE, INC., Et Al.*. ORDER GRANTING PLAINTIFF'S MOTION FOR A STAY, 12 Oct. 2006.

[442] Crabb, Gregory. "A Start - Breaking into 2 so Attachments Not Too Much." Received by Douglas Jackson, *A Start - Breaking into 2 so Attachments Not Too Much*, 27 Mar. 2006.

287

fashion. I have a small list of e-gold accounts that trace to individuals that are tied to these credit card organizations. This will be a place for us to start:

Akihikotobe: 1315932
zo0mer: 826191
Smash: 1671595
Tron: 588095
Archi: 317802
Nikiforov: 291618
Raghu: 985132
cc--trader: 1259368
uBuyweRush: 950023
Maksik: 1751848

The documents that I have provided to Main Department of Justice request the account information for these e-gold accounts. The documentation is going to ask for the following:

    - e-gold account profile information for the e-gold account number;
    - transaction history information for the e-gold account numbers;
    - information on any other accounts owned or controlled by the individual; and
    - counter account profile information.

As we begin to examine the activity of these individuals, I expect that we will begin to find some striking patterns. XXXXX and I have accumulated over ten thousand e-mail addresses of subjects that are engaged these credit card fraud activities. It may be useful for us to provide you with these e-mail addresses to assist in our examination of this activity. I will call you after my meetings this afternoon. It will take me a few hours to prepare my computer to communicate via Skype and PGP. Take care,

Greg

        Attachments:
        Akihikotobe 1315932.xls
        Archi 317802.xls
        cc--trader 1259368.xls
        Corporate Gz 966750.xls
        DeluzioNFX 1539702.xls
        denisabi 986677.xls
        johndillinger 2963049.xls[443]

---

[443] Ibid

288

Here is Jackson's email response.

First pass - I'm saving these as Excel 4 worksheets since I figure whatever version Excel you are working with should be able to open. I could also do csv (or you could convert) - let me know which most expedient.

First glance at 1315932, one might say:
- who is this 966750?, and
- how far removed from 950023 is Akikikotobe?
Answer,
- 966750 is another bad guy, and
- one hop.

But darn, even a superficial glance at 966750 begs the question, what's with this 2196759 counterparty, who he is buying UK data from and also splitting loot with? Does napalm ring a bell? But I digress...

Zo0mer leads right to Maksik, but both bring up this 2464856 (hardware?) guy I was mentioning last week who particularly irks me since he obviously makes sooo much more money than me. **I called him Stephen Ceres but I think segvec (from Drax.. whatever Drax is) is probably a better nym.**[444]

When you see an incriminating memo like "cut", it is just too compelling. So segvec segues into DeluzioNFX, 1539702.

I'm also throwing in one of the little johndillnger accounts because it is interesting to see yet another illustration of how things flow through 950023.

Same with Karma, 1633978, he's just so tied in with all the others.

Plus a first round of one of the more recent kaisersose accounts for reasons apparent at a glance. I forwarded requests to two exchangers this am with whom I see hc has done exchanges to see how good their data is on his ID/location.

On this Nikiforov, from what I see, he appears to be a legitimate exchanger. If so, it might be best for me to ask him for whatever data is needed or to get Estonia to subpoena him directly. If he is legitimate, and I see no reason to doubt it, he will be delighted to aid

in investigation. If you have reason to suspect otherwise, like you know he participates in criminal forums etc. I can dump his data to you easy enough.

His contact info:

---

[444] In 2020, Jackson added: Perhaps this sentence should be highlighted since from that moment forward "segvec" became a primary target of international law enforcement agencies (except the USSS and Peretti - who had long known who segvec was).

3235521   1   291618   Vitali Nikiforov   Asula 2-7   Saku Harjumaa
Estonia/75501 info@webmoney.ee   +(372)5218877   False

On this cc--trader: 1259368 guy, I remember asking XXXXX back in Feb for data about this guy because he had 3 debit cards through them. She wrote back and said their company was in some disarray because of the abrupt cancer illness/death of the principal. I'll remind her again because I know debit card vendors always have data on where the cards were originally sent and every place they've been used.

Looking at Carranza's account, I see he is recently doing some largish exchanges with the Bullion exchange 2325383. They are entirely legitimate.

Looking at the most recent Carranza tx's, I ran 3018183 who then exchanged onto a debit card via Cashcards, 274303. I've queried cashcards for records before - they have excellent records and they love to help catch bad guys. Running memos from their history I see this 3018183 guy used to use e-gold account 1763802 to fund the same card. This guy is (or is in league with - no time to go back and recollect unless important to you) holy_father - the hxdef rootkit guy (1669902 not to my knowledge part of this ring, but considered to be a bad person nonetheless. OmniPay, btw, has a good address in CZ for this guy. Taking break, been at it non-stop 4.5 hrs.[445]

About an hour later, Jackson sent another email to the USPIS that included scanned copies of a French government-issued ID. Jackson's message read:

> Got some absolute positive ID on one of the guys, kaisersose, who also (coincidentally) absolutely positively turns out to be that 'napalm' character who, by mere stint of his prominence, I had sent on impulse in earlier batch. Low hanging fruit, but a prolific one man crime wave.[446]

After requesting information from an e-gold® exchange provider, Jackson received documents and details identifying the person using the alias "Lord Kaisersose."

> Dear Doug,
> Following our conversation earlier today, please find herewith the information I was able to get from XXXXX
> This individual's name is Ali BELDJOUHEUR attached pdfs are front & back of his

---

[445] Jackson, Douglas. "Re: A Start - Breaking into 2 so Attachments Not Too Much." Received by Gregory S Crabb, *Re: A Start - Breaking into 2 so Attachments Not Too Much*, 27 Mar. 2006.

[446] Jackson, Douglas. "Re: A Start." Received by Gregory S Crabb, and Agent X, *Re: A Start*, 27 Mar. 2006.

ID, and Driver's license. Addresses on them appear to be current (10 rue Ranque, Marseille 1er, France)

(his gCard had been sent to that address)

gCArd informed me that he had been arrested by the (Marseille) French Financial police about a Month ago, on "illegal Banking activity" charges, and interrogated for 48 hours... ("garde a vue") He now apparently is "mis en examen" by a French "Juge d'instruction" (most probably from Marseille), who is conducting a full criminal enquiry on the case. No doubt the French Police, as well as the Judge will be most interrested about his relationship to the carder ring!

The Cell Phone I have for him (from card funding orders) is: +33-610.21.11.83

If I can be of further help, please do not hesitate to say. In case you need to reach me again, and I'm not available at +33-494.XX.XX.XX (where you left the message earlier today), you can call me on my Cell: +33-611.XX.XX.XX

XXXX@mutemail.com is my personal private e-mail[447]

The next day, Jackson sent Crabb another email with additional documents and details on the target   suspects.

I'll be doing spring break stuff with our kids (mostly driving a gang of them to Orlando) until after noon but I'll have cell 321 XXX XXXX with me.

I'm attaching a few stragglers I was working on later in afternoon yesterday. Pudu, a carder himself, exchanges carders' physical cash for e-gold, a sort of exchange middleman. Barboza also launders for them - still learning details on him. There are of course scores of very prolific players we haven't talked about yet. I'm also attaching confirmed identity info on Ali BELDJOUHEUR, aka kaisersose, aka napalm

Attached pdfs are front & back of his ID, and Driver's license.

Addresses on them are believed current (10 rue Ranque, Marseille 1er, France) - he had a debit card from gcard sent to that address.

Per gCArd he had been arrested by the (Marseille) French Financial police about a Month ago, on "illegal Banking activity" charges, and interrogated for 48 hours... ("garde a vue")

He now apparently is "mis en examen" by a French "Juge d'instruction" (most

[447] Patrick. "Acct # 2567183 Case." Received by Douglas Jackson, *Acct # 2567183 Case*, 27 Mar. 2006.

probably from Marseille), who is conducting a full criminal enquiry on the case. The Cell Phone he has used with exchangers for card funding orders is +33-610.21.11.83

Email contained the following files:[448]
Luis Barboza 2136572.xls
Pudu Bol 1772946.xls
earlier Pudu and Bol 1236175.xls
driving_licence_ front.JPG
driving_licence_back.bmp
ID_back.JPG
ID_front.JPG

Jackson had identified Ali Beldjouheur, aka Lord Kaisersose, to the USPIS in March 2006.

In June 2007, nearly one year after Jackson had given the information to Crabb identifying Beldjouheur, French agents from the Central Office for Combating Crime Related to Information and Communication Technologies (OCLCTIC)[449], along with dozens of armed officers, assaulted addresses in Marseilles and outside of Paris. Law enforcement agents in France arrested Ali Beldjouheur in a central Marseilles apartment. Lord Kaiserose purchased stolen credit card information from the Ukrainian criminal kingpin Maksik. The individual behind the alias Maksik was one of the world's largest vendors of stolen credit card information. For over two years, Maksik had sold Beldjouheur the details of at least 28,000 credit cards, which had a cash-out value of $10 to $14 million.

Shortly after these arrests, news reports chronicled how the United States Secret Service had carried out "Operation Lord Kaisersose." The media illustrated how USSS Special Agents in the Miami office had identified a suspect using the alias Lord Kaisersose and provided the French National Police with information to make the arrests. There was no mention of e-gold's help. Furthermore, no evidence of Jackson's contribution was ever acknowledged or presented to the Court.

Withholding details about Jackson's cooperation allowed the prosecution to claim that e-gold® was ignoring the alleged criminal activity taking place on the platform. By not acknowledging e-gold's assistance, Jackson alleged that the USSS was purposely creating a

---

448 Jackson, Douglas. "Stragglers from Yesterday." Received by Gregory S Crabb, and Agent X, *Stragglers from Yesterday*, 28 Mar. 2006.
449 The Central Office for Combating Crime Related to Information and Communication Technologies (OCLCTIC) merged and is now the Sub-Directorate for the Fight Against Cybercrime (SDLC), the body of the French police dedicated to the fight against cybercrime and a branch of the Central Directorate of the Judicial Police

fake e-gold profile of the company to aid in a successful criminal prosecution. Jackson was not surprised to learn that the Miami office of the USSS had conducted operation "Lord Kaisersose."

On June 25, 2007, the USSS issued a press release entitled "United States Secret Service Targets Cyber Criminals." It included the tag line, "Recent operations and arrests demonstrate the importance of international law enforcement partnerships."

(Washington, D.C.) – The United States Secret Service today made public multiple international arrests as part of ongoing anti-cyber crime initiatives. These covert Internet based investigations target individuals who involve themselves in various types of illegal activities to include the manufacture, purchase, sale, and exploitation of various financial instruments and personal identification information and documents.

Operation Lord Kaisersose
Operation Lord Kaisersose is an ongoing covert Internet investigation based out of the Secret Service's Miami Field Office. In conjunction with this investigation, agents were able to identify an individual known as "Lord Kaisersose." "Lord Kaisersose" was associated with Internet sites known for identity theft and financial fraud activities. The Secret Service investigation uncovered online transactions with "Lord Kaisersose" including the sale of access device numbers compromised through commercial databases.

Operation Hard Drive
Operation Hard Drive is an ongoing covert operation being coordinated by the U.S. Secret Service's Buffalo Field Office. With the cooperation of the French National Police (FNP) and the Calgary Police Service, the operation has led to arrests in France and Canada of individuals who together are responsible for more than $1 million in fraud losses.

Investigation uncovered an individual using the screen name "THEEEEL," a resident of Marseille, France, through his association with Internet sites known for illegal carding activity. Investigators discovered online transactions conducted by "THEEEEL," including the purchase of thousands of dollars worth of stolen access device numbers.

On June 12, 2007, acting on the information provided by the U.S. Secret Service, the

FNP executed arrest and search warrants upon "THEEEEL" and his residence, recovering evidence and/or contraband associated with illegal carding activity including multiple external hard drives, skimming and encoding devices, counterfeit identification and counterfeit credit cards.

Nicholas Joehle, of Calgary, Alberta, Canada, using the screen name "Dron" was identified as a primary suspect in the sale of high-quality "skimmers" over the Internet. Over the past year, Operation Hard Drive investigators discovered numerous global online sales of these skimmers by Joehle. On May 25, 2007, Secret Service agents from the Buffalo and Vancouver offices assisted Calgary Police Service officials in executing a search warrant. One hundred skimmers in various stages of production, a skimmer manufacturing lab and $30,000 in genuine U.S. and Canadian currency were recovered as a result of the search.

Joehle has since been charged by Canadian officials with violating Canadian statutes governing the import and export of credit card alteration/forgery devices, possession of credit card alteration/forgery devices and possession of criminal proceeds. "The success of these investigations is a direct result of the excellent partnerships that exists between the Secret Service and our international law enforcement partners," said Assistant Director Stenger.[450]

The press release did not mention e-gold®. Neither the media nor the USSS made any statement about e-gold® or Jackson as having assisted the investigation. To add insult to injury, specific news articles published on the operation included comments suggesting that e-gold® may have hindered law enforcement's investigative efforts.

The media attempted to portray the protection afforded by e-gold's international legal structure as having hampered or obstructed "Operation Lord Kaisersose." The irresponsible description of e-gold® appeared in multiple articles of similar content, including PCWorld, InfoWorld, ZDnet, and other popular online magazines. "A probe into unauthorized electronic funds transfer via e-gold service became complex because the company registration is at Nevis, West Indies, although its assets are wholly established in Florida."[451]

None of these articles included any mention of how Jackson had first identified the French suspect almost one year earlier. A June 27, 2007, article from SecurityFocus.com,

[450] "UNITED STATES SECRET SERVICE TARGETS CYBER CRIMINALS." *US Secret Service*, United States Secret Service Office of Government and Public Affairs, 25 June 2007, secretservice.gov.
[451] Lemos, Robert. "Cybercrime Busts Net Data-Theft Suspects." *Cybercrime Busts Net Data-Theft Suspects*, 27 June 2007, www.securityfocus.com/brief/536.

framed the USSS's actions in similar glowing tones and tried to cast doubt on the e-gold® operation.

Cybercrime busts net data-theft suspects
Published: 2007-06-27
Two operations run by the the U.S. Secret Service led to the arrests of French and Canadian citizens on charges stemming from the theft of user names and passwords and illegal carding activity, the federal agency said this week.

In Operation Lord Kaisersose, the Secret Service's Miami field office identified an individual, known online as "Lord Kaisersose," that had allegedly stolen more than 28,000 compromised accounts and used the information to commit more than $14 million in fraud. The investigation led the French National Police to arrest a French citizen and three associates, the Secret Service said in a statement. A second operation led the Calgary Police Service to arrest an Alberta resident on charges of possessing and trading credit-card skimming devices and a French resident on charges of illegal carding activities.

The Secret Service stressed that the operations, as with most other Internet investigations, would not have been successful without international cooperation.

"Technology has forever changed the way commerce is conducted, virtually erasing geographic boundaries," Michael Stenger, assistant director of the U.S. Secret Service Office of Investigations, said in a statement (PDF). "While these advances continue to have a profound impact on the financial crimes we investigate, sharing information and resources through international partnerships is the best way to combat these types of crimes."

Most cybercrime investigations have had international components. An investigation into online funds transfer service e-gold has been complicated by the fact that the company is registered in Nevis, West Indies, even though the company's assets appear to be entirely based in Florida. Operation Cardkeeper -- an FBI investigation into the illegal trading of credit-card numbers, so-called "carding" -- led to the arrest last year of three people in the U.S. and another 13 in Poland.

The U.S. Secret Service is developing the curriculum for the National Computer Forensics Institute in Hoover, Alabama, which will train both U.S. and international law enforcement personnel.[452]

After the Lord Kaisersose arrest, in fall 2007, Jackson discovered that the criminal mastermind, Ali Beldjouheur, had never stopped his recidivist online activity. Upon his release, Ali continued trying to open new e-gold® accounts and transact illegal carder business. This USSS arrest was another case where Special Agents received critical information provided by Jackson that identified, located, and supported the arrest a significant carder. However, no mention of this assistance or cooperation ever made it into the e-gold® Court case, nor appeared in the news media.

In 2007-2008, many insiders believed that the USSS had recruited Ali as a confidential informant. However, a year of research turned-up no evidence this allegation was true. In 2020, French Police know Ali Beldjouheur as the "forger linked to organized crime." Between 2006 and 2016, he accumulated ten convictions in French courts, including fines and prison time.[453]

In 2007, a Washington Post reporter named Brian Krebs told Jackson that he had verbally confirmed the USSS directly learned of Lord Kaisersose through e-gold's original information.[454]

Jackson sent an email to Agent Crabb on August 4, 2006, expressing concern that the USSS may try to portray e-gold as "turning a blind eye." Jackson complained to Inspector Crabb:

> Regarding these carders...
> For months I've held off on exorcising them on the informal understanding that you guys prefer we allow them to continue a while for track/trace purposes.
>
> But is there an end in sight? I am concerned that:
> a) I don't want these guys continuing to infest e-gold, on general principles
> b) conceivably, their continuing activity could even be construed as complicity on our part by someone with a particularly twisted agenda I need either explicit instruction to let things go on, or a sense of when I can drop the hammer on them. I have a file of every account yet identified and can pull the trigger on them in

[452] Lemos, Robert. "Cybercrime Busts Net Data-Theft Suspects." *Cybercrime Busts Net Data-Theft Suspects*, 27 June 2007, www.securityfocus.com/brief/536.

[453] Charlet, Denis. "Trial of Counterfeiters in Marseille: the Main Suspect Denies Everything in Block." *LaDepeche.fr*, ladepeche.fr, 23 Nov. 2017, www.ladepeche.fr/article/2017/10/23/2671196-proces-faux-monnayeurs-marseille-principal-suspect-nie-tout-bloc.html .

[454] Jackson, Douglas. "Narrative - Lord Kaisersose." Received by Machalagh Carr, *Narrative - Lord Kaisersose*, 25 Oct. 2008.

minutes. If this was done in a coordinated fashion, btw, with a court order to freeze, a fair amount of value could also be locked down, further hurting these dudes. Even if we do it on our own, our plan is to have a rolling follow-up designed to uncover their yet-unknown accounts as they scurry around trying to find an account that accepts value from blocked accounts. This would hold value in the system for as long as we run the program but in effect would also more or less violate our user agreement that we don't outright freeze without due process.[455]

Crabb emailed his response five days later.

> Subject: RE: cardersmack
> From: "Crabb, Gregory S" <XXXXX@uspis.gov>
> Date: Wed, 9 Aug 2006 08:32:20 -0400
> To: "Douglas Jackson" <djackson@e-gold.com>
> CC: "Agent X" <XXXXX@uspis.gov>, "Agent Y" <XXXXX@uspis.gov>
> Doug,
> Sorry for the delay in my response. I have been out of the office for about a week and a half.
> We have been progressing on some foreign operations based, in part, on the information that you have provided. We expect that these operations will yield very positive results in the coming months.
> I just made an inquiry to a couple of assistant US Attorney's familiar with these issues. Pending their response, I will provide you with an explicit statement one way or the other.
> Take care,
> Greg[456]

Additionally, hiding critical case details and evidence from the Court, such as not disclosing e-gold's assistance or Jackson's cooperation, suggests a malicious prosecution. Why was there no mention of e-gold's direct interaction in these significant cases? Why did prosecutors and the USSS downplay e-gold's participation? In the same letter to John Roth at DHS, Jackson revealed some additional thoughts.

> Convinced the data I had provided had constituted the breakthrough, in my sentencing memorandum I detailed the information I had uncovered and supplied to

[455] Jackson, Douglas L. "Subject: Cardersmack." Received by Gregory S. Crabb, *Subject: Cardersmack*, 4 Aug. 2006.

[456] Crabb, Gregory S. "RE: Cardersmack." Received by Douglas Jackson, *RE: Cardersmack*, 9 Aug. 2006.

law enforcement. At my sentencing hearing, Peretti's associate Laurel Rimon denied the significance of my efforts (Exhibit 26): "He relates in his papers that his work led to the arrest and indictment of Segvec and Maksik, two computer criminals who broke into a restaurant chain of Dave and Buster's cash registers, had stole credit card information and sold that credit card information.

This case happens to be handled by Kim Peretti my colleague is the lead prosecutor on that case and was very intimate and familiar with it. The postal service is not an investigative agency on this case, it's a pure U.S. Secret Service case. The information that Dr. Jackson may have provided to Agent Crabb did not factor into this investigation at all."

On December 1, 2008 (Exhibit 27), I related the prosecution's comments to USPIS Agent X,[law enforcement agent working closely with Jackson], "At sentencing, the gov lawyer said my assistance to LE had been of no or at most trivial benefit, that the USSS had already gleaned anything that might have been useful to them directly from our database. But as of about August 2006 they still hadn't managed to even mount it on a server in a way that would enable queries." Agent X replied "Being off the record, regarding that comment, I would completely disagree.   I know wholeheartedly how many investigations you assisted us on and how much it helped for us referring cases to international LE based off of your work. There are still cases ongoing today that are as a direct result of your help."[457]

e-gold® Pushback

Within the e-gold® community, there was a growing awareness of the company performing in-house investigations on potential bad actors. Many of e-gold's oldest customers and exchange providers were upset that Jackson may have ignored terms of the e-gold® Account User Agreement[458] and shared users' personal information   with "the government." Explicitly, section 3.7.2 of the Privacy Policy contained in the User Agreement stated:

> "3.7.2. Unless (1) otherwise approved by User or (2) ordered by a court or arbitration body of acceptable jurisdiction, as determined by Issuer, Issuer shall not reveal User's contact or identifying information or transaction history to any third party."[459]

---

[457] Ibid

[458] "e-gold Account User Agreement." Edited by Douglas Jackson, e-gold.com, e-gold Ltd., 2002, web.archive.org/web/20021217010505fw_/www.e-gold.com/unsecure/e-g-agree.htm.

How e-gold® had used private customer information to identify bad actors buying and selling stolen credit card information (Carders) appeared in a December 11th, 2006, Wired.com article. The report elaborated on e-gold's investigations into potential misuse of the platform. From December 2006, article entitled *e-gold Gets Tough on Crime*, this content appeared one year after the 2005 G&SR search warrants.

> "The founder of PayPal competitor e-gold® has grown tired of the government characterizing his business as a haven for money launderers, terrorists, child pornographers and credit card thieves. So a year after the Department of Justice raided his offices, Douglas Jackson, president of Gold and Silver Reserve, which operates e-gold®, has been wading deep into his customer transaction logs to identify and fight back against people who misuse his system. In the last month, he's blocked about 2,000 accounts from his system, and he's voluntarily turned over detailed account and transaction histories to federal law enforcement."[460]

In the same 2006 Wired.com article, attorney for the Defendants, Andrew Ittleman, commented about the relationship between e-gold® and the law enforcement community. The primary point of contention was that federal agents were receiving private details on e-gold® customers when there had been no legal court order.[461]

> "Jackson acknowledges some discomfort over the decision to give information to the feds without legal process -- a move that could save e-gold® from further law enforcement aggression, while tarnishing its libertarian sheen. His lawyers aren't bothered by the move, however. They say agents repeatedly promised to provide Jackson with court orders since last February but have not come through. "You have a very strong documented relationship with these agents asking about particular people with the promise that they are going to be subpoenaing," says Jackson attorney Andrew Ittleman. "Just because they never ultimately gave him a subpoena doesn't put the fault on Jackson -- it's on the agents. He was acting in good faith."

> His lawyers also say that once the company discovered possible wrongdoing, it had no choice but to hand over information to the government. The government could

---

[459] Ibid

[460] *e-gold Gets Tough on Crime,* December 11th, 2006, Wired.com https://www.wired.com/2006/12/e-gold-gets-tough-on-crime/

[461] Ibid

have charged Jackson with aiding and abetting money launderers under federal statutes if he didn't report the suspicious activity.

"e-gold®, because of the way in which it operates, creates the potential for a misuse," says lead attorney Mitchell Fuerst. "And to the extent that that can happen, I think the company has an ethical and a legal obligation to prevent those crimes from being committed."

But the company thinks it's unlikely that anyone involved in illicit activity would sue e-gold® for blocking their account or giving their data to law enforcement."[462]

The same article drew immediate criticism and condemnation from defenders of Internet privacy, such as Kevin Bankston, a staff attorney for the Electronic Frontier Foundation. He was quoted in Wired.com saying that e-gold® was "violating its privacy policy, which states that the company won't hand over data except under court order. Its actions could open it to liability under contract violation and false advertising and unfair competition claims."[463]

Bankstron was not alone; a chorus of other serious objections appeared across the Internet, labeling Jackson's "snooping" as unethical. That chorus included an article from Claire Wolfe. In a December 12, 2006, post, popular author and well-known privacy advocate Claire Wolfe attacked e-gold's warrantless searches. She published this piece in her Wolfesblog.

e-gold Spreads its Legs for the Feds
by Claire Wolfe from Wolfesblog 12/12/2006 Archived Entry

e-gold, UNDER PRESSURE, lies down and spreads its legs for the feds. Heck, it even goes out trolling for fed "customers," which it services for free (no warrant or subpoena required for the fed big boys).

So much for e-gold's "libertarian image." If you deal with e-gold in the future, be sure to have yourself checked for STDs afterwards -- that is Statist Transmitted Despotisms.

No big surprise -- and no big deal, I suppose. Just one more corporate sellout, one more act of data mining snoopery by a private business on behalf of its federal partner. One more unsurprising revelation of who the real customer is. Ho hum, what's on the other channel?

---

[462] Zetter, Kim. "e-gold Gets Tough on Crime." *Wired.com*, 11 Dec. 2006.
[463] Ibid

Though Wolfesblog has an e-gold link for donations and the annual book sale, I believe it's been used just once in the last three years. Getting money into and out of e-gold was always such a bitch it seems few people ever got around to it. I'd close my e-gold account, except it's hardly worth bothering for the hundred bucks or so worth of metals that have been sitting idly in it all these years. Still, you hadda kinda hope that a business, started by alleged freedom lovers, and dealing internationally in metal money, would be prepared to hold out, and wouldn't cave so spectacularly and so cravenly.[464] (http://ClaireWolfe.com)

♦

Senate Testimony on Deleting Commercial Child Pornography

On September 21, 2006, Jackson visited Washington, D.C, and testified on behalf of e-gold Ltd. and Gold & Silver Reserve, Inc. He participated in a House Hearing before the Subcommittee on Oversight and Investigations of the Committee on Energy and Commerce for the House of Representatives, One Hundred Ninth Congress, Second Session. The hearing was entitled "Deleting Commercial Child Pornography Sites From the Internet: The U.S. Financial Industry's Efforts To Combat This Problem."[465]

During his testimony, Dr. Jackson told Congress there were over 60 million e-gold transactions at that time, and transfers worth over $2 billion per year. E-gold was the largest digital currency operating over the internet.[466]

Just before the hearing, a member of the subcommittee, U.S. Congressman Michael C. Burgess from the 26th district of Texas, published this statement. The document's content revealed the members' ignorance regarding the e-gold® platform, its operation, benefits, and

[464] Wolfe, Claire. "e-gold Spreads Its Legs for the Feds." Billstclair.com, 12 Dec. 2006, doi:https://billstclair.com/clairewolfe/wolfesblog/00002336.html Clairewolfe.com

[465] "DELETING COMMERCIAL PORNOGRAPHY SITES FROM THE INTERNET: THE U.S. FINANCIAL INDUSTRY'S EFFORTS TO COMBAT THIS PROBLEM." - DELETING COMMERCIAL PORNOGRAPHY SITES FROM THE INTERNET: THE U.S. FINANCIAL INDUSTRY'S EFFORTS TO COMBAT THIS PROBLEM HEARING BEFORE THE SUBCOMMITTEE ON OVERSIGHT AND INVESTIGATIONS OF THE COMMITTEE ON ENERGY AND COMMERCE HOUSE OF REPRESENTATIVES ONE HUNDRED NINTH CONGRESS SECOND SESSION SEPTEMBER 21, 2006 Serial No. 109-141 Printed for the Use of the Committee on Energy and Commerce Available via the World Wide Web: http://www.access.gpo.gov/Congress/House U.S. GOVERNMENT PRINTING OFFICE 31-467 WASHINGTON : 2006, [House Hearing, 109 Congress] [From the U.S. Government Printing Office], 21 Sept. 2006, www.govinfo.gov/content/pkg/CHRG-109hhrg31467/html/CHRG-109hhrg31467.htm. Serial No. 109-141

[466] Docket No. CR 07-109. UNITED STATES OF AMERICA vs. E-GOLD LTD, GOLD & SILVER RESERVE LTD, DOUGLAS L. JACKSON, BARRY K. DOWNEY, REID A. JACKSON. TRANSCRIPT OF SENTENCE BEFORE THE HONORABLE ROSEMARY M. COLLYER UNITED STATES DISTRICT JUDGE, 20 Nov. 2008. Statement by Laurel Loomis Rimon Esquire during Dr. Jackson's sentencing November 20, 2008

safeguards. No subcommittee member, or staff present at the hearing, had ever opened an e-gold® account or completed a Spend transaction. Jackson had a difficult time energetically discussing the e-gold® system and responding to the members' awkward questions.

Statement by the Honorable Michael C. Burgess, M.D.
Deleting Commercial Child Pornography Sites from the Internet:
The U.S. Financial Industry's Efforts to Combat this Problem
September 21, 2006
Thank you Mr. Chairman, and thank you for the continuation of this important series of hearings.

Over the past few months, our committee has taken up the important cause of protecting our children from sexual exploitation over the Internet. My emotions on this horrific issue have ranged from shock to disgust to a strong desire to completely eradicate this problem. I, for one, have learned a great deal more than what I ever wanted to know about this topic. However, it is crucial for the safety of our children for all of us to know about these evils so that we can help end this abusive and dangerous practice. While the pedophiles are our biggest enemy, we must also continue to look and combat everyone associated with this crime.

I am glad that today we are focusing on the efforts of the financial industry. The representatives from reputable credit card companies will provide a valuable insight into what their respective companies are doing. I am also very interested in discussing with Dr. Douglas Jackson his company, e-gold. I do not understand the need for an anonymous digital currency, and I look forward to hearing from Dr. Jackson about his company's due diligence and role in stopping illegal activities like child pornography.

Today, we also have with us Mr. Ernie Allen, President and CEO of NCMEC, who will be discussing the creation and role of The Financial Coalition Against Child Pornography at NCMEC. From my understanding, it has been reported the Mr. Allen believes that the Financial Coalition can eradicate commercial child pornography by 2008. I think I can speak on behalf of the rest of the committee that we would all like to learn more about how he thinks this goal is attainable.

Mr. Chairman, thank you again for your continued leadership and dedication to this grave situation. I look forward to working with you and others on the committee as we continue to seek solutions to this most horrid problem. It is my sincere hope that this hearing will be a catalyst for more legislation aimed at curbing this problem.[467]

---

[467] "DELETING COMMERCIAL PORNOGRAPHY SITES FROM THE INTERNET: THE U.S. FINANCIAL INDUSTRY'S EFFORTS TO COMBAT THIS PROBLEM." - DELETING COMMERCIAL PORNOGRAPHY SITES

On September 29, 2006, after his Washington testimony, Jackson sent a private letter to representatives that included his open offer of support. Jackson also detailed additional measures that e-gold® was undertaking to prevent the platform from being used by bad actors.

The Honorable Ed Whitfield, Chairman
The Honorable Bart Stupak, Ranking Member
The Committee on Energy and Commerce
Subcommittee on Oversight and Investigations
2125 Rayburn House Office Building
Washington, DC 20515

Honorable Congressmen Whitfield and Stupak:

I would like to thank you again for allowing me to participate in your hearing on Thursday, September 21 on stopping child pornography on the Internet. Anything and everything we can do to eradicate this crime is worthwhile.

After reviewing the collective testimony and comments from the Subcommittee, my fellow participants, and myself, I believe it would be worthwhile to clarify several items. I would also like to share with you additional actions we are taking to do our part in eliminating child pornography from the Internet completely.

One specific question was raised as to how many buyers of child pornography e-gold® investigators had turned over to law enforcement. The simple answer is at least 2,000 (in the US), and more likely more than 3,000. This spans the entire interval since September 2004, when these criminals first started to abuse e-gold®, to the present, when such abuse has been driven down to a negligible level. Generating an exact total would be time consuming, and it may be more productive to relate the evolution of mechanisms whereby such data is supplied.

FROM THE INTERNET: THE U.S. FINANCIAL INDUSTRY'S EFFORTS TO COMBAT THIS PROBLEM HEARING BEFORE THE SUBCOMMITTEE ON OVERSIGHT AND INVESTIGATIONS OF THE COMMITTEE ON ENERGY AND COMMERCE HOUSE OF REPRESENTATIVES ONE HUNDRED NINTH CONGRESS SECOND SESSION SEPTEMBER 21, 2006 Serial No. 109-141 Printed for the Use of the Committee on Energy and Commerce Available via the World Wide Web: http://www.access.gpo.gov/Congress/House U.S. GOVERNMENT PRINTING OFFICE 31-467 WASHINGTON : 2006, [House Hearing, 109 Congress] [From the U.S. Government Printing Office], 21 Sept. 2006, www.govinfo.gov/content/pkg/CHRG-109hhrg31467/html/CHRG-109hhrg31467.htm. Serial No. 109-141

In the earlier version of NCMEC's CyberTipline, available to e-gold® investigators from late summer 2005 until around January 2006, the Tipline design was oriented toward identifying sites and sellers with little provision for uploading information regarding buyers. It is my understanding that this was partly due to reticence (or even inability) on the part of the credit card associations to blacklist card holders who had made such purchases. During this phase, the e-gold® interdiction protocol consisted of:

- Identifying and blocking not only sellers, but investigating buyers as well, performing queries to identify any other e-gold® accounts controlled by the buyers and blocking them, thereby preventing them from ever receiving further e-gold® payments. During this phase, it was found that the best way to find CP sellers was to look via an iterative process at all other accounts to which CP buyers had spent their e-gold®.
- Non-identifying buyer data revealing the city and state of buyers was uploaded in order for NCMEC to aid in distributing the data to whichever law enforcement agency was likely to have jurisdiction.
- Based on the general location data supplied, a subpoena would be returned enabling e-gold® investigators to provide detailed CP buyer data, including name, address, phone, log-in IPs and timestamps, and email accounts.

During this phase, although accounts were blocked to prevent buyers from receiving further payments, it was still possible for them to spend value already in their accounts.

In Spring 2006, a system-wide change was implemented, making it possible for an e-gold® account user to refuse to accept payments from blocked accounts. This was primarily for the benefit of exchange services who did not wish to unwittingly receive e-gold® payments that might constitute the proceeds of crime. The account setting to refuse payment from blocked accounts was made active by default, so that a user would have to actively change the setting in order to accept such payments, thereby enabling investigators to query for accounts which had changed this setting and subject them to closer scrutiny. In addition, the system would not allow new accounts to change the setting at all until they were a month old. These latter details were designed to strengthen this feature—to more nearly approximate freezing an account but stopping short of transgressing the e-gold® Account User Agreement which allows e-gold® to refuse to do business on the basis of a right of association but prohibits e-gold® from outright freezing value without due process.

Around this time, the CyberTipline was between generations and there were virtually no notifications from NCMEC to e-gold® (though we did continue to receive notifications at an already decreasing rate from other sources). In March 2006, e-gold® investigators rolled out a new capability for screening transactions directly from the transaction database, based on pattern recognition algorithms. This enabled a step change advance in interdiction, starting a shift from reliance on notification from external parties such as NCMEC or ASACP, instead enabling identification of CP seller accounts directly from the e-gold® database as early as their first inbound payment.

In summer 2006, the next generation CyberTipline was deployed, but it made essentially no provision for uploading buyer information. By this time, however, e-gold® investigators had enough personal contacts within the law enforcement community to have a sense as to which individuals might actually do something if notified of CP buyers. Since this time, the expedient mechanism has been for e-gold® investigators to provide intelligence directly to law enforcement and aid them in preparing subpoenas that enable the most complete release of information.

The e-gold® detection and interdiction protocols continuously evolve. More recent, highly effective changes have included:

- With every purchase event, the ultimate exchange source of the e-gold® is identified and the exchange service notified, enabling them to blacklist the buyer and upload data to shared fraud databases developed for the joint use of independent exchangers.
- Seller accounts are frozen, if value remains. This turns into a race between the e-gold® investigators who find the new seller account upon its first payment, and the CP seller who as quickly as possible seeks to spend the e-gold® to an innocent third party, most usually an exchange service providing automated exchange from e-gold® into Webmoney. Therefore, with each escape event, Webmoney investigators are informed within hours or even minutes of the payment, enabling hot pursuit to continue within Russia. Data returned from this intelligence channel is then forwarded to U.S. law enforcement.

Additional refinements are continuously being developed. One ongoing project has been a case-by-case review of buyer accounts, re-querying to assure that all other e-gold® accounts controlled by the same people are identified and added to the buyer master list and freezing any buyer-controlled accounts (initially) with value over AUG 0.05 (5 cg of gold, equivalent to about $30 at current exchange rates). In addition, the most effective and timely screening tool for finding actual CP payments, first deployed in August and resulting in a second step change reduction in escape payments [currently down to below $1000 per week and still dropping] up until now has been run manually about 10 times each day and night. This tool has reached the point of effectiveness that it is being reconfigured to run in a fully automated manner, countering the tendency for CP sellers to empty their account immediately after receiving a payment.

For the past year, there has been only a handful of remaining CP sellers, all of them from Russia. Each payment system uses techniques suited for their specific nature, which for credit cards requires looking for websites. For e-gold®, looking at websites is now the least timely and effective detection mechanism, the safety net for re-acquiring the scent of a seller in the event that they shape shift so effectively as to evade the database detection protocols. The database queries are nearing 100% effectiveness. Now, notifications from third parties are for sites whose every attempt to receive payment by e-gold® has already been found and blocked. In addition, based on the procedures e-gold® uses to "punish" the buyer, we are rapidly reaching the point where the only e-gold® users capable of buying CP will be law enforcement investigators, because they are the only CP-buying e-gold® users left who have not been dealt with severely.

Several times in the hearings, it was noted that credit cards have been the major source of payments for this illegal activity, but their efforts are pushing sellers to alternative means of accepting payment. I would like to emphasize that among all possible "alternative" payment systems, e-gold® is the first to become so actively involved in the fight against child pornography. To note Mr. Allen's comments, we are being very aggressive. As the hard data in the submitted written testimony demonstrates, the e-gold® story, with respect to eradicating the commercial viability of child pornography, is one of resounding success.

The hearings highlighted several areas where I believe we or the coalition can take additional steps to solve this problem.

We recognize that our payment system is new and unique. It is not simple to understand. We would like to offer our time to more fully explain how e-gold® operates, its benefits, why it is not a good vehicle for crime, and how it can actually help. We would be more than happy to host your representatives at our headquarters so they can gain a thorough understanding. As an example, we recently had representatives from the NTFIU unit of Scotland Yard hosted by the FBI in Melbourne to educate them on e-gold®. Using several test cases they presented, we were able to demonstrate how we could track and identify their suspects. In these examples we did see that e-gold® was used in a very limited manner by their targets.

> This educational offering has for years been extended to all law enforcement and remains an open invitation.

Congressman Stupak made an interesting observation that all the panel participants indicated their systems saw low use for buying child pornography, so how was so much being spent? I have contacted all the financial partners in the coalition, requesting that we collectively address this question and will follow the issue through our future meetings.

I have also initiated several actions internal to e-gold®.

- We have had a project to move to a user-based log-in system that enables systematic, stronger validation of customer identity in conjunction with an enhanced (two-factor) authentication protocol. This project was scheduled to be complete by now, but was seriously delayed as the government action taken in December, which consumed both management focus and financial resources. Financial resources remain a problem as our funds remain seized and we are facing high legal costs, but we intend to accelerate this project.
- The effort to change over to user-based log-in is not simple or quick. In parallel, we are adapting the postal validation process developed and used by OmniPay for use with e-gold. e-gold's unparalleled existing capability with regard to traceability will be complemented by this and other market driven evolutionary enhancements in knowledge of customers.

I am continuing to coordinate interdiction efforts with exchange services. These independent businesses have enthusiastically embraced our efforts to expel and blacklist anyone who has ever purchased child pornography and have themselves become a very valuable source of intelligence.

Finally, in reviewing the webcast of my testimony, I noticed that I became somewhat defensive in my answers at times, and I apologize. Unlike my colleagues on the panel, I take this issue personally. I conceived e-gold®, founded it, and have endured hardships to my family's life to keep it going through some very troubled times. I have two children not much older than the children we see exploited. I have a dedicated team of people working who have children, several of whom have done part-time work with us. With any sense that we are being accused of complicity, I do take it personally.

We are available to support your efforts in any way we can, and will stay actively engaged with the NCMEC until this crime is eliminated.

Sincere regards,
Dr. Douglas Jackson
Chairman, e-gold Ltd.
CEO, OmniPay
djackson@e-gold.com

Jackson invited Committee members and staff to visit the offices of e-gold® in Florida.

From: Douglas Jackson <djackson@e-gold.com>
Sent: Tuesday, October 17, 2006 12:06 PM
To: Andrews, Kelli
Cc: XXXXX@jcwatts.com
Subject: reply to Rep. Stupak's inquiry
Kelli
Sorry this took so long - the consulting firm that I have engaged to advise us in these and related matters, JC Watts Co., was sidetracked by the Foley thing and that delayed their review.
Could you forward this to Rep. Stupak's office?
I reiterate my invitation that some tech savvy staffer on Whitfield's, Stupak's or the committee staff spend a day in our shop in order to get up to speed on our CP [Child Pornography] detection and interdiction capabilities. We really have driven CP purchases involving e-gold® down to a minuscule volume. If "$20 billion" of this stuff was/is being bought/sold each year then about $20 billion of that total was/is happening somewhere other than e-gold.

sincere regards,
Douglas Jackson

After appearing in Washington before the subcommittee and answering questions, Jackson concluded that representatives of other banks and payment companies, that testified, did not honestly want to solve the child pornography payment issues. Jackson believed that the bank and payment company representatives were engaged in a public relations campaign with the government. Based on their statements, Jackson concluded that the big banks and credit card processors were presenting data only to mask the ineffectiveness of the measures being used by their organizations to combat child pornography payments.

Regarding e-gold®, Jackson later confided that he also believed the committee was never interested in the efficacy of e-gold® to identify and prevent child pornography payments. In a January 15, 2019 email, Jackson recalled his Commission testimony.

> "Just like Bank of America's.[Testimony] Only later did I realize the whole purpose of Coalition was to advance the PR efforts of big banks and card associations and deflect attention from fact that for every buck that went through e-gold® for this illicit purpose, 10,000 went through credit cards. And that was before we completely successfully eradicated."[468]

Regarding testimony from Bank of America's Kim Mowder[469], Jackson offered this insight in a 2019 email. "Bank of America - no data, only description of their due diligence which obviously was routinely circumvented by every CP seller as described in my Ernie letter."[470]

Jackson considers the entire Washington event to have been a PR stunt by the big banks and payment companies.

---

[468] Jackson, Douglas. "Fw: [Fwd: Visa's Testimony]." Received by Carl Mullan, *Fw: [Fwd: Visa's Testimony]*, 15 Jan. 2019.

[469] "DELETING COMMERCIAL PORNOGRAPHY SITES FROM THE INTERNET: THE U.S. FINANCIAL INDUSTRY'S EFFORTS TO COMBAT THIS PROBLEM." - DELETING COMMERCIAL PORNOGRAPHY SITES FROM THE INTERNET: THE U.S. FINANCIAL INDUSTRY'S EFFORTS TO COMBAT THIS PROBLEM HEARING BEFORE THE SUBCOMMITTEE ON OVERSIGHT AND INVESTIGATIONS OF THE COMMITTEE ON ENERGY AND COMMERCE HOUSE OF REPRESENTATIVES ONE HUNDRED NINTH CONGRESS SECOND SESSION SEPTEMBER 21, 2006 Serial No. 109-141 Printed for the Use of the Committee on Energy and Commerce Available via the World Wide Web: http://www.access.gpo.gov/Congress/House U.S. GOVERNMENT PRINTING OFFICE 31-467 WASHINGTON : 2006, [House Hearing, 109 Congress] [From the U.S. Government Printing Office], 21 Sept. 2006, www.govinfo.gov/content/pkg/CHRG-109hhrg31467/html/CHRG-109hhrg31467.htm. Serial No. 109-141

[470] Ibid

e-gold® Sheriff-Bot

The fourth quarter of 2006 ushered in several innovative e-gold® protocol enhancements that the company designed to combat or block potential bad actors using the e-gold® system.

- Sheriff-Bot deployed that captured transaction data in real-time before a seller could exchange e-gold® value for WebMoney.
- Routine screening of new accounts looking for password hashes with high specificity for sellers.
- Draconian reduction of value pool potentially available for CP purchase by detection of historic yet-unfrozen buyer accounts and freezing them.

E-gold® had started deploying a useful new tool in the fight against crime. It was called the "sheriff-bot." This software tool monitored customer Spends in real-time and detected transactions with indices of illicit activity. Once triggered, the sheriff-bot could "arrest" the account value leaving the payer account and the recipient account frozen. The Sheriff flagged both items by the nature of the suspected offensive activity. This trigger event also created a permanent discoverable record that investigators could later use to facilitate a legal seizure and forfeiture of the account value. The tool's activity became so sophisticated; there were circumstances where the first incoming or outgoing transaction would trigger a sheriff-bot arrest. The software proved to be exceptionally accurate and rarely produced a false positive.

♦

In late October, Jackson's patience ran out. Government investigators that had promised court orders and legal paperwork on suspicious e-gold accounts, had not delivered on their commitments. The straw that broke the camel's back was delivered by the press.

From: Douglas Jackson [mailto:djackson@e-gold.com]
Sent: Monday, October 23, 2006 9:40 PM
To: Agent X [USPIS] Cc: Crabb, Gregory S [USPIS]
Subject: [left blank]
Please call me this week for coordination- I have had more than enough of these people using e-gold. Lacking a trap and trace or equivalent court order this week they will be exorcised, using something more excruciating to them than freezing. I will not tolerate one more shitty little article like
http://www.darkreading.com/document.asp?doc_id=107516&WT.svl=news1_1   or

http://www.itpro.co.uk/internet/news/96333/online-crime-more-profitable-than-drugs.html [471]

The USPIS Special Agent immediately responded. The author changed the agent's name for privacy.

> Agent X [USPIS] wrote:
> Doug,
> I am currently coordinating the FBI unit I have been assigned to via Greg[USPIS Agent Crabb] to start working on drafting a court order on carders using egold. I am out of the office until next week (on vacation). I will attempt to coordinate some of this while I am out of the office. Is it possible for you to hold off on freezing the accounts at least until I can get back into the office next week?
> Thanks, Agent X[472]

The following day, October 24, 2006, Jackson followed up with this email. He eluded to e-gold's in-house program to end potential carder activity called the "Cardersmack Initiative."

> From: Douglas Jackson [mailto:djackson@e-gold.com]
> Sent: Tuesday, October 24, 2006 2:04 PM
> To: Agent X [USPIS]
> Subject: Re: Digits, that is, Karma, Ethereal
> I'll hold off. The thing we have designed for them is pretty devious though and I'm anxious to spring it.[473]

The USPIS Special Agent immediately responded.

> Agent X wrote:
> Thanks, Doug. I'll get with you next week about the court order.
> Bill[474]

Jackson sent a final email three days later, explaining his frustration.

---

[471] Jackson, Douglas. "Chunk 10." Received by Carl Mullan, *Chunk 10*, 31 Mar. 2020.
[472] Ibid
[473] Ibid
[474] Ibid

Subject: regarding e-gold brand damage
Douglas Jackson <djackson@e-gold.com>
Fri 10/27/2006 4:15 PM
To: Agent X <XXXX@uspis.gov>; Crabb, Gregory S <XXXXX@uspis.gov>
Bcc: Kim Zetter <kzetter@gmail.com>; Barry K. Downey
<bdowney@smithdowney.com>; Bill Cunningham <bcunningham@gsr.com>; Reid
Jackson-OP <rjackson@omnipay.com>; Mitchell Fuerst
<MFuerst@FUERSTLAW.COM>; Andrew Ittleman
<AIttleman@FUERSTLAW.COM>; Kevin.Zuccato@afp.gov.au

Agent X, Greg
Cutting to the chase, I am loathe to permit e-gold to be exposed to further damage to
its brand name by continuing to allow notorious carders and their accomplices to
openly use e-gold. It is impossible for e-gold to grow, to garner significant merchant
usage, strategic allies, or even (on the average) a better class of users when the press
is filled with stories depicting e-gold as the payment mechanism of choice for
criminals.

Since 2001, this sort of negative press - largely (at least initially) attributable to a
disgruntled former employee exerting himself in conjunction with an unscrupulous
would-be competitor to defame e-gold to anyone who would listen, with his message
falling on especially receptive ears in the US Secret Service, who amplified the
reputation attacks both with their actions and explicit statements in the press - has
functioned as a self-fulfilling prophecy, discouraging legitimate businesses from
embracing e-gold and encouraging criminals to abuse the system. Further
compounding this damage over the years has been a practice among law enforcement
agencies, again chiefly the USSS, to subordinate actual crime fighting efforts to their
agenda of (falsely) portraying e-gold as "anonymous, untraceable and inaccessible to
law enforcement", going so far as to keep their knowledge of criminal abuses secret
from e-gold, rather than engaging with e-gold's superb in-house investigative
capability.   Enough is enough.

At the same time, I am happy to continue my cooperative efforts, and, in the context
of a legal writ to also mobilize e-gold's investigative staff to perform the complex
iterative tracking and tracing, in liaison with your staff and with e-gold exchangers
around the world that has proven to be highly productive over the past 8 months or
so. As always, e-gold records are permanent and the data which has already lead to

the location and apprehension of numerous criminals long thought to be virtually uncatchable can continue to be mined.

The immediate context is the trap and trace order which we first discussed 3/1/06. Yes, we need a court order to satisfy the e-gold Account User Agreement which requires that we do not release customer information without due process. I have been going bare for the past eight months, exposed to liability with the > 500 hours I have devoted to this investigation. If, however, this order goes further and requires us to continue to be presented to the world as complicit in credit card fraud that would seem nothing more than an unconstitutional taking, causing us to bear these costs (the opportunity costs and brand damage) without compensation. It would only be fair for e-gold to receive compensation for this substantial investment, as I propose below.

I do not doubt that Bank of America already has a similar order. I can't otherwise conceive, for instance, how the notorious money launderer in California who we have discussed, the guy who deals with all the major ringleaders of this scheme, could continue to operate. But BoA is not damaged by such an arrangement. I've never seen an article portraying them as the bitch of criminals. The public works off a different set of memes in its reactions to long established institutions than it does with something as innovative and potentially disruptive [to the existing economic-evolutionary fitness landscape] as e-gold.

When I asked you to call, it was for the purpose of further explicating the nuances of the "exorcism" I have been waiting to unleash these recent months. The process I propose to launch within e-gold does not violate the e-gold Account User Agreement by overtly freezing any accounts. The authority for it derives entirely from e-gold's explicitly stated Right of Association that allows e-gold to refuse to do business with someone for any reason or without cause. Under this provision we cannot prevent a User from spending the e-gold already in their account without due process. However we can prevent the account from ever receiving any more incoming transfers. Strengthening this is a feature we deployed about 6 months ago that allows e-gold users to refuse to accept transfers from such blocked accounts. [It is set by default to refuse Spends from blocked accounts - a User would have to actively flip the switch to accept such transfers]. One major purpose of this is so that exchangers can avoid unwittingly receiving tainted value that might constitute the proceeds of crime. So, the tricky tweak we are prepared to unleash starts with a list of accounts that we

313

suspect of involvement in this illegal carder activity. All of these accounts will be blocked, that is, set so as to prevent their ever receiving another e-gold transfer. Moreover, since we also don't want to do business with any User who would willingly and knowingly accept transfers form this cohort, the mechanism will also automatically block accounts that receive payment from any account in this group... and add the newly blocked accounts to the list, seeding an iterative process. Part of the logic of this is that the bad guys will squirm around trying to move the e-gold into accounts they might secretly control, in hopes they can then exchange the value out through exchange portals, thereby uncovering more accounts heretofore occultly controlled by the bad guys. Likewise, it will expose third parties who would knowingly accept value from accounts that they knew e-gold had seen fit to block.

I see little or no downside to proceeding both with the trap and trace - as a means of relieving e-gold's liability for continuing release of data - AND the e-gold rolling blocklist. The bad guys in their squirming are likely to generate a lot of good forensic data that we could all sort out at will.

If, however, the Gov is intent on including provisions in this order that force us to continue to do business with these people... and not tell anyone, there needs to be some carrot with that stick besides the rosy glow of having continued to do our civic duty. It could all be a worthwhile investment if:
a) it is for a fixed limited time interval,
b) during that time some effort is made to discretely try to tone down the adverse press,
c) at the designated end point, e-gold gets some REALLY NICE press recognition of having been good guys all along, who went along with a sting because they recognized the once-in-a-lifetime opportunity for taking down a worldwide network of otherwise uncatchable bad guys by this means,
d) this turns into a springboard for a mutually beneficial strategic relationship with at least one big brand name institution that (in my opinion, and I can convincingly develop this case, given the chance) really needs us anyway, namely the USPS.

If we do end up in another three months or so of sting, that interval will hopefully suffice for e-gold to complete its switch-over from account-based to user-based log-in, the foundation of our next generation user validation and authentication protocols. That of course would have been complete already had not the USSS stolen the development budget war chest we had assiduously marshaled to enable us to

develop/effect and survive that transition. With User-based log-in and related enhancements it will become safe for an entity like the USPS (and the postal services of other countries - they're all in the same boat, business obsolescence-wise) to offer over the counter exchange from cash to e-gold and v.v. with no risk whatsoever of facilitating money laundering. Imagine postal services in multiple countries doing that --> bye-bye expensive abuse-ridden Western Union. [That's what I mean by disruptive, btw.]
sincere regards,
Doug[475]

e-gold's Cardersmack Initiative

This content, copied from the 2008 Court Sentencing Memorandum, accurately describes e-gold's struggle to combat bad actors, including carders, attempting to use the platform.

"None of the founders of e-gold, Ltd. or G&SR were people with unlimited resources; the resources they have been able to invest in these businesses have therefore been limited. They have had a limited number of employees whom they could dedicate to police the system for fraud and unlawful activity and limited dollars to expend on software enhancements to pursue these objectives. Indeed, G&SR's struggle for existence has been one of triage, seeking to focus the few available resources on the issues requiring the most immediate attention.

Unfortunately, in addition to struggling to simply underwrite day-to-day operating expenses, the Companies were repeatedly confronted by a parade of horrible circumstances that continuously drained further resources that the Companies did not even have. These included litigation concerning claims of patent infringement, garnishment, and the storage of precious metals, as well as actions against persons who sought, fraudulently, to take advantage of the Companies.[476]

G&SR instructed its employees to root out criminal activity in the egold system. Even with its limited resources, G&SR made it clear to its employees that they should not countenance any use of e-gold® or OmniPay for criminal purposes and worked to do what it could to shut down such activity.

---

[475] Ibid

[476] G&SR Sentencing Memorandum. *UNITED STATES OF AMERICA V. E-GOLD LIMITED, GOLD & SILVER RESERVE, INC., DOUGLAS L. JACKSON, BARRY K. DOWNEY and REID A. JACKSON.* Nov. 2008.

Past carder investigations, in collaboration with the U.S. Postal Inspection Service, had led to dozens of arrests and successful prosecutions of international bad actors known as carders. However, by November 2006, after ten months of examining e-gold® customer accounts without a Court Warrant, the e-gold® team could not wait any longer. During this period, e-gold® had delayed expunging a litany of carder activity at the request of law enforcement. By November, the promises of warrants and action remained unfulfilled. Instead of continuing the wait, e-gold® launched a highly focused internal initiative called "Cardersmack" that was designed to eradicate all carder abuse of the e-gold® system."[477]

◆

On October 13, 2006, the Financial Action Task Force (FATF)[478] published the *Report on New Payment Methods*. The document included a summary of information on new technology & products labeled "Digital Precious Metals" that included e-gold®.

"The FATF has examined the way in which money can be laundered through the exploitation of new payment technologies (prepaid cards, Internet payment systems, mobile payments, and digital precious metals). The report found that, while there is a legitimate market demand for these payment methods, money laundering and terrorist financing vulnerabilities exist. Specifically, cross-border providers of new payment methods may pose more risk than providers operating within a particular country. The report recommends continued vigilance to further assess the impact of evolving technologies on cross-border and domestic regulatory frameworks."[479]

The same October 2006 FAFT Report indicated that U.S. money transmitters were among the money-services businesses required to register with the FIU (FinCEN). The report also stated that U.S. Money transmitters were subject to AML reporting and record-keeping requirements and needed to be licensed by the state at every level. "Whether an online payment system or digital precious metals dealer meets the definition of a money transmitter pursuant to the relevant regulations, though, depends upon its location and the ways in which it participates in or conducts transactions."[480] [481]

---

[477] Ibid

[478] In response to mounting concern over money laundering, the Financial Action Task Force on Money Laundering (FATF) was established by the G-7 Summit that was held in Paris in 1989. Recognizing the threat posed to the banking system and to financial institutions, the G-7 Heads of State or Government and President of the European Commission convened the Task Force from the G-7 member States, the European Commission and eight other countries.

[479] Financial Action Task Force. *REPORT ON NEW PAYMENT METHODS. REPORT ON NEW PAYMENT METHODS*, 2006 FATF/OECD, 2006.

However, the only response from the Financial Action Task Force in 2006 on Digital Precious Metals was "continued vigilance." In 2006, there were no existing laws registered anywhere in the world that accurately identified and regulated e-gold®.

Iranian e-gold® Accounts

From 1996 through 2006, anyone from any country could have operate an e-gold® account. The e-gold® Terms of Service contained no restrictions on account holders or where they could live. That e-gold® policy changed in 2006.

On November 24, 2006, e-gold® closed thousands of user accounts because the e-gold® software had determined the account user was either resident in or accessing the system from Iran. Data generated through the user logins recorded an Iranian IP address, and that flagged the account. E-gold froze the online value without the users being warned or notified. Immediately following the freeze, the e-gold service department emailed all of the Iranian e-gold® account owners with this statement.

> "Your account has been frozen in compliance with the laws which govern e-gold, Ltd. and its managers. e-gold, Ltd. has taken this step in strict compliance with the law. No further information is available at this time. When additional information is available it will be provided upon account login. Thank you."[482]

Many of the Iranian accounts had e-metal balances that were inaccessible. The Iranians loudly complained and posted comments on popular Internet discussion forums. There were no further actions or comments from e-gold® or G&SR, and the precious metal balances disappeared along with the Iranian e-gold® online accounts. Online rumors presented multiple alleged reasons for the frozen Iranian accounts. However, there was no press release or public notification from e-gold®.

The event remained a mystery until spring 2007. On June 6, 2007, about seven months after e-gold® had frozen the Iranian e-gold® accounts, documents uncovered from the Director of the OFAC solved the mystery. Due to Iran's support for international terrorism, the United States Government had imposed unilateral sanctions on Iran. Individuals found to have breached the economic restrictions faced a fine of up to $250,000 and 20 years in jail; per violation.

[480] Financial Action Task Force, FATF. "Report on New Payment Methods." *Documents - Financial Action Task Force (FATF)*, 13 Oct. 2006, www.fatf-gafi.org/documents/documents/reportonnewpaymentmethods.html.

[481] G&SR Sentencing Memorandum. UNITED STATES OF AMERICA V. E-GOLD LIMITED, GOLD & SILVER RESERVE, INC., DOUGLAS L. JACKSON, BARRY K. DOWNEY and REID A. JACKSON. Nov. 2008.

[482] Herpel, Mark. "Digital Currency Magazine." DGC Magazine, Sept. 2008, issuu.com/dgcmagazine/docs/digital-gold-currency-magazine-september-2008.

The OFAC documents disclosed that Gold & Silver Reserve, Inc., the contractual Operator for the system, was being fined by the OFAC for violating Iranian sanctions. A Prepenalty Notice [Fine] for $5,000,000 had been issued to G&SR by the OFAC. The notice stated, G&SR was guilty of "exportation of financial services in the form of 56,739 e-currency accounts through its website for persons located in Iran."[483]

Before the Prepenalty Notice, in December 2006, following weeks of efforts to achieve substantive engagement with the OFAC, G&SR was served by the OFAC with a paired set of two documents – a Cease and Desist Order, and, a License. The Cease and Desist Order formalized: "GSR is hereby ordered to cease and desist from providing any further services to persons in Iran in violation of the prohibitions set forth in Part 560, and is directed to provide confirmation in writing to such effect, identifying the actions it has taken to end such activity."

On December 7, 2006, the Defendants' attorney, Andrew Ittleman, received a Cease and Desist Order from the Department of the Treasury. The Order was directed to "President Gold & Silver Reserve, Inc."

Dear Sir or Madam:

It has come to the attention of the Office of Foreign Assets Control (OFAC) that Gold & Silver Reserve Inc. (G&SR) operates "e-currency" accounts for persons located in Iran.

As a U.S. person, G&SR is subject to the comprehensive prohibitions on trade with Iran set forth in the Iranian Transactions Regulations, 31 C.F.R. Part 560 (the Regulations) U.S. persons are prohibited, unless specifically authorized by OFAC, from engaging in actions that include, but are not limited to: the importation and exportation of goods and services from and to Iran, see§§ 560.201 and 560.204, see also § 560.306; any transaction or dealing in or related to goods, technology, or services for exportation, re-exportation, sale or supply, directly or indirectly, to Iran (including, but not limited to, purchasing, selling, transporting, swapping, brokering, approving, financing, facilitating, or guaranteeing), see§ 560.206; facilitating transactions by foreign persons that U.S. persons are prohibited from engaging in themselves, see§§ 560.208 and 560.417; and undertaking new investment in Iran, see § 560.207. We suggest you consult Part 560 in its entirety, which more comprehensively addresses the prohibitions.

G&SR's provision of services to persons in Iran without OFAC's authorization, including the maintaining and servicing of "ecurrency" accounts for persons located in Iran, appears to be in violation of the Regulations, specifically 31 C.F.R. §

[483] Szubin, Adam. "PENALTY NOTICE." Received by Gold & Silver Reserve, Inc. Attn: Carol R. Van Cleef, Patton Boggs L.L.P. 2550 M Street, N.W., 6 June 2007, Washington, D.C.

560.204. G&SR is hereby ordered to cease and desist from providing any further services to persons in Iran in violation of the prohibitions set forth in Part 560, and is directed to provide confirmation in writing to such effect, identifying the actions it has taken to end such activity, see Part 560, and section 501.602 of the Reporting, Procedures and Penalties Regulations, 31 C.F.R. Part 501.

G&SR is directed to mail this information to OFAC within four weeks of the date stamped above to OFAC's Special Investigations Section, U.S. Department of the Treasury, 1500 Pennsylvania Ave., N.W., Washington, DC 20220.

Please be advised that violation of the International Emergency Economic Powers Act (IEEPA) and OFAC's implementing regulations could result in criminal prosecution and/or fines of up to $250,000 per violation and up to 20 years in jail for individuals, and up to $500,000 per violation for corporations, and/or the imposition of a $50,000 per violation civil penalty by OFAC. In addition, failure to respond to this Requirement to Furnish Information pursuant to section 501.602 may result in a significant civil penalty.

G&SR also is directed to ensure that it is in compliance with the other regulations administered by OFAC (see www.treas.gov/ofac for details on all of OFAC's sanctions programs). For example, the Cuban Assets Control Regulations, 31 C.F.R. Part 515, require that any accounts held by Cuban residents or nationals living outside the United States must be blocked and reported to OFAC; and any accounts held by Specially Designated Nationals and Blocked Persons (SDNs) 1 must be blocked and reported to OFAC.

Thank you for your cooperation on this matter. If you have any questions regarding any aspect of this order, please contact Alison Cooper at 202/622-2430 or alison.cooper@do.treas.gov.

Sincerely,

Daryl L. Johnston

Acting Assistant Director for Enforcement

Office of Foreign Assets Control[484]

Attached to the Order was an "Iranian Transactions Regulations LICENSE" (License No. IA-9010)

The License, with a termination date of February 28, 2007, provided: "Gold & Silver Reserve, Inc. (the "Licensee") is hereby authorized to engage in all transactions necessary to

[484] Johnston, Daryl L. "CEASE AND DESIST ORDER." Received by President Gold & Silver Reserve Inc., 175 E. Nasa Blvd., 7 Dec. 2006, Melbourne, Florida. DEPARTMENT OF THE TREASURY WASHINGTON, D.C. 20220 FAC No. IA-312338, COMPL 0600978

close e-currency accounts of persons located in Iran held by the Licensee and to effect lump sum transfers of funds held in such accounts to the account holders provided the transfer does not involve an account of an Iranian bank on the books of a U.S. bank" as well as "the transfer of funds through the U.S. financial system pursuant to the authorization…should reference the number of this license to prevent the blocking of this transfer."

The License seemingly provided a solution that would enable G&SR as the contractual Operator for e-gold, in tandem with G&SR's exchange division, OmniPay, to exchange frozen e-gold and send the proceeds to the Iranian customers. But there was a hitch. License or no license, none of G&SR's banks were willing to be involved in any way with payment to an Iranian recipient.

About two months later, in January 2007, the Department of the Treasury followed up with G&SR's attorneys requesting information regarding the Iranian e-gold accounts. This request included information requests for any accounts held by nationals of Cuba.

January 29, 2007
Dear Mr. Ittleman:
Thank you for your letter of January 24, 2007, in response to our Cease and Desist Order to Gold & Silver Reserve Inc. (G&SR) of December 7, 2006.

Pursuant to the Iranian Transactions Regulations, 31 C.F.R. Part 560 (the "ITR"), the Cuban Assets Control Regulations, 31 C.F.R. Part 515 (the "CACR"), and section 501.602 of the Reporting, Procedures and Penalties Regulations, 31 C.F.R. Part 501, you are directed to provide the Office of Foreign Assets Control (OFAC) with the following information:

- The number of E-Gold accounts as of January 1, 2007 held by persons in Iran or the Government of Iran
- The number of E-Gold accounts as of January 1, 2007 held by nationals of Cuba

G&SR is directed to fax this information to OFAC (fax 202-XXX-XXXX) by the close of business on Friday, February 2, 2007.
Please be advised that violation of the International Emergency Economic Powers Act (IEEPA) and the ITR could result in criminal prosecution and/or fines of up to $250,000 per violation and up to 20 years in jail for individuals, and up to $500,000 per violation for corporations, and/or the imposition of a $50,000 per violation civil penalty by OFAC.
Violation of the Trading with the Enemy Act (TWEA) and the CACR could result in criminal prosecution and/or fines of up to $250,000 per violation and up to 10 years

in jail for individuals, and up to $1 million per violation for corporations, and/or the imposition of a $65,000 per violation civil penalty by OFAC.

In addition, failure to respond to this Requirement to Furnish Information pursuant to section 501.602 may result in a significant civil penalty.

Thank you for your cooperation on this matter. If you have any questions regarding any aspect of this Requirement to Furnish Information, please contact me at 202/XXX-XXXX or XXXX@do.treas.gov.

Sincerely,

Alison L. Cooper

Chief, Special Investgations Section

Office of Foreign Assets Control[485]

While the penalty was a massive hit to G&SR, later, the company received a reduction in the $5,000,000 proposed amount. The court provided consideration for other payments G&SR was to make under other unrelated U.S. government enforcement actions. Accordingly, a civil penalty for $2,950,000.00 was imposed upon G&SR pursuant to 31 C.F.R. § 560.705.

On July 11, 2008, a document published by OFAC shed light on the Iranian issue by listing financial enforcement actions for two tiny cases that occurred in June and August 2006. There had been two cited U.S. persons that received fines for alleged violation of the prohibitions in Iranian Transaction Regulations.

These cited persons lived in the United States and had been buying e-gold® from a popular online exchange provider operating from Kish Island, Iran. Me-gold was the name of the independent exchange provider business, that had likely serviced hundreds or thousands of U.S. based customers. None of the customers had any idea they were violating U.S. Sanctions. The entities' website had openly listed the business' professional information and Iranian address.[486]

- Business Name: Me-gold Kish Co.
- Mr. Soleiman Founder & CEO
- Legal status: Private joint-stock co.
- Registration no.: 3641

[485] Cooper, Alison L. "REQUIREMENT TO FURNISH INFORMATION." Received by Andrew S. Ittleman Fuerst Humphrey Ittleman PL, 1001 Brickell Bay Dr., Suite 2002, 29 Jan. 2007, Miami, Florida. DEPARTMENT OF THE TREASURY WASHINGTON, D.C. 20220 FAC No. IA-312338, COMPL 0600978

[486] "Me-gold Company Page." Me-gold.com, 2006, web.archive.org/web/20061202164802/www.me-gold.com/company.php

- P.O. Box 1167, Venus Center,
- Kish Island, Iran

No U.S. e-gold® customers noticed or cared. Copied below are a few details from each OFAC Enforcement action.

> One individual has agreed to a settlement totaling $840 for alleged violation of the prohibitions in the Iranian Transactions Regulations: OFAC alleged that in August 2006, the individual attempted to transfer funds to Me-gold Kish, Co. in Iran in an apparent attempt to purchase electronic gold without an OFAC license. The individual did not voluntarily disclose this matter to OFAC.[487]

> One individual has agreed to a settlement totaling $400 for alleged violation of the prohibitions in the Iranian Transactions Regulations: OFAC alleged that in June 2006, the individual attempted to purchase electronic gold from Me-gold Kish Co. in Iran in apparent violation of §§ 560.201, 560.203 and 560.204 of the Iranian Transactions Regulations. The individual did not voluntarily disclose this matter to OFAC. [488]

With this additional information, e-gold's reason for closing all Iranian accounts was evident. The mistake had cost G&SR $2,950,000.

The November 14th, 2008 Memorandum in Aid of Sentencing for e-gold Ltd. explained more details about these events. [Partial text]

> (d)   OFAC compliance e-gold, Ltd. agreed that within ninety days of the Plea Agreement all of its existing and newly created accounts would be in compliance with the U.S. Department of Treasury's Office of Foreign Asset Control (hereinafter "OFAC") regulations or closed. In August, 2008, OFAC issued a license to e-gold, Ltd. and G&SR, thereby empowering them to dispose of the value frozen in e-gold accounts since 2006 relating to country sanctions. The license imposes an August 2009 deadline for final disposition of this frozen value. Counsel has been in ongoing discussions with Laurel Loomis Rimon and Victoria Rosenthal, general counsel for OFAC, regarding the most expeditious way to dispose of current accounts that are

---

[487] "Sanctions Information." Treasury.gov, Resource Center, 2008, www.treasury.gov/resource-center/sanctions/Documents/07312008.pdf
488 Ibid

closed but not yet liquidated.[489]

In an effort to fully comply with this section of the plea agreement without running afoul of OFAC regulations, counsel for defendant spoke with AUSA Laurel Loomis Rimon and Victoria Rosenthal, Counsel for OLFAC twice in the past ten days. The purpose of this call was to determine the best way to liquidate e-gold, Ltd. accounts held by individuals in Iran without violating the terms of the plea agreement or OFAC regulations. On the call, OFAC counsel explained she had to meet with her client before she could give defendants specific instructions on how to comply with this section of the plea agreement. As of the date of the filing of this Memorandum[Nov.14, 2008], defendant's have not received instructions from OFAC; however, in an effort to expedite compliance, e-gold, Ltd. has begun the process of moving all the identified Iranian accounts into one single account so it is easier to liquidate when OFAC provides instructions for how to execute this liquidation.[490]

e-gold® Milestone: Ten Years Online

On November 27th, 2006, e-gold® celebrated a milestone. The business had been operating online for the past ten consecutive years. Jackson posted comments on the e-gold® website, including the following statements.

> While other payment systems have come and gone, losing millions of investment dollars, e-gold has continued to successfully serve its customers. It has flourished due to its strong fundamental principles of freedom from default and finality of settlement. e-gold has always held true to meeting its User obligations. When merchants are paid they stay paid, and consumers can make payments without compromising their personal information online.

> Operational since 1996, e-gold has settled over 70M transactions, serves customers in 165 countries, and holds nearly 3.5 metric tonnes of gold.[491]

Unfortunately, Jackson's celebratory tone did not last long. The following month, in

[489] Case 1:07-cr-00109-RMC Document 176 . UNITED STATES OF AMERICA v. E-GOLD, LTD. E-GOLD, LTD.'S MEMORANDUM IN AID OF SENTENCING AND INCORPORATED POSITION WITH RESPECT TO SENTENCING FACTORS, 14 Nov. 2008.

[490] Ibid

[491] e-gold Ltd. (2006). *e-gold® Celebrates Ten Year Anniversary* [Press Release]. Retrieved from https://web.archive.org/web/20070104151105if_/http://www.e-gold.com:80/tenyears.html

mid-December, the federal government unveiled a pending indictment of e-gold Ltd., Gold & Silver Reserve Inc., and the company's co-founders.

Plead guilty. Plead early.

In the federal court system, around ninety-seven percent of criminal defendants plead guilty and waive their constitutional right to a jury trial in exchange for sentencing concessions.

> In 2016, 97.3% of defendants in the federal criminal justice system accepted a plea instead of going to trial. The following year, the figure was 97.2% and the number of federal criminal cases going to trial in 2020 remains around just 3%. A trail by a jury of peers is one of America's most crucial constitutional right.[492]

Over the last fifty years in America, trial by jury has declined at a rapid pace. This decrease has considerably lessened the role of jury trials in protecting individual American liberties. The public rarely exercises its oversight function envisioned by the Framers inherent in jury service. Citizens no longer identify trial by jury as one of their principal mechanisms for public participation in the criminal justice system.

In exchange for prosecutorial concessions, such as dropped charges or shorter sentences, defendants are pleading guilty and avoiding a trial. The Federal Rules of Criminal Procedure acknowledge and sanction "plea bargaining."

Charged individuals do not want to risk a more severe post-trial sentence and decide to plead guilty out of fear. Consequently, most defendants opt for the lesser penalty by agreeing to plead guilty.

Known as the "trial penalty," this sentencing differential between defendants pleading guilty by agreement and defendants found guilty in a jury trial, underpins the entire U.S. legal system. The trial penalty is a price prosecutors extract from defendants for exercising their right to trial, and it is widespread in America's court system.[493]

Federal defendants exercising their right to a trial guaranteed by the Sixth Amendment, which are eventually found guilty, encounter precipitately stiffer punishment because they rejected the prosecution's offer. Recognizing the more massive potential trial penalty, federal defendants plead guilty and plead early.

Ultimately these bargains also require defense lawyers to spend a large share of their

---

[492] Jones, Rick, et al. THE TRIAL PENALTY: The Sixth Amendment Right to Trial on the Verge of Extinction and How to Save It. National Association of Criminal Defense Lawyers®, 2018, pp. 3–3, THE TRIAL PENALTY: The Sixth Amendment Right to Trial on the Verge of Extinction and How to Save It.

[493] "AN OFFER YOU CAN'T REFUSE How US Federal Prosecutors Force Drug Defendants to Plead Guilty." *Human Rights Watch*, Human Rights Watch, 2013, www.hrw.org. ISBN: 978-1-62313-0824

time negotiating the plea deal. Because defense lawyers haggle with prosecutors outside of court, defendants often enter a guilty plea without any real comprehension of their sentencing exposure.

When confronted with a sizable post-trial sentence, most federal defendants accept the nearly sure thing with the guilty plea because they believe that their life is on the line. Confronted by the massive trial penalty, risk-averse innocent defendants may also plead guilty. The threat of an excessive trial penalty is contrary to a defendants' rights and inconsistent with the right to a fair trial.

Problem with Courts

The bargaining process incentivizes guilty pleas. The result from engineering more guilty pleas empties the courtrooms enabling prosecutors and judges to clear more cases. Courts rely on plea bargaining to keep the number of jury trials to a manageable level.

"The federal system as currently funded could not handle the strain of trying every case."[494]

It is apparent in the e-gold case that prosecutors, and even the judge, may have deliberately positioned the case timeframe to encourage the plea agreement and avoid a trial.

Prosecutors

Prosecutors hold all the cards during plea negotiations and serve in an adversarial role. The bargaining process revolves around the prosecutors charging decisions. In other words, federal prosecutors strongly influence sentences by the charges they select. Prosecutors have unsupervised discretion over the selection of charges, any threats or promises made during the bargaining process, and ultimately what threats to pursue if a defendant does not plead. In most cases, any number of criminal statutes could apply to a defendant's conduct, and each might carry a different potential sentence. Ultimately, these charges significantly affect the penalty. Prosecutors are sentencing convicted defendants according to the charges they bring.

During a plea bargain, the federal prosecutor's actions are largely unchecked by the court. Prosecutors have no sympathy for defendants that reject a guilty plea and demand a jury trial. As a reward for accepting their plea, prosecutors can adjust the defendant's penalty by (1) agreeing to recommend or not oppose a sentence; or (2) deciding not to argue for or against the application of particular sentencing factors.[495] As retribution for not accepting a

---

[494] McConkie, Daniel S. "JUDGES AS FRAMERS OF PLEA BARGAINING." *STANFORD LAW & POLICY REVIEW*, vol. 26, no. 61, 2015.

plea, federal prosecutors may also threaten additional charges or recommend increased sentences. Government lawyers take this aggressive action to ensure that future defendants are more inclined to accept a plea.

The prosecutor's advantage includes broad discretion over information and potential evidence during the preliminary stages of criminal proceedings. There is an incentive for prosecutors to overstate the strength of their case to compel the defendant's acceptance of a guilty plea. One illustration of this situation might be when a prosecutor quietly holds evidence not discoverable to the defendant that bears on the likelihood of the defendant's acquittal at trial. Did this action occur in the e-gold case?

Mandatory Sentences

Legal experts believe the rising number of guilty pleas is the direct result of U.S. legislation. These newer laws include the Sentencing Reform Act of 1984, the Guidelines' adoption, and minimum sentencing in 1986 and 1988. Mandatory minimum sentencing provisions, activated solely by the prosecutor's charging decisions, have been a primary driver of reducing the trial rate. Judges are required to impose the minimum sentences on guilty defendants convicted with a prosecutor's mandatory penalties.

The D.O.J. frequently pushes Congress and the Sentencing Commission for higher and higher penalties, further evidencing a strong desire to enhance the government's negotiating leverage.[496] The D.O.J. also has a habit of using these provisions to compel guilty pleas, and punish defendants who have the "chutzpah" to exercise their right to trial.[497]

Guidelines

The Sentencing Guidelines offer severe sentencing ranges that encourage plea deals when mandatory sentences do not. The federal Sentencing Guidelines create cut-and-dried calculations for sentencing defendants. Prosecutors exploit minimum sentences and leverage this advantage during the plea bargaining process. The outcome of this activity usually results in criminal penalties out of proportion with a defendant's actual liability.

Inflated Sentencing Guidelines and statutes create a distinct advantage for the prosecution. The results: plead guilty early in the process and receive a light sentence. Reject the prosecutor's deal by demanding a jury trial, get penalized, and receive a sentence multiple times greater than deserved. Guidelines calculations are protected from reversal on

---

[495] "AN OFFER YOU CAN'T REFUSE How US Federal Prosecutors Force Drug Defendants to Plead Guilty." *Human Rights Watch*, Human Rights Watch, 2013, www.hrw.org. ISBN: 978-1-62313-0824

[496] "THE TRIAL PENALTY: The Sixth Amendment Right to Trial on the Verge of Extinction and How to Save It." *National Association of Criminal Defense Lawyers*, National Association of Criminal Defense Lawyers, 2018, www.nacdl.org/trialpenaltyreport.

[497] Ibid

appeal.

Economic Crimes As an Example of the Guidelines' Overreach
One of the most flagrant examples of how the Guidelines call for the imposition of excessive sentences is Section 2B1.1, the Guideline that applies to economic crimes. Section 2B1.1 has long been criticized for resulting in sentences that are grossly disproportionate to a defendant's actual culpability. Judges have referred to sentences under this Guideline as "patently absurd on their face," "a black stain on common sense," and, "fundamentally flawed." Because defendants' sentences are so inflated under the Guidelines, prosecutors have enormous leverage in economic crime cases to force guilty pleas.[498]

As in Douglas Jackson's case:

> Under these Guidelines, a fixed plea/trial differential has been formalized, in part, as the "acceptance of responsibility" reduction, amounting to two or three offense levels. That reduction tends to be about one-third of the post-trial sentence for those who accept responsibility for their crimes by pleading guilty. The reduction— designed to encourage guilty pleas—is virtually assured when the defendant pleads guilty and virtually unheard of otherwise.[499]

On February 9, 2007, the initially proposed plea agreements arrived by fax. The letters originated from the office of U.S. Attorney for the District of Columbia, and Assistant United States Attorney Laurel Loomis Rimon signed the documents.

> **Aceptance of Responsibility: 3-point reduction**:   Assuming Dr. Jackson clearly demonstrates acceptance of responsibility, to the satisfaction of the Government, through Dr. Jackson's allocution and subsequent conduct prior to the imposition of sentence, the Government agrees that a 2-level reduction would be appropriate, pursuant to U.S.S.G. § 3E1.1(a). Furthermore, assuming Dr. Jackson has accepted the responsibility as described in the previous sentence, the Government agrees that an additional 1-level reduction would be appropriate, pursuant to § 3E1.1(b), U.S.S.G., because Dr. Jackson has assisted authorities by providing timely notice of his intention to enter a plea of guilty, thereby permitting the Government to avoid

---

[498] Ibid
[499] McConkie, Daniel S. "JUDGES AS FRAMERS OF PLEA BARGAINING." *STANFORD LAW & POLICY REVIEW*, vol. 26, no. 61, 2015.

preparing for trail and permitting the Court to allocate its resources efficiently. [footnote proposed plea Feb 9, 2007]

C.   **Applicable Guideline Range**

Based up the calculations set forth above, Dr. Jackson's stipulated Sentencing Guidelines range is 30 to 37 months (the "Stipulated Guidelines Range"). The parties agree that under the Sentencing Guidelines Range set forth above is warranted. Accordingly, neither party will seek such a departure or seek any adjustment not set forth herein. Nor will either party suggest that the Court consider such a departure or adjustment. Additionally, if Dr. Jackson is sentenced to any period of probation or supervised release, the parties agree that terms of this plea agreement contained in paragraphs 14 to 20 below may be included by the Court as conditions of probation and/or supervised release.[500]

Judges

Cases resolved by plea bargaining require minimal judicial control and contribution. This lack of judicial supervision can lead to questions of transparency and fair sentencing.

The combination of fewer jury trials and a higher plea/trial differential commands a more significant number of plea bargains, which helps contend with heavier case backlog. Based on the number of proceedings, judges can signal an average length for the plea/trial differential, incentivizing an optimal amount of guilty pleas. This high incidence of guilty pleas decreases oversight and lessens the supervisory capacity of the judge.

◆

Indictment Letter & Proposed Plea Agreements

On December 15, 2006, the Miami attorney's for Douglas Jackson, Barry Downey, Reid Jackson, Gold & Silver Reserve, Inc. and e-gold, Ltd. received several faxed documents from the office of Jeffrey A. Taylor, United States Attorney District of Columbia.[501] The letters were not items that anyone would want to receive ten days before Christmas.

Assistant United States Attorney Laurel Loomis Rimon [signed letter] and Kimberly Kiefer Peretti, Senior Counsel for the United States Department of Justice, sent the message.

---

[500] Taylor, Jeffrey A., et al. "Re: Dr. Douglas L. Jackson." Received by Mitchell Fuerst, Esq., Andrew Ittleman, Esq. Fuerst Humphrey Ittleman, Judiciary Center 555 Fourth St. N.W., 9 Feb. 2007, Washington, District of Columbia.

[501] Jeffrey A. Taylor is the former interim United States Attorney for the District of Columbia appointed by Alberto Gonzales on September 22, 2006 and resigned May 28, 2009.

Dear Messrs Fuerst and Ittleman:

As you know, your clients, Douglas Jackson, Barry Downey, Reid Jackson, Gold & Silver Reserve, Inc., and e-gold, Ltd. are the targets of a criminal investigation that has been conducted by agents from the United States Secret Service and the Federal Bureau of Investigation, in conjunction with the United States Attorney's Office for the District of Columbia and the Criminal Division of the United States Department of Justice. This investigation is now substantially completed and shows that your clients have committed violations of the federal criminal code, including violations involving 18 U.S.C. S 1956 (money laundering) and 18 U.S.C. § 1960 (operation of an unlicensed money transmitting business).

This letter is to inform you that the Government anticipates asking the grand jury to return a criminal indictment in the very near future. We would like to afford your clients an opportunity to discuss the potential of criminally resolving the matter short of indictment. Accordingly, please contact the undersigned if your client has an interest in doing so. Any such meeting must occur on or before Wednesday, January 3, 2007.[502]

Interpreting this letter as a possible offer of a Deferred Prosecution Agreement (DPA), the parties met in DC on December 29, 2006. As Jackson later related:

"Prior to the meeting our attorneys made it clear that none of the defendants should speak. They explained that Martha Stewart, who everyone assumed had been convicted of some sort of securities/insider trading violation, had instead gone to jail for obstruction of justice, making false statements and conspiracy for lying to investigators. All because of trying to explain to prosecutors her side of the story in a meeting like this.[503]

We therefore sat mutely as the prosecutors produced a draft indictment that listed a number of criminal transactions, all of which had been detected by our investigators and the accounts blocked. It didn't seem to describe any criminal activity on our part but nevertheless called for prolonged jail time and multi-million dollar fines. Our attorneys pointed out that it didn't seem to specify any crime on our part. Rimon

[502] Rimon, Laurel Loomis, and Kimberly Kiefer Peretti. "Letter from the U.S. Department of Justice Regarding Anticipated Indictment." Received by Mitchell Fuerst, Esq., Andrew Ittleman, Esq., at Fuerst Humphrey Ittleman, 15 Dec. 2006, Miami, FL.

[503] Isidore, Chris. "Trump May Pardon Martha Stewart. Here's Why She Went to Jail." *CNNMoney*, Cable News Network, 31 May 2018, money.cnn.com/2018/05/31/news/companies/trump-martha-stewart-pardon/index.html.

seemed flustered and didn't have a coherent answer. At this point, another attorney—an older man [John Roth] who seemed to be the boss—intervened, saying he knew we weren't "bad guys" and that no one was going to jail. I distinctly recall thinking 'These clowns have put us through all this and probably spent a few million bucks in the process and now, for the first time, there is an adult in the room. I wish I could listen in on the fireworks when he reams them out.' As we left, I felt incredible relief, believing the ordeal of the past year was finally over."

Reid Jackson memorialized Jackson's and the other directors' state of mind in an email. Reid had not attended the conference but had gotten a phone briefing immediately afterward. His reaction:

"*** PGP SIGNATURE VERIFICATION ***
*** Signer: Reid Jackson (0x93A2D0DF) ***
Signed: 12/29/2006 8:20:08 PM
*** BEGIN PGP DECRYPTED/VERIFIED MESSAGE ***
Further thoughts/comments... [feel free to shoot down at will] The reason why the boss stepped into the process today and removed the jail time part from their original draft indictment is in no sense because he is a good guy looking to do the right thing. Rather...
1. He really wants to make a deal because he knows they have no case, or a prayer of ever having a case, in the absence of manufacturing evidence.
2. He knows that there is no way in hell we are going to agree to jail time for crimes we did not commit, and in a move ***calculated to make sure he did not lose the opportunity for negotiation***, he removed that part from the draft. [If you ask for too much at the start of a negotiation, the other party generally walks]
3. He fully expects that we will not accept their proposal as is (unless we're really dumb and he's really lucky).
****
We shouldn't be editing the draft. We should be re-writing it from scratch - a process that all of us need to participate in every step of the way. Towards that end, I think the current (soon to be gutted) draft should be circulated to all.
Goals:
1. *None* of the entities are indicted (corporate or individual) since none of them committed any crimes. In this scenario, the glory to the Justice Dept should come from prosecuting any actual bad guys they are able to identify from the e-gold data their accomplices illegally seized. Perhaps they could claim to have busted more

330

Shadow Crew types from data that could have been more easily obtained with a subpoena.

2. There should be no government monitoring of the e-gold system.

3. GSR should get all of its money back since it did not commit any crimes.

4. Access is given to the appropriate people to discuss appropriate regulation of "new paradigm" entities.

****

Anything less than all of the above is not a victory. Ultimately making money is not a victory. If that were the prime directive, there would have been considerably easier paths to follow.

****

Fallback position:

* Goal 1 is subverted to agree to indictment of GSR (but no other entity).

* Goal 3 is subverted to agree to the return of GSR's money minus the fine for whatever crime it did not actually commit.

* A new goal is added of making sure that the indictment of GSR for the crime it did not commit does not result in damage to innocent third parties (see prior e-mail).

- Reid –

*** END PGP DECRYPTED/VERIFIED MESSAGE ***[504]

But, as will be detailed in a later chapter, the relief was short-lived when, weeks later, the prosecutors reneged on everything Roth had said.

2007

Though a continuing effort to operate within existing U.S. regulations, during the first months of 2007, e-gold® and G&SR began employing a new software tool that allowed any user, particularly those located outside of the United States, to block incoming Spends from any account operated by a U.S. person. This robust tool empowered legal foreign casinos to comply with newly enacted 2006 federal law by providing non-US casino operators, accepting e-gold®, a method to block U.S. players from making e-gold® deposits, and illegally accessing casino play from the United States.

The e-gold® website published the following statement in February 2007 detailing the use of this new mechanism.

e-gold Empowers Online Gambling Sites to Refuse Payments from US Persons

---

[504] Jackson, Reid. "Post Meeting Notes." Received by Douglas Jackson, *Post Meeting Notes*, 29 Dec. 2006.

On October 12, 2006, the Safe Ports Act was signed into law in the United States. As a result of the Safe Ports Act and the Unlawful Internet Gambling Enforcement Act of 2006 contained in the Safe Ports Act, the facilitation of many forms of Internet gambling by persons located in the United States has become a proscribed activity. With the objective of preventing the use of e-gold by United States persons for unlawful online gambling, e-gold has deployed a feature whereby any e-gold account holder may configure their e-gold account(s) to block incoming e-gold Spends from accounts controlled by Users residing inside the United States or who are accessing the Internet from within the United States. Online gambling businesses using e-gold are now required to enable this new account attribute.[505]

♦

Sexual Exploitation of Children Over the Internet

In January 2007, the United States House of Representatives Energy Committee published a staff report on Sexual Exploitation of Children Over the Internet prepared for the Committee on Energy and Commerce.[506] The report highlighted financial regulatory problems that existed in 2006-2007 and possible solutions. The report underscored the current reality that U.S. financial regulations were out-of-date and inadequate for governing the Internet's new digital currency technology.

In a significant statement, the document addressed digital currencies such as e-gold® and concluded "Digital currencies that do business in the United States are not subject to any of the U.S. banking requirements."[507] The report recognized "the lack of regulation of digital currencies by any government entity, domestic or foreign."[508]

The U.S. Government had not yet written laws governing the supervision and regulation of value moving on the Internet outside of banks. The United States did not have financial definitions or rules encompassing the e-gold® business model.

Below are select examples of content taken from the report. This material demonstrates the absence of any 2007 U.S. financial regulations governing digital currency businesses.

---

[505] "e-gold Empowers Online Gambling Sites to Refuse Payments from US Persons." *e-gold News*, Apr. 2007, web.archive.org/web/20071005000424/http://www.e-gold.com/news.html.

[506] United States, Congress, COMMITTEE ON ENERGY AND COMMERCE. "Sexual Exploitation of Children over the Internet: a Staff Report Prepared for the Use of the Committee on Energy and Commerce, U.S. House of Representatives, 109th Congress." *Sexual Exploitation of Children over the Internet: a Staff Report Prepared for the Use of the Committee on Energy and Commerce, U.S. House of Representatives, 109th Congress*, U.S. G.P.O., 2007, pp. 3–39. 109-F.

[507] Ibid

[508] Ibid

The report also concluded that government agencies, such as the U.S. Department of the Treasury, should amend or introduce modern legislation capable of supervising and regulating digital currency products.

Digital currency products were beyond the scope of existing U.S. financial regulations, and companies such as e-gold® were operating in a gray area. This new legal reality had created the opportunity for misuse of these platforms.

> The Subcommittee's investigation into the use of financial instruments to purchase child pornography over the Internet revealed a much larger problem touching upon the burgeoning industry of digital currencies: the lack of regulation of digital currencies by any government entity, domestic or foreign. Digital currencies that do business in the U.S. are not subject to any of the U.S. banking requirements. This has created a dangerous loophole in commercial transactions occurring on the Internet with virtually no accountability. It is imperative that the U.S. and other countries address the rise of digital currency and begin to subject this industry to some form of oversight and regulatory consistency. As of now, operations such as e-gold are available to individuals who wish to transfer money anonymously for any purpose, whether legal or illegal.

4) Digital currencies are being used more frequently on commercial child pornography websites and provide another layer of anonymity to the purchaser and seller of these materials. Digital currencies on the Internet are not regulated anywhere in the world.

5) The U.S. Department of Treasury and the U.S. Department of Justice should propose legislation to Congress aimed at providing effective controls over the burgeoning digital currency industry over the Internet.

> The second panel was comprised of witnesses from the credit card associations, including American Express, MasterCard, and VISA, and other payment companies, including e-gold and PayPal. The purpose of this panel was to examine the payments industry's efforts to prevent individuals from using their systems to process child pornography transactions.

> Like the credit card associations, PayPal and e-gold, which are alternative payment mechanisms or digital currencies, have also adopted policies and procedures that prohibit their users from using their account to purchase child pornography. PayPal, a subsidiary of eBay, has taken steps to identify and minimize the use of its services for illegal transactions. For example, PayPal's policies state that its users may not use their accounts to purchase "any obscene or sexually oriented goods or

services.

While e-gold is also a digital currency, it operates differently from PayPal in that its accounts are purportedly backed by actual gold reserves. To establish an account, an individual completes a short form online, including some identifying information. However, e-gold does not verify this identification information or require that a credit card or other financial instrument be presented to verify identity. Further, e-gold does not maintain sufficient records reflecting the activity of e-gold accounts or, unlike credit card associations and merchant banks, conduct any due diligence on the merchants that accept e-gold.[509]

The report's ultimate conclusion stated: "Clearly, neither current legal requirements nor voluntary action have been apparently sufficient to put a significant dent in the problem of sexual exploitation of children over the Internet."[510]

The report ignored the extensive testimony and documentary evidence Dr. Jackson had provided the Subcommittee, choosing to draw from other conclusions that might as well have been drafted by the high paid lawyers and lobbyists employed by the credit card industry.

♦

Reality Sets In

By February 2007, the felony charges and pending indictments shifted ominously closer to becoming a reality for the defendants. On February 9, 2007, the proposed plea agreements arrived by fax from the DOJ. The letter originated from the office of U.S. Attorney for the District of Columbia and signed by Assistant United States Attorney Laurel Loomis Rimon.

> Re: e-gold, Ltd., et al.
> Dear Messrs. Fuerst and Ittleman:
> Enclosed please find draft plea agreements for your clients, Douglas L. Jackson, Barry K. Downey, Reid A. Jackson, e-gold, Ltd., and Gold & Silver Reserve, Inc. We have also sent a copy of Mr. Downey's agreement to Aron Raskas, Esq. These agreement are drafts because we have not yet included specific amounts for fines, forfeiture, and/or restitution. Although some financial penalty will be required, the

---

[509] Ibid
[510] Ibid

exact amount and form of that penalty will be determined after we receive information from your clients concerning their current assets and financial status. After specific amounts have been determined, we will provide final plea agreements to be executed by both parties. Please note that the "Statement of Offense and "Consent Order of Forfeiture" referred to in the plea agreements are not included in this transmission, but will be forwarded at a later time.

The plea offer will expire on February 16, 2007. Please inform us on or before that date if your client(s) will accept the agreement. We expect, however, that it may take some additional time to finalize certain details, particularly the financial provisions, in order for both parties to execute the agreement and present it to the Court. Accordingly, we have left the date of expiration of the plea agreement in the enclosed drafts blank until we have received your initial response. I will be calling your office shortly after I fax these agreements to you, but please feel free to contact myself or Kim Peretti if you would like to discuss this further.

Sincerely,

Laural Loomis Rimon

Assistant United States Attorney

Kimberly Keifer Peretti

Senior Counsel

United States Department of Justice

The proposed February plea agreement for Douglas Jackson has been summarized below in highly abbreviated fashion. The original document is fourteen pages long.[511]

Re: e-gold, Ltd.

Dear Messrs. Fuerst and Ittleman:

This letter sets forth the full and complete plea offer to your client, e-gold, Ltd. (referred to herein as "Company" or defendant). This offer is by the Criminal Division of the United States Attorney's Office for the District of Columbia (the "Office") and the Criminal Division of the U.S. Department of Justice ("Department") and is binding upon both. This plea offer will expire on February __, 2007. Upon receipt, the executed letter will itself become the plea agreement. The terms of the offer are as follows:

1.   **Charges and Statutory Penalties**

Dr. Jackson agrees to waive Indictment and to plead guilty to a two-count

[511] Rimon, Laurel Loomis. "Draft Plea Agreements." Received by Mitchell Fuerst, and Andrew Ittleman, *Draft Plea Agreements*, 9 Feb. 2007.

information charging violations of Title 18, United States Code, Sections 1956(h) (Conspiracy to Engage in Money Laundering) and 1960(b)(1)(A), (B), and (C) (Operation of an Unlicensed Money Transmitting Business). Dr. Jackson understands that, pursuant to 18 U.S.C. § 1956, the maximum sentence that can be imposed is twenty (20) years imprisonment, a fine of $500,000, or a fine of twice the value of the property involved in the transaction pursuant to 18 U.S.C. §1956(a)(1), a $100 special assessment, a five-year term of supervised release, an order of restitution, and an obligation to pay any applicable interest or penalties on fines or restitution not timely made. Dr. Jackson understands that, for a violation of 18 U.S.C. § 1960, the maximum sentence that can be imposed is five (5) years imprisonment, a fine of $250,000, or a fine of twice the pecuniary gain or loss pursuant to 18 U.S.C. § 3571(d), a $100 special assessment, a three-year term of supervised release, an order of restitution, and an obligation to pay any applicable interest or penalties on fines or restitution not timely made. In consideration of Dr. Jackson's plea to the above offenses, Dr. Jackson will not be further prosecuted criminally by this Office or the Department for the conduct set forth in the attached Statement of Offense.

3. **Sentencing Guidelines Stipulations**

Dr. Jackson understands that the sentence in this case will be determined by the Court, pursuant to the factors set forth in 18 U.S.C. X 3553(a), including a consideration of the guidelines and policies promulgated by the United States Sentencing Commission, Guidelines Manual 2005 (hereinafter "Sentencing Guidelines" or "U.S.S.G."). Pursuant to Federal Rule of Criminal Procedure 11(s)(1)(B), and to assist the Court in determining the appropriate sentence, the parties stipulate to the following:

A. **Offense Level Under the Guidelines**

Money Laundering

§ 2.S1.1

(a) Base Offense Level		8
Value of laundered funds of more than $10,000		4
(b) Specific Offense Characteristics		
2S1.1 (b)(1) – knowledge or belief that funds were involved in child exploitation		6
2S1.1(b)(2) – conviction under 18 USC 1956		2

§ 3B1.1

Organizer or leader of criminal activity with less than 5 participants	2
TOTAL:	22

Money Transmitting
§ 2S1.1

(a) Base Offense Level	8
Value of laundered funds of more than $10,000	4
(b) Specific Offense Characteristics	
2S1.1 (b)(1) – knowledge or belief that funds were involved in child exploitation	6

§ 3B1.1

Organizer or leader of criminal activity with less than 5 participants	2

Acceptance of Responsibility: 3-point reduction: Assuming Dr. Jackson clearly demonstrates acceptance of responsibility, to the satisfaction of the Government, through Dr. Jackson's allocution and subsequent conduct prior to the imposition of sentence, the Government agrees that a 2-level reduction would be appropriate, pursuant to U.S.S.G. § 3E1.1(a). Furthermore, assuming Dr. Jackson has accepted the responsibility as described in the previous sentence, the Government agrees that an additional 1-level reduction would be appropriate, pursuant to § 3E1.1(b), U.S.S.G., because Dr. Jackson has assisted authorities by providing timely notice of his intention to enter a plea of guilty, thereby permitting the Government to avoid preparing for trail and permitting the Court to allocate its resources efficiently.

In accordance with the above, the applicable Guidelines Offense Level for the money laundering violation is 19 and for the money transmitting violation is 17. he parties agree that the offenses of money laundering and operation of an unlicensed money transmitting group under USSG § 3D1.1, resulting in a total offense level of 19.

C.   **Applicable Guideline Range**

Based up the calculations set forth above, Dr. Jackson's stipulated Sentencing Guidelines range is 30 to 37 months (the "Stipulated Guidelines Range"). The parties agree that under the Sentencing Guidelines Range set forth above is warranted. Accordingly, neither party will seek such a departure or seek any adjustment not set forth herein. Nor will either party suggest that the Court consider such a departure or adjustment. Additionally, if Dr. Jackson is sentenced to any period of probation or supervised release, the parties agree that terms of this plea agreement contained in paragraphs 14 to 20 below may be included by the Court as conditions of probation and/or supervised release.

On February 16, 2007, the expiration date of the DOJ offer, attorney for the Defendants, Mitchell S. Fuerst, Esq. responded to Laurel Loomis Rimon, Assistant United States Attorney.

__Sent via Facsimile and United States Mail__
Laurel Loomis Rimon, Esquire
Assistant United States Attorney
Office of the United States Attorney
555 Fourth Avenue, N.W.
Washington, D.C. 20530

Re: *e-gold, Ltd., et al.*

Dear Laurel:
We have received and reviewed your cover letter of February 9, 2007, along with the 14-page draft plea agreements that you enclosed for each of our five clients. Quite frankly, as we told you when you called our office on February 9, 2007 to confirm our receipt of the letter, we are dumbfounded by the materials that we received from you.
Preliminary, while speaking in one sentence about requiring "additional time to finalize certain details," you unambiguously state that the "plea offer will expire on February 16, 2007." That is incredible on a number of levels.
First, the government has been investigating this matter for well over a year. In December, 2006, you advised us that you intended to present an indictment to the grand jury, and you then met with us on December 29, 2006 to discuss your perspective of a reasonable plea agreement. You advised that you wished to put your offer into a written form and that you would send it to us to review with our clients. You then waited six weeks to transmit your draft plea offers to us, and in the same breath demanded that we respond to you in just one week. Your statement that your "offer" is merely a draft is similarly curious. Are you expecting an acceptance of your draft offer to be a draft as well? Or would such an acceptance be something to

338

which our clients would be bound?

Second, you have demanded that we respond to you within a week, yet you offer no details about several major aspects of the plea agreement into which you would have our clients enter. You want a response to the offer, yet you provide no "Statement of Offense," which will unquestionably shape each sentence. You wish to know whether our clients will accept your offer, yet you have "not yet included a specific amount of the fine, forfeiture, and/or restitution." Indeed, you have not even advised us as to the method by which you would determine appropriate financial penalties or against which putative defendants you intend to seek them. Without such basic information, it is impossible for us to reasonably advise our clients and respond to your offer. No competent professional would be able to do so in such a situation. Aside from the timing of your letter and the deadline that you arbitrarily set for the expiration of your draft plea offers, we are even more troubled by the substance of your letters. When we met with you, Mr. Roth, Ms. Peretti and your agents on December 29, 2006, Mr. Roth specifically acknowledged that "nobody was saying that [our clients] are bad people," but they were simply individuals who had "gotten in over their heads." Yet, your plea offer requests that they plead to criminal charges carrying substantial penalties and potential sentences of incarceration, with statements of the offense that you have yet to even address, and requirements for fine, forfeiture, and/or restitution that remain still to be asserted. All of this appears wholly at odds with the perspectives that Mr. Roth shared at our meeting; your proposals astounded us and our clients and have, very candidly, led everyone on our side to substantially question the government's good faith in these discussions. That is particularly troubling when considering that you are asking us to rely upon the government's "good faith" in moving for the proposed 5K1.1 departures and, presumably, in setting the as yet unstated "Statement of Offense" and specific amounts of a fine, forfeiture, and/or restitution.

Yes, our clients are interested in a resolution of this matter through appropriate plea agreements. But "appropriate," in this case, means agreements that are consistent with your stated perspective that these are not "bad people." We are willing to entertain further discussions, but we believe that it would be more productive conducting them in person rather than through these types of written communications.[512]

The proposed plea agreement included a suggested minimum prison sentence of thirty

---

[512] Fuerst, Mitchell S. "Re: e-Gold, Ltd., Et al." Received by Laurel Loomis Rimon, Esquire Assistant United States Attorney, 1001 Brickell Bay Drive, Ste. 2002, 16 Feb. 2007, Miami, Florida.

to thirty-seven   months and a maximum of twenty years. However, as in all federal criminal cases, the non-mandatory sentencing guidelines were not binding on the Court. The sentence to be imposed upon Dr. Jackson would be determined solely by the Court Judge on the day of sentencing. Court documents copied here illustrate these conditions.

> Dr. Jackson acknowledges that his entry of a guilty plea to the charged offenses authorizes the sentencing court to impose any sentence, up to and including the statutory maximum sentence, which may be greater than the applicable Guidelines range. The Government cannot, and does not, make any promise or representation as to what sentence Dr. Jackson will receive. Moreover, it is understood that Dr. Jackson will have no right to withdraw his plea of guilty should the Court impose a sentence outside the Guidelines range.[513]

The terms listed below were also a part of the agreement:

> Dr. Jackson understands and acknowledges that this Agreement and any plea of guilty which he may enter pursuant to this Plea Agreement are contingent upon the entry of guilty pleas by co-defendant[s], Barry K. Downey, Reid A. Jackson, e-gold, Ltd., Gold & Silver Reserve, Inc., in this case. If these co-defendants fail to enter a guilty plea, this Plea Agreement and any proceedings pursuant to this Plea Agreement may be withdrawn or voided at the discretion of the Government.[514]

In this initial proposed plea agreement, the three Defendants were all facing prison time. This shocking proposal caught all of the men by surprise.

- Based up the calculations set forth above, Dr. Jackson's stipulated Sentencing Guidelines range was 30 to 37 months
- Based up the calculations set forth above, Mr. Downey's stipulated Sentencing Guidelines range was 6 to 12 months
- Based up the calculations set forth above, Reid Jackson's stipulated Sentencing Guidelines also included prison time.

Andrew Ittleman, one of the defense counsel team, immediately replied, pointing out:

---

[513] Ibid

[514] Rimon, Laurel Loomis. "Draft Plea Agreements." Received by Mitchell Fuerst, and Andrew Ittleman, *Draft Plea Agreements*, 9 Feb. 2007.

"All of this appears wholly at odds with the perspectives that Mr. Roth shared at our meeting; your proposals astounded us and our clients and have, very candidly, led everyone on our side to substantially question the government's good faith in these discussions."[515]

As previously discussed, in late December 2006, the Defendants Barry Downey, Reid Jackson, and Douglas Jackson met in person with the team of attorneys for the prosecution, along with Mr. John Roth, an Assistant U.S. Attorney for the District of Columbia working on fraud and public corruption cases.[516] Jackson stated that Roth had been present during this face-to-face meeting. "Roth had played a key role in the December 2006 meeting. But then when their subsequent written offer arrived in Feb 2007 it seemed like a bombshell, completely different from what we were led to expect at the December meeting."

In an August 2017 letter, Jackson expressed his disbelief with the government's more aggressive approach that arrived with the new Plea Agreements. This text is from a letter to Roth, who held the position in 2017 as Inspector General, U.S. Dept. of Homeland Security.

As you may recall, 6 weeks later (February 9, 2007) we [Defendants] were presented with a draft plea agreement that included a lengthy (30-37 month) term of incarceration for me [Douglas Jackson]. Our counsel called you directly to try to understand this apparent about-face and escalation in ferocity. He related to us that you [Roth] said that you had been overruled in this matter, that the decision to continue/intensify this shock and awe campaign had "come from the highest levels".[517]

Just a month later, in March 2007, e-gold® had recorded the highest level of activity in the company's history. E-gold® was holding 3.8 metric tonnes of stored gold on behalf of account holders. The size of these precious metal bullion reserves exceeded the official gold reserves of many nations, including Canada and Mexico.

◆

---

[515] Fuerst, Mitchell S. "Re: e-Gold, Ltd., Et al." Received by Laurel Loomis Rimon, Esquire Assistant United States Attorney, 1001 Brickell Bay Drive, Ste. 2002, 16 Feb. 2007, Miami, Florida.

[516] In 2004, Mr. Roth became an Assistant U.S. Attorney for the District of Columbia. In 2007, he served as Deputy Assistant Attorney General for the Criminal Division and became chief of staff to the Deputy Attorney General in 2008; then assumed the post of Inspector General of the Department of Homeland Security (DHS) on March 10, 2014.

[517] Jackson, Douglas. "Prefatory Letter to John Roth." Received by Inspector General John Roth, 1020 Steven Patrick Avenue, 24 Aug. 2017, Indian Harbour Beach, Florida. Origins and motives behind the USSS campaign to destroy e-gold, Gold & Silver Reserve, Inc.

Fox TV

The Defendants 2008 sentencing memorandum stated:

> Indeed, as they continued to operate the businesses, the belief that they were not subject to the existing laws and regulations for money transmitting businesses regularly appeared to them to be corroborated by many different government agencies and representatives.[518]

For example:
- A Special Agent of the FBI's Cyber Crimes Unit, when questioned by Fox News about the government's investigation of the e-gold business, stated that: "At this point it is not illegal, it operates in an area of the law where there is no law."[519] [520]

In March 2007, e-gold Ltd and G&SR had requested for the court to issue a subpoena to preserve and obtain exculpatory evidence that may be beneficial to their criminal case. The court granted their request. Here is the partial text from that order.

> ORDER GRANTING CLAIMANT GOLD & SILVER RESERVE, INC.'s UNOPPOSED REQUEST FOR PERMISSION TO ISSUE SUBPOENA FROM STAYED CASE THIS MATTER came before the Court on the Claimant's Unopposed Request for Permission to Issue a Subpoena from this Stayed Case. Being fully advised in the premises, it is hereby ordered and adjudged that Claimant's unopposed motion is hereby GRANTED.
> The Claimant may serve a subpoena on Fox TV in Los Angeles for purposes of recovering the video footage of FBI Special Agent Ken McGuire as outlined in the claimant's motion.
> SIGNED and ORDERED in Chambers this _____ day of March, 2007.[521]

---

[518] G&SR Sentencing Memorandum. *UNITED STATES OF AMERICA V. E-GOLD LIMITED, GOLD & SILVER RESERVE, INC., DOUGLAS L. JACKSON, BARRY K. DOWNEY and REID A. JACKSON.* Nov. 2008.

[519] Interview available at: http://www.myfoxla.com/myfox/pages/Home/Detail;jsessionid=CE5F83220C 1D2FOAA94771245 5408C DF?contentld=252103 8&version=3&locale=EN-US&layoutCode=VSTY &pageld= 1.1.1 (last visited September 10, 2008) (emphasis added).

[520] G&SR Sentencing Memorandum. *UNITED STATES OF AMERICA V. E-GOLD LIMITED, GOLD & SILVER RESERVE, INC., DOUGLAS L. JACKSON, BARRY K. DOWNEY and REID A. JACKSON.* Nov. 2008.

[521] U.S. District Court for the District of Columbia. *ALL FUNDS SEIZED FROM OR ON DEPOSIT IN SUNTRUST ACCOUNT NUMBER 1000028078359, IN THE NAME OF GOLD AND SILVER RESERVE, INC. AND ALL FUNDS ON DEPOSIT IN REGIONS BANK ACCOUNT NUMBER 67-0919-4851, IN THE NAME OF GOLD AND SILVER*

Earlier, in February 2007, FOX 11, a local television news station for the Greater Los Angeles area, aired a video story that discussed e-gold® digital currency. During the taping of that story, FBI Special Agent Ken McGuire discussed legal aspects of the digital gold business and made certain statements on video. While the footage that included his comments was recorded and later cut from the piece the station aired on Fox, attorney's for the Defendants felt his recorded statements could be helpful to their clients. G&SR lawyers asked the court to issue a warrant to obtain the video evidence. The following are details of that civil case.[522]

> District Of Columbia District Court, Case No. 1:05-cv-02497-RMC
> UNITED STATES OF AMERICA v. ALL FUNDS SEIZED FROM OR ON
> DEPOSIT IN SUNTRUST ACCOUNT NUMBER 1000028078359, IN THE NAME
> OF GOLD AND SILVER RESERVE, INC. et al[523]
>
> CLAIMANT GOLD & SILVER RESERVE, INC.'s UNOPPOSED REQUEST FOR
> PERMISSION TO ISSUE SUBPOENA FROM STAYED CASE COMES NOW, the
> Claimant, GOLD & SILVER RESERVE, INC., and respectfully requests permission
> from this Court to issue a subpoena out of this stayed case and to hold an oral hearing
> on the matter.
>
> IN SUPPORT THEREOF, the Claimant respectfully submits to the Court:
> 1. On February 27, 2007, Fox TV in Los Angeles aired an investigative news report
> on e-gold and other digital currencies and currency providers.[524] Undersigned
> counsel has recorded the Fox TV report as a Windows Media Audio/Video file and
> may furnish it to the Court upon request.
> 2. During that report, FBI Special Agent Ken McGuire discussed the digital currency
> industry. He stated that "[a]t this point it is not illegal...It operates in an area of the
> law where there is no law."
> 3. These statements are highly relevant to the instant case. Indeed, if one federal
> agent (who is also a Certified Public Accountant) is on the record stating that the
> digital currency industry "operates in an area of the law where there is no law," it

---

RESERVE, INC. Defendants. . Case 1:05-cv-02497-RMC Document 37-2 Filed 03/16/2007, 16 Mar. 2007
[522] Ibid
[523] Ibid
[524] That report may be found at the following URL:
http://www.myfoxla.com/myfox/pages/Home/Detail;jsessionid=1E280B208A6234CADCD8D10A1C603473?contentId=2521038&version=3&locale=EN-US&layoutCode=VSTY&pageId=1.1.1. [no longer available]

becomes highly unlikely that the claimant's business could subsequently be painted as a money transmitting business as defined in 31 U.S.C. § 5330.

4. Accordingly, the claimant is very interested in other statements that Special Agent McGuire may have made that were not aired on the Fox 11 report.

5. On March 12, 2007, undersigned counsel spoke with counsel for Fox TV, David Keneipp, Esq., about the unused footage at issue *sub judice*. During that conversation, Mr. Keneipp advised undersigned counsel that Fox TV would not turn over any footage without a subpoena. However, Mr. Keneipp also advised undersigned counsel that it was Fox TV's policy to destroy unused footage on a regular basis.

6. Accordingly, based on the statements made by Special Agent McGuire, the claimant believes that the unused McGuire footage is crucial, and based on Fox TV's policy of destroying unused footage, the claimant believes that a subpoena directed to Fox TV in Los Angeles is urgent. It is based on those considerations that the claimant requests that the stay in this case be lifted exclusively for purposes of subpoenaing Fox TV in Los Angeles.

7. Prior to the filing of this motion, undersigned counsel conferred with AUSA Laurel Loomis Rimon as to whether the government would have any objection. AUSA Rimon has advised undersigned counsel that the government has no objections. Accordingly, this motion is filed without opposition.

8. Counsel for Fox TV, David Keneipp, Esq., has been copied on this motion. Undersigned counsel respectfully requests that the Court copy Mr. Keneipp on any resulting orders.

9. Upon receipt of any subpoenaed footage from Fox TV, undersigned counsel will make such footage available to counsel for the government.

The Defendants' lawyers never recovered the footage.

◆

In April 2007, e-gold® was still engaged in a significant war against fraud. The business introduced a new tool for customer account protection against phishing attacks. The Account Sentinel™ (a.k.a. AccSent™) arsenal of security features hosted the device, and the e-gold® website described its new protection.

Using DNS blacklist data published by well known third parties, AccSent now blocks account access from IPs identified as open proxies, insecure web servers, or otherwise open to exploitation by criminals. For the sake of brevity, e-gold refers to such blacklisted IPs as "blips".

As always, the AccSent advantage is that e-gold Users need not take any action - or even understand what an IP address, an open proxy, or a phishing attack is - to immediately benefit from this innovative new feature. However, as powerful as AccSent is, the best protection against phishing and other criminal attacks is user education. For this reason e-gold urges its Users to carefully read and practice the Security Recommendations published on the e-gold.com website.[525]

♦

Sealed Indictment

Defendants e-gold, Ltd., Gold & Silver Reserve, Inc., Douglas Jackson, Barry Downey, and Reid Jackson were indicted by a District of Columbia federal grand jury on April 24, 2007. The government charged all Defendants with conspiracy to launder money instruments (from about 1999 through December 2005), in violation of 18 U.S.C. §§ 1956, 1957 (Count One); conspiracy to operate an unlicensed money transmitting business (from October 26, 2001, through December 2005), in violation of 18 U.S.C. § 371 (Count Two); operation of an unlicensed money transmitting business (from October 26, 2001, through (at least) December 2005), in violation of 18 U.S.C. §§ 2, 1960 (Count Three), and money transmitting without a license (from May 14, 2002, through at least March 23, 2003), in violation of D.C. Code § 261002 (Count Four).

The indictment contained a forfeiture allegation seeking all assets of the defendant corporations based on the money laundering and operation of an unlicensed money transmitting business violations.[526] [527]

A Motion accompanied the Federal Indictment to seal, and a Memorandum Of Points and Authorities in Support of Government's Motion to Seal. The Government requested that the Court place the Indictment, the Bench Warrant, the Motion to Seal, and the Court's Order under seal. Prosecutors had asked that all information regarding this case remain private, and provided the following statement as grounds for secrecy.

---

[525] Jackson, Douglas. "e-gold News." *e-gold.com*, Appearing in Web Archive, Sept. 2008, web.archive.org/web/20070426074040/www.e-gold.com:80/news.html

[526] GOVERNMENT'S RESPONSE TO DEFENDANTS' MOTION TO VACATE SEIZURE WARRANT AND TO MODIFY RESTRAINING ORDER AND REQUEST FOR AN EVIDENTIARY HEARING. *UNITED STATES OF AMERICA Criminal No. 07-109 (RMC) v. E-GOLD, LTD. GOLD & SILVER RESERVE, INC., DOUGLAS L. JACKSON, BARRY K. DOWNEY, and REID A. JACKSON, Defendants.* 15 June 2007.

[527] Sealed Indictment. *U.S.A. v. e-gold, Ltd., Gold & Silver Reserve, Inc. Douglas L. Jackson, Barry K. Downey, and Reid A. Jackson, Defendants.* Criminal No. 07-109, 24 Apr. 2007.

1. There is a compelling public interest in sealing these records, because the records relate to an ongoing sensitive law enforcement investigation, and because disclosure of the existence of the information contained in the Indictment and Bench Warrants could alert the defendants and frustrate execution of the Warrants. Additionally, the United States anticipates filing within the next day applications for the seizure of approximately 57 digital currency (e-gold, Ltd.) accounts, and a motion to restrain of all assets of the defendant corporations, e-gold, Ltd. and Gold & Silver Reserve, Inc.[528]

The Court granted the motion and sealed the case. The Federal Grand Jury Indictment identified property subject to forfeiture under 18 U.S.C. § 982(a)(l) and established sufficient probable cause for the issuance of the restraining order. Because the case was sealed, on April 24, 2007, the Defendants were unaware of the criminal charges.

♦

Section 1960

Section 1960 was not widely used for prosecution until the 2001 Patriot Act added significant amendments to the statute. Title III of the USA PATRIOT Act amended Section 1960 to modify the scienter requirement under the statute's licensing prong. Whereas before, the Government had to prove that a defendant operated a business intentionally without a license. Under the Patriot Act provision, the intent element was omitted, negating any "mistake of law" defense. H.R. Rep. No. 107250, at 54 (2001). Additionally, subsection (C), which makes it illegal to transmit funds derived or in aid of unlawful activity. *Id.* was also added.*529*

> 18 U.S.C. § 1960 ("Section 1960") imposes criminal penalties on anyone who knowingly conducts, controls, manages, supervises, directs or owns all or part of an unlicensed money transmitting business." 18 U.S.C. § 1960(a) (2008). It also provides that:
> As used in this section —
> (1) the term "unlicensed money transmitting business" means a money transmitting business which affects interstate or foreign commerce in any manner or degree and

---

[528] Case 1:07-cr-00109-RMC Document 2-2. *U.S.A. v. e-gold, Ltd., Gold & Silver Reserve, Inc. Douglas L. Jackson, Barry K. Downey, and Reid A. Jackson, Defendants.* Memorandum of Points and Authorities in Support of the Government's Motion to Seal, 24 Apr. 2007.

[529] Linn, Courtney J. "One-Hour Money Laundering, Prosecuting Unlicensed Money Transmitting Businesses Under 18 U.S.C. § 1960." U.C. Davis Bus. L.J. , vol. 8, no. 138, ser. 2007, 28 Jan. 2008. 2007.

(A) is operated without an appropriate money transferring license in a State where said operation is punishable as a misdemeanor or a felony under State law, whether or not the defendant knew that the operation was required to be licensed or that the operation was so punishable;

(B) fails to comply with the money transmitting business registration requirements under section 5330 of title 31, United States Code, or regulations prescribed under such section; or

(C) otherwise involves the transportation or transmission of funds that are known to the defendant to have been derived from a criminal offense or are intended to be used to promote or support unlawful activity;

(2) the term "money transmitting" includes transferring funds on behalf of the public by any and all means including but not limited to transfers within this country or to locations abroad by wire, check, draft, facsimile, or courier. [. . .][530]

The indictment focused on e-gold® customer Spend transactions. The government was alleging that the transfer of e-gold® from one account to another had facilitated criminal activity. The alleged criminal activity included the sale of child pornography, stolen credit and debit card information, and various types of investment fraud, such as Ponzi schemes and illegal high-yield investment programs.[531] If found guilty, defendants were facing decades in prison.[532]

Seizure Warrant & Post-Indictment Restraining Order

On April 25, 2007, while the indictment remained sealed, the United States filed an ex parte application and a supporting affidavit with the United States District Court. The government sought to seize, for forfeiture, the value of property stored in the business' two e-gold® operating accounts. E-gold Ltd. (544179) and Gold & Silver Reserve, Inc. DBA OmniPay (109243).[533]

---

[530] No. 07-3074. UNITED STATES of America, Appellee v. E-GOLD, LTD., Et Al., Appellants. U.S. V. E-GOLD, LTD, 521 F.3d 411 (D.C. Cir. 2008), 11 Apr. 208AD.

[531] *Id. At 7-8.*

[532] Larry Greenemeier & Sharon Gaudin, *Law Abiding ... or Criminal Enabler?*, INFORMATIONWEEK, May 7, 2007, at 20.

[533] U.S. District Court for the District of Columbia. E-GOLD *LIMITED, GOLD & SILVER RESERVE, INC., DOUGLAS L. JACKSON, BARRY K. DOWNEY and REID A. JACKSON Related Case In the Matter of the Seizure of Any and All Property in/Underlying e-gold Account 544179 and in/Underlying E-GOLD CASE NUMBER account 109243, Held by e-gold, Ltd. or 07-167-M-01 Gold & Silver Reserve, Inc. on Behalf of e-gold, Ltd.* DEFENDANTS' MOTION TO VACATE SEIZURE WARRANT AND TO MODIFY RESTRAINING ORDER AND REQUEST FOR AN EVIDENTIARY HEARING, 6 Jan. 2007.

The entire basis of the government's application was the allegation that the accounts constituted "property involved in an unlicensed money transmitting business" in violation of 18 U.S.C. § 1960.

On April 26, 2007, federal agents served this and multiple other Seizure Warrants on G&SR.[534] With these warrants, the Court essentially deputized G&SR, as contractual Operator of the e-gold system, to freeze numerous e-gold accounts, including both its own company accounts and those of e-gold Ltd. G&SR was also ordered to exchange the frozen and seized e-gold for U.S. dollars within twenty-four hours.

These two accounts contained $1,481,976.38 worth of e-gold, and the government eventually received these funds on May 11, 2007, in bank transfers. The government could not seize any of e-gold's physical precious metal[535] from the secure international storage vaults. The Court had to rely on G&SR to freeze the e-gold accounts, exchange the e-gold for USD, redeem the e-gold, sell the precious metal which had backed the digital balances in these accounts, and then send the government a bank payment. USSS Special Agent Dotson's Seizure Affadivit detailed these fund transfers.

> "To obtain the value subject to seizure in these accounts pursuant to the requested seizure warrant, it will be necessary to require e-gold, Ltd. and/or Gold & Silver Reserve, Inc. to convert the "egold" in the accounts specified to United States dollars or physical precious metals before turning the funds over to the United States."[536]

If the government's prosecution ended in a conviction, e-gold® would have to forfeit the monetary value of precious metal held in these accounts to the government, according to 18 U.S.C. § 982(a)(l).

Additionally, back on December 30, 2005, in Civil Action No. 05-02497, the Clerk had signed a Warrant of Arrest in Rem, which resulted in the arrest of two bank accounts containing approximately $850,000 owned by Gold & Silver Reserve, Inc.

Consequently, without ever having been heard on the merits of the seizures, the Defendants lost e-gold® and U.S. Dollars with an approximate total value of Three Million

---

[534] Any and all property in/underlying e-gold account 544179 and in/underlying e-gold account 109243, held by e-gold, Ltd. or Gold & Silver Reserve, Inc. on behalf of e-gold, Ltd. *U.S.A. v. e-gold, Ltd., Gold & Silver Reserve, Inc. Douglas L. Jackson, Barry K. Downey, and Reid A. Jackson, Defendants.* SEIZURE WARRANT, CASE NUMBER: 07-167-M-01, 26 Apr. 2007.

[535] PLAINTIFF'S MOTION TO STAY AND SUPPORTING MEMORANDUM. *UNITED STATES OF AMERICA, v. ALL PROPERTY IN/UNDERLYING e-gold ACCOUNT NUMBERS 544179 AND 109243.* Case 1:07-cv-01337-RMC Document 18, 5 Feb. 2008.

[536] U.S. District Court for the District of Columbia. *U.S.A. v. e-gold, Ltd., Gold & Silver Reserve, Inc. Douglas L. Jackson, Barry K. Downey, and Reid A. Jackson, Defendants.* . AFFIDAVIT IN SUPPORT OF SEIZURE WARRANT (18 U.S.C. §§ 981, 1960), Apr. 2007.

Fifty-Five Thousand Eight Hundred Sixteen Dollars ($3,055,816.00). As a result of the government's actions, the Defendants did not have money to operate their businesses, pay attorney fees, or pay for reasonable operating and living expenses.[537]

Additionally, prosecutors served G&SR with another twenty-four seizure warrants on more than fifty other e-gold® accounts operated by well-known independent exchange providers. Prosecutors alleged that the e-gold® value held in those accounts (estimated at $14 million) was involved in money laundering and the operation of an unlicensed money transmitting business. The proceeds of exchange from these accounts were also turned over by G&SR on May 11.

The government base the GS&R Seizure Warrant on an Affidavit signed by U.S. Secret Service Special Agent Roy Dotson.[538] The Affidavit alleged that thirty-six e-gold® transactions, between August 2000 and December 2005, had been connected to crimes. The Spend transactions ranged in value from $40 to $725,000.00. The government claimed that these transfers had supported illegal activity.[539] This fact was clear, the alleged involvement in operating an unlicensed money transmitting business was the sole basis for the Seizure.

> 4. Based upon the evidence uncovered, there is probable cause to believe that the property contained in the above identified e-gold accounts is involved in a violation of Title 18, United States Code, Section 1960, and is therefore subject to seizure and forfeiture pursuant to 18 U.S.C. § 981(a)(1)(A).[540]

Surrendering to the Feds

In a May 6, 2007 email, to Dan Kaplan reporter for SC Magazine (Haymarket Media Inc.), Jackson discussed his ugly experience with federal authorities upon surrendering to the Court. Copied below are partial email sections from the email.

> I'm so sorry for my delay in responding to these follow-up questions. I needed to fly to DC to "surrender to Federal authorities". While there I had no Internet [and in fact

---

[537] U.S. District Court for the District of Columbia. E-GOLD *LIMITED, GOLD & SILVER RESERVE, INC., DOUGLAS L. JACKSON, BARRY K. DOWNEY and REID A. JACKSON Related Case In the Matter of the Seizure of Any and All Property in/Underlying e-gold Account 544179 and in/Underlying e-gold CASE NUMBER account 109243, Held by e-gold, Ltd. or 07-167-M-01 Gold & Silver Reserve, Inc. on Behalf of e-gold, Ltd.* DEFENDANTS' MOTION TO VACATE SEIZURE WARRANT AND TO MODIFY RESTRAINING ORDER AND REQUEST FOR AN EVIDENTIARY HEARING, 1 June 2007.

[538] U.S. District Court for the District of Columbia. *U.S.A. v. e-gold, Ltd., Gold & Silver Reserve, Inc. Douglas L. Jackson, Barry K. Downey, and Reid A. Jackson, Defendants.* AFFIDAVIT IN SUPPORT OF SEIZURE WARRANT (18 U.S.C. §§ 981, 1960), Apr. 2007.

[539] *Id. At 14-18.*

[540] Ibid

349

spent several hours being held incommunicado in government holding cells and also had the novel experience of being paraded handcuffed through the streets of DC, despite solemn assurances of the prosecutor that wouldn't happen. But that was relatively trivial compared to another deceitful last minute change they pulled - more on this below...] Having returned in the wee hours Saturday morning I'm just now scrambling to triage the hundreds of emails. In passing, I would like to comment on that "surrender" expression. In the past, when I'd seen "surrender to Federal authorities" it evoked an image of someone on the lam, a fugitive, weary of fleeing justice who finally turns himself in. Now I realize that my experience is probably the more typical one. It means taking time off work and traveling at one's own expense to whatever place one's case is being adjudicated in order to participate in a carefully orchestrated formality. In addition, since an arraignment is a pretty significant life event, I felt like my wife and kids should see what was happening, even though that meant the additional expense of flying them to DC.

As it turned out, it was probably good they were there. My two boys got a real world lesson on how agents of the government behave when they set out to damage or destroy someone.

Going in to the hearing, or at least the stated government position the day before, we were told:
1. I and the other named defendants would be released "on our own recognizance" [i.e., no need to post bail], and
2. The only restriction on my continued ability to conduct business, which is rather more difficult anyway given the repeated asset seizures and irresponsible recent government propaganda depicting e-gold as faulty in its efforts to detect and interdict payment for child pornography, would be that I surrender my passport and apply to the USSS whenever I need to travel abroad.

So, a remarkable thing happened at the arraignment.

My attorney leaped to his feet and told the judge these assertions could not be allowed to pass unchallenged and that I would waive my 5th amendment rights on the spot in order to respond.

For about the next 15 minutes, the Judge asked me questions. For the first time since

12/05 [actually before that I guess, since the government organized its secret task force - apparently for the single purpose of destroying e-gold - and also was pursuing a secret grand jury investigation], we were able to offer facts to a Judge to counter the deceitful claims that have been submitted in sealed affidavits and ex parte proceedings.

His response was measured but I could tell he was listening. He took pains, twice, to point out that his involvement was extremely limited since he was only presiding over the arraignment. He made it clear that the actual trial judge would have the power to alter any pretrial conditions and would very likely be interested in addressing that issue.[541]

◆

Post-Indictment Restraint of Assets (PIRO)

In addition to the seizure warrant, the District Court contemporaneously issued a Post-Indictment Restraint of Assets (PIRO), against the five criminal Defendants, applicable to the assets and records of transactions of the corporate entity. To prevent the dissipation of e-gold® account value, the PIRO required the Defendants to provide information about assets subject to forfeiture and comply with specific notice and approval requirements before disposing of their physical precious metal holdings. This order also imposed restrictions on further transactions by the Defendants. The following text was copied from the PIRO and detailed a critical issue affecting e-gold's daily business.

> IT IS FURTHER ORDERED that upon receipt of this Order, the defendants are required to (insert) freeze – that is, not conduct or allow any further transactions in (delete) that is, to freeze e-gold accounts that the e-gold operation itself has already identified as being used for criminal activity. Defendants shall continue to freeze all accounts that have been frozen (or in any way suspended from conducting further transactions) by the e-gold operation on the basis that they have been involved in (delete) either child pornography, or credit card, or identity fraud.[542] [This section contains had hand-written corrections initialed by Judge Rosemary M Collyer.]

---

[541] Jackson, Douglas. "Re: Question." Received by Dan Kaplan, et al., *Re: Question*, 6 May 2007.

[542] https://legalupdate.e-gold.com/2007/04/post-indictment.html. U.S.A. v. e-gold, Ltd., Gold & Silver Reserve, Inc. Douglas L. Jackson, Barry K. Downey, and Reid A. Jackson, Defendants. POST-INDICTMENT RESTRAINING ORDER, 26 Apr. 2007.

The PIRO created the following realities.

- Deputized e-gold's in-house investigators to freeze any e-gold® accounts they suspected of criminal activity without legal, due process.
- Crippled exchange markets by requiring the prosecutor's permission to redeem e-gold®
- Reduced circulation in response to decreased demand for e-gold®

The document included a restriction that the Court termed, "a controlled ability to sell precious metals" for customer accounts. This statement meant that bullion sale transactions could take place only after pre-approval from the Court.[543] The PIRO detailed how the government expected e-gold® to satisfy all customer outexchange transactions in non-seized accounts with existing funds.

The Defendants moved quickly to vacate the seizure warrant, modify the restraining order, and seek an evidentiary hearing. In the absence of the seized assets, the Defendants alleged an inability to pay for counsel of their choice. The following text, copied from the Motion, illustrates the consequence of the PIRO.

> Despite persuading the Court to sign the Post-Indictment Restraining Order stating that "the order requested is narrowly tailored to allow orderly continuation of defendants' business activities as well as the ability of the defendants' customers to access their funds through it," (Post-Indictment Restraining Order, ¶ 7), the government failed to advise the Court that because the seizure warrant issued in Case No. 07-167-M-01 (the "Primary Seizure Warrant") ordered the seizure of "[a]ny and all property" in the primary operating accounts of e-gold Ltd. and G&SR, the Defendants would be left incapable of continuing the orderly operation of the business and of allowing customers the ability to access their funds.[544]

The combined asset seizures and PIRO ended exchange operations and redemption through G&SR/OmniPay, along with the company's capacity to generate a monthly income.

---

[543] "Digital Currency Business e-gold Indicted for Money Laundering and Illegal Money Transmitting." *U.S. Department of Justice*, DOJ, 27 Apr. 2007, www.justice.gov/archive/opa/pr/2007/April/07_crm_301.html.

[544] U.S. District Court for the District of Columbia. *E-GOLD LIMITED, GOLD & SILVER RESERVE, INC., DOUGLAS L. JACKSON, BARRY K. DOWNEY and REID A. JACKSON Related Case In the Matter of the Seizure of Any and All Property in/Underlying e-gold Account 544179 and in/Underlying e-gold CASE NUMBER account 109243, Held by e-gold, Ltd. or 07-167-M-01 Gold & Silver Reserve, Inc. on Behalf of e-gold, Ltd.* DEFENDANTS' MOTION TO VACATE SEIZURE WARRANT AND TO MODIFY RESTRAINING ORDER AND REQUEST FOR AN EVIDENTIARY HEARING, 1 June 2007.

While e-gold® had been fully operational from November 1996 through April 2007, by May, the PIRO had interrupted e-gold's ability to generate steady revenue.

After OmniPay exchange operations halted, G&SR revenues declined quickly. Mounting legal expenses from the Government's case overwhelmed the Defendants. In 2007, G&SR had two sources of monthly income. The first revenue stream came from benefits paid by e-gold, Ltd., to G&SR, according to rights granted on its e-gold® account number one (1). This account was known as Super Originator Right Number 1 ("SO 1").[545] This paid income was calculated on a specified percentage of gross Spend fees collected from e-gold® payees that have SOI as their "Super Originator." E-gold identified this plan as the Account Referral Incentive Program. After May 2007, the total number of Spends and Spend fees, which generated the small referral payments, declined precipitously. As the number of Spends plummeted, so did G&SR's SO 1 receipts. The Defendants' lawyers presented these examples to illustrate the lost revenue stream.[546]

In May, 2007, G&SR had SO 1 receipt of $44,462.97 for SO 1 benefits accrued in April 2007. This period was before the impact of the indictment affected the e-gold® and G&SR businesses. In 2008, G&SR's monthly SO 1 receipt fell to the $1,000. level.

January: $19,359.35
February: $21,268.86
March: $19,755.40
April and /May: $28,260.95
June: $11,592.67
July: $11,514.39
August: $8,966.55
September: $3,120.62
October: $1,735.78[547]

---

[545] Every e-gold account has an Originator and a Super Originator. The Super Originator receives, for each Spend to each account for which it is designated as Super Originator, a specified percentage of the gross Spend fees arising from that e-gold account. Account-holders who refer new account holders to e-gold become Originators and those new accounts inherit the Super Originator of their Originator. When a new e-gold account is opened without a referring party being designated, the e-gold computer system randomly assigns to the new e-gold account an Originator (and thereby a Super Originator) from a specified pool of e-gold accounts, some of which have SOI as their Super Originator. G&SR is the owner of the SO 1 right and the recipient of its benefits.

[546] CASE NUMBER: 07-167-M-01. *UNITED STATES OF AMERICA V. E-GOLD LIMITED, GOLD & SILVER RESERVE, INC., DOUGLAS L. JACKSON, BARRY K. DOWNEY and REID A. JACKSON.* SENTENCING MEMORANDUM OF GOLD & SILVER RESERVE, INC., Nov. 2008.

[547] Ibid

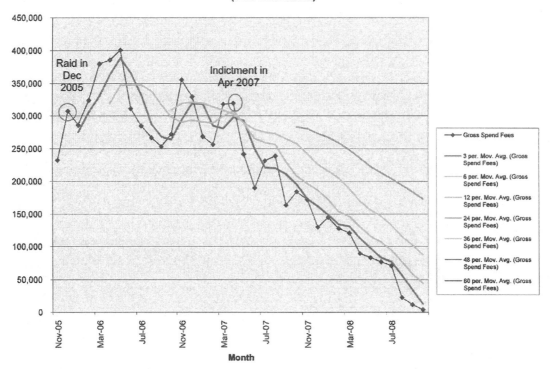

e-gold Gross Spend Fee Revenue (USD Cost Basis)

G&SR lost revenue stream presented by Defendants' lawyer January – October 2008[548]

G&SR's other single revenue steam came through payments it received from e-gold, Ltd. according to an agreement for services provided by G&SR in its capacity as Operator of the e-gold® system. These payments were made by e-gold, Ltd. to G&SR on a "cost-plus" basis to cover operating expenses and   compensate G&SR for its expenses and undertakings as Operator of the e-gold® system.[549] Of note, while the prosecutors set out to misrepresent e-gold Ltd. and G&SR, Inc. as if a single entity, G&SR, had been paying corporate income tax on all revenues received from e-gold Ltd. since the latter company had become operational in 2000.

On April 30, 2007, Jackson published a strong denial of any wrongdoing on the e-gold®

[548] Case 1:07-cr-00109-RMC Document 176. *United States of America.* E-GOLD, LTD.'S MEMORANDUM IN AID OF SENTENCING AND INCORPORATED POSITION WITH RESPECT TO SENTENCING FACTORS, 17 Nov. 2008.

[549] CASE NUMBER: 07-167-M-01. *UNITED STATES OF AMERICA V. E-GOLD LIMITED, GOLD & SILVER RESERVE, INC., DOUGLAS L. JACKSON, BARRY K. DOWNEY and REID A. JACKSON.* SENTENCING MEMORANDUM OF GOLD & SILVER RESERVE, INC., Nov. 2008.

website.[550]

e-gold® Founder Denies Criminal Charges

On April 24, 2007, a Federal Grand Jury handed down an indictment charging e-gold Ltd., Gold & Silver Reserve, Inc., and the Directors of both companies with money laundering, operating an unlicensed money transmitter business, and conspiracies to commit both offenses.

Dr. Douglas Jackson, Chairman and Founder of e-gold®, speaking on behalf of his fellow Directors and both companies vigorously denies the charges, taking particular exception to the allegations that either company ever turned a blind eye to payments for child pornography or for the sale of stolen identity and credit card information.

Dr. Jackson states, "With regard to child pornography, the government knows full well that their allegations are false, yet they highlight these irresponsible and purposely damaging statements in order to demonize e-gold® in the eyes of the public. During the Inquisition, accusations of witchcraft and heresy were used to sanctify torture and seizures of property. In post 9-11 America, child porn and terrorism serve as the denunciations of choice. e-gold®, however, as a matter of incontrovertible fact, is the most effective of all online payment systems in detecting and interdicting abuse of its system for child pornography related payments. e-gold Ltd. is a founding member of the National Center for Missing and Exploited Children's (NCMEC) Financial Coalition to Eliminate Child Pornography. e-gold® is the only member institution to demonstrate with hard, audit-able data a dramatic reduction of such payments to virtually zero, while billions of child porn dollars continue to flow through other (heavily regulated) payment systems. [Most members, that is, all the banks and credit card associations are utterly unable to even provide an estimate of the volume of such payments processed by their systems. eBay's PayPal subsidiary, who may have the ability to make such a determination, has refused to do so and has indicated they destroy payment records after two years.] What is worse, until August 2005 when NCMEC courageously broke ranks with US law enforcement agencies and began directly notifying e-gold® of criminal sites via the CyberTipline, component agencies of the US Department of Justice purposely concealed their knowledge of child pornography abuses from e-gold's investigators, subordinating actual crime fighting to a policy agenda designed to dirty up e-gold."

---

[550] Jackson, Douglas. "e-gold Founder Denies Criminal Charges." *e-gold*, e-gold.com, 30 Apr. 2007, web.archive.org/web/20071227093207if_/www.e-gold.com:80/letter3.html.

In December 2005, the Secret Service (USSS) deceived a Federal Magistrate judge with bogus testimony in order to obtain search and seizure warrants authorizing the government to seize the US bank accounts of Gold & Silver Reserve, Inc. The seizure, which netted the government about $ 0.8 million, was designed to put e-gold® out of business without due process, since G&SR serves as the contractual Operator of the e-gold® system. At a subsequent emergency hearing, the government made no effort to defend their (sealed) allegations of lurid criminality, falling back to a position that their action was warranted because of a licensure issue. At the hearing, G&SR described its ongoing dialog with the Department of Treasury, initiated by formal request of the company in Spring 2005, to determine a possible basis for regulating the company's activities, since it was patently clear to competent authorities that G&SR's exchange service was not encompassed within any existing regulatory rubric [subsequently re-confirmed by experts at the Federal Reserve]. The US Attorney for the District of Columbia, responsible for the prosecution, was completely unaware of this orderly proceeding, as well as Treasury reports issued the same week that acknowledged e-gold® as an innovation not meeting definitions of a money services business or a money transmitter.

Since this time, the government has been confronted with overwhelming evidence that the USSS had made a horrible mistake in its attack on the e-gold® system and its repeated defamatory claims in the media that e-gold® is anonymous, untraceable, and inaccessible to US law enforcement. They have concealed the fact that Dr. Jackson had personally arranged to come to USSS headquarters to train the USSS cybercrime squad in December 2004 (along with agents of the UK's National High Tech Crime Unit, and the Australian Federal Police) on advanced techniques, particularly in the area of efficient interaction with e-gold's in-house investigative staff, but was prevented when senior USSS management learned of the initiative and forbade the training on the grounds of a policy declaring e-gold® as their designated bogey man.

The Department of Justice has had to determine whether to continue to stand behind their component agency. Their decision to close ranks has directly resulted in a gross mis-allocation of resources, with the result that vicious criminals who might have been brought to justice remain at large. An example of this is the Shadowcrew investigation, hyped by the USSS as a major success in disrupting international credit card thieves. The USSS did not subpoena records from e-gold® at any time in their investigation, or engage with e-gold's superb in-house investigative staff, with the result that the sophisticated hierarchy of the ring was unmolested and probably strengthened while the USSS hauled in the low hanging fruit, "a dime a dozen and relatively easy to track down and pop".

Similarly, there is compelling evidence that the international cartel of commercial vendors of child pornography continues to operate because the FBI Innocent Images Unit and Special Agents within the Immigration and Customs Enforcement Agency have been forbidden to follow investigative protocols developed by Dr. Jackson, apparently for fear of further belying the party line that e-gold® is itself a nefarious operation.

With regard to allegations of money laundering, Dr. Jackson notes "G&SR's online exchange service, OmniPay, has for years followed stringent customer identification procedures and an absolute policy of only accepting money payments by bank wire. If bank wires aren't already "clean" then what is? Furthermore, e-gold Ltd. can scarcely be construed as a money launderer since it does not accept money payments from anyone in any form and has never owned a single dollar, yen, euro or any other brand of legacy money. As far as the possibility of a criminal successfully obfuscating a money trail, e-gold® is a closed system. The only way to obtain e-gold® is by receiving a transfer from someone who already has some. e-gold® is also the only payment system accessible by the public that maintains a permanent record of all transfers."

On April 27, 2007, the government served seizure warrants on G&SR ordering it to freeze, liquidate and turn over to the government the operating e-gold® accounts of G&SR and e-gold Ltd. The value seized, about $762 thousand worth of e-gold® from e-gold Ltd. and about $736 thousand worth of e-gold® from G&SR [on top of the $0.8 million seized from G&SR in 2005, and the approximately $1 million spent by G&SR so far in its defense] constitutes the bulk of the liquid assets of both companies. Perplexingly, a post-indictment restraining order states "Nothing in the provisions of this restraining order shall be construed as limiting the e-gold® operation's ability to use its existing funds to satisfy requests from its customers to exchange e-gold® into national currency, or its ability to sell precious metals to accomplish the same once approval has been obtained." Having taken virtually the entire operating funds of G&SR and e-gold Ltd., that is, the e-gold® in both companies' own e-gold® accounts, it is unclear if the government has even a basic grasp of the operations it has been investigating for three years at a taxpayer expense

357

in the millions.

The most remarkable element of the restraining order is that the US government deputizes e-gold® with plenipotentiary powers to act as judge, jury and executioner against any account user e-gold® itself has deemed to be a criminal: "It is further ordered that upon receipt of this order the defendants are required to freeze, that is, not conduct or allow any further transactions in e-gold® accounts that the e-gold® operation itself has identified as being used for criminal activity". Although not accompanied by an outright letter of marque, this commission (the financial equivalent to double ought status?) would appear to be an acknowledgment that e-gold's 'Know Your Customer' prowess far exceeds that of any regulated financial institution, who would be obliged to rely on court orders or other legal writs to determine if freezing an account is warranted.

Concurrent with this latest attempt to knock e-gold Ltd. and G&SR out of business and thereby effectively deny them due process, the government also attacked other prominent exchange services that deal in e-gold®; IceGold, The Bullion Exchange, Gitgold, Denver Gold Exchange, AnyGoldNow, and Gold Pouch Express, plus a sophisticated and secure alternative payment system called "1MDC". All of the listed exchange services also follow stringent Customer Identification Programs congruent with what would be required of a currency exchange business, if the law supported such a classification. Two of the services, IceGold and AnyGoldNow, are located in Europe and deal primarily with non-US customers. As a direct and immediate result of the seizures, these companies, all of who had built a reputation for honoring their obligations to customers in a timely fashion, have been disrupted, and, at least in the case of Gitgold, checks to customers issued in fulfillment of exchanges have bounced. This is a repeat of what happened to G&SR as a direct result of the 2005 seizure, when over 200 checks to customers bounced and refunds had to be sorted out with severely crippled liquidity and without a US bank account.

It must not be overlooked that the search warrant obtained by misrepresentations before a magistrate judge in 2005 resulted in the government helping themselves to the financial records of hundreds of thousands of American citizens [plus citizens of virtually every other country] who had not been accused of any wrongdoing. Since the initial raid, the prosecutor has caused the Grand Jury to order complete dumps of the e-gold® data base on three additional occasions.

This case has nothing to do with criminal activity, at least not on the part of e-gold Ltd., G&SR, the named individuals or these other exchange services of high reputation. It is about a Department of Justice that is out of control, cognizant of having made a horrible mistake but determined at all costs to preserve its turf. In a meeting at the US Attorney's office in Washington on December 29, 2006, a Chief Assistant US Attorney told us that the United States knew we weren't "bad guys" and that the United States had no interest in sending any of us to prison or causing e-gold® to go out of business. This was in virtually the same breath as proposing that the current defendants plead guilty to Federal felony charges.

The plain fact is that the repeated statements and actions of the government since 2001, especially the USSS, are directly responsible for crippling e-gold's ability to market its service to mainstream businesses and consumers, slowing [but fortunately not stopping] e-gold's continuous development of advanced anti-crime capabilities, subordinating US law enforcement's cybercrime fighting efforts to the forlorn hope of destroying e-gold®, driving market share to non-US based alternative payment systems and making the US law enforcement community the laughingstock of competent cybercrime fighting agencies worldwide because of its obstinate inability to back down from the USSS's longstanding e-gold® vendetta.[551]

An indictment is merely an allegation, and all defendants are presumed innocent unless and until proven guilty beyond a reasonable doubt in a court of law. After all, this is still America.

This statement is a standard "disclaimer" that appears on the bottom of all DOJ press releases that announce a new federal indictment. However, this text is never a part of any articles or followup statements by federal agents that are published by the media.

The April 27, 2007, DOJ press release falsely characterized Jackson, a former doctor, as an evil criminal mastermind.

"As alleged in the indictment, the e-gold® payment system has been a preferred means of payment for child pornography distributors, identity thieves, online scammers, and other criminals around the world to launder their illegal income anonymously," said Assistant Attorney General Alice S. Fisher of the Criminal Division. "This indictment demonstrates that the Department of Justice, in cooperation with its law enforcement partners, will aggressively identify and

---

[551] Jackson, Douglas. " e-gold Founder Denies Criminal Charges." *e-gold*, e-gold.com, 30 Apr. 2007, http://web.archive.org/web/20070502021439if_/http://www.e-gold.com:80/letter3.html

prosecute those who knowingly enable and profit from transmitting the proceeds of criminal activity, online or offline."[552]

"Douglas Jackson and his associates operated a sophisticated and widespread international money remitting business, unsupervised and unregulated by any entity in the world, which allowed for anonymous transfers of value at a click of a mouse," said U.S. Attorney Jeffrey A. Taylor for the District of Columbia. "Not surprisingly, criminals of every stripe gravitated to e-gold® as a place to move their money with impunity. As alleged in the indictment, the defendants in this case knowingly allowed them to do so and profited from their crimes."[553]

Assistant Director James E. Finch, of the FBI's Cyber Division, tried his best to associate e-gold® with terrorists by stating for the media:

"The advent of new electronic currency systems increases the risk that criminals, and possibly terrorists, will exploit these systems to launder money and transfer funds globally to avoid law enforcement scrutiny and circumvent banking regulations and reporting."[554]

The DOJ's press release, and all of the vengeful accusations that followed, failed to mention critical facts. The government had not yet written the laws and regulations that would eventually supervise digital currency products. These laws did not go into effect until 2010-2011.

◆

As of May 2007, immediately following the formal indictment, GS&R stopped all exchange services. During the last days of April 2007, those involved with the regulation of financial products in the State of Florida began discussing the new e-gold® federal charges. These persons are previously identified individuals.

From: Mike Ramsden
Sent: Monday, April 30, 2007 9:17 AM
To: John Harper; Rick White; Robert Rosenau; Robert Beitler

---

[552] "Digital Currency Business e-gold Indicted for Money Laundering and Illegal Money Transmitting." *U.S. Department of Justice*, DOJ, 27 Apr. 2007, www.justice.gov/archive/opa/pr/2007/April/07_crm_301.html
[553] Ibid
[554] Ibid

Cc: Chris Hancock; Mark Mathosian; Peter Fisher
Subject: FW: [ACAMS] Digital Currency Business e-gold Indicted

Perhaps we should revisit?[555]

From: Peter Fisher
Sent: Mon 5/21/2007 4:44 PM
To: Mike Ramsden; Robert Rosenau
Cc: John Harper; Chris Hancock; Mark Mathosian; Robert Beitler; William Oglo
Subject: RE: [ACAMS] Digital Currency Business e-gold Indicted

Bob and Mike,
I am in the process of reviewing some open case files, one of which includes e-gold. The e-gold legal file was opened originally based on a request for opinion from each of you. While an initial opinion was drafted there was still considerable discussion about the draft ongoing, and a reply to the request was not made. Do you still want an opinion? Is there some additional follow up needed at this point? I am presuming not based on our last discussion and the intervening events that have occurred, so I would like to have the file closed unless you find some additional follow-up necessary at this point.
Please let me know your thoughts.[556]

From: Robert Rosenau
Sent: Friday, May 25, 2007 9:50 AM
To: Peter Fisher; Mike Ramsden
Cc: John Harper; Chris Hancock; Mark Mathosian; Robert Beitler; William Oglo
Subject: RE: [ACAMS] Digital Currency Business e-gold Indicted

I think we need an OFR position on this issue. It appears the Feds decided that e-gold is a money transmitter. It appears logical that OFR could conclude that other entities using a similar business model would be a money transmitter.
r[557]

[555] "Subject: FW: [ACAMS] Digital Currency Business E-Gold Indicted." Received by John Harper, et al., Subject: FW: [ACAMS] Digital Currency Business E-Gold Indicted, 30 Apr. 2007. Ref. (Emails Redacted.pdf)

[556] Fisher, Peter. "RE: [ACAMS] Digital Currency Business e-Gold Indicted." Received by Mike Ramsden, and Robert Rosenau, *RE: [ACAMS] Digital Currency Business e-Gold Indicted*, 21 May 2007.

[557] Rosenau, Robert. "[ACAMS] Digital Currency Business e-Gold Indicted." Received by Peter Fisher, and Mike Ramsden, *[ACAMS] Digital Currency Business e-Gold Indicted*, 25 May 2007.

From: Robert Beitler
Sent: Friday, May 25, 2007 9:59 AM
To: Robert Rosenau; Peter Fisher; Mike Ramsden
Cc: John Harper; Chris Hancock; Mark Mathosian; William Oglo
Subject: RE: [ACAMS] Digital Currency Business e-gold Indicted

Bob:

This is all fact intensive. I haven't a clue what evidence the feds have. As I recall, just about all the facts that we received from you for this opinion was what you pulled off the e-gold web site. And that information was insufficient for us to conclude that this was a money transmitter. Even if we had all the fed's info, we might reach the same conclusion.

Everyone knows why they went after e-gold, but as you are aware the filing of charges is not determinative of anything. In addition, any opinion which we reach in e-gold, especially based on such skeletal information as you have been able to provide, is unlikely to provide useful guidance for most other companies, as each will be dependent on the facts available regarding that enterprise and its method of operation.
Rob[558]

From: Peter Fisher
Sent: Thursday, May 31 , 2007 2:56 PM
To: Robert Rosenau; Mike Ramsden
Cc: John Harper; Robert Beitler; William Oglo
Subject: RE: [ACAMS] Digital Currency Business e-gold Indicted

Bob and Mike -
Based on my conversations with each of you it is my understanding that we're in agreement as to our closing the legal file on Egold, and that if a similar factual situation arises in the future we will review the facts and circumstances at that time. If my understanding is incorrect, please let me know as soon as possible, otherwise by this email I am asking Bill to close the legal file. Thanks.
  – Peter[559]

---

[558] Beitler, Robert, and Peter Fisher. "RE: [ACAMS] Digital Currency Business e-Gold Indicted." Received by Robert Rosenau, and Mike Ramsden, *RE: [ACAMS] Digital Currency Business e-Gold Indicted*, 25 May 2007.

In Jackson's May emails with Dan Kaplan, a reporter for SC Magazine (Haymarket Media Inc.) Jackson responded to questions and clarified e-gold Ltd.'s regulatory licensing.

> -----Original Message-----
> From: Douglas Jackson
> Sent: Wednesday, May 02, 2007 9:05 AM
> To: Dan Kaplan
> Subject: question
>
> Hi Dan
> There has been no claim or charge that e-gold Ltd. requires any license or registration. Or if there is, it is news to me.
> There is a charge that Gold & Silver Reserve, Inc.(G&SR) is operating an unlicensed money transmitting business.
> This is incorrect.
> For details you may contact the attorneys.
> It is also laid out definitively in our motions from the first emergency hearing before Judge Facciala 12/29/05 and reviewed in oral discussion (the transcript).
> There are also court filings from later hearings. This part is open and shut.
> Specifically because G&SR does not fit under any existing reg, and this is immediately apparent to anyone familiar with the relevant law, G&SR had reached out to and engaged with Treasury in Spring 2005 to try to discover/determine some suitable regulatory rubric.
> The USSS and the US Atty for DC, despite their "investigation" of G&SR were completely unaware we had been talking to Treasury for 8 or 9 months on this very subject.
> Please read the transcript linked from my posted response.
> sincere regards,
> Douglas Jackson[560]

♦

Child Pornography and The NCMEC

[559] Fisher, Peter. "RE: [ACAMS] Digital Currency Business e-Gold Indicted." Received by Robert Rosenau, and Mike Ramsden, *RE: [ACAMS] Digital Currency Business e-Gold Indicted*, 31 May 2007.

[560] Jackson, Douglas. "Re: Question." Received by Dan Kaplan, et al., *Re: Question*, 6 May 2007.

Despite all of Jackson's voluntary work with law enforcement agencies, the media had presented a steady stream of abusive and even ridiculous allegations painting e-gold® as having turned a blind eye to crime. The one shining beacon of truth proving e-gold's aggressive fight against corruption was its founding membership in the Financial Coalition Against Child Pornography (FCACP) through the NCMEC. As a founding Coalition member and in partnership with the NCMEC, e-gold® was able to develop solutions for detection, investigation, interdiction, and reporting of suspicious payment activity, including CP payments.

On May 1, 2007, the National Center for Missing and Exploited Children published a statement on its website regarding the organization's expulsion of e-gold® from the Financial Coalition Against Child Pornography (FCACP).

> Statement Regarding e-gold Expulsion from Financial Coalition[561]
> Alexandria, VA - April 30, 2007.   The National Center for Missing and Exploited Children, together with its sister organization, the International Center for Missing & Exploited Children today announced that e-gold has been expelled from the membership of the Financial Coalition Against Child Pornography (FCACP). e-gold had been a member of FCACP since 2006. [e-gold was a charter member of, and an active participant in, the FCACP, dating back to summer 2005, nine months before its formal announcement].
> Upon learning that an indictment had been returned against e-gold alleging that e-gold has been a highly favored method of payment by operators of investments scams, credit card and identify fraud, and sellers of online child pornography, and that the company conducted funds transfers on behalf of their customers knowing that the funds involved were the proceeds of unlawful activity including child exploitation and as a result violated money laundering statutes, e-gold was immediately expelled from the Coalition.
> "We were shocked and disappointed to learn of these allegations," said Ernie Allen, President and CEO. "The work the Coalition is doing is of tremendous importance and will not be impacted in any way by the expulsion of e-gold."
> The Financial Coalition Against Child Pornography was formed to address the alarming growth of commercial child pornography over the Internet, which has become a multi-billion dollar enterprise.   The Coalition is comprised of twenty-nine

[561] "Statement Regarding e-gold Expulsion from Financial Coalition." *Statement Regarding e-gold Expulsion from Financial Coalition*, http://www.ncmec.org, 30 Apr. 2007, http://web.archive.org/web/20071019032038/www.ncmec.org/missingkids/servlet/NewsEventServlet?LanguageCountry=en_US&PageId=3150

leading banks, credit card companies, third-party payment companies, and Internet services companies which have pledged to work towards eliminating the commercial viability of child pornography on the Internet. The members of the Coalition represent 90% of the U.S. payments industry, as well as several leading international financial and Internet companies.

Through the Coalition, the flow of funds is being disrupted and payment accounts are being shut down, making the business of selling and purchasing child pornography much more difficult. However, commercial distributors of child pornography are constantly creating new types of currencies. In addition to eliminating the ability to use traditional payment methods such as credit cards, FCACP is working to curtail the use of alternative payment mechanisms to purchase child pornography.

About the National Center for Missing and Exploited Children

NCMEC is a 501(c)(3) nonprofit organization that works in cooperation with the U.S. Department of Justice's Office of Juvenile Justice and Delinquency Prevention. NCMEC's congressionally mandated CyberTipline, a reporting mechanism for child sexual exploitation, has handled more than 475,000 leads. Since its establishment in 1984, NCMEC has assisted law enforcement with more than 127,900 missing children cases, resulting in the recovery of more than 110,200 children. For more information about NCMEC, call its toll-free, 24-hour hotline at 1-800-THE-LOST or visit its website at www.missingkids.com.

About the International Center for Missing and Exploited Children

ICMEC is a private, 501(c)(3) nonprofit nongovernmental organization. It is the leading agency working on a global basis to combat child abduction and exploitation. It is the sister organization of the National Center for Missing and Exploited Children.

On May 25th, 2007, Dr. Jackson responded to Ernie Allen in a blistering twenty page private letter.

♦

In 2006, G&SR had engaged a DC lobbying and public relations company, JC Watts. In summer 2007, Jackson elected to rely on the Watts firm to re-engage with NCMEC and to serve the letter. NCMEC counsel Carlos Ortiz stonewalled these efforts. In September 2007, a perfunctory meeting finally occurred. Meeting notes provided by a Watts staff member who had been in attendance reported: "As the meeting concluded, Ernie indicated a willingness to work with E-Gold directly. We believe that this will not actually come to fruition."

The letter was also supplied to Brian Krebs, at that time at the Washington Post, on July 11, 2007. Krebs indicated he would incorporate the data into an expose he was working up that would reveal the government's misinformation campaign against e-gold concerning carders and CP investigations. The article was to come out in August. No such news item was ever published, and all of Jackson's subsequent calls to Krebs, and a follow-up email on August 16, 2007, went unanswered.[562]

On June 4, 2007, William Oglo wrote a brief memo regarding the status of e-gold® with the State of Florida in light of the federal indictment. His message ended with this recommendation, "Both the Money Transmitter's Unit and the Bureau of investigations agree that is it appropriate to close this matter at this time subject to reopening at a later date if warranted."

[State of Florida]
INTEROFFICE COMMUNICATION OFFICE OF FINANCIAL REGULATION
LEGAL SERVICES
DATE: June 4, 2007
TO: File
FROM: William Oglo [Initialed]
RE: Requests for Informal Opinion on e-gold-closing memo

e-gold is a digital currency which purportedly can be used as a store of value or a method of payment to certain companies operating online. Both the Money Transmitter Unit and the Bureau of Investigations requested that Legal provide an informal opinion regarding whether the Office can regulate companies that exchange dollars for e-gold. The matter was assigned to me.

After I had a chance to research and review the legal issues, a decision was made to have a meeting with representatives of Legal, the Money Transmitter's Unit, the Division of Securities and Finance, and the Bureau of Investigations, prior to the issuance of an informal opinion. This was because the Bureaus wanted to exchange their ideas on whether the Office could legally regulate e-gold and/or whether the Office should regulate e-gold. On January 18, 2007, a meeting was held where a number of issues were discussed. The decision whether the Office should regulate e-gold was postponed in part so that the newly reorganized Finance Division would have time to familiarize itself with the issues. On or about April 30, 2007, the Office

[562] Jackson, Douglas. "Chunk 6." Received by Carl Mullan, *Chunk 6*, 3 Mar. 2020. DJ redlines 6

became aware that U.S. Justice Department issued an indictment charging e-gold with money laundering, conspiracy, operating an unlicensed money transmitter business, and other violations of law. Thus, it appears that the Justice Department is addressing concerns of the manner in which e-gold is operating. Both the Money Transmitter's Unit and the Bureau of Investigations agree that it is appropriate to close this matter at this time subject to reopening at a later date if warranted.[563]

♦

Database Update

The e-gold® operation provided a second update of the full customer database information (by copying the database to an external hard drive) for the period of October 2006 through March 2007 in response to a grand jury subpoena issued on March 6, 2007.

♦

The Battle for an Evidentiary Hearing

"we know that many of the rules and devices of adversary litigation as we conduct it are not geared for, but are often aptly suited to defeat, the development of the truth."[564]

The strategies of the prosecution and defense attorneys in the e-gold case were straightforward. The defense sought to introduce evidence and testimony to acquaint the judge with the companies' actual business model and operations. Failure to do so would lead to an outcome based on uncontested assertions of probable cause and the "assumed facts" of the criminal complaint. The prosecution strategy was to prevent the introduction of evidence (which could be challenged) or testimony (which would be subject to cross-examination) - improving their chances of achieving victory during the pre-trial "motions practice" of the proceedings. Rulings on pre-trial motions are informed by a different logic than the "presumption of innocence" that comes into play should a criminal case proceed to trial, i.e., the "evidentiary phase."

Throughout June 2007 and continuing into July, the e-gold case hinged on defense efforts to obtain an evidentiary hearing to challenge the allegations of probable cause in the

---

[563] Oglo, William. "Requests for Informal Opinion on e-Gold-Closing Memo." Received by File, *Requests for Informal Opinion on e-Gold-Closing Memo*, 4 June 2007. State of Florida interoffice Communication Office of Financial Regulation Legal Services

[564] "The Search For Truth: An Umpireal View" MARVIN E. FRANKEL (35th Benjamin Cardozo Lecture, 1975.)

asset seizure/forfeiture case (a so-called "Monsanto hearing"[565]), and efforts by the prosecution to prevent such a hearing.

The defense made the initial request for an evidentiary hearing in late May 2007. Judge Collyer set a tentative court date of June 25-26 pending submission and court review of arguments in favor/opposition of the hearing.

In June, the Defendants filed Court documents attempting to reverse the previous seizures and resolve pivotal Court issues.[566] The Defendants moved to vacate the civil seizure warrant and modify the restraining order to permit inter alia and the use of the seized assets to retain defense counsel. Defendants filed the Motion to Vacate Seizure Warrant and to Modify Restraining Order and Request for an Evidentiary Hearing on June 1st. The motion was fully briefed, with affidavits submitted by both sides. The content from Court documents copied here details how the Defendants challenged the government's basis for the forfeiture. Also included is information SA Dotson never disclosed to the Court.[567]

III. THE GOVERNMENT LACKED PROBABLE CAUSE TO BELIEVE THAT THE DEFENDANTS COMMITTED ANY CRIMES THAT WOULD PROVIDE THE BASIS FOR FORFEITURE

On May 22, 2007, nearly one month after the execution of the seizure warrants and Post-Indictment Restraining Order, the government first made available to Defendants a copy of the government's affidavit submitted to the Court in support of the seizure warrants issued in these matters. That affidavit makes clear that the seizure warrants were sought, and issued, solely on the basis of the allegation that the property subject to the Primary Seizure Warrants "was involved in the operation of an unlicensed money transmitting business in violation of Title 18, United States Code, Section 1960.

See Affidavit in Support of Seizure Warrant ("Dotson Affidavit"), ¶ 6; see also ¶¶ 4, 22-26.

The affidavit was purportedly prepared and signed by Roy Dotson, a Special Agent with the United States Secret Service who has – at least based on a plain

---

[565] A "Monsanto hearing" is "a hearing at which the government must establish that there is probable cause to believe the property will be forfeited if the defendant is convicted". Asset Forfeiture Law in the United States - Second Edition By Stefan D. Cassella, pp. 520-522.

[566] Case 1:07-cr-00109-RMC Document 35 . *UNITED STATES OF AMERICA v. E-GOLD LIMITED, GOLD & SILVER RESERVE, INC., DOUGLAS L. JACKSON, BARRY K. DOWNEY and REID A. JACKSON In the Matter of the Seizure of Any and All Property in/Underlying e-gold Account 544179 and in/Underlying e-gold CASE NUMBER Account 109243, Held by e-gold, Ltd. or 07-167-M-01 Gold & Silver Reserve, Inc. on Behalf of e-gold, Ltd.* DEFENDANTS' MOTION TO VACATE SEIZURE WARRANT AND TO MODIFY RESTRAINING ORDER AND REQUEST FOR AN EVIDENTIARY HEARING, 1 June 2007.

[567] Ibid

reading of his affidavit – never previously investigated either a licensed or unlicensed money transmitting business; Dotson Affidavit, at ¶ 1. Strikingly, SA Dotson was either unaware, or, if aware, failed to disclose to the Court, that his conclusion about the supposed illegality of Defendants' operations is rebutted by many other government authorities who have previously stated that existing federal laws and regulations do not apply to digital age businesses such as e-gold® and G&SR. For example:

- A January, 2007 United States House of Representatives Energy Committee staff report, addressing digital currencies such as e-gold, concluded that: "Digital currencies that do business in the United States are not subject to any of the U.S. banking requirements." Indeed, the staff report noted "the lack of regulation of digital currencies by any government entity, domestic or foreign."

- A Special Agent of the FBI's Cyber Crimes Unit, when questioned by Fox News about the government's investigation of the e-gold business, stated that: "At this point it is not illegal, it operates in an area of the law where there is no law."[568]

- In a December, 2005 report titled U.S. Money Laundering Threat Assessment, issued jointly by a number of government agencies, including the Department of Treasury and Department of Justice, those agencies observed that "[w]hether an online payment system or digital currency service meets the definition of a money transmitting business pursuant to BSA regulations . . . depends upon its location and the ways in which it participates in or conducts transactions."[569]

- In its October 13, 2006 Report on New Payment Methods, the Financial Action Task Force (FATF) indicated that in the United States, money transmitters are among moneyservices businesses that are required to register with the FIU (FinCEN), they also are subject to AML reporting and recordkeeping requirements and are often required to be licensed on the state level. "Whether an online payment system or digital precious metals dealer meets the definition of a money transmitter pursuant to the relevant regulations, though, depends upon its location and the ways in which it participates in or conducts transactions."[570]

---

[568] Interview available at: *FOX 11 Los Angeles*, FOX 11 Los Angeles, 11 Feb. 2020, www.myfoxla.com/myfox/

[569] MONEY LAUNDERING THREAT ASSESSMENT WORKING GROUP. "U. S. Money Laundering Threat Assessment." District of Columbia, Washington, D.C., Dec. 2005.

[570] While not technically a federal department or agency, the FATF is an inter-governmental body which sets standards and develops and promotes policies to combat money laundering and terrorist financing; see, www.fatf-gafi.org.

- Additionally, on May 3, 2007 – the date on which the Defendants were all arraigned in this case based on an indictment which alleged that they conspired to participate in an unlicensed money transmitting business – the Department of Justice announced the release of the 2007 National Money Laundering Strategy (the "2007 Strategy");[571] [572]
- The 2007 Strategy, which is signed by the Secretary of the Treasury (Henry Paulson, Jr.), the Attorney General (Alberto Gonzales), and the Secretary of Homeland Security (Michael Chertoff), "is a direct response to the first U.S. Government wide money laundering threat assessment released in December 2005. In addition to following this new methodology, **the 2007 Strategy for the first time focuses exclusively on money laundering**." 2007 Strategy, at v; [Emphasis added].[573]
- The 2007 Strategy specifically references e-gold in its discussion of "online payment systems" and "digital currency dealers;" *id.*, at 43-45. According to the 2007 Strategy, "[t]he oldest and best known of the **digital currency services** is e-gold Ltd., licensed in Nevis, with almost 2 million accounts." *Id.,* at 43-44; [Emphasis added]. The Strategy, in its discussion of Regulation and Public Policy, continues:
- In the United States, money transmitters are among MSBs required to register with FinCEN, are subject to AML reporting and record keeping requirements, and are often required to be licensed on the state level. **Whether an online payment system or digital currency service meets the definition of a money transmitter pursuant to BSA regulations, though, depends upon its location and the ways in which it participates in or conducts transactions.**
- *Id.,* at 45; [Emphasis added].
- In each of the above-referenced reports, the authors have expressly stated that they are on notice that **(a)** e-gold exists and that **(b)** money transmitters exist.

---

[571] "2007 National Money Laundering Strategy Released." Edited by Molly Millerwise, #07-325: 05-03-07 2007 *National Money Laundering Strategy Released*, DOJ, 3 May 2007, www.justice.gov/archive/opa/pr/2007/May/07_opa_325.html. Treasury Contact: Molly Millerwise

[572] [Given the breadth and depth of the 2007 Strategy, one must reasonably conclude that its findings were already available to Department of Justice and Department of Homeland Security personnel the week previously, when the government submitted the Dotson Affidavit to the Court.]

[573] The 2007 Strategy was authored jointly by the Drug Enforcement Agency, the National Drug Intelligence Center, the Department of Justice, the Department of the Treasury, the U.S. Department of Homeland Security, the Board of Governors of the Federal Reserve System, the United States Postal Service, the Federal Bureau of Investigations, the Department of State, the Comptroller of the Currency, the Federal Deposit Insurance Corporation, and the Internal Revenue Service. (The foregoing agencies delineated in bold print each have members on the team of government agents investigating and prosecuting this case, all of whom have repeatedly appeared for each proceeding before this Court.

However, not one such author or report has labeled e-gold as a money transmitting business, licensed or otherwise. Rather, each author states that whether a company like e-gold, Ltd. or G&SR is a money transmitting business depends on the way that it participates in or conducts transactions; *id.*

The Defendants' motion sought an evidentiary hearing as to the suitability of the seizure of assets, and individually as to the existence of probable cause to believe that the Defendants had committed an offense warranting the issuance of the seizure warrant and restraining order.

The Defendants' June 1st, 2007 argument to the Court for an Evidentiary Hearing is one of the most influential elements in the Defendants' criminal case. Below is the partial text from that sixty-seven page Court filing.

II. DEFENDANTS MUST BE AFFORDED AN EVIDENTIARY HEARING BASED UPON THE DUE PROCESS CLAUSE OF THE FIFTH AMENDMENT

The question which this Court must first resolve is whether – and upon what basis – the Defendants are entitled to an evidentiary hearing before trial to challenge the seizure warrants and post-indictment restraining order which currently restrain the Defendants' assets and impair their livelihood and ability to retain counsel. Based upon the grounds and authorities discussed below, the Court must find that Defendants are to be afforded such a hearing. Following that hearing, the Court should enter an order vacating the Primary Seizure Warrant and appropriately modify the restraining order.

A. The Defendants' Fifth Amendment Due Process Rights Have Been Triggered by the Government's Seizure of the Defendants' Property

It is well recognized that a pre-trial seizure of assets in a criminal case constitutes an impairment on property triggering the Due Process Clause of the Fifth Amendment of the United States Constitution, which provides that "no person shall…be deprived of life, liberty, or property, without due process of law." *See, Connecticut v. Doehr, 501 U.S. 1, 12 (1991); United States v. Crozier*, 777 F.2d 1376, 1383 (9 Cir. 1985). The United States Supreme Court has gone so far as to describe pretrial asset restraints as the "nuclear weapon of the law." *Grupo Mexicano de Deasarrollo, S.A. v. Alliance Bond Fund, Inc.*, 527 U.S. 308, 332 (1999).

The federal courts have consistently recognized that particular attention must be paid when dealing with this "severe remedy," *United States v. Razmilovic*, 419 F.3d 134, 137 (2d Cir. 2005). This is particularly so because asset restraints are

371

imposed on an ex parte basis and without the benefit of an adversarial process and because the government has a strong pecuniary interest in the outcome. *E.g., United States v. James Daniel Good Real Property*, 510 U.S. 43, 56 n.2 (1993) (extent of government's financial stake in forfeiture has produced a concomitant lack of neutrality); *Krimstock v. Kelly*, 306 F.3d 40, 63 (2d Cir. 2002) (there is a need for greater procedural safeguards – here, an early, pretrial adversary hearing – where the government has a pecuniary interest in the outcome of forfeiture proceedings), *cert. denied*, 539 U.S. 969 (2003); 1 David B. Smith, *Prosecution and Defense of Forfeiture Cases*, §§1.01-1.02 (2006 ed.).

B. The Triggering of the Defendants' Fifth Amendment Rights Necessitates a Post-Deprivation, Pre-Trial Hearing Where the Defendants May Challenge the Government's Restraint of Their Assets

The protection afforded by the Due Process Clause's plain text applies whenever the government has "deprived" a person "of…property." U.S. Const. Amend. V; [Emphasis added]. Nothing in that clause limits the Fifth Amendment's protections to only those persons who need to use their seized property or who are indigent. Accordingly, the federal courts have held that, when the government restrains a criminal defendant's assets before trial on the assertion that they may be subject to forfeiture, due process requires that the defendant be afforded a post deprivation, pre-trial hearing to challenge the restraint if certain minimal conditions are satisfied.[574]

IV. THE DEFENDANTS – AS THE NECESSARY AND PROXIMATE RESULT OF THE PRE-TRIAL RESTRAINTS LEVIED UPON THEM IN THIS CASE – HAVE BEEN RENDERED UNABLE TO PAY   FOR COUNSEL AND FOR REASONABLE LIVING AND OPERATING EXPENSES

As previously stated, without so much as a hearing, and based on a legitimate question of law which would be far more appropriately resolved in a declaratory judgment action, the government has seized from the Defendants e-gold Ltd. and G&SR bank accounts and e-gold accounts with an aggregate value of approximately USD $3,055,816. In this case, attorneys fees, together with litigation, discovery management, travel and related expenses, will cost the companies far in excess of $3.5 million.

---

[574] Because the seizure warrants in this case were unmistakably punitive in nature, the government should not be permitted to argue that the Defendants are not yet entitled to challenge the pretrial restraints in this case because their assets were seized "civilly." As the Tenth Circuit has observed "[t]he wholesale use of civil forfeiture proceedings [should cause] grave concern when the Government has clearly focused its law enforcement energies and resources upon a person and attempts to restrain his property in anticipation of formal criminal proceedings." *United States v. $39,000 in Canadian Currency*, 801 F2d 1210, 1219 n.7 (10th Cir. 1986); *see also United States v. Nichols*, 654 F. Supp 1541, 1545 (D.Utah 1987).

V. CONCLUSION

Based upon an incomplete and at times inaccurate ex parte presentation, the government has persuaded the Court in this case and in the stayed civil action to legitimize the seizure from the Defendants of more than Three Million Dollars ($3,000,000) of their assets without any opportunity for the Defendants to be heard on the merits of those seizures. Those seizures are rapidly precipitating the ruin of two legitimate and innovative businesses, creating substantial hardship on the Individual Defendants and their families and will leave Defendants unable to retain counsel to respond to the baseless charges brought in this action.

The seizures and pre-trial restraints are particularly shocking and inappropriate in this case where (a) there is a substantial good faith disagreement about the applicability of the law – the very law upon which the government sought the seizure warrants -- to the Defendants' businesses; (b) other government authorities have themselves questioned the applicability of that law to the Defendants' businesses; (c) Defendants have since the inception of the businesses worked hand-in-hand with government agents to root out fraud and illicit activity perpetuated by people using the e-gold system for improper purposes; and (d) have fully cooperated with the investigators and prosecutors in this case during the course of the government's nearly three-year investigation.

For all of these reasons, and the reasons more fully set forth above, the Court should grant Defendants an evidentiary hearing through which Defendants may challenge the seizures and pre-trial restraints in place in this case. Following that hearing, the Defendants request that the Court enter an order vacating the seizure warrant and modifying the post indictment restraining order.

WHEREFORE, for the foregoing reasons, the Defendants respectfully request that this Court hold a hearing whereby the Defendants may challenge the seizures and pre-trial restraints in place in this case, and, upon holding such a hearing, enter an order vacating the seizure warrant in Case No. 07-167-M-01 and modifying the post indictment restraining order.[575]

On June 15, 2007, the Government filed a response to the Defendants Motion to Vacate

---

[575] Case 1:07-cr-00109-RMC Document 35. *UNITED STATES OF AMERICA vs. E-GOLD LTD, GOLD & SILVER RESERVE LTD, DOUGLAS L. JACKSON, BARRY K. DOWNEY, REID A. JACKSON Related Case: In the Matter of the Seizure of Any and All Property in/Underlying E-GOLD, Account 544179 and in/Underlying E-GOLD Account 109243, Held by E-GOLD, Ltd. or Gold & Silver Reserve, Inc. on Behalf of E-GOLD, Ltd.* DEFENDANTS' MOTION TO VACATE SEIZURE WARRANT AND TO MODIFY RESTRAINING ORDER AND REQUEST FOR AN EVIDENTIARY HEARING, 1 June 2007.

the Seizure Warrant and to Modify the Restraining Order and to Request an Evidentiary Hearing, with a list of arguments in opposition.

The Government's response emphasized: "Defendants admittedly have not applied for or received a license in either the District of Columbia or Florida, and thus violate 18 U.S.C. 1960(b)(1)(A)." This item was accompanied by citations of the relevant state statutes, District of Columbia Money Transmitters Act, D.C. Stat. §§ 26-1001 - 26-1026 and the Florida Money Transmitter's Code, Fla. Stat. §§ 560.101-560.408.[576]

Five days later, on June 20, 2007, the Defendants added their reply.[577] The following day, June 21, there was a Court hearing with oral arguments on this motion. From the onset, the discussion went poorly for the defense. The first issue addressed was that defendant Barry Downey was not present. Downey's wife was diagnosed two days before with malignancy and required immediate hospital admission and chemotherapy. Barry missed the oral arguments to be with his wife.

The Judge prefaced her remarks with the statement, "I think you're starting from a negative position." Next, Judge Collyer enumerated multiple legal risks by proceeding with one of the Defendants absent. In a precursor to her 2008 observations noting "bad legal advice," she called each member of the defense team to the microphone inquiring whether they even practiced criminal law or had prior experience in Federal court, concluding "I can see a whole host of problems from this legal team. That causes me palpitations. And so I think that I am not overreacting when I say it causes me a lot of concern."[578] In emails, Jackson later recalled his thoughts from that hearing.

> In the view of the defendants present, the crux of the matter that needed to be brought to the attention of the court was the segregation of roles between e-gold Ltd. and G&SR (dba OmniPay). The most distinctive element of what we had built and refined over the years was our institutional arrangements that ring-fenced off the core functions of a monetary authority—issuance and settlement—from the business risks of currency exchange. To us, the cardinal deceit of the prosecution in the criminal complaint had been the artifice that framed the companies as if a single "e-gold

---

[576] Jackson, Douglas. "Chunk 7." Received by Carl Mullan, *Chunk 7*, 15 Mar. 2007. DJ redlines 7.pdf

[577] U.S. District Court for the District of Columbia. *U.S.A. v. e-gold, Ltd., Gold & Silver Reserve, Inc. Douglas L. Jackson, Barry K. Downey, and Reid A. Jackson, Defendants. Related Case: In the Matter of the Seizure of Any and All Property in/Underlying e-gold Account 544179 and in/Underlying e-gold Account 109243, Held by e-gold, Ltd. or Gold & Silver Reserve, Inc. on Behalf of e-gold, Ltd.* DEFENDANTS' REPLY MEMORANDUM IN SUPPORT OF MOTION TO VACATE SEIZURE WARRANT AND TO MODIFY RESTRAINING ORDER AND REQUEST FOR AN EVIDENTIARY HEARING, 20 June 2007.

[578] Docket No. CR 07-109. *UNITED STATES OF AMERICA vs. E-GOLD LTD, GOLD & SILVER RESERVE LTD, DOUGLAS L. JACKSON, BARRY K. DOWNEY, REID A. JACKSON.* TRANSCRIPT OF EVIDENTIARY HEARING BEFORE THE HONORABLE ROSEMARY M. COLLYER UNITED STATES DISTRICT JUDGE, 21 June 2007.

Operation." But the reality was that e-gold Ltd. did not receive or make money payments or transfers of value in any form, to or from customers. G&SR, on the other hand, did receive money payments (bank wires only), but exclusively for buying or selling e-gold, which the authorities were reticent to classify as money. Our defense attorneys did not ever seem to grasp the actual institutional arrangements or business model of the companies and dismissed our entreaties to articulate them in their pre-trial motions. Their stated rationale was that such explanations constituted evidence and, absent an evidentiary hearing, an attempt to introduce such arguments could antagonize the judge if they were perceived as a stratagem to sneak evidence into the record.[579]

The emphasis of the defense attorneys was always on the peculiarities of 18 USC 1960 and the related statutes. In aggregate, the interpretation of these items defined a "Money Transmitting Business" that hinged on whether either or both the companies accepted cash or other bearer instruments that would require the filing of Currency Transaction Reports (CTRs).

As the hearing went on, several opportunities arose to bring the institutional arrangements and transaction models of the companies to the attention of the Court and explain that the so-called "e-gold Operation" was a figment.

The most critical moment occurred when it became evident the judge did not understand the difference between G&SR (dba OmniPay) and e-gold Ltd. This opportunity allowed AUSA Laurel Rimon to reinforce critical misinformation:

"As we indicated in our papers we believe that is one operation and the distinction is not a real distinction here, but they are two different names on the accounts themselves. But they are operating accounts for the transmitting business of e-Gold."[580]

By this time in the proceedings, it had become painfully evident that defense counsel was incapable of seizing such opportunities to clearly articulate the roles of e-gold Ltd. and G&SR (dba OmniPay). The judge. observing my consternation, directed our counsel:

---

[579] Jackson, Douglas. "Chunk 7." Received by Carl Mullan, *Chunk 7*, 15 Mar. 2007. DJ redlines 7.pdf
[580] Ibid

"There are negative shakings of head, go confer again."[581]

I then urged our counsel to put me on the stand to testify. We firmly believed that if the judge could understand the actual functioning of the companies, the Court would dismiss the case. I reminded him that I had spoken in Court to the judge who presided over our arraignment and that the effect had seemed to be beneficial.[582]

After conferring, defense counsel proposed:
"Your Honor, would you allow Dr. Jackson to speak to that. I think he's far more --
THE COURT: Would you allow? Yes, if he wants to get up on the stand and take an oath. But we have to take a break, the Court Reporter needs a break for her fingers, so we'll take a break and Dr. Jackson can then get up on the stand.[583]

During this break, it became evident the defense attorneys felt unprepared to deal with possible cross-examination and when court resumed there was no further mention of putting me on the stand. There was never another opportunity for me to say anything in court until the day of sentencing, November 2008. Nevertheless, during this hearing yet another opportunity arose for counsel to plainly state that e-gold Ltd. did not receive or make money payments or transfers of value of any kind to or from customers. Instead, the best counsel could manage to argue was the following statement.[584]

"MR.ITTLEMAN: Whether the company -- even accepting, even accepting the government's definition of what a money transmitting business is i.e. a business that transmits money. Even under that definition e-Gold Ltd. couldn't possibly be a business that transmits money. It couldn't be. E-Gold Ltd. doesn't do any of that. E-Gold Ltd. – all right Judge, you have an e-Gold account hypothetically of course.
THE COURT: I understand -- what your argument is going to be.
MR. ITTLEMAN: So E-Gold Ltd. takes no part in, when you and I perform an e-Gold exchange, it doesn't do anything. It's not transmitting anything, it couldn't even be alleged."[585]

[581] Ibid
[582] Ibid
[583] Docket No. CR 07-109. *UNITED STATES OF AMERICA vs. E-GOLD LTD, GOLD & SILVER RESERVE LTD, DOUGLAS L. JACKSON, BARRY K. DOWNEY, REID A. JACKSON.* TRANSCRIPT OF EVIDENTIARY HEARING BEFORE THE HONORABLE ROSEMARY M. COLLYER UNITED STATES DISTRICT JUDGE, 21 June 2007.
[584] Jackson, Douglas. "Chunk 7." Received by Carl Mullan, *Chunk 7*, 15 Mar. 2007. DJ redlines 7.pdf
[585] Docket No. CR 07-109. *UNITED STATES OF AMERICA vs. E-GOLD LTD, GOLD & SILVER RESERVE LTD,*

With defense counsel electing to perseverate primarily on the language of the various statutes, not only was the opportunity to introduce clarity lost. Additionally, the Judge appeared to hold the impression that the defense's reasoning for wanting an evidentiary hearing so severely was so that it could introduce evidence that neither company accepted cash. Ironically, as later became apparent in the Judge's (May 2008) denial of the Motion to Dismiss, her interpretation of the law did not even hinge on whether either company accepted cash but rather on the tortuous hypothetical emphasized by Middlebrook et al. in their 2014 analysis of the case.[586]

With the defense counsel focus on dissecting the relationship of the 18 USC 1960 statute to related statutes, neither counsel nor the defendants seem to recognize the significance of AUSA Laurel Rimon's additional argument: "They still violated 1960 by not having a license in the states where they operated…"[587]

The following day, June 22, 2007, after hearing oral arguments,[588] the Court denied both the motion and the hearing request.[589] Defense counsel immediately began to explore avenues for appealing the Judge's decision to deny the defendants an evidentiary hearing. The Defendants engaged the law firm Robbins, Russell, Englert, Orseck, Untereiner & Sauber LLP. A firm that specialized in appeals to the D.C. Federal Court of Appeals and the U.S. Supreme Court.

A few days later, on June 26, 2007, there was a telephone conference with all parties regarding whether the Government would consent to stay the criminal case pending an appeal of the June 22 ruling denying an evidentiary hearing.[590] AUSA Rimon stated that the Government would not agree to stay the case. The newly retained attorney, Lawrence (Larry) Robbins, then spoke up. [bolding added for emphasis]

"I'm frankly really surprised that the government takes that position because while

DOUGLAS L. JACKSON, BARRY K. DOWNEY, REID A. JACKSON. TRANSCRIPT OF EVIDENTIARY HEARING BEFORE THE HONORABLE ROSEMARY M. COLLYER UNITED STATES DISTRICT JUDGE, 21 June 2007.

[586] Jackson, Douglas. "Chunk 7." Received by Carl Mullan, *Chunk 7*, 15 Mar. 2007. DJ redlines 7.pdf

[587] Docket No. CR 07-109. *UNITED STATES OF AMERICA vs. E-GOLD LTD, GOLD & SILVER RESERVE LTD, DOUGLAS L. JACKSON, BARRY K. DOWNEY, REID A. JACKSON.* TRANSCRIPT OF EVIDENTIARY HEARING BEFORE THE HONORABLE ROSEMARY M. COLLYER UNITED STATES DISTRICT JUDGE, 21 June 2007.

[588] U.S. District Court for the District of Columbia. *U.S.A. v. e-gold, Ltd., Gold & Silver Reserve, Inc. Douglas L. Jackson, Barry K. Downey, and Reid A. Jackson, Defendants.* . TRANSCRIPT OF EVIDENTIARY HEARING BEFORE THE HONORABLE ROSEMARY M. COLLYER UNITED STATES DISTRICT JUDGE, 21 June 2007.

[589] Minute Entry Order at 1, United States v. e-gold Limited, Gold & Silver Reserve, Inc., Douglas L. Jackson, Barry K. Downey, and Reid A. Jackson, Crim. No. 07-109 (D.D.C. June 22, 2007).

[590] U.S. District Court for the District of Columbia. *U.S.A. v. e-gold, Ltd., Gold & Silver Reserve, Inc. Douglas L. Jackson, Barry K. Downey, and Reid A. Jackson, Defendants.* . TRANSCRIPT OF TELEPHONE CONFERENCE BEFORE THE HONORABLE ROSEMARY M. COLLYER UNITED STATES DISTRICT JUDGE, 26 June 2007.

they may prevail on the appeal and they may not, if they don't and the criminal case moves forward, I suspect that **Court of Appeals were they to agree with us on the merits will regard the error as structural error in nature not subject in other words to a harmless error inquiry.**

Which means that if the case on merits goes forward on judgment or for that matter any significant ruling is made, I think the Court of Appeals would likely reverse almost per se any such ruling on the ground that the Defendants should have been entitled to the seized assets to pay for the counsel of their choice.

If as a result of the denial of a Monsanto hearing and the concomitant finality of the seizure of assets, the Defendants are thereby deprived of counsel of their choice, which is almost surely what will happen in this case, I can't imagine the government would be happy about that. Because what they would discover is that any judgment they get on the merits or for that matter **even any significant ruling this court makes at a time when the defendants have been deprived of counsel of their choice is almost surely going to be set aside.**"[591]

If Robbins was correct, it is possible that a year later, when Judge Collyer ruled to deny the Defendant's Motion to Dismiss, that critical, case-ending ruling could have been appealed. But instead, the Defendants were strongly encouraged by their (by that time) court-appointed counsel to enter into plea negotiations.[592]

On June 29, 2007, the Defendants filed a five-page Notice of Interlocutory Appeal and Request for Expedited Consideration with the Court.[593] Also, on the 29th, the Government responded by submitting a Memorandum of Points and Authorities Regarding a Stay of This Criminal Case Pending an Appeal by Defendants.[594] The Government's lawyers outlined reasons why they believed a stay of the case pending an interlocutory appeal would not be appropriate. Prosecutors argued that the defendants were not able to satisfy the criteria

---

[591] Jackson, Douglas. "Chunk 7." Received by Carl Mullan, *Chunk 7*, 15 Mar. 2007. DJ redlines 7.pdf

[592] Ibid

[593] Case 1:07-cr-00109-RMC Document 48 Filed 06/29/2007 Page 1 of 5 6-29-Not-of-Interlocutory-Appeal.pdf (DEFENDANTS' NOTICE OF APPEAL AND REQUEST FOR EXPEDITED CONSIDERATION Account 544179 and in/underlying e-gold account 109243, CASE NUMBER: 07-167-M-01) Case 07-167-M-01, Defendants' notice of appeal and request for expedited consideration]   5pgs   filed 6/29/2007   Case 1:07-cr-00109-RMC Document 48 (-gov.uscourts.dcd.125293.48.0)

[594] U.S. District Court for the District of Columbia. *U.S.A. v. e-gold, Ltd., Gold & Silver Reserve, Inc. Douglas L. Jackson, Barry K. Downey, and Reid A. Jackson, Defendants.* GOVERNMENT'S MEMORANDUM OF POINTS AND AUTHORITIES REGARDING A STAY OF THIS CRIMINAL CASE PENDING AN APPEAL BY DEFENDANTS, 29 June 2007.

required to be entitled to a stay of the criminal case proceeding against them. The Government respectfully requested the Court deny defendants' motion to stay and reasoned that the Defendants' arguments on appeal were not likely to be successful, and there was a lack of a threat of irreparable harm. On July 9th, 2007, the Court received the Defendants' Memorandum of Points and Authorities in Support of a Stay of This Case Pending Defendants' Interlocutory Appeal.[595]

The Defendants were respectfully requesting that the Court enter an order staying this case pending the resolution of the Defendants' appeal of the Court's June 22, 2007 order denying the defendants' request for an evidentiary hearing. The Defendants' lawyers presented the following arguments. [Partial text from the filing]

> In this case, the denial of the defendants' motion to vacate the seizure warrant and modify the post indictment restraining order will be tantamount to the denial of the defendants' counsel of their choice.
>
> The Court's decision on whether or not to enter a stay of this case pending the resolution of the defendants' interlocutory appeal will have a profound effect upon the defendants' rights to the counsel of their choice.
>
> The defendants are already substantially indebted to counsel for work performed to date, and are unable to pay undersigned counsel to enter a permanent appearance in this case to defend them at trial, where fees and costs are expected to exceed $3.5 million. With such uncertainty about how they will defend themselves in this Court, the defendants cannot hope to move forward on an additional front while fees are still owed from the district court proceedings.
>
> The harm that the defendants will suffer is real, extreme and imminent. In support of their motion to vacate the seizure warrants and modify the restraining order and their subsequently filed reply, the defendants filed a total of ten affidavits which showed the prejudice that they face as a result of the seizure of the G&SR and e-gold Ltd. operating accounts. Although this Court never ruled on the issue of the prejudice faced by the defendants, those affidavits showed how and why   the defendants have been rendered incapable of paying for attorneys fees in this case. There are simply

---

[595] U.S. District Court for the District of Columbia. *U.S.A. v. e-gold, Ltd., Gold & Silver Reserve, Inc. Douglas L. Jackson, Barry K. Downey, and Reid A. Jackson, Defendants.* DEFENDANTS' MEMORANDUM OF POINTS AND AUTHORITIES IN SUPPORT OF A STAY OF THIS CASE PENDING DEFENDANTS' INTERLOCUTORY APPEAL, 9 July 2007.

insufficient assets with which to do so, much less to hire an outside vendor to assist the defendants in managing and reviewing the three terabytes of discovery recently provided to the defendants by the government. Now the defendants face the prospect of moving forward in two cases – one before this court and one before the D.C. Circuit – without the resources necessary to appropriately be heard in one. Accordingly, should this court refuse to stay this case for the pendency of the (expedited) appellate proceeding, there exists a strong likelihood that the defendants would receive insufficient representation in either case. Should that occur, the harm that would befall the defendants would be severe and irreparable, and the defendants therefore implore this Court to stay this case until their interlocutory appeal has been resolved.

The issuance of a stay of this case pending a resolution of defendants' expedited interlocutory appeal will preserve the defendants' constitutional rights.

Should a stay of this case not be granted, there exists a very serious threat of irreparable harm to the Defendants. The Defendants simply cannot afford to fight a single war on two fronts and continue their efforts to keep their businesses alive if this case is not stayed.

In actuality, should this Court deny the defendants' request for a stay, the defendants would be necessarily and irreparably injured by being forced into litigation on multiple fronts without the benefit of the vast majority of their assets.

Finally, despite the government's tortured understanding of the "public interest," the public interest actually supports a stay of this case so that the defendants can adequately defend themselves before both this Court and the Court of Appeals, while continuing to try to keep their businesses, their families and themselves alive.[596]

On July 20, 2007, the Judge denied the defense motion to stay the criminal case, noting among her reasons; "Defendants' likelihood of success on appeal [on the issue of whether they were entitled to an evidentiary hearing] is very narrow."[597]

---

[596] U.S. District Court for the District of Columbia. *U.S.A. v. e-gold, Ltd., Gold & Silver Reserve, Inc. Douglas L. Jackson, Barry K. Downey, and Reid A. Jackson, Defendants.* DEFENDANTS' MEMORANDUM OF POINTS AND AUTHORITIES IN SUPPORT OF A STAY OF THIS CASE PENDING DEFENDANTS' INTERLOCUTORY APPEAL, 9 July 2007.

[597] Case 1:07-cr-00109-RMC Document 52 . *UNITED STATES OF AMERICA vs. E-GOLD LTD, GOLD & SILVER RESERVE LTD, DOUGLAS L. JACKSON, BARRY K. DOWNEY, REID A. JACKSON.* MEMORANDUM OPINION,

♦

2007 G&SR Company Status

From a July 9th, 2007 filing, the partial text summary for e-gold® and G&SR copied from the Defendants' Memorandum of Points and Authorities in Support of a Stay of this Case Pending Defendants' Interlocutory Appeal is reproduced below.[598]

> As a direct result of the government's actions, G&SR lost its banking relationships and presently has no bank account suitable for supporting exchange operations. G&SR's OmniPay business has therefore not been operational since May 25, 2007. Multiple prominent independent exchange services have also had their assets seized with no timely possibility of defending themselves in open court.
>
> Likewise, subsequent to May 25 there has been no functional Primary Dealer for e-gold, i.e., an entity credentialed to and capable of undertaking the steps required to effect an increase or decrease in the total quantity of e-gold in circulation. At the same time, government attacks against e-gold in the media have created a panic environment that could be characterized as a "run" on e-gold. In normal circumstances, a run on e-gold would constitute a somewhat salutary occurrence because e-gold is designed to operate without disruption even if/as circulation winds down to zero, thereby demonstrating to the public the existence and importance of a 100% reserve. Under the present circumstances, i.e. a crippled and essentially nonfunctioning exchange market combined with an overtly stated U.S. Secret Service intent to "shut down" e-gold, there is widespread public perception that e-gold has failed and is no longer able to meet its primary obligation of redeeming e-gold gram for gram.[599]

On July 10, 2007, the Defendants' requested that the Court hold an oral hearing on the matter of the Defendants' entitlement to a stay of this case pending the Defendants' interlocutory appeal.[600]

Ten days later, on July 20th, 2007, without an oral hearing, the Court issued a Memorandum Opinion and Order denying the defendants' request for a stay. Below is a

20 July 2007.

[598] Ibid

[599] Ibid

[600] Ibid

partial text from that document stating, "no basis to grant a stay pending appeal."

> *U.S. v. e-gold Limited*
> United States District Court, D. Columbia Jul 20, 2007
> Criminal Action No. 07-109 (RMC). (D.D.C. Jul. 20, 2007)
> MEMORANDUM OPINION
> ROSEMARY COLLYER, District Judge
> The criminal Defendants in this case — two corporations and three individuals —
> have sought a stay of the prosecution while they appeal this Court's denial of their
> motion to release funds seized by the Government. See June 22, 2007, Minute Entry
> Order. The Court admittedly was so inclined at the end of the motions hearing on
> Defendants' Motion to Vacate Seizure Warrant and to Modify Restraining Order and
> Request for an Evidentiary Hearing, but after careful review of the parties' briefs, it
> concludes that there is no basis to grant a stay pending appeal.
>
> The Court's Memorandum Opinion, addressing the question of whether a Stay of this
> case's proceedings should be granted pending an appeal of its decision not to grant an
> Evidentiary Hearing on the merits of the hitherto unchallenged seizure of assets from
> the Defendants, accompanied by its Order denying the Defendants' Oral Motion for
> such a Stay, were both filed on 2007-07-20.
>
> The Court's Order also denied Defendants' Request for Oral Hearing on the Matter of
> the Entry of a Stay of this Case Pending their Interlocutory Appeal (2007-07-10) as
> moot.[601]

The eventual verdict of this paramount digital currency legal case was significant to the
government for several critical reasons.

- A failure to clarify the evolving "money transmitter" laws, or a not guilty verdict in
  this highly publicized criminal prosecution, could have disrupted the advancing
  regulated electronic money industry.
- Failure to interpret and precisely define money transmitting regulations would have
  skyrocketed   compliance costs for emerging online payment technologies.

---

[601] U.S. District Court for the District of Columbia. *U.S.A. v. e-gold, Ltd., Gold & Silver Reserve, Inc. Douglas L. Jackson, Barry K. Downey, and Reid A. Jackson, Defendants.* MEMORANDUM OPINION, 20 July 2007.

The majority of U.S. states, including Florida, and the District of Columbia required money transmitting businesses to obtain a license and comply with applicable regulations for such licensed entities. Additionally, the federal government requires new money transmitting businesses to register with the Financial Crimes Enforcement Network (FinCEN), a branch within the U.S. Department of the Treasury, within 180 days after the date the business was established.

According to the government, G&SR had failed to register with FinCEN and failed to obtain a money transmitter's license in the District of Columbia;[602] as is required by law.[603] Prosecutors also alleged that G&SR ignored federal requirements to implement an anti-money laundering program[604] and to file reports of suspicious transactions (so-called "Suspicious Activity Reports" or "SARs") with the U.S. Department of the Treasury.[605]

The Defendants expressly disagreed with the government's allegations and charges. Lawyers for the Defendants attacked SA Dotson's Affidavit by declaring that neither G&SR nor e-gold Ltd. was required to obtain a money transmitting license in any U.S. State. According to the Defendants, not only did existing money transmitter laws not apply to its businesses, but several government officials and law enforcement members agreed with the company's position. Text from Court documents explains the Defendants' view.

> In fact, the manner in which Defendants conduct their transactions renders them outside the ambit of the statutes and regulations applicable to "money transmitting businesses." Many in the United States government apparently concur. Yet, SA Dotson never addressed the findings, reports, statements and conclusions reached by other government officials on this issue.[606]

The Defendants claimed that Dotson's affidavit lacked the proper legal terminology. Text from Court documents, submitted by the Defendants, argued that Dotson had failed to discuss the collection of laws governing and defining the money transmitting business. Defendants' lawyers were forthright in establishing this position, as shown in the statements

---

[602] Id. at 22.

[603] Id. at 26 (citing D.C. CODE ANN. § 26-1001(10) (LexisNexis 2001)).

[604] Id. at 5 (citing 31 U.S.C. § 5318(h) (Supp. IV 2004) and its implementing regulations (31 C.ER. § 103.125 (2007)).

[605] Id. (citing 31 U.S.C. § 5318(g) (Supp. IV 2004) and its implementing regulations (31 C.ER. § 103.20 (2007)).

[606] Case 1:07-cr-00109-RMC Document 35 . *UNITED STATES OF AMERICA v. E-GOLD LIMITED, GOLD & SILVER RESERVE, INC., DOUGLAS L. JACKSON, BARRY K. DOWNEY and REID A. JACKSON Related Case: In the Matter of the Seizure of Any and All Property in/Underlying E-GOLD Account 544179 and in/Underlying E-GOLD Account 109243, Held by E-GOLD, Ltd. or Gold & Silver Reserve, Inc. on Behalf of E-GOLD, Ltd.* DEFENDANTS' MOTION TO VACATE SEIZURE WARRANT AND TO MODIFY RESTRAINING ORDER AND REQUEST FOR AN EVIDENTIARY HEARING, 1 June 2007.

copied here.

> 18 U.S.C. § 1960 does not define the term "money transmitting business." As such, SA Dotson's description of "money transmitting laws" is inexcusably incomplete[607] According to SA Dotson,
>> [t]he term "money transmitting" under Section 1960(b)(2) includes "transferring funds on behalf of the public by any and all means including but not limited to transfers within this country or to locations abroad by wire, check, draft, facsimile, or courier."[608]
> SA Dotson leads the reader to believe that so long as a person, business or other entity transmits money, that person, business or other entity automatically becomes a money transmitting business. Federal regulation 31 U.S.C. § 5330 is entitled "Registration of money transmitting businesses." The statute advises "money transmitting businesses" that if they are such a business then they must register with the Secretary of the Treasury, the state in which they operate, or both; see, § 5330(a)(1).[609]

The G&SR legal team argued that to fully articulate probable cause that the Defendants were operating an unlicensed money transmitting business, Dotson first needed to fully articulate that the Defendants were indeed running a money transmitting business. Accordingly, because Dotson failed in this task, his Affidavit was insufficient, and probable cause was never truly established. The Defendants argued these points in Court. The 2014 document: *Regulating Cryptocurrencies in the United States: Current Issues and Future Directions* by Stephen T. Middlebrook and Sarah Jane Hughes contains a significant discussion of e-gold entitled Precursors to Regulation--The Government's Prosecution of e-gold.

> Defendants argued that within federal law, the term "money transmitting business" is only defined at 31 U.S.C. § 5330, which provides that a business can be considered a "money transmitting business" only if it is required to file cash transaction reports under 31 U.S.C. § 5313." Section 5313, in turn, places a reporting requirement only

---

[607] See, Dotson Affidavit, at ¶¶ 22 – 23.

[608] See, Dotson Affidavit, at ¶ 23;

[609] Although SA Dotson never cited to this statute in his affidavit, he was clearly on notice that it existed. In his affidavit, at ¶ 11, he advised the Court that "the federal government requires money transmitting businesses to have registered with the Financial Crimes Enforcement Network (FinCEN), a bureau of the Department of the Treasury, by December 31, 2001 if they were in existence before that date, and, otherwise, within 180 days after the date the business was established."

upon domestic financial institutions involved in transactions of "United States coins or currency (or other monetary instruments the Secretary of the Treasury prescribes)." Accordingly, e-gold argued that because § 5330 applies only if § 5313 is triggered, and § 5313 requires the handling of cash or coin[610], § 5330 also must require the handling of cash or coin.

To be sure, the Government has long since acknowledged that the Defendants do not accept cash as part of their business. Consistent with that acknowledgement, SA Dotson wrote in his affidavit as follows:

> To obtain e-gold through OmniPay, a customer is required to wire national currency, in an amount greater than $1,000, to a bank account specified by the e-gold operation. Thereafter, the customer's e-gold account would be credited for the amount of the wire, minus an exchange fee collected by OmniPay.

Dotson Affidavit, at ¶ 29.[611] Therefore, even had SA Dotson attempted to take the Court through § 5330's three-prong definition of "money transmitting business," he could never have done so. Per SA Dotson's own writing, the Defendants are not required to file reports under 31 U.S.C. § 5313. Section 5313 is entitled "Reports on domestic coins and currency transactions." In its opening paragraph, that statute provides as follows:

> (a) When a domestic financial institution is involved in a transaction for the payment, receipt, or transfer of United States coins or currency (or other monetary instruments the Secretary of the Treasury prescribes), in an amount, denomination, or amount and denomination, or under circumstances the Secretary prescribes by regulation, the institution and any other participant in the transaction the Secretary may prescribe shall file a report on the transaction at the time and in the way the Secretary prescribes.

In other words, § 5313 provides that when a person is engaged in a transaction involving currency, a certain form must be filed. Pursuant to 31 U.S.C. § 5313, currency transaction reports need only be filed when a **transaction in currency** is performed. It naturally follows that entities that do not – as a matter of practice – engage in transactions in currency need not file reports under 31 U.S.C. § 5313;

---

[610] e-gold, Ltd., 550 F. Supp. 2d at 87-88.

[611] SA Dotson's use of the word "currency" in this paragraph, while colloquially acceptable, is legally inapt. 31 C.F.R. § 103.11(h) defines "currency" as "[t]he coin and paper money of the United States or of any other country that is designated as legal tender and that circulates and is customarily used and accepted as a medium of exchange in the country of issuance. Currency includes U.S. silver certificates, U.S. notes and Federal Reserve notes. Currency also includes official foreign bank notes that are customarily used and accepted as a medium of exchange in a foreign country." By its very definition, currency cannot be wired. This issue is crucial and must neither be confused nor overlooked.

Therefore, the Defendants in this case – who, as a matter of practice, do not engage in transactions in currency and are therefore not required to file reports under § 5313 – cannot be defined as a money transmitting business under 31 U.S.C. § 5313. Accordingly, so long as e-gold, Ltd. and G&SR do not deal in currency, they cannot be required to file currency transaction reports under § 5313. And, so long as neither company is required to file currency transaction reports under § 5313, they cannot be described as "money transmitting businesses" under § 5330, the sole federal statute which actually defines that term. SA Dotson and the prosecutors in this case, who travel under an overly-narrow reading of the law, stand alone in their contentions. The Defendants in this case do not operate a money transmitting business and do not purport to do so and the government cannot establish that it does.[612]

Neither G&SR nor e-gold had ever accepted cash (currency) from any customer. E-gold Ltd. had never even had a bank account. Defense counsel argued because neither G&SR nor e-gold Ltd. handled cash, the Court should dismiss the indictment. The Court took a different view.

Interlocutory Appeal

Defense lawyers filed an expedited request for Interlocutory Appeal to overturn Judge Collyer's denial of the Defendants' request for an evidentiary hearing on July 16, 2007. On July 27, the Appellate court granted the request. It established an expedited schedule requiring the Appellant brief to be filed August 20, the Government response on September 10, the Appellants reply on September 20. Oral argument was then scheduled for October 26, 2007, allotting 15 minutes each for the Appellant and Respondent counsels to argue their case.

◆

Resignation of Escrow Agent

On October 10, 2007, concerned by the adverse publicity surrounding the e-gold case, the Escrow Agent—attorney James Baker of the Baltimore law firm of Baker, Baxter, Sidle, Conn, and Jones, P.A. —resigned. Baker had performed this role since 2000. The Post-Indictment Restraining Order (PIRO) of April 2007 had already crippled e-gold exchange markets by requiring prosecutorial approval of any redemptions of e-gold that would result

---

[612] Hughes, Sarah Jane and Middlebrook, Stephen T., "Regulating Cryptocurrencies in the United States: Current Issues and Future Directions" (2014). Articles by Maurer Faculty. Paper 2096. http://www.repository.law.indiana.edu/facpub/2096

in the release of bullion bars from the reserve. Now, lacking an Escrow Agent, even if the prosecutor allowed release of some bullion, the required second signatory for such a release to be authorized was absent.

This emergency was resolved in mid-November when FarmWinds Advies & Beheer BV, a Netherlands-based Accounting firm, agreed to appointment as Escrow Agent. But with the PIRO still in place, what could have been a salutary "run" on e-gold, that is, a drastic decline in the amount of e-gold in circulation with no effect on its value relative to gold, could not occur. Some enterprising exchange services elected to offer bids to buy e-gold at deep discounts and managed to find some sellers.

The e-gold® prosecution was straight out of the DOJ's playbook. Through its prosecutorial powers, the government had succeeded in blocking the Defendants' income, seizing the Defendants' liquid assets, and vilifying the Defendants through the media. Without being convicted of any crime, the DOJ's combined assault had isolated e-gold® from any future business relationships. These tactics are a lethal   combination that pressures defendants to accept a plea agreement in more than 97% of all federal court cases.

Remarkably, in August, amidst all the controversy, Douglas Jackson created the e-gold® blog. This piece was the first post from August 2007.

August 1, 2007
Hi, I'm Douglas Jackson and this is the first entry of the e-gold blog. Welcome! My goal in this first note is not to introduce myself - I'll surely get to that by and by - but rather to scope out my/our blogatorial intentions.

I will write from a personal perspective but will mostly talk about e-gold. Given that e-gold.com has been online since November 1996, that means I have a lot of catching up to do. The story that I will relate will therefore not be told chronologically. What I have in mind instead is to explain e-gold, its doctrine and logic, my vision of how the emergence of e-gold can advance the material welfare of mankind. Sometimes, for instance when describing the rationale that informed various decisions or policies, this will entail recreating a historic context. At other times, for example when I compare e-gold to legacy monetary institutions such as government central banks or the various historic flavors of gold standards, this will require some teaching. It probably also goes without saying but I will make no pretense of objectivity. I believe e-gold can serve as a fulcrum for a better future. I can do no other than to speak as advocate - apologist and polemicist - for e-gold.

We [Reid, Barry and I] debated whether to start a personal (Douglas Jackson) vs. an outright corporate (e-gold Ltd.) blog. The fact that the URL you entered to reach this page contains "e-gold" indicates which arguments prevailed. My sense and expectation though is that the personal vs. corporate thing will not greatly influence the voice with which I post. I am the Chairman of e-gold Ltd. and it is appropriate to call me the "Founder" of e-gold. I could offer a disclaimer protesting that I am offering opinions that are mine alone and do not reflect the official position of e-gold but I can't think of an edifying instance wherein the two viewpoints diverge. Nonetheless, I don't want to hog the mike either since the health and future of e-gold depend on the expertise and best efforts of many people.

A final (for now) comment... Anyone remotely familiar with e-gold knows that it is currently, August 2007, under legal (and reputation) attack by the United States Secret Service.   I intend though to stick to the affirmative message of e-gold in this blog - to undertake to do a better job telling the e-gold story and to become more visible as the human being primarily responsible for e-gold. The legal wrangle will be the subject matter for a separate legal blog.[613]

Shortly after that, on July 31, the defendants respectfully requested that this Court reconsider its July 20, 2007 order denying the defendants' request for a stay of this case pending their interlocutory appeal.

In support of this motion, the defendants state as follows: (this is the partial text from Document 54)

I. The Court's Decision was Based Upon Findings of Fact Based Exclusively Upon Controverted Affidavits and Without the Benefit of an Evidentiary Hearing.

On June 21, 2007, this Court held an oral argument on the issue of whether the Defendants were entitled to an evidentiary hearing on the Defendants' motion to vacate the seizure warrant and to modify the restraining order entered in this case. At that hearing, this Court ruled that the Defendants were not entitled to such a hearing and concluded that they "were totally unable to make any showing of any kind that the Omnipay[614] operating accounts did not contain monies entirely resulting from the exchange business which the Government asserts is an unregistered and unlicensed money exchange business." Memorandum Opinion, at 4-5.

---

[613] Jackson, Douglas. "e-gold Blog." *e-gold Blog*, e-gold.com, 1 Aug. 2007, web.archive.org/web/20071012223611/blog.e-gold.com/2007/08/welcome-to-the-.html.

[614] The Defendants respectfully note that the accounts seized were not "Omnipay operating accounts." Of the two seized accounts, one is owned by e-gold Ltd. and the other is owned by Gold & Silver Reserve, Inc. OmniPay is simply the name of the e-gold exchange service offered by Gold & Silver Reserve, Inc. This confusion is also present in the seizure warrant affidavit, where Special Agent Dotson swears, at p.2, that both of the seized e-gold accounts were owned by e-gold Ltd.

Several factors present during the June 21, 2007 oral arguments contributed to the Defendants' inability to make such a tracing showing. First, in its seizure warrant affidavit, the government attacked all of the Defendants' activities as proscribed under 18 U.S.C. § 1960. During oral arguments, the Court accepted the government's allegations as true and refused to receive evidence concerning any of the following issues:

> a) that e-gold Ltd. and Gold & Silver Reserve, Inc. are distinct businesses;
>
> b) that e-gold Ltd. does not offer an exchange service;
>
> c) that none of e-gold Ltd.'s seized e-gold (from e-gold account no. 544179) was traceable to an exchange service; and
>
> d) whether the e-gold seized from the Gold & Silver Reserve, Inc. e-gold account (account no. 109243) was traceable to exchange activities.

Thus, once the Court accepted the government's allegations as true and refused to permit the Defendants to explain why the government's presentation was inaccurate, the Defendants were left with no meaningful way to make such a showing.[615]

II. The Court's Decision was Based Upon Erroneous Calculations of the Defendants' Available Assets.

In its Memorandum Opinion filed on July 20, 2007, at p.9, this Court found, based upon the aggregation of four (4) categories of "funds" listed by the government in its memorandum in opposition to the defendants' request for a stay, that the Defendants had $3,856,669 with which to pay for attorneys fees. However, because none of the four (4) listed categories accurately reflects the Defendants' (or any individual Defendant's) available assets, the cumulative value is also inaccurate. The $3.86 million figure is the result of double counting and a grossly incomplete presentation of facts filed by the government.

To prevail on the motion for reconsideration, the Court stated that the Defendants "must demonstrate that there has been 'an intervening change in controlling law,' there is 'new evidence,' or there is a 'need to correct clear error or prevent manifest injustice.'"[616] On August 10, 2007, Government lawyers responded to the Defendants' request.

GOVERNMENT'S RESPONSE TO DEFENDANTS' REQUEST FOR

---

[615] The only showing that the Court would have permitted the Defendants to make was described as follows: "[U]nless you can make a showing, some kind of a proffer that some of these monies did not derive from either of those operations, then I don't think we have any place to go." June 21, 2007 Hearing Transcript, at 65:8 – 65:11.

[616] Case 1:07-cr-00109-RMC Document 59 . *UNITED STATES OF AMERICA v. E-GOLD LIMITED, Et Al.* ORDER, 13 Aug. 2007.

RECONSIDERATION OF JULY 20, 2007 MEMORANDUM OPINION AND ORDER DENYING DEFENDANTS' REQUEST FOR STAY

…

For the foregoing reasons, including defendants' failure to present any argument regarding a change in the law, new evidence, or clear error, the Government respectfully requests that the Court deny Defendants' Request for Reconsideration of This Court's July 20, 2007, Memorandum Opinion and Order.

ARGUMENT

A. The Defendants Have Not Demonstrated Proper Grounds For Reconsideration Of The Order Denying A Stay

1.   There Has Been No Intervening Change In Law
2.   Defendants Have Not Presented Any New Evidence
    a. There Is No Controverted Evidence
    b. The Court Did Not Miscalculate
3.   Defendants Have Not Established Any Clear Error Of Law Or Manifest Injustice
4.   (B.) The Court Properly Denied A Stay[617]

Judge Collyer denied the request on August 13th, 2007 stating:

> In any event, Defendants have failed to muster any basis, on any standard, for the Court to reconsider its prior ruling. This request, the request for a stay in the proceedings, and the motion to vacate the seizure warrant all rest on Defendants' disagreement with the underlying indictment. The Court has expressed its willingness to accept a motion to dismiss and has noted that Defendants can present their case to a jury. The request for reconsideration is DENIED.[618]

On August 15, 2007, Department of Justice Trial Attorney Michelle Kane filed a notice of appearance as the co-counsel who would be arguing on behalf of the United States in the impending appeal.[619]

Kavanaugh

---

[617] Ibid

[618] Ibid

[619] U.S. District Court for the District of Columbia. *UNITED STATES OF AMERICA : CRIMINAL NO. 07-109 (RMC) v. E-GOLD, LTD., Et Al, Defendants.* NOTICE OF APPEARANCE AS CO-COUNSEL, 15 Aug. 2007.

The Court scheduled oral argument on the Defendants' appeal for an evidentiary hearing on October 26, 2007. One of the Judges that heard the case is now on The Supreme Court of the United States.

> It is ORDERED, by the Court on its own motion, that the above entitled case be scheduled for oral argument on Friday, October 26, 2007 at 9:30 AM before Circuit Judges Sentelle and Kavanaugh and Senior Judge Williams.[620]

Oral argument occurred as scheduled on October 26, 2007. Fifteen minutes were provided for counsel for the opposing sides to make their opening arguments, followed by direct questioning from the Appeals Court judges. No transcript is known to exist. The Appellate Court handed down its decision in April 2008.

◆

In September 2007, industry blogs confirmed that Google had banned all e-gold® advertising. E-gold vendors questioned the ban, because other popular digital currency, including trademarked names, were still permitted to advertise. A blog post from September 2007 discussed Google's ban.

> Google is stating that the word 'egold' is a trademark and banning it from their ads. One popular exchange provider which had ads canceled posted this email.

> > *Thank you for advertising with Google AdWords. After reviewing your account, we've found that one or more of your ads or keywords does not meet our guidelines. You can see your disapproved ad(s), the reason for disapproval, and editorial suggestions, from the Disapproved Ads page within your account.*
> > *Ad Status: Suspended Pending Revision*
> > *Ad Issue(s): Trademark in Ad Content*
> > *SUGGESTIONS:*
> > *Ad Content: Please remove the following trademark from your ad: egold.*

> It's also an odd thing that all of these other digital currencies GoldMoney, Pecunix, ebullion, Webmoney, Liberty Reserve are also trademarked names…but they were

---

[620] No. 07-3074. *United States of America, Appelle v. e-gold, Ltd., Et Al., Appellants.* Order, 5 Sept. 2006.

not banned.[621]

Meanwhile, in September, e-gold® published its bullion statistics proving beyond a doubt that the company's e-metal had always been 100% backed by weight in precious metals.

> September 17, 2007
> e-gold® Releases Audit Report on Gold Holdings
> FOR IMMEDIATE RELEASE
> September 11, 2007
> [Melbourne, FL] -- e-gold Ltd today released an audit report corroborating the Gold, Silver, Palladium, and Platinum held by the e-gold Bullion Reserve Special Purpose Trust stored in London and Dubai. All e-metals are 100% backed by the physical metal held by the Trust. The audit was conducted by Stout, Causey & Horning, P.A. who noted in their Independent Auditor's Report, that the Summaries of stored metal as of April 30, 2007 fairly represented the physical amount of metals by repository. The audit report can be viewed from the Examiner page on the e-gold® website.[622]

Unfortunately, after the Indictment in this case was unsealed, in April 2007, customer activity within the e-gold system plummeted. As a result, both G&SR's and e-gold Ltd.'s revenues radically declined. The loss of income and soaring legal expenses threatened to exhaust the working capital of both companies. The dwindling revenue on top of the asset seizures left the defendants unable to afford counsel of their choice. Therefore, the Court assigned the Defendants new counsel. The first appointment was September 26, 2007, with Assistant Federal Public Defender Michelle Petersen designated to represent Reid Jackson.[623] About a week later, the Court designated Barry Pollack of Kelley Drye & Warren LLP to represent Barry Downey.[624] The Court appointed Joshua Berman of Sonnenschein Nath & Rosenthal LLP to Douglas Jackson.[625] Petersen, Pollack and Berman are all highly accomplished attorneys. Machalagh Carr was Berman's associate at Sonnenschein.

---

[621] Herpel, Mark. "Digital Money World." *Digital Money Worlds RSS*, B5media, 5 Sept. 2007, web.archive.org/web/20071228182038/www.digitalmoneyworld.com/google-drops-all-e-gold-ads-adwords/.

[622] Jackson, Douglas. "e-Gold Blog." *e-Gold Blog*, Internet Archive, 17 Sept. 2007, web.archive.org/web/20071012223134/blog.e-gold.com/2007/09/e-gold-releases.html.

[623] A.J. Kramer & Michelle Peterson, Office of the Federal Public Defender, 625 Indiana Avenue N.W. Suite 550 Washington, D.C. 20004, Attorneys for Reid A. Jackson

[624] Barry J. Pollack, Kelley Drye & Warren LLP, 3050 K Street, N.W., Suite 400, Washington, D.C. 20007, Attorneys for Defendant Barry K. Downey

[625] Joshua G. Berman & Machalagh Proffit-Higgins, Sonnenschein Nath & Rosenthal LLP, 1301 K Street, N.W., Suite 600, East Tower, Washington, DC 20005-3364, Attorneys for Defendant Douglas L. Jackson

Trial Date

An October 2007 Court docket entry showed that the Court had scheduled the e-gold Defendants' trial to begin on October 27th, 2008. Other Court documents from March 7th, 2008, renewed the government's focus.

> At trial in this case, the government intends to prove that, from about 1999 through December, 2005, the defendants, through e-gold and GSR, publicly offered and operated an Internet-based e-gold digital currency system as a payment mechanism that facilitated several different types of criminal activity, including investment fraud, credit card and identity fraud, and child pornography. In doing so, the e-gold system became the most popular and prominent digital currency for transmitting funds using Internet-based accounts.
>
> Additionally, in operating the e-gold system without complying with either state licensing or federal registration requirements, and by transferring funds defendants knew and believed to be involved in criminal activity, defendants avoided compliance and reporting requirements applicable under federal laws to money transmitting businesses, and aided criminals in avoiding detection of their activities by law enforcement. By widely offering their services to individuals whom the defendants knew to be engaged in criminal activity and using e-gold to transfer illicit funds, and by choosing not to comply with state and federal requirements for money transmitting businesses that would have brought the criminal activity to light, defendants drastically increased the volume of transactions in their system and made the e-gold system dominant among internet based digital currencies.[626]

The U.S. Court of Appeals for the D.C. Circuit held oral arguments before the three Judges Sentelle, Kavanaugh, and Williams on October 26, 2007.[627] That eventual ruling by the Appeals Court was in the Defendants' favor.

However, by November 6, 2007, the government was turning up the heat on the Defendants. Court documents reveal that just ten days later, on November 15, 2007, Prosecutors convened a brand new Federal Grand Jury in the District of Columbia.[628] The

---

[626] Case 1:07-cr-00109-RMC Document 99. *UNITED STATES OF AMERICA vs. E-GOLD LTD, GOLD & SILVER RESERVE LTD, DOUGLAS L. JACKSON, BARRY K. DOWNEY, REID A. JACKSON.* GOVERNMENT'S RESPONSE TO DEFENDANTS' MOTION TO DISMISS COUNTS TWO, THREE AND FOUR OF THE INDICTMENT, 7 Mar. 2008.

[627] Entry in Docket 07-3074, D.C. Circuit Court of Appeals, 2007-10-26.

[628] Case 1:07-cr-00109-RMC Document 104. *UNITED STATES OF AMERICA v. E-GOLD, LTD. GOLD & SILVER RESERVE, INC. DOUGLAS L. JACKSON, BARRY K. DOWNEY, and REID A. JACKSON.* SUPERSEDING

Government had requested updated SQL Database copies, an additional new trial Attorney, Assistant United States Attorney Jonathan W. Haray[629], filed his appearance with the Court, and a government moved to amend the PIRO.[630]

Changes to the Post-Indictment Restraining Order are illustrated by text from that document.[631]

GOVERNMENT'S MOTION TO AMEND POST-INDICTMENT RESTRAINING ORDER

COMES NOW the United States, by and through the United States Attorney for this District and by the United States Department of Justice, and hereby respectfully moves this Court to amend the Post-Indictment Restraining Order to require the defendants to provide to the United States (i) within five (5) days of this order an electronic copy of the SQL server databases and/or files reflecting transactions conducted, and account owner or operator information, for all e-gold, LTD. and GOLD & SILVER RESERVE, INC. transactions from May 1, 2007 through the date of this order, and (ii) every thirty (30) days thereafter until the start of trial in this criminal proceeding an updated electronic copy of such databases and/or files. As grounds therefor, the Government states as follows:

1. That on April 24, 2007, E-GOLD, LTD., GOLD & SILVER RESERVE, INC., DOUGLAS L. JACKSON, BARRY K. DOWNEY, and REID A. JACKSON were indicted by a federal grand jury for this district on charges of money laundering conspiracy and operation of an unlicensed money transmitting business in violation of 18 U.S.C. §§ 1956 and 1960.

> 2. That, previously on April 26, 2007, based upon an Affidavit submitted by the United States detailing ongoing and widespread use of the e-gold system by those engaged in criminal activity, this Court has ordered the corporate defendants to produce to the Government copies of their transactional

---

INDICTMENT, 3 Apr. 2008.

[629] Case 1:07-cr-00109-RMC Document 76 . UNITED STATES OF AMERICA v. E-GOLD, LTD. GOLD & SILVER RESERVE, INC. DOUGLAS L. JACKSON, BARRY K. DOWNEY, and   REID A. JACKSON. NOTICE OF ASSIGNMENT AND APPEARANCE AS CO-COUNSEL, 30 Nov. 2007.

[630] Case 1:07-cr-00109-RMC Document 79 . *UNITED STATES OF AMERICA v. E-GOLD, LTD. GOLD & SILVER RESERVE, INC. DOUGLAS L. JACKSON, BARRY K. DOWNEY, and REID A. JACKSON.* GOVERNMENT'S MOTION TO AMEND POST-INDICTMENT RESTRAINING ORDER, 30 Nov. 2007.

[631] U.S. District Court for the District of Columbia. *UNITED STATES OF AMERICA Criminal No. 07-109 (RMC) v. E-GOLD, LTD. GOLD & SILVER RESERVE, INC. DOUGLAS L. JACKSON, BARRY K. DOWNEY, and REID A. JACKSON, Defendants.* GOVERNMENT'S MOTION TO AMEND POST-INDICTMENT RESTRAINING ORDER, 3 Nov. 2007.

databases.

3. That the defendants have never filed a single Suspicious Activity Report (SAR), a form that licensed and registered money services business, banks, commodities dealers, and other financial institutions are obligated to file with the Department of Treasury to notify law enforcement of transactions they know or suspect are suspicious. In fact, defendants have taken the position that they are not required to make such reports at all.

4. That the Affidavit of United States Secret Service Special Agent Roy Dotson, attached as Exhibit 1, identifies several e-gold® accounts currently or recently involved in child pornography, credit card or identity fraud, and investment fraud, demonstrating that significant criminal activity continues to be facilitated by the e-gold system.

5. That the Jury Trial in this criminal proceeding has been set for October 27, 2008, which will allow the criminal activity within the e-gold system to continue unabated without the Government's ability to detect and investigate such activity in any meaningful way for one year.

Wherefore, for the foregoing reasons, the Government requests this Court to amend said Post-Indictment Restraining Order to require defendants e-gold, LTD., GOLD & SILVER RESERVE, INC., DOUGLAS L. JACKSON, BARRY K. DOWNEY, and REID A. JACKSON to provide to the United States (i) within five (5) days of this order an electronic copy of the SQL server databases and/or files reflecting transactions conducted, and account owner or operator information, for all e-gold, LTD. and GOLD & SILVER RESERVE, INC. transactions from May 1, 2007 through the date of this order, and (ii) every thirty (30) days thereafter for the duration of the criminal proceeding an updated electronic copy of such databases and/or files.

JONATHAN HARAY
Assistant United States Attorney
U.S. Attorney's Office, Criminal Division

e-gold Ltd. filed an answer to the Government's Verified Complaint for Forfeiture in Rem (2007-07-24) on November 30th, 2007.[632] At the insistence of the Defendants, defense counsel was finally seeking to object to the prosecution's device of depicting both

[632] Case 1:05-cv-02497-RMC Document 14. *UNITED STATES OF AMERICA v. ALL FUNDS SEIZED FROM OR ON DEPOSIT IN SUNTRUST ACCOUNT NUMBER 1000028078359, IN THE NAME OF GOLD AND SILVER RESERVE, INC. AND ALL FUNDS ON DEPOSIT IN REGIONS BANK ACCOUNT NUMBER 67-0919-4851, IN THE NAME OF GOLD AND SILVER RESERVE, INC.*. CLAIMANT GOLD & SILVER RESERVE, INC.'s ANSWER TO THE PLAINTIFF'S VERIFIED COMPLAINT FOR FORFEITURE, 12 Jan. 2006.

companies as a combined fictitious "e-gold operation."

CLAIMANT E-GOLD LTD.'s ANSWER TO THE PLAINTIFF'S VERIFIED COMPLAINT FOR FORFEITURE

COMES NOW, Claimant E-GOLD LTD., by and through its undersigned counsel, and files this Answer to the Plaintiff's Verified Complaint for Forfeiture *In Rem*. In support of this Answer, Claimant e-gold Ltd. states as follows:

GENERAL OBJECTION AND DENIAL

Throughout the Complaint the Government uses the terms "e-gold operation" and "e-gold system." These terms are vague, ambiguous and undefined. e-gold Ltd. is a Nevis corporation and is the Claimant/Respondent filing this Answer. Gold & Silver Reserve, Inc. ("G&SR") is a Delaware corporation. G&SR is one of a number of entities that offers e-gold exchange services. Only e-gold Ltd. is filing this Answer. Accordingly, all of the responses to this Answer are those of e-gold Ltd., not those of G&SR or any other entity. e-gold Ltd. denies the existence of any entity known as the "e-gold operation" or "e-gold system" and each of the responses below should be read to incorporate this denial.[633]

Amid this dramatic Court battle, e-gold released some supporting facts about the Company's participation with the law enforcement community. Here is that post from the e-gold blog.

December 12, 2007

e-gold® Assists Law Enforcement, Bringing Hundreds of Criminals to Justice
[Melbourne, FL] -- Since its inception in 1996, e-gold® has settled over 85 million payments and extended its customer base to more than 165 countries. It currently receives nearly one million visits to its website weekly and settles over $1 billion worth of payments annually. It provides a valuable service for many individuals and companies doing business online. e-gold® usage offers significant advantages over credit cards. Besides the obvious advantages to merchants (reduced cost and instantaneous settlement with no risk of chargeback), e-gold® is not as subject to the risk of exposing personal information over the Internet (an identity theft risk), while still maintaining full identifying information as part of the record for every

---

[633] U.S. District Court for the District of Columbia. *UNITED STATES OF AMERICA, V. ALL PROPERTY IN/UNDERLYING E-GOLD   ACCOUNT NUMBERS: 544179 and 109243 Defendant.* ANSWER OF CLAIMANT GOLD & SILVER RESERVE, INC. TO PLAINTIFF'S VERIFIED COMPLAINT FOR FORFEITURE IN REM, 30 Nov. 2007.

transaction.

e-gold® is always vigilant to assist federal law enforcement in bringing criminals to justice. Regrettably, e-gold's work with the FBI, FTC, IRS, DEA, SEC, USPS, and other government agencies has gone widely unnoticed. The e-gold® staff has participated in hundreds of investigations in support of law enforcement. In addition, e-gold® maintains an active investigations staff using numerous automated system protocols to work proactively to identify and stop unwanted activity. e-gold's investigative capability has not only made it one of the poorest choices for illicit activity, but has directly provided extraordinary data that has lead to the identification, apprehension, and conviction of cyber criminals.[634]

2008

As the legal case began to overwhelm the Defendants in Court, the e-gold® platform and business had continued updating its procedures with the future goal of operating as a fully regulated U.S. financial business.

The Appearance of Bernie Grimm

The Court appointed counsel for Dr. Jackson and the other individual defendants. However, companies are not entitled to court-appointed representation, and both G&SR and e-gold Ltd. lacked funds to retain such counsel. Aron Raskas, who had previously represented G&SR in other matters, agreed to represent the company at a discounted rate. An additional attorney was needed to represent e-gold Ltd.

On January 25, 2008, Barry Pollack circulated a proposal to retain Bernie Grimm, a renowned criminal defense attorney. Pollack's email read:

> "I just got off the phone with Bernie Grimm. As I think you all know, Bernie is a very talented criminal defense lawyer (who Collyer knows and respects). Bernie is interested in representing e-gold in the criminal case. However, he does not think he can do it for $100k. He suggested that he appear at the status conference on Monday and tell Collyer he is interested, but that e-gold does not have unfrozen funds sufficient to retain him. He will suggest to Collyer to suggest to the Government that the Government allow currently frozen funds to be used to pay his fees. He thinks that Collyer may well pressure the Government to agree to do so. Bernie can come for part of our meeting before the status conference to meet everyone. What do people think of this idea?"[635]

---

[634] Jackson, Douglas. "e-gold Blog." *'e-gold Blog'*, e-gold.com, 12 Dec. 2007, blog.e-gold.com/2007/12/e-gold-assists.html.

On March 5, the defense and the government petitioned the court to release $275,000 of the funds that had been seized from G&SR to pay Grimm's retainer. Redemption of the e-silver seized in G&SR's e-metal account would generate the amount. The funds were released, and Grimm filed an Order of Appearance on April 11, 2008.[636]

♦

February 2008 - Motion to Dismiss

The Defendants took one of their last significant legal actions on February 11, 2008, when Defense Counsel filed a Motion to Dismiss the three licensing charges.

- Conspiracy (to operate an unlicensed money transmitting business) per 18 USC 371 (Count Two),
- Operation of an unlicensed money transmitting business per 18 USC 1960 (Count Three), and,
- Money Transmission without a License per DC Code 26-1002 (Count Four).

The Defendants did not move to dismiss Count One, which charged a money laundering conspiracy. There was no need to seek dismissal of Count One—the money laundering charge (19 USC 1956)—because all parties recognized the only possible way for that charge to succeed was if the companies were found guilty of the licensing charge. If found guilty of the licensing charge, that would mean the companies were financial institutions and therefore required to file Suspicious Activity Reports (SARs) where failure to file SARs is listed in the 1956 statute as an act of money laundering.

Any Motion to Dismiss filed with the Court had to conform to a highly stylized logic. These details were copied from the "Trial Manual 6 for the Defense of Criminal Cases" promulgated by the American Law Institute.

> "20.4.1 Failure to Charge Acts That Are Criminal in Nature
> The allegations may state fully and clearly what specific acts the defendant is charged with doing, but these acts may be no crime... A motion to dismiss or demurrer here tests the prosecution's legal theory... Ordinarily, the sole focus of this species of motion to dismiss is the text of the charging paper: Do the actions and circumstances which the charging paper sets forth constitute a crime or do they not?"[637]

---

[635] Jackson, Douglas. "Chunk 8." Received by Carl Mullan, *Chunk 8*, 27 Mar. 2020.
[636] Ibid

In other words, a Motion to Dismiss is constrained by the requirement to only work with "assumed facts," as alleged in the indictment and statement of offense. The major problem with that restriction in the e-gold case—as later (2017) claimed by Jackson in his letter to DHS, was the prosecutor's purposeful obfuscation of the distinction between e-gold Ltd. and G&SR (dba OmniPay), characterizing them as a blended "e-gold operation."

> "I will argue that Ms. Peretti went beyond non-disclosure of material information and in fact, informed by that very material [information revealed by the Florida Office of Financial Regulation in 2017], purposely set out to craft an erroneous and misleading mischaracterization of the business model, institutional arrangements and transaction logic of the defendant businesses in the criminal complaint as to trick the court into working with assumed facts that she knew to be spurious."[638]

But having missed the opportunity to put Jackson on the stand during the June 21, 2007 hearing to testify as to the institutional arrangements, all defense counsel had to work with for drafting the Motion to Dismiss was the charging papers and the law.

The legal argument

The principal argument for the February 11, 2008, defense Motion to Dismiss the three licensing charges, proposed that while 18 USC 1960 makes the operation of unlicensed money transmitting business a federal crime, it does not define a "money transmitting business."[639] 18 USC 1960 points to and relies on the definition found in 31 USC 5330, which is the only definition of "money transmitting business" in the United States Code.

Section 5330(d)(1)(B)[640] provides, in part, that a business can constitute a money transmitting business only when it is required to file reports under 31 USC 5313. Section 5313, in turn, makes clear that such reports must be filed only by domestic financial institutions involved in transactions "for the payment, receipt, or transfer of United States coins and currency (or other monetary instruments the Secretary of Treasury prescribes."

The "currency transaction reports," referred to in Section 5330(d)(1)(B) (Department of the Treasury FinCEN Form 104), contain the following definitions.

---

[637] Anthony G. Amsterdam & Randy Hertz, Trial Manual 6 for the Defense of Criminal Cases § 15.4 (6th ed. 2016).

[638] Jackson, Douglas. "Investigation Request." Received by John Roth, Inspector General, US Dept. of Homeland Security, 1020 Steven Patrick Avenue, 24 Aug. 2017, Indian Harbour Beach, Florida.

[639] "18 U.S. Code § 1960 - Prohibition of Unlicensed Money Transmitting Businesses." Legal Information Institute, Legal Information Institute, 1992, www.law.cornell.edu/uscode/text/18/1960.

[640] "31 U.S. Code § 5330 - Registration of Money Transmitting Businesses." Legal Information Institute, Legal Information Institute, 1994, www.law.cornell.edu/uscode/text/31/5330.

Currency. The coin and paper money of the United States or of any other country which is circulated and customarily used and accepted as money.

Transaction in Currency. The physical transfer of currency from one person to another. This does not include a transfer of funds by means of a bank check, bank draft, wire transfer or other written order that does not involve the physical transfer of currency.

Having noted the direct language of the relevant United States Code provisions, defense counsel then reminded the court, "Because the Indictment Does Not Allege That the Defendants Engaged in Cash Transactions, It Fails to Establish That They Operated a "Money Transmitting Business."

Unexpectedly, in April 2008, yet one more opportunity would indeed arise for defense counsel to exploit a chance to explain the actual organization and operations of the companies to the court. And, once again, counsel was unprepared to seize the opportunity.[641]

Fair Warning of the Conduct it Proscribes

A second argument of the Motion to Dismiss addressed the "vagueness" and "ambiguity" of 18 USC 1960, the statute on which all charges ultimately rested. The Legal Research Tools from Casetext explained:

> "A criminal statute that fails to provide fair warning of the conduct it proscribes violates the Due Process Clause of the United States Constitution.[642] [citing two precedent cases]...This "fair warning requirement" manifests itself in three ways:

> First, the vagueness doctrine bars enforcement of "a statue that either forbids or requires the doing of an act in terms so vague that men of common intelligence must necessarily guess at its meaning and differ as to its application"...Second, as a sort of "junior version of the vagueness doctrine"...the rule of lenity ensures fair warning by so resolving ambiguity in a criminal statute as to apply it only to conduct clearly covered...Third,...due process bars courts from applying a novel construction of a criminal statute to conduct that neither the statute nor any prior judicial decision has fairly disclosed to be within its scope.[643]

---

[641] Jackson, Douglas. "Chunk 8." Received by Carl Mullan, *Chunk 8*, 27 Mar. 2020.

[642] U.S. v. E-Gold, Ltd., 550 F. Supp. 2d 82 (D.D.C. 2008)

[643] Collyer, Rosemary M. "U.S. v. E-Gold, Ltd." *Legal Research Tools from Casetext*, 8 May 2008, casetext.com/case/us-v-e-gold.

While unknown to the defense or the court, this argument and its detailed explication in the Motion to Dismiss, eerily mirrored the 2007 Middlebrook analysis of the e-gold case which highlighted the "ambiguities in the law pertaining to 'money transmission' busineses."[644]

Analysis of Stephen T. Middlebrook, US Dept. of the Treasury

Unknown to Defendants or the Court at the time, in November 2007, Stephen T. Middlebrook published an analysis of the e-gold® case. His work specifically examined 18 USC 1960, which was the statute at the core of the government's case. Stephen T. Middlebrook was at the time Senior Counsel at the U.S. Department of the Treasury, Financial Management Service.[645] Jackson later shared his thoughts on the analysis.

> The take home message of Middlebrook's analysis was that the "'money transmitter' laws" contained "inconsistencies" and "ambiguities" rendering it impossible for any attorney to advise a client whether their business activities fell within the scope of the statute.[646]

> In the defendants' Motion to Dismiss Counts 2, 3 and 4, a key argument was that 18 USC 1960 fails to provide fair warning of the conduct it proscribes. Defense counsel made reference to the vagueness doctrine and rule of lenity. Had we known that the leading government expert in this field agreed we would have had a much persuasive argument. The case was lost when this motion was denied. Middlebrook specifically stated, "Based on the indictment, it appears that the government's theory of this case is that e-gold constitutes a money transmitter under 18 U.S.C. § 1960, and that fact triggers compliance obligations with money transmitter requirements found in 31 U.S.C. §§ 5330, 5318(g) and (h), and 31 C.F.R. part 103.

---

[644] Middlebrook, Stephen T., et al. Developments in the Law Concerning Stored-Value Cards and Other Electronic Payments Products. Indiana University Maurer School of Law, 2007, Developments in the Law Concerning Stored-Value Cards and Other Electronic Payments Products. http://www.repository.law.indiana.edu/facpub/174

[645] Stephen T. Middlebrook was Senior Counsel, U.S. Department of the Treasury; he is co-chair of the Working Group on Electronic Payments Systems, ABA Cyberspace Law Committee (2006–present). He is responsible for Part III.A.1 titled "The Prosecution of e-gold Ltd. and the Definition of Money Transmitter" and for Part III.B. Mr. Middlebrook's research is current through July 9, 2007. The views in this Article are those of Mr. Middlebrook alone and do not necessarily reflect the views of the U.S. Department of the Treasury. In 2019 Stephen T. Middlebrook is an attorney at Womble Bond Dickinson in Atlanta, Georgia. He has over more than 20 years of experience with complex regulatory and compliance matters.   womblebonddickinson.com/us/people/stephen-t-middlebrook

[646] Middlebrook, Stephen T., et al. *Developments in the Law Concerning Stored-Value Cards and Other Electronic Payments Products*. Indiana University Maurer School of Law, 2007, *Developments in the Law Concerning Stored-Value Cards and Other Electronic Payments Products*.

e-gold's position is that it is not a money transmitter under any definition and thus is not subject to any of these requirements. Resolution of the debate is hampered by the fact that §§ 1960, 5318, 5330, and 31 C.F.R. part 103 all contain different definitions of "money transmitter." The concept in each of the laws is similar, but the details are not the same. Because e-gold is operating outside the traditional realm of money transmitters, it is necessary to explore the nuances of the statutory definitions in order to determine whether the laws encompass e-gold. The inconsistencies in the statutes, coupled with potential criminal penalties in § 1960(a), make advising clients who want to implement novel new payment mechanisms a difficult task."

Later, the analysis concludes by saying: "e-gold is being prosecuted, it appears, on an amalgam of all four laws. Because 18 U.S.C. § 1960 exposes individuals to criminal as opposed to civil liability for the business decisions of their companies, resolution of the ambiguities is essential for the market of electronic payment products to mature. At a technical level, failure to clarify the scope of the "money transmitter" laws—all four of them— coupled with criminal prosecution of businesses and their owners who run afoul of these laws will likely stifle the development of new electronic money products or raise compliance costs for new businesses."[647] [648]

◆

On March 7th, 2008, the Government filed a thirty-one-page response to the Defendants' Motion.[649] A summary of this response is below.

Summary of Argument

Defendants have moved to dismiss Counts Two, Three, and Four of the indictment. Specifically, defendants contend that Counts Two and Three, which charge them with conspiracy to operate an unlicensed money transmitting business and operation of an unlicensed money transmitting business under 18 U.S.C. § 371 and 18 U.S.C. § 1960 respectively, fail to state an offense and should be dismissed pursuant to

[647] Jackson, Douglas. "Investigation Request." Received by John Roth, Inspector General, US Dept. of Homeland Security, 24 Aug. 2017, Indian Harbour Beach, FL.

[648] Middlebrook, Stephen T., et al. *Developments in the Law Concerning Stored-Value Cards and Other Electronic Payments Products*. Indiana University Maurer School of Law, 2007, *Developments in the Law Concerning Stored-Value Cards and Other Electronic Payments Products*.

[649] GOVERNMENT'S RESPONSE TO DEFENDANTS' MOTION TO DISMISS COUNTS TWO, THREE AND FOUR OF THE INDICTMENT. *UNITED STATES OF AMERICA v. E-GOLD, LTD. GOLD & SILVER RESERVE, INC. DOUGLAS L. JACKSON, BARRY K. DOWNEY, and REID A. JACKSON.* Case 1:07-cr-00109-RMC Document 99, 7 Mar. 2008.

Federal Rule of Criminal Procedure 12(b)(3)(B). Defendants' central argument is that 18 U.S.C. § 1960 ("Section 1960"), the statute that prohibits operation of an unlicensed money transmitting business, only applies to businesses that engage in cash transactions. Defendants argue that Counts Two and Three are defective because these charges do not specifically allege that defendants accepted cash from customers, and because Section 1960 is unconstitutionally vague as to whether it applies to non-cash businesses. However, as is explained below, defendants are mistaken in their view that Section 1960 only applies to businesses engaged in cash transactions. Defendants have taken a reference to 31 U.S.C. § 5330 ("Section 5330") found in one subpart of Section 1960 and applied it to the entire statute. Defendants do not appear to dispute that their activity falls within Section 1960's definition of "money transmitting." Nor do defendants appear to dispute that they operate or manage a business whose activities fall within Section 1960's definition of "money transmitting." Nevertheless, defendants urge the Court to invalidate the government's effort to prosecute them under Section 1960 because, they insist, the statute does not contain a separate definition for the phrase "money transmitting business." Absent that, defendants maintain, the Court must either: (1) borrow a definition for the same phrase from another statute – which definition, defendants maintain, they fall without; or (2) declare Section 1960 void for vagueness. But, defendants' tortured reading of Section 1960 is purely self-serving and lacks any support in logic or the rules of statutory construction. Further, it is not the case that Section 5330 is, in fact, limited only to businesses that actually accept cash. Nor does the indictment limit the government's ability to submit proof at trial that defendants actually engaged in cash transactions. Additionally, Section 1960, which contains its own definition of "money transmitting," is clear on its face as to the conduct that is prohibited and is therefore unambiguous and comports with Due Process. Only defendants' determined attempt to create an inconsistency suggests vagueness. As an alternative basis for dismissal, defendants contend that Counts Three and Four are insufficient because they merely track the language of the statute and do not make any independent factual allegations. However, except in limited circumstances where the conduct forming the basis for the charge would not be evident from the statutory language, thereby depriving the defendant of notice of the basis for their indictment, it is sufficient for an indictment to simply track the statutory language. Here, Counts Three and Four both track the statute and contain factual allegations sufficient under Federal Rule of Criminal Procedure 7. Last, with respect to Count Four, defendants argue simply that the judicial economy that permits charging a state offense in this federal case does not apply if the Court dismisses Counts Two and Three, and, therefore Count Four should be dismissed at the same time. But, not only is there no basis to dismiss Counts Two or Three, there is still an unchallenged Count One. Thus, the legal basis for defendants' assertion that Count Four should be dismissed does not exist.[650]

About two weeks later, on March 19th, 2008, the Defendants filed a Reply to the Government's Opposition to Defendants' Motion.

The defendants have moved to dismiss Counts Two, Three and Four of the Indictment. The Government has opposed the defendants' motion. In doing so, the Government ignores the statutory definition of "money transmitting business" and supplants it with a definition created by the Government out of whole cloth. Indeed, the Government argues that 18 U.S.C. § 1960 suffers no vagueness problems, because the statute purportedly gives plain and unambiguous notice that the reader is to ignore the statutory definition of the term "money transmitting business" and, instead, import a definition that has never appeared in any statute, regulation, or anywhere else - until it was articulated by the Government in its opposition to the defendants' motion. The Government's argument should be squarely rejected.

Separately, the Government implicitly concedes that because it failed to incorporate any factual allegations in Counts Three and Four of the Indictment, those counts must rise or fall on the Government's mere recitation of the statutory language. The Government fails to overcome the well-established rule that an indictment must allege the facts and circumstances that give rise to the alleged statutory violation. The Indictment's failure to do so in Counts Three and Four is fatal to those counts.

Finally, the Government contends that the dismissal of Counts Two and Three would not warrant the dismissal of Count Four. In making this argument, the Government simply ignores the fact that federal courts should be reluctant to try local District of Columbia offenses in the absence of a strong nexus between the local offense and a charged federal offense. The presumption is against - not in favor of - a federal court exercising jurisdiction over a local District of Columbia offense. Once the federal money-transmitting-business offenses in Counts Two and Three have been dismissed, the Court should exercise its discretion to dismiss the related local money-transmission offense in Count Four.

---

[650] Ibid

First, the Government argues that, whether or not they actually deal in cash, all "financial institutions" are required to file reports under Section 5313. See Gov't Opp. at 10. And, as a result, opting out of accepting cash does not relieve e-gold and G&SR - which the Government asserts are "financial institutions" - of Section 5330's registration requirements. Id. As a threshold matter, the Government is incorrect that e-gold and G&SR are "financial institutions." However, even assuming, *arguendo,* that e-gold and G&SR are "financial institutions," the Government's argument ignores the plain language of Section 5313. Section 5313 clearly states that "financial institutions" are required to file reports only if "involved in a transaction for the payment, receipt, or transfer of *United States coins and currency* (or other monetary instruments the Secretary of Treasury prescribes)." 31 U.S.C. § 5313(a) (emphasis added). The Indictment fails to allege that the defendants actually engaged in cash transactions. Thus, they were not required to file reports under Section 5313, which means they do not qualify as "money transmitting businesses" for the purposes of Section 5330.[651]

Request to Modify Downey's Conditions of Release

On February 27, 2008, the court had permitted Jackson to travel to Canada for G&SR company business. Later, in May 2008, an additional unopposed motion was submitted to the court:

> Dr. Jackson's United States Passport ("Passport") is set to expire May 29, 2008. Dr. Jackson may have a need to travel for business purposes and has recently traveled internationally for business purposes with this Court's permission and without incident. Accordingly, he hereby seeks to have his Passport released temporarily for the sole purpose of renewing the Passport.[652]

This motion was granted as well.

Defense counsel filed with the Court a similarly innocuous motion to modify

---

[651] DEFENDANTS' REPLY TO THE GOVERNMENT'S OPPOSITION TO DEFENDANTS' MOTION TO DISMISS COUNTS TWO, THREE AND FOUR OF THE INDICTMENT. *UNITED STATES OF AMERICA v. E-GOLD, LTD. GOLD & SILVER RESERVE, INC., DOUGLAS L. JACKSON, BARRY K. DOWNEY, REID A. JACKSON.* Case 1:07-cr-00109-RMC Document 100, 19 Mar. 2008.

[652] Case 1:07-cr-00109-RMC Document 115. UNITED STATES OF AMERICA vs. E-GOLD LTD, GOLD & SILVER RESERVE LTD, DOUGLAS L. JACKSON, BARRY K. DOWNEY, REID A. JACKSON. DEFENDANT DOUGLAS L. JACKSON'S UNOPPOSED MOTION TO MODIFY ORDER SETTING CONDITIONS OF RELEASE, 28 May 2008.

Downey's conditions of release on March 20, 2008:

> Pursuant to [the original Conditions of Release entered by Magistrate Judge Kay on May 3, 2007], Mr. Downey may travel for business with notification to Pretrial Services, but otherwise is to stay within 50 miles of home and work. Mr. Downey has relatives, including his wife's parents who live in Martinsburg, West Virginia, who live slightly more than 50 miles from Mr. Downey. Mr. Downey wishes to visit his relatives for Easter. In addition, he likely will in the future desire to see his relatives. Accordingly, he hereby seeks to modify the Order Setting Conditions of Release to allow travel within 75 miles of his home or work. It is the understanding of undersigned counsel that Pretrial Services has no objection to this modification. Similarly, undersigned counsel has confirmed with counsel for the Government that it does not oppose this motion.[653]

Surprisingly, the Court immediately denied the request. The Court rejected this motion by minute order entered the same day. As will be seen below, this was not the end of this seemingly trivial incident.

♦

Superseding Indictment

On April 3rd, 2008, the day before oral arguments were to be held on Defendants' Motion to Dismiss; the Government filed a twenty-eight-page Superseding Indictment. A second Grand Jury, sworn in on November 15th, 2007, had returned the new Indictment. It bolstered the large-scale nature of e-gold's "money transmitting business" by alleging it maintained "a cadre of employees" and transferred "approximately $145,535,374.26" in funds. The Government argued that, together, e-gold® and G&SR had a large number of employees supervised by three primary managers, Jackson, Downey, and Reid Jackson. It also alleged that more than $145 million had been transferred through the combined "e-gold operation"[654] collectively, constituting an operation of "major proportions" within Congress's intended meaning of the term "business." Furthermore, if the Government proved that e-gold® and G&SR engaged in money transmitting, then e-gold® and G&SR were, in fact, money transmitting businesses.

---

[653] Case 1:07-cr-00109-RMC Document 101. *UNITED STATES OF AMERICA vs. E-GOLD LTD, GOLD & SILVER RESERVE LTD, DOUGLAS L. JACKSON, BARRY K. DOWNEY, REID A. JACKSON*. DEFENDANT BARRY K. DOWNEY'S UNOPPOSED MOTION TO MODIFY ORDER SETTING CONDITIONS OF RELEASE, 20 Mar. 2008.

[654] Case 1:07-cr-00109-RMC Document 104. *UNITED STATES OF AMERICA v. E-GOLD, LTD. GOLD & SILVER RESERVE, INC. DOUGLAS L. JACKSON, BARRY K. DOWNEY, and REID A. JACKSON*. SUPERSEDING INDICTMENT, 3 Apr. 2008.

UNITED STATES OF AMERICA v. e-gold, LTD. GOLD & SILVER RESERVE, INC. DOUGLAS L. JACKSON, BARRY K. DOWNEY, and REID A. JACKSON, VIOLATIONS:

- 18 U.S.C. § 1956 (Conspiracy to Launder Monetary Instruments);
- 18 U.S.C. § 371 (Conspiracy);
- 18 U.S.C. § 1960 (Operation of Unlicensed Money Transmitting Business);
- D.C. Code § 26-1002 (Money Transmitting Without a License)
- 18 U.S.C. § 2 (Aiding and Abetting and Causing an Act to be Done); and
- 18 U.S.C. § 982(a)(1) (Criminal Forfeiture)[655]

April 2008 Hearing for Motion to Dismiss

At a hearing on April 4, 2008, counsel for Mr. Downey orally moved for the Court to reconsider its March 20, 2008, Minute Order restricting his travel. The Court took the motion under advisement. At the following status conference, held on May 19, 2008, defense counsel renewed the motion and filed a proposed order that same day. The Judge ruled on this motion on June 10, 2008.

On April 4, 2008, the Court held a Motion Hearing Before The Honorable Rosemary M. Collyer, on the Defendants' Motion to Dismiss.[656] Attorneys present for the government were Laurel L. Rimon, Esquire U.S. Department of Justice, Kimberly K. Peretti, Esquire Department of Justice, and Jonathan W. Haray, Esquire Assistant United States Attorney. Mr. Barry J. Pollack, Esquire, representing Defendant Downey, was speaking directly to the court. Also present was Michelle Peterson, Esquire Assistant Federal Public Defender representing Reid Jackson, and Joshua Berman, Esquire serving Douglas Jackson. A fifty-eight-page transcript of the event is available online.

Early in the e-gold Hearing it became evident that the Judge interpreted the requirement contained in 31 USC 5330,[657] "is required to file reports under section 5313" as applying to the defendant companies on the basis that they might hypothetically accept cash in the future. The Judge came to this conclusion even though the requirements to file a Currency Transaction Report had never been triggered, and neither company's business model encompassed the acceptance of cash in any circumstance..

[655] Ibid

[656] Docket No. CR 07-109. *UNITED STATES OF AMERICA v. E-GOLD, LTD. GOLD & SILVER RESERVE, INC. DOUGLAS L. JACKSON, BARRY K. DOWNEY, and REID A. JACKSON.* TRANSCRIPT OF MOTION HEARING BEFORE THE HONORABLE ROSEMARY M. COLLYER UNITED STATES DISTRICT JUDGE, 4 Apr. 2008.

[657] "31 U.S. Code § 5330 - Registration of Money Transmitting Businesses." *Legal Information Institute*, Legal Information Institute, 1994, www.law.cornell.edu/uscode/text/31/5330.

One of the three criteria that must all be met for a business to fulfill the 5330 statute definition of a "money transmitting business" is that the business "is required to file reports under section 5313."[658] However, the Judge interpreted the statute in the other direction. She started on the premise that the business was a money transmitting business because it was a business that, in her view, engaged in Money Transmission. She believed that e-gold had a "legal obligation" to file Currency Transaction Reports: "You're required to file reports if you're a money transmitting business."[659] As the argument continued. Defense counsel reiterated:

> "The only place there is a definition of money transmitting business is in 5330(d). 5330(d) does not say that I have to be a category of business that if I do something in the future I'd be required to do something. It is on the present tense that I have to be a business that is required to file reports.
> And your honor that makes sense. It does make sense. It makes sense that we're not worried about businesses that do not engage in these kind of transactions. We don't have a law enforcement interest in tracking transactions that aren't occurring. It's only if you're engaging in those transactions that you become a money transmitting business that we want to to regulate."
>   The Court: "I think, I think that that is actually misreading the statute. I think that if you are engaged in a money transmitting business as described in A, you have a legal obligation to file reports under B, capital letter B on the occasions in which you deal in cash."[660]

The discussion then turned once again to the nature of OmniPay's transaction model. Defense counsel sought to contrast e-gold with the operation of a hawala.

> "What GSR is doing is taking national currency and converting that to e-gold, not giving somebody else money. Not transmitting money to somebody else through a financial information [sic] or in any other manner. It's a one way transaction and a one way transaction back to same person. It's not transmitting from person A to person B.
>
> The only transmission from person A to person B is in E-gold where one person gets

[658] Ibid
[659] TRANSCRIPT OF MOTION HEARING BEFORE THE HONORABLE ROSEMARY M. COLLYER UNITED STATES DISTRICT JUDGE. UNITED STATES OF AMERICA vs. E-GOLD LTD, GOLD & SILVER RESERVE LTD, DOUGLAS L. JACKSON, BARRY K. DOWNEY, REID A. JACKSON. Docket No. CR 07-109, 4 Apr. 208AD.
[660] Ibid

E-gold transmitted from their account to another account."[661]

During the Hearing, Judge Collyer incorrectly illustrated the funds flow in an OmniPay transaction.

> THE COURT: "So I wire some money to G&SR OmniPay. OmniPay turns it into E-gold, puts it in my account in E-gold. E-gold transfers my money from my account to somebody else's account in E-gold.
>
> That person in the second account gets it somehow downloaded to OmniPay which turns it back into money, right? And sends it back to the home bank account of the second person.
>
> Now you would admit that if OmniPay had an office in which I could walk in and hand them my money and we went through that entire regimen and that it came out the other end and the second person walked in and got the money that it would be a money transmitting business."

Given this unexpected additional opportunity to precisely clarify the actual transaction models of e-gold and OmniPay, counsel instead responded with: "I would admit that it has characteristics that are similar to a money transmitting business."[662]

Dr. Jackson, offered this subsequent commentary regarding this critically important statement.

> "This was the closest our counsel ever came in their arguments in open court to describing the distinct roles of the companies. To his credit, Barry Pollack did point out that an OmniPay transaction always involved a single customer. Unfortunately, as always occurred with our lawyers, he scrupulously confined his remarks to only use the (purposely misleading) language of the criminal complaint, specifically their weasel-word "convert."
> The critical insight that needed to be, but wasn't, conveyed was that in buying and selling e-gold—the only transactions OmniPay engaged in—it was not "converting" national currency into e-gold. e-gold was a closed system; no exchange transaction with a customer resulted in money or value in any form entering or exiting the e-gold system. Every time OmniPay sold or bought e-gold to/from a customer, it was itself

[661] Ibid
[662] Ibid

409

acting as an e-gold customer, making or receiving a Spend of *already existing* e-gold respectively from or to its own e-gold account.

A Spend, in turn, was the only transaction that could be executed in the e-gold system. The only way any customer could obtain a quantity of e-gold was to receive a Spend from another e-gold customer who already had some. Exchange from or to conventional money was not an obligatory starting or endpoint of an e-gold transaction. The starting point of every e-gold Spend was a prospective payer - some e-gold customer with e-gold. The endpoint of every e-gold Spend was the e-gold customer who had received the Spend of e-gold.

While this may seem a hair-splitting subtlety, the importance of this lost opportunity to achieve clarity was demonstrated a minute later when the Judge recited back her understanding of an e-gold transaction as starting with conventional money and ending up as conventional money, based on her misunderstanding that an exchange transaction in which an OmniPay customer is buying e-gold results in money being 'turned into' e-gold."[663]

Appeals Court Ruling On Right to an Evidentiary Hearing

On April 11, 2008, the United States Court of Appeals for the District of Columbia Circuit handed down its ruling overturning Judge Collyer's decision denying the evidentiary hearing to challenge ex parte allegations of probable cause warranting in the second round of asset seizures.

" Defendants moved to vacate the seizure warrant and to modify the restraining order, and sought an evidentiary hearing. In support of their motions, the individual appellants alleged an inability to pay for counsel of their choice in the absence of the seized assets. The district court denied the motions. Appellants brought the present appeal, arguing that the seizure warrant and restraining order without at least a post-seizure evidentiary hearing violated their due process rights and right to counsel under the Fifth and Sixth Amendments to the Constitution. For the reasons stated below, we agree with appellants and vacate the order of the district court and remand the case for further proceedings."[664]

When this news became public, it was a ray of sunshine to the e-gold community.

[663] Jackson, Douglas. "Chunk 7." Received by Carl Mullan, *Chunk 7*, 15 Mar. 2020.

[664] No. 07-3074. UNITED STATES of America, Appellee v. E-GOLD, LTD., Et Al., Appellants. U.S. V. E-GOLD, LTD, 521 F.3d 411 (D.C. Cir. 2008), 11 Apr. 208AD.

e-gold® Wins Appeal in D.C. Circuit for Hearing on Asset Seizure
April 21, 2008, FOR IMMEDIATE RELEASE
[Melbourne, FL] -- e-gold Ltd is pleased to announce a favorable ruling from The United States Court of Appeals for the District of Columbia Circuit in the matter of whether it, Gold & Silver Reserve, Inc., and Directors of both corporations are entitled to a hearing in the Federal district court regarding whether there was sufficient probable cause to justify seizures of assets from the corporations in December 2005 and April 2007. The higher court concluded:
"In short, we hold that where the government has obtained a seizure warrant depriving defendants of assets pending a trial upon the merits, the constitutional right to due process of law entitles defendants to an opportunity to be heard at least where access to the assets is necessary for an effective exercise of the Sixth Amendment right to counsel."
The complete text of the court's opinion is available online: Opinion for the Court, filed by Chief Judge Sentelle.
This ruling will ultimately prove to be beneficial to all Americans whose Fourth, Fifth and Sixth Amendment rights have been increasingly encroached upon in the name of fighting domestic wars du jour - whether or not they use e-gold.
e-gold Ltd, Gold & Silver Reserve, Inc., and their Directors believe there was insufficient probable cause for the seizure warrants at issue and look forward to finally having their day in court on this matter.[665]

Though the appeals court ruled that the defendants were entitled to an evidentiary hearing to challenge the allegation of probable cause that had resulted in the seizure of their assets, the Hearing never occurred. Judge Collyer quickly countered with an action that ensured no such hearing would ever take place.

Weeks later, on May 8, 2008, the Court issued an Order denying Defendants' Motion to Dismiss Counts Two, Three, and Four of the Indictment. The Order was filed simultaneously with Judge Collyer's Memorandum Opinion[666] elucidating reasons for finding the Defendants' argument unsound.

ORDER
For the reasons stated in the Memorandum Opinion filed simultaneously with this

---

[665] Jackson, Douglas. "Gold Wins Appeal in D.C. Circuit for Hearing on Asset Seizure." *e-gold Blog*, e-gold.com, 21 Apr. 2008, blog.e-gold.com/2008/04/e-gold-wins-app.html.

[666] U.S. District Court for the District of Columbia. *United States of America v. e-gold, Ltd, Et Al., Defendants*. MEMORANDUM OPINION, 8 May 2008.

Order, it is hereby
ORDERED that Defendants' Motion to Dismiss Counts Two, Three and Four of the
Indictment is DENIED.
SO ORDERED.
Date: May 8, 2008 /s/
ROSEMARY M. COLLYER[667]

The Court had developed the position that the Defendant companies, e-gold Ltd. and G&SR Inc., operated as one collective entity. The Court viewed the companies as being managed by the same individuals and labeled it the "e-gold operation." The ruling considered this non-existent amalgam, created only by the illocutionary speech of the government's indictment, to be a money transmitting business. Consequently, with the Court's recognition, the "e-gold operation" required U.S. financial licenses and regulatory supervision. After this Opinion, the Defendants' arguments fell silent.

"Without effective defense presentation of exculpatory and mitigating evidence, there can be no counterpunch to the prosecution's heavy blows."[668]

In 2018 emails, Jackson shared his insight.

> To preview a critical aspect of the legal case…The indictment portrayed a fictional entity called the "e-gold operation". It was a mishmash that smooshed together-gold Ltd. and Gold & Silver Reserve Inc. (dba OmniPay) as if one entity, and mischaracterized the fundamental transaction of e-gold, which was a Spend. As with how most white collar criminal cases go, there was never an opportunity to present or examine evidence that would have enabled explication of the actual organization or transaction logic.[669]

Judge Collyer's May 8th Opinion was an accurate summary of digital currency technology's future as online payments in the United States. From this argument, the court concluded that e-gold® was a "money transmitter business." Furthermore, the court held that without ever handling government currency or coin, e-gold® was a money transmitter and

---

[667] U.S. District Court for the District of Columbia. United States of America v. e-gold, Ltd, Et Al., Defendants. ORDER, Defendants' Motion to Dismiss Counts Two, Three and Four of the Indictment [Dkt. # 93] is DENIED., 8 May 2008.

[668] Stephanos Bibas, Plea Bargaining Outside the Shadow of Trial, 117 HARV. L. REV. 2464 (2004) [hereinafter Bibas, Plea Bargaining Outside]; Albert W. Alschuler, The Defense Attorney's Role in Plea Bargaining, 84 YALE L.J. 1179 (1975).

[669] Jackson, Douglas. "Chunk 8." Received by Carl Mullan, Chunk 8, 27 Mar. 2020.

subject to reporting requirements.

The District Court Judge Rosemary M. Collyer held that:
1. "money transmitting business" in the governing criminal statute was not restricted to business that handled cash;
2. defendants operated "money transmitting business" within meaning of Money and Finance Code provision mandating registration of such businesses;
3. the criminal statute was not void for vagueness;
4. rule of lenity was not applicable; and
5. no novel statutory construction was involved in the instant prosecution.

Defendants' motion to dismiss Counts Two and Three because the underlying criminal statute is void for vagueness, ambiguous, or because the Government's interpretation of the statute poses a novel construction of a criminal offense, each in violation of the Due Process Clause of the Constitution, will be denied.[670]

The opinion was around thirty pages long. Selected portions are below.[671]

MEMORANDUM OPINION

Title 18 of the United States Code ("U.S.C.") sets out federal law covering Crimes and Criminal Procedure. Title 31 of the U.S.C. sets out federal law covering Money and Finance, including the Internal Revenue Code. 18 U.S.C. § 1960 makes it a crime to operate an unlicensed money transmitting business. Section 1960 defines what it means to be unlicensed and what it means to engage in money transmitting. By those definitions, a business can clearly engage in money transmitting without limiting its transactions to cash or currency and would commit a crime if it did so without being licensed. The only definition in the United States Code for a "money transmitting business" *per se* is at 31 U.S.C. § 5330. Section 5330 defines a money transmitting business as one that, *inter alia*, is required to report certain cash or currency transactions to the Internal Revenue Service ("IRS").

Before the Court is a motion to dismiss filed by the criminal defendants in this case. They have all been charged with operating an unlicensed money transmitting business in violation of Section 1960. They contend that Section 1960 does not apply

---

[670] Ibid

[671] U.S. District Court for the District of Columbia. *United States of America v. e-gold, Ltd, Et Al., Defendants.* MEMORANDUM OPINION, 8 May 2008.

413

to their operations because they never deal in cash or currency. Since they are not required to file reports with the IRS concerning cash transactions, they argue that they do not operate a "money transmitting business" and, therefore, cannot be an "unlicensed money transmitting business" within the scope of Section 1960. They further argue that even if one could distinguish Section 1960 and Section 5330, Section 1960 is unconstitutionally vague as to the meaning of the term "money transmitting business," and therefore violates Defendants' rights under the Due Process Clause of the Constitution, or at least is ambiguous as to the meaning of that term, and the rule of lenity requires dismissal of most of the counts in the criminal indictment.

The Defendants have moved, pursuant to Federal Rule of Criminal Procedure 12(b)(3)(B), to dismiss Count Two of the Indictment for failure to state an offense under 18 U.S.C. § 371, and to dismiss Count Three for failure to state an offense under 18 U.S.C. § 1960. The Defendants also move to dismiss Count Four, based on the Court's discretion not to exercise jurisdiction over an alleged state offense, Money Transmission Without a License in violation of D.C. Code § 26-1002. Alternatively, the Defendants move to dismiss Counts Three and Four for failure to comply with Federal Rule of Criminal Procedure 7(c)(1).₁ Whether the Defendants' business activities, described below, are criminal in nature has been orally contested since the Indictment was obtained. The Court is now advantaged by the written arguments presented by the parties, as well as a spirited oral argument, and finds that Counts Two and Three properly allege offenses of 18 U.S.C. §§ 371 and 1960. Since the Indictment remains intact, the Court will maintain the state-law count in Count Four. The motions to dismiss are based on a mis-reading of the statutory text and will be denied.

Along with e-gold and G&SR, three individual Defendants are named in the Indictment. These three are alleged to have varying management roles in e-gold and G&SR and to have an ownership interest in G&SR. Id. ¶¶ 16-18. Specifically, Defendant Douglas L. Jackson is alleged to be co-founder, Chairman, and Chief Executive Officer of e-gold and GS&R and majority owner of GS&R; Defendant Barry K. Downy is alleged to be co-founder, Secretary, and a Director of e-gold and GS&R and an owner of 20 percent (20%) of GS&R; and, finally, Defendant Reid A. Jackson is alleged to be the Managing Director of e-gold and GS&R and owner of three percent (3%) of GS&R. All Defendants are charged with conspiracy to launder money instruments (from about 1999 through December 2005), in violation of 18 U.S.C. §§ 1956, 1957 (Count One); 3 conspiracy to operate an unlicensed money transmitting business (from October 26, 2001 through December 2005), in violation of 18 U.S.C. § 371 (Count Two); operation of an unlicensed money transmitting business (from October 26, 2001 through (at least) December 2005), in violation of 18 U.S.C. §§ 2, 1960 (Count Three); and money transmitting without a license (from May 14, 2002 through at least March 23, 2003), in violation of D.C. Code § 26-1002 (Count Four).[672]

Defendants argue:

> By its terms, Section 1960 applies only to "money transmitting business[es]." 18 U.S.C. § 1960. . . .[I]n order to qualify as a "money transmitting business," a business must engage in cash transactions. Because the Indictment fails to allege that either e-gold or G&SR engages in cash transactions – and indeed specifically alleges that e-gold merely transfers e-gold between accounts and that G&SR transacts in wires – they cannot constitute a money transmitting business, either individually or collectively. Thus, under the terms of the Indictment, the defendants could not have violated the law by operating an unlicensed money transmitting business, or by conspiring to operate an unlicensed money transmitting business. Accordingly, Counts Two and Three of the Indictment must be dismissed.

Defs.' Mem. at 5; see also Defs.' Reply at 7 ("the statutory definition of 'money transmitting business' encompasses only businesses that engage in cash transactions"). Stated in the reverse, Defendants argue that one cannot be engaged in a money transmitting business unless one engages in cash transactions. In support of their position, Defendants rely on Section 5330(d)(1)(B), which defines money transmitting businesses, in part, as those required to file cash transaction reports under Section 5313. Defs.' Mem. at 7 ("a business can constitute a money transmitting business only when it is required to file reports under 31 U.S.C. § 5313"). Defendants submit that Section 5313 "in turn, makes it clear that such reports must be filed only by domestic financial institutions involved in transactions 'for the payment, receipt, or transfer of United States coins and currency (or other monetary instruments the Secretary of Treasury prescribes).'" Id. (citing 31 U.S.C. § 5313(a) (emphasis added)). For a definition of "currency" and "transaction in currency," Defendants refer the Court to the "currency transaction reports" referred to in Section 5330(d)(1)(B) which define these terms as follows:

> **Currency.** The coin and paper money of the United States or any other country, which is circulated and customarily used and accepted as money.

Currency Transaction Report at 3 (Department of Treasury FinCEN Form 104)

---

[672] Ibid

(emphasis added).

> **Transaction in Currency.** The physical transfer of currency from one person to another. This does not include a transfer of funds by means of bank check, bank draft, wire transfer or other written order that does not involve the physical transfer of currency.

Id. (emphasis in original).

Defendants contend that, taken together, these statutory provisions establish that an entity is a "money transmitting business" only if it engages in the physical transfer of currency, and because the Government failed to allege that Defendants engaged in the physical transfer of currency, Defendants cannot be a money transmitting business, or consequently, an unlicensed money transmitting business, for purposes of Section 1960. Defs.' Mem. at 8 ("in order to qualify as a 'money transmitting business,' a business must be required to file reports under 31 U.S.C. § 5313, and a business is only required to file reports under § 5313 if it engages in cash (coin and paper money) transactions"). In the alternative, Defendants argue that because the term "money transmitting business" is only defined in Section 5330, and that definition purportedly conflicts with the definition of "money transmitting" in Section 1960(b)(2), Section 1960 is unconstitutionally vague, or "at best," ambiguous as to the proper meaning of the term "money transmitting business," and the rule of lenity dictates that the Court should "resolve the ambiguity" in Defendant's favor. Id. at 12 (citing *United States v. Granderson, 511 U.S. 39, 54 (1994)*).[673] [674]

The document offered these detailed explanations.

> But does Section 1960's reference to Section 5330 in Section 1960(b)(1)(B) limit its scope to businesses that handle cash? The answer is no – for two reasons: (1) Section 1960 does not borrow the definition of "money transmitting business" from Section 5330, and (2) Section 5330's definition of "money transmitting business" is not limited to cash transactions, but rather includes transmissions of funds by any means.[675]

---

[673] Ibid

[674] U.S. v. E-Gold, Ltd., 550 F. Supp. 2d 82 (D.D.C. 2008)

[675] Because the Court holds that the definition of "money transmitting business" in Section 5330 does not control the interpretation of Section 1960, the scope of Section 5330's definition of "money transmitting business" is relevant only to whether the Government has properly alleged that Defendants e-gold and G&SR (together and/or separately) are required to register with the Secretary of Treasury pursuant to 31 U.S.C. § 5330. If Defendants do constitute a money transmitting business under Section 1960, and if they are required to comply with the business registration requirements under Section 5330 (or the regulations promulgated thereunder), then their failure to do so could constitute a crime in violation of 18 U.S.C. § 1960(b)(1)(B).

The court also held that even though e-gold had never handled currency or coin, it was still subject to the currency reporting requirements: "**A money transmitting business is no less a transmitter of money just because it does not deal in currency. Rather, Section 5313 comes into force and will require a report if, when, and as the transmitter does engage in currency transactions.**" In conclusion, the court was very clear in its view that handling cash is not the touchstone of being a money transmitting business under federal law. "The term 'money transmitting business' as used in Section 5330 includes all financial institutions that fall outside of the conventional financial system (and that are not a 'depository institution'), not just those that engage in cash transactions."[676] [Emphasis added]

On May 30th, 2008, the Defendants filed a Motion To Dismiss Count Four Of The Superseding Indictment for failure to state an offense under D.C. Code § 26-1002. The partial text is below.

> Pursuant to Rule 12(b)(3)(B) of the Federal Rules of Criminal Procedure, defendants egold, Ltd., Gold & Silver Reserve, Inc., Douglas L. Jackson, Barry K. Downey, and Reid A. Jackson, through their attorneys, respectfully submit this memorandum of law in support of their motion to dismiss Count Four (Money Transmission Without a License in violation of D.C. Code § 26-1002) of the Superseding Indictment ("the Indictment"). The District of Columbia's money transmission laws regulate only persons or businesses that have a physical presence in, or other substantial nexus to, the District of Columbia. The Indictment does not allege, nor could it, that any of the defendants conducted a business with a physical presence in the District of Columbia or that they otherwise had a substantial nexus to the District. Accordingly, Count Four of the Indictment must be dismissed for failure to state an offense.
>
> The crux of Count Four is that the defendants operated a money transmitting business without obtaining a license to do so from the Office of Banking and Financial Institutions of the District of Columbia pursuant to D.C. Code § 26-1002. Superseding Indictment at ¶ 80. However, Section 26-1002 is inapplicable to the defendants' business activities as it is intended to be a licensure provision only for individuals and businesses that have a significant physical presence in the District of Columbia or other substantial nexus to the District.[677]

---

[676] U.S. District Court for the District of Columbia. *United States of America v. e-gold, Ltd, Et Al., Defendants.* MEMORANDUM OPINION, 8 May 2008.

The Defendants' lawyers argued that the State of New York had previously supported their conclusion.

> This conclusion is further bolstered by authority from New York involving a statute analogous to Section 26-1002. New York's money transmission licensing statute is similar to the District's, stating broadly that "[n]o person shall engage in the business of ... receiving money for transmission or transmitting the same, without a license therefore obtained from the superintendent." N.Y. Banking Law § 641(1). In a 2000 letter opinion, however, counsel for the New York Banking Department - the state agency charged with regulating money transmitters - clarified that PayPal, a California-based corporation with no physical presence in New York, which offered money transmitting services exclusively through the Internet to residents of the United States, was *not* required to obtain a license under that statute. 2000 N.Y. Bank. LEXIS 1, at *3 (July 18, 2000) ("the Banking Department will interpose no objection at this time to your client offering PayPal services to New York customers without being licensed under [the money transmitting statutes]). [678]

> e-gold, Ltd. was incorporated in the British West Indies and has no physical presence in the District. Gold & Silver Reserve, Inc., the operator of e-gold, Ltd., which has its offices in Florida, likewise is not alleged to have a physical presence in the District of Columbia. In addition, like PayPal at the time that it sought guidance from New York with respect to the need for New York licensure, e-gold, Ltd. conducts its business wholly through the Internet and offers its services to residents of the United States at a national level. The New York Banking Department's opinion that under these circumstances no state license is required, is instructive with respect to Section 26-1002.

> Based on the statute's failure to include language stating that it applies to non-residents, the District of Columbia Court of Appeals' reading of a similar District of

---

[677] U.S. District Court for the District of Columbia. *United States of America v. E-gold, Ltd, Et Al., Defendants.* MOTION TO DISMISS COUNT FOUR OF THE SUPERSEDING INDICTMENT, 30 May 2008.

[678] In reaching its conclusion, the Banking Department noted: The definition of "money transmission" in Article XIII-B of the New York Banking Law is very broad. The intent of the New York legislature was to, among other things, minimize the risk of loss to New York customers who utilize third parties to transmit funds and ensure that persons and entities which engage in money transmission activities do not utilize their services to facilitate the conduct of illegal activities. *Id.* at *2-3. However, despite the broad goals of consumer protection, the New York Banking Department concluded that the statute was not intended to require registration by a company that, by virtue of its use of the Internet, had customers in New York, but did not have a physical presence in the State or specifically target New York residents.

Columbia licensure requirement, and New York's interpretation of its money transmission statute analogous to Section 26-1002, the Court should find that Section 26-1002 does not apply to non-resident companies and individuals with no substantial nexus to the District of Columbia and dismiss Count Four of the Indictment since it does not allege that the defendants had such a presence in or nexus to the District of Columbia.[679]

As it turned out, no ruling was ever made, or needed, regarding this motion to dismiss the DC charge. Instead, the Judge issued a ruling on June 10th that resulted in defense counsel revealing to the defendants, for the first time, the facts of life regarding the criminal justice system in the United States.

Specifically, the defendants learned why virtually all parties charged in federal court with white-collar crimes plead guilty. From June 10th onward, the Defendants' task became to seek the least onerous terms for a Plea Agreement.

That dreadful day, June 10, 2008, the Court returned an adverse ruling denying Defendant Downey's request to modify the conditions of his release. As previously discussed, Barry Downey had requested modification to his conditions of release in March and again in April 2008. The original conditions authorized travel within a 50-mile radius of his home and office. His Counsel had requested, and the government did not oppose, expanding his travel to a 75-mile radius, which would enable Downey to drive his wife and family to her parent's home in Martinsburg, West Virginia. The ruling ended up being highly material to the Defendants' near-term decision to enter into plea negotiations.

Judge Collyer denied Downey's request and issued an Order on Motion to Modify Conditions of Release.[680] Once again, the Judge's response appeared to "turn up the heat" and steer the Defendants towards a plea. The critical takeaway message from Collyer's Order included the following text:

> In the average case, a criminal defendant ceases his alleged criminal behavior upon arrest and/or indictment. **Defendants here vigorously deny the charges but heretofore have done so relying entirely on a legal challenge to the Government's interpretation of the criminal statute; the basic facts as to how the e-Gold operation is conducted are not much in dispute. Their legal argument has been rejected by this Court.** Defendants' situation has thus altered

---

[679] U.S. District Court for the District of Columbia. *United States of America v. e-gold, Ltd, Et Al., Defendants.* MOTION TO DISMISS COUNT FOUR OF THE SUPERSEDING INDICTMENT, 30 May 2008.

[680] Case 1:07-cr-00109-RMC Document 122. UNITED STATES OF AMERICA vs. E-GOLD LTD, GOLD & SILVER RESERVE LTD, DOUGLAS L. JACKSON, BARRY K. DOWNEY, REID A. JACKSON. ORDER ON MOTION TO MODIFY CONDITIONS OF RELEASE, 10 June 2008.

since their arraignments and detention hearings.

> These circumstances affect the analysis here. The Court concludes that the risk of flight by Mr. Downey has increased since the rejection of the statutory defense and that the continued operation of e-Gold and Gold & Silver Reserve poses some risk to the community at large from the allegedly illegal nature of those businesses and alleged use of E-gold by pornographers and other illicit sales operations. Notably, Mr. Downey lives in Maryland, not in this jurisdiction. The minor inhibition on Mr. Downey's personal travel, therefore, will remain in place.[681]

In other words, the Judge had signaled to the Defendants that they were effectively guilty. Barry Downey, a respected attorney, devoted husband, and father, and a conscientious steward of the value entrusted to e-gold Ltd. by its customers, was suddenly deemed an unacceptable flight risk? No circumstances had changed in Downey's life, employment, or financial situation during the previous months.

Had some new event or evidence caused the Judge to view Downey as a possible threat or risk? With statements such as "alleged use of E-gold by pornographers," was the Court "turning up the heat" and pressing the Defendants to accept a plea? Is it the place of a District Court Judge to rearrange the pieces on the board and influence whether a Defendant exercises their Constitutional right to a fair trial? Was Jackson correct in questioning the Judge's motivation for a fast resolution and plea?

The combination of two highly prejudicial rulings—the denial of the Motion to Dismiss and the even more clear signal of this denial—raised a grave risk. If finally allowed to present evidence such as the actual organization and function of the companies, the distinct nature of an e-gold Spend and, the OmniPay exchange operations business model, would the introduction of such evidence even be tolerated? It appeared very clear that "the basic facts as to how the e-Gold operation is conducted are not much in dispute." The Court had rejected the Defendants' legal argument.[682]

Similarly, it would be difficult to envision a judge instructing jurors to consider whether the companies were indeed distinct, per the traits that differentiated e-gold from would-be imitators, or if the "e-gold Operation" was indeed one business.

It was at this time the Defense Counsel also revealed to the defendants the doctrine of Relevant Conduct and the role of Federal Sentencing Guidelines.

And the overly-broad definition of "relevant conduct" allows prosecutors to introduce evidence of conduct that was not previously charged or of which the defendant was actually

---

[681] Ibid
[682] Jackson, Douglas. "Chunk 8." Received by Carl Mullan, Chunk 8, 27 Mar. 2020.

acquitted. This doctrine was discussed by Kevin Dowd in *New Private Monies*.

> Dr Jackson was right to be worried. As Chetson (2011) explains, the concept of relevant conduct 'allows the judge to punish the defendant for uncharged crimes, or crimes for which a jury acquitted (found not guilty!) the defendant, when sentencing the defendant following the conviction on even tenuously related charges.' The implications are disturbing, to say the least. For instance, if a defendant goes to trial and is acquitted by a jury of his peers of trafficking, he may be punished for trafficking by the judge if he's convicted of any tangentially related charge by the jury. The system is so absurd – it fundamentally turns the putative Constitutional 5th, 6th, 8th and 14th Amendments on their heads – that it creates a system where about 98 per cent of all defendants plead guilty as part of agreements out of fear that even if they were to win everything (except a minor related charge), they would be sentenced by the judge in spite of those acquittals (Chetson 2011).[683]

In light of this perceived stacked deck, the Defendants decided to enter into plea negotiations.

Given Bernie Grimm's high reputation and established goodwill within the DC Circuit, the Defendants elected to take advantage of his recent addition to the team by having him approach the government.[684]

♦

On June 20, 2008, the Department of the Treasury's receipt was filed with the Court documenting the seized property in e-gold accounts 544179 and 109243. The seized property was described as "$1,481,976.38 in U.S. Currency."[685]

♦

While still fighting in the Court, e-gold's management had to also contend with the everyday business issues such as its website and the thorny press. Because of an overnight DDOS attack, on July 6th, 2008, the e-gold® website access was temporarily degraded, and

---

[683] "Chapter 3." *New Private Monies: a Bit-Part Player?*, by Kevin Dowd, Institute of Economic Affairs, 2014, pp. 32–33.

[684] Ibid

[685] Jackson, Douglas. "Service of Verified Complaint for Forfeiture in Rem ('All Property in e-gold [Sic] Account Numbers 544179 and 109243') (2008-06-20)." *e-gold*, e-gold.com, 20 June 2008, legalupdate.e-gold.com/2008/06/service-of-verified-complaint-for-forfeiture-in-rem-all-property-in-e-gold-sic-account-numbers-544179-and-109243-2008-.html.

the site went offline for several hours.[686]

A few days later, on July 9th, 2008, an unknown party published a fake press release appearing to be from e-gold®. It falsely stated that both e-gold Ltd. and Gold & Silver Reserve, Inc. had filed for bankruptcy. The fake news rumor spread quickly across the Internet. After recovering from the DDOS attack, the e-gold® website carried this disclaimer about the fake release.

> Fraudulent "Press Release" and accompanying DDoS attacks
> Beginning July 7, 2008 a fraudulent press release was sent to multiple online publication services claiming that e-gold Ltd. and Gold & Silver Reserve, Inc. had filed for bankruptcy. The announcement was a fraud and did not come from either company or anyone associated with either company. Concurrent with the fraudulent press release there have also been intermittent denial-of-service attacks against the e-gold.com website, probably originating from the same perpetrator. An investigation is underway seeking to discover the source of both this malicious misinformation and the denial of service attacks.[687]

◆

The Guilty Pleas

The Defendants used the weeks after June 10th to evaluate their position. While they had vigorously contested the Government's interpretation and application of 18 U.S.C. § 1960 to their businesses, the arguments were over. Attorneys had litigated the case, and once the Court interpreted the statute, Dr. Jackson and his co-defendants moved towards closure.[688]

In the November 2008 sentencing transcript, Attorney Pollack representing Defendant Downey discussed with the Court, the Defendants' actions after the Memorandum Opinion of May 8th, 2008.

> MR. POLLACK: and when the Court made that determination[May 8th Memorandum Opinion], obviously Mr. Downey, all of the defendants could have

[686] Jackson, Douglas. "e-gold Blog." 'e-gold Blog', e-gold.com, 6 July 2008, web.archive.org/web/20081013193730/blog.e-gold.com/2008/07/e-gold-web-site.html.

[687] Jackson, Douglas. "e-gold Blog." 'e-gold Blog', 9 July 2008, web.archive.org/web/20081219140050/blog.e-gold.com/2008/07/fraudulent-pres.html.

[688] Case 1:07-cr-00109-RMC Document 176 . UNITED STATES OF AMERICA v. E-GOLD, LTD. E-GOLD, LTD.'S MEMORANDUM IN AID OF SENTENCING AND INCORPORATED POSITION WITH RESPECT TO SENTENCING FACTORS, 14 Nov. 2008.

gone to trial. They could have appealed that issue. It was a pure legal ruling.[689]

Okay, but they didn't. They moved with incredible speed. As the Court knows within two months we were back before the Court entering guilty pleas. That included the commitment to immediately get the businesses registered with the federal government, apply for licenses in states where licenses were needed and not to do any business in any state until that had been accomplished.[690]

On July 21, 2008, the Defendants signed plea agreements. That same day, e-gold, Ltd. suspended new e-gold account creation pending development and deployment of its new, compliant Customer Identification Program.

Barry Downey Plea Agreement

Plea as to 26 D.C. Code § 1002 by Barry K. Downcy (2008-07-21) [partial content]
On 2008-07-21, Mr. Downey agreed to plead guilty to the charge of Engaging in the Business of Money Transmission Without a License, in violation of 26 D.C. Code § 1002 (Count Four of the Superseding Indictment (2008-04-03)). Mr. Downey was also required to allocute, undergoing formal questioning by the Court as to his offense.[691]

e-gold® Plea Agreement

On July 21, 2008, Defendant, e-gold, Ltd., through its organizational representative Douglas Jackson, pled guilty to one count of conspiracy in violation of Title 18, United States Code, Section 371 and one count of conspiracy to launder monetary instruments in violation of Title 18, United States Code, Section 1956.[692]

Plea as to 18 U.S.C. §§ 1956(h) and 371 by e-gold, Ltd. (2008-07-21) [partial content]
On 2008-07-21, e-gold, Ltd. agreed to plead guilty to charges of Conspiracy to Launder Monetary Instruments, in violation of 18 U.S.C. § 1956(h) (Count One of

---

[689] Docket No. CR 07-109. UNITED STATES OF AMERICA vs. E-GOLD LTD, GOLD & SILVER RESERVE LTD, DOUGLAS L. JACKSON, BARRY K. DOWNEY, REID A. JACKSON. TRANSCRIPT OF SENTENCE BEFORE THE HONORABLE ROSEMARY M. COLLYER UNITED STATES DISTRICT JUDGE, 20 Nov. 2008.

[690] Ibid

[691] Ibid

[692] Case 1:07-cr-00109-RMC Document 176 . *UNITED STATES OF AMERICA v. E-GOLD, LTD.* E-GOLD, LTD.'S MEMORANDUM IN AID OF SENTENCING AND INCORPORATED POSITION WITH RESPECT TO SENTENCING FACTORS, 14 Nov. 2008.

the Superseding Indictment (2008-04-03)), and Conspiracy to Operate an Unlicensed Money Transmitting Business, in violation of 18 U.S.C. § 371 (Count Two of the Superseding Indictment (2008-04-03); see also 18 U.S.C. § 1960). e-gold, Ltd. was also required to allocute, or respond to questions from the Court as to the offenses charged. Douglas L. Jackson spoke on behalf of e-gold, Ltd. for the purposes of the allocution.[693]

Dr. Douglas Jackson's Plea Agreement

"I think that Dr. Jackson has suffered, will suffer, will continue to suffer and may never be successful at E-Gold, but I think that that factor suggests that a jail term is not necessary."
Judge Collyer's statement at the sentencing November 20, 2008.[694]

Plea as to 18 U.S.C. §§ 1956(h) and 1960(b)(1)(A), (B), and (C) by Douglas L. Jackson (2008-07-21) [partial content]
On 2008-07-21, Dr. Jackson agreed to plead guilty to charges of Conspiracy to Launder Monetary Instruments, in violation of 18 U.S.C. § 1956(h) (Count One of the Superseding Indictment (2008-04-03)), and Operation of an Unlicensed Money Transmitting Business, in violation of 18 U.S.C. § 1960(b)(1)(A), (B), and (C) (Count Three of the Superseding Indictment (2008-04-03)). Dr. Jackson was also required to allocute, undergoing formal questioning by the Court as to his offense.[695]

Each Plea Agreement also included a series of requirements that effectively represented a bespoke regulatory 'blueprint' designed to enable the companies to resume operations as regulated financial institutions. Since e-gold® was still in operation, the companies, including the primary exchange, were required to register as an MSB. Additionally, the business would have to create an Anti-Money Laundering Program with OFAC compliance, file Suspicious Activity Reports (SAR), and employ third-parties to conduct regular precious metal audits. E-gold was required to complete all of these additions within ninety days.

e-gold, OmniPay or other digital currency accounts must be brought into compliance with 31 U.S.C. § 5318(1) and 31 C.F.R. § 103.125 or closed within ninety (90) days.[696]

---

[693] Taylor, Jeffrey A., et al. "Plea Agreement." Received by Barry J. Pollack, Esq, *U.S. Department of Justice*, United States Attorney, 21 July 2008, pp. 1–10.

[694] Ibid

[695] Peretti, Kimberly Kiefer. "Plea Agreement." Received by Bernard S. Grimm, Esq., *Department of Justice*, United States Attorney, 18 July. 2008, pp. 1–13.

Jackson also agreed that e-gold® and G&SR, or any other entity through which he offered a digital currency, would submit to supervision by the Internal Revenue's Bank Secrecy Act Division. Additionally, he was bound by the Plea Agreement not to make any public statements that contradicted the Statement of Offense or Plea Agreement for the next three years. A violation of this would constitute a breach of the Agreement.

While sentencing commonly occurs within three months of entry of a guilty plea, in the e-gold cases it was scheduled for November 2008 – affording an additional month for the companies to work through their challenging list of mandated reforms.

On July 21, 2008, the same day of the Plea Agreements, Jackson published an astonishing blog post on the e-gold® website entitled "A New Beginning." The lengthy text included an acknowledgment that the e-gold® Defendants had accepted the DOJ plea agreements and recognition that e-gold® was a Financial Institution. Partial content from this blog post is below.

> The criminal case has been resolved. The resolution of the criminal case however provides for a second chance, an opportunity to address the flaws embedded in the e-gold® system and to transform the "e-gold Operation" into the institutions I, the other directors, and our longsuffering employees and contractors have always envisioned, one that serves to advance the material welfare of mankind.

> In harmony with this transformation, we acknowledge that e-gold® is indeed a Financial Institution or Agency as defined in US law and should be regulated as a Financial Institution. e-gold Ltd. has submitted an application to FinCEN to be registered as a Money Services Business and will be seeking licensure in all states that require it. Most importantly, working in conjunction with US government agencies, we will be exerting every effort to bring e-gold® into compliance with US law and regulation as quickly as possible.[697]

The final paragraph included an apology that was surprisingly upbeat.

> Looking Forward
> We are confident that a regulated e-gold® rebuilt to a more systematic specification

[696] Taylor, Jeffrey A., and Jonathan Haray. "Re: e-gold, Ltd." Received by Bernard S. Grimm, Esq., 1627 I Street, NW, 21 July 2008, Washington, D.C.

[697] Jackson, Douglas. "e-gold Blog." *'e-gold Blog'*, e-gold.com, 21 July 2008, web.archive.org/web/20100126034650/blog.e-gold.com/2008/07/a-new-beginning.html.

will be less hospitable to criminals, and more attractive to mainstream business use without being less accessible to those disregarded by legacy payment systems. Please accept our apologies for the occasional turbulence you may experience on this journey. And, as always...Thank you for using e-gold®.[698]

After resolution of the criminal case, the directors of e-gold, Ltd. vowed to continue operations and follow all of the Court's required new federal guidelines. Jackson affirmed to the world that e-gold, Ltd. was a financial institution as defined by U.S. law and regulated as such. Company statements advised that e-gold, Ltd. had submitted an application to FinCEN (Financial Crimes Enforcement Network) to be registered as a money services business and would be seeking licensure in all states that required it.

In a grand gesture, one statement stood out above all others. It explained that e-gold, Ltd. and G&SR wanted to "make something clear that should have been made more emphatically clear long ago. Use of the e-gold system for criminal activity will not be tolerated."[699]

The company amended the e-gold Account User Agreement to include provisions that an e-gold "user agrees to not use e-gold in any manner that violates the laws of whatever jurisdiction to which the User is subject" and to give e-gold, Ltd. the right to freeze and take other actions relating to accounts suspected of criminal activity.[700] [701]

Around one week after the e-gold® plea agreements, Jackson learned of the Government indictment against Albert Gonzalez, aka segvec.

Consent Order of Forfeiture

Also, on July 21st, 2008, the Government filed a Consent Order of Forfeiture.[702] The value of the forfeiture was not to exceed $1,750,000.00.

CONSENT ORDER OF FORFEITURE

WHEREAS, a written plea agreement was filed with this Court and signed by defendants **E-GOLD, LTD.** and **GOLD & SILVER RESERVE,** INC., and their respective counsel, Bernard Grimm and Aron Raskas, in which defendants E-GOLD,

---

[698] Ibid

[699] Jackson, Douglas. "A New Beginning." *e-Gold Blog*, e-Gold Ltd., 21 July 2008, blog.e-gold.com/2008/07/a-new-beginning.html.

[700] For specific provisions added to the User Agreement, see the Status Report on Activities Undertaken by Defendants to Comply with All Provisions of Plea Agreements, page 8-9.

[701] Case 1:07-cr-00109-RMC Document 176 . UNITED STATES OF AMERICA v. E-GOLD, LTD. E-GOLD, LTD.'S MEMORANDUM IN AID OF SENTENCING AND INCORPORATED POSITION WITH RESPECT TO SENTENCING FACTORS, 14 Nov. 2008.

[702] U.S. District Court for the District of Columbia. *U.S.A. v. e-gold, Ltd., Gold & Silver Reserve, Inc. Douglas L. Jackson, Barry K. Downey, and Reid A. Jackson, Defendants.* . CONSENT ORDER OF FORFEITURE, 21 July 2008.

LTD. and GOLD & SILVER RESERVE, INC. agreed to plead guilty to felony violations, that is, money laundering conspiracy and operation of an unlicensed money transmitting business in violation of 18 U.S.C. §§ 1956 and 1960;

WHEREAS, the Indictment also alleged the forfeiture of certain property, which property is subject to forfeiture, pursuant to Title 18, United States Code, Section 982(a), as property involved in the commission of the offenses set forth above;

WHEREAS, in its plea agreement, the defendants expressly agreed and consented to the entry of an Order of Forfeiture, under Fed. R. Crim. P. 32.2(b) (2), concerning certain property subject to forfeiture, as property involved in its violations of 18 U.S.C. §§ 1956 and 1960; and

WHEREAS, this Court has determined, based on the evidence set forth during the defendants' guilty pleas, that the "Subject Property" is subject to forfeiture pursuant to Title 18, United States Code, Section 982, and that the Government has established the requisite nexus between such property and violation of Title 18, United States Code, Sections 1956 and 1960;

NOW THEREFORE, IT IS HEREBY ORDERED, ADJUDGED AND DECREED:

1. That the following property is declared forfeited to the United States, pursuant to Title 18, United States Code, Section 982:

MONEY JUDGMENT: not to exceed $1,750,000.00 for which defendants E-GOLD, LTD. and GOLD & SILVER RESERVE, INC. are jointly and severally liable (One Million, Seven Hundred Fifty Thousand U.S. Dollars). The United States agrees that it is in possession of all funds to be forfeited.

Four days later, Kim Zetter wrote an article for Wired.com about the e-gold® guilty pleas. In her article, Zetter quoted Jackson as opting to resolve the case in a way that enabled e-gold® to move ahead as a licensed institution. Instead of dragging out the legal situation, Jackson had chosen to rebuild and overcome the past hits to e-gold's reputation. Text from Zetter's article entitled *e-gold Founder Pleads Guilty to Money Laundering* quoting Jackson is below.

From our perspective, the possibility of resolving the legal case in a manner that allows for a path forward, that provides an explicit roadmap enabling e-gold to emerge as a regulated financial institution in full compliance with US law is greatly preferred over continued conflict," he wrote. "We acknowledge that we made mistakes and fully accept responsibility for those mistakes. Our goal throughout these recent negotiations was to set the stage for e-gold to get a second chance and to get it right this time, to emerge as an institution that can become an integral and vital part of the financial and commercial mainstream.[703]

KPMG

Since the plea he[Douglas Jackson] has spent almost every waking minute with KPMG, with Cyveillance, with his brother, with Mr. Downey in trying to put together an absolute compliance plan. It won't be perfect. He will do his absolute true to the heart best.[704]
Statement by Attorney Joshua Berman representing Douglas Jackson at sentencing.

On September 3, 2008, Jackson received a brief letter from KPMG LLP in Boston, amending a previously signed agreement to assist e-gold® and G&SR. KPMG's 2008 agreement included audits that the company would present to the DOJ, and KPMG also would help in creating an Anti-Money Laundering (AML) program.

September 3, 2008[705]
Private
Dear Dr. Jackson:
On behalf of KPMG LLP ("KPMG"), we are providing an amendment to our original engagement letter dated August 20, 2008 in which we were retained to assist e-gold, Ltd. and Gold & Silver Reserve, Inc. (hereinafter referred to collectively as "the Companies") with the development of its Anti-Money Laundering (AML) program. The purpose of this letter is to set forth an amendment to the terms of the engagement specifically regarding the number of deliverables we would expect to provide you. All other terms remain the same.

Deliverables
Upon completion of the work, and as previously indicated, KPMG will deliver the following previously articulated deliverables to the Companies with the following amendments:

With regard to Task 1(A), KPMG will deliver to the Client two independent reports, one regarding e-gold, Ltd. and the other regarding G&SR. The final versions of both

[703] Zetter, Kim. "e-gold Founder Pleads Guilty to Money Laundering." *Wired.com*, 25 July 2008, www.wired.com/2008/07/e-gold-founder/.

[704] Docket No. CR 07-109. UNITED STATES OF AMERICA vs. E-GOLD LTD, GOLD & SILVER RESERVE LTD, DOUGLAS L. JACKSON, BARRY K. DOWNEY, REID A. JACKSON. TRANSCRIPT OF SENTENCE BEFORE THE HONORABLE ROSEMARY M. COLLYER UNITED STATES DISTRICT JUDGE, 20 Nov. 2008.

[705] KPMG LLP. "Private." Received by Dr. Jackson, KPMG LLP, 3 Sept. 2008, Boston, MA.

of these reports will be delivered to the US. Department of Justice, United States Attorney, District of Columbia and the Internal Revenue's Bank Secrecy Act Division.

With regard to Task (2), KPMG will deliver two projects plans (one for each entity) for the development of an AML Program, to include AML and OFAC program enhancements as recommended in accordance with the detailed report.

Later that month, on September 29, 2008, the following release appeared on the e-gold® website.

e-gold® Engages KPMG to Assist e-gold® in its Development of AML Program Improvements[706]

[MELBOURNE, FL] -- e-gold Ltd. announced today that it has retained KPMG LLP to assist e-gold Ltd. in its development of an improved Anti-Money Laundering Program. KPMG's Advisory Services practice brings significant industry knowledge and experience that will greatly benefit e-gold Ltd., e-gold Ltd. announced. Dr. Douglas Jackson, e-gold Ltd. Founder, said, "e-gold Ltd. is seeking to have one of the market's most effective Anti-Money Laundering Programs." Dr. Jackson said e-gold Ltd.'s goal is to implement significant enhancements to its Anti-Money Laundering Program in the next 30-60 days.

Ironically, between 1996 and 2007, KPMG had never accepted an employment offer from e-gold®. It wasn't until after e-gold® halted their business, that KPMG accepted e-gold's invitation. In 2019 emails, Douglas Jackson commented on this critical milestone.

We[e-gold] were never able to secure a relationship with one of the big accounting firms until 2008 when KPMG was only too happy to take $500k from us to perform virtually worthless work in fulfillment of Plea requirements.[707]

By October 19th, 2008, e-gold, Ltd. had effectively frozen all accounts. The plan was to verify all users and be in compliance with 31 U.S.C. § 5318(l) and 31 C.F.R. § 103.125. As of November 14, 2008, customers were only allowed to upload identification documents. Spends were not possible.[708]

[706] Jackson, Douglas. "e-gold Blog." *'e-gold Blog'*, e-gold.com, 29 Sept. 2008, web.archive.org/web/20081002040642/blog.e-gold.com/2008/09/e-gold-engages.html.
[707] Jackson, Douglas. "Chunk 8." Received by Carl Mullan, *Chunk 8*, 27 Mar. 2020.

The Defendants Attorney stated, in the November 2008 Sentencing Memorandum, how e-gold® and G&SR had upgraded their services and platform to comply with U.S. financial regulations.

> G&SR has made herculean efforts to reshape its business and ensure that it is in compliance with the undertakings it assumed in the plea agreement and with all applicable laws and regulations.
>
> Even before the plea agreements were signed, defendants began working earnestly to change the nature of the Companies to bring them into compliance with all applicable laws and regulations. They have expended hundreds of thousands of dollars and thousands of hours of manpower to meet this goal.
>
> It is fair to say that today these are far different companies than those that existed a mere four months ago. The Companies have sought to make it clear to all users of the e-gold and OmniPay services that neither company will tolerate criminal abuse of their systems and that the Companies will continue to work proactively with law enforcement officials to ensure that the Companies retain this new reputation.[709]

Sentencing

A lot was riding on this case. There is ample evidence that suggests Prosecutors were pushing hard to increase the Defendants' sentences. This production is their job. Here are some statements from the government's team that demonstrate why DOJ Prosecutors wanted a significant victory.

> The E-Gold prosecution makes it clear that the DOJ is willing to prosecute businesses aggressively under the anti-money laundering laws, whether these businesses operate online or offline, when a risk of money-laundering is created by a company's service offerings.[710]

> Adequate deterrence to criminal conduct is the really difficult one on which I really needed to pause because the government makes a very good argument that others

[708] Case 1:07-cr-00109-RMC Document 176 . UNITED STATES OF AMERICA v. E-GOLD, LTD. E-GOLD, LTD.'S MEMORANDUM IN AID OF SENTENCING AND INCORPORATED POSITION WITH RESPECT TO SENTENCING FACTORS, 14 Nov. 2008.

[709] CASE NUMBER: 07-167-M-01. *UNITED STATES OF AMERICA V. E-GOLD LIMITED, GOLD & SILVER RESERVE, INC., DOUGLAS L. JACKSON, BARRY K. DOWNEY and REID A. JACKSON.* SENTENCING MEMORANDUM OF GOLD & SILVER RESERVE, INC., Nov. 2008.

[710] Bunnell, Steve, et al. "Internet Businesses Beware: Aggressive Enforcement of Money Laundering Laws Targets Online Payment Systems." *O'Melveny & Myers LLP*, 21 July 2008. E-Gold Criminal Indictment Resolved in a Plea Agreement

need to understand that this new day of internet crime is going to be as vigorously prosecuted as the old day of, you know, the mob or something in, in, we won't pick a state, never mind. So we need to send a message out.[711]

On the day of sentencing, Assistant United States Attorney Jonathan W. Haray made this statement to the Court:

> I think it's especially important in a field like this, Your Honor. I mean, the banking field itself, the brick and mortar banking field is a well established field where people know for the most part how they need to keep their businesses in compliance.
>
> This is a field that is developing and the fact that it's developing means that it's open to people who would take advantage of it to do so. Unless they know that there's a penalty at stake, a real penalty, then I think it runs the risk of just emboldening people to commit the same offense that this company, this defendant has committed.[712]

During the sentencing, DOJ Prosecutor, Laurel Rimon, openly acknowledged that the federal government intended to make an example of e-gold® and send a message to any future digital currency platforms intending to operate in the United States. She stated:

> This is a particularly significant case. Digital currencies are on the forefront of international fund transfers. E-Gold is the most prominent digital currency out there. It has the attention of the entire digital currency world. That world is a bit of a wild west right now. People are looking for what are the rules and what are the consequences. Criminal activity runs rampant. It's important that this case be seen as making a clear statement that if you are a person who knowingly facilitates and conducts funds transfers with dirty money, you're going to pay the price.[713]

After the guilty verdict, U.S. Attorney Jeffrey Taylor observed: "Because of the successful prosecution of these defendants, digital currency providers everywhere are now on notice that they must comply with federal banking laws or they will be subject to

---

[711] Ibid

[712] Docket No. CR 07-109. UNITED STATES OF AMERICA vs. E-GOLD LTD, GOLD & SILVER RESERVE LTD, DOUGLAS L. JACKSON, BARRY K. DOWNEY, REID A. JACKSON. TRANSCRIPT OF SENTENCE BEFORE THE HONORABLE ROSEMARY M. COLLYER UNITED STATES DISTRICT JUDGE, 20 Nov. 2008

[713] Ibid

prosecution."[714]

November 20th, 2008, was sentencing day for the three persons and two corporations charged in the e-gold case. In preparation for that event, Prosecutors and Defense Lawyers filed crucial Memorandums with the Court.

#174
UNITED STATES OF AMERICA v. E-GOLD, LTD,
GOVERNMENT'S MEMORANDUM IN AID OF SENTENCING[715]

In this filing, the Prosecutors tried to focus the Court on the Defendants' crimes with the intent of increasing the final penalties handed down by the Judge. However, the Prosecutors' argument opened with some seemingly insignificant evidence. On page two, in the "BACKGROUND" section, the Government presented items from the mainstream media in support of their case. The Government's Memorandum, document # 174, headlines a Businessweek article and two misguided Fox News stories alleging malicious activity with e-gold.

Hearing Prosecutors mention Brian Grow's Businessweek article was no surprise for the Defendants. In these articles, Grow had colluded so closely with the USSS, Jackson agrees that he should have been on their payroll. Over past decades, Businessweek has acted as a government mouthpiece with scarcely more nuance than Pravda for the USSR. Grow's performance is no exception and hearing the Prosecutor retort his claims only verified further their relationship.[716] Below is content from the Government's filing.

> A January 9, 2006 Business Week article entitled "Gold Rush: Online Payment Systems Like E-gold Ltd. Are Becoming The Currency of Choice for Cybercrooks," stated:
>
> > A tour of some outlaw corners of the Internet illustrates why [law enforcement was interested in the E-gold system]. One Web site called CC-cards -- where cyberthieves sell pilfered bank account and credit-card information -- often asks for payment via e-gold. Some sites pushing child

---

[714] Justice, Department of. "Digital Currency Business E-Gold Pleads Guilty to Money Laundering and Illegal Money Transmitting Charges." *#08-635: Digital Currency Business E-Gold Pleads Guilty to Money Laundering and Illegal Money Transmitting Charges (2008-07-21)*, DOJ, 21 July 2008, www.justice.gov/archive/opa/pr/2008/July/08-crm-635.html.

[715] GOVERNMENT'S MEMORANDUM IN AID OF SENTENCING. *UNITED STATES OF AMERICA v. E-GOLD, LTD.* Case 1:07-cr-00109-RMC Document 174 , 14 Nov. 2008.

[716] Jackson, Douglas. Received by Carl Mullan, *316-351*, 22 May 2020. p. 316 - 351.docx

pornography have dropped Visa and MasterCard recently in favor of e-gold, according to the National Center for Missing & Exploited Children, which tracks underage porn. These examples were not unique.* Indeed, the E-gold system's own computer records demonstrated how popular E-gold became among criminal users.

*[footnote from Document #174]As further example, Fox News ran two stories (1 in early 2004 and 2006) on the potential, and in some circumstances actual, use of e-gold as a payment mechanism for, among other things, online investment scams online child pornography.[717]

Other content in this Memorandum reiterated many of the government's original accusations. Prosecutors effectively concluded their argument with the following recommendation. The phrase "deter others" is present.

CONCLUSION
The United States respectfully requests that E-gold be sentenced to a term of probation of three years, and to some amount of a fine that is commensurate with its ability to pay over a period of time, to punish it for its conduct and to deter others who might consider committing similar misconduct.[718]

Attorneys prosecuting the case that contributed to this filing included:

- Jonathan W. Haray, Assistant United States Attorney, Fraud & Public Corruption Section
- Kimberly Kiefer Peretti, Senior Counsel, U.S. Department of Justice, Computer Crime and Intellectual Property Section, Criminal Division
- Laurel Loomis Rimon, Deputy Chief for Litigation, U.S. Department of Justice, Asset Forfeiture and Money Laundering, Section, Criminal Division

The Government also submitted a Memorandum in Aid of Sentencing of Defendant Gold & Silver Reserve Inc.[719]   Except for the name change, this filing, including the Conclusion, was nearly identical to the previous E-gold Memorandum document.

[717] Ibid
[718] Ibid
[719] Case 1:07-cr-00109-RMC Document 175 Filed. *UNITED STATES OF AMERICA v. GOLD & SILVER RESERVE, INC.* GOVERNMENT'S MEMORANDUM IN AID OF SENTENCING, 14 Nov. 2008.

That same day, Defense Attorney Bernard Grimm filed a lengthy Memorandum on behalf of E-gold, Ltd.[720] In the case of E-gold, Ltd., a virtual company, that contracted with other businesses to perform the actual operational and fiduciary roles, Grimm was arguing to reduce or eliminate the Government's monetary fine.

Document #176

UNITED STATES OF AMERICA v. E-GOLD, LTD

E-GOLD, LTD.'S MEMORANDUM IN AID OF SENTENCING AND INCORPORATED POSITION WITH RESPECT TO SENTENCING FACTORS

Defendant, e-gold, Ltd. through undersigned counsel, hereby files this memorandum in anticipation of its sentencing on November 20, 2008.

On July 21, 2008, defendant, e-gold, Ltd., through its organizational representative Douglas Jackson, pled guilty to one count of conspiracy in violation of Title 18, United States Code, Section 371 and one count of conspiracy to launder monetary instruments in violation of Title 18, United States Code, Section 1956. The advisory sentencing guideline calculation is undisputed and places the defendant at offense level 32. Pursuant to U.S.S.G. § 8C3.3, e-gold,

Ltd. requests this Court waive the Stipulated Fine ($3,738,387.30) so that it can continue to operate in compliance with applicable laws and its Plea Agreement with the government. As articulated in the status report filed on November 6, 2008 the costs associated with compliance efforts commenced prior to the plea in this case has consumed a considerable portion of e-gold, Ltd.'s working capital. A fine in **any** amount will "substantially jeopardize the continued viability of the organization."[721]

On November 14th, Defense Attorney Aron Raskas filed a Sentencing Memorandum on behalf of Gold & Silver Reserve, Inc.[722] In preparation for sentencing, this defense filing highlighted positive actions and outcomes caused by the Defendants throughout their e-gold business. This defense argument sought to lessen the Defendants' final penalties handed down by Judge Collyer on sentencing day. The fifty-five-page filing contained and an

---

[720] Case 1:07-cr-00109-RMC Document 176 . *UNITED STATES OF AMERICA v. E-GOLD, LTD*. E-GOLD, LTD.'S MEMORANDUM IN AID OF SENTENCING AND INCORPORATED POSITION WITH RESPECT TO SENTENCING FACTORS, 14 Nov. 2008.

[721] Ibid

[722] CASE NUMBER: 07-167-M-01. *UNITED STATES OF AMERICA V. E-GOLD LIMITED, GOLD & SILVER RESERVE, INC., DOUGLAS L. JACKSON, BARRY K. DOWNEY and REID A. JACKSON*. SENTENCING MEMORANDUM OF GOLD & SILVER RESERVE, INC., Nov. 2008.

extensive amount of factual information relating to the Sentencing of the Defendants.

> Document #177
> *UNITED STATES OF AMERICA V. E-GOLD LIMITED, GOLD & SILVER RESERVE, INC., DOUGLAS L. JACKSON, BARRY K. DOWNEY and REID A. JACKSON*
> *SENTENCING MEMORANDUM OF GOLD & SILVER RESERVE, INC.*
> Criminal No. 07-109 – RMC
> related case:
> In the Matter of the Seizure of Any and all property in/underlying E-GOLD Account 544179 and in/underlying E-GOLD account 109243, held by E-GOLD, Ltd. or Gold & Silver Reserve, Inc. on behalf of E-GOLD, Ltd.
> CIVIL CASE NUMBER: 07-167-M-01

Raskas' primary arguments in this filing were two-fold. The first point was to acknowledge the Defendants' guilt and responsibility for their actions.

> G&SR does not seek to justify or excuse its unlawful conduct in any fashion. Yet, counsel believe that it is important - and appropriate - that the Court view these offenses in the context in which they occurred. That context suggests that G&SR did not intentionally seek to engage in criminal activity and, in fact, took steps to act as required.[723]

The second point Raskas illustrated was how G&SR's financial constraints had hampered the Defendants' "ability to improve its system and better restrict unlawful use of the e-gold system."[724] In the opening paragraph, Defense Attorney Raskas respectfully asks the Court to afford particular consideration to the "circumstances that G&SR confronted along the road that it has traveled from its founding to this date."[725]

> We ask that, in sentencing G&SR, the Court take into account the good faith beliefs under which G&SR operated; the many positive efforts that it did make to combat unlawful activity; the legal and severe financial constraints under which it operated its businesses, which limited its ability to more forcefully combat fraud and illegality; the substantial forfeiture of assets to which it has already agreed; and the manner in

[723] Ibid
[724] Ibid
[725] Ibid

which it has reshaped its business since the Court ruled that it is a money transmitting business.

In particular, we ask that the Court recognize the great loss of business and income which G&SR has already suffered as a result of this matter. On the basis of all this information, we ask that the Court find that G&SR lacks the ability to pay a fine, and that it fashion a sentence that will not require G&SR to pay a fine, but which will allow it to continue serving the public and operating its business in compliance with all applicable laws and the undertakings that it assumed in its plea agreement with the government.[726]

Raskas hoped to convince the Court, "to recognize the state of mind with which G&SR pursued its business model and appreciate the understandings upon which that state of mind developed."[727] He argued for the Court to "consider all of the efforts that G&SR *did* take to work with law enforcement personnel and combat fraud and illegal activity that developed in the e-gold system."[728]

so that the Court may appreciate the reasons why G&SR acted as it did. We also hope that it will allow the Court to learn about the many things that G&SR did do right along the path that it took to grow its business and how it has responded since this Court's substantive ruling on the issue of whether G&SR was in fact a money transmitting business.[729]

The filing (Document #177) had thirteen separate Exhibits.

◆

November 20, 2008 Sentencing Hearing
Criminal action 07-109, United States of America versus E-Gold Limited, Gold & Silver Reserve, Limited, Douglas L. Jackson, Barry K. Downey and Reid A. Jackson.
- For the government Kimberly Peretti, Laurel Rimon and Jonathan Haray.
- For the defense, Bernie Grimm, Aaron Raskas, Machalagh Carr, Joshua Berman, Barry Pollack and Michelle Peterson.

[726] Ibid
[727] Ibid
[728] Ibid
[729] Ibid

- From the probation office Renee Moses Gregory and Kelly Kramer-Soares. Defendants Barry K. Downey, Reid A. Jackson, and Douglas Jackson were present in the courtroom.[730]

After the three-year gag order had elapsed, Jackson shared this memory of his day in court.

"Heading into the sentencing hearing, the expectation was that I would be sentenced to incarceration for a year and a day."[731]

During the hearing, Jackson observed Charles Evans and his ex-wife (divorced seven years previously) seated two rows back from the prosecutors, in chairs behind the USSS Special Agents. Repeatedly Evans was observed to scribble notes on paper, which he would then pass to the USSS Special Agents who, after scanning them, would pass them on to AUSAs Rimon and Peretti. As the hearing began, Dr. Jackson's attorney, Joshua Berman, addressed the court:

Some final points, Your Honor, about the family. In the courtroom today we have Dr. Jackson's wife, we have his two adopted sons, Ben and Sam. We have his sister, and obviously one of his brothers who is a co-defendant. His father is here and his father's current wife. He has got his brother-in-law and a sister-in-law I believe. I believe he has at least three nieces and nephews. This is a group of folks who cares deeply   for this man. But perhaps more importantly recognizes what he means to his family. Putting him in jail will have significant emotional and financial consequences to the family.[732]

The transcript for the Sentencing Hearing reveals that the Judge questioned the Prosecutor's depiction of e-gold as based on some anti-government philosophy:

THE COURT "You say E-Gold was found[ed] at least in part based upon a philosophy that opposed government regulation of financial institutions and the banking industry. …What do you mean when you say that it was founded on a philosophy that opposed government regulations?[733]

[730] Ibid
[731] Jackson, Douglas. "Chunk 8." Received by Carl Mullan, *Chunk 8*, 27 Mar. 2020.
[732] Docket No. CR 07-109. UNITED STATES OF AMERICA vs. E-GOLD LTD, GOLD & SILVER RESERVE LTD, DOUGLAS L. JACKSON, BARRY K. DOWNEY, REID A. JACKSON. TRANSCRIPT OF SENTENCE BEFORE THE HONORABLE ROSEMARY M. COLLYER UNITED STATES DISTRICT JUDGE, 20 Nov. 2008.
[733] Jackson, Douglas. "Chunk 8." Received by Carl Mullan, *Chunk 8*, 27 Mar. 2020.

In response, AUSA Jonathan Haray cited Brian Grow's Business Week article of December 2005 that Jackson, and others in the industry, believed was produced with aid and input directly from USSS Special Agents. Referencing Brian Grow, the word "shill" comes to mind. Yet, even Grow's article had contained no claims that Jackson "opposed government regulation of financial institutions and the banking industry." The only reference to Jackson's "philosophy" had been:

[Grow] What's the philosophy behind e-gold?
[Jackson] My concern...was that historically it looked like a lot of the suffering of recent centuries -- some of the scale of wars, some of the economic dislocations -- could be traced back to credit cycles, and that credit cycles could be traced back to monetary manipulation. I wanted to try to create a system that was not subject to discretion, that was rules-based and predictable.[734]

In this article, rather than expressing resistance to government regulation, the piece quoted Jackson saying:

We want the regulatory focus to be on OmniPay, because OmniPay is where money or value -- as it's defined in regulation and legislation – comes into play. We've been making the case that OmniPay is really not a money-service business either, but we are close enough to it that it makes sense for it to observe the spirit of the Bank Secrecy Act as it has been modified by the Patriot Act.

Some of these things get into the area of legal opinion and regulatory questions, which I believe are a little bit complex. We have been in this process of dialogue and discussion with [regulators] as we try to assess what is the appropriate way to regulate e-gold vis-à-vis U.S. regulations.[735]

In a 2020 email, Jackson explained what occurred next in the hearing.

For the first hour or so of the hearing, all was playing out according to that script. But around noon, Rimon once again launched into her gratuitous sniping seeking to play up allegations that we had turned a blind eye to child pornography – the attack that had served the prosecution so well in its years of efforts to demonize and isolate the

[734] Ibid
[735] Ibid

companies with reputation attacks. But this was in violation of the mutual agreement that she would not go there at sentencing since, after all, all parties knew all along it was a propagandistic lie.

Joshua Berman immediately stood up and objected, basically forcing her to eat her words. Then shortly afterward was my opportunity to speak for the first time in the nearly two years we had litigated before Judge Collyer.[736]

The first Defendant to be sentenced was Reid Jackson followed by Barry Downey, who was convicted of the exact same charges as Reid Jackson. Reid's Attorney, Ms. Michelle Peterson had a chance to address the Court before sentencing:

He's[Reid] pled guilty to a crime that does not require that he knew that he was breaking the law and that's why he was able to plead guilty to it. He knew and he fully accepts it, he knew how E-Gold, GSR, OmniPay, how they operated. He was aware that there were requirements for companies to be licensed. He just didn't put those two together. He didn't believe that the way OmniPay, GSR and E-Gold operated required a license and he based that on the information that he was receiving from counsel.

The company received bad legal advice. And they based their belief that they could continue to act the way they were on advice that there was no way they could lose the motion to dismiss that would ultimately be filed before Your Honor.

And because of that bad legal advice, combined with, I think the government also pointed out the criminal activity that they had to be aware of because they saw it on Foxx news, I'm not going to go there. I'd love to go there but I won't. But you can't assume that because you see allegations on Fox News that Mr. Jackson knew that there was criminal activity going on in the company.

In fact, he was assured repeatedly that his brother, Dr. Jackson, was doing everything in his power to assist law enforcement. That wasn't something that Mr. Reid Jackson was tasked with, but he saw the public persona of his brother testifying in Congress assisting M.C. Mack, assisting law enforcement, doing everything in his power to make sure that bad people who use the system were being dealt with. That's what he saw. At the same time that he heard the company's lawyers telling him you're not a

---

[736] Jackson, Douglas. "Chunk 8." Received by Carl Mullan, *Chunk 8*, 27 Mar. 2020.

money transmitting business, you don't deal in cash, you will win this argument.[737]

Moments before delivering Reid Jackson's final sentence, Judge Collyer spoke directly to him, and his Attorney Ms. Peterson, regarding Reid's activity while working at e-gold & G&SR. The Judge said:

> And so I also accept her[Peterson's] you had no intentions of violating the law, that you were being a systems analyst in trying to grow a business.[738]

Here is a brief section[Partial Text] of the Judge's statement concerning Reid Jackson's sentencing.

> THE COURT: ...So what it seems to me the thing to do is to sentence you to six months but to suspend execution of sentence and place you on probation for 36 months. That way you are sentenced, but you don't go to jail. Your sentence is suspended and unless you do something else that's illegal in connection with this effort, it will remain suspended.
> THE COURT: It's the judgment of the Court that you, Reid A. Jackson, are hereby committed to the custody of the U.S. Bureau of Prisons to be imprisoned on Count IV for 180 days. Execution of sentence is suspended as to all 180 days and the Court places you on probation for a term of 36 months. During the course of your term of probation, you shall perform 300 hours of community service, at least 100 hours in each year of your probation. You are further ordered to pay a $100 special assessment and a $2500 fine.
> -You shall pay the balance of the fine owed at a rate of no less than $100 each month and shall provide verification of payment to the Probation Office.
> -You shall provide the Probation Office with your income tax returns, authorization for release of credit information, and any other business or financial information which you have a control or interest. The Probation Office shall release the presentence investigation report to all appropriate agencies in order to execute the sentence of the Court.[739]

Towards the end of the sentencing hearing, while providing details of Reid's sentence,

---

[737] Ibid

[738] Docket No. CR 07-109. UNITED STATES OF AMERICA vs. E-GOLD LTD, GOLD & SILVER RESERVE LTD, DOUGLAS L. JACKSON, BARRY K. DOWNEY, REID A. JACKSON. TRANSCRIPT OF SENTENCE BEFORE THE HONORABLE ROSEMARY M. COLLYER UNITED STATES DISTRICT JUDGE, 20 Nov. 2008. p.24

[739] Ibid

the Judge added this statement about Reid Jackson and also invited later counsel or other parties to rely on this statement, if ever needed:

> [...] everything about that I know about him and sort of almost conceded by the government is that his intent was not to violate the law. That's for Mr. Reid Jackson if anybody ever needs it.[740]

The Judge then called for a short break. After a brief recess, the Judge returned and the Court began sentencing Defendant Barry Downey. Judge Collyer asked if Downey wanted to make a statement to the Court.

> THE COURT: Mr. Downey, did you want to say something?
> DEFENDANT DOWNEY: Good morning, Your Honor.
> THE COURT: Good morning, sir.
> THE DEFENDANT: I do appreciate the opportunity to say something to you. I appreciated all along the time you put into this in preparing and obviously reading the voluminous documents that have been submitted, I truly appreciate that. You treated me with respect and everyone else here with respect. I appreciate that deeply. I hope you also, and I think you have indicated that you understand none of us, I did not intend to do anything that would be out of compliance with any applicable rules or laws or regulations. But as you ruled earlier this year, I was wrong and obviously, I stand here before you admitting that on this D.C. statute and regulation on the licensing for the company for D.C. I would ask, Your Honor, that in your sentencing of me that, I would ask that you at least give me the ability to continue practicing in that area where I could continue to support my family, stand with my wife for the care that she needs without interruption and that I be able to continue to provide for my family and community in the area that I practice, I truly appreciate that.
> THE COURT: Thank you, sir.

Next, Defense Attorney Barry Pollack, representing Downey, addressed the Court submitting that Downey's culpability was at most comparable to Reid Jackson and did not exceed it. He concluded that any sentence the Court imposes on Downey would be comparable to Reid's penalty. Pollock expressed that as a licensed attorney, Downey had additional restrictions and consequences.

He self-reported to the bars of the District of Columbia and Maryland of that fact,

---

[740] Ibid p.57

and as a result, will have to fight to retain his law license which means retaining his livelihood.

It means retaining medical coverage for his family. There is no question that Mr. Downey regardless of what this Court does today will have suffered enormous consequences as a result of the facts that bring us here.[741]

The Judge continued:

For Mr. Barry Downey, the seriousness of the offense remains serious although what we're talking about is the failure to register. Now the failure to register is what leads to the ability of criminals to make use of the E-Gold system for nefarious purposes and abuse the system if you want.[742]

The plea agreements that were extended by the government certainly reflect that. The plea agreement   that was extended to Mr. Downey was identical to the plea agreement that was extended to Mr. Jackson. The government's sentencing recommendation reflects that. The sentencing recommendation by the government is the same for Mr. Downey as it is for Mr. Jackson.[743]

Defense Attorney Pollock stated:

Mr. Downey as a result of his failure in judgment, not his criminal intent, but his failure in judgment, has suffered and will suffer lasting consequences, financially, emotionally, reputationally, he will suffer. And that his sentence should be the same; that is, six months suspended with three years of probation and 300 hours of community service, a fine of $2500 and a special assessment of $100.

Judge Collyer handed down the final sentence for Downey:

THE COURT: All right. It's the judgment of the Court that you, Barry K. Downey, are hereby committed to the custody of the U.S. Bureau of Prisons to be imprisoned on Count IV for 180 days. Execution of sentence is suspended as to all 180 days and the Court places you on probation for a term of 36 months. You are further ordered to pay $100 special assessment and a $2500 fine and to perform 300 hours of

---

[741] Ibid
[742] Ibid
[743] Ibid

442

community service, at least 100 hours in each year.[744]

After passing down this sentence, the Judge made additional statements regarding Downey that included, "And I believe him when he says that he didn't intend to violate the law. It happened that way, it came out that way. He didn't intend it to be a violation."[745]

Reid Jackson, Douglas' brother, and e-gold® co-founder/Director Barry Downey were each sentenced to three years of probation, 300 hours of community service, and ordered to pay a $2,500 fine and a $100 assessment.

The next Defendant to face sentencing was Dr. Douglas Jackson. Defense Attorney Joshua Berman represented Jackson and addressed the court.

> THE COURT: All right. Are we ready to proceed to Mr. Douglas Jackson?
> MR. BERMAN: Yes, Your Honor. I believe I can now say good afternoon.
>
> MR. BERMAN: I expect you will hear from Dr. Jackson. I believe he will make remarks to this Court and I anticipate knowing how he feels about this case and having spoken with him for hundreds of hours that he's incredibly sorry for what he did for his role in E-Gold and GS&R's inability to stem the misuse of the platforms that he conceived of and that he built.[746]

Jackson addressed the Court, delivering this emotional statement.

> THE COURT: All right. Does Dr. Jackson want to speak?
> MR. BERMAN: I believe so, Your Honor.
> DEFENDANT DOUGLAS JACKSON: Good afternoon, Your honor.
> THE COURT: Good afternoon, sir.
> DEFENDANT DOUGLAS JACKSON: Thank you very much for this opportunity to speak. I will be brief. But there are several things I wanted you to hear from my heart. First, I want you to know that I take absolute full responsibility for my actions. As I told you when I stood here at the guilty pleas, E-Gold and GS&R were companies that I founded, I conceived and I take responsibility for their failures and my criminal conduct. I apologize for violating the law, for not licensing these entities and for profiting from the proceeds of criminal conduct.

---

[744] Ibid

[745] Ibid p.58

[746] Docket No. CR 07-109. UNITED STATES OF AMERICA vs. E-GOLD LTD, GOLD & SILVER RESERVE LTD, DOUGLAS L. JACKSON, BARRY K. DOWNEY, REID A. JACKSON. TRANSCRIPT OF SENTENCE BEFORE THE HONORABLE ROSEMARY M. COLLYER UNITED STATES DISTRICT JUDGE, 20 Nov. 2008.

I also want to apologize to my family. I have hurt and disappointed those I love the most. And for this, I am truly sorry. My family has always trusted me to support them, provide for them, do the right thing and I let them down. My actions have caused us great financial pain, and emotional pain. I've shamed my family. I will have to live with this every day. I'm desperate to put this behind us. While I have said it to her many times in private, I want to publicly apologize to ███████, my faithful and true wife of 30 years. I know this has been an extraordinary financial and emotional burden on her. I am so sorry I caused this pain.

I also want to let my boys Ben and Sam know how much I love them, care for them, and will always be there for them. ███████ and I brought them into our home. Those are the single greatest decisions we ever made in our lives. There aren't words for the love I feel for them. They're good boys. And they have shown a great deal of courage throughout this entire process. I wouldn't ever want to do them, to cause them pain and I am so sorry I have put you boys through this. I apologize for taking up this Court's and Your Honor's valuable and significant time, energy and resources in dealing with this matter. I also want the government to know that I respect their efforts and apologize to them for having to expend resources on the companies.

Having served this country for 16 years in the U.S. Army I have an honest respect for those who serve the public like Ms. Rimon, Ms. Peretti, Mr. Haray and their team. I want to also express my remorse for the harm I have visited on my dear friends Reid and Barry because of their years of sacrifice to support E-Gold, my life's work. Your Honor, I have always tried to do the right thing. For over a decade I tried to save and help lives as a radiation oncologist. I then founded E-Gold because I believe that a currency backed by gold is safer, more secure, more stable than a currency that does not have the same backing.

But I didn't do the things I should have done to make the payment system less vulnerable to abuse and I'm very sorry for that. Looking forward, I am grateful and hopeful for another chance to do it right.

I welcome the compliance regime that will establish to do everything we can to ensure that never again is E-Gold a system abused by criminals. I promise to undertake to do everything humanly possible to make it work. One final comment. I want to thank my lawyers, Machalagh and Josh, for the hundreds of hours they have volunteered on this effort. I'm very grateful that the Court appointed them.[747]

At 2:45pm that day, after Dr. Jackson addressed the court, Judge Collyer took an abrupt break and retired to her chambers. She stated, "I'm going to step down for a few minutes. I want to review some things before I finalize a decision on this."[748]

Jackson recalls she was gone between 30 and 45 minutes. Upon her return, he observed a "dramatic turnaround" in her behavior.[749] He recalled, that the first part of the of the hearing had felt scripted and in his opinion, "all was playing out according to that script."[750]

After this dramatic break, Jackson sensed that "everything had changed,"[751] and he described the Judge as having "deviated from the show trial script."[752] Jackson recalled:

> When she returned it was immediately apparent that something had changed and that she had even gone so far as to write up different working notes. She took pains to state for the record:
>
> "I have no doubt that Dr. Jackson has respect for law."
>
> "I will note that in terms of the anonymity and the privacy the very fact that E-Gold kept such credible records does as argued by counsel have some impact on whether or not this was a business that was really trying to operate in the shadows or not."
>
> "he did have bad legal advice on the question of whether or not the businesses needed to be registered and licensed."
>
> "the intent was not there to engage in illegal conduct."
>
> And finally, with respect to a sentence of incarceration for Dr. Jackson she observed: "The government's arguing for 14 months…[but taking the concept of "related conduct", synonym for "relevant conduct" into account] makes for a guideline range

[747] Docket No. CR 07-109. UNITED STATES OF AMERICA vs. E-GOLD LTD, GOLD & SILVER RESERVE LTD, DOUGLAS L. JACKSON, BARRY K. DOWNEY, REID A. JACKSON. TRANSCRIPT OF SENTENCE BEFORE THE HONORABLE ROSEMARY M. COLLYER UNITED STATES DISTRICT JUDGE, 20 Nov. 2008.

[748] Docket No. CR 07-109. UNITED STATES OF AMERICA vs. E-GOLD LTD, GOLD & SILVER RESERVE LTD, DOUGLAS L. JACKSON, BARRY K. DOWNEY, REID A. JACKSON. TRANSCRIPT OF SENTENCE BEFORE THE HONORABLE ROSEMARY M. COLLYER UNITED STATES DISTRICT JUDGE, 20 Nov. 2008. p.108

[749] Jackson, Douglas. "P.352 to End." Received by Carl Mullan, P.352 to End, 23 May 2020.

[750] Jackson, Douglas. "Chunk 8." Received by Carl Mullan, Chunk 8, 27 Mar. 2020.

[751] Ibid

[752] Jackson, Douglas. "P.352 to End." Received by Carl Mullan, P.352 to End, 23 May 2020.

of a 108 to a 135 months."

After careful analysis of multiple factors, her startling conclusion was:
"I cannot find that it's appropriate to incarcerate him just to send a signal to other people when that's the only reason that would be, that would make at all sense to send him to a term in jail."[753] [754]

His final sentence included:

- Time served;
- A three year term of supervised release, on each Count I and III, served concurrently;
- 300 hours of community service, with a minimum of 100 hours in each year up until 300;
- A six month term of home detention with electronic monitoring[Ankle] to be paid by the defendant;
- Special assessment that was immediately payable to the Clerk of the D.C. District Court[755]

Additionally, the Court found that Jackson could not pay a fine and therefore waived the imposition of a fine in his case.[756] Jackson's total out of pocket expense from the guilty plea was $200, to cover the cost of the electronic monitoring service.

For six months, Jackson was restricted to his residence at all times except for employment, education, religious services, and other activities required to be pre-approved by the probation officer. During the November 20, 2008 sentencing, the Judge made the following statements about Dr. Jackson and e-gold.

To provide just punishment for the offense. Just punishment here does not require a sentence of incarceration. I think that Dr. Jackson has suffered, will suffer, will continue to suffer and may never be successful at E-Gold, but I think that that factor suggests that a jail term is not necessary.
The Court shall also consider the nature and circumstances of the offense and the

---

[753] Jackson, Douglas. "Chunk 8." Received by Carl Mullan, Chunk 8, 27 Mar. 2020.
[754] Docket No. CR 07-109. UNITED STATES OF AMERICA vs. E-GOLD LTD, GOLD & SILVER RESERVE LTD, DOUGLAS L. JACKSON, BARRY K. DOWNEY, REID A. JACKSON. TRANSCRIPT OF SENTENCE BEFORE THE HONORABLE ROSEMARY M. COLLYER UNITED STATES DISTRICT JUDGE, 20 Nov. 2008.
[755] Ibid
[756] Ibid

history and characteristics of the defendant. The history and characteristics of the defendant are for all intents and purposes up to this period of time and this moment in my courtroom, the history and characteristics of the defendant have been very admirable.

He's an educated man who has used his brain for the benefit of other people. He's adopted two children who he loves, he has a close family relationship to which he's been a good father. He has used his imagination and his intelligence to come up with the concepts that he's dealing with now. And all of those things are positives. He also has no prior criminal record.

The nature and circumstances of the offense we're back into this sort of gray, funny, sort of difficult area where the intent was not there to engage in illegal conduct. It was at least naivety about this all. The ability of others to work and use what was intended to be a sort of perfectly good system for their own ill-conceived purposes and then the desire of the inventor to protect that system and not let the government take it apart, to keep it as intended, to keep it private and maybe anonymous.

I will note that in terms of the anonymity and the privacy the very fact that E-Gold kept such credible records does as argued by counsel have some impact on whether or not this was a business that was really trying to operate in the shadows or not.[757]

Douglas Lee Jackson, M.D., was sentenced on November 20, 2008. The digital currency pioneer had faced a maximum sentence of twenty years in prison and a $500,000 fine.[758]

G&SR forfeited $1,750,000 of funds to the government. A DOJ letter, outlining the Plea Agreement, detailed these terms. [Partial text]

9. Forfeiture

Criminal Forfeiture. The Company agrees to criminal forfeiture in the form of a money judgment of $1,750,000.00, which it agrees constitutes an amount of funds involved in the offenses to which it will plead guilty. The Company agrees that it and defendant Gold & Silver Reserve, Inc. will be jointly and severally liable for satisfaction of the money judgment.

[...]

The Government agrees that $1. 75 million will constitute the total amount

---

[757] CASE NUMBER: 07-167-M-01. *UNITED STATES OF AMERICA V. E-GOLD LIMITED, GOLD & SILVER RESERVE, INC., DOUGLAS L. JACKSON, BARRY K. DOWNEY and REID A. JACKSON.* SENTENCING MEMORANDUM OF GOLD & SILVER RESERVE, INC., Nov. 2008.

[758] Zetter, Kim. "e-gold Founder Pleads Guilty to Money Laundering." *Wired.com*, 25 July 2008, www.wired.com/2008/07/e-gold-founder/.

forfeitable to the Government as a result of the crimes to which the defendant will plead guilty.[759]

On July 21, 2008, the law firm of Fuerst Humphrey Ittleman submitted to the Department of the Treasury registration forms on behalf of the Companies registering them as Money Services Businesses. On August 8, 2008, the Department of Treasury sent notices acknowledging the registrations.[760]

Within thirty days, Fuerst Humphrey Ittleman sent each state an application for a license or a letter seeking an advisory opinion on the Companies' obligations to be licensed in the respective state. In the advisory opinion requests, the letters explained how each company operated and sought an opinion as to whether the state required licensure under those circumstances.[761]

The period between July 2008 and April 2009, kept Jackson busy upgrading the e-gold® platform to conform with U.S. financial regulations. It was an optimistic time, and he posted many upbeat progress reports on the e-gold blog.

> September 19, 2008
> Enhancements to e-gold's Customer Identification Program[762]
> October 10, 2008
> e-gold® update: U.S. State Licensing and Customer Identification[763]
> October 19, 2008
> e-gold® update: Customer Identification, Identity Document Review[764]

Day by day, Jackson and the other company executives still operating e-gold® were preparing to reopen the company, to the public, as a licensed and regulated U.S. Financial business.

However, Jackson's plan was never realized and due to the inability to obtain state licensing as required under the Plea Agreement. E-gold® voluntarily halted the execution of Spend instructions in January 2009. The section of the agreement outlining federal

---

[759] Peretti, Kimberly Kiefer. "Plea Agreement." Received by Bernard S. Grimm, Esq., *Department of Justice*, United States Attorney, 18 Jan. 2008, pp. 1–13.

[760] Jackson, Douglas. "Chunk 8." Received by Carl Mullan, *Chunk 8*, 27 Mar. 2020.

[761] Ibid

[762] Jackson, Douglas. "Enhancements to e-gold's Customer Identification Program." *'e-gold Blog'*, Archive.org, 19 Sept. 2008, web.archive.org/web/20090626091831/blog.e-gold.com/2008/09/enhancements-to.html.

[763] Jackson, Douglas. "e-gold Update: U.S. State Licensing and Customer Identification." *'e-gold Blog'*, Archive.org, 10 Oct. 2008, web.archive.org/web/20091125044023/blog.e-gold.com/2008/10/e-gold-update.html.

[764] Jackson, Douglas. "e-gold Update: Customer Identification, Identity Document Review." *'e-gold Blog'*, Archive.org, 19 Oct. 2008, web.archive.org/web/20091224044855/blog.e-gold.com/2008/10/e-gold-update-c.html.

registration and state licensing was copied below from a DOJ letter.

10. **Registration as a Money Services Business**

The Company agrees that it and Gold & Silver Reserve, Inc. are "financial institutions" as defined in 31 U.S.C. § 5312(a)(2) and are money services businesses under 31 C.F.R. § 03.1 l(uu)(5). Further, the Company agrees that the e-gold operation (including both e-gold, Ltd. and Gold & Silver Reserve, Inc. doing business as OmniPay) is a money transmitting business within the meaning of 18 U.S. C. § 1960, and, as such, may not operate without a money transmitting license in States that require licensing of businesses engaged in money transmitting and without   registration with the Department of Treasury (FinCEN) pursuant to 31 U.S.C. § 5330 and 31 C.F.R.§ 103.41.

Accordingly, the Company will not engage in operation of the e-gold digital currency system, or any other digital currency system, until it has registered with FinCEN. In addition, within thirty (30) days of entering this Plea Agreement, the Company will submit applications to obtain State licenses in States that require licensing of businesses engaged in money transmitting or submit a request for an advisory opinion from such a State that the Company is not required to be licensed. The Company shall obtain any State license to engage in money transmitting (or advisory opinion stating that a license is not required) within six (6) months of entry of this Plea Agreement or stop conducting business in any State where such money transmitting license (or advisory opinion) has not been obtained.[765]

Florida Denies Money Transmitter License

In April 2009, the State of Florida denied e-gold's Money Transmitter license application because of Jackson's criminal conviction. When the plea agreements were signed, Jackson and the other Defendants were unaware that pleading guilty to a felony conviction would bar them from receiving a Money Transmitter license. Jackson explained the situation in a 2020 email.

> More importantly, though the defendants were unaware of it at the time, there was another, more nuanced, Catch-22. The fact that the companies had been compelled to declare themselves "financial institutions" and to register with FinCEN as "Money Services Businesses," not only freed the Florida Office of Financial Regulation from any obligation to make a determination whether license was required but also

---

[765] Peretti, Kimberly Kiefer. "Plea Agreement." Received by Bernard S. Grimm, Esq., *Department of Justice*, United States Attorney, 18 Jan. 2008, pp. 1–13.

precluded the OFR from making a determination that license was not required. The full irony of this did not become apparent until May 2017.[766]

In June, Kim Zetter wrote another article for Wired.com entitled *Bullion and Bandits: The Improbable Rise and Fall of e-gold.*

> After the years of investigations and legal pressure from all sides, two facts were apparent, e-gold's governance model had resisted all attempts by the IRS, USSS, DOJ, and others to seize the physical gold bullion and the government's massive legal assault never forcibly closed e-gold Ltd. or G&SR. Furthermore, both companies continued to meet financial obligations and G&SR never bounced a payroll check.[767]

Douglas Jackson's six-month-long house arrest ended in June 2009. A November 2013 Financial Times article by Stephen Foley stated: "For several years, Mr. Jackson had hoped to resurrect e-gold himself, but it became clear he would not be able to obtain the money transmitter licenses required in most US states."[768]

Community service

The Judge sentenced the three individual Defendants to 300 hours of community service. Attorney Barry Downey fulfilled his community service obligation within the first year, providing at least ten hours per week of pro bono legal services in a Baltimore community-based legal aid clinic. Reid Jackson took on a research project for the Economic Development Commission of Florida's Space Coast, evaluating the prospects for establishing and fostering a renewable energy industry cluster in Brevard County, Florida. Douglas Jackson assisted his brother with the research, analysis, and document drafting for his first 150 hours of service. But he was then offered the opportunity to fulfill his remaining 150 hours with a single week of full-time physical labor in a joint program organized by the United States Probation Office for the Middle District of Florida. As Dr. Jackson later related:

> The Probation Offices throughout the Middle District had worked out an arrangement for maintenance and improvement projects in the Ocala National Forest. Due to the

[766] Jackson, Douglas. "Chunk 8." Received by Carl Mullan, *Chunk 8*, 27 Mar. 2020.

[767] Zetter, Kim. "Bullion and Bandits: The Improbable Rise and Fall of e-gold." *Wired.com*, 6 Sept. 2009, www.wired.com/2009/06/e-gold/.

[768] Foley, Stephen. "e-gold Founder Backs New Bitcoin Rival." *Financial Times*, Financial Times, 28 Nov. 2013, www.ft.com/content/f7488616-561a-11e3-96f5-00144feabdc0.

fact that it was residential, that is, since we were housed on-site, they were able to credit participants with 24 hours per day. I liked to joke with my family that I was working on the chain gang but in reality this was far from some "Cool Hand Luke" gulag. The food was good and the work was paced as to avoid risk of heat injury. The overall experience reminded me of what I had read about with Civilian Conservation Corp projects back during Roosevelt's New Deal Program in the 1930s. In fact, some of the facilities we were working to refresh involved CCC-era infrastructure.

Overall, it was a godsend for me because the ongoing EDC project had been such a drain on my creative energies as to hamper efforts that were just getting underway to re-engineer e-gold from the ground up.[769]

♦

A new 'gotcha' emerged

After the legal case, Judge Collyer, having already stated "the [e-gold] system conceptually, is not illegal" had mandated:

> Now that legal issues are resolved, he [Douglas Jackson] has committed e-gold and G&SR to a vigorous compliance and oversight program which could only succeed if he were there to head the companies. Since there is no reason to shut down e-gold and G&SR, and every reason to have them come into legal compliance, a sentence of incarceration for Dr. Jackson would be counterproductive.[770]

In keeping with this constructive prospect, new counsel was retained[771] with the expertise required to guide the companies as they navigated their re-emergence as licensed financial institutions.

But by mid-2009 it became apparent that e-gold would be unable to obtain the required state licenses. The Jacksons had to face the realization there was no alternative but to permanently suspend execution of customer Spend orders, wind down the system, liquidate the bullion reserves and distribute the proceeds in the form of conventional money payments to customers. Technically this could be accomplished in a straightforward fashion since exchanges from e-gold to conventional government currencies had comprised a major

---

[769] Jackson, Douglas. "Chunk 9." Received by Carl Mullan, Chunk 9, 29 Mar. 2020. DJ redlines 9.pdf

[770] Ibid

[771] In light of Judge Collyer's repeated and pointed observations that the companies had received bad legal advice, G&SR and e-gold Ltd. filed a malpractice suit against the attorneys retained in 2005. This case settled in 2013.

component of OmniPay's normal business. But there was a catch.

Counsel advised that the companies were not allowed to give the customers their money back. To do so could be deemed a violation of parole, a recidivist provision of unlicensed money transmitting services. The only apparent solution was to re-engage with the US government and persuade them to act as middleman for the distribution of funds. As it turned out, this gave the USSS—stung by their failure to seize and forfeit the bullion reserves in accordance with their original design[772]—another bite at the apple.[773]

♦

Value Access Plan (VAP)

Eventually, Jackson's Value Access Plan allowed many past e-gold® account holders, but not all of them, to claim and access the stored value trapped in the platform during the legal case. The idea was to identify two account groups. The first was accounts frozen by e-gold for suspected criminal activity. The second group consisted of accounts that belonged to regular customers entitled to recover the account value. The plan would process suspected illegal accounts first, enabling the early forfeiture of that tranche. The figure represented about five percent of all stored customer value.

Because of gold's price appreciation during the legal case, e-gold® account holders who were able to access their account through the VAP received a value that was two to five hundred percent higher than the account's previous unlocked amount. Here is a chart showing the price of gold in USD from around 1996 – 2013.

---

[772] Per both the 2007 indictment and the PIRO: "the defendants…shall forfeit to the United States any property, real or personal, involved in, or traceable to such property involved in money laundering, in violation of Title 18, United States Code, Section 1956, and in operation of an unlicensed money transmitting business, in violation of Title 18, United States Code, Section 1960; including, but not limited to the following…all precious metals, including gold, silver, platinum, and palladium, that "back" the emetal electronic currency of the E-GOLD operation, wherever located."

[773] Jackson, Douglas. "Chunk 9." Received by Carl Mullan, *Chunk 9*, 29 Mar. 2020. DJ redlines 9.pdf

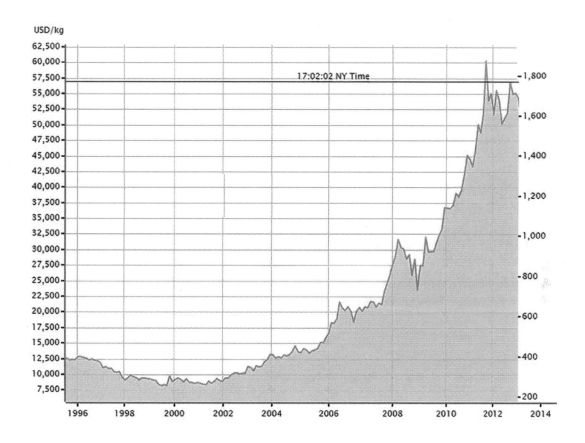

Historic USD price of gold chart from 1995 through 2013.

Rust Consulting

The Court ordered Rust Consulting, a private company located in Maryland, to organize refunds to e-gold® account holders able to prove a legitimate source of e-gold® funds.

In March 2012[774], e-gold® sold all bullion reserves and forwarded approximately $92-95 million to the new government-appointed Claims Administrator. The VAP offered a three-month window for claims. From June 3, 2013, to October 1, 2013, past e-gold® account holders were able to submit a request to claim their frozen value. The firm extended the term to December 31, 2013.[775] In later 2019 emails, Jackson commented on the VAP and

[774] Jackson, Douglas. "Gold Value Access Plan - Monetization Progress Report." *e-Gold Blog*, e-Gold Ltd., 12 Mar. 2012, blog.e-gold.com/2012/03/e-gold-value-access-plan-monetization-progress-report.html.

[775] Jackson, Douglas. "Gold Value Access Plan - Monetization Complete." *e-gold Blog*, e-gold.com, 21 Aug. 2013, blog.e-

the USSS.

> Thanks to the impediments and delays thrown in the way of the e-gold Value Access Plan by the USSS, the residual unclaimed amount the USSS obtained by forfeiture at the end of the Claims window was $45 million.[776]

> $12 million that was the accumulated total of account balances frozen over the years in cases of suspected criminal activity and $1 million that was in a special pot to be distributed in relation to people who had gotten caught up in OFAC country sanctions (but was never distributed because no bank or government agency would assist in disbursing it).[777]

As Jackson later related in a March 2020 email:

> "It would be hard to imagine a situation so fraught with conflict of interest as we encountered when we tried to give customers their money back. Our (i.e. the defendants') understanding when we approached the DOJ was that they would simply act as the middleman for distributing value back to the e-gold customers. But immediately it became apparent they were entering into this arrangement under the auspices of the USSS once again being their "client". And to our horror, the only legal mechanism that was presented as an option was a negotiated consensual forfeiture action. The gist was that the USSS would appoint its own contractor to disburse the funds and any unclaimed amounts at the end of the process would be forfeited to the USSS. So it was immediately obvious that the USSS's pecuniary interest would be best served by making the claims process as difficult as possible, with maximum delay - making it harder when the time came to track down claimants and shepherd them through the process.

> We negotiated a "Letter Agreement" that prescribed a process for liquidating bullion reserves, validating customer claims and distributing proceeds of the liquidation. This was the basis for the subsequent "e-gold Value Access Program" or "e-gold VAP". Under this agreement, the "reasonable expenses" borne by G&SR, which turned out to be well in excess of five million dollars, would be reimbursed by the government at the conclusion. But the overall process was reminiscent of the

gold.com/2013/04/new-post-now-that.html.

[776] Jackson, Douglas. "Re: Quick Question." Received by P. Carl Mullan, *Re: Quick Question*, 12 July 2019.

[777] Ibid

"Gingerbread Man" story in which the Gingerbread Man has no recourse but to cross the stream riding on the fox's snout.

Negotiating the Letter Agreement alone took nearly a year, with the meter running the whole time with very costly legal expenses and the need to maintain sufficient customer service staff to validate claimants once the process commenced.

Then there was another two years, largely consisting of conference calls between the G&SR team[778], our outside counsel, the DOJ's AUSA and the USSS contractor - Rust Consulting. Additionally, a USSS agent would sit in on the calls. His role seemed to be that of the Muppet characters Statler and Waldorf, to chime in from time to time with irrelevant and disruptive insults that seemed designed to impede constructive efforts. One result was that it took years to reach sign-off on the protocol that would enable e-gold software engineers to create the interface and backend code for validating claims and handing them off to Rust for them to sort out bank coordinates and execute the disbursements. By the time the claims process began in 2013, we had been forced to retain support and technical staff sufficient to re-ramp up at scale – a four-year interval. What could have been completed in a few weeks or months in 2009 via OmniPay's normal course of business, with a substantially higher proportion of value disbursed, instead took nearly five years with six million USD out-of-pocket costs for the companies.

The bigger issue was that, as a result of USSS obstructionism, more than three years elapsed before the notification process to potential claimants, which Rust Consulting was tasked with performing, got underway. But this was an interval during which nearly everyone was ditching landlines and switching over to mobile phones, making much contact information useless. Also, with so much time elapsed, it was only natural that many email addresses were no longer valid, thousands of people would have moved and no small number from such a large cohort would have died. Compounding the ineffectiveness of Rust's notification process was the fact that it was postal. Customers who had moved more than a year previously would no longer have mail forwarding and postal notifications in general in such matters are hard to distinguish from the official-looking junk mail notifications we are all deluged with.

A further complicating factor was people spreading disinformation online alleging

---

[778] Reid Jackson oversaw the VAP process. Other members of the G&SR team included Jay Wherley (Lead Developer)_and Randy Trotter (Head of Customer Service, Due Diligence and Investigations)

that the claims process was a trick to lure people into supplying their names and other personal identifying information (including bank account coordinates) to either or both a government list or criminal fraudsters. The result was that tens of thousands of people with modest but by no means trivial balances in the 100-400 USD range apparently elected not to bother revalidating their identities given what they perceived as uncertainties.

About six weeks before the end of the claims window, we were able to ascertain that many thousands of account holders, some with quite significant balances, had not finished the claims process. We obtained an extension and began a feverish effort to contact customers ourselves.
I personally began working through a list starting with higher value accounts and working downward. Many of them took significant time and effort to work through. For instance there was a man who had obtained e-gold by exchange in the late 1990s and hadn't logged in in nearly fifteen years, during which time the value of his e-gold had increased five-fold to exceed twenty thousand USD-equivalent. I ended up needing to check real-estate records, contacting a former business partner of his who had subsequently moved to India and started a boutique distillery, and finally talking with the doorman of the building where I learned he had moved over ten years prior.

In another case, I found through obituary records that an account holder whose account held over 40 thousand worth of e-gold had died two weeks after her initial exchange order had been fulfilled. I tracked down the pastor who had spoken at the funeral who put me in touch with the executor of her estate and finally was able to reach family members.

Through my personal efforts I was able to shepherd account holders who together had aggregate holdings of over 4 million USD through the process.

The last infuriating aspect was that in 2016 I had occasion to reach out again to some of the people I had helped compete the process. Three different individuals claimed they never did receive their distribution - even after jumping though all the hoops, the final one of which was to validate their bank coordinates with Rust."[779]

---

[779] Jackson, Douglas. "Chunk 9." Received by Carl Mullan, *Chunk 9*, 29 Mar. 2020. DJ redlines 9.pdf

2010 - 2011
The MSB Rule & The Prepaid Access Rule

The Judge sentenced e-gold Defendants in November 2008. FinCEN began a public discussion to change the U.S. regulations governing digital currency issuers and exchangers (MSBs) a few months later on May 12, 2009.

> FinCEN Proposes Amendments to MSB Definition
> *Public comments sought for important refinements*
> FinCEN is proposing to revise the MSB definition by describing with more clarity the types of financial activity that will subject a business to the Bank Secrecy Act (BSA) implementing rules.[780]

Recognizing that the Internet and other advances, such as smartphone payments, made it possible for foreign-located MSBs to offer services in the U.S., FinCEN extended the BSA rules to all persons engaging in MSB activities within the U.S. regardless if a person's physical location. The U.S. laws were beginning to catch up with the new technology. The MSB Rule offered this definition of an MSB, "person wherever located doing business, whether or regularly or as an organized or licensed business concern, wholly or in substantial part within the United States."[781] The text below is from the FinCEN website and described the agency's focus.

> In direct support of its BSA Efficiency and Effectiveness Initiative to craft a more narrow definition of MSBs, FinCEN announced a Notice of Proposed Rulemaking (NPRM) designed to make the determination of which businesses qualify as MSBs more straightforward and predictable. FinCEN is proposing to revise the MSB definition by describing with more clarity the types of financial activity that will subject a business to the BSA implementing rules. This proposal will incorporate past FinCEN rulings and policy determinations into the regulatory text and will make it easier for MSBs to determine their responsibilities.[782]

On June 21, 2010, FinCEN announced another proposed rule. The takeaway from

[780] "FinCEN Proposes Amendments to MSB Definition." *Financial Crimes Enforcement Network*, 12 May 2009, edocket.access.gpo.gov/2009/pdf/E9-10864.pdf.

[781] "31 CFR § 1010.100 - General Definitions." Legal Information Institute, Legal Information Institute, 2011, www.law.cornell.edu/cfr/text/31/1010.100.

[782] "Regulatory Efficiency and Effectiveness - 2009." *Regulatory Efficiency and Effectiveness - 2009 | FinCEN.gov*, U.S. Department of the Treasury, 12 May 2009, www.fincen.gov/regulatory-efficiency-and-effectiveness-2009.

this proposed rule change: Digital currency a/k/a "stored value" was re-classified as "prepaid access" and would now be heavily regulated.

> In a Notice of Proposed Rulemaking (NPRM) entitled Amendment to the Bank Secrecy Act Regulations – Definitions and Other Regulations Relating to Prepaid Access, the Financial Crimes Enforcement Network (FinCEN) today proposed new rules that would establish a more comprehensive regulatory framework for non-bank prepaid access.[783]

This change became known as the Prepaid Access Rule, and significant features of this proposal included:[784]

- Renaming "stored value" as "prepaid access" without intending to broaden or narrow the term and defining the term to allow for future changes in technology and prepaid devices;
- Deleting the terms "issuer" and "redeemer" of stored value and adding the terms "provider" and "seller";
- Placing registration requirements on providers of prepaid access and suspicious activity reporting, customer information record keeping, and new transactional record keeping requirements on both providers and sellers of prepaid access; and
- Exempting certain categories of prepaid access products and services posing lower risks of money laundering and terrorist financing from certain requirements.

On July 18, 2011, FinCEN published a final rule (the MSB Rule)[785], updating the regulations regarding money services businesses. The MSB Rule became effective on September 19, 2011. FinCEN did not require compliance with the MSB Rule until January 23, 2012. The MSB Rule clarified that a person's activities, not their formal business status, could allow FinCEN to categorize a person as an MSB. Whether a person engages in Regulated MSB Activity is dependent on the facts and circumstances of each case.

---

[783] Ibid

[784] "FinCEN Proposed Rule Seeks Greater Transparency for Prepaid Access to Help Curb Money Laundering, Terrorist Financing." *FinCEN Proposed Rule Seeks Greater Transparency for Prepaid Access to Help Curb Money Laundering, Terrorist Financing | FinCEN.gov*, U.S. Department of the Treasury - FinCEN, 21 June 2010, www.fincen.gov/news/news-releases/fincen-proposed-rule-seeks-greater-transparency-prepaid-access-help-curb-money.

[785] "FinCEN Clarifies Money Services Businesses Definitions Rule Includes Foreign-Located MSBs Doing Business in U.S." *Financial Crimes Enforcement Network*, FinCEN, 18 July 2011, www.fincen.gov/news/news-releases/fincen-clarifies-money-services-businesses-definitions-rule-includes-foreign.

On July 26, 2011, FinCEN published a final rule (the Prepaid Access Rule)[786] to amend the BSA regulations applicable to MSBs concerning stored value or "prepaid access." The Rule's effective was September 27, 2011. The compliance deadline for 31 C.F.R. § 1022.380 (registration of money services businesses) was January 29, 2012.

The MSB Rule and the Prepaid Access Rule, changed the landscape for all centralized digital currency in the United States and effectively shut-out both foreign and domestic unregulated entities. For the first time, FinCEN required certain foreign-located MSBs with a US presence[any U.S. customers] to follow the BSA rules.

Foreign-operated centralized digital currency companies, such as WebMoney Transfer and GoldMoney, located outside of the U.S., and servicing residents in America, had to comply with these new BSA regulations or withdraw entirely from the U.S. market. Everyone pulled out.

Digital Currency Issuers
Obligations of a Provider of Prepaid Access as an MSB[787]

Registration as an MSB—Non-bank providers of prepaid access are required to register as an MSB with FinCEN[788] and are subject to BSA regulations, including the maintenance of an anti-money laundering ("AML") program, the filing of suspicious activity reports, and the recordkeeping and customer identification requirements described below. On the other hand, if a bank issuer is designated the provider of prepaid access, then neither the bank nor any other participants in that particular prepaid program will be required to register with FinCEN.[789] This exemption for banks does not, however, exempt bank-issued prepaid access or the other participants (e.g., sellers of prepaid access) in that particular prepaid program from their obligations specified in the Final Rule. For example, in a prepaid program in which a bank issues the prepaid access and a retailer sells the prepaid access, the retailer would still be deemed a seller of prepaid access and would be subject to the obligations of a seller of prepaid access.

AML Program—A provider of prepaid access must: (i) establish procedures to verify

---

[786] "FinCEN Issues Prepaid Access Final Rule Balancing the Needs of Law Enforcement and Industry." *Financial Crimes Enforcement Network*, 26 July 2011, www.fincen.gov/news/news-releases/fincen-issues-prepaid-access-final-rule.

[787] "FinCEN's Prepaid Access Rule." *Morrison & Foerster LLP*, By L. Richard Fischer, Obrea O. Poindexter and M. Sean Ruff, 5 Aug. 2011, mofo.com.

[788] 31 C.F.R. § 1022.380.

[789] As noted above, the supplementary information accompanying the Final Rule states that banks that serve as providers of prepaid access are not subject to the Final Rule because FinCEN has excluded banks from the definition of an MSB. In addition, FinCEN states that by "virtue of the regulatory definition of a money services business, neither a bank nor any other participants in the bank-centered prepaid program would be required to register with FinCEN."

the identity of a person who obtains prepaid access under a prepaid program and obtain identifying information concerning that person, including name, date of birth, address and identification number; and (ii) retain access to such identifying information for five years after the last use of the prepaid access device.[790]

Suspicious Activity Reporting—A provider of prepaid access must file with the Treasury Department a report, to the extent and in the manner required under Section 1022.320, of any suspicious transactions relevant to a possible violation of law or regulation.[791]

Recordkeeping—A provider of prepaid access must maintain access to transaction records for a period of five years that are generated in the ordinary course of business and that would be needed to reconstruct prepaid access activation, loads, reloads, purchases, withdrawals, transfers, or other prepaid-related transactions.[792] [793]

Independent Digital Currency Exchange Providers
Seller of Prepaid Access[794]

Under Section 1010.100(ff)(4)(7), a "seller of prepaid access" is defined as any person that receives funds or the value of funds in exchange for an initial loading or subsequent loading of prepaid access if that person triggers coverage under (i) or (ii) below because it either:

(i) Sells prepaid access offered under a prepaid program that can be used before verification of customer identification under Section 1022.210(d)(1)(iv).

- For example, if a business sells closed-loop prepaid access to funds that exceed $2,000 on an individual access device or vehicle, then such business would be a "seller of prepaid access." Similarly, if a business were to sell prepaid access to funds from which more than $1,000 can be initially or subsequently loaded, used or withdrawn, then such business would be a "seller of prepaid access."

- Also, if a business sells immediately usable prepaid access that is open loop, it should not be regulated as a "seller of prepaid access" if at the time of the sale, and before the collection of customer identification material, the prepaid access does not permit: (i) access to funds in excess of $1,000; (ii) international use or person-to-person transfers; or (iii) additional loading of

---

[790] 31 C.F.R. § 1022.210.

[791] 31 C.F.R. § 1022.320.

[792] 31 C.F.R. § 1022.420.

[793] "FinCEN's Prepaid Access Rule." *Morrison & Foerster LLP*, By L. Richard Fischer, Obrea O. Poindexter and M. Sean Ruff, 5 Aug. 2011, mofo.com.

[794] Ibid

the cards at non-depository sources.

(ii) Sells prepaid access (including closed-loop prepaid access) to funds that exceed $10,000 to any person during any one day and has not implemented policies and procedures reasonably adapted to prevent such a sale.

o Coverage as a seller of prepaid access based on selling access to funds that exceed $10,000 to any person during any day can be triggered by the sale of any "prepaid access" regardless of whether such prepaid access is part of a covered "prepaid program." For example, even if a business sells closed-loop cards in which the prepaid access is not to exceed $2,000 and, therefore, is not considered part of a covered "prepaid program," the business still would need to have in place "policies and procedures reasonably adapted to prevent" a sale of prepaid access exceeding $10,000.[795]

Money Transmitter[796]

Under the MSB Rule, a person who provides money transmission services or any other person engaged in the transfer of funds is a money transmitter.[797] The term money transmission services means the acceptance of currency, funds, or other value that substitutes for currency from one person and the transmission of currency, funds, or other value that substitutes for currency to another location or person by any means. The phrase "any means" includes, but is not limited to, "through a financial agency or institution; a Federal Reserve Bank or other facility of one or more Federal Reserve Banks, the Board of Governors of the Federal Reserve System, or both; an electronic funds transfer system network; or an informal value transfer system" (such as a hawala).[798]

Whether a person is a money transmitter is a matter of facts and circumstances.[799] The term money transmitter does not include a person who only:

[795] Ibid

[796] Santangelo, Betty, et al. "FinCEN Issues Final Rules Relating to Money Services Business (MSB) Definitions." *Journal of Investment Compliance*, vol. 13, no. 1, ser. 2012, 2012, pp. 17–22. *2012*, doi:10.1108/15285811211216655.

[797] 31 C.F.R. §1010.100(ff)(5)(i)(A). "An 'informal value transfer system' refers to any system, mechanism, or network of people that receives money for the purpose of making the funds or an equivalent value payable to a third party in another geographic location, whether or not in the same form ... 'Hawala' is one name for a type of informal value transfer system that operates outside of, or parallel to, 'traditional' banking or financial channels." 76 Fed. Reg. at 43,592, n. 50.

[798] 31 C.F.R. §1010.100(ff)(5)(i)(A). "An 'informal value transfer system' refers to any system, mechanism, or network of people that receives money for the purpose of making the funds or an equivalent value payable to a third party in another geographic location, whether or not in the same form ... 'Hawala' is one name for a type of informal value transfer system that operates outside of, or parallel to, 'traditional' banking or financial channels." 76 Fed. Reg. at 43,592, n. 50.

[799] 31 C.F.R. §1010.100(ff)(5)(ii).

1. Provides the delivery, communication, or network access services used by a money transmitter to support money transmission services;
2. Acts as a payment processor to facilitate the purchase of, or payment of a bill for, a good or service through a clearance and settlement system by agreement with the creditor or seller;
3. Operates a clearance and settlement system or otherwise acts as an intermediary solely between BSA regulated institutions. This includes but is not limited to the Fedwire system, electronic funds transfer networks, certain registered clearing agencies regulated by the SEC, and derivatives clearing organizations, or other clearinghouse arrangements established by a financial agency or institution;[800]
4. Physically transports currency, other monetary instruments, other commercial paper, or other value that substitutes for currency as a person primarily engaged in such business, such as an armored car, from one person to the same person at another location or to an account belonging to the same person at a financial institution, provided that the person engaged in physical transportation has no more than a custodial interest in the currency, other monetary instruments, other commercial paper, or other value at any point during the transportation;
5. Provides stored value (now referred to as prepaid access under the Prepaid Access Rule), whether it is opened or closed loop;[801] or
6. Accepts and transmits funds only integral to the sale of goods or the provision of services, other than money transmission services, by the person who is accepting and transmitting the funds.[802]

---

[800] "Persons who solely provide a clearance and settlement system or act as intermediaries between BSA regulated institutions and do not provide other types of money transmission services are mere instrumentalities that the financial institutions use to process their transfers . . . [T]hese instrumentalities, such as the credit card networks, are not included in the definition of 'money transmitter.'" 76 Fed. Reg. at 43,593.

[801] FinCEN intends that both entities involved in the sale and management of stored value programs be excluded. " For example, a department store that offers gift cards that only may be used at that department store, a convenience store that sells network branded cards that may be used anywhere like a credit card, or a program manager who organizes a stored value program and facilitates loading the stored value device are not subject to the MSB rules as money transmitters." 76 Fed. Reg. at 43,594.

[802] 31 C.F.R. §1010.100(ff)(5)(ii)(A)-(F). FinCEN notes that, similar to circumstance (B), " persons that sell goods or provide services other than money transmission services, and only transmit funds as an integral part of that sale of goods or provision of services, are not money transmitters. For example, brokering the sale of securities, commodity contracts, or similar instruments is not money transmission notwithstanding the fact that the person brokering the sale may move funds back and forth between the buyer and seller to effect the transaction." FinCEN also indicates that a similar limitation would apply to "a debt management company that made payments to creditors as the conduit for a negotiated schedule of payments from the debtor to its creditors." 76 Fed. Reg. at 43,594.

After all of these events, Jackson shared these thoughts.

> The e-gold development team went on to establish a next generation system merging the proven monetary and transactional principles of e-gold with much more robust and scalable technology, innovative features and innumerable safeguards that meet not only applicable regulatory requirements but define a new standard for security and prevention of abuses. Even now as I address these questions we are also in the midst of a corporate restructuring designed to generate value for the long suffering shareholders of G&SR. It is definitely "too early to say" how the e-gold initiative plays out.[803]

CMO, Inc. and COEPTIS

The Internet technology that launched e-gold® in the mid-nineties continued to live and grow beyond 2013. The next generation of centralized compliant digital currency based on the concept of e-gold® was Coeptis.

Coeptis is dba of CMO, Inc., a Delaware Corporation (46-2070657) incorporated on February 8th, 2013. CMO, Inc. applied as a foreign corporation[i.e., Delaware] to transact business in Florida on June 10th, 2013. The company provided a Satellite Beach, Florida address for the filing. William A. Cunningham was the Chief Executive Officer. Coeptis/CMO Inc., 927 E New Haven Avenue, Melbourne, Florida 32901, was registered as a payment processing service with the Better Business Bureau.[804] The website address was http://www.globalstandard.com and also http://www.coeptis.com An archived website copy from December 2014, described membership to this platform.

> ### Global Standard Payment System
> COEPTIS provides its Members exclusive access to a unique payments system, which mobilizes the value of gold for electronic payments. Members can use Global Standard Currency in the same manner as any other currency to make direct, immediate, final, secure, and low-cost transactions across a closed platform.
> ### Becoming a Member
> COEPTIS members are required to complete simple yet robust customer identification, verification, and due diligence procedures. Businesses and financial

---

[803] Jackson, Douglas. "A New Beginning." *e-Gold Blog*, e-Gold, 21 July 2008, blog.e-gold.com/2008/07/a-new-beginning.html.

[804] Bureau, Better Business. "Coeptis/CMO Inc.: Better Business Bureau® Profile." *BBB*, 2013, www.bbb.org/us/fl/melbourne/profile/payment-processing-services/coeptiscmo-inc-0733-90330066.

institutions are required to complete a more rigorous review and must agree to protocols designed to enhance consumer safety.

Security Benefits

Members have confidence that they are transacting with the person or business with whom they intend. COEPTIS has already validated the identity of each of its Members. Conversely, members will never have to provide personal or financial information when specifying a Spend instruction. Identity and Privacy are very secure on this closed system.[805]

The COEPTIS organization had applied for a Money Transmitters License in all required U.S. States and did not operate a client account in unlicensed states. In thirty-six U.S. States, COEPTIS was either granted a license or provided a determination indicating that a license was not required.

District of Columbia Money Transmitters License for COEPTIS

In his August 2017 letter to John Roth, regarding issues with the e-gold® case, Jackson compared the 2016 licensing requirements of CMO/Coeptis in the District of Columbia with details from the e-gold® case.

> A further indication of the materiality, if outcome of determinations is held to be the standard, is that in 2016 the DC Department of Insurance, Securities and Banking (DISB) made a determination (Exhibit 7) that neither CMO Inc., nor an exchange service affiliated with CMO, required licensing as a money transmitter under the DC statutes. This is relevant in that every aspect of the system deployed by CMO had been invented and developed by Douglas Jackson, duplicating the business model, institutional arrangements and transaction logic of the e-gold system. Similarly, the affiliated exchange business, Fidelis FX was modeled after the OmniPay business of Gold & Silver Reserve in that every exchange conducted by Fidelis or Omnipay entailed the purchase or sale of the digital currency issued and circulated by CMO or e-gold respectively.

> The difference between the 2016 DC DISB determination and the judicial opinion issued in this case was entirely due to the DISB basing their 2016 determination on facts and circumstances.[806]

---

[805] Inc., CMO. "COEPTIS." *COEPTIS*, CMO, Inc., 17 Dec. 2014, web.archive.org/web/20141217034458/coeptis.com/.

[806] Jackson, Douglas. "Investigation Request." Received by John Roth, Inspector General, US Dept. of Homeland Security, 24 Aug. 2017, Indian Harbour Beach, FL.

On October 14, 2015, Bill Cunningham sent a letter to the Department of Insurance, Securities and Banking for the District of Columbia. This department is responsible for a money transmitter license in Washington, D.C. Cunningham requested an official opinion as to whether CMO, Inc. (dba COEPTIS) would need to obtain a money transmitter license in the District of Columbia. Washington, D.C. is the jurisdiction in which the federal government had charged e-gold® for operating an unlicensed money transmitting business. The institutional arrangements, business model, and transaction logic of CMO/Coeptis was designed, developed, and subsidized by e-gold Ltd's successor company, Fulcrum IP Corporation. CMO/Coeptis was nearly identical to e-gold®.

Amazingly, on June 23, 2016, Assistant General Counsel for District of Columbia, Charlotte W. Parker, responded to Bill Cunningham. In her letter, she stated, "Therefore, based on the position of the Banking Bureau and an analysis of Exhibits A, B, and C, CMO, Inc., dba COEPTIS does not require a money transmitter license."

> June 23, 2016
> William A. Cunningham
> Chief Executive Officer
> COEPTIS
> 927 New Haven Avenue, Suite 209
> Melbourne, Florida 32901
>
> Re: Money Transmitter License
>
> Dear Mr. Cunningham:
>
> This is in response to your letter, dated October 14, 2015 in which you request an opinion as to whether the company of CMO, Inc., dba COEPTIS (COEPTIS)[807] needs to obtain a money transmitter license in the District of Columbia, which would be issued by the Department of Insurance, Securities and Banking.
>
> According to the COEPTIS' Global Standard System Overview, which is attached hereto as Exhibit A and incorporated herein by reference, COEPTIS intends to launch a Global Standard System (System) which will use a privately issued currency (AUG) that will be 100% reserved by physical gold. The System will only

---

[807] Per an e-mail dated June 16, 2016, Carol Van Cleer, a partner at Manatt, Phelps & Phillips, LLP informed the Department of Insurance, Securities and Banking (Department) that CMO, Inc. had decided to use Global Standard System as the dba and not COEPTIS. However, since the standard system overview, submitted to the Department, uses the term COEPTIS throughout, that term will be employed herein.

operate online and will not have any physical locations in the District of Columbia, but it will conduct business with District of Columbia residents.

As described in Exhibit A, the System will use a closed/centralized settlement platform (Settlement Platform) to make internet payments. National currency will not be received, dispensed, or used on the Settlement Platform. COEPTIS will not provide for any conversion of AUG to national currency or national currency for AUG. Further, according to Exhibit A, exchange transactions, using national currency, will only be conducted by independent financial institutions that are engaged in exchange services. These financial institutions, which will be independent, will be appropriately licensed or authorized in the states(s) and/or country in which they conduct business.

Based on both Exhibit A and Exhibit B, which is attached hereto and incorporated herein by reference, the Department's Banking Bureau has concluded that COEPTIS does not require a money transmitter license pursuant to the District of Columbia Money Transmitters Act of 2000, D.C. Official Code 26-1001 et. Seq. (2012 Repl.), because "the transactions as described to not involve the transmission of money." See email from Tiwana Hicks, Department Licensing Manager, attached hereto as Exhibit C and incorporated herein by reference. In Exhibit C Ms. Hicks, citing Exhibit B, notes that "COEPTIS is engaged in a two party business model that does not involve the transfer of 'money' or a 'a medium of exchange authorized or adopted by a government as part of its currency.'"

Therefore, based on the position of the Banking Bureau and an analysis of Exhibits A, B, and C, CMO, Inc., dba COEPTIS does not require a money transmitter license.

If, however, any of the facts in the attached Exhibits change, including any change in ownership or name, CMO, Inc., dba COEPTIS, shall submit those changes to the Department for further review and analysis.

Thank you.

Charlotte W. Parker

Assistant General Counsel

Attachments:

Exhibit A – COEPTIS' Global Standard System Overview

Exhibit B – Memorandum to Chester McPherson, Acting Commissioner for the Department of Insurance, Securities and Banking, from Christopher Weaver, Associate Commissioner for Banking

Exhibit C – E-mail from Tiwana Hicks, Licensing Manager, Banking Bureau, Department of Insurance, Securities and Banking.

Cc: Carol R. Van Cleet
Manatt, Phelps & Phillips, LLP
1050 Connecticut Avenue, NW, Suite 600, Washington, DC 20036[808]

◆

Texas

On December 8, 2015, the Texas Department of Banking sent COEPTIS a determination letter stating:

"The Texas Department of Banking has determined that your proposed activity does not require a money transmission license."[809]

Once again, this was in marked contrast with the Texas Department of Banking actions in February 2010. As e-gold Ltd. and G&SR were struggling to survive in the aftermath of the e-gold case, Texas had fined the companies (jointly) $135,525 "for conducting an unlicensed money services business in Texas."[810]

◆

The United States Secret Service

The following paragraphs describe the work of the U.S. Secret Service. This content appeared in Verizon's 2010 Data Breach Investigations Report, Study conducted by Verizon RISK Team in cooperation with the United States Secret Service.[811]

Background on USSS

[808] Parker, Charlotte W. "Re: Money Transmitter License." Received by William A. Cunningham, *Government of the District of Columbia*, CMO, Inc., 23 June 2016, pp. 1–3.

[809] Wood, Daniel C. "RE: Money Transmission Licensing Inquiry." Received by William Cunningham, CEO · CMO, Inc. d/b/a Coeptis, 2601 N. Lamar Blvd, 8 Dec. 2015, Austin, TX. Daniel C. Wood Assistant General Counsel, Texas Department of Banking

[810] Loomis, Deborah H. "Re: Egold Ltd. and Gold & Silver Reserve, Inc. Penalty." Received by Ms. Carol R. Van Cleef, Esq. Patton Boggs LLP, 2550 M Street, N.W., 5 Feb. 2010, Washington, District of Columbia.

[811] Baker, Wade, et al. *2010 Data Breach Investigations Report, Study Conducted by Verizon RISK Team in Cooperation with the United Stated Secret Service*. Verizon Business, 2010, *2010 Data Breach Investigations Report, Study Conducted by Verizon RISK Team in Cooperation with the United Stated Secret Service*, securityblog.verizonbusiness.com. https://www.wired.com/images_blogs/threatlevel/2010/07/2010-Verizon-Data-Breach-Investigations-Report.pdf

Over the last 145 years, our investigative mission and statutory authority have expanded, and today the Secret Service is recognized worldwide for our expertise and innovative approaches to detecting, investigating and preventing financial and cyber fraud.

Cyber Intelligence Section

The Cyber Intelligence Section (CIS) of the Secret Service was founded in 2005 to combat trends in fraud and identity theft. The CIS serves as a central repository for the collection of data generated through the agency's field investigations, open source Internet content and a variety of information obtained through financial and private industry partnerships as it relates to identity theft, credit card fraud, bank fraud, and telecommunications fraud.[812]

CIS leverages technology and information obtained through private partnerships, to monitor developing technologies and trends in the financial payments industry that may enhance the Secret Service's abilities to detect and mitigate attacks against the financial and telecommunications infrastructures. CIS penetrates, disrupts and dismantles online criminal networks, investigates and coordinates network intrusion investigations, and provides case agents with actionable intelligence to support their investigations.[813]

The Secret Service is the only entity within the Department of Homeland Security that has the authority to investigate violations of Title 18, United States Code, Section 1030 (Computer Fraud). Congress also directed the Secret Service in Public Law 107-56 to establish a nationwide network of Electronic Crimes Task Forces (ECTFs) to "prevent, detect, and investigate various forms of electronic crimes, including potential terrorist attacks against critical infrastructure and Financial payment systems."[814]

The USSS is an extraordinary agency regarded as one of the preeminent law enforcement organizations in the world. However, based on his experiences, Jackson holds a very different opinion about some former members of this organization and their activities relating to his investigation, interaction, and prosecution.

In his letter to John Roth, dated August 24, 2017, Jackson explained his frustrations about the USSS's alleged misconduct.[815] He made the following statements and allegations about the USSS to the Inspector General of the US Department of Homeland Security, John

---

[812] Ibid

[813] Ibid

[814] Ibid

[815] Jackson, Douglas. "Investigation Request." Received by John Roth, Inspector General, US Dept. of Homeland Security, 1020 Steven Patrick Avenue, 24 Aug. 2017, Indian Harbour Beach, Florida. 14pgs

Roth, whom he had previously met during the e-gold® criminal case. Partial text from the letter included the following statements by Jackson.

> Following the more concrete assertions of misconduct and the related Exhibits, I will offer a synopsis that I believe encapsulates the actual sequence of events and agency motives that not only impelled the USSS and Peretti to perpetrate this injustice but progressed to involve successively higher elements of DHS and DOJ as they closed ranks to protect these rogue elements in order to avoid revealing their malice and incompetence to Congress and the American public.[816]

> By way of context, we had, for several preceding years, observed indications that there was a rogue element within the USSS operating "off the reservation," which we knew had initially been goaded into acts of aggression against e-gold by a particular private cabal driven by malice, the interests of would-be competitors and a desire for informant rewards.

> As I relate in the attached materials, it is likely that senior echelons elected to close ranks with their rogue subsidiary to avoid the embarrassment that would result were the funding subcommittee that had been suckered into funding this misadventure circa 2003 learned the USSS had willingly been recruited by a private cabal that had deceived them into acting as their all-too-willing cat's paw. Had Congressional oversight officials realized that e-gold—instead of being some sort of shadowy arch-villainous cybercrime organization as depicted by erroneous and fabricated testimony—was rapidly evolving the most effective anti-crime countermeasures in the payments industry, they might have been receptive to more constructive engagement with respect to appropriate regulation for such an innovation.[817]

G&SR had been in contact with the USSS multiple times over many years. Jackson had offered to explain the e-gold® platform, share critical data, and cooperate with the agency through legal channels.

As early as 2001, G&SR was willing to illustrate e-gold's advanced protocols for interdiction and investigation. Jackson has well documented his treatment by the USSS. The following text includes some items extracted from the Sentencing Memorandum of Gold & Silver Reserve, Inc. Case Number 07-167-M-01.[818] Within this Court document, Counsel for

---

[816] Ibid
[817] Ibid
[818] CASE NUMBER: 07-167-M-01. *UNITED STATES OF AMERICA V. E-GOLD LIMITED, GOLD & SILVER*

G&SR, discussed several of Jackson's unfortunate interactions with the USSS.

> In 2004, Dr. Jackson initiated on behalf of the Companies a dialogue with the United States Secret Service to discuss further measures that could be implemented to locate abusers of the e-gold system.[819]

> Dr. Jackson personally arranged to visit Secret Service headquarters in Washington, D.C. to acquaint the Secret Service (along with agents of the United Kingdom's National High Tech Crime Unit and the Australian Federal Police) with e-gold and show them how they could most efficiently interact with e-gold's in-house investigative staff. *Id.* The Secret Service, however, cancelled that meeting at the last minute on grounds that were never plausibly explained.[820]

From April 2003 to October 2004, the USSS Shadow Crew investigation had been underway, and despite e-gold® volunteering its full assistance, the USSS did not engage e-gold® investigators. On multiple occasions, Jackson had explained, with a proper subpoena from the USSS, that e-gold® could obtain detailed information from the e-gold® database that could significantly assist in their investigations. Throughout the G&SR's history, the executives cooperated with numerous other law enforcement agencies and expeditiously answered subpoenas. However, the USSS had always refused to interact with e-gold® on any open investigation. The refusal of this agency to accept valuable intelligence cautioned the e-gold® operators to a possible issue with the USSS. In a November 5th, 2008 email, Jackson explained his distrust toward members of this agency, and briefly elaborated on actions taken by USSS Special Agents.

> Since Spring 2001, the USSS had repeatedly manifested antipathy toward e-gold, with USSS spokesmen periodically making statements in the press characterizing e-gold as anonymous and, as we long perceived, undermining our existing relationships and efforts to establish constructive relationships with other law enforcement agencies.[821]

In 2017, Jackson further detailed his experiences "the USSS had always stood out as obtusely refusing to engage with our investigators, on several occasions appearing to prefer

RESERVE, INC., DOUGLAS L. JACKSON, BARRY K. DOWNEY and REID A. JACKSON. SENTENCING MEMORANDUM OF GOLD & SILVER RESERVE, INC., Nov. 2008.

[819] Ibid

[820] Ibid

[821] Jackson, Douglas. "USSS Blurb." Received by Machalagh Carr, *USSS Blurb*, 5 Nov. 2008.

to turn a blind eye to criminal exploits rather than engage with us to bring identified perpetrators to justice."[822]

In 2004, John Roth became an Assistant U.S. Attorney for the District of Columbia. By 2007, Roth had served as Deputy Assistant Attorney General for the Criminal Division U.S. Attorney's Office in the District of Columbia and became chief of staff to the Deputy Attorney General in 2008. He later assumed the post of Inspector General of the Department of Homeland Security (DHS) on March 10, 2014. In November 2017, Roth stepped down from his position as the Department of Homeland Security's inspector general and retired after thirty-two years of federal service. Jackson was familiar with Roth from his involvement in the e-gold® case. Jackson stated that Roth had been present with prosecutors during a December 2006 plea agreement meeting in Washington, DC.[823] Jackson described his previous contact with Roth in the 2017 letter shown below, stating "[Roth]...played a direct role in this case at perhaps its most critical juncture."[824]

> To: John Roth (Personally)
> Inspector General, US Dept. of Homeland Security,
> From: Dr. Douglas Jackson
> XXXXXXXX, Indian Harbour Beach, FL 32937-4276
> Regarding:
> Corruption and misconduct on the part of USSS and DOJ officials in relation to the 2007-08 prosecution of e-gold Ltd., Gold & Silver Reserve, Inc. (and the directors of both companies) as well as the asset seizures and forfeiture actions undertaken in conjunction with the case. These allegations center on actions taken by Kimberly Kiefer Peretti and her associates and superiors at the USSS, DHS and DOJ.
>
> Ms. Peretti is currently employed by Alston Bird, LLC, The Atlantic Building, 950 F Street, NW, Washington, DC 20004-1404. This request for investigation is in regard to her tenure as Senior Counsel, U.S. Department of Justice Computer Crime and Intellectual Property Section, Criminal Division 1301 New York Ave., NW, Suite 600 Washington, D.C.   20530
> Date: August 24, 2017
>
> Dear Inspector General Roth,

---

[822] Jackson, Douglas. "Investigation Request." Received by John Roth, Inspector General, US Dept. of Homeland Security, 1020 Steven Patrick Avenue, 24 Aug. 2017, Indian Harbour Beach, Florida.

[823] Ibid

[824] Ibid

With the enclosed narrative and Exhibits I am alleging corruption and (possibly criminal) misconduct on the part of certain elements of the United States Secret Service (USSS)—in league with Kimberly Kiefer Peretti and her associates/superiors, circa 2003-2010—and requesting investigation by your office. The misconduct I allege was undertaken in relation to the prosecution of e-gold Ltd., Gold & Silver Reserve, Inc. and the directors of both companies.

I am prefacing these allegations with a note to you personally because you played a direct role in this case at perhaps its most critical juncture.

In December 2006, the directors of e-gold Ltd. and G&SR, along with their counsel, were summoned to Washington to meet with DOJ prosecutors as well as representatives of federal law enforcement agencies. A draft indictment had been prepared and we were presented with the option of entering into a plea agreement. You were present but in the initial portion of the day's proceedings your role in this matter was unclear to me.

I read the draft indictment and, though not permitted to speak directly, expressed my outrage and incredulity (albeit toned down by counsel). I saw my life's work misrepresented with a distorted description of our business and transaction model as well as the institutional arrangements, safeguards and crime fighting capabilities we had pioneered. Moreover, the criminal complaint, while describing criminal activity on the part of customers, falsely alleged that we turned a blind eye to such activities.

In response to our outrage you intervened and spoke up. This is what I then perceived…

By way of context, we had, for several preceding years, observed indications that there was a rogue element within the USSS operating "off the reservation", which we knew had initially been goaded into acts of aggression against e-gold by a particular private cabal driven by malice, the interests of would-be competitors and a desire for informant rewards. Therefore, when on December 29, 2006 you intervened in the discussion, I felt for the first time that finally there was going to be some responsible adult supervision. It seemed that you yourself were hearing for the first time the full extent to which this rogue element had squandered resources pursuing their counterfactual agenda to portray e-gold as criminal-friendly. I perceived that you realized how off base these people had been and had stepped in to try to mitigate an absurd mess that was likely to expose the USSS as incompetent bunglers with a dysfunctional corporate culture.

In your comments you observed, "nobody is saying you are bad people" followed by the assurance that the government would not be seeking jail time . I

472

recall describing my relief to my wife after the meeting, expressing my hopes that the surreal nightmare we had been living might finally be concluding.

But instead the decision was made by senior officials to close ranks with their rogue agency rather than to yank their antenna and clean house.

As you may recall, 6 weeks later (February 9, 2007) we were presented with a draft plea agreement that included a lengthy (30-37 month) term of incarceration for me. Our counsel called you directly to try to understand this apparent about-face and escalation in ferocity [Exhibit 41]. He related to us that you said that you had been overruled in this matter, that the decision to continue/intensify this shock and awe campaign had "come from the highest levels".

As I relate in the attached materials, it is likely that senior echelons elected to close ranks with their rogue subsidiary to avoid the embarrassment that would result were the funding subcommittee that had been suckered into funding this misadventure circa 2003 learned the USSS had willingly been recruited by a private cabal that had deceived them into acting as their all-too-willing cat's paw. Had Congressional oversight officials realized that e-gold—instead of being some sort of shadowy arch-villainous cybercrime organization as depicted by erroneous and fabricated testimony—was rapidly evolving the most effective anti-crime countermeasures in the payments industry, they might have been receptive to more constructive engagement with respect to appropriate regulation for such an innovation.

But this tragic turn set the stage for the subsequent misconduct and the decade-long cascade of harmful consequences that have ensued. To maintain the fiction of alleged criminality on the part of e-gold et al, the USSS itself turned a blind eye to serious crime in a coverup that escalated to cross DHS agency boundaries.

I believe that at that time (and afterward), Peretti and her USSS co-conspirators kept you and your superiors in the dark with respect to the Gonzalez matter detailed in my narrative and exhibits. Similarly, the *Brady* violations that I will relate had not yet occurred and I have no reason to think you were party to them.

It would however strain credulity to extend this benefit of the doubt to your Acting Assistant, Laurel Loomis Rimon. Perhaps she actually was out of the loop regarding the Gonzalez matter. But she was wholly complicit in the willful *Brady* violations I will document. And if she did in fact know the facts of the Gonzalez coverup, she willfully perjured herself in open court. For this reason, I would suggest taking any recollections and assertions she may offer in relation to these matters with a grain of salt.

You were correct in your characterization that we weren't bad guys. But when

473

our own government elected to make us enemies of the state, the consequences that resulted from this, some of which may not have become fully manifest yet, were dire. They were of course ruinous for the defendants. But, worse than that, our absence from the marketplace directly led to the emergence of Bitcoin and the various other flavors of blockchain or "distributed ledger" systems now so in vogue with herd-like investors. I can detail, if interested, the monumental malinvestment and waste of resources due to this technological dead-end fad. You may also be aware of the strong anonymity baked into these systems. Yet these systems are celebrated for this purposeful ability to defy governments, sometimes by the same pundits who had parroted false accusations that e-gold provided anonymity and a platform conducive to criminal exploits. And if you think Bitcoin is criminal friendly, wait until you witness what is possible with Zcoin, already the favored medium of shadowbrokers and other vendors of criminal goods and services.

But there are other potential consequences, not yet manifest, orders of magnitude worse.

When I walked away from a successful practice of medicine over twenty years ago in order to create an alternative global currency and settlement facility, I was primarily impelled by a perception of systemic monetary and financial risks that could not be resolved by any process of reform. At best, consequences of their deeply embedded flaws could only be deferred. But deferral carried the certainty that when they could no longer be contained, the disruption that would ensue would be all the more devastating. I perceived a Gordian Knot-cutting solution, which I have continued to refine to this day.

Consequences of these systemic risk factors have in fact been deferred. So far. Now, however, the world may be on the brink of renewed financial crisis. Yet none the "unconventional monetary policies" deployed in the aftermath of the so-called GFC have yet been unwound. Government central banks and fiscal policy leaders may shortly enter into a maelstrom of financial contagion with no countercyclical policy instruments left in their arsenal. In less than three years there is a strong likelihood that helicopter money, originally framed as a tongue-in-cheek rhetorical device, will take center stage as the logical escalation of monetary/fiscal stimulus.

Had we not been (in effect) murdered, our continued growth and maturation would have already established safeguards to attenuate what may be coming. Even yet, an urgent program of deployment could both mitigate the most extreme systemic risks and establish a sort of safety net affording emergence of more stable arrangements in the aftermath.

But we are not in the market, as a direct consequence of the actions undertaken by parties unknown in the USSS, in league with Kimberly Kiefer Peretti, dating back to 2003.

If you take up this matter, I would be honored to describe what we could yet do, systematic remedies that could not be implemented by all the king's men and horses, even if the understanding and will to do so existed. The most critical precursor to this, however, would be to undo, at this late hour, the lingering harm of this unjust prosecution.

My agenda and goals in reaching out to you, as usual, are transparent. My ask is that if you look into this matter and corroborate the misconduct and outright conspiracy I allege that you undertake for the DHS or DOJ to petition the court to retroactively dismiss all charges, perhaps on the basis of a Writ of Error Coram Nobis.

My work has the potential to afford great benefit to society but the lingering consequences of this prosecutorial misadventure make my task almost impossible.
Enclosures
Request for investigation, with specific allegations and guide to Exhibits.
Synopsis of origins of the case (that may provide useful context to frame investigation).[825]

The Tangled Web - Part One

During the sentencing hearing on November 20, 2008, DOJ Attorney Laurel L. Rimon, made several insincere remarks to Judge Collyer's Court. Rimon's statements referenced evidence voluntarily provided by Jackson to Agent Crabb of the United States Postal Inspection Service in June 2006. Jackson's evidence should have helped law enforcement agents to track down the most wanted hacker "segvec" easily. Instead, Rimon asserted that Jackson had not provided any assistance and that his gathered intelligence had not factored into any other criminal investigation. [Partial text copied below]

> He[Jackson] has argued for a sentence of no jail time on large part based on what he says is extraordinary cooperation to the government. The fact is that he has not provided extraordinary or substantial cooperation.[826] p.86

The other thing that is important to note is the vast majority of his cooperation related

---

[825] Jackson, Douglas. "Investigation Request." Received by John Roth, Inspector General, US Dept. of Homeland Security, 1020 Steven Patrick Avenue, 24 Aug. 2017, Indian Harbour Beach, Florida.

[826] Docket No. CR 07-109. UNITED STATES OF AMERICA vs. E-GOLD LTD, GOLD & SILVER RESERVE LTD, DOUGLAS L. JACKSON, BARRY K. DOWNEY, REID A. JACKSON. TRANSCRIPT OF SENTENCE BEFORE THE HONORABLE ROSEMARY M. COLLYER UNITED STATES DISTRICT JUDGE, 20 Nov. 2008. pg.86

to two particular individuals with the U.S. Postal Inspection Service, Agent Crabb and Agent X. Dr. Jackson developed a collegial relationship with those individuals but it's important to note that **the utility of what he provided was very limited.** There was no cooperation agreement. There was no need for a cooperation agreement.

Based on his relationship with those two individuals, Dr. Jackson takes credit for some very significant things and some very significant investigations and he's again misstating and overstating what he did.

I'd just like to give you a couple of examples related to what was submitted by Dr. Jackson submitted in his papers and explain to you that when he said his work has led to significant results, it's just not true.

He relates in his papers that his work led to the arrest and indictment of Segvec and Maksik, two computer criminals who broke into a restaurant chain of Dave and Buster's cash registers, had stole credit card information and sold that credit card information.

This case happens to be handled by Kim Peretti my colleague is the lead prosecutor on that case and was very intimate and familiar with it. **The postal service is not an investigative agency on this case, it's a pure U.S. Secret Service case. The information that Dr. Jackson may have provided to Agent Crabb did not factor into this investigation at all.**

The fact is that at the time of this investigation we already had the data base [e-gold's Db] **that we had seized in December of 2005. Secret Service agents were able to review it and analyze and get the information they needed.**

And even after that, the E-Gold part of the case is just one part. So I just bring that up to point out that he's overstating, Dr. Jackson is overstating what he's done.[827] p.86-88 [Emphasis added]

Evidence from past emails and personal communications between USPIS Agents and Jackson, tend to prove that Rimon's November 2008 statements to the Court were untrue. Her criticisms are examined and discussed here:

---

[827] Ibid

Rimon: The postal service is not an investigative agency on this case, it's a pure U.S. Secret Service case.[828] p.88

Agents of the USPIS emailed Jackson, asking him to research specific e-gold account numbers and provide the USPIS with any uncovered transactional data and crucial details. After receiving the e-gold intelligence from Jackson, USPIS Agents would pass credible data to the United States Department of Justice for possible prosecution. Jackson followed these instructions and fulfilled the Agents' requests. Here are the background details and full email chains showing the activity. These correspondences indicate that, through his work, Jackson uncovered and shared a significant amount of critical intelligence material. The emails also prove that USPIS Agents acknowledged Jackson's work was beneficial and were pleased to work with him.

Thursday, February 9, 2006 17:30 -0500 [829]
From: Douglas Jackson
Subject: e-gold service of process
Dear Inspector Crabb,
Thank you for your call and your interest in busting this international ring of "carders." I think a major key to this group, in terms of verifying physical locations and identifying assets in banks, is an entity who started out making purchases of physical goods on behalf of group members buy over time has modulated into spending money into Bank of America bank accounts on their behalf. I can't tell for sure if he knows what they are up to or even that he is engaged in ML but I can see he explicitly charges 6% for making deposits. [Looking again just now I see some of his earliest transactions involved selling "MSR 206" units...he knows!] The tough call will be how best to approach him, but however done I think he should be approached (or collared or whatever) first before the group knows they are compromised.
I'm virtually certain he is in Long Beach, CA and that we have a good name, address and phone.
The best catch-all for the group I've seen is "cardersyndicate." I'd suggest the order be worded to order us provide data and stabilize value pertaining to the network known as 'cardersyndicate'." The actual discovery of this ring started as we were

[828] Ibid
[829] Jackson, Douglas. *"e-gold Service of Process."* Received by Gregg Crabb, et al., e-gold Service of Process, 9 Feb. 2006.

477

looking for a trojan-writing ring called 'ratsystems'. We've failed to find them (yet) but that string was the actual initial rossetta stone – a ratsystems wannabee turned out to be a small-time carder.

I think the key that gives us the broadest mandate for tracing all their connections is for the court to order us to specify that we do all the bullet points below, plus words to the effect of "traffic and transaction analysis to identify counterparties (an counterparties of the counterparties) who appear to be engaged in buying or selling credit card data, log-ins to transaction systems or other identify theft data".

[A section of this email was removed]

In order to ensure you get all pertinent information when issuing court orders or subpoenas to e-gold Ltd please:

- Ask for the e-gold account profile information for the e-gold account number
- Ask for transaction history information for the e-gold account number
- Ask for information on any other accounts owned or controlled by the individual
- Ask for counter account profile information. This is the account profile information for any accounts that made payments into or received payments from the subpoenaed account
- If applicable, ask for stabilization of the funds in question "freezing of the account if the funds are still under the control of the perpetrator"

This is going to take a lot of work from our investigators and I'm thinking there may be a strategically efficient way of proceeding in stages, like nailing the Long Beach guy, then freezing beacoup accounts [it involves over 300 e-gold accounts], then chasing down best possible physical location data [which will come from exchange services that have been used by these people – I've already spot checked several with various of the exchange services and they have excellent data – in many cases they know specific bank accounts used by these guys].

Sincere regards, Dr. Douglas Jackson, Chairman, e-gold Ltd., CEO, Gold & Silver Reserve, Inc.[830]

Thursday, February 9, 2006 21:38 -0500
From: "Crabb, Gregory S" [USPIS]
Subject: RE: e-gold service of process
Mr. Jackson,
Thank you for bringing this organization to our attention. I believe that I familiar

[830] Ibid

with the activities of some of the individual that you are suggesting. This "carder syndicate" has been operating in a variety of countries from the last several years. **The law enforcement investigators that I am bringing together in Lyon would greatly benefit from your information concerning the flow of funds.**

I will provide this information to the Postal Inspection Service's Economic and Financial Crime Task Force in L.A. I will provide them with instructions on how to obtain a court order (as opposed to a grand jury subpoena – as we discussed) for the financial transaction information that you are suggesting below. It will likely time them a week or more to work through the court process to obtain the order; however, I will ask for a rush on the processing of this legal process.

Postal Inspection Service Intelligence Analyst Agent X will be assisting me in further this investigative inquiry.

Thank you,

Gregory S. Crabb, Program Manager, Postal Inspector Group – 5, International Affairs

U.S. Postal Inspection Service[831] [emphasis added]

Thursday, February 9, 2006 17:01:59 -0500

From: "Crabb, Gregory S"

Subject: Interpol Operation Gold Phish Meeting

Mr. Jackson,

I wanted to follow-up with you concerning more information on the event at Interpol next week. I apologize for the short notice. **I am certain that we could use e-gold's assistance in support of this meeting. The law enforcement/private industry meeting is going to be held at Interpol in Lyon, France** on February 16th to discuss phishing, pharming and other high technology account takeover and laundering activities and the resources that you have to help combat the problem. If you are able to attend, the International community would be very grateful. Additionally, if you would be willing to provide a presentation at the event, the international community would be grateful to learn how to obtain records from e-gold.

Under the name Operation GoldPhish, Interpol is organizing an International inquiry into phishing, pharming, spyware, remote access trojans, keystroke logging and other high technology crimes to facilitate identity related financial crimes. Interpol is rallying the support of private industry and the international law enforcement together to tackle identity theft crimes.

---

[831] Crabb, Greg. "RE: e-gold Service of Process." Received by Douglas Jackson, *RE: e-gold Service of Process*, 9 Feb. 2006.

[...]

In addition to the Postal Inspection Service's International Affairs Group, agents from the FBI's National Cyber Forensic and Training Alliance are invited. In a law enforcement only meeting on February 14 and 15, the representatives from these countries will hold an operational meeting concerning these crimes.[832]

In a February 14, 2019, email, Jackson discussed this situation:

Then, January 2006, when I acquired the capability to do full text search and found the "Rosetta stone" carder account, I again reached out to the SS. Rebuffed again by them, a banking industry investigative contact referred me to Greg Crabb of the USPIS, who I'd worked with years before on another case. That was extremely productive but there was an element of being screwed by them too.[833]

Jackson and the USPIS Inspectors' emails laid the groundwork for future collaboration.[834] In a 2019 email, Jackson explained the launch of these investigations:

I didn't resume direct investigative activity myself until 2006 when we found the Rosetta stone for detecting and tracing carders (after we installed multi-core processors in the database server – I have the emails time stamping that event). Since we had no legal cover[legal protection] for that work (we were repeatedly promised a pen register type writ, but never received it) he [e-gold's head of investigations Mr. Trotter] preferred not to act in what amounted to violation of our User Agreement so I took that on myself. He[Trotter] continued to handle all the subpoena and court order work while I spent over 500 hours on investigative work in 2006.[835]

The event in Lyon, France, was held on February 16, 2006, and Jackson was in attendance. On February 23, 2006, Jackson sent another email to Agent Crabb requesting a subpoena for pending e-gold investigations.

From: Douglas Jackson [mailto:djackson@e-gold.com]

[832] Crabb, Gregory S. "Subject: Interpol Operation Gold Phish Meeting." Received by Douglas Jackson, *Subject: Interpol Operation Gold Phish Meeting*, 9 Feb. 2006.

[833] Ibid

[834] Crabb, Gregory S. "Interpol Operation Gold Phish Meeting." Received by Douglas Jackson, Interpol Operation Gold Phish Meeting, 9 Feb. 2006.

[835] Jackson, Douglas. "Re: Attached for Short Important Read." Received by Carl Mullan, *Re: Attached for Short Important Read*, 13 Feb. 2019.

Sent: Thursday, February 23, 2006 8:45 AM
Subject: carder ring
Greg

So far I've held off on blocking the e-gold accounts of the carder ring we talked about in order to maximize the possibilities for asset recovery. But I am getting anxious to lower the boom on these people and expel them from the e-gold universe. Our initial discovery of this ring, and attempt to engage law enforcement in the matter [email/phone to WayneXXXX@usss.dhs.gov] was 1/24/06.

Can you offer an estimate of when a subpoena might be forthcoming, especially with a view to picking up the Long Beach, CA kingpin who I believe has data regarding the various carder stashes at BoA?

Peter [Bank of America] - if delays are expected, is there a chance that BoA could proceed with a John Doe civil case? e-gold can certainly comply with civil subpoenas as well.

sincere regards, Douglas Jackson[836]

Wednesday, March 1, 2006 17:38:05 -0500
From: "Crabb, Gregory S"
Douglas,

Could you please review the attached court order language for us? It is probably broader in scope than other orders that you have received in the past. I would like to be able to view Carranza's accounts for some time before we take specific action. Please let me know your opinion, if we are to present you with such an order.

Thanks, Greg
Attachment: Court Order – Carranza e-gold.doc [837]

Wednesday, March 1, 2006 21:43:02 -0500
From: Douglas Jackson
Subject: Re: FW: eGold Court Order
Greg,

Trap and trace is what WE do...

We of course capture a permanent record of IP numbers (and a lot of other information) with every transaction written to the database (plus with certain events such as log-in attempts even if no transaction occurs) and have since 1996. I'll bring a printout of the most useful fields of his data tomorrow and if you can provide me

---

[836] Jackson, Douglas. "Carder Ring." Received by Gregory S. Crabb, *Carder Ring*, 23 Feb. 2006.

[837] Crabb, Gregory. "FW: EGold Court Order." Received by Douglas Jackson, *FW: EGold Court Order*, 1 Mar. 2006.

Internet access [alternatively we can walk over to a hotspot] I can walk you through some of our existing real time capabilities for traffic/transaction analysis. I believe it would be best to compare notes in that fashion first before specifying the monitoring methodology

See you tomorrow, 1:30'ish

Douglas Jackson[838]

As previously discussed, on March 27, 2006, USPIS Investigator Greg Crabb had emailed Jackson to   request assistance with several investigations. Jackson provided the USPIS with preliminary intelligence on the required high-priority target e-gold® accounts. He later followed up with additional evidence obtained through e-gold's in-house investigative work.

Doug,
Thank you for taking the time to examine this activity with us in this iterative fashion. I have a small list of e-gold accounts that trace to individuals that are tied to these credit card organizations. This will be a place for us to start:
Akihikotobe: 1315932
zo0mer: 826191
Smash: 1671595
Tron: 588095
Archi: 317802
Nikiforov: 291618
Raghu: 985132
cc--trader: 1259368
uBuyweRush: 950023
Maksik: 1751848
The documents that I have provided to Main Department of Justice request the account information for these e-gold accounts. The documentation is going to ask for the following:
    - e-gold account profile information for the e-gold account number;
    - transaction history information for the e-gold account numbers;
    - information on any other accounts owned or controlled by the individual; and
    - counter account profile information.

[838] Jackson, Douglas. "Re: FW: EGold Court Order." Received by Gregory Crabb, *Re: FW: EGold Court Order*, 1 Mar. 2006.

As we begin to examine the activity of these individuals, I expect that we will begin to find some striking patterns. XXXXX and I have accumulated over ten thousand e-mail addresses of subjects that are engaged these credit card fraud activities. It may be useful for us to provide you with these e-mail addresses to assist in our examination of this activity. I will call you after my meetings this afternoon. It will take me a few hours to prepare my computer to communicate via Skype and PGP. Take care, Greg

> Attachments:
> Akihikotobe 1315932.xls
> Archi 317802.xls
> cc--trader 1259368.xls
> Corporate Gz 966750.xls
> DeluzioNFX 1539702.xls
> denisabi 986677.xls
> johndillinger 2963049.xls[839]

Jackson quickly responded with an enormous amount of detailed evidence on the e-gold accounts and the users' activity.

> Subject: Re: A Start - breaking into 2 so attachments not too much
> From: Douglas Jackson <djackson@e-gold.com>
> Date: Mon, 27 Mar 2006 13:29:31 -0500
> To: "Crabb, Gregory S" <GSCrabb@uspis.gov>
> First pass - I'm saving these as Excel 4 worksheets since I figure whatever version Excel you are working with should be able to open. I could also do csv (or you could convert) - let me know which most expedient.
> First glance at 1315932, one might say:
> - who is this 966750?, and
> - how far removed from 950023 is Akikikotobe?
> Answer,
> - 966750 is another bad guy, and one hop.
> But darn, even a superficial glance at 966750 begs the question, what's with this 2196759 counterparty, who he is buying UK data from and also splitting loot with? Does napalm ring a bell? But I digress...
> Zo0mer leads right to Maksik, but both bring up this 2464856 (hardware?) guy I was mentioning last week who particularly irks me since he obviously makes sooo much

[839] Ibid

more money than me. I called him Stephen Ceres but I think segvec (from Drax.. whatever Drax is) is probably a better nym. When you see an incriminating memo like "cut", it is just too compelling. So segvec segues into DeluzioNFX, 1539702. I'm also throwing in one of the little johndillnger accounts because it is interesting to see yet another illustration of how things flow through 950023.

Same with Karma, 1633978, he's just so tied in with all the others. Plus a first round of one of the more recent kaisersose accounts for reasons apparent at a glance. I forwarded requests to two exchangers this AM with whom I see he has done exchanges to see how good their data is on his ID/location. On this Nikiforov, from what I see, he appears to be a legitimate exchanger. If so, it might be best for me to ask him for whatever data is needed or to get Estonia to subpoena him directly. If he is legitimate, and I see no reason to doubt it, he will be delighted to aid in investigation. If you have reason to suspect otherwise, like you know he participates in criminal forums etc. I can dump his data to you easy enough.

His contact info:

3235521 1 291618 Vitali Nikiforov Asula 2-7 Saku

Harjumaa Estonia/75501 info@webmoney.ee +(372)5218877 False

On this cc--trader: 1259368 guy, I remember asking xlcard.com back in Feb for data about this guy because he had 3 debit cards through them. She wrote back and said their company was in some disarray because of the abrupt cancer illness/death of the principal. I'll remind her again because I know debit card vendors always have data on where the cards were originally sent and every place they've been used.

Looking at Carranza's account, I see he is recently doing some largish exchanges with the Bullion exchange 2325383. They are entirely legitimate.

Looking at the most recent Carranza tx's, I ran 3018183 who then exchanged onto a debit card via Cashcards, 274303.

I've queried cashcards for records before - they have excellent records and they love to help catch bad guys. Running memos from their history I see this 3018183 guy used to use e-gold account 1763802 to fund the same card. This guy is (or is in league with - no time to go back and recollect unless important to you) holy_father - the hxdef rootkit guy (1669902), not to my knowledge part of this ring, but considered to be a bad person nonetheless. OmniPay, btw, has a good address in CZ for this guy. Taking break, been at it non-stop 4.5 hrs.[840]

On April 10, Jackson volunteered another intelligence package to the USPIS, that

[840] Jackson, Douglas. "Re: A Start - Breaking into 2 so Attachments Not Too Much." Received by Gregory S. Crabb, Re: A Start - Breaking into 2 so Attachments Not Too Much, 27 Mar. 2006.

contained expanded information on transactions involving segvec; including debit cards and bank transfers obtained exclusively through e-gold's in-house investigations.

♦

Prosecuting Attorney Laurel R. Rimon had stated to the Court, at Jackson's Sentencing Hearing, that USSS Agents had uncovered all relevant information from the subpoenaed e-gold hard drive. However, Jackson's third-party data was never in the e-gold database copied by the USSS in late 2005. Jackson retrieved this critical evidence through his in-house investigation. Rimon's statements to the Court were untrue. She claimed, "The fact is that at the time of this investigation we already had the data base that we had seized in December of 2005. Secret Service agents were able to review it and analyze and get the information they needed."[841]

> Subject: Re: Maksik's Big Mover
> From: Douglas Jackson <djackson@e-gold.com>
> Date: Mon, 10 Apr 2006 08:59:19 -0400
> To: "Agent X"
> CC: "Crabb, Gregory S" <GSCrabb@uspis.gov>
> This is an expansion of previous file titled Stephen Ceres. This combines several segvec accounts. He used a debit card issued by 385775 but I'm unfamiliar with them and have held off on asking them for the card data until I have a sense of whether they are/were OK.
> I also see Vadim Vassilenko did several wires in fulfillment of segvec exchanges from several of these accounts. I don't know who if anybody is minding the store at WesternExpress these days now that Vadim is in jail - maybe the exchange/wire records are well enough understood/organized by whichever agency is doing the Vassilenko case to get that data. I wouldn't be surprised if I just tried a generic customer service email to WesternExpress that they would still track and supply the info – but I don't really know that and it probably isn't worth the risk. [attached files]
> **segvec multiple - supersedes Stephen Ceres.xls**
> **Segvec universe ins and outs.xls**
> **Segvec counterparties.xls**[842]

[841] Docket No. CR 07-109. UNITED STATES OF AMERICA vs. E-GOLD LTD, GOLD & SILVER RESERVE LTD, DOUGLAS L. JACKSON, BARRY K. DOWNEY, REID A. JACKSON. TRANSCRIPT OF SENTENCE BEFORE THE HONORABLE ROSEMARY M. COLLYER UNITED STATES DISTRICT JUDGE, 20 Nov. 2008.

[842] Jackson, Douglas. "Re: Maksik's Big Mover." Received by USPIS Agent X, Re: Maksik's Big Mover, 10 Apr. 2006.

One email chain began on May 3, 2006, between Jackson and a USPIS Agent, referred to as Agent X, to conceal his real identity. Here is the first email of the chain followed by responses from Jackson.

Agent X wrote:

Doug,

Thank you for that e-mail earlier concerning Valenzuela and Carranza. Extremely interesting.

Also, of other note, there is a connection between Valenzuela, Carranza, and one of the counterparties known as Nicole Hixson, e-gold number: 1761885. Hixson runs a company called: Sales on the Move. They are all intertwined with Carranza as he is the figurehead of both Valenzuela and Hixson.

>From what we have been noticing, Carranza has been directing "carders" to Valenzuela, but the money laundering is going on through Valenzuela and going back eventually to Carranza.

To let you know, e-gold account number: 2299815, Jamie Hopper was the subject of a large FBI arrest recently. Hopper was involved with many major carders as a cashout artist. He was laundering a lot of money back to Eastern Europe due to cashing out "dumps and pins" at ATMs and sending back hundreds of 1,000's of dollars back to the hackers in Eastern Europe.

You pose a good question about Eskalibur and his relationship with these individuals. Eskalibur is a savvy hacker from the Ukraine who is one of the largest dump sellers on the internet. He is always online.

Excellent work on the Postal Money Orders. We cannot thank you enough for that lead. We will certainly run that information through our money order coordinator at USPIS.

Agent X[843] [emphasis added]

Minutes later, Jackson responded:

Subject: Re: Also...
From: Douglas Jackson <djackson@e-gold.com>
Date: Wed, 03 May 2006 07:45:10 -0400
To: "Agent X"
CC: "'Crabb, Gregory S'" <GSCrabb@uspis.gov>

[843] Jackson, Douglas. Received by USPIS Agent X, 3 May 2006.

Something I hadn't re-realized with last note regarding Carranza/Esk flows is that youngdon 2143273 [previously sent as "biggest Carranza out-conduit] also sends virtually all of his e-gold to Esk. It was not apparent at the time I first sent it because I didn't yet know that 1097167 was an Esk account (created by him and under his direct control) and that 1283948 (littlefish) was also a conduit to Esk.
Another one I need to look at in this whole area of analysis now is another pass at Segvec, Carranza's second largest outflow, after youngdon. Segvec is sending largest tranche (197k) to an offshore debit card guy in Ireland (2417121 XXXXXX.com) I hadn't previously noticed. Memos indicate three accounts with XXXXXX.com. I'm going to check with the guy for details of where the value goes then. I don't know him but he has provided good contact info that matches his website and is virtually certain to want to help. I'll look at these ones you mention today.[844]

This email detailed the start of Jackson's investigation with a third-party financial services company. That foreign business had legally provided customer ATM debit cards that accepted e-gold and deposited USD to the card. Jackson reached out to the company for information on his e-gold account holder "segvec."

Wednesday, May 3, 2006, 8:18:07 PM, you wrote:
DJ> Douglas Jackson here, Chairman of e-gold.
DJ> I tried calling you just now, 08:11 eastern US time, but your listed voice line is hooked up to your fax machine.
DJ> I need to speak to you, rather urgently, regarding one of your customers. He is acting as a conduit for three ringleaders of the most infamous credit card ring in the entire world. I am hoping for your assistance in investigating this ring.
DJ> Please email with a good voice contact number. My cell is +1 321 271 7440. You can corroborate that by contacting e-gold investigations at the number listed on the contact page of the e-gold website, ext. 106. My extension [though I'm working from home this morning] is 114.
DJ> sincere regards,
DJ> Douglas Jackson[845]

After Jackson's request, that same day, an employee of the company responded:

███████████████

---

[844] Jackson, Douglas. "Re: Also..." Received by USPIS Agent X, and Gregory Crabb, Re: Also..., 3 May 2006.
[845] Jackson, Douglas. "Re: Pursuing a Criminal." Received by ███████, *Re: Pursuing a Criminal*, 3 May 2006.

Hello Douglas,
Happy to help in any way we can. However we are traveling and   currently in Asia.
The time change is a huge difference where you are and where we are i.e. its night
time here now, morning for you.
Please provide full details of the party in question, your complaint etc. and all
relevant information and we'll assist to the best of our ability via e-mail. I'll stay on-
line for the next half hour.
Regards[846]

Next, Jackson sent his request for information to the third-party financial service.

Subject: Re: pursuing a criminal
From: Douglas Jackson <djackson@e-gold.com>
Date: Wed, 03 May 2006 08:39:44 -0400
I greatly appreciate your prompt response.
Here are the recent transactions:
12/7/2005 8:11 72.138.206.55[IP] 1956825 2417121 24   52247127 6687.43
█ 00000406
[...]

Every bit of this guy's [calls himself Segvec] incoming e-gold comes from notorious
carders. Some he proceeds to exchange on their behalf via WM exchangers. But this
197k has come your direction.
Anything you can provide that would aid in confirming his identity, the identity of
these three profiles, the disposition of where the value went [for instance if he funded
debit cards, detailed history of where cards were delivered, and subsequent usage
history, or if it has gone to other dispositions, by other means etc. At the moment,
during intelligence and investigations phase my correspondents have trusted me to
proceed without subpoena. If prosecutions result, the agencies I'm working with can
of course provide any necessary legal cover for us to avoid liability under our
respective user agreements.
Douglas[847]

Finally, Jackson shared the intelligence he uncovered about the carders with USPIS Crabb
and his associate.

---

[846] ██████████. Received by Douglas Jackson, 3 May 2006.
[847] Jackson, Douglas. "Re: Pursuing a Criminal." Received by ████████, *Re: Pursuing a Criminal*, 3 May 2006.

Subject: a particle
From: Douglas Jackson <djackson@e-gold.com>
Date: Wed, 03 May 2006 10:18:28 -0400
To: "Agent X"
CC: "Crabb, Gregory S" <GSCrabb@uspis.gov>
I heard back quickly from ███████████████████████████ privacy service.
He is traveling and did not have full access to data. Plus, they are currently
transitioning to tighter AML rules (promulgated by CardOne of Canada), some of
which go into effect 5/12 but have in the past deleted data after 90 days. That being
said, he believes the bank that actually does the debit cards in question, Royal Bank
of Montreal, may have the full data set. What he did have was a few email addresses:
"Card nrb. 6220983033000000406 was suspended and presumed cancelled last year
due to the customers failure to provide ID for the bank when the bank requested it.
████ nrb. 6220983033000000612 has an e-mail address of
=pedrosanchezmorales2@yahoo.com attached to it
████ nrb. 6220983033000000604 with an e-mail address of
=symanuellee@yahoo.com"
[no hits in e-gold in these emails, btw]
But, and this is the possibly interesting part:
"for Card nrb. 6220983033000000612 took place as follows:
Apr 10, 2006 WEST KENDALL #2 01L5 ATM Withdrawal Fee for about
US$2,000
The last withdrawal on Apr 28, 2006 REGIONS BANK FC26 ATM Withdrawal
of US$600. Unless I am mistaken, that is in the South Florida USA area."[848]
[Emphasis added]

From: Douglas Jackson
Sent: Sunday, May 07, 2006 1:23 PM
To: Crabb, Gregory S: Agent X
Subject: CardOne of Canada
Greg
One of last week's possible breakthroughs was some further data from ███████████
████████ regarding Segvec activities [but I was waiting/hoping for more – see below].
Looking at the Segvec constellation, (1632310, 1956825, 2132095, 2464856,
2996438), the largest outflow (about $197,000 US) had been to three cards arranged

---

[848] Jackson, Douglas. "a Particle." Received by Agent X, and Gregory Crabb, *a Particle*, 3 May 2006.

via XXXXX with CardOne. One 6220983033000000406 was apparently Segvec himself, using his alias Stephen Ceres. That one had been suspended last year because he failed to provide adequate contact info to CardOne.

The other two 6220983033000000604 and 6220983033000000612 have remained active and received about $90,000 US each.

I don't know understand who the beneficiaries of these funds are yet but we have some names or aliases (see attached), and recent usage history and CardOne certainly has additional data.

XXXXX provided me with the attached screenshots of their CardOne history but when I asked him to go further and click the URL of the names to get the contat data and a longer dropdown than 10 days he got a case of cya and instead dumped it off on CardOne investigatios like MLA regs apparently require. So unless CardOne exhibits a little flexibility they are sure to cancel the cards, balk on providing data without writ and serve merely to tip off whoever that they have been detected/traced. I just found out this morning that ███████ felt obliged to dump this on CardOne and I'm bcc'ing you on my note to CardOne.

But for what its worth, Here is some stuff, about "Sy Lee" and "Pedro Morales", guys who received value via Segvec and CardOne of course also has usage history on the $17,000 that went to Cares/Segvec before they canceled his card.

Doug[849]

Subject: RE: CardOne of Canada
From: "Crabb, Gregory S"
Date: Sun, 7 May 2006 21:12 -0400
Doug,

This information on Segvec is outstanding. Do you mind sharing your contact at CardOne with me? I think that we can definitely get the legal process in place to go after segvec and other related accounts info. I don't want the account to be suspended, if we can moniter it, then we can get a physical body behind the ATM withdrawals.

Could you refresh my memory on how we have established that segvec and Stephen Cares are one in the same?

Thanks,
Greg[850]

[849] Jackson, Douglas. "CardOne of Canada." Received by Gregory Crabb, CardOne of Canada, 7 May 2006.

[850] Crabb, Gregory. "RE: CardOne of Canada." Received by Douglas Jackson, and "Agent X", *RE: CardOne of Canada*, 7 May 2006.

From May 3, through May 16, 2006, Jackson shared an extensive amount of high-priority target intelligence with the USPIS and Agent Crabb. Most of the shared information identified segvec activity. **SIA EKOSISTEMS LV** is a direct reference to a company bank account in Latvia that segvec was known to use.

Subject: s____c constellation
From: Douglas Jackson <djackson@e-gold.com>
Date: Wed, 10 May 2006 12:58:37 -0400
To: "Crabb, Gregory S" <GSCrabb@uspis.gov>, "Agent X"
reviewing to make sure I still believe this list is all segvec and nothing but segvec
1632310, 1956825, 2132095, 2464856, 2996438 none show indication of hijacking
[and 2132095 was never really used] these couplets establish:
2464856 and 1632310 are same
10/18/2005 2:17:02 PM 24.154.14.51[IP] 2464856 415814 24
50267441 5986 egold to wire transfer
10/18/2005 2:20:36 PM 24.154.14.51[IP] 1632310 415814 24
50267540 8083 egold to wire transfer
1632310 and 1956825 are same
6/28/2005 8:48:08 PM 69.208.191.218[IP] 1956825 1632310
23 46295048 9901 contract 839JJ
6/28/2005 8:51:15 PM 69.208.191.218[IP] 1956825 291618
24 46295094 9900 **SIA EKOSISTEMS LV**36UBAL145812409100
1956825 and 2996438 are same
3/19/2006 10:52:52 PM 83.149.74.43[IP] 1956825 2996438
23 57777066 98.926769
3/20/2006 10:59:21 PM 83.149.74.43[IP] 1956825 2996438
24 57843109 100 yo
here are his poc records
Account_ID Name Addr1 Addr2 Addr3 Addr4 Email Phone Fax
1632310 Christopher G. Teptitov 1868 Lee Road Winter Park FL USA/32789
cgt@hotbox.ru 321-299-3595
1956825 **segvec** 483 Mkdlvic Circle Brooklyn NY 10092
segvec@fromru.com 212-384-3948
2132095 Andrew Montesani 239 Broadway Ave New York NY 10022
nukes@land.ru 212-348-9382
2464856 **Segvec** Mihali 839 N Brown ST Brooklyn NY 11182

nukes@land.ru 212-384-3970

2996438 Andrew Mckenzie Swallow age str. 3-10 Portland OR 32134

spike_spiegel@safe-mail.net 823565674

and his User account_id user_name user_descr auth_expr master_passwordhash emergency_passwordhash Last_Failed_Login Last_Access_Time

1632310 cgt 3AA1F1676B54EAE3124251420C338D82

11DBCAE45A14B2A98C08C968083F3DA6

55CD46A7AC2B0F855D11C74A4115F134

2/25/2005 6:30:29 PM 3/18/2006 6:15:18 PM

1956825 **segvec segvec** 1E9BB3E80B8D8D862705731A1EC87213

5CF80860E3180A1E74923459534AB8DD

5CF80860E3180A1E74923459534AB8DD

3/7/2006 6:00:04 PM 4/18/2006 11:15:07 AM

2132095 nukes EAC661B0B29B94E7D74E03E07D476CB7

855423C8B05886D6E2CDE6EAC2D7ECD0

FE9ABEFE81FF87C4C13EC167CB9F6072

12:00:00 AM 12:00:00 AM

2464856 **Segvec** 0EBBCBDFE04DB5550DC6CD8C5122A37C

CD9F13B7941B7CCE73A896C65B464A8C

42D8AA7CDE9C78C4757862D84620C335

12:00:00 AM 5/10/2006 7:52:24 AM

2996438 Spike B3BA03050F641D50663ED9FC21773D9C

3A8340788A5332547AB61419557DC8B4

C8837B23FF8AAA8A2DDE915473CE0991

4/25/2006 5:43:21 PM 4/24/2006 2:51:15 PM

I note his password_hashes changed since last time I captured it [this field, unfortunately, overwrites]

2996438

Spike B3BA03050F641D50663ED9FC21773D9C

F3BAD77C8FAFECE33E8A62441C26C1B0

2DB229E6236C0A3F531E2C2F48D7E260

12:00:00 AM 3/31/2006 12:24:46 PM

and accounts tables

account_id acct_name descr1 descr2

1632310 cgt

1956825 **segvec segvec segvec**

2132095 nukes

2464856 **segvec**
2996438 Spike[851]

During May 2006, Jackson delivered clear evidence capable of exposing the segvec suspect's true identity to government investigators. Jackson's intelligence included segvec's mailbox information in Miami and confirmed the use of segvec@fromru.com email address on the debit card registrations. Jackson was able to cross-reference this data and identify other alias used by segvec, including "Ceres" and "Sy Lee."

On or about May 12, 2006, USPIS Agent Gregory Crabb, emailed Jackson, requesting information on segvec e-gold accounts. As he often did, Jackson quickly replied with details on the request accounts.

> Crabb, Gregory S wrote:
> Doug,
> Could you give us a refresh on segvec accounts?
> 1632310
> 1956825
> 2132095
> 2464856
> 2996438
> Your last cut to us ran through 4/7... Time flies when you are having fun and he is a very hot topic.[852]

Jackson's response:

> Subject: Re: Maksik's Big Mover
> From: Douglas Jackson <djackson@e-gold.com>
> Date: Fri, 12 May 2006 10:20:02 -0400
> Looks like he hasn't been terribly busy this month - only about another 40k in. I ran it in overlap fashion so this includes/supersedes the prior. Spotcheck today shows he is holding 980 oz. in account 2464856. At this moment's exchange rate that's about $708 k worth. He also has about another 20k worth scattered in other accounts, apparently on his behalf
> [Attached file data shown below]

---

[851] Jackson, Douglas. "s____c Constellation." Received by Gregory Crabb, and Agent X, *s____c Constellation*, 10 May 2006.

[852] Crabb, Gregory. "Maksik's Big Mover." Received by Douglas Jackson, *Maksik's Big Mover*, 12 May 2006.

Segvec, updated 5.12.06 accts 1632310, 1956825, 2132095, 2464856, 2996438.xls[853]

Four days later, Jackson emailed Agent Crabb with some astonishing new segvec data obtained through e-gold in-house investigations with a third-party exchange provider.

Subject: more S----c data
From: Douglas Jackson <djackson@e-gold.com>
Date: Tue, 16 May 2006 08:18:19 -0400
I noticed yesterday that Segvec's 5th largest outbound, to account 108179, is another XXXXX account [Third-party financial services company].
XXXXX had this additional data filed under that profile, including not only a Tokyo maildrop but the next hop (in FL) for where mail from that drop was to be forwarded. I'm pasting that   part first, but all the data is pretty interesting, including confirmation that Ceres and Sy Lee are indeed Segvec nyms
****
Regarding the mail drop details:
Below is the confirmation e-mail from the Tokyo mail accommodation address provider to us confirming the order along with our e-gold batch details paying the Tokyo provider for the service.
Hello.
We got your payment.
Thank you very much.
The maildrop account is ready.

Mr. Sy Manuel LEE
502 Hillsidekagurazaka,
3-6-10 Kagurazaka,
Shinjyuku-ku,
Tokyo 162-0825
JAPAN

Weekly forwarding to

Leo Peralta
PMB #118

[853] Jackson, Douglas. "Re: Maksik's Big Mover." Received by Gregory Crabb, and Agent X, *Re: Maksik's Big Mover*, 12 May 2006.

11762 S.W. 88 Street
Miami,FL 33186
USA
****

1. Remittance on 11/21/2005 was for a XXXXX from "Ceres," number 0406 and shipped to Florida, USA on November 22nd, 2005. No other information available on this other than what I previously gave you.
2. Remittance on 2/1/2006 was an order for misc items, i.e.
1 x Panama bearer share company @ $1935
3 x bank accounts @ $5550
4 x XXcards @ 5280
6 x Travel Cards @ $6000
1 x maildrop @ $500
shipping @ $128
See notes below on the above.

To the best of my recollection, the above products were shipped to a Florida address, probably Ceres'. The bank account application forms were emailed. The Panama company was an off the shelf bearer share company and after looking for the name for you, I couldn't locate it. Those kind of companies come with apostille papers, English translations and a blank power of attorney where the customer writes in the persons name to operate the company. Other than fulfilling that order I have no other information regarding that.

Be advised that I informed XXXXX Security there is approximately US$14,500 waiting for load on XXCard number 0604 and approximately US$14,500 for card number 0612 for a total of US$29,000. Those funds were not loaded when the US$50,000 loads for each card were received because XXXXX had recently lowered the daily/monthly load limits on all their cards from the previous amounts XXXXX allowed, i.e. US$300,000 per month per card.

The customer/s sent US$50,000 e-gold load for each card before they learnt of these lower

loading amounts. Card holder/s inquired about why the cards were only loaded with only US$30,000 and was the limits for their cards only? I informed the cardholder/s of the recently lower amounts allowed by XXXXX ($9500 per day -$ 30,000 per 30 day month per card,) for all cards and they requested 2 other XXXXX. When asked for a delivery address they instructed that I e-mail them the card numbers and pins as they can replicate the cards, which I did as no delivery was provided by them. Those cards has not been activated.

A week or so later I emailed them again requesting instructions for loading for the remaining balances. I have not contacted them again nor have I heard back from them or received any further communications from them. Those funds, i.e. approximately US$14,500 for each card (total US$29,000 plus or minus) are still sitting in the XXXXX merchant account pending further instructions. I do not know how XXXXX is going to proceed nor what they intend to do regarding those funds. Be advised that to the best of my knowledge, I do not have any other information regarding these cardholders/customers. I have complied with XXXXX's and your/e-gold requests to the best of my ability.

I will contact XXXXX and you in the event I receive any communications from the above cardholders/customers as I previously promised you. I trust this information will be of help to you.

Regards

XXXXX

****

notes

The below "Travel Cards" cards are denominated in euro and are issued from PrivatBank

Evpatoriya in the Ukraine.

6762 4620 1233 7520 - sold - Feb 1 2006 - ███ - egold - Ceres - segvec@fromru.com

6762 4620 1233 7512 - sold - Feb 1 2006 - ███ - egold - Ceres - segvec@fromru.com

6762 4620 1233 8197 - sold - Feb 1 2006 - ███ - egold - Ceres - segvec@fromru.com

6762 4620 1233 8098 - sold - Feb 1 2006 - ███ - egold - Ceres - segvec@fromru.com

6762 4620 1233 8106 - sold - Feb 1 2006 - ███ - egold - Ceres - segvec@fromru.com

6762 4620 1233 8189 - sold - Feb 1 2006 - ███ - egold - Ceres - segvec@fromru.com

….

The below are XXXXX. To the best of my knowledge, cards number 0596 and 0620 have not

been activated.

6220983033000000596 - sold - Feb 1 2006 - ███ - egold - Ceres - segvec@fromru.com

6220983033000000604 - sold - Feb 1 2006 - █████ - egold - Ceres -
segvec@fromru.com
6220983033000000612 - sold - Feb 1 2006 - ████ - egold - Ceres -
segvec@fromru.com
6220983033000000620 - sold - Feb 1 2006 - ███ - egold - Ceres -
segvec@fromru.com[854]

Another email from Jackson to USPIS Crabb, received by this government investigator on Thursday, June 22, 2006, 1:09 PM, and soon after copied to DOJ Prosecutor Peretti, identified segvec as having been previously arrested and released. This fact explicitly matched Albert Gonzalez, who had been previously arrested by authorities in 2003 for carder related crimes and released. Jackson's information was another tell-tale signal leading straight to Albert Gonzalez. USPIS investigators received Jackson's intelligence that was capable of identifying Gonzalez in June 2006. By July, DOJ Attorney Kimberly Peretti had received that same evidence.

Here is a copy of that email chain including segvec's partial header.[855]

Subject: RE: s____c [segvec]
From: "Agent X" <XXXXX@uspis.gov>
Date: Thu, 22 Jun 2006 13:31:06 -0400
Doug,
Very interesting. Thank you for sending this over. Very very interesting...

-----Original Message-----
From: Douglas Jackson [mailto:djackson@e-gold.com]
Sent: Thursday, June 22, 2006 1:09 PM
To: Agent X
Cc: Crabb, Gregory S
Subject: s____c
Agent X, ████████████ received this email from his customer, who I thought he had previously known only as Stephen Ceres, Sy Lee or Pedro Morales. **The critical bit - apparently, someone had arrested segvec but let him out.**
Doug[856]

[854] Jackson, Douglas. "More S----c Data." Received by Gregory S. Crabb, *More S----c Data*, 16 May 2006.
[855] Jackson, Douglas. "s____c." Received by Gregory S Crabb, *s____c*, 22 June 2006.
[856] Ibid

Received: from www3.pochta.ru [81.211.64.23];
Tue, 20 Jun 2006 14:13:34 +0200
Received: (from www@localhost) by www3.pochta.ru (8.13.1/8.13.1) id
k5KCDZ4R050672;
Tue, 20 Jun 2006 16:13:35 +0400
(MSD) (envelope-from segvec@fromru.com)
Date: Tue, 20 Jun 2006 16:13:35 +0400
(MSD) Message-Id: <200606201213.k5KCDZ4R050672@www3.pochta.ru>
 From: segvec@fromru.com
To: XXXXXX.com
X-Mailer: Free mail service Pochta.ru;
WebMail Client; Account: segvec@fromru.com
X-Proxy-IP: [85.216.54.253]
X-Originating-IP: [85.216.54.253]
Subject: Re: egold => ███ #2
X-IMAIL-SPAM-DNSBL: (fiveten,e66e1eef010a48c1,127.0.0.9)
X-RCPT-TO: XXXXXX.com

With Jackson's in-house investigative work, by June 2006, government agents had direct evidence identifying segvec was operating in Miami, not Europe. Furthermore, Jackson had supplied segvec's local Miami mailbox drop address and two recent locations of ATM card withdrawals through local Miami area banks. Indeed, this ATM footage would have shown a person making the segvec debit card withdrawals. Finally, Jackson profiled the segvec suspect as having been previously arrested and released! This detail matched Gonzalez.

However, no one arrested Gonzalez or even questioned him! Furthermore, Peretti's office seems to have buried and ignored Jackson's evidence. Why would DOJ prosecuting attorneys and USSS Special Agents ignore or conceal this critical information? Only years later, the world would learn that "segvec" was the alias used by hacker Albert Gonzalez. In June 2006, when government agents received Jackson's evidence, Gonzalez was a paid confidential informant for the USSS.

In July 2006, this e-gold® evidence that Jackson had shared with the USPIS, including all email correspondences, was forwarded to Kimberly Peretti at the Department of Justice. Based on her request, Jackson estimates that Kimberly Peretti received the following information in the second week of July 2006.

1. The alias used to set up the Miami box, Leo Peralta
2. The address and post box number of his Miami maildrop
3. The debit card information [Functioning cards being used by segvec]
4. The last locations of cash withdrawals at two South Florida bank ATMs
5. The fact that segvec had previously been arrested and released.

Jackson believes, and the evidence suggests, that Peretti knew segvec's true identity and did not arrest or charge Gonzalez because he was a paid USSS informant. No arrest occurred after July 2006. It seems possible that the emails and information arrived at Peretti and went no further. Did Kimberly Peretti bury this critical intelligence?

Later that year, in mid-October, Jackson followed up with the USPIS Agents and supplied additional updated segvec intelligence. This information also came from e-gold in-house investigations.

Subject: segvec update 10.19.06
From: Douglas Jackson <djackson@e-gold.com>
Date: Thu, 19 Oct 2006 17:56:25 -0400
To: "Agent X", "Crabb, Gregory S" <GSCrabb@uspis.gov>
1632310, 1956825, 2132095, 2464856, 2996438, 3584031, 3584940, 3463311, 3479376, 3463311 and 3479376 are new Segvec accounts
Someone in our Due Diligence Unit blocked the primary Segvec account, 2464856, on 8/25 for false ID, apparently in relation with blocking 2132095 for same and noting both were controlled by same person Segvec or someone closely associated with him hijacked 1336546 and used it as conduit for sending value to Bart Bogers 1111355, an Irish guy who I've encountered before [the NTFIU Mazhar thing] who sort of poses as an exchanger? but is looking more and more like a money launderer. Bogers sends value out through IceGold so I've asked IceGold to figure out if Bogers is directing value for the benefit of third parties.
10/2/2006 8:21:37 AM 66.227.136.32 2464856 1336546 24
      68578604 1 50000 intercambio urgente para
10/2/2006 8:23:29 AM 84.197.6.3 1336546 1111355 24
      68578652 85 39428 Exchange for Abdulgadir (URG 02/10) thnx
Segvec or someone closely associated with him also hijacked 1115523 and used it as conduit for sending value to 3584031 and 3584940 [both of which still contain all the value - he apparently bobbled the passphrase for 3584940 (see below)]. 3584031, 3584940 solely hold segvec value and are almost certainly controlled by him.
9/13/2006 3:03:25 PM 69.151.61.14[IP] 2464856 1115523 24

67737870 1   300000 repayment of debt
9/13/2006 3:05:06 PM 85.17.6.159[IP] 1115523 3584940 24
    67738154 1   299000 for down payment of offshore property #8972-2006
9/13/2006 3:08:01 PM 69.151.61.14[IP] 2464856 1115523 24
    67738628 1   17001 last payment
9/13/2006 3:10:36 PM 69.151.61.14[IP] 2464856 1115523 24
    67739056 1   5 egold fees
9/13/2006 3:11:19 PM 85.17.6.159[IP] 1115523 3584031 24
    67739174 1 18000 Shipment #2908D&G
The e-gold Customer Service staff received this note which I'm sure was from
Segvec:
From: michaelspropertyinvestments@yahoo.com
Sent: Thursday, September 28, 2006 9:20 AM
To: J8TCwJsg_service@e-gold.com
Subject: [e-gold-service] I can't access my account for so ... [PR:ESSAPTVP]
Submitter IP: 66.188.84.252
CATEGORY: CUSTOMER SUPPORT
Customer Name:
Email: michaelspropertyinvestments@yahoo.com
e-gold Batch:
e-gold Account: 3584940
Question: I can't access my account for some reason. Please advise what the problem
is."
Linking transactions:
8/4/2006 12:05:52 PM 75.3.142.227[IP] 2464856 3463311 24
    65791584 1 3200
8/4/2006 12:10:35 PM 75.3.142.227[IP] 3463311 3129497 24
    65791874 1 3096 two new servers payment
8/9/2006 5:50:06 PM 64.85.230.235[IP] 3463311 3479376 24
    66072691 1 1000 2nd payment
8/9/2006 5:51:42 PM 64.85.230.235[IP] 3479376 1461558 24
    66072727 1 1329.98
8/21/2006 9:06:38 PM 68.32.69.184[IP] 2464856 3463311 24
    66684686 1 5150 exchange #06-2989
8/21/2006 9:07:33 PM 68.32.69.184[IP] 3463311 3472732 24
    66684705 1 5150
1632310 Christopher G. Teptitov 1868 Lee Road Winter Park FL USA/32789

cgt@hotbox.ru   321-299-3595

1956825 segvec 483 Mkdlvic Circle Brooklyn NY 10092

segvec@fromru.com 212-384-3948

2132095 Andrew Montesani 239 Broadway Ave New York NY 10022

nukes@land.ru 212-348-9382

2464856 Segvec Mihali 839 N Brown ST Brooklyn NY 11182

nukes@land.ru 212-384-3970

2996438 Andrew Mckenzie Swallow age str. 3-10 Portland OR 32134

spike_spiegel@safe-mail.net 823565674

3463311 Stephen K 63 Canterbury Rd Newton Highlands MA 02461

stephenk@mail333.com 617-916-2081

3479376 jcjethro jcjethro New York NY 10098

jcjethro@pisem.net 212-390-2985

3584031 John Doe Guang Hua Lu Beijing China 00000

johndoe46@safe-mail.net 6524-5521

3584940 Harry Michaels 208 29th St NW Bradenton FL 34205-3409

michaelspropertyinvestments@yahoo.com (941) 747-6225

[Parts of this email were removed for brevity]

[Attached files][857]

Segvec update 10.19.06 transactions.xls

Segvec update 0.19.06 ins and outs.xls

Segvec update 10.19.06 counterparties.xls

As previously shown, these are statements to the Court by Prosecuting Attorney Laurel Rimon during the November 2008 Sentencing Hearing.

> The information that Dr. Jackson may have provided to Agent Crabb did not factor into this investigation at all.[858]

> We[The prosecution] intentionally did not seek a cooperation agreement or offered a cooperation agreement in this case because we don't need his[Jackson] cooperation. We needed the account information and we have it.[859]

---

[857] Jackson, Douglas. "Segvec Update 10.19.06." Received by Gregory Crabb, and Agent X, *Segvec Update 10.19.06*, 19 Oct. 2006.

[858] Docket No. CR 07-109. UNITED STATES OF AMERICA vs. E-GOLD LTD, GOLD & SILVER RESERVE LTD, DOUGLAS L. JACKSON, BARRY K. DOWNEY, REID A. JACKSON. TRANSCRIPT OF SENTENCE BEFORE THE HONORABLE ROSEMARY M. COLLYER UNITED STATES DISTRICT JUDGE, 20 Nov. 2008.

[859] Ibid

The fact is that at the time of this investigation we already had the data base that we had seized in December of 2005. Secret Service agents were able to review it and analyze and get the information they needed.[860]

And in any event, what he can provide and what he has provided is quite limited. As we've talked about most of the accounts, **a vast majority of the accounts don't have good identifying information.** If we get information from Dr. Jackson that an account has an IP address in Estonia, even if we get a post office box on a corner, street corner in Estonia, that means absolutely nothing if you have no where to trace to an individual and that's what we found over and over again.[861]

The evidence that identified segvec's location as being Miami, Florida and not eastern Europe came from Jackson's June 2006 information. Segvec's registered Miami mailbox address came from Jackson's third-party industry contacts responding to his information requests. None of this critical intelligence or evidence was in the e-gold database copied by the USSS in 2005. The government investigators did not retrieve any of this data before Agent Crabb had received it from Jackson.

That facts and dates in these emails prove beyond a shadow of a doubt that Dr. Jackson shared a vast amount of detailed intelligence with the USPIS. Jackson's information originated with third-party exchange providers, debit card issuers, and licensed financial service companies. Any law enforcement organization could have benefited from this comprehensive intelligence and by working directly with e-gold. Furthermore, because the volume of identifying information users would leave behind after every Spend transaction was so large, it was also evident that e-gold not anonymous.

In 2006, the Court had not charged the company or its operators with a crime. Given this innocence, some fundamental questions emerge:

- From 2005 until 2007, why didn't the U.S. Secret Service acknowledge the benefits of Jackson's fruitful assistance?
- When the investigative tools and evidence were available, why didn't the USSS, an agency charged with arresting criminals, use the available e-gold data and stop the illegal carder operation?
- Jackson was offering e-gold inside information with no strings attached. Why didn't the U.S. Secret Service work with him and arrest more criminals?

[860] Ibid
[861] Ibid

Hindsight being 20/20, the answer to these questions appears to be a simple one. In e-gold's case, the U.S. Secret Service seemed to have only been concerned about convicting the e-gold defendants and seizing the e-gold bullion reserves. Prosecutors sought the shortest path to the prize. Any detours outside of that focus may have weakened their case against Jackson.

In July 2006, Peretti received Jackson's in-house intelligence on segvec from USPIS Agent Crabb. After reviewing the information, she may have realized the criminal responsible for her two career-building cases, was the same confidential informant they had released in 2003.

Who knows what occurred after that revelation. Did Jackson's crucial evidence identifying Gonzalez get buried in a drawer or dropped in a shredder? The world may never know. This evidence disappeared because the Defendants never received credit for their work, and Gonzalez continued committing crimes.

Until the publication of *Better Money*, that critical July 2006 email evidence disappeared.

The USSS had similar motivations. If Jackson was able to prove that his voluntary assistance cracked the segvec case, then the resulting e-gold praise may have weakened the USSS's chance to seize the bullion. By any means possible, convicting Jackson was the only way to guarantee forfeiture of the nearly $50 million in precious metal. If Jackson and e-gold had avoided the charges altogether or prevailed in court, the USSS would not have received their monetary prize.

A Tangled Web Part Two

From September 2005 through November 2007, during the e-gold case, Laurel Loomis Rimon was an Assistant United States Attorney in Washington, D.C.

For 37 months, from January 2015 through January 2018, Laurel Loomis Rimon served as General Counsel for the third-largest federal Office of Inspector General in Washington, D.C. From January to September 2017, her title was Acting Assistant Inspector General for Inspections.[862]

Rimon's employment profile reads like Peretti's CV. Each of the former DOJ lawyers' profiles tends to boast about their achievements in the e-gold case. Rimon's LinkedIn profile states:

Served as an AUSA in the Fraud and Public Corruption Section.

[862] Rimon, Laurel L. "Laurel Loomis Rimon." *LinkedIn*, LinkedIn Corporation, 2020, www.linkedin.com/in/laurel-loomis-rimon-58655323/.

Successfully led prosecution of "e-gold" enterprise, a novel on-line digital currency service used to fund various criminal enterprises, under money laundering and money transmitting statutes.[863]

Surprisingly, Rimon also had been employed at The Department of Homeland Security when Jackson's August 24, 2017, personal letter, on corruption and misconduct by USSS & DOJ officials, arrived at the DHS Office of the Inspector General. As Jackson later indicated in this February 2019 email, when his letter arrived, Rimon was working for DHS under John Roth, as Acting Assistant Inspector General for Inspections. It is unknown if Rimon received a copy or read Jackson's letter.

02/15/2019
Oh and then Laurel Loomis-Rimon went on to a gig as counsel for the ID of DHS, John Roth, who had been involved in our case at a critical juncture, late December 2006, when they were deciding whether to press ahead and indict.

It is no wonder the ID of DHS refused to so much as acknowledge my detailed complaint after I learned (summer 2017) critical facts revealing prosecutorial misconduct, though I have the delivery confirmation that they received my extensive hard copy complaint and supporting exhibits.[864]

On or about December 1, 2008, former United States Postal Inspection Service Agent X, now working in the private sector, sent this email to Jackson warning of active new malware. Jackson had already pleaded guilty, and the Court had sentenced him earlier that year.

Agent X wrote:
Doug,
Not sure if you are aware or not, but there is a trojan called Zeus that is very popular among the hackers/carders. I just got the configuration file for the trojan and it has e-gold and Webmoney listed in the trojan as sites to keylog the user from once they visit it. We've seen very large botnets using Zeus where they are harvesting a large amount of gigabytes of raw data. If you can bridge the relationship between myself and Peter [of WebMoney Transfer] (asking for his PGP), I can send him such type information directly. Please see the config file below and take note, Agent X[865]

[863] Ibid
[864] "Re: K. Peretti." Received by Carl Mullan, *Re: K. Peretti*, 15 Feb. 2020.

Jackson responded to the email later that day.

> On 12/1/08 1:19 PM, "Douglas Jackson" < djackson@e-gold.com> wrote:
> * PGP Signed by an unmatched address: 12/01/08 at 13:19:51, Decrypted
> Hi ██████,
> Much appreciated.
> I passed it on the Peter D with my recommendation that he sync up with you. I see the USSS is persisting in their false advertising today in the guise of a Symantec whitepaper
> http://eval.symantec.com/mktginfo/enterprise/white_papers
> /b-whitepaper_underground_economy_report_11-2008-14525717.en-us.pdf
> Its tempting to run the numbers retrospectively to see how many orders of magnitude they are inflating by. My experience with the CP topic with NCMEC was that they implied that e-gold had seen about 10,000 times [that's actual] the volume it really had. At sentencing, the gov lawyer said my assistance to LE had been of no or at most trivial benefit, that the USSS had already gleaned anything that might have been useful to them directly from our database. But as of about August 2006 they still hadn't managed to even mount it on a server in a way that would enable queries.
> Doug[866]

Minutes later, Agent X sent this email reply discussing Jackson's previous USPIS assistance on international criminal investigations.

> Subject: Re: For e-gold and may want to share this with Peter at WM
> From: Agent X
> Date: Mon, 1 Dec 2008 14:05:32 -0500
> To: Doug Jackson <djackson@e-gold.com>
> I'm letting the whitepaper load and I'll take a look at it and give some thoughts later.
>
> Being off the record, regarding that comment, I would completely disagree. I know wholeheartedly how many investigations you assisted us on and how much it helped for us referring cases to international LE based off of your work.

[865] X, Agent. "Re: For e-Gold and May Want to Share This with Peter at WM." Received by Douglas Jackson, *Re: For e-Gold and May Want to Share This with Peter at WM*, 1 Dec. 2008.
[866] Jackson, Douglas. "Re: For e-Gold and May Want to Share This with Peter at WM." Received by Agent X, *Re: For e-Gold and May Want to Share This with Peter at WM*, 1 Dec. 2008.

There are still cases ongoing today that are as a direct result of your help. Several cyber-criminals would not have been identified without your assistance. Another story for a different setting/time however.

PGP key. Thanks, Agent X[867]

In September 2009, Agent X emailed Jackson and shared his thoughts. Jackson has never before made these emails public. The information presented in these short emails categorically proves that the segvec evidence Jackson provided the USPIS, was forwarded to the Miami USSS office and shared with Special Agents.

While a paid USSS Confidential Informant, Albert Gonzalez, a/k/a segvec, was under the USSS Miami office's full-time supervision.

On Wednesday, September 2, 2009, Jackson sent this email to the former USPIS Agent X.

> Subject: Esk
> From: Douglas Jackson <djackson@e-gold.com>
> Date: Wed, 02 Sep 2009 17:33:23 -0400
> I see Esk indeed turned out to be Egor Shevelev of Kiev.
> http://manhattanda.org/whatsnew/press/2009-08-31.shtml
> At my sentencing, the prosecution indicated that my investigative efforts were of little consequence, that the USSS had already culled all the useful data, for example in the Segvec case, from the seized e-gold database. They described that the USPIS has no role in the Gonzalez or Carranza cases - that they were strictly USSS ops. They've now not only taken credit but have also gratuitously badmouthed e-gold in the cases of:
> - Blinky,
> - Kaisersose,
> - Segvec,

[867] X, Agent. "Re: For e-Gold and May Want to Share This with Peter at WM." Received by Douglas Jackson, *Re: For e-Gold and May Want to Share This with Peter at WM*, 1 Dec. 2008.

- Esk

I guess they didn't take credit for Jilsi who I only recently learned really was Renu Subramanian.[868]

Later that same day, the former USPIS Agent replied to Jackson.

> Wednesday, September 02, 2009
> Agent X wrote:
> Doug,
> I still wish I had my government e-mails to show you some of the stuff. On the Segvec stuff, where we worked with you and the exchanger out of Salt Lake, we sent all of that stuff to our Miami office to work it. They sent an Inspector with the information (unbeknownst to us) to a USSS task force meeting in Miami where all of that info was brought up in the meeting. The Inspector said "The SS there was really interested in all that information. They seemed like they had a handle on it so I turned it over to them."
>
> We were not pleased with this at all and this was part of the problem we were running into at our HQ at the time. If the case was domestic US, we had to send everything out to our field offices and help them with it. If it was international, then we were to work directly with the international LE agency.
>
> I can tell you that it was USPIS providing the information to SOCA regarding Jilsi.
>
> We'll have to chat sometime, Doug. We by no means had what happened to you happen to us by the people you're talking about but it wasn't a pleasant working experience either.[869]

Jackson responded the following day.

> From: Douglas Jackson [mailto:djackson@e-gold.com]
> Sent: Thursday, September 03, 2009 9:27 AM
> Subject: Re: Esk
> Old Signed: 09/03/09 at 09:27:03, Decrypted
> Agent X,

[868] Jackson, Douglas. "Esk." Received by Agent X, *Esk*, 2 Sept. 2009.
[869] X, Agent. "RE_Esk2.Pdf." Received by Douglas Jackson, *RE_Esk2.Pdf*, 2 Sept. 2009.

I greatly appreciate this insight. I have a transcript of our sentencing hearing that you might find parts of which interesting.

I know Kim Zetter is still keenly interested in the whole Gonzalez story and many of the others but there is so little I can tell her for fear of something possibly being construed as contradicting my plea or statement of offense. I still suspect that one of the tasks Gonzalez's USSS handlers assigned him was to recruit his criminal community to use e-gold and thereby dirty up e-gold, which agenda may even help account for how they could have been blind to his involvement in both the TJX and then the Heartland capers while he was their boy.

That assignment, if it occurred, would have been pursuant to an established agenda relating to... Throughout the process we intuited and also had data snippets supporting our hypothesis that a pathologically embittered ex-employee named Charles Evans who we had fired in 2000 was deeply involved, dating back to 2001, in initially suckering the USSS into thinking we could be their career-making poster child of criminality, garnering them the status and funding as the NetForce-like lead US agency of cybercrimefighting [that was SOCA's theory, more or less, regarding USSS adherence to this ever weirder agenda even as the exculpatory evidence was becoming so overwhelming that any idiot could see how ridiculous the whole thing was], That was never fully corroborated until sentencing when, there he[Evans] was in the courtroom!, passing notes to the USSS agents who in turn passed them to the prosecutors. How a nutcase like him could recruit an agency of the US gov into serving as the cat's paw of his vengeance [and the furtherance of the goals of the would-be competitor to e-gold that he had gone to work for in 2001] is not a pretty thing to contemplate.
Doug[870]

Shortly after that dialog, Agent X sent this final email in this chain. [Portions redacted]

Subject: RE: Esk
From: "Agent X"
Date: Thu, 3 Sep 2009 13:04:00 -0400
To: Doug Jackson <djackson@e-gold.com>
* PGP Signed by an unverified key: 09/03/09 at 13:04:00, Decrypted
(Sorry, the e-mails I sent were supposed to be encrypted. I think I fixed that issue now.)

[870] Jackson, Douglas. "Re: Esk." Received by Agent X, *Re: Esk*, 3 Sept. 2009.

Yes, I have similar reservations in talking about anything with anyone from the media about this. I do not trust what someone would do in trying to make another example out of someone, if you catch my drift. What I do know is you helped on countless numbers of investigations. There are some things that I'd rather not put in writing about how Greg and I tried helping you when all this went down and it was like pleading your case to a wall. Some would listen (probably just to appease us) and some would look at us like why are we going to bat for you. It was a really messed up situation. Like I said, probably better to be discussed over Pina Coladas sometime.

As for your final thoughts in the past message regarding nutcases. You have Gonzalez, Brett Johnson, who were CIs and doing crime on the side, including one of Zetter's favorites (David Thomas aka El Mariachi). Sometimes nutcases are much better at their game than the people supposed to arrest them.[871]
[from Agent X]

USSS Origins and Motives

In 2019 emails, Jackson expressed that e-gold's story could have turned out very differently. Dr. Jackson encapsulates the events and outcome in terms of lessons learned, an 'if only I had known then what I know now' saga.

Only if relevant documents and testimony were to surface, could the true motives and origins of the USSS campaign be definitively established. However, available artifacts and records provide a pretty clear picture. He described much of the company's legal battles as having "stemmed from the USSS misguided agenda of treating us like criminals to advance their own agency's interests."[872]

Reviewing the origins and alleged motives for the USSS targeting e-gold®, as Jackson

---

[871] X, Agent. "RE: Esk." Received by Douglas Jackson, *RE: Esk*, 3 Sept. 2009.

[872] Jackson, Douglas. "2019.8.23 Observations and Comments." Received by Carl Mullan, 2019.8.23 *Observations and Comments*, 23 Aug. 2019.

perceived them, provides crucial insight into the agency's alleged misconduct. This section offers additional facts, information, and background. Many of these facts support Jackson's claims directly, and others are circumstantial.

Origins

Jackson alleges that a covert campaign by certain USSS Special Agents, to close down and prosecute e-gold®, began in early 2001. On many occasions, Jackson has shared his belief that a private cabal of individuals was engaged allegedly in a malicious campaign against e-gold®. Ex-employee Charles Evans, competitor James Turk, and previous litigant Ian Grigg were allegedly participating in the conspiracy.

Seeking to malign e-gold®, Jackson claims that these parties may have supplied the USSS with false and misleading information about e-gold®. The cabal's ultimate goal was to shut down e-gold® and create unnecessary legal trouble for Jackson. He further explained these menacing roles in a 2020 email.

> The role of James Turk was pretty straightforward – to destroy the competitor that was preventing his business from attracting any usage as a payment system. But what caused Charles Evans and Ian Grigg to change from trusted allies to bitter enemies, set on seeking vengeance and informant rewards? They would later claim to have acted out of conscience[873], appalled by what they described as a lax permissive attitude on the part of the e-gold principals, causing them to turn a blind eye toward illicit usage of the system. But there is no record of such concerns being registered during 2000, as e-gold usage exploded and as rapid and continuous evolution of policies and countermeasures to combat illicit usage ensued. No disagreements surfaced in relation to development and implementation of appropriate anti-crime responses and both Grigg and Evans had already departed before the intensive arms race between e-gold developers and investigative staff and the online hackers and fraudsters escalated.

> So the question arises as to the extent to which Evans and Grigg came to be driven by personal malice and how much by economic motives, i.e. a desire for greater financial gain than they thought would accrue from their continued participation with the e-gold effort. And, to the extent personal malice played a role, the question that

---

[873] In 2016, in a conversation with attorney Carol Van Cleef at a payments conference in Orlando FL, Evans spun his motives in a different way, claiming "I did what I did because, if I had not, there would have been four defendants rather than three". This would imply the USSS had initiated the contact, a thesis that is highly implausible given the fact that the cabal was hiding out offshore at the time of their initial contacts with the IRS and the USSS, first in Anguilla, later in the Bahamas, in order to evade service of process in the civil suit G&SR brought against Evans.

comes into focus is: what was the origin of their alienation – the grievances, real or imagined, that impelled them to devote nearly two years of their lives (and those of the three other members of their shared household) to their campaign to destroy e-gold, even as their perseverance in such efforts drove all of them to the brink of destitution?[874]

Relationship with Charles Evans
As recalled by Dr. Jackson:

> "At no other time in my life, then or since, had I experienced personal interactions with anyone like Charles Evans. In his direct interactions with me he would engage in flattery slathered on so thick it reminded me of 'Lefou' in Disney's "Beauty and the Beast". Except I was no 'Gaston', a fact that seemed to bother him. On multiple occasions, he would urge me to project a more alpha male style of leadership, particularly like Larry Ellison of Oracle who he seemed to regard as the paradigm of how a captain of industry should come across. Evans was also given to using harsh metaphors, his favorite being the admonition to "ream him a new one" [i.e. a new asshole]. He also felt I was seriously deficient in the guile and deceit department and even gifted me a copy of Machiavelli's "The Prince" for remedial reading.
>
> But with people he perceived as lower in the pecking order he was supercilious, mocking and cruel. For instance, when Reid began taking a more active role in the company, he misperceived Reid's low-key mannerisms as an indication of weakness. It was disorienting to Charles to discover that Reid could not be bullied and he became increasingly resentful as he perceived Reid's growing influence.[875]

"Three Ends-of-the-World"
In this same April 8, 2020 email Jackson delved further into Evans' mind.

> Charles described "THREE (3) Ends-of-the-World" in his "sharp little pieces" threat email. This was a reference to a recurring pattern Charles perceived of being shafted by previous employers or superiors jealous or fearful his brilliance might eclipse theirs. The first such had been when either Professor Tyler Cowen or Randall Kroszner of George Mason University had allegedly blackballed him, preventing his matriculation into the PhD program in the George Mason Economics Department.

[874] Jackson, Douglas. Received by Carl Mullan, Evans and Grigg Analysis and Write-Up, 8 Apr. 2020.
[875] Ibid

Another had been alleged treachery of some sort at the hands of James C. Bennett, in relation to a late-90's project called Internet Transactions Transnational Inc.[876] Over time, I had growing concerns that Charlie exhibited signs of what the DSM IV termed "Antisocial Personality Disorder". He was a charming, even brilliant, conversationalist. But his effect on organizations, at least ours, was to sow discord. His standard MO was to denounce and undermine person A to person B, typically telling person B that person A was saying bad things about her while at the same time maligning person B to person A. This was most evident with his drumbeat of criticism (expressed to me) of Ian Grigg as milking us for money that was being wasted on an economically worthless scheme. I can only imagine what he was saying about me to Grigg.

By summer 2000, especially after Charles had made his "sharp little pieces" threat, we attempted to convince the principals of Standard Reserve—Elwyn Jenkins, Jack Jones and Glen Hammer—to take him on as CEO. Our hope was that perhaps if he was appointed top dog of some hierarchy, as he always seemed to aspire to, that what we perceived as dysfunction might be channeled into a more constructive, perhaps even Larry Ellison-like, flowering of fulfilled potential. But Jenkins et al wanted no part of him."[877]

At least two of these individuals, in the presupposed conspiracy, were alleged to be motivated by revenge and personal profit. All three individuals had previous legal action with Jackson, G&SR, or e-gold®.

- Ian Grigg: Arbitration Case Case 50 T 117 00265 01 May 2001.
- Charles Evans: California Civil Case 322321 June 2001.
- G.M. Network Ltd. [Goldmoney/Turk] Case 01 CV 9621 November 2001.

Case 50 T 117 00265 01
Ian Grigg, Systemics, Inc.
Downey & Jackson, DigiGold Inc.
Arbitration Case

Around May 29, 2001, DigiGold.net Inc.[Jackson] filed claims and asked for injunctive relief against Systemics Inc.[Grigg] though the Courts of Anguilla. The Arbitrator delivered

---

[876] A search for the pre-October 1999 website for Bennett's transnational.net website on archive.org occasionally redirects to the "chyden.net" servers established and maintained by Evans since the 90's https://web.archive.org/web/19990208010623/http://www.chyden.net/index.html

[877] Jackson, Douglas. Received by Carl Mullan, Evans and Grigg Analysis and Write-Up, 8 Apr. 2020.

the Final Award on August 28, 2002. The Court rejected the claims brought by DigiGold and ordered DigiGold to pay all of the Arbitration costs to Systemics[878] The Arbitrator's award to Systemics was paid out in full by DigiGold, by late January 2003.

Case 322321
Charles Evans, personally
Downey & Jackson, Gold & Silver Reserve, Inc.

After being terminated by Jackson, G&SR sued Charles Evans. On June 21, 2001, Charles Evans received a Summons and Complaint in California alleging misappropriated trade secrets, tortious interference, unfair business practices, and breach of loyalty. G&SR was seeking a judgment against Defendant Charles Evans.[879] On May 23, 2002, G&SR filed a 2nd Amended Complaint in the same suit, adding two additional names to the legal case, including Ian Grigg. Evans, however, could not be located having fled the country to evade service of process. [Not until 2007 did Jackson learn Evans had holed with Grigg and other cabal members, first in Anguilla, later in the Bahamas where they were living on funds Jackson had provided Grigg for the Ricardo/Digigold development project]. Therefore, on August 30, 2002, unable to serve the amended complaint, G&SR withdrew their complaint against Evans et al. from the California court, and the judge dismissed the case without prejudice.

Case 01 CV 9621
James Turk/GoldMoney
e-gold Ltd. & DigiGold.net Ltd

In early November 2001, G.M. Network Ltd. [Goldmoney/Turk] announced the business was suing e-gold Ltd. and DigiGold Ltd. for patent infringement.

> November 5th, 2001 - G.M. Network Ltd., the company that has developed GoldMoney, today announced that it is defending in the US District Court in New York City its digital gold currency patents against infringement by e-gold Ltd. and DigiGold Ltd. e-gold and DigiGold are reportedly owned, operated and controlled by Doug Jackson and Barry Downey and related family trusts, all of whom were named in the Complaint. The Trustees of the e-gold Special Purpose Trust, the Escrow Agents used by that trust, and Gold & Silver Reserve Inc. (d/b/a OmniPay) were also

---

[878] Grigg, Ian. "Anguilla Shutdown of DigiGold Servers." *DigiGold.net Ltd versus Systemics Inc,* www.systemics.com, May 2001, www.systemics.com/legal/digigold/#anguilla.

[879] Grigg, Ian. "G&SR v. Evans." *DigiGold.net Ltd versus Systemics Inc*, http://www.systemics.com, June 2001, www.systemics.com/legal/digigold/#evans.

named in the Complaint.[880]

Eventually, the Court dismissed this case without prejudice, and each side claimed partial victory. Of note, in 2011-12 the US Patent Office performed an Inter Partes Reexamination of Turk's 7206763 patent. On reexamination, all claims were denied making the patent invalid.[881] The two page Reexamination Certificate dated April 3, 2012 concludes: "The patent is hereby amended as indicated below. As a result of reexamination, it has been determined that: Claims 1-30 are canceled."

Jackson proposes that in late 2001 or early 2002, this private cabal initiated contact with the USSS and also approached the IRS intending to focus misleading attention on Jackson and malign e-gold's business. He believes that the secret cabal had the following impetus.

- Personal malice against the principals of e-gold®
- Monetary rewards as a government informant
- Desire to advance the prospects of would-be competitors

Jackson wrote, "At least one such competitor acted as a sort of silent partner, launching reputation attacks through additional channels intended to complement the direct efforts of the cabal."[882] There is evidence to suggest that this statement is true.

On April 24, 2002, an attorney working for Mr. James Turk at the law firm of Conyers Dill & Pearman in Bermuda, sent an inflammatory letter to attorney Michael J. Mello, a partner in the Bermuda law firm Mello Jones & Martin. Mello was an attorney for The e-gold Bullion Reserve Special Purpose Trust registered in Hamilton, Bermuda. This Trust was the legal entity holding title to all of e-gold® customer bullion.

The company behind GoldMoney, GM Network Ltd., sent the letter. The letter contained incendiary remarks attacking Jackson's character and the reputations of G&SR, Inc. and e-gold Ltd. The letter also included a laundry list of alleged wrongdoing intended to reflect poorly on Jackson's character and present e-gold's business in a negative light. The letter's first paragraph read:

Our client [GM Network Ltd./GoldMoney] has become increasingly concerned by

[880] Grigg, Ian. "Goldmoney Patent v. G&SR, e-gold Ltd, DigiGold.net Ltd, Et Al." *DigiGold.net Ltd versus Systemics Inc,* Nov. 2001, www.systemics.com/legal/digigold/#evans.

[881] Turk, James J. *METHOD AND SYSTEM FOR COMMODITY-BASED CURRENCY FOR PAYMENT OF ACCOUNTS.* 17 Apr. 2007. https://bit.ly/2P2Jn6R

[882] Jackson, Douglas. "Origins and motives behind the USSS campaign to destroy e-gold." Received by John Roth, Inspector General, US Dept. of Homeland Security, 24 Aug. 2017, Indian Harbour Beach, FL.

recent reports in the Press concerning the propriety of the activities and management of the e-gold system, and the effect of these activities on public confidence in digital gold currency systems.[883]

The letter that had originated from Turk's lawyers set out to attack the e-gold® business from within; through the legal party responsible for the bullion trust. As a competitor in the new digital gold industry, GoldMoney would have benefited directly from the closure of e-gold®. Furthermore, any possible adverse action against Jackson, resulting from the letter, could have helped members of the plot.

Jackson later alleges that Turk's dirty tactic had been an attempt to intimidate the law firm into severing their relationship with e-gold®. The facts and evidence related to this attack support Jackson's claims. Jackson also shared this information in a 2019 email.

> "it was the off-the-reservation actions of a rogue agency[USSS] that had been goaded into destroying us by the Evans/Grigg/Turk cabal (and the incompetence of our own attorneys who were ignorant of the actual realities of how to interpret the post-PATRIOT Act money transmitter laws/landscape).[884]

Jackson stated in the same 2019 email that the funding behind the cabal originated from e-gold®.

> The cabal was financed by money that had been provided by the e-gold founders themselves to support an additional development initiative (Digigold, based on a digital cash protocol) but ended up largely diverted to fund cabal activities. These funds enabled the cabal to maintain a household, initially in Anguilla, later in the Bahamas where the principals had fled to evade service of process in a related matter.[885]

This claim by Jackson, regarding funds received by cabal members as originated from e-gold®, appears to be accurate and is backed up by evidence. Jackson's funding reference was an estimated $400,000 lawfully received by Grigg. The funds were a licensing fee between Jackson's company DigiGold and Grigg's company Systemics. Archived documents

883 Pearman, Conyers Dill. "e-gold Bullion Reserve Special Purpose Trust." Received by Michael Mello, *e-gold Bullion Reserve Special Purpose Trust*, 24 Apr. 2002.

884 Jackson, Douglas. "2019.8.23 Observations and Comments." Received by Carl Mullan, 2019.8.23 *Observations and Comments*, 23 Aug. 2019.

885 Jackson, Douglas. "Origins and motives behind the USSS campaign to destroy e-gold." Received by John Roth, Inspector General, US Dept. of Homeland Security, 24 Aug. 2017, Indian Harbour Beach, FL.

indicate that around eighty percent of a $500,000 licensing agreement was paid by DigiGold and received by Systemics. The deal was compensation for licensing of the Ricardo software and operation of the DigiGold servers. In a spring 2020 email, Jackson confirmed the payment amount to Grigg.

> In the aftermath of the firing of Evans and his co-conspirators, Ian Grigg announced that G&SR was in breach of its licensing agreement, having paid only[approximately] $370 thousand (that could be accounted for) of the specified $500 thousand (that we discovered had been written into a draft contract as due by June 2000). Just as the software that had been developed to support commercial operations with Digigold was finally becoming available, Grigg indicated he was going to pull the plug on the servers (operated by Systemics in Anguilla) where the Digigold application was hosted. For the e-gold principals, this breach in relations came as a complete surprise. They interpreted the break as stemming from bad feelings relating to the dismissal of Evans.[886]

As previously stated, this agreement ended up in arbitration with Grigg's company prevailing. A legal summary of the pleadings revealed this transaction.

> The Demand alleged, *inter alia*: (a) In or about August 1999 DigiGold entered into a Software License Agreement with Systemics under which Systemics agreed to develop the DigiGold product, i.e. a gold-backed digital currency which can be e-mailed between users and used to purchase items on the Internet; (b) Claimants provided $400,000 in funds and materials to initiate and continue the operation of Systemics for which Claimants were to receive 25% of the shares of Systemics; (c) Systemics used said funds to develop the DigiGold product and a settlement server and a market server for use in connection with DigiGold transactions, and (d) Systemics wrongfully sought to terminate its contractual and business relationship with Claimants, including its support for the DigiGold product.[887]

Jackson contends that cabal members realized the USSS would be receptive to their false portrayal of e-gold® as a shadowy offshore organization. Grigg's protégé, Jeroen, Jeroen van Gelderen, provided evidence in support of Jackson's claims during a May 29,

[886] Jackson, Douglas. "Evans and Grigg Analysis and Write-Up." Received by Carl Mullan, *Evans and Grigg Analysis and Write-Up*, 8 Apr. 2020.

[887] "DigiGold.net Ltd versus Systemics Inc." *DigiGold.net Ltd versus Systemics Inc*, May 2001, www.systemics.com/legal/digigold/.

2007, face-to-face meeting between Jackson, Bill Cunningham, and Jeroen van Gelderen in Vero Beach, Florida. Jeroen stated that he was aware that Ian Grigg and Charles Evans had engaged in malicious attacks against e-gold®. Statements copied from a memo supplied by Jackson dated May 29, 2007, seem to confirm Jackson's claims.

> Bill Cunningham and I[Jackson] met with Jeroen van Gelderen for about three hours at the Cracker Barrel at jct of Rt 60 and I-95 near Vero, Fl.. The meeting was May 29, 2007 from about 7- 10 pm.
>
> to describe his suspicions that Charles Evans and Ian Grigg had been involved in the origins of the USSS vendetta against e-gold. He described that shortly after G&SR had fired Charles Evans [late 2000, around late October] that Charles and ████ went to LA to work for Jim Fayed who was organizing e-bullion. After the brief LA sojourn, Charles and his [newly ex-]wife ████ relocated to Anguilla to live in the house that Ian was renting [which was being paid for by funds e-gold and I had provided to finance the continued development of the Ricardo payment mechanism, an amount exceeding $450,000 from 98-2000].... Sometime in 2001, Ian, Charlie, ████ and Jeroen moved to Freeport in the Bahamas where they leased a house: Waterfall Drive, possibly number 7A, a 2 story peach colored duplex....Early during this interval, Charlie was employed by James Turk for a period of several months.... Jeroen describes that Ian exerted a lot of effort to get e-gold in trouble with various US government agencies, primarily by claiming that e-gold's policy toward hyips and Ponzi's was insufficiently strict/effective.
>
> He also indicates that early on, Ian had attempted to attack the e-gold Bullion Reserve Special Purpose Trust, not clear on whose behalf, via his role as Protector. This was apparently thwarted by e-gold changing the Protector.
>
> Ian at one point asked Jeroen to try to penetrate the decryption of the e-gold backups that for a period had been backed up to Anguilla. I[Jackson] failed to ask on whose behalf Ian was seeking to decrypt the e-gold database. Jeroen says he refused and that was the first he began to suspect that Ian was perhaps not entirely an innocent victim of harsh dictatorial arrogant Doug... as Ian had led him to believe.[888]

Other evidence that confirms Jackson's allegation that Charles Evans had been feeding

---

[888] Jackson, Douglas. "Crackers in the Gtloaming." Received by Douglas Jackson, et al., *Crackers in the Gtloaming*, 29 May 2007.

the USSS false e-gold® information were statements from G&SR employees present in the Melbourne office during December 2005, execution of the USSS Search Warrant.

On December 16, 2005, the USSS executed a Search Warrant for the offices of Gold & Silver Reserve, Inc. DBA OmniPay, located in Melbourne, Florida.[889] During the warranted search, United States Secret Service Special Agents surprised OmniPay employees by making verbal references to conversations they had with fired employee Charles Evans. For several years, Jackson had been alleging Evans collaborated with the USSS, and this witness testimony seems to confirm Jackson's claims.

One of the more exciting events supporting Jackson's allegations that the USSS was receiving information from this private cabal, happened on the day of his sentencing in Federal Court. Jackson stated that he could see Charles Evans present in the courtroom seated two rows back from the prosecutors, in the chairs directly behind USSS Special Agents.

The Court had not subpoenaed Evans, and he was not required to be present. Furthermore, during the proceedings, Evans could be seen scribbling down notes on pieces of paper, then passing the notes forward to the USSS Special Agents and Prosecutors. On the day of sentencing, this appearance in Court is clear proof that Evans had a close relationship with the USSS, and very likely, also the DOJ Prosecutors in the e-gold case.

Jackson claims that the USSS had allegedly welcomed any incoming malicious intelligence on e-gold®. He provided these two critical points, which affirm his claims. First, depicting e-gold® as a shadowy offshore organization supported USSS claims that e-gold® offered anonymous payments. Secondly, the clever depiction of e-gold® as uncooperative, foreign, and inaccessible to law enforcement, would aid the USSS in its criminal case and the DOJ prosecution.

There is evidence that USSS Special Agents engaged and even coached the media claiming that e-gold® had been uncooperative and turned a "blind eye" to criminal activity on the platform. Next, because the USSS could benefit significantly from positive media exposure, Jackson alleges that the agency had a strong motivation to present a high-profile e-gold® prosecution. Jackson asserts that prominent USSS headlines in the mainstream press and larger forfeitures could have afforded the USSS a higher allocation of budgeted funds from the federal government. In support of his claims, Jackson offered the items shown below.

They[Cabal Members] encountered a USSS that was receptive due to a combination

---

[889] Gold & Silver Reserve, Inc "Gold & Silver Reserve, Inc." included the following parties Barry K. Downey, Director, Jackson Trading Company; Douglas L. Jackson, President, Jackson Trading Company; Barry K. Downey, Director, Gold & Silver Reserve, Inc.; Douglas L. Jackson, President, Gold & Silver Reserve, Inc.

of factors, organizational and circumstantial:

- Organizational – a dysfunctional corporate culture that severely impaired USSS competence with respect to cybercrime exploits,
- Circumstantial – an agency in crisis due to restructuring as USSS was moved from Treasury to the newly forming DHS.

This combination made the USSS receptive as it appeared to afford a path to greater resources. The USSS was enticed with the prospect of :

- preeminence as the lead agency for cybercrime matters,
- a special appropriation to fund the initiative (giving rise to the SCIRS-SS Task Force.
- A larger share of the DHS budgetary pie.
- Tens of millions of dollars' worth of assets that could potentially be seized and subjected to forfeiture action

After committing to the effort, a secret appropriation was secured on the basis of representations to the Congressional Subcommittee tasked with funding such initiatives depicting e-gold as shadowy criminal masterminds.[890]

Jackson explained possible allegations that may have motivated or helped to frame the USSS's attitude and actions toward e-gold®.

> Post-911, the USSS was an agency in crisis, having lost its niche within Treasury and facing severe challenges in its struggle for resources in the newly forming DHS. A core group within USSS convinced its superiors that e-gold could serve as their meal ticket, garnering prestige as the preeminent cybercrime agency, a larger share of the DHS budget and, icing on the cake, posing a potentially lucrative target for seizure and forfeiture actions.[891]

The Cover-up Phase

In his 2017, private letter to John Roth, Jackson proposed that a new USSS dynamic emerged late in the case, which may have included DOJ Prosecutor Kimberly Kiefer Peretti.

> It became apparent that the USSS had been duped, and had become the all too willing cat's paw serving the agenda of the private cabal. The major fly in the

---

[890] Jackson, Douglas. "Origins and Motives behind the USSS Campaign to Destroy e-gold." Received by Carl Mullan, *Origins and Motives behind the USSS Campaign to Destroy e-gold*, 26 July 2017. 2017.07.26 Timeline of the USSS campaign.docx

[891] Ibid

ointment was realization, especially after the initial search warrants and seizures of December 2005, that e-gold was highly motivated and active in its crime fighting efforts and had developed (and was continuously evolving) increasingly effective capabilities to prevent, detect, interdict, investigate, report and resolve customer activities involving the e-gold platform that bore indices of possible criminal activity.

Rather than back off and seek to mitigate the damage done to e-gold, at repeated critical junctures the decision was made to close ranks and carry on. Each critical juncture involved successively higher and broader echelons and in each case the decision was made to press on with the campaign even after it was fully recognized that the entire underlying premises were false.

The USSS approached their funding committee and secured a secret appropriation that enabled them to establish the SC-IRSSS Task Force in 2003, with its principal target e-gold. Kim Peretti was seconded to USSS and the working group also availed itself of the services of Albert Gonzales, a Criminal Informant.

Moreover, the mis-characterization of e-gold as turning a blind eye to criminal abuses was belied by e-gold's record of effective and timely support of law enforcement agencies around the world.

So the USSS undertook to dirty up e-gold, with a steady steam of defamatory media allegations depicting e-gold as criminal friendly - in effect soliciting criminals to matriculate to e-gold. Possibly these efforts were more overt; it is for you to determine exactly what Gonzalez's (and perhaps other CIs) marching orders consisted of...[892]

Peretti

Allegedly, because of Gonzalez's participation as a confidential informant, Peretti deferred prosecution for his 2003 felony charges. Furthermore, the government did not indict him for any of the additional crimes committed through ShadowCrew and was not incarcerated. Gonzalez was allowed to walk free under court supervision.

Below is Jackson's email from May 2006 sent to USPIS Agent Crabb.[893] This email is one of several containing verified evidence, obtained by Jackson, that helped identify segvec

[892] Jackson, Douglas. "Origins and motives behind the USSS campaign to destroy e-gold." Received by John Roth, Inspector General, US Dept. of Homeland Security, 24 Aug. 2017, Indian Harbour Beach, FL.
[893] Jackson, Douglas. "More S----c Data." Received by Gregory S Crabb, et al., *More S----c Data*, 16 May 2006.

was operating in Miami, including the identification of two other aliases he was using, "Ceres" and "Sy Lee." Peretti's office received this email and had this information about the suspect segvec[Albert Gonzalez] in 2006, around two years before Gonzalez's arrest.

> **Subject:** more S----c[Segvec] data
> **From:** Douglas Jackson <djackson@e-gold.com>
> **Date:** Tue, 16 May 2006 08:18:19 -0400
> **To:** "Crabb, Gregory S" <GSCrabb@uspis.gov>, "Agent X" <XXXXX@uspis.gov>
> **BCC:** Mitchell Fuerst <MFuerst@MFUERSTLAW.COM>, Andrew Ittleman <AIttleman@MFUERSTLAW.COM>
>
> I noticed yesterday that Segvec's 5th largest outbound, to account 108179, is another ███████ account.
> ███████ had this additional data filed under that profile, including not only a Tokyo maildrop but the next hop (in FL) for where mail from that drop was to be forwarded. I'm pasting that part first, but all the data is pretty interesting, including confirmation that Ceres and Sy Lee
> are indeed Segvec nyms

Additional information on Gonzalez, generated from his 2003, arrest included:

1. 2003 forensic analysis of a computer used by Albert Gonzalez indicated he had also used the email address soupnazi@efnet.ru. Other USSS confidential informants also linked Gonzalez to the screen name "soupnazi."
2. From Gonzalez's July 2003 arrest, agents seized numerous computers. One of the units contained logs of his ICQ chat conversations from 2000. During the ICQ chat, Gonzalez had used the alias "soupnazi."

The November, 2010 article in The New York Times, by James Verini, entitled The Great Cyberheist discussed Gonzalez's screen name.

3. Gonzalez worked alongside the agents[USSS], sometimes all day and into the night, for months on end. Most called him Albert. A couple of them who especially liked him called him Soup, after his old screen-name soupnazi. "Spending this much time with an informant this deeply into a cybercrime conspiracy — it was a totally new experience for all of us," one Justice Department prosecutor says. "It was kind of a

bonding experience. He and the agents developed over time a very close bond. They worked well together."[894]

4. Following the 2003 discovery that one of the hacked retailers had discovered his database intrusion, Gonzalez changed his email from soupnazi@efnet.ru to segvec@fromru.com Later, during interviews with law enforcement officials, Gonzalez admitted that he had used the nicknames "soupnazi" and "segvec."

5. On several occasions, Gonzalez's chat logs indicated that he had instructed associates to wire his share of the proceeds from the sale of stolen cards to a bank account in Latvia. Other USSS confidential informants stated that Albert Gonzalez also instructed them to wire the illegal proceeds of their criminal activity to a Latvia bank account under the company name SIA Ekosistems.[895]

6. Records supplied by e-gold to the USSS contained transaction information from an e-gold account registered using segvec@fromru.com.[896] At least one e-gold transaction moved value from this account to a Latvian company called SIA Ekosistems.[897]

Here is one of the DOJ press releases on Gonzalez's participation as a paid USSS confidential informant while he was committing "the largest hacking and identity theft case ever prosecuted by the Department of Justice."[898] [Partial text from the 2008 release]

FOR IMMEDIATE RELEASE
Tuesday, August 5, 2008
WWW.USDOJ.GOV
Department of Justice AG

Retail Hacking Ring Charged for Stealing and Distributing Credit and Debit Card Numbers from Major U.S. Retailers

894 Verini, James. "The Great Cyberheist." *The New York Times*, The New York Times, 10 Nov. 2010, www.nytimes.com/2010/11/14/magazine/14Hacker-t.html.

895 Jackson, Douglas. Received by Gregory S. Crabb, *Subject: Segvec Update 10.19.06*, 19 Oct. 2006.

896 Jackson, Douglas. "More S----c Data." Received by Gregory S Crabb, et al., *More S----c Data*, 16 May 2006.

897 Jackson, Douglas. "s____c Constellation." Received by Gregory S Crabb, et al., *s____c Constellation*, 10 May 2006. Exh_17-5-10-2006-SIA-segvec-constellation.pdf

898 "Retail Hacking Ring Charged for Stealing and Distributing Credit and Debit Card Numbers from Major U.S. Retailers." *Department of Justice*, 14 Nov. 2008, www.justice.gov/archive/criminal/cybercrime/press-releases/2008/gonzalezIndict.pdf.

More Than 40 Million Credit and Debit Card Numbers Stolen

BOSTON – Eleven perpetrators allegedly involved in the hacking of nine major U.S. retailers and the theft and sale of more than 40 million credit and debit card numbers have been charged with numerous crimes, including conspiracy, computer intrusion, fraud and identity theft, Attorney General Michael B. Mukasey, U.S. Attorney for the District of Massachusetts Michael J. Sullivan, U.S. Attorney for the Southern District of California Karen P. Hewitt, U.S. Attorney for the Eastern District of New York Benton J. Campbell and U.S. Secret Service Director Mark Sullivan announced today. The scheme is believed to constitute the largest hacking and identity theft case ever prosecuted by the Department of Justice.

…

In an indictment returned on Aug. 5, 2008, by a federal grand jury in Boston, Albert "Segvec" Gonzalez, of Miami, was charged with computer fraud, wire fraud, access device fraud, aggravated identity theft and conspiracy for his role in the scheme. Criminal informations were also released today in Boston on related charges against Christopher Scott and Damon Patrick Toey, both of Miami.
The Boston indictment alleges that during the course of the sophisticated conspiracy, Gonzalez and his co-conspirators obtained the credit and debit card numbers by "wardriving" and hacking into the wireless computer networks of major retailers — including TJX Companies, BJ's Wholesale Club, OfficeMax, Boston Market, Barnes & Noble, Sports Authority, Forever 21 and DSW. Once inside the networks, they installed "sniffer" programs that would capture card numbers, as well as password and account information, as they moved through the retailers' credit and debit processing networks.
The indictment alleges that after they collected the data, the conspirators concealed the data in encrypted computer servers that they controlled in Eastern Europe and the United States. They allegedly sold some of the credit and debit card numbers, via the Internet, to other criminals in the United States and Eastern Europe. The stolen numbers were "cashed out" by encoding card numbers on the magnetic strips of blank cards. The defendants then used these cards to withdraw tens of thousands of dollars at a time from ATMs. Gonzalez and others were allegedly able to conceal and launder their fraud proceeds by using anonymous Internet-based currencies both within the United States and abroad, and by channeling funds through bank accounts in Eastern Europe.
Gonzalez was previously arrested by the Secret Service in 2003 for access device

fraud. **During the course of this investigation, the Secret Service discovered that Gonzalez, who was working as a confidential informant for the agency, was criminally involved in the case.** Because of the size and scope of his criminal activity, Gonzalez faces a maximum penalty of life in prison if he is convicted of all the charges alleged in the Boston indictment.[899]

On April 29, 2010, BankInfoSecurity.com published an interview with Kim Peretti, who was then a former DOJ senior counsel. Tom Field conducted the meeting and entitled his article *Inside the TJX/Heartland Investigations.*[900] Peretti offered several insights on Gonzalez's identification.

> PERETTI: Well, there were three really challenging aspects to this. One was the identification of the individuals. The second was building on developing cases just based on technical facts and forensic information.
>
> PERETTI: Sure, sure. The way I think of it is it unfolds very, very slowly. You know it's piece by piece; it's just like a puzzle maybe a 500-piece puzzle. You get little pieces of data along the way, and what has been significant in these cases and solving these cases is working with historical data.
>
> Again, a couple a more examples: registration data on one of the chat accounts that was used. There was registration data on there that two pieces of registration data and one from early on had matched, it was an email address that Albert Gonzalez had used when we first arrested him in 2003, and that was on his laptop. That was sort of one of those critical moments -- we're sort of in the right direction now.[901]

The interview contained no mention of Jackson's assistance or the critical segvec information he supplied in 2006.

On May 20, 2010, the Miami New Times published an article by Tim Elfrink entitled *Hack Pack*. This material provided some information about how the USSS and Peretti fit those puzzle pieces together and identified Gonzalez.[902] There was no mention of Jackson or e-gold® in this article. The content refers to Maksym, a hacker who bought vast quantities of stolen credit cards from Miami's most wanted hacker, USSS confidential informant Albert Gonzalez. The following text came from the *Hack Pack* article.

[899] Ibid
[900] Field, Tom, and Kim Peretti. "Inside the TJX/Heartland Investigations." *BankInfoSecurity.com*, Information Security Media Group, 29 Apr. 2010, www.bankinfosecurity.com/interviews/inside-tjxheartland-investigations-i-500. Accessed 4 Jan. 2018.
[901] Ibid
[902] Elfrink, Tim. "Hack Pack." *Miami New Times*, 20 May 2010, www.miaminewtimes.com/news/hack-pack-6379188.

Detectives focused on Maksym's chats with one American — 201679996 — who had sold him millions of stolen credit card numbers. They spent the next few months studying the data with experts at Carnegie Mellon University. By late 2007, they[USSS] had linked the numbers to a Russian email address with a startling name: soupnazi@efnet.ru.

Alarm bells rang across the Secret Service. Was their prize informant playing them? Then investigators found a chat in which 201679996 referred to himself as "segvec" — another nickname Albert had used in his ShadowCrew days. That sealed it. The Secret Service immediately began investigating Albert.[903]

After authorities arrested Gonzalez in May 2008, dozens of online articles discussed how the USSS had tracked and captured. None of these articles or interviews mentioned Jackson's assistance or e-gold's database contributions. None of this information made it into the Court record.

In one case, investigated by the F.B.I., there was a wireless intrusion at Target's headquarters originating through a Miami store location. The building was in the line of sight of Gonzalez's condo and a valuable spot for a war-driving attack.

In his August 2017, letter to Roth, Jackson alleged some of the possible reasons behind Peretti's actions, or lack of action regarding Gonzalez.

> The essence of my allegation is that Ms. Peretti et al, having learned (from the work product of egold's own in-house investigatory unit, headed up by me) no later than July 2006 that their own CI was the perpetrator of the largest "cybercrime heist" on record, purposely delayed the arrest and prosecution of Gonzalez for nearly two years in order to cover up that it was my personal efforts that cracked the case. During this two year delay, and while continuing to operate under the noses of Peretti and his USSS handlers, Gonzalez perpetrated additional massive cybercrime exploits eclipsing his own personal world's record.[904]

Furthermore, Jackson alleges that Peretti hid the knowledge that Gonzalez was Miami's most wanted hacker for over a year, allegedly to engage in a cover-up.

---

[903] Ibid

[904] Jackson, Douglas. "Investigation Request." Received by John Roth, Inspector General, US Dept. of Homeland Security, 1020 Steven Patrick Avenue, 24 Aug. 2017, Indian Harbour Beach, Florida.

And finally, Peretti herself then insisted the USPIS forward to her all of their data that I had supplied in our joint efforts. I strongly suspect she did that to determine whether I had figured out yet that segvec was their very own Gonzalez. Satisfied I had not figured out that last critical bit, she and her superiors elected to cover it up, allowing his crime spree to continue for another year and half (during which interval he did the Heartland breach), in order to complete our destruction and silencing to avoid exposing SS incompetence.

After stealing hacked data from approximately 130 million credit and debit card customers, the USSS finally charged him. Gonzalez collected Indictments from New Jersey, New York, and Massachusetts. The prosecution later consolidated these cases into just one. He received a twenty-year sentence. Accounting for good behavior, Gonzalez could emerge from prison as early as 2025.

On March 24th, 2011, after being convicted, Albert Gonzalez filed a Habeas Petition (Petition Under 28 USC § 2255 to Vacate, Set Aside, or Correct Sentence By a Person in Federal Custody). Among other claims, Gonzalez declared, in this filing, that every criminal act he committed, while a USSS Confidential Informant, had been authorized by his USSS handlers. Shown here is the related text copied from that Court filing. [Partial Text from the document]

PETITION UNDER 28 USC § 2255 TO VACATE, SET ASIDE, OR CORRECT SENTENCE BY A PERSON IN FEDERAL CUSTODY
United States District Court, Boston, Massachusetts
Case No. 1:08-cr-10223-PBS and 1:09-cr-10262-PBS
Date of conviction: March 25, 2010,
Length of sentence: 240 months.
Nature of Offense involved (all ccunts): (Ct 1) 18:371 Conspiracy; (Ct2-6) 18:1030 Damage to Computer Systems; (Ct7-10) 18:1343 Wire Fraud; (Ct11-15) 18:1029 Access Device Fraud; (Ct16-19) 18:1028A Aggravated Identity Theft (Ct1) 18:1349 Conspiracy to commit Wire Fraud
Prisoner 25702-050
United States of America V. Albert Gonzalez

GROUND NUMBER TWO: My guilty plea was not knowingly and voluntarily entered because I did not know I had an available defense to all the charges under "Public Authority." My trial counsel was ineffective for failing to present Public Authority Defense.

FACTS THAT SUPPORT GROUIID NUMBER TWO:
If a person is acting under the actual or believed exercise of public authority on behalf of a law enforcement agency he has a public authority defense against any illegal conduct arising from his actions.

When I committed the illegal acts to which I plead guilty I believed I was acting under the grant of authority from Agents of the United States Secret Service to engage in the conduct that were violations of the laws of the United States, which included Conspiracy, Wire Fraud, Access Device Fraud, Conspiracy To Commit Wire Fraud and Aggrevated Identity Theft. (See Indictments).

The facts that support my claim of a public authority defense were never revealed during the proceedings of my case and exist outside the motions, files and records of the case. The following is a narrative of the unrevealed facts that led me to believe that I was acting as an Agent of the Secret Service and authorized by the Secret Service to conduct the illegal acts to which I plead guilty in the United States District Courts for the District of Massachusetts.

In 2003, after my arrest for access device fraud, Agents of the United States Secret Service convinced me to become a Confidential Informant for the Secret Service. I reluctantly agreed to become a Confidential Informant for the Secret Service.

I was provided with a CI Kumber and indocturinated as to what was expected of me as a CI for the Secret Service. An Agent by the name of David Esposito was assigned as my handler. Another Agent named Steve Ward who was Agent Esposito's supervisor also assisted in handling me. Eventually Agent Ward became my sole handler. I also worked with other Secret Service Agents on numerous investigation.

Because of my skills and information I possessed about computers and hacking the Agents were anxious to work with me and learn what I know about hacking. Apparently I made quite an impression on the Agents I was working with and they took me into their confidence and trusted me. They treated me like one of their own and I began to feel like part of the Secret Service Agency. As I provided invaluable assistance on a number of cases that resulted in indictments and convictions the trust and bond between me and the Agents grew stronger.

I was allowed to sit in on confidential briefings and asked my opinion on issues, I was provided with access to highly confidential information. I was asked to commit acts I knew were illegal but I complied in order to please the Agents who had shown me such respect and friendship. When I commented on something being illegal they told me "don't worry we got your back." At that point I would have done anything they asked me to do. I was overwhelmed and felt like I could do no wrong.

The Agents had me infiltrating chat rooms setting people up and then the Agents would bust them. A lot of arrests were made because of the work I was doing. I was taken to different parts of the country to help with undercover operations. On one occasion I was taken to California for a week to help Agents there with an undercover operation that resulted in arrests and convictions. In 2003, I was taken to a military base in Cavens Point, NJ and assisted in a sting named "Operation Firewall" that resulted in the arrest and conviction of more than 20 persons involved in computer crimes.

When the days work was done the Agents took me bike riding with them. We went bar hopping together and partying together. They provided me with a salary of $1200 a month and occasionally provided me with additional cash to help cover my expenses. I was instructed not to say anything about the cash payments as that money was not supposed to exist. They gave me my own computer to work with but eventually asked for it back. They told me to continue my game in an effort to make contact with more hackers involved in computer crimes. They told me do what you have to do just try not to get caught. All the time I was educating the Agents as to hacking methods and computer crimes. They treated me like, one of their own and did everything but give me a gun and a badge. On one occasion even the possibility of a gun for protection was discussed if the need ever arose.

In 2004 and 2005 my handler Agent Steve Ward escorted me to Secret Service Headquarters in Washington D. C. to give presentations on the Evolution of Malicious Software and 0-day Vulnerabilities. These presentations were attended by at least 50 Secret Service Agents and a number of persons who were not Agents.

While in Washington D.C. the USSS, Criminal Intelligence Section (CIS) conducted confidential meetings with me to obtain from me information and methods of intelligence gathering via computer.

All of this inflated my ego and made me feel very i.mportant and made it feel like I was really a part of the Secret Service with the backing and support of that Government Agency. One day I was unknown and nothing and the next day I am being hailed as a genius and giving presentations to Secret Service Agents in Washington D.C. All of this was mind boggling for me.

At one point Secret Service Agents took me to Chicago, Illinois to give Secret Service Agents there technical assistance in setting up a "honeypot." A honeypot is used utilized to observe hackers committing computer fraud in order to learn how the hackers operate and track their origins. During the Chicago trip the Agents had me attend a Information Security Conference hosted by ABM Amro LaSalle Bank to obsrve security measures being discussed. In 2003, before "Operation Firewall" and before I became a Confidential Informant, I owed a Russian "carder" $5,000 and he was prcssing me for the money. I told Agent Steve Ward that I needed $5,000 to pay the Russian or I would loose credability with him and others. Agent Ward made it clear they were not going to pay the $5,000 debit and that I would have to take care of it myself.

I told Agent Ward I did not have the money to take care of the debit. Agent Ward told me "go do your thing and pay the debit, just don't get caught.   I did my thing and payed off the $5,000 debit. Later Agent Ward asked me if I took care of the debt, I told him yes.

In 2003, my parents were very nervous about my involvement with the Secret Service Agents. An Agent by the name of Robert Villanueva who was of Cuban descent as my parents called my parents and arranged a meeting for Agents Steve Ward and David Esposito with my parents to discuss my involvement with the Secret Service. At the meeting with my parents the Agents told my parents that my knowledge and skills with computers was very important to the Secret Service and that I had a future with them depending on me. (SEE AFFIDAVIT OF MOTHER EXHIBIT A)

After I was issued my Confidential Informant number I was told to take a bigger role in obtaining information concerning international cyber crime. To seek out persons in other countries who were involved in cyber crime. We discussed methods and ways of doing this. After I made contact with persons in other countries who were involved with cyber crime it became apparent that I would have to participate in illegal activity and give them something in order to gain their confidence and trust. I contacted persons here in the United States who I had been involved with prior to becoming a Confidential Informant. Through them I made contacts with other persons involved in cyber crime and furthered my reputation as someone who could be trusted. In order to establish trust I had to become involved in the same illegal activities they were involved in. I had to become involved in order to be accepted into the operation. During this time the Agents were encouraging me to gather intelligence. They explained the difference between intelligence that could be used to establish probable cause legally in court and intelligence that could not legally be used in court. Some of the intelligence gathering activity I was conducting occured during Operation Firewall. After Operation Firewall was completed I was moved to Miami, Florida and was instructed to continue my operation from there. At all time my handler Agent Steve Ward and higher-ups in GID/CIS knew exactly what I had been instructed to do and what I was doing. I firmly believed I was authorized to engage in the cyber crimes I was participating in in order to gather intelligence on National and International cyber criminals and I was doing my job to the best of my abilities. When I was arrested and charged with numerous offenses against the United States I was shocked and did not understand what was happening. I was expecting Secret Service to come ard take custody of me and squash the charges. But that never happened. I had been instructed by Agent Steve Ward that if I ever got arrested by authorities not to say anything but request that he be called and made aware of my arrest. But at the time of my arrest Steve Ward was no longer a Secret Service Agent. When I was arrested by the Secret Service I was placed in isolation in the Special Housing Unit (SHU) at the Federal Detention Center in Miami, FLorida for protection due to my status as a Confidential Informant for the Secret Service.

I retained attorney Rene Palomino to represent me in this case. I explained my status as a Confidential Informant working for the Secret Service and explained about Operation Firewall and my involvement in that operation. I even explained to Mr. Palomino about an incident where a Secret Service employee out of the Washington D.C. headquarters was fraudulently using my CI Number to steal confidential informant funds for her own personal use. The person was fired from the Secret Service and criminally prosecuted. I do not remember everything I told Mr. Palomino about my involvement as a CI for the Secret Service. But it was enough to alert him to the fact that he should have conducted a further investigation of a Public Authority Defense. I did not know that such a defense of Public Authority existed. I did not know that due to the Secret Service Agents directing me to participate in cyber crime that I had a Public Authority defense available to me against the charges.

The Government obtained the services of Mark J. Mills, JD, MD. to conduct a psychiatric evaluation of me. During my evaluation session with Dr. Mills I tried to explain to him how the Secret Service Agents had authorized me to commit the criminal acts I had engaged in in order to gather intelligence and infiltrate cyber crime operations as a participant. Dr. Mills told me we could not discuss the charges or why I committed the crimes. (See Exhibit B, letter from Mark J. Mills M.D.) During the time I was giving a proffer my attorney Martin Weinberg who was lead counsel on the Massachusetts case told me he overheard the prosecutors and Agents talking about giving me immunity. Mr. Weinberg told me immunity was on the table but that he didnt think they would give it to me. Mr. Weinberg asked me why would they give you immunity.

I told him because they know the Agents instructed me to commit the acts that I am now being charged with and they know what I did was part of the operation named "Shadow Ops" being conducted out of the Miami field office. The Agents who arrested me were not the Agents who were conducting Shadow Ops operations. I tried to tell the arresting Agents that I was one of the Secret Service's Confidential Informants.

I gave them my number and told them I was involved in Shadow Ops operation. I asked them to call my handlers and verify that I was an active registered CI engaged in intelligence gathering for the Secret Service. They told me don't worry we will sort it all out we are just doing what we have been told to do so just relax we know who you are we just don't know whats going on at this point.

I still believe that the actions I took in engaging in various cyber crimes were authorized by Agents of the Secret Service. I still believe that I was acting on behalf of the United States Secret Service and that I was authorized and directed to engage in the conduct I committed as part of my assignment to gather intelligence and seek out international cyber criminals. I now know and understand that I have been used as a scapegoat to cover someone's mistakes. If I had known that my case presented a "Public Authority" defense I would never have entered a guilty plea to the charges unjustly brought against me. I request that I be allowed to withdraw my guilty plea in all three cases that I was prosecuted in based on the foregoing claim and facts. I believe I am actually innocent of the charges brought against me because I was

531

authorized by the Secret Service to commit the acts that constitute the charges.[905]

◆

In his 2018 letter, Jackson offers his opinion and thoughts on the cause and effects of the mistakes made by USSS Special Agents in their prosecution of e-gold®.

> Had the decision not been made by the USSS in 2003 to anchor its ambitions for preeminence as the lead cybercrime agency on a campaign to demonize and destroy e-gold, the world would be a safer place from the standpoint of systemic risk. As matters stand, no systematic alternative has been advanced to forestall or attenuate economic disruption should the unprecedented distortions arising from unconventional monetary policies culminate in financial (possibly even monetary) collapse.
>
> Instead, as a direct result of misperceptions arising from this case, anonymous digital cash, resurrected in the form of cryptocurrencies, gained a foothold. This has led to monumental levels of malinvestment in a technology that rests on monetary fallacies, poorly conceived institutional arrangements and technical deficiencies with respect to efficiency, scalability and security. Though avidly embraced (for now) by avaricious institutions, the prototypical instrument, Bitcoin, excels only as a vehicle for ransomware payments and as fuel for a speculative bubble.[906]

Profit motive

In a 2019 email, Jackson explained his thoughts on a possible profit motive that could have been driving the USSS. The following text is a partial copy of the original document.

> Asset seizure and forfeiture actions by law enforcement agencies are inherently tinged by an ethical slippery slope. The fact that such agencies are not only permitted but encouraged to supplement their operational budgets with the proceeds of asset forfeitures inevitably introduces a conflict of interest predisposing the agency to err on the side of avidity rather than restraint. The very origins of forfeiture law, derived from the admiralty laws that governed the activities of privateers on the high seas, stand in stark contrast with the constitutional safeguards and common law traditions

---

[905] Case 1:08-cr-10223-PBS Document 121 Filed 03/24/11 25pgs. *United States of America V. Albert Gonzalez.* PETITION UNDER 28 USC § 2255 TO VACATE, SET ASIDE, OR CORRECT SENTENCE BY A PERSON IN FEDERAL CUSTODY, 24 Mar. 2011, pp. Case No. 1:08-cr-10223-PBS and 1:09-cr-10262-PBS.

[906] Ibid

that theoretically assure presumption of innocence.

It would require willful blindness[907] to not recognize the likelihood that the USSS and especially the cabal goading them was motivated to significant degree by the prospect of seizing and bringing forfeiture actions to take all of the customer value circulating within the e-gold system.[908]

In the e-gold case, the gold reserves constituting the basis of value underlying the money in all customer accounts was an enticing target. At exchange rates prevailing at the time of indictment, the reserves (having already been drawn down in relation to a flurry of asset seizures undertaken in conjunction with indictment) were worth over $50 million US. Three aspects or phases can be identified with respect to USSS efforts to take this money for themselves (and to reward their CIs):

- Preemptive strike
- PIRO-related
- e-gold VAP

Before proceeding with discussion of these phases, it is instructive to note the irony inherent in the contrast between the decade long fiduciary integrity of the defendants vs. the rapacious avarice of this government agency and the -Grigg cabal with whom they were collaborating. A fundamental distinctive of the e-gold model was carefully designed efforts to safeguard reserves. We realized the imperative of implementing institutional arrangements which, by protecting the reserves from potential malfeasance of company insiders, would also aid in securing against error or external coercion. To cite a horrifying hypothetical, even if one of the signatories empowered to authorize a release and specify the disposition of reserve assets was kidnapped and tortured, that individual – in fact no single individual – would be able to breach these safeguards. Protective measures were multiple and interlocking:

- Reserve assets were titled to a purpose trust that held them for the exclusive benefit of all e-gold account holders.
- Any release of reserves had to be authorized by two signatories, a company representative and an independent third party escrow agent.
- The only permissible disposition was intra-vault delivery, moving bullion from the allocated holdings of the Trust to the custody of either a Primary Dealer or their designate, who was additionally required to have undergone the stringent due diligence measures specified by the custodial facility, which in all cases was a treasury-grade vault used by government central banks and

---

[907] In a March, 2020 email, Jackson shared that that he had written this statement before he "...realized their design to steal all the bullion via forfeiture was overtly stated in the indictment and in the PIRO."

[908] Jackson, Douglas. "Chunk 10." Received by Carl Mullan, *Chunk 10*, 31 Mar. 2020.

international gold banks for housing their gold bullion.

- Vault personnel, long familiar with the patterns of a legitimate delivery order, followed a protocol of contacting the company to verify the legitimacy of any order that was remotely unusual, as for example occurred after the indictment when e-gold and G&SR were compelled to exchange millions of dollars worth of e-gold seized by the USSS from multiple entities at the time of the e-gold indictment, for US dollars

These safeguards withstood the repeated efforts of the USSS and its co-conspirators to steal the reserves. When the criminal case was resolved by plea agreement, full control over the disposition of reserves was restored to the designated fiduciaries. Sadly, however, having won the battle, our customers ultimately lost the war.

Phase 1 – preemptive strike

As noted in the notes memorializing disclosures made by a junior subordinate in the -Grigg cabal (Jeroen Van Gelderen), Ian Grigg had tried to compromise e-gold system assets on two occasions. The first had been at the behest of the IRS and entailed an effort to crack the encryption of back-up copies of the entire e-gold database – personal identifying information of the customers as well as all transaction records. Later, when the cabal had modulated into collaboration with the USSS, Ian Grigg, who had initially been designated as the "Protector" of the Trust, undertook to trigger emergency provisions designed to afford continuity of fiduciary integrity in order to breach the trust so as to enable the USSS to seize the entire stock of reserves. This failed immediately because after the company became aware of Grigg's treachery in 2001 arrangements had been made to appoint a replacement to serve as Protector.[909]

Evidence recovered in email documents, supplied by Jeroen Van Gelderen, supports Jackson's claim that Grigg had attempted to control the bullion trust.[910]

◆

In 2020, Ian Grigg appeared in another digital currency-related legal case. The plaintiffs filed this case in the United States District Court for the Southern District of New York. The plaintiffs are all persons or entities who purchased or acquired EOS tokens during the period between June 26, 2017, and the present. The case is captioned: Crypto Assets Opportunity Fund LLC and Johnny Hong v. Block.one, Brendan Blumer, Daniel Larimer,

---

[909] Jackson, Douglas. "Origins and Motives behind the USSS Campaign to Destroy e-gold." Received by Carl Mullan, *Origins and Motives behind the USSS Campaign to Destroy e-gold*, 26 July 2017. 2017.07.26 Timeline of the USSS campaign.docx

[910] Ibid

Ian Grigg, and Brock Pierce, 1:20-cv-3829 (S.D.N.Y.). The case is related to the earlier action Williams et al. v. Block.One et al., 1:20-cv-02809 (S.D.N.Y.) that is pending before Judge Lewis A. Kaplan in the United States District Court for the Southern District of New York.

The Block.one website touts itself as "[...] a leader in providing high-performance blockchain solutions."[911]

The plaintiffs announced the new legal action on May 18, 2020. The complaint is an effort to hold Block.one and its leadership accountable for allegedly duping global investors in what may be "the biggest of all crypto frauds." According to the press release:

> Today's filing is Block.one's second legal challenge over its ICO. Last September, the company agreed to a $24 million settlement with the Securities and Exchange Commission — a relative slap on the wrist that did little to promote investor protection.
>
> In asserting violations by Block.one of Sections 5, 12(a)(1)-(2), and 15 of the 1933 Securities Act and Sections 10(b) and 20(a) of the 1934 Securities Exchange Act, the lawsuit alleges breach of fiduciary duty and unjust enrichment by defendants, who comprise both current and former company executives. They include co-founders Brendan Blumer and Daniel Larimer, who remain with Block.one, and co-founder Brock Pierce, who has since departed. Also named is former partner Ian Grigg.
>
> Block.one, founded in 2017, has operations in Virginia and Hong Kong but is registered in the Cayman Islands. Starting in June 2017 and over the course of almost a year, it sold 900 million EOS cryptocurrency tokens by aggressively marketing to investors in the United States and other countries.
>
> Announced with great fanfare and publicized as a means of funding a new open-source software and superior competitor to the Bitcoin and Ethereum blockchains, the offering was accompanied by a Times Square billboard ad, a bullish white paper, presentations by company principals at blockchain conferences and meet-ups, and promotion via crypto-focused online news and investor outlets. As the complaint states, "defendants worked cooperatively to promote EOSIO as the next, superior version of the existing blockchain...."
>
> As the complaint notes, however, at no time during all of this fanfare did Block.one register its offering with the SEC, as required by U.S. securities law, nor seek an exemption from registration (for which it did not qualify).

[911] "Executive Team." *Block.one*, 1 May 2020, block.one/team/.

The complaint alleges that the consequence of this willful evasion of regulations – expressly established to promote fairness and investor confidence – was to blind the ICO's investors, depriving them of disclosures regarding Block.one's financial history, operations and budget, executive compensation, material trends, risk factors, and other information required by law. In essence, the complaint alleges, Block.one made a wild-card coin offering that profited the company handsomely but ultimately left investors holding little more than crypto-dust. In September 2019, the SEC issued a cease-and-desist order against further sale of Block.one's tokens, determining they were securities under the law and had been sold without proper registration. At no time had the company disclosed that it was subject of a government investigation.

Attorneys representing investors note that Block.one's $24 million settlement with the SEC represents a meager 0.6% of the $4 billion Block.one raised through its ICO. Unusually, the settlement did not require registration of the tokens going forward, or reimbursement or rescission for investors; nor did it disqualify Block.one from making securities offerings in the future. The lawsuit argues that the company's minor mea culpa was only a tiny speed bump in what remains a successful scheme to defraud investors.

"Institutional funds that were lied to by Block.one have a duty to all their investors – large and small – to take action against fraudsters and con artists," said James Koutoulas, CEO of hedge fund Typhon Capital Management and securities lawyer who formed the nonprofit Commodity Customer Coalition and led the 101% recovery of $6.7 billion for victims of the MF Global bankruptcy. He continued, "We believe in the cryptocurrency space, which is why those who exploit it for naked personal gain need to be held accountable. Where the SEC only dipped a toe into upholding securities laws and protecting investors, our action encourages those who were swindled by this biggest of all crypto frauds to join us in pressing the courts for justice and restitution."

Daniel Berger, a director at Grant & Eisenhofer and veteran class action litigator, said, "Investors of all types deserve to be treated equitably and honestly. This lawsuit is an important means to redress the brazenly unlawful conduct that Block.one exhibited in defrauding investors through its EOS token offering."[912]

[912] P.A., Grant & Eisenhofer. "Investors Bring Class Action Lawsuit against Block.one for 'Biggest of All Crypto Frauds' - Coin-Offering Scam Netted Company Billions." *PR Newswire: News Distribution, Targeting and Monitoring*, 18 May 2020, www.prnewswire.com/news-releases/investors-bring-class-action-lawsuit-against-blockone-for-biggest-of-all-crypto-frauds--coin-offering-scam-netted-company-billions-301061047.html.

This lawsuit, naming Ian Grigg, is merely a claim or accusation and has not been proven in a court of law. In America, anyone can sue anyone else.

♦

Interaction Between the USSS and the State of Florida

A timeline created from files provided by the Florida Office of Financial Regulations and delivered to Jackson, in response to his 2017 public records requests, revealed some astonishing facts about the interaction between the USSS and Florida officials. Emails and interoffice communications show that the USSS directed state investigators and regulators not to engage in any dialogue with Jackson or e-gold®. These directions contributed significantly to the lack of regulatory guidance on financial licensing from the State Office of Financial Regulations.

These newly uncovered internal communications provide an extraordinary look at the federal government's investigative process leading up to the 2007 criminal indictment.

The following text includes emails, and interoffice communications exchanged during 2006 and mid-2007. As indicated by the message dates, most of these exchanges took place before the criminal indictment in April 2007. These messages, and others, confirm two critical points that support Jackson's claims.

#1 In 2007, the State of Florida did not target e-gold® or G&SR for violations of the state's Money Transmitter regulations.

#2 The USSS and Federal government's criminal case against e-gold® may have hinged on receiving a Money Transmitter violation from Florida, which would have created a mechanism for the federal charges. One thought echoes throughout this communication, "A violation of State law is a violation of Federal law."

A batch of uncovered documents and emails from May 2006, between Florida regulators, showed an official request, from the Office of Financial Regulation, for an opinion as to whether G&SR Inc. or e-gold Ltd. required a state license. The state was requesting a possible classification of e-gold® as a Money Transmitter with the State of Florida. This legal opinion would have determined whether e-gold® was required to obtain a State Money Transmitter License. Attorney William Oslo, Assistant General Counsel, State of Florida Office of Financial Regulation (OFR), was assigned the task of writing this legal opinion.

INTEROFFICE COMMUNICATION OFFICE OF FINANCIAL REGULATION

DATE: May 15, 2006
TO: Jo Schultz, Attorney Supervisor
FROM: Mike Ramsden, Financial Administrator
THRU: Rick White, Director
Issue: Legal Opinion Regarding e-gold
Recommended Action:
Assign an attorney to review the concept of e-gold and give an opinion on whether companies that offer e-gold should register to be a licensed Money Transmitter.[913]

On Friday, May 19, 2006, USSS Special Agent Roy Dotson, employed in the Orlando Field Office, sent an email to Investigator David Burley of the Florida Office of Financial Regulation. Dotson shared a simple request from an Assistant United States Attorney, inquiring if any notes were available from a meeting between Jackson and State of Florida officials. He asked if Burley could share any records with the USSS and the AUSA.[914] As previously discussed, here is a critical part of Burley's email.

> We have not interviewed Douglas Jackson or any of the employees at G&SR or OmniPay due to your request in late January to not correspond with Mr. Jackson or his staff. You explained that your investigative team did not want to give Mr. Jackson the opportunity to boast about his cooperation in resolving complaints and assisting government regulators.[915]

In this message, Burley indicated that during an earlier communication in January 2006, USSS Special Agent Dotson had instructed the State of Florida financial regulators not to correspond with Douglas Jackson or the e-gold® staff. These Florida employees were the very people responsible for the supervision and licensing of Money Transmitter businesses within the State.

Dotson's instructions were to block Jackson from receiving any critical licensing information and financial guidance, from Florida Regulators, on whether Florida statues governed e-gold's business. Burley's message also revealed that the USSS did not want to provide an opportunity for Jackson to cooperate or assist law enforcement agents and government regulators. This email shows that the United States Secret Service directed officials within the Florida Office of Financial Regulations not to provide a legal opinion on

---

[913] Ramsden, Financial Administrator, Mike. "Legal Opinion Regarding e-gold." Received by Jo Schultz, Attorney Supervisor, *Legal Opinion Regarding e-gold*, 15 May 2006.

[914] Dotson, Roy Daniel. "Interviews." Received by David Burley, *Interviews*, 19 May 2006. 12:58 PM

[915] Burley, David. "RE: Interviews." Received by Roy Daniel Dotson, *RE: Interviews*, 19 May 2006. 3:04 PM

state financial regulations.

These email exchanges are astonishing! USSS Special Agent Roy Dotson advised the Florida Office of Financial Regulations not to interact with the company, thus blocking proper guidance and potential licensing. In May 2006, there were no outstanding criminal charges against e-gold®, and it would be more than a year later, in 2007, before the federal government filed a formal indictment. One year was ample time for Florida regulators to render an opinion and issue a money transmitter license to G&SR if required by Florida. This single email exchange is sufficient evidence to support Jackson's claim of malicious treatment by the USSS.

Three days later, after learning that the State of Florida was seeking a legal opinion on e-gold®, federal prosecutors and DOJ attorneys requested a phone call with officials in Florida.

> From: Roy Dotson, Daniel
> Sent: Monday, May 22, 2006 11:08 AM
> To: David Burley
> Subject: Legal Contact
> David,
> The AUSA and DOJ attorney would like a contact in your legal department to reference determining where e-gold falls. Can you send me a name and number please?
> Thanks,
> Roy[916]

Three hours later, Dotson received an email response from Burley.

> Money Transmitter's Unit and the Bureau of investigations
> From: David Burley
> Sent: Monday, May 22, 2006 3:10 PM
> To: 'Roy Dotson, Daniel'
> Cc: Jo Schultz; Peter Fisher; Mike Ramsden
> Subject: RE: Legal Contact
> Importance: High
> Roy:
> I spoke with Mike Ramsden, the Administrator of our Money Transmitter Unit, regarding his referral to our Legal Department for an opinion on whether the business

[916] Dotson, Roy Daniel. "Legal Contact." Received by David Burley, *Legal Contact*, 22 May 2006.

operations of e-gold, Ltd, and the e-gold exchange outlets, fall under our money transmitter statutes found in Chapter 560, of the Florida Statutes. He advised that you should refer your AUSA and the DOJ attorneys to our General Counsel's office in Tallahassee, more specifically to either of the following persons:
Ms. Jo Schultz, Chief Counsel
(850) 410 - XXXX
XXXX@FLDFS.com

Peter Fisher, Chief Counsel
(850) 410 – XXXX
XXXX@FLDFS.com
Take care,
David[917]

On June 5th, 2006, the Florida Office of Financial Regulation received a fax on the Department of Justice letterhead from the Criminal Division of Computer Crime and Intellectual Property Section in Washington, DC, which identified the sender Kimberly Peretti. The receiver listed on the fax was Peter Fisher, Chief Counsel for the Division of Financial Services for the State of Florida.

Records indicate that the original document contained three pages. However, the FL OFR only provided the cover sheet in response to Jackson's Public Records request. This June 5th fax cover sheet timestamps the DOJ's formal request for a State of Florida legal opinion on whether e-gold Ltd. and G&SR were engaged in unlicensed money transmission under Florida law.

---

[917] Burley, David. "RE: Legal Contact." Received by Roy Daniel Dotson, et al., *RE: Legal Contact*, 22 May 2006.

URGENT: PLEASE DELIVER IMMEDIATELY   6/5/06

FROM: Department of Justice
           Criminal Division
           Computer Crime and Intellectual Property Section
           1301 New York Ave., Suite 600
           Washington, D.C. 20005

           Fax No.   (202) 514-6113
           Voice No.   (202) 514-1026

SENT BY: Kimberly Peretti

TO: Mr. Peter Fisher
           Chief Counsel
           Division of Financial Services
           State of Florida

FAX No.   850-410-9645

NUMBER OF PAGES SENT (INCLUDING COVER PAGE): 3

SPECIAL INSTRUCTIONS:

    This document was obtained by Jackson after the case, from the Florida Office of Financial Regulation. It was discovered through a series of three FL Public Records requests.

    After the communication, official documents show that Florida financial lawyers performed the research and analysis of facts and circumstances to inform their opinion determining the status of e-gold® under Florida law. The conversation started a long chain of interoffice communications between officials in the Office of Financial Regulation (OFR), that were all asking a very similar question.

A draft final opinion from the OFR, on e-gold's business, requested on May 15, 2006, was produced and circulated in December 2006. In his draft opinion, Attorney William Oglo, acting as Assistant General Counsel, State of Florida Office of Financial Regulation, concluded that e-gold® did not need a money transmitter license to do business in the State of Florida.[918]

Smoking Gun

The following text is a full copy of the Interoffice communication dated December 5, 2006, containing the draft opinion.

draft
OFFICE OF FINANCIAL REGULATION
TO: Bob Rosenau, Chief, Bureau of Investigations, Mike Ramsden, Financial Administrator, Money Transmitter Regulation Unit
FROM: William Oglo, Assistant General Counsel
THROUGH: Peter Fisher, Chief Finance Attorney
SUBJECT: Informal opinion regarding whether the activities of e-gold, Ltd. and Gold &
Silver Reserve, Inc. are subject to regulation by Chapter 560, Florida Statutes
Legal file no. 0009-M-6/06
DATE: December 5, 2006

e-gold and Gold & Silver Reserve, Inc. (G&SR) purportedly provide consumers and merchants with "digital currency" backed by gold which can be used as an online payment system and a store of value. The system works in the following manner. A customer creates an account with e-gold, a "digital currency" dealer. He then funds his account by paying domestic or foreign currency to G&SR, a digital currency exchange service, in exchange for units of e-gold. Units of e-gold are measured in troy ounces or grams. G&SR performs this service for a percentage fee. The customer cannot purchase units of e-gold directly from e-gold.

918 Rosenau, Robert J. "Request for Legal Opinion – E Gold/Gold & Silver Reserve." Received by Bob Reitler, *Request for Legal Opinion – E Gold/Gold & Silver Reserve*, 14 Sept. 2006.

The value of the customer's e-gold units, as expressed in domestic or foreign currency, fluctuates according to the market value of the metal. The customer can purportedly redeem his e-gold units for actual gold metal. The customer can make purchases online using his e-gold units with merchants who accept consideration in e-gold and have accounts with e-gold. e-gold charges a fee for the purchasing transaction. e-gold also charges a maintenance fee on accounts. Merchants can exchange e-gold units for domestic or foreign currency through a digital currency exchange service. G&SR is e-gold's primary digital currency exchange service. Merchants or customers can also exchange their units of e-gold through independent digital exchange services.

G&SR is the parent corporation of e-gold and is responsible for the administration of e-gold's accounts. G&SR's business offices are located in Melbourne, Florida. The e-gold accounts are in a server located in Orlando, Florida. e-gold is a corporation registered in the Caribbean Island of Nevis, near Antigua. The founder of e-gold says that he was guided by high principles of libertarianism to remove a "currency" from what he calls the detrimental influences of governments. Government regulators are concerned that e-gold can be used to launder money anonymously.

Pursuant to Sections 560.204(1) and 560.303(1), Florida Statutes, e-gold and G&SR cannot engage in the businesses of exchanging foreign currency, acting as funds transmitters, or selling payment instruments, among other things, without first being registered with the Office.

Neither e-gold nor G&SR are engaging in the business of exchanging foreign currency. A "foreign currency exchanger" exchanges currency of the United States or a foreign government to currency of another government pursuant to Section 560.103(6), Florida Statutes. "Currency" is defined in Section 560.103(6), Florida Statutes, as money of the United States or of any other country which is designated as legal tender. There is no evidence that e-gold is money of the United States or of any other country which is designated as legal tender. Thus, when G&SR takes currency from a customer and exchanges it for e-gold units, this activity is not encompassed by the definition of Section 560.103(6), Florida Statutes. This is because G&SR is not exchanging currency of one government for currency of another government.

There are two positions as to whether e-gold or G&SR are engaging in the activity of a funds transmitter. A "funds transmitter" engages in the receipt of currency or payment instruments for the purpose of transmitting to another location by wire, electronic transmission, or otherwise. The first position on whether e-gold and G&SR are funds transmitters maintains that G&SR is receiving domestic currency from a customer and is "exchanging" it for e-gold units, a non currency commodity. G&SR is not transmitting it. Once the currency is exchanged fore-gold units, the e-gold units would no longer be considered currency. While a customer may use egold units to purchase things from merchants, the e-gold units are not actual currency. Thus, there would be no transmission of currency from G&SR or e-gold to the merchant. The transaction would be a barter exchange, where a merchant agrees to accept e-gold units for his goods or services. If G&SR received e-gold units from a merchant for conversion to domestic currency, it would not be not receiving currency that is the legal tender of a government. Thus, G&SR would not be operating as a transmitter of funds from the merchant either.

The second position on whether e-gold and G&SR are funds transmitters maintains that the above-referenced transaction is in effect the transmission of funds. The currency provided by the consumer to G&SR would be in effect transmitted to a merchant in payment for the goods or services. The parties may describe the transaction as a purchase of goods for e-gold units, but the transaction was always intended to be a purchase of goods for currency. To the extent that courts do not reject e-gold's and G&SR's business model as a sham transaction, currency converted into e-gold units is still being transmitted as currency, and the Money Transmitter's Code covers the transmission of it. Based upon the description of the e-gold business model as it is currently known and described herein, this writer believes first position, that funds are not being transmitted, is more appropriate. This is based upon the possibility that a court might determine that the statute authorizing the Office to seek fines for unregistered money transmitting is a penal statute. Penal statutes are strictly construed.

The remaining issue is whether the activities of e-gold or G&SR fall within the definition of payment instrument, as opposed to "currency", such that e-gold or G&SR would be acting as funds transmitters. Section 560.103(15), Florida Statutes, defines "payment instrument" as:

> a check, draft, warrant, money order, travelers check or other instrument or payment of money, whether or not negotiable.

Chapter 560, Florida Statutes, does not directly require that the term "payment instrument", involve the currency of a government. However, the terms in the definition of "payment instrument" require that the instrument involve money. For instance, the term "draft" is defined in the Law Dictionary, 2nd Ed., as:

> an order in writing directing a person other than the maker to pay a specified sum of *money* to a named person; *(emphasis supplied)*

Money is defined in the Law Dictionary, 2nd Ed., as:
> coined metal, usually gold or silver, upon which a government has impressed its stamp to designate it's value. While money was once limited to coin of the realm," in common usage the term refers to any currency, tokens, bank notes or the like accepted as a medium of exchange. *Under the Uniform Commercial Code, money is defined as "a medium of exchange authorized or adopted by a domestic or foreign government as a part of its currency.* "U.C.C. Section 1- 201(24) *(emphasis supplied)*

Most of the instruments mentioned in the Section 560.103(15), Florida Statutes, definition of "payment instrument", such as check and draft, are governed by the U.C.C., adopted as Chapters 670 through 679, Florida Statutes. Thus, when G&SR converts e-gold units into domestic or foreign currency for a merchant, it is not receiving a "payment instrument"-which needs to be money-for purposes of transmission to another location.

Based upon the foregoing, the activities of e-gold and G&SR are not subject to regulation through Chapter. 560, Florida Statutes. This opinion is based upon the following materials provided to Legal. The Money Transmitter Regulation Unit provided a Business Week magazine article about e-gold as well as copies of material from e-gold's website. Investigations provided Legal with an operational summary of e-gold, Ltd. Prepared by an investigator, printouts of a digital currency exchange service's website, and a chapter about online payment systems from the 2005 Threat Assessment, among other things. ·

Approved by:
Robert B. Beitler, General Counsel
Mike Ramsden, Financial Administrator, Money Transmitter Regulation Unit

Robert Rosenau, Chief, Bureau of Investigations
Rick White, Director of Securities and Financial Regulation[919]
[Document was not signed]

In 2006, this document demonstrates that the State of Florida had determined, e-gold and G&SR were not considered money transmitters under Chapter 560, Florida Statutes. The following text is the explanatory statement from that document, "Based upon the foregoing, the activities of e-gold and G&SR are not subject to regulation through Chapter 560, Florida Statutes."

On February 6, 2007, Investigator Burley had a phone call regarding the federal investigation of e-gold with USSS Special Agent Dotson and Kim Peretti, DOJ Attorney. On that day in February 2007, it should have been painfully obvious, to the USSS and the DOJ, that no State of Florida financial related criminal charges for money transmitting would be available for Federal prosecutors in the e-gold case. Many people have argued that because the state where e-gold had operated for more than a decade, did not require a money transmitter license, there should not have been any federal money transmitting charge. The timeline of these events also appears to confirm Jackson's claims. After Florida's draft opinion that e-gold was operating legally in their state, the USSS began shopping for a willing jurisdiction to produce the charge.

If the federal case was to proceed, it seems plausible that DOJ prosecutors had to seek out another state that would produce the unlicensed money transmitter charge. Without a state violation, the government could not file the federal money transmitter violation. The timeline and the evidence uncovered suggest that the e-gold federal charge had initially relied on a State of Florida violation that never surfaced.

The fax cover sheet evidencing the February 2007 phone call between prosecutors and Florida financial regulators appears to confirm this claim. It seems likely, by February 2007, federal prosecutors recognized that no violations were coming from Florida, and the federal government changed their game plan. Other interoffice communications show that after receiving the draft opinion, the DOJ officials directed Florida regulators not to discuss or release that draft opinion and not make any declaration about e-gold. Here is the critical line from that February 6, 2007, email.

Agent Dotson and AUSA Predi requested that OFR and the State of Florida continue

[919] Oglo, William. "Informal Opinion Regarding Whether the Activities of e-gold, Ltd. and Gold & Silver Reserve, Inc. Are Subject to Regulation by Chapter 560, Florida Statutes Legal File No. 0009-M-6/06." Received by Bob Rosenau, and Mike Ramsden, *Informal Opinion Regarding Whether the Activities of e-gold, Ltd. and Gold & Silver Reserve, Inc. Are Subject to Regulation by Chapter 560, Florida Statutes Legal File No. 0009-M-6/06*, 5 Dec. 2006. OFFICE OF FINANCIAL REGULATION, THROUGH: Peter Fisher, Chief Finance Attorney

to delay any declarations or Orders regarding the regulatory status of e-gold and related entities as possible money transmitters.[920]

The question arises, if the State of Florida Office of Financial Regulation had this draft opinion and was ready to provide requested financial guidance to the decade-old Florida company, why did the USSS direct them not to release it? The following text is the full email.

> From: David Burley
> Sent: Tuesday, February 06, 2007 11:12 AM
> To: Alex Toledo   [Investigations Manager at Florida Office of Financial Regulation, Orlando]
> Subject: e-gold case status
> Alex:
> I just spoke this morning with SA Roy Dotson with the U.S. Secret Service and Kim Predi[Peretti], U.S. Attorney (Washington, D.C.) for the Dept. of Justice regarding their investigation of e-gold and several other digital currencies. Agent Dotson and AUSA Predi requested that OFR and the State of Florida continue to delay any declarations or Orders regarding the regulatory status of e-gold and related entities as possible money transmitters. Their actions are still under seal though they did want us to pass along to Tallahassee that their grand jury investigation is almost wrapped up, and they believe the final resolution will be very beneficial to the federal agencies and each of the states with money transmitter regulations. Agent Dotson will keep us updated as their investigation and the DOJ's prosecution concludes.[921]

This email, from February 6, 2007, clarifies events.

a) Peretti, the USSS, and the DOJ prosecutors had received the draft legal opinion that e-gold and G&SR were not subject to Florida statutes. Agents of the federal government were aware that the State of Florida had drafted a legal opinion that stated e-gold and G&SR were not violating FL Statutes on money transmitting.
b) Federal prosecutors requested that the State of Florida Office of Financial Regulation bury the draft legal opinion, delay any release of other opinions or guidance, have no contact with e-gold, and keep the Feds agenda secret.

About fifteen minutes later, on February 6, 2007, Alex Toledo, Investigations Manager

---

[920] Burley, David. "e-gold Case Status." Received by Alex Toledo, *e-gold Case Status*, 6 Feb. 2007.
[921] Ibid

at Florida Office of Financial Regulation, Orlando sent an email to Chris Hancock in the OFR disclosing that G&SR was willing to register as a Money Transmitter in the State of Florida and potentially other states.

This next email, also demonstrates that Florida officials knew e-gold was willing to register as a Money Transmitter in Florida; had the state instructed the company to get the license. These items demonstrate Florida's intent not to charge the company and e-gold's willingness to register and become licensed in February of 2007. All of this documented evidence is "on the record" in recovered official State of Florida documents and emails.

> From: Alex Toledo
> Sent: Tuesday, February 06, 2007 11:26 AM
> To: Chris Hancock
> Subject: FW: e-gold case status
> Chris:
> Please see David's communication below. It appears the company is showing a willingness to register as a money transmitter in Florida and potentially other states. An agreement appears to be in the works though it, and the information below, is still a part of the USDOJ's confidential investigation. Let's discuss when you have an opportunity.
> Alex[922]

This email also provides a possible explanation of why the December 2006 informal opinion issued by the State of Florida was not signed or released. A legal conclusion that e-gold had not violated Florida statues, from qualified financial regulators responsible for supervising the e-gold business, would have delivered a knock-out punch to the federal government's criminal case.

It is critical to note that Jackson did not uncover these email and interoffice communications until years after the guilty plea agreements. It is also crucial to understand that the DOJ prosecuting attorneys did not disclose any of this information or any of the documents to the Court in the DOJ's letter regarding *Brady* materials.

Government disclosure of material exculpatory and impeachment evidence is part of the constitutional guarantee to a fair trial. *Brady v. Maryland*, 373 U.S. 83, 87 (1963); *Giglio v. U.S.*, 405 U.S. 150, 154 (1972). The law requires the disclosure of exculpatory and impeachment evidence when it is material to guilt or punishment. *Brady*, 373 U.S. at 87; *Giglio*, 405 U.S. at 154. Prosecutors must provide this substantial evidence according to their *Brady* and *Giglio* constitutional obligations. *Brady* materials must be disclosed

---

[922] Toledo, Alex. "FW: e-gold Case Status." Received by Chris Hancock, *FW: e-gold Case Status*, 6 Feb. 2007.

regardless of whether the defendant makes a request for exculpatory or impeachment evidence. *Kyles v. Whitley*, 514 U.S. 419, 432-33 (1995).

AUSAs [Assistant United States Attorneys] in the criminal division must be familiar with and fully comply with their discovery obligations under Federal Rule of Criminal Procedure 16, the Jencks Act, Federal Rule of Evidence 404(b), the *Brady/Giglio* line of cases, and Department of Justice policies.

On April 7, 2008, the US Department of Justice Senior Counsel Kimberly Peretti sent a letter to all attorneys involved in the criminal case (*United States v. e-gold, Ltd., et al.*, Cr. No. 07-109 (RMC)). The document was composed in accordance with the amended Scheduling Order responding to Item #2, which requires the Government to produce, to the extent it has not already been produced, all material pursuant to *Brady v. Maryland, Giglio v. United States*, and their progeny by April 7, 2008. The four-page letter stated, "Although we do not believe that the following information is materially exculpatory, we disclose it out of an abundance of caution."[923]

All of these newly uncovered communications between the USSS, DOJ, and Florida officials occurred before April 2007. However, none of this material, Jackson discovered in later years, was included in the prosecutor's *Brady* material. Neither Kim Peretti nor Lauren Lomis disclosed anything regarding their communications with officials from Florida's Office of Financial Regulations, the USSS, or any information about the Florida's draft legal opinion. Although the documents and communications existed, the Prosecutors did not present this material.

By burying these State of Florida documents and correspondence, the Prosecutors had owned   information, not discoverable to the Defendants, that increased the possibility of an acquittal at trial. By hiding this DOJ interaction with Florida Lawyers and Regulators, Prosecutors undoubtedly exaggerated the strength of their case and forced the plea.

Did the DOJ Prosecutors, including Kimberly Peretti, purposely bury these documents to bolster their prosecution and build their careers? The world may never know.

Even a novice legal mind might conclude that these communications were material to the e-gold case. Jackson proposes, and the circumstances dictate, that prosecutors should have disclosed this evidence of interactions between the DOJ, USSS, and Florida to the Court in the *Brady* material.

This disclosure is part of the U.S. Constitution's guarantee to a fair trial. Jackson zeros in on these questions in his 2017 letter to John Roth.

Material information not disclosed in the *Brady/Giglio* letter

---

[923] Peretti, Kimberly Kiefer. "Re: United States v. e-gold, Ltd., Et al., Crim. No. 07-109 (RMC)." Received by Joshua G. Berman, et al., *Re: United States v. e-gold, Ltd., Et al., Crim. No. 07-109 (RMC)*, 7 Apr. 2008.

[*Brady* letter is Exhibit 2]. The case against e-gold et al was a complex case of first impression with regard to novel and innovative monetary and payments systems.

The core of the case was a charge of violations of 18 USC 1960, Operation of an Unlicensed Money Transmitting Business. The companies (and I) were also charged with violations of 18 USC 1956 (money laundering). No legal theory was advanced to support the money laundering charge but it was evident the success of 1956 was dependent on the 1960 charge.

As noted by the competent Florida regulators in the attached materials, the determination of whether a company requires licensing as a money transmitter is a fact-intensive evaluation. A cornerstone of the defense strategy was therefore to obtain a Monsanto hearing as a means of introducing the court to the relevant facts and circumstances. The goal of the prosecution was to prevent such a hearing and force an outcome based on the assumed facts of the criminal complaint. This is indeed what happened – the case never reached an evidentiary phase (despite an Appeals Court ruling that we were entitled to an evidentiary hearing) and was effectively lost when Judge Collyer issued a strongly worded ruling denying the Motion to Dismiss the 1960 charge.

Had the information suppressed by the prosecution been available, a much more persuasive argument could have been made in the Motion to Dismiss that 18 USC 1960 fails to provide fair warning of the conduct it proscribes. Unbeknownst to us, the competent authorities in our home state of Florida had examined the question at the behest of Ms. Peretti and concluded:

"Based upon the foregoing, the activities of e-gold and G&SR are not subject to regulation through Chapter 560, Florida Statutes. This writer has no knowledge that any other federal or state regulator has held that this activity is within the jurisdiction of their money transmitter code."[924]

In a 2018 email, Jackson discussed these details.

Only at the same time in 2010 did we learn that the SS had then (2005-6) proceeded

---

[924] Jackson, Douglas. "Prefatory Letter to John Roth." Received by Inspector General John Roth, 1020 Steven Patrick Avenue, 24 Aug. 2017, Indian Harbour Beach, Florida. Origins and motives behind the USSS campaign to destroy e-gold, Gold & Silver Reserve, Inc.

to "shop" other jurisdictions to find one more amenable. Hence the involvement of DC, where at no time in prior history had the Money Transmitter label been applied to any entity lacking a physical presence in DC and that did not transact in paper cash.

In 2019, Jackson shared an additional revelation regarding the District of Columbia Department of Insurance, Securities and Banking (DISB) in the e-gold case:

> As you know, when I made my records request to the DC DISB in 2017 they denied having any record of communications with anyone regarding e-gold circa 2006-2007.[925] I thought maybe they had destroyed the documents as is routine with record retention requirements/policies since more than a decade had since elapsed. But I just got off the phone from a call with [attorney who represented the companies on regulatory matter from 2009 - 2015] and she told me she met with the DC DISB last week in relation to another client. She asked [a senior official who had been there at the time] about the discrepancy of how Reid and Barry had been charged with, and convicted for, violations of the DC Money Transmitter statutes but COEPTIS had been told in 2016 that no license was required. They told her that no one had ever contacted the DISB in relation to the e-gold case.[926]

Another exchange from Attorney Oglo, in early May 2007, summarized the new e-gold® indictment and appeared to back up the State's draft legal opinion that e-gold® was not operating as an unlicensed money transmitter. This email stated, "Since the federal definition of a money transmitting business is different than the Chapter 560 definition, this count does not appear to offer support for the Office[Florida OFR] to take action under Chapter 560."

> **From:** William Oglo
> **Sent:** Tuesday, May 01, 2007 11:11 **AM**
> **To:** Peter Fisher
> **Subject:** RE: [ACAMS] Digital Currency Business e-gold Indicted
> Peter,
> Here are a couple of thoughts on this article. The article can be summed up in one of

---

[925] Alula, Claudine. "FOIA Tracking # 2017-FOIA-02650 Final Response Letter. NO RECORDS." Received by Douglas Jackson, and Charlotte Parker, *FOIA Tracking # 2017-FOIA-02650 Final Response Letter. NO RECORDS*, 2 May 2017.

[926] Jackson, Douglas. "Chunk 10." Received by Carl Mullan, *Chunk 10*, 31 Mar. 2020.

its paragraphs:

Count 1-conspiracy to launder monetary instruments
-While one of the goals of Chapter 560 is to reduce money laundering, money laundering, in and of itself, does not trigger jurisdiction of the Office of Financial Regulation. Chapter 560, Florida Statutes, is designed to require businesses operating as money transmitters to obtain registration and comply with the provision of Chapter 560, Florida Statutes. Specifically, the Office needs evidence that e-gold® is violating Section 560.204 (1), Florida Statutes, which provides "No person shall engage for consideration, nor in any manner advertise that they engage in the selling or issuing of payment instruments or in the activity of a funds transmitter, without first obtaining registration under the provisions of this part." There is no clear evidence that the elements to prove: money laundering are exactly the same as the elements to prove jurisdiction under Chapter 560.

Count 3-operating a unlicensed money transmitting business under federal law -31 U.S.C. Section 5330(a) requires any person who owns or controls a money transmitting business to register the business with the Secretary of the Treasury. 31 U.S.C. Section 5330(d) provides the following definitions:

(1) Money transmitting business.- The term "money transmitting business" means any business other than the United States Postal Service which-

(a) provides check cashing, currency exchange, or money transmitting or remittance services, or issues or redeems money orders, traveler's checks, and *other similar instruments or any other person who engages as* a *business in the transmission of funds, including any person who engages as* a *business in an informal money transfer system or any network of people who engage as* a *business in facilitating the transfer of money domestically or internationally outside of the conventional financial institutions system; (emphasis supplied)*

* * *

(2)	Money transmitting service.- The term " money transmitting service" includes accepting currency or funds denominated in the currency of any country and transmitting the currency of funds, or the value of the currency or funds, by any means through a financial agency or institution, a Federal reserve bank or other facility of the Board of Governors of the Federal Reserve System, or an electronic funds transfer network.

The italicized portion was added by the 2001 Patriot Act. It used to read "and other similar instruments." It is not clear whether e-gold units, which are not currency, would be covered by the italicized language. However, the italicized language is substantially dissimilar to the Chapter 560 definition of a funds transmitter which "means a person who engages in the receipt of currency or payment instruments for the purpose of transmission by any means, including transmissions within this country or to or from locations outside this country, by wire, facsimile, electronic transfer, courier, or otherwise." Since the federal definition of a money transmitting business is different that the Chapter 560 definition, this count does not appear to offer support for the Office to take action under Chapter 560.[927]

However, this draft legal opinion, along with the other uncovered communications, was never released, never provided to the Court, and never shown to the Defendants. At least partially because of the DOJ and USSS, no guidance from the State of Florida or legal opinions were discussed or offered to e-gold®. Nor, as required by *Brady/Giglio*, was this information disclosed by the prosecution to the Court. This draft legal opinion remained in the private files of the OFR hidden until Jackson uncovered it in 2017 through Florida's version of the freedom of information act.

The next email, sent about three months later in May 2007, was between the same Florida OFR employees and attorneys. This email is very revealing for two reasons.

1. The sender, General Counsel Robert Beitler, appears to cast doubt on the previous draft legal opinion.
2. Beitler reveals the possible USSS hidden agenda saying, "Everyone knows why they went after e-gold[...]"

From: Robert Beitler
Sent: Friday, May 25, 2007 9:59 AM
To: Robert Rosenau; Peter Fisher; Mike Ramsden
Cc: John Harper; Chris Hancock; Mark Mathosian; William Oglo
Subject: RE: [ACAMS] Digital Currency Business e-gold Indicted

Bob:
This is all fact intensive. I haven't a clue what evidence the feds have. As I recall, just about all the facts that we received from you for this opinion was what you pulled off the e-gold web site. And that information was insufficient for us to conclude that this was a money transmitter. Even if we had all the fed's info, we might reach the same conclusion.

---

[927] Oglo, William. "RE: [ACAMS] Digital Currency Business e-Gold Indicted." Received by Peter Fisher, *RE: [ACAMS] Digital Currency Business e-Gold Indicted*, 1 May 2007.

Everyone knows why they went after e-gold, but as you are aware the filing of charges is not determinative of anything. In addition, any opinion which we reach in e-gold, especially based on such skeletal information as you have been able to provide, is unlikely to provide useful guidance for most other companies, as each will be dependent on the facts available regarding that enterprise and its method of operation.
Rob[928]

After the DOJ formally indicted e-gold® in April 2007, based on their correspondence, the Office of Financial Regulation appeared to be purposely lost. OFR members and attorneys seemed as though they were working in circles, to avoid discussing e-gold's status and produce the legal opinion. On June 4th, Attorney Oglo recorded a cryptic memo to the document file and closed the case.

DATE: June 4, 2007
TO: File
FROM: William Oglo
INTEROFFICE COMMUNICATION OFFICE OF FINANCIAL REGULATION
LEGAL SERVICES
RE: Requests for Informal Opinion on e-gold-closing memo

e-gold is a digital currency which purportedly can be used as a store of value or a method of
payment to certain companies operating online. Both the Money Transmitter Unit and the Bureau of Investigations requested that Legal provide an informal opinion regarding whether the Office can regulate companies that exchange dollars for e-gold. The matter was assigned to me.

After I had a chance to research and review the legal issues, a decision was made to have a meeting with representatives of Legal, the Money Transmitter's Unit, the Division of Securities and Finance, and the Bureau of Investigations, prior to the issuance of an informal opinion. This was because the Bureaus wanted to exchange their ideas on whether the Office could legally regulate e-gold and/or whether the Office should regulate e-gold. On January 18, 2007, a meeting was held where a

[928] Bietler, Robert. "RE: [ACAMS] Digital Currency Business e-Gold Indicted." Received by Robert Rosenau, et al., *RE: [ACAMS] Digital Currency Business e-Gold Indicted*, 25 May 2007.

number of issues were discussed. The decision whether the Office should regulate e-gold was postponed in part so that the newly reorganized Finance Division would have time to familiarize itself with the issues. On or about April 30, 2007, the Office became aware that U.S. Justice Department issued an indictment charging e-gold with money laundering, conspiracy, operating an unlicensed money transmitter business, and other violations of law. Thus, it appears that the Justice Department is addressing concerns of the manner in which e-gold is operating. Both the Money Transmitter's Unit and the Bureau of Investigations agree that it is appropriate to close this matter at this time subject to reopening at a later date if warranted.[929]

♦

Invisible Assistance

Before the investigation of e-gold® had progressed to an indictment, Jackson had responded to hundreds of court requests and actively aided the law enforcement community. However, at no time did the USSS ever give Jackson credit for his contributions. Nor was Jackson's assistance presented to the Court. Data extracted from the e-gold® database by e-gold's in-house investigative staff and by Dr. Jackson himself delivered critical help with the identification and interdiction of numerous high-profile transnational criminals and criminal organizations. Yet, the USSS never acknowledged Jackson's support.

This May 19, 2006, email from USSS Special Agent Dotson to David Burley, in the OFR acknowledges one prime reason that the USSS did not want to release the truth about Jackson's assistance. Burley wrote: "You explained that your investigative team did not want to give Mr. Jackson the opportunity to boast about his cooperation in resolving complaints and assisting government regulators."[930]

In a 2020 email, Jackson noted another example of a government prosecutor's denying his assistance in any government investigations. Below is a December 1, 2008 email exchange with Agent X (USPIS), who was in the private sector by this time.

> On December 1, 2008 (Exhibit 27), I related the prosecution's comments to Agent X[USPIS], "At sentencing, the gov lawyer said my assistance to LE had been of no or at most trivial benefit, that the USSS had already gleaned anything that might have been useful to them directly from our database. But as of about August 2006 they still hadn't managed to even mount it on a server in a way that would enable queries."

---

[929] "Requests for Informal Opinion on e-Gold-Closing Memo." Received by William Oglo, *Requests for Informal Opinion on e-Gold-Closing Memo*, 4 June 2007. INTEROFFICE COMMUNICATION OFFICE OF FINANCIAL REGULATION LEGAL SERVICES

[930] Burley, David. "RE: Interviews Importance: High." Received by Roy Daniel Dotson, *RE: Interviews Importance: High*, 19 May 2006.

Agent X replied "Being off the record, regarding the prosecutor's comment, I would completely disagree. I know wholeheartedly how many investigations you assisted us on and how much it helped for us referring cases to international LE based off of your work. There are still cases ongoing today that are as a direct result of your help."[931]

Many law enforcement agents and investigators welcomed critical data scraped from the e-gold® database. The USSS had always acted very differently to offers of aid from Jackson. He proposes that the lack of acknowledgment regarding his assistance was a ploy by the USSS to strengthen their future criminal case against e-gold®. If the agency ignored and downplayed Jackson's aid, the USSS could continue presenting the false narrative that e-gold® turned a blind eye to crime.

Additionally, in a 2019 email, Jackson shared his concern that e-gold, at the request of law enforcement, had held off for most of 2006 on "dropping the hammer" on carder accounts was being exploited by the USSS to portray the companies as "turning a blind eye."

On August 4, 2006 (Exhibit 23), concerned with mounting indications that the USSS was exploiting the fact that, at the request of law enforcement, we had not lowered the boom on the carders in order to portray us as "turning a blind eye."

Indeed, Jackson raised this concern in his August 4, 2006 email:

From: Douglas Jackson [mailto:djackson@e-gold.com]
Sent: Friday, August 04, 2006 9:34 AM
To: [XXX]
Cc: [XXX]
Subject: cardersmack
[XXX]
Regarding these carders...
For months I've held off on exorcising them on the informal understanding that you guys prefer we allow them to continue a while for track/trace purposes.
But is there an end in sight? I am concerned that:
a) I don't want these guys continuing to infest e-gold, on general principles
b) conceivably, their continuing activity could even be construed as complicity on our part by someone with a particularly twisted agenda I need either explicit

[931] Jackson, Douglas. "PGP Message Decrypted." Received by William Crabb, *PGP Message Decrypted*, 1 Dec. 2008.

instruction to let things go on, or a sense of when I can drop the hammer on them. I have a file of every account yet identified and can pull the trigger on them in minutes. If this was done in a coordinated fashion, btw, with a court order to freeze, a fair amount of value could also be locked down, further hurting these dudes. Even if we do it on our own, our plan is to have a rolling follow-up designed to uncover their yet-unknown accounts as they scurry around trying to find an account that accepts value from blocked accounts. This would hold value in the system for as long as we run the program but in effect would also more or less violate our user agreement that we don't outright freeze without due process.[932]

Between December 2005 and April 2007 included dozens of negative press attacks against the company and Jackson. E-gold®, OmniPay, and G&SR were targets of malicious items planted in the news. Jackson's personal life was also interrupted by multiple false allegations leaked through the press. Many people, close to the case, shared impressions that rogue USSS Special Agents allegedly created the regular false claims appearing in the media. Their supposed goal for leaking the information was to bolster the DOJ's criminal case against e-gold®.

On more than one occasion, Jackson stated that the USSS incorrectly represented facts about e-gold® to the media. He claims that the USSS withheld critical information on e-gold® to advance a misleading and malicious profile of the e-gold® business. In 2019, Jackson shared these items.

In their[USSS] first slur of e-gold, with "have allowed online criminals to…" they are essentially saying we turned a blind eye and knowingly permitted. This isn't true. When I became aware there was such a things as carders (Tom Zeller's NYT articles summer 2005), I immediately called the USSS.[933]

Then, January 2006, when I acquired the capability to do full text search and found the "Rosetta stone" carder account, I again reached out to the USSS. Rebuffed again by them, a banking industry investigative contact referred me to Greg Crabb of the USPIS, who I'd worked with years before on another case.[934]

They[USSS] are definitely twisting the narrative to the extent that it amounts to lying

[932] Jackson, Douglas. "Cardersmack." Received by Gregory S. Crabb, *Cardersmack*, 4 Aug. 2006.
[933] Jackson, Douglas. "Re: Attached for Short Important Read." Received by Carl Mullan, *Re: Attached for Short Important Read*, 12 Feb. 2019.
[934] Ibid

in the sense that a reader would conclude things that are not true.[935]

There were several instances where Jackson had made a significant contribution of information that identified and located suspects resulting in high-profile arrests.

The USSS investigation of Lord Kaisersose is an excellent example of Jackson's claims. News reports chronicled how the United States Secret Service carried out "Operation Lord Kaisersose" and reported how Special Agents in the USSS Miami office had identified a suspect using the alias Lord Kaisersose and provided French National Police with information to make the arrests. There was no mention of e-gold's direct assistance. Furthermore, there was no evidence of Jackson's critical cooperation ever presented to the Court. Another essential item that illustrates how the USSS worked to vilify e-gold® surfaced in a June 21, 2005, article written by Tom Zeller Jr., for the New York Times entitled *Black Market in Stolen Credit Card Data Thrives on Internet.* In the piece, Zeller writes that USSS Special Agents, talking with him, had expressed skepticism that e-gold® was storing any gold bullion backing the digital units! Despite Jackson's elaborate auditing functions and public display of all precious metal balances backing the digital currency, the USSS was busy spreading malicious rumors about e-gold®. These facts also back up Jackson's claims.

> Payments often change hands in relative anonymity (and with little regulation) by, an electronic currency that purports to be backed by gold bullion and issued by e-gold Ltd., a company incorporated on the island of Nevis in the Caribbean. (Secret Service agents have expressed skepticism over the gold backing.)[936]

Zeller's article demonstrates how common it was for the USSS to attempt and discredit e-gold® or vilify Jackson.

During his interaction with the law enforcement community, Jackson had requested the proper legal paperwork and Court orders before sharing e-gold® client information. However, an event eventually occurred when Jackson complied with the information requests before the paper warrants were delivered. In some instances, the Court document authorizing the search of an e-gold® customer's account never arrived. However, Jackson had already complied and released the customer account information.

In a 2006 Wired.com article, Jackson's attorney, Andrew Ittleman, commented about search warrants and the relationship between e-gold® and law enforcement agents. The point

---

[935] Ibid

[936] Zeller, Tom. "Black Market in Stolen Credit Card Data Thrives on Internet." *The New York Times*, 21 June 2005, www.nytimes.com.

of contention had occurred after a government agent promised Jackson a pending court order. Jackson delivered the requested database details on e-gold® customers, then never received the guaranteed Court order.

Jackson's attorney, Andrew Ittleman, explained that while this event upset Jackson, his actions were legal and proper. Ittleman's comments on the matter appeared in an article entitled *e-gold® Gets Tough on Crime,* written by Kim Zetter and published on December 11, 2006, in Wired.com. The following partial text is from the article.

> His[Jackson] lawyers aren't bothered by the move, however. They say agents repeatedly promised to provide Jackson with court orders since last February but have not come through.
>
> "You have a very strong documented relationship with these agents asking about particular people with the promise that they are going to be subpoenaing," says Jackson attorney Andrew Ittleman. "Just because they never ultimately gave him a subpoena doesn't put the fault on Jackson -- it's on the agents. He was acting in good faith."
>
> His lawyers also say that once the company discovered evidence of possible wrongdoing, it had no choice but to hand over information to the government. Jackson could even have been charged with aiding and abetting money launderers under federal statutes if he didn't report the suspicious activity.[937]

The government's failure to deliver a court order opened Jackson's eyes in 2006. Government investigators had requested that he allow the activity to continue unabated in several suspicious accounts. In some cases, Jackson complied with their requests. However, without court orders, and no valid documents stating that government agents had directed him to leave the accounts untouched, Jackson realized these actions might further the false characterization that e-gold® was "turning a blind eye." Had USSS Special Agents been setting Jackson up to promote the government's criminal case? He later described this situation in 2018 emails.

> That[working with law enforcement] was extremely productive but there was an element of being screwed by them too. From day 1 (in our meeting at their Reston,

---

[937] Zetter, Kim. "Gold Gets Tough on Crime." *Wired.com*, Internet Archive, 11 Dec. 2006, web.archive.org/web/20080513004819/http://www.wired.com/science/discoveries/news/2006/12/72278?currentPage=2
.

VA HQ) I indicated I needed a trap and trace court order (once known in the phone industry in relation to wiretaps as a "pen register") or some sort of due process to cover my liability stemming from releasing such extensive and ongoing investigative data/work product. They promised but never came through with one. Moreover, they asked me not to block or freeze any of the accounts while we were working together (see attached). So from January to November 2006 I left these accounts open while I compiled and provided thousands of pages of investigative material.[938]

Attempts to associate e-gold® with child pornography

It is important to note that neither the April 2007 Federal Indictment nor the final Superseding Indictment contained any formal charges related to child pornography payments. The DOJ did not ever file any criminal charges related to child pornography against e-gold® or the other defendants.

One of the first Court documents made public in the legal proceedings against e-gold®, way back in December 2005, contained details falsely attempted to portray e-gold® as a favored mainstream method used to pay for child pornography.

Jackson stated later, "Prior to this time,[939] law enforcement agencies had been concealing knowledge of the use of e-gold® for CP per a hidden agenda to portray e-gold® as complicit in the activity." Jackson explained further:

> I have seen press releases where the Government describes the conviction of a CP buyer as deriving from "records seized from e-gold" when in actuality the man was approached in a 'knock-and-talk' after e-gold investigators supplied his identity to law enforcement in response to a subpoena that e-gold itself had solicited.[940]

E-gold® was a founding member of the NCMEC's Financial Coalition to Combat Child Pornography, and Jackson was deeply committed to eradicating online payments used in these crimes. In a May 25, 2007, letter to Ernie Allen, CEO, National Center for Missing & Exploited, Jackson proposes that the USSS had been concealing knowledge of CP abuses from e-gold investigators. He labeled Phase One of the alleged USSS operation as "The conspiracy of silence." The following text includes some of Jackson's comments on Phase One.

---

[938] Jackson, Douglas. "Re: Attached for Short Important Read." Received by Carl Mullan, *Re: Attached for Short Important Read*, 13 Feb. 2019.

[939] Jackson commented that "this time" was a reference to before July 2005, when NCMEC finally responded to him and invited him to be a charter member of their newly forming FCACP.

[940] Jackson, Douglas. "Dear Ernie C.doc." Received by Ernie Allen, *Dear Ernie c.doc*, 25 May 2007AD.

Phase 1, the conspiracy of silence

The first phase is the interval from August 2003, the first instance [as we subsequently learned] these criminals undertook to abuse e-gold for this purpose, until August 2005, when e-gold was invited to join the newly forming FCACP. Until the formation of the FCACP, there as a conspiracy of silence with the intent of damaging e-gold. We had no way of knowing it at the time but law enforcement (at the behest of the USSS), and NCMEC itself, was concealing knowledge of CP abuses from e-gold investigators. In some instances, agents of the US government, rather than notifying e-gold or requesting data by subpoena, elected instead to plant stories in the media describing e-gold as a major player in CP payments. This may have begun as early as 2004 when the CP sellers were much less sophisticated and a collaborative effort with e-gold's investigators might have located them easily.[941]

One possible connection that may support Jackson's claim is the close association between the USSS and the NCMEC. At the time, e-gold® was a member of the Financial Coalition Against Child Pornography, a former head of the USSS Brian Stafford, who was an NCMEC Vice-Chairperson and Board Member.[942] The relevance of this association is unknown.

Jackson had been a staunch opponent of child pornography and was deeply against any child endangerment. E-gold® issued the following statement, in September 2006. The company was an active member of the Financial Coalition Against Child Pornography, a coalition organized by the National Center for Missing and Exploited Children (NCMEC).

The NCMEC's Financial Coalition is demonstrating how a strong level of cooperation can lead to the reduction and hopefully elimination of crime on the Internet. It is certainly e-gold's objective, working with the NCMEC and our coalition partners to completely eradicate child pornography on the Internet.[943]

---

[941] Ibid

[942] "Senator Dennis DeConcini Named Chairman of the Board of Directors for the National Center for Missing & Exploited Children." *Business Wire*, 6 Jan. 2004, www.businesswire.com/news/home/20040106005468/en/Senator-Dennis-DeConcini-Named-Chairman-Board-Directors.

[943] "DELETING COMMERCIAL PORNOGRAPHY SITES FROM THE INTERNET: THE U.S. FINANCIAL INDUSTRY'S EFFORTS TO COMBAT THIS PROBLEM." - DELETING COMMERCIAL PORNOGRAPHY SITES FROM THE INTERNET: THE U.S. FINANCIAL INDUSTRY'S EFFORTS TO COMBAT THIS PROBLEM HEARING BEFORE THE SUBCOMMITTEE ON OVERSIGHT AND INVESTIGATIONS OF THE COMMITTEE ON ENERGY AND COMMERCE HOUSE OF REPRESENTATIVES ONE HUNDRED NINTH CONGRESS SECOND SESSION SEPTEMBER 21, 2006 Serial No. 109-141 Printed for the Use of the Committee on Energy and Commerce Available via the World Wide Web: http://www.access.gpo.gov/Congress/House U.S. GOVERNMENT PRINTING OFFICE 31-467 WASHINGTON : 2006, [House Hearing, 109 Congress] [From the U.S. Government Printing Office], 21 Sept. 2006, www.govinfo.gov/content/pkg/CHRG-109hhrg31467/html/CHRG-109hhrg31467.htm.

Jacksons makes a reasonable claim about the USSS using the press in a failed attempt to associate e-gold® with child pornography payments closely. Evidence and information support Jackson's statements. Also, Jackson has shown that the USSS used inaccurate statements, regarding e-gold's alleged association with child pornography, to deceive the original Federal Magistrate Judge that issued the 2005 warrant.

Early in the criminal case, the USSS had falsely labeled e-gold® as a primary payment tool used in the online sale of child pornography, despite a mountain of evidence to the contrary. The 2007 indictment highlighted this sinister undertaking.

26. "e-gold" has been a highly-favored method of payment for sellers of child pornography over the Internet. In some instances, "e-gold" has been the only method of payment available on websites offering child pornography for sale.[944]

This evidence found in Court documents does support the allegation that USSS Special Agents tried to use child pornography payments to craft a malicious image of e-gold®.

The original December 2005, seizure froze the bank accounts of e-gold's primary exchange provider. This tactic is a legal mechanism regularly used in federal cases that works to separate a Defendant from regular income and access to funds.

In this case, the allegation e-gold® was deeply involved with child pornography was the critical information that influenced the Judge to issue the warrant. The frozen accounts also were targeted for seizure. This first December 2005 warrant that presented a false connection to child pornography was an all-out attempt to close down e-gold®.

The Federal Magistrate Judge that signed this original December 2005 search warrant, authorizing the government's seizure, stated that government prosecutors had deceived him. The Judge said that he was reluctant to undertake such a drastic and potentially damaging action on an ex parte basis. However, that following day, he had granted the seizures when the US Attorney and USSS Special Agents alleged that e-gold® was complicit in child pornography. In the August 2017 letter to John Roth, Jackson detailed part of this alleged deception.

The pattern of misleading the court that I allege in this document was first evident in relation to the December 2005 asset seizures and search warrant that preceded the

Serial No. 109-141

[944] Holding a Criminal Term Grand Jury Sworn in on May 11, 2006. *UNITED STATES OF AMERICA v. E-GOLD, LTD. GOLD & SILVER RESERVE, INC.DOUGLAS L. JACKSON, BARRY K. DOWNEY, and REID A. JACKSON Defendants.* 24 Apr. 2007.

indictment. It is my belief—evidenced by the remarks of Magistrate Judge Facciola at an emergency hearing on December 29, 2005, in which he expressed indignation and outrage at the willful deceit of the government attorneys—that the government attorneys knowingly misled him in their allegations of probable cause. At the outset of the hearing, speaking of the government's application for the search and seizure warrants, Magistrate Judge Facciola related (Exhibit 39) The Judge stated:

> "In the ordinary course I would review it on the spot and sign it or not sign it. But in that particular instance I immediately expressed to Mr. Cowan my concern with this matter, because it seemed to be a quite unusual matter.", going on to relate "I anticipated a day like today would come."[945]

According to the National Association of Criminal Defense Lawyers® and an NACDL Trial Penalty Recommendation Task Force report entitled *THE TRIAL PENALTY: The Sixth Amendment Right to Trial on the Verge of Extinction and How to Save It:*

> A grand jury presentation can consist entirely of information that would be inadmissible at trial. A prosecutor may knowingly use illegally-obtained evidence to obtain an indictment, and if she has evidence in her possession that substantially exculpates the target, she may withhold it from the grand jury. The presentation need only establish probable cause to believe the target committed the crime. If 11 of the 23 grand jurors are unconvinced that even that low threshold has been met, an indictment can still be obtained. And of course it's all ex parte, so no one is even there to question the prosecutor's presentation.[946]

At the emergency hearing, Government lawyers asserted that the arcane licensing issue had been the actual basis for seizures and that their child pornography allegations were not relevant to the seizure activity. The Judge replied:

> It's not irrelevant in the sense of the representations that were made to me with the search warrant. This was part of an investigation into what I was told was related to a child pornography ring … It [also] never occurred to me in my wildest dreams that far from operating surreptitiously, there have been negotiations with this company

[945] Jackson, Douglas. "Investigation Request." Received by John Roth, Inspector General, US Dept. of Homeland Security, 24 Aug. 2017, Indian Harbour Beach, FL.

[946] Jones, Rick, et al. THE TRIAL PENALTY: *The Sixth Amendment Right to Trial on the Verge of Extinction and How to Save It.* National Association of Criminal Defense Lawyers®, 2018, pp. 3–3, THE TRIAL PENALTY: *The Sixth Amendment Right to Trial on the Verge of Extinction and How to Save It.*

and the Internal Revenue Service as to the precise issue you raise about transmitting money and being subject to that statute, the Bank Secrecy Act.[947]

Judge Facciola's declaration regarding the DOJ claims from December 2005, verified that USSS Special Agents had made misleading statements and Prosecutors presented information to the Court. This evidence supports Jackson's allegations that the USSS had wrongly tried to paint e-gold® as a significant player in child pornography payments.

In February 2009, letter to a G&SR defense attorney, Jackson communicated his strong desire to correct the misleading public record on e-gold® and child pornography.

> From: Douglas Jackson <djackson@e-gold.com>
> Sent: Thursday, February 12, 2009 11:32 AM
> To: Van Cleef, Carol
> Cc: rjackson@g-sr.com
> Subject: add'l backgrounders
> Carol
> In Barry's case, bar counsel was recently in contact with prosecutor who gave communication designed very deceitfully to suggest that Barry was complicit in "turning a blind eye" crap with regard to CP.
> This is a reminder of our eventual need to correct the record as it relates to CP, the most egregious element of the injustice that was perpetrated against us.
> I am attaching a letter I had worked up summer 07, a comprehensive expose of the state of how CP is actually paid for etc., originally intended for publication. We were maneuvered out of sending it, as was usual in our every effort to dispel the vicious lies.
> The letter may be imperfect in tone but every factual assertion in it is verifiable.
> I am also attaching an interim report I had prepared and submitted to NCMEC in preparation for the January 07 quarterly Financial Coalition meeting. It constitutes the only instance where any financial firm ever provided a report, verifiable or otherwise, of actual retrospective historic data. The graph was an update of one I'd produced for a report I had prepared for my Congressional testimony in Sep 06. The attached NCMEC Q406 report was copied and re-distributed to all attendees of the

---

[947] Case 1:05-cv-02497-RMC Document 31-2 . *UNITED STATES OF AMERICA vs. ALL FUNDS ON DEPOSIT ON OR BEFORE DECEMBER 19, 2005 IN REGIONS BANK ACCOUNT NO. 6709194851, REGIONS BANK ACCOUNT NO. 6709194878 AND SUNTRUST BANK ACCOUNT NO. 1000028078359 IN THE NAME OF GOLD & SILVER RESERVE, INC., d/b/a OMNIPAY, in Rem, .* Case 1:05-cv-02497-RMC Document 31-2 , 14 Sept. 2006, pp. TRANSCRIPT OF MOTIONS HEARING BEFORE THE HONORABLE JOHN M. FACCIOLA UNITED STATES MAGISTRATE JUDGE .

January 07 meeting.
One of the biggest reasons I wanted to go to trial was to expose the purposeful foulness of the government's lies in this area.
Doug[948]

The "e-gold Operation"

One striking example of unusual legal activity in the e-gold® case was the government's use of the term "e-gold operation." This phrase improperly combined two distinct and separate legitimate companies, Gold & Silver Reserve, Inc. (Delaware Corporation) and e-gold Ltd. a Nevis, West Indies company. Dotson's depiction of one organization running two separate and distinct business was utterly incorrect. However, in many instances, Court documents evidence that DOJ prosecutors and USSS Special Agents aggregated the two companies into one combined organization. In USSS Special Agent Dotson's 2005 and 2007 Affidavit(s) in Support of Seizure,[949] he repeated the term "e-gold operation." This phrase appears around thirty separate times in the 2007 Affidavit document. However, there was no attempt by Dotson or any DOJ lawyer to legally define the term "e-gold operation" or the individual entities represented in the government's illusionary description.

Jackson offered these thoughts on the rise and fall of the e-gold platform in a 2019 email. He states that e-gold's executives were never opposed to financial regulations.

> Moreover, the financial regulations are ok as they are. Our mistake was in not conforming to them from early on. Then, once we did finally understand they would interpret us as a financial institution subject to regulation, we never got the chance to re-emerge as a licensed financial institution. But that was more of a one-off comedy of Catch-22 errors, stemming from the USSS mis-guided agenda of treating us like criminals in order to advance their own agency's interests. The successor system we have built robustly conforms to laws and regs and that conformity is actually beneficial as a means of preventing abuses (that would give rise reputation attacks) and enhancing the security of customer accounts.

Internal Revenue Service

Without a proper summary, it is challenging to comprehend G&SR's long-running IRS audit and settlement. In a 2019 email, Jackson provided these details along with his

---

[948] Jackson, Douglas. "Add'l Backgrounders." Received by Carol Van Cleef, *Add'l Backgrounders*, 12 Feb. 2009.

[949] U.S. District Court for the District of Columbia. *U.S.A. v. e-gold, Ltd., Gold & Silver Reserve, Inc. Douglas L. Jackson, Barry K. Downey, and Reid A. Jackson, Defendants.* . AFFIDAVIT IN SUPPORT OF SEIZURE WARRANT (18 U.S.C. §§ 981, 1960), Apr. 2007.

allegations regarding the IRS.[950]

- It appears G&SR's accountant had already met once with the examiner in the local (Melbourne) IRS office. The 4/8 email subject was "Items needed for IRS audit." The question arises as to the [IRS] motives/origin. We[Jackson] believe that Ian[Grigg] and Charles[Evans] had reached out to the IRS (they were denouncing us to anyone and everyone circa 2002-2003 in their efforts to throw nails under our tires and, we believe, garner some sort of informant rewards). There are three primary bases for this belief:
- In response to our 7206(c) filing with the IRS of 7/18/2003 requesting list of all third parties they had been in contact with, Ian and Charles were listed. There was also one additional, a university professor whose name was unfamiliar to us.
- We also had the "Amzallag" email of 6/9/2003 (which I suspect was sent by Jeroen who, unbeknownst to us at that time, was part of the Grigg/Evans cabal household) claiming "Mr. Evans while working with Bob Nugent has been supplying information to the IRS about GSR and Egold."[951] Given that that email also said "Mr. Evans is broke and without funds. Mr. Evans is actively speaking to people in your office and has an active campaign to destroy you.", I think it likely they were seeking informant rewards in case an IRS fishing expedition led to some sort of windfall of unreported income on the part of e-gold customers. Somewhat supportive of this, I was later told in 2008 at the IMTC conference I attended in Miami that the IRS had previously managed to pressure all banks operating in the Caymans to informally provide any and all records regarding US taxpayers without need for any legal writ. It is possible some IRS manager simply wanted a feather in his cap by getting us to give them carte blanche as well.
- There was also Jeroen's statements [memorialized in my note "Crackers in the Gloaming"] indicating such when he came to us in April 2007.

The first email document, referencing the IRS, was recovered from May 2002. This inquiry focused on G&SR's financial statements from the tax year 1999. Jackson stated: "As early as 5/6/2002, it was already evident the IRS did not really think G&SR had any material inaccuracies in its tax filings."[952]

Below is a copy of a private decrypted email from G&SR's accounting firm showing

[950] "Re: Update." Received by P. Carl Mullan, *Re: Update*, 25 July 2019.

[951] Amzallag, William. "Charles Evans Has Been Supplying the IRS with Information." Received by Douglas Jackson, *Charles Evans Has Been Supplying the IRS with Information*, 9 June 2003.

[952] Jackson, Douglas. "Chunk 10." Received by Carl Mullan, *Chunk 10*, 31 Mar. 2020.

that G&SR did not have an issue with the IRS at that time.

> Decrypted email from our accountant
> 2002.06.02 IRS tax examination & request for info
> Doug & Barry
> Good morning! I just wanted to update you on the status of the IRS audit.   I am scheduled to meet with the IRS auditor (Mr. Ganesh) on June 5 & 6th.   During our initial meeting with Mr. Ganesh, he requested additional information over and above what was on their original document request. I have spoken with both Reid & XXXX and they have been working to gather the documentation.   The only issue we have come across relates to the customer list.   As we all know, providing this information would be in violation of OmniPay's user agreement.   Mr. Ganesh's request for the customer list can be considered normal audit process and in no way reflects animosity towards OmniPay and/or the firm.
>
> Apart from the issue mentioned above, I feel that the audit is progressing well. Although Mr. Ganesh initially was adamant about OmniPay providing a customer list, he did not include this in the final document request. His comment just before leaving our offices, was "if you can provide all the information for 1999, I will not have to review the 2000 return."
>
> On the final verbal document request, Mr. Ganesh asked for a transaction history on Barry & Doug's personal e-gold accounts for 1999.   If Mr. Ganesh asks for this information on Wednesday, I would like to have this available to him.   Rhonda said that this information can be exported from e-gold to an excel spreadsheet.   Can each of you email me that information?   As I said earlier, it is quite possible that IRS will not examine 2000 if we can provide everything for 1999.
>
> Please let me know if you have any comments or questions.
> Sincerely,
> Reed, Henzell & Shott, PA
> Melbourne, FL 32901[953] [954]

Jackson further explained that, while the IRS focused on e-gold's customer and transaction

[953] "Re: Update." Received by P. Carl Mullan, *Re: Update*, 25 July 2019.

[954] "IRS Tax Examination & Request for Info." Received by Douglas Jackson, and Barry Downey, *IRS Tax Examination & Request for Info*, 2 June 2002.

data, the agency's reasons for requesting the information were unclear.

> They wanted G&SR's customer list. During this initial phase, the year under
> examination was 1999, prior to when G&SR devolved the core functions of e-gold to
> e-gold Ltd. So it seemed as if they wanted a list of e-gold customers though it is
> possible they were only looking for information on customers who had used
> G&SR/OmniPay for exchange services. Our position was per the attached email of
> 5/6/2002 "req for information."[955]

This following letter is a followup email from Downey to the accounting firm.IRS Response
Letter

May 2002.06.02
Barry K. Downey <bdowney@smithdowney.com>
Mon 5/6/2002 3:28 PM received
To: XXXX@rhscpa.com Reid Jackson <rjackson@omnipay.net>; Douglas Jackson
<djackson@OmniPay.net>;
Rhonda and Jannine:
We should tell the IRS the following about their request for the G&SR client list:
The terms of the G&SR User Agreement provide:
"17.2. Unless (i) necessary for completing payments, (ii) otherwise approved by
User, (iii) ordered by a court or arbitration body of acceptable jurisdiction, as
determined by G&SR, or (iv) required for the submission of a U.S. Department of the
Treasury Form 8300, G&SR shall not reveal User's contact or identifying
information or transaction history to any third party."

Therefore, G&SR will disclose its customer list upon receipt of an appropriate court
order. Alternatively, it may be possible to provide certain transaction information or
selected types of transaction information without revealing User's contact or
identifying information or transaction history. Or, the agent may wish to request a
court order for selected customers' information instead of the entire customer list.
If the agent decides to obtain a court order to obtain the customer list, to allow us to
respond as quickly as possible, the court order should be as specific as possible as to
the exact information that needs to be provided. For example, if the agent wants to
look at transactions over a certain amount during a specific period of time, the order
should request something like the following:
"All information concerning exchange transactions (national currency to e-gold or e-

---

[955] "Re: Update." Received by P. Carl Mullan, *Re: Update*, 25 July 2019.

gold to national currency) in excess of $10,000 during the period March through June 1999, including the type of the transaction, any bank wire information for the wire to or from the customer, the amount of the transaction (in USD and in e-gold), and any point of contact information for the customer or the recipient of payment."
Please contact me if you have any questions.
Barry[956]

In 2019 emails, Jackson looked back at probable reasons for the IRS to request client data. These 2019 statements do not lessen the involvement of Ian Grigg and Charles Evans in alleged malicious activity.[957]

> In retrospect, at that stage it was possible however that the request for some customer data was innocent and was merely for purposes of spot checks to track flow of funds for purposes of validating how money received in a currency exchange transaction tied to fulfillment of the exchange order. In retrospect, it probably would have been a better idea to work out a way of providing some way of supporting such spot checks. Instead what was threatened was to treat any money received by OmniPay as income, disregarding the fact that only about 2% of such money received (i.e. the spread between spot and ask) represented income since the cost of fulfilling the exchange was roughly 98%, not even counting overhead such as staff, facility, hosting etc.

> What perhaps could have been done was to modify Omnipay customer agreement (a little) as to allow auditor to see (but not retain a copy of) a list, in the office, enabling him to select some test transactions, which could then be tracked by some non-identifying number, and to provide all documentation from inbound wire (with appropriate redaction) to outbound Fulfillment Spend.

> Instead, as months passed and we spent many tens of thousands on accountants and tax attorneys, and we responded to over a dozen IDRs (Information Document Requests), the IRS ambit expanded both in terms of years under audit and in terms of efforts to see the entire e-gold database even though only G&SR dba OmniPay was under audit.[958]

Jackson further explained that by 2003, the IRS audit had expanded to include an

[956] "Req for Information." Received by Jannine Henzell, and Rhonda Reed, *Req for Information*, 6 May 2002.
[957] "Re: Update." Received by P. Carl Mullan, *Re: Update*, 25 July 2019.
[958] "Re: Update." Received by P. Carl Mullan, *Re: Update*, 25 July 2019.

international IRS team. The following October 8th, 2003 email from G&SR's accountant is a snapshot detailing the expanded scrutiny.

> From: Rhonda Reed
> Sent: Wed Oct 08 10:43:53 2003
> To: 'Miriam L. Fisher'   Cc: 'Jannine Henzell'
> Subject: GSR Audit
> Hello Miriam -
> Dino[IRS Agent] is here today and is being difficult! TODAY, he has lost all knowledge of the e-gold system and we had to go through the process again. He is not grasping the fact that transactions can occur that do not go through the banks and appear on the bank statements... However, his stand today is two-fold:
> 1.) All deposits made to the banks are income - no expenses will be recognized unless we can prove them by invoice or identify individuals so that he may track (on a customer basis by individual customer) the fulfillment or cost of sale...
> 2.) Transfer of IP - talking valuation of IP transferred to e-gold Ltd on spin off...
> He brought up the customer list and a stratification of customer transaction history to identify largest value volume customers and continues to talk about a John Doe Summons...
> Also, for what it is worth, an International Agent (Linda Dawson) was supposed to meet him here today and so far has not shown up... I was unaware that she was supposed to be here.
> AND - he is saying that the IRS has the right to require GSR to report as a cash basis tax payer even though the IRC requires the accrual basis...
> Right now he is going through the sample of invoices he selected to review. I will keep you posted as the day progresses.
> Rhonda K. Reed, CPA
> Reed, Henzell & Shott, P.A.
> Melbourne, Florida 32901[959]

Jackson claims that new IRS issues with G&SR evolved from broad observations and bizarre inquiries.

> All deposits on the bank statements will be considered as income - Any expenses we want <u>to be considered</u>[960] by the IRS as legitimate expense must be proven by an

[959] "GSR Audit." Received by Miriam L Fisher, and Jannine Henzell, *GSR Audit*, 8 Oct. 2003.
[960] Jackson noted that this statement is an extract from the accountant's email dated 10/9/2003.

invoice and in the case of exchange fulfillment we must be able to show him an exact trail tying that fulfillment to the income wire (in other words - identify the customer by name or number) if we can not do that then they will disallow the fulfillments as business related transactions. This seems to be a ploy to get the customer list! He said over and over again that he believes that the accounting and tax returns are correct and there are no problems with them... So why is he going to disallow all expenses?"[961]

Another email on November 4th, 2003, from G&SR's tax attorney made a similar observation.

It's just this continuing bizarre scenario where he does not really think the tax returns are materially inaccurate, but he is not satisfied that he has sufficient information to "test" the books. There HAS to be a compromise short of getting a summons, which is where we are headed.[962]

A particularly suspicious event came to our attention in December 2004. As per the attached "Exh_1 2004.12.27 e-gold Ltd IRS Notice.pdf", on December 24, 2004 we received "a notice from the IRS requesting the tax returns (Form 1120) for e-gold Ltd for the tax periods: 12/31/01 12/31/02 12/31/03."
This was bizarre because e-gold Ltd. was not a US company. Moreover, it maintained no office and had no paid employees. It outsourced all operational tasks to G&SR which in turn reported all revenues received as Operator (the bulk of its overall revenues – more than it made providing exchange services as OmniPay) as taxable income. An especially fishy aspect was noted; "Apparently they have also assigned e-gold Ltd a TIN which is **-******. This is the first I have seen or heard of this - do any of you have any further information on this request for tax returns?" Some unknown person had obtained a US TIN for e-gold Ltd. Despite later FOIA requests, we were never able to learn who applied or this Taxpayer Identification Number. We did discover that whoever applies for a TIN must provide their own SSN and if applying online, the interface explicitly warns "If a third party designee (TPD) is completing the online application on behalf of the taxpayer, the taxpayer must authorize the third party to apply for and receive the EIN on his or her behalf." In 2007, after the indictments, the IRS suspended its active audit and instead sent

---

[961] "Finally." Received by Barry K. Downey, et al., *Finally*, 4 Nov. 2003. Miriam L. Fisher, Hogan & Hartson LLP, NW Washington, DC 20004
[962] Ibid

"30-day letters" to G&SR demanding about 20 million or whatever the gross amount of money received from OmniPay customers during the years in question had been, as if people sent us money for no reason and all they sent was profit. That would be a nice business model! Oh wait, that IS Ripple's business model.

Barry and I also received 30 day letters that totaled the same amount, proportionate to our respective % ownership in G&SR, on basis that as largest owners of G&SR all that free money flowed directly to our benefit. I can't find mine but it was for well over 10 million. We didn't bother to respond to the stupid letters; there was no point. Eventually, around 2012, all parties finally settled with the IRS for about 100k, which also wasn't owed but was simply an extorted amount to close out the matter.[963]

♦

Final note:

On July 2nd, 2020, the former e-gold Defendants filed a Petition for Writ of Error Coram Nobis asking the Court to vacate, with prejudice, the former Defendants' convictions.

Criminal Action No. 07-109-RMC
IN THE UNITED STATES DISTRICT COURT FOR THE DISTRICT OF COLUMBIA
UNITED STATES OF AMERICA
v.
E-GOLD LIMITED, GOLD & SILVER RESERVE, INC. DOUGLAS L. JACKSON,
BARRY K. DOWNEY, and REID A. JACKSON

PETITION FOR WRIT OF ERROR CORAM NOBIS

Defendant-Petitioners e-gold, Ltd., Gold & Silver Reserve, Inc., Douglas L. Jackson, Barry K. Downey, and Reid A. Jackson (collectively, "Petitioners"), hereby petitions this Court to issue a writ of error coram nobis pursuant to the All Writs Act, 28 U.S.C. § 1651(a), and vacate, with prejudice, Petitioners' convictions in this proceeding for the reasons set forth in the accompanying Memorandum of Points and Authorities.

Dated: July 2, 2020

A copy of this sixty-two page document can be found on the e-gold website.

---

[963] Ibid

https://legalupdate.e-gold.com/2020/07/petition-for-writ-of-error-coram-nobis.html

THE END

Alphabetical Index

A

B

C

D

E

F

G

H

I

K

L

M

N

O

P

R

S

T

U

W

X

Z